Moses Maimonides

Moses Maimonides

The Man and His Works

Herbert A. Davidson

OXFORD
UNIVERSITY PRESS
2005

OXFORD
UNIVERSITY PRESS

Oxford New York
Auckland Bangkok Buenos Aires Cape Town Chennai
Dar es Salaam Delhi Hong Kong Istanbul Karachi Kolkata
Kuala Lumpur Madrid Melbourne Mexico City Mumbai Nairobi
São Paulo Shanghai Taipei Tokyo Toronto

Published by Oxford University Press, Inc.
198 Madison Avenue, New York, New York 10016

www.oup.com

Library of Congress Cataloging-in-Publication Data
Davidson, Herbert A. (Herbert Alan), 1932–
Moses Maimonides : the man and his works /
Herbert A. Davidson
p. cm.
Includes bibliographical references and index.
ISBN 0-19-517321-X
1. Maimonides, Moses, 1135–1204. 2. Rabbis—Egypt—Biography.
3. Jewish scholars—Egypt—Biography. 4. Maimonides,
Moses, 1135–1204—Teachings. I. Title.
BM755.M6D38 2004
291.1'81—dc22
[B] 2003069098

2 4 6 8 9 7 5 3 1

Printed in the United States of America
on acid-free paper

IN MEMORIAM

Avigdor and Genesia Bernstein

Louis and Ettabelle Davidson

PREFACE

If we were charged with listing the two or three medieval figures who have had the greatest impact on Jewish history, we would have to include the name of Moses Maimonides. If it were a question of the two or three most intriguing figures in medieval Jewry, his name would have to appear there too. And if we had to identify the single medieval figure who had the greatest impact on Jewish history or to identify the single most intriguing figure in medieval Jewry, a very strong case could be made for awarding Maimonides the palm on each score.

He is moreover the medieval Jewish author about whom most has been written. The following pages nonetheless attempt to do something that, as far as I know, has not yet been done—to limn in one volume a complete and comprehensive picture of Maimonides' life, personality, literary oeuvre, and thought. My assumption has been that the life he led and the writings he produced in disparate areas were the expression of a single, complex person and not the expressions of several distinct personas who somehow had gotten bundled uncomfortably and awkwardly into a single human frame.

As I delved deeper and deeper into the subject, I was repeatedly surprised to find information about Maimonides that has for decades or centuries been treated as common knowledge and that I also hitherto accepted without question to be supported by no credible evidence at all. Still more disconcerting, supposed facts concerning Maimonides and his writings sometimes turn out, on careful inspection, to be not only unsupported but to be patently incorrect. Instances will come up throughout the book.

In the hope that the book may be of interest to persons of different backgrounds, I have included explanations of terms, such as Oral Torah, mishna, midrash, halaka, and aggada, which some may regard as superfluous. I ask the indulgence of those readers.

Maimonides' law code, the *Mishneh Torah*, is gradually being translated into English in a series of volumes published by Yale University Press. Since each volume in the series has its own translator and date, and citing them is therefore cumbersome, and since the footnotes already threatened to get out of hand, I do not give references to the Yale translations in the notes. I trust that readers who wish to will be able to find the appropriate volumes without too much trouble. References are also omitted to English translations of the works of well known writers, such as Aristotle, which can easily be found. BT signifies "Babylonian Talmud," and PT, "Palestinian Talmud." The entire Babylonian Talmud is available in English in the well-known Soncino translation. The newer Steinsaltz and Schottenstein translations are better; as of this writing the latter is approaching completion, while

approaching completion, while the former has a considerable way to go. I have opportunity to cite the midrashic compilations known as *Genesis Rabba*, *Leviticus Rabba*, and *Ecclesiastes Rabba*, and these are available in English in the Soncino translation of *Midrash Rabba*. I cite Maimonides' *Guide for the Perplexed* from the Arabic edition of S. Munk (Paris 1856–1866), as republished with minor corrections by I. Joel (Jerusalem 1929). Joel indicates the original pagination of the Munk edition. Ordinarily I cite the *Guide* by Part and Chapter; where I thought it necessary to include page references as well, they are to Munk's pagination, as reproduced by Joel. The best English translation of the *Guide for the Perplexed* is that of S. Pines (*Guide of the Perplexed*, Chicago 1963), and Pines too indicates the pagination of Munk's Arabic edition. Everyone who possibly can should use Munk's French translation of the *Guide*. It is a monument of Jewish scholarship and remains, after a century and a half, one of the two or three best translations ever made of a medieval Hebrew or Arabic philosophic text into a Western language.

With the exception of the foregoing, the footnotes provide information about published English translations of texts that I cite or refer to. All the translations into English from documents and from rabbinic, philosophic, or medical works are nevertheless my own. When quoting Scripture, I wherever feasible follow the old Jewish Publication Society translation of the Hebrew Bible, which is essentially the King James translation.

Two good and faithful friends, David Hirsch and Tzvi Langermann, have aided me in numerous ways and on numerous occasions, and I wish to express my deepest appreciation to them. I began work with the help of a fellowship from the National Endowment for the Humanities, and I extend my appreciation to that institution. My wife, Kinneret, has subjected every sentence in the book to repeated, meticulous scrutiny. Whatever clarity is to be detected in the following pages is due to my implacable and best-loved critic.

Shelli we-shellakem, shellah hu.

CONTENTS

Moses Maimonides

1

MAIMONIDES' LIFE

> I am astonished at great men who have been blinded by comfort, deny the truth, and accustom themselves to take wages for issuing legal decisions and for teaching. (Maimonides, Commentary on the Mishna: *Nedarim* 4:3)

> If a person undertakes to study the Torah, forgo gainful employment, and support himself through charity, that man profanes the divine name, shows contempt for the Torah, extinguishes the light of religion, brings evil upon himself, and removes his life from the world to come. For it is forbidden to derive benefit from the Torah in this world . . . . Torah unaccompanied by labor will in the end be rendered as naught. It leads to sin, and the man will eventually rob his fellow creatures. (Maimonides, *Mishneh Torah*: *H. Talmud Torah* 3.10, incorporating language from Mishna *Abot* 2:2)

More information is available regarding the life of Moses ben Maimon, or Maimonides—known in Hebrew by the acronym RaMBaM—than that of any other medieval Jewish figure. The data are nevertheless still too meager to allow one to contemplate anything resembling the highly detailed biographies of nineteenth- and twentieth-century personages, and sometimes of personages from earlier periods as well, with which we have been graced in recent years. Jews in Maimonides' time did not write autobiographies or biographies, and documents in which they refer to incidents from their own or others' personal lives are rare. Biography happens to be a genre that was pursued intently, if not always critically, by medieval Muslim writers, and the Muslim biographical dictionary of al-Qifṭī, a man who was on friendly terms with Maimonides' favorite student, has an entry on Maimonides. The entry is only two pages long, however. And while it supplies several particulars unknown from any other source, they cannot be accorded unqualified credibility; for Qifṭī's book, which is preserved in a reworked and abbreviated form made after the author's death by another writer, is not reliable, at least in its present form.

The genuinely reliable data regarding Maimonides' life are primarily those that can be drawn from his own books and letters, and it is mainly thanks to them that he is the medieval Jewish figure about whom most is known. The number of letters of Maimonides' which have been preserved is, I believe, greater than that preserved from any other medieval Jewish figure. They contain material of a personal character and are especially valuable in the light they cast on his life as well as the glimpses they offer into traits—some of which might not be expected—of his personality. Further details can be culled from documents relating to Maimonides which come from the hands of contemporaries. What is known about Maimonides has moreover increased in recent decades, thanks to the publication of fragments of letters either written by him or referring to him which have been uncovered in the Cairo Geniza, the treasure trove of discarded documents discovered over a century ago in a closed chamber of the Fustat, or Old Cairo, synagogue. In contrast to the information supplied by Maimonides and his contemporaries, supposed facts reported by authors who lived centuries after his death must be used with the greatest circumspection.

When everything is put together, large gaps remain. Since Maimonides is a highly intriguing figure and scholarship abhors a vacuum, scholars during the past century or so have filled some of the gaps with conjectures—regarding places where he resided before reaching Egypt, dates, teachers with whom he studied, books that he read, offices that he held in Egypt, and more. Many of the conjectures are, to borrow a rabbinic phrase, "like mountains hanging from a hair." I shall try to restrict myself to what can be stated about him with a fair degree of certainty.

He styled himself "Moses, the son of Maimon the rabbinic judge [*dayyan*], the son of Joseph the scholar [or: rabbi (*ḥakam*)], the son of Isaac the rabbinic judge, the son of Joseph the rabbinic judge, the son of Obadia the rabbinic judge, the son of Solomon the rabbi, the son of Obadia the rabbinic judge."[1] He thus saw himself as the scion of a line of rabbinic scholars who were sufficiently conscious of their distinction to preserve a genealogy, with titles, extending back seven generations. When signing his name, he would often identify himself as "the Cordovan," and a

[1]Colophon to his Commentary on the Mishna (=*Mishna* ᶜ*im Perush R. Moshe ben Maimon*), Arabic original and Hebrew trans. J. Kafah [Jerusalem 1963–1968]) 6.738.

note ascribed to his grandson explicitly gives Cordova as his birthplace.[2] Cordova, Spain, was an Arabic metropolis in Maimonides' day.

His father was an accomplished rabbinic scholar and a rabbinic judge. Nothing is known of his mother, although fanciful legends exist about her.[3] He had a single, younger brother, David, of whom he was extremely fond and whose education he undertook.[4] And there is evidence that he had more than one sister. Qifṭī's biographical dictionary, which was just mentioned, reports that a sister of his was married to an Egyptian Jew who held a position in Saladin's court.[5] A letter to Maimonides from his brother, who was then on a business trip, sends good wishes to David's "sisters," in the plural.[6] Then there is a curious letter, discovered in the Cairo Geniza, which was sent to Maimonides by a woman named Miriam, who identifies herself as his sister. The letter was written after Maimonides' father had died, and it speaks of Maimonides as a person possessing important status; he was therefore apparently already in Egypt and well established in Fustat, the city in which he spent the second half of his life. The woman concludes with greetings for David and for Maimonides' "sisters." The term *sister* in the letter, as in the letter from Maimonides' brother, could conceivably have the broad sense of female relation rather than female sibling, but if all the sisters in the woman's letter—the writer herself and those whom she greets side by side with Maimonides' brother—were genuine siblings of Maimonides', we have evidence of at least three. As for the letter's content, the woman complains, or has the scribe to whom she dictated the letter complain, that she was in a "wretched state," "weeping and fasting," because her son, who had left home, had for some time failed to write. She pleads with Maimonides for help in searching the young man out and asks him to inform her by letter where and how her darling was.[7] *Plus ça change, plus c'est la même chose.*

[2]Commentary on *Rosh ha-Shana*, ed. S. Sachs in *Jen Libanon* (*Yen Lebanon*) (Paris 1866) 1. Reprinted in M. Zacks, *Ḥiddushe ha-Rambam la-Talmud* (Jerusalem 1963) 58–98. I checked the text against Paris MS 336.

[3]The story, in various versions which cannot all be harmonized, was that Maimon followed instructions he received in a dream and married a butcher's daughter. See Gedalia Ibn Yaḥya, *Shalshelet ha-Qabbala* (Jerusalem 1962) 104; W. Fischel, "*Maqama ᶜal ha-Rambam we-Abiw*," *Tarbiz* 6 (1934–1935) 423–24; T. Alexander and E. Romero, *Erase una vez . . . Maimonides* (Cordoba 1988) 47–54 (four versions).

[4]Maimonides, Letter to Japhet ben Elijah, in I. Shailat, *Letters and Essays of Moses Maimonides* (in Hebrew) (Jerusalem 1987–1988) 230; English translation: F. Kobler, *A Treasury of Jewish Letters* 1 (London 1952) 192–93. A document published by J. Mann, *The Jews in Egypt and in Palestine* (Oxford 1920–1922) 2.319, shows that David was Maimonides' only brother.

[5]See below, p. 37.

[6]S. Goitein, *Letters of Medieval Jewish Traders* (Princeton 1973) 211.

[7]S. Goitein, "*Otograf shel ha-Rambam u-Miktab elaw me-et Aḥoto Miryam*," *Tarbiz* 32 (1962–1963) 188–91. On p. 189, Goitein draws the conclusion that Maimonides must have been in Fustat. He also makes the observation that the sender could conceivably have been a female

An eighteenth-century Latin volume dealing with antiquities reproduces a medallion on which a purported portrait of the adult Maimonides is engraved. The medallion is adorned with a scrolled Latin inscription, the figure portrayed in it wears a large turban, the style of which may or may not be historically accurate, but around his neck there hangs a ribbon to which another medallion is, anachronistically, appended. The portrait in the Latin volume inspired additional minor artists to create other pictures of Maimonides in a similar style.[8] There is not the slightest reason to suppose that the portrait engraved on the medallion, not to speak of the derivative pictures, has any basis in reality. The handsome statue of Maimonides recently erected in Cordoba is likewise the product of an artist's imagination. No written description of Maimonides' external appearance has come to light, nor was any to be expected, since medieval Jewish writers did not discuss matters of the sort. What he looked like is therefore unknown.

A number of dates have been recorded for his birth. One sixteenth-century writer cites sources giving 1131, 1132, and 1135 as the date, and then he quotes without comment a statement by Maimonides which, as will be seen, indicates still another year.[9] Until recently, 1135 was generally accepted as the correct date, and biographers of Maimonides would often add the exact day of the month, the day of the week, and even the time of day when he was born.

The date of 1135 for Maimonides' birth is, in the first place, found in a note that one or two[10] manuscripts append to a medieval commentary on the tractate *Rosh ha-Shana* of the Babylonian Talmud. Most manuscripts containing the commentary do not have the note. The manuscript or manuscripts that do have it, as well as most of those that do not, are problematic in their own right. They attribute the commentary that they contain to "the great rabbi, our master . . . light of Israel, R. Moses, son of his honor, the judge Ibn Maimon, of Granada [*Rimmon*], Spain." Maimonides is plainly the person intended. We know, however, that his father's name was not Ibn Maimon, but Maimon. When Maimonides refers to his city of origin, as he often does, he invariably identifies himself as a citizen of Cordova; nothing known connects either him or his father to Granada. And the manuscripts' attribution of the commentary on the tractate *Rosh ha-Shana* which they contain to Maimonides is also in error, for Maimonides could not possibly

---

relation other than a sibling.

[8]R. Cohen, "*We-hayu* ^{c}*Eneka Ro'ot et Moreka*," *Zion* 58 (1993) 443–44.

[9]Gedalia Ibn Yaḥya, *Shalshelet ha-Qabbala*) 96. S. Havlin, "*Le-Toledot ha-Rambam*," *Da*^{c}*at* 15 (1985) 74, writes that the date of 1131 is due to an error in a text from which Gedalia worked. Havlin surveys the medieval sources for Maimonides' birth as well as the postmedieval sources—which are plainly derivative—and he arrives at the conclusion that will be given below. Unfortunately, his article is marred throughout by typographical errors.

[10]*Jen Libanon* (n. 2 above), page 5 of the unpaginated introduction, implies that the note appears in two manuscripts of the commentary on BT *Rosh ha-Shana*. I found the note only in Paris, Bibliothèque Nationale, Hebrew MS 336, a microfilm of which I examined in the Institute of Microfilmed Hebrew Manuscripts, Jerusalem.

have been the author.[11] We are thus dealing with a document preserved in a context that commands little credibility.

As for the note itself, the scribe responsible for it relates that a previous scribe "copied the following from the hand of our master, the Nagid R. David, R. Moses' descendant [*nin*]." The David referred to was Maimonides' grandson, and the ascription to him appears to be basically genuine. For the note records—albeit with gaps in the preserved version—the dates of the birth and death of David's father and Maimonides' son, Abraham, calling them the days on which "my father" was born and died, as well as David's own birth date, calling it the day "when I, David, was born."[12]

The note reports: "Rabbi Moses was born to his father Rabbi Maimon, in Cordova, on the fourteenth day of the month of Nisan in the year 1446 of the Seleucid chronology, which corresponds to the year 4893 after the creation of the world. He departed this world and gained everlasting life on Sunday night, the twentieth day of the month of Tebet, in the year 1516 of the Seleucid chronology." There is a glaring inconsistency here. The month of Nisan of the year 1446 of the Seleucid chronology fell within the year 1135 of our Western calendar, whereas Nisan of 4893 in the creation chronology fell within 1133. The note thus tells us in a single breath that Maimonides was born both in 1133 and in 1135. The full date for Maimonides' death—the night of 20 Tebet, 1516 of the Seleucid chronology—corresponds to December 12, 1204, and that, the note states correctly, was indeed a Sunday night.[13]

The first source of the date of 1135 for Maimonides' birth is, then, a copy of a report that very likely originates with his grandson but that in the preserved form contradicts itself by giving the year both as 1133 and 1135. The report moreover has come to us in a manuscript or manuscripts that are highly problematic.

A second medieval source for the date of Maimonides' birth, this one anonymous, avoids the discrepancy in the preserved version of David's account by reporting the year only according to the Seleucid chronology; it gives the Seleucid equivalent of 1135 and nothing more. It adds a new detail, informing us that Maimonides died "in Egypt [or: in Fustat; Hebrew: *Miṣrayim*; the name designates both the city and the country] and he was buried . . . in the city of Tiberias." But all the other information it furnishes agrees precisely with what the note attributed to

[11]Below, pp. 144-46.

[12]The scribe who produced the manuscript published in *Jen Libanon*, writes that he was copying from a prior manuscript that had been written in Acre, Palestine; see *Jen Libanon* 1. That detail is compatible with David Maimonides' authorship of the note in question, since he is known to have lived for a period in Acre; see J. Mann, *Texts and Studies* (New York 1972) 1.419–21. A Geniza document corroborates the dates given by the note for Abraham Maimonides' death and David Maimonides' birth; see Shailat, *Letters and Essays of Moses Maimonides* (n. 4 above) 170.

[13]For converting dates, I used A. Akavia, N. Fried, and D. Zakai, *Calendar for 6000 Years* (in Hebrew) (Jerusalem 1976).

Maimonides' grandson said. Furthermore, it uses telltale phraseology that betrays a direct or indirect connection with the grandson's note, for it too speaks of Maimonides' having "departed this world . . . and . . . gained everlasting life."[14] The two sources—whether the anonymous source is later than the grandson's report, as seems probable, or earlier—do not, therefore, look like independent witnesses.

A third source, the earliest supplying the day of the week and time of day on which Maimonides supposedly was born, is a chronicle written by a fifteenth-century Spanish Jewish scholar, Saadia Ibn Danan. Ibn Danan records the two different years for Maimonides' birth which the note attributed to David Maimonides gave—one according to the Seleucid chronology and the other according to the creation chronology—and he adds that Maimonides was born on a Saturday afternoon; in the year 1135, 14 Nisan was a Saturday. He thereupon introduces a new discrepancy, now in regard to Maimonides' death. For he again records the year according to both the Seleucid and the creation chronologies, and the years he records in the two chronologies again do not agree. Not only that: Both of the dates for the year of Maimonides' death in the preserved text of Ibn Danan differ from the year given by Maimonides' grandson. And the Ibn Danan document does not stop there. It compounds the disarray by giving as a month and day for Maimonides' death the month and day that David Maimonides' note had given for the death of Maimonides' son and David's father, Abraham.[15] Ibn Danan's account thus lacks all credibility.

What we have seen so far is that the commonly accepted date of 1135 for Maimonides' birth goes back to three sources. The first is a note attributed to Maimonides' grandson, very likely written by him, but preserved in a copy made by another party. The copy gives not merely 1135, but 1133 as well, for the year

[14]The passage also commits a slip of the pen, in calling Maimonides' father "Moses." The passage reads: "R. Moses . . . son of the rabbi and rabbinic judge R. Moses . . . departed this world in Miṣrayim [which can mean either the city Fustat, not far from Cairo, or the country of Egypt] and was buried in . . . the city of Tiberias. And he gained everlasting life on Sunday night, the twentieth day of the month of Tebet, in the year 1516 of the Seleucid chronology. His birth date was the fourteenth day of the month of Nisan in the year 1446 of the Seleucid chronology. His lifespan was therefore seventy years." Quoted in A. Freimann, "*Shalshelet ha-Yaḥas shel Mishpaḥat ha-Rambam*," *Alumma* (1936) 18. The passage is taken from Vatican Heb MS 303, 125a, which I checked.

[15]Ibn Danan writes: "Maimonides was born in Cordova, on Saturday afternoon, the fourteenth day of Nisan in the year 1446 of the Seleucid chronology [equivalent to 1135], which is the year 4893 of the creation chronology [equivalent to 1133]. He *departed to everlasting life* in Fustat, Egypt, on Sunday night, the eighteenth day of Kislev in the year 1517 of the Seleucid chronology [equivalent to 1205], which is 4964 of the creation chronology [equivalent to 1203]. His lifespan was thus almost seventy-two years." Published by S. Edelmann, *Ḥemda Genuza* (Königsberg 1856) 30b, which I corrected using Bodleian MS 108 (=Neubauer 2233) 18b. Shailat, *Letters and Essays of Moses Maimonides* 520, checked two additional manuscripts and found that they agree with the version I have given. In 1203, 18 Kislev did fall on Sunday night.

of Maimonides' birth, and the context in which it is found is careless regarding other information about Maimonides. The second source has only the date of 1135 yet does not appear to be independent of the David Maimonides report. The third, Ibn Danan's report, is useless. The 1135 date therefore does not have impeccable legs to stand on. As several scholars in recent decades have realized, it cannot outweigh the explicit information furnished by Maimonides himself concerning the year in which he was born.

At the conclusion of his Commentary on the Mishna, Maimonides writes: I "began the composition of this commentary when I was twenty-three years old and I completed it in Fustat [or: in Egypt] when I was thirty years old, in the year 1479 of the Seleucid chronology." In the fifteenth century, a meticulous scribe collated one of the manuscripts containing the statement with Maimonides' own handwritten copy of the Commentary on the Mishna.[16] The statement's accuracy can therefore not be doubted. The year 1479 in the Seleucid chronology corresponds to the last quarter of 1167 and the first three quarters of 1168. Maimonides was thus thirty years old on the day within that period when he completed his Commentary on the Mishna; but we do not know whether he had just passed his thirtieth birthday or was approaching his thirty-first. If we accept 14 Nisan as the day on which he was born, he entered this vale of tears on either April 7, 1137, or March 28, 1138. If we choose to reject the testimony of the David Maimonides note completely and question even the dating of Maimonides' birth to the month of Nisan, he could have been born on any day between the beginning of September 1136 and the first week of September 1138.[17]

What has just been seen in regard to Maimonides' birth date is emblematic of other details of his life. Information that biographies of him purvey as common knowledge is not necessarily borne out by the evidence.

It was an unsettled time. The Almoravids, a confederation of Berber tribes whose roots lay in the Sahara region, were nominally in control of Muslim Spain and western North Africa. But Almoravid power in Spain was crumbling under the pressure of Muslim chieftains seeking freedom of action within and of Christian forces conducting incursions from without. More ominously, a new Berber power, the Almohads, had begun to stir out of the Atlas mountains in what is today

[16] J. Kafah's introduction to edition of Maimonides, Commentary on the Mishna (n. 1 above) 6, pp. 7–8; S. Sassoon, *A Comprehensive Study of the Autograph Manuscript of Maimonides' Commentary to the Mishnah* (Jerusalem 1990) chapter 6. Kafah, ibid., p. 5, recognizes 1137–1138 as the date of Maimonides' birth, as does S. Goitein, "Moses Maimonides, Man of Action," *Hommages à Georges Vajda*, ed. G. Nahon and C. Touati (Louvain 1980) 155.

[17] The same observation is made by M. Friedman, "Social Realities in Egypt and Maimonides' Rulings on Family Law," in N. Rakover, *Maimonides as Codifier of Jewish Law* (Jerusalem 1987) 225. For a strained attempt to harmonize the date of birth that Maimonides indicates and the year 1135, which had become generally accepted, see A. Geiger, *Nachgelassene Schriften* 3 (Berlin 1876) 86.

southwestern Morocco. The founder of the Almohad movement, Ibn Tumart, was a student of theology and a preacher, and his movement was professedly driven by religious motives. Its primary declared grievance was the failure of many Muslims, most notably the Almoravids, to uphold the absolute unity of God, and its declared aim was eradication of the error.[18] The Almohads eradicated religious error as fanatical religious groups have eradicated it in other periods of history and as we still see such groups doing in our own day. They drowned it in blood[19]—the blood of their Almoravid enemies, of Muslim chieftains who failed to do obeisance, of Spanish Christian forces probing from the north, and of unfortunate bystanders. By the early 1150s, the Almohads had conquered a wide swath of North Africa extending from the Atlantic Ocean through most of present-day Algeria—an area known in Arabic as the Maghrib, "the West"—as well as the western portion of Muslim Spain, including the city of Cordova. By 1160, they had expanded their control of North Africa beyond areas that had been ruled by the Almoravids, to include Tunisia and Tripoli. Ten years later they completed their conquest of Muslim Spain.[20] Jewish communities were among those trampled under foot.

An Egyptian Jew writing in 1148 reports eyewitness descriptions of Almohad ferocity in areas that are today Morocco and western Algeria and, what is of interest for us, actions the Almohads took toward the Jewish population: When ᶜAbd al-Mu'min, the successor of Ibn Tumart, conquered Oran, he put the Almoravid garrison to death, killed the Almoravid governor, and gibbeted the latter's body. In Fez, he slaughtered a total of 100,000 persons and in Marrakesh, a total of 150,000—numbers that are scarcely imaginable. He killed the entire population of Tilimsen, with the exception of Jews who converted to Islam. After occupying Sijilmasa, a city that did not resist, the Almohads tried to persuade the Jewish inhabitants to convert to Islam. Nothing came of the negotiations for seven months, whereupon a new governor appeared and presented the Jewish population with an ultimatum: conversion or death—this although Islamic legal doctrine of the time rejected the validity of coerced conversions.[21] Some 150 Jews were thereupon put to death for their obstinacy, while the remainder, led by the local rabbinic judge, accepted the cordial invitation to embrace the majority faith. From the city of Bejaïa (Bougie) on the eastern Algerian coast to Gibraltar, no one professing "the name Jew . . . remains; he who was killed was killed, he who sinned [by converting to Islam] sinned."[22]

[18]H. Terrasse, *Histoire du Maroc* (Casablanca 1949) 266–67.

[19]The medieval historian al-Baiḍaq speaks of one purge that resulted in 32,000 deaths; see A. Huici Miranda, *Historia política del imperio almohade* 1 (Tetuán 1956) 154–56.

[20]R. Le Tourneau, *The Almohad Movement in North Africa in the Twelfth and Thirteenth Centuries* (Princeton 1969) 2, 52–57.

[21]A. Fattal, *Le statut légal des non-Musulmans en pays d'Islam* (Beirut 1958) 165; M. Abumalham, "La conversión según formularios notariales andalusíes," *Miscelanea de estudios arabes y hebraicos* 34 (1985) 76, 77, 79.

[22]Cited by H. Hirschberg, "*ᶜAl Gezerot ha-Meyaḥadim*," *Sefer ha-Yobel le-Yiṣḥaq Baer*,"

Abraham Ibn Daud, a Spanish Jewish chronicler writing in or after 1161,[23] relates that with the Almohad conquest, "years of calamity, evil decrees, and religious persecutions [*shemad*][24] befell Israel." To the troubles that had been visited upon Jews from of old, a new calamity had been added, the calamity of those who "were marked for leaving the faith at the threat of the sword. . . ." The Almohad leader Ibn Tumart, who appeared on the world scene "in 1113, . . . decreed that Israel should leave its faith"; he declared: "come let us cut them off from being a nation, so that the name of Israel may be no more in remembrance"; he "left them neither name nor remnant in his entire kingdom."[25]

138–40, 142, 147–48; summarized in H. Hirschberg, *A History of the Jews in North Africa* 1 (Leiden 1974) 127–28. The pertinent part of the letter is translated by S. Goitein, *Mediterranean Society* 5 (Berkeley 1988) 60–61. The religious judge from Sijilmasa who converted to Islam may later have returned to the Jewish faith; see Hirschberg, *History of the Jews in North Africa* 353.

[23]Abraham Ibn Daud, *The Book of Tradition*, ed. and trans. G. Cohen (Philadelphia 1967), English section 43.

[24]In talmudic literature, the term *shemad* is applied to situations in which gentile authorities were understood to have issued a general prohibition against the observance of Jewish religious commandments (Tosefta *Shabbat* 15.17, and BT *Sanhedrin* 74a, manuscript reading; censors objected to the term *shemad*, and here as elsewhere printed editions of the Babylonian Talmud replace *shemad* with a less offensive synonym); to have prohibited circumcision, the study of the Law, and observance of the Sabbath (BT *Rosh ha-Shana* 19a, manuscript reading); to have required Jews to perform labor on the Sabbath (YT *Ḥagiga* [Venice 1523/Krotoschin 1866] 2.1, 77b; to have prohibited the observance of the Day of Atonement while nonetheless permitting observance of the Jewish Sabbath (BT *Ḥullin* 101b); to have taken unspecified anti-Jewish measures while permitting religious services on Jewish holy days (BT *Rosh ha-Shana* 32b); to have taken unspecified anti-Jewish measures while exempting Samaritans (YT *Qiddushin* 4.1, end); to have required Jews to worship idols (Tosefta, *ᶜAboda Zara* 5.6, combined with YT *ᶜAboda Zara* 5.8); or to have given district military commanders the right to sexual relations with Jewish brides (YT *Ketubbot* 1.5). Even in the instance where the term *shemad* is employed for the coercion of Jews to worship idols, it does not necessarily involve the renunciation of Jewish religious affiliation and formal adoption of a different religious affiliation. Maimonides, *Mishneh Torah, H. Yesode ha-Torah* 5.3 (Frankel edition), defines *shemad* as a situation wherein "a wicked king such as Nebuchadnezzar and the like arise and issue a decree against Israel in order to extirpate the Jewish religion or to prohibit observance of one of the religious commandments." He uses the term in a similar sense in *Epistle to Yemen*, Arabic and Hebrew versions, ed. A. Halkin, with English trans. B. Cohen (New York 1952) 22; English translation [v].

The term *meshummad*, a passive participle from the root *sh-m-d*, is commonly translated as "apostate." But BT *Ḥullin* 3a, 17a, in the reading preserved by the first Venice edition, 1520, recognizes a type of *meshummad* who is a sinner yet retains his privileges as a member of the Jewish faith. In paraphrasing the talmudic passage, Maimonides recognizes the same type of *meshummad*; see his Commentary on the Mishna, *Ḥullin* 1:2, in Kafah's edition, and *Mishneh Torah*: *H. Sheḥiṭa* 4.14, in the Frankel and Kafah editions.

[25]Abraham Ibn Daud, *The Book of Tradition*, Hebrew section 65–66; English section 88. The quotations incorporate phraseology from Psalms 83:5 and Isaiah 14:22. Although Ibn Daud credits Ibn Tumart with the persecutions, the conquest of North Africa and Muslim Spain did not begin until the accession of Ibn Tumart's successor, ᶜAbd al-Mu'min.

Testimony is also furnished by a poetic elegy composed by the Spanish Jewish scholar Abraham Ibn Ezra, whose life covered the first half, and the beginning of the second half, of the twelfth century. Ibn Ezra laments the destruction of a dozen Jewish communities in Spain and North Africa, two of which are particularly pertinent, namely, Cordova and Fez. The opening lines of the elegy give 1139—or in another reading 1141—as the year in which one Jewish community was overrun, so that Ibn Ezra undoubtedly has suffering sowed by the Almohads in view. He speaks of death, devastation, and captivity inflicted on Jewish communities but significantly mentions no forced conversions to Islam.[26]

Alternate versions of Ibn Ezra's poem offer further information. One of them appends a stanza, clearly from another hand, at the end; the supplement apostrophizes Ibn Ezra and asks him why he had forgotten six North African communities that had likewise been laid waste. A second alternate version, also probably the handiwork of someone other than Ibn Ezra, interpolates two stanzas into the body of the poem which lament the destruction of a dozen additional communities in Spain, the Mediterranean islands, and North Africa. None of the additions makes any mention of forced conversions.[27] Still another version of the poem, which could have been composed by either Ibn Ezra or someone else, reworks the poem rather than adding to it. In the reworked guise, the poem tells of a single instance of forced conversion and it describes the fate of Fez: The Jews of Dar^ca, an area in present-day southwestern Morocco which was close to the Almohad heartland, were given the choice of converting to Islam or being killed; when they refused to convert, ninety-four members of the community were put to death. And the Jewish community of Fez, which had prided itself on its scholars and other religious functionaries, was, according to the present version of the poem, destroyed.[28]

Maimonides too took oblique notice of Almohad persecutions. In the early 1170s, he sent a public letter to the Yemenite Jewish community, a community that was itself staggering under measures taken to force its conversion to Islam. The circular letter grieves at news that a ruler "in the Land of Yemen . . . has decreed religious persecution [*shemad*] upon Israel and forced [the inhabitants of] all places where he exercised sovereignty to leave their religion, as the African did in the land of the West."[29] The letter makes no further mention of the persecution of Jews in the western lands. A different letter of Maimonides', written in 1199, bewails the

[26] D. Kahana, *Qobeṣ Ḥokmat R. Abraham Ibn Ezra* (Warsaw 1894) 140–42; Hirschberg, *History of the Jews of North Africa* (n. 22 above) 1.123–24.

[27] Kahana 143, 250. D. Cazès, "Antiquities judaiques en Tripolitaine," *Revue des études juives* 20 (1890) 82–87.

[28] H. Schirmann, "*Qinot* ^{c}*al ha-Gezerot*," *Qobeṣ* ^{c}*al Yad* 3 (13) (1939) 33–35. D. Corcos, "*Yeḥasam shel Shalliṭe ha-al-Muwaḥadun la-Yehudim*," *Zion* 32 (1967) 147, note, writes, without citing a source, that when the Almohads took Fez, they pronounced a general amnesty on all inhabitants except the Almoravids.

[29] Maimonides, *Epistle to Yemen* (n. 24 above) 4; English translation [ii].

decline of rabbinic studies throughout the world and in that connection makes the obscure remark: "As for the cities of the West, it is well known what, as a consequence of our sins, has been decreed against them."[30] In neither context does Maimonides suggest that he had himself experienced Almohad persecution.

Further references to the grief visited upon the North African Jewish communities are found in two works of Joseph Ibn ᶜAqnin, a Jewish writer living in Morocco in the twelfth century. Ibn ᶜAqnin is of special interest, since he was personally acquainted with Maimonides during the time when the latter sojourned in North Africa. Both of Ibn ᶜAqnin's works bemoan the Almohad persecutions, one more somberly than the other.

The more somber account reports the confiscation of Jewish inheritances, the preventing of Jews from engaging in trade, a prohibition against their possessing slaves, the requirement that Jews wear distinctive clothing, the removal of Jewish children from their parents' hands and the raising of them as Muslims on the basis of an old Muslim tradition that "every child is by nature born a Muslim" and only its two parents train it to be a Jew, a Christian, or a Magian.[31] A silver lining in the situation was that by God's grace, "the more we obey them . . . the more heavy they make the yoke," with the consequence that Jews were discouraged from "betraying and leaving the Jewish religion completely." In another manifestation of God's grace, the descendants of even those who converted to Islam two or three generations earlier had been subjected to such discrimination that many returned to their ancestral faith.[32] Ibn ᶜAqnin accuses coreligionists who did not flee the country when conditions permitted of desecrating God's name, and the context and tone indicate that he is referring to persons who had converted to Islam as a result of persecution and now had the opportunity to escape.[33] Although the picture is bleak and although it alludes to conversions to Islam resulting from persecution, Ibn ᶜAqnin does not, as far as I could see from the available fragments, speak of a general campaign to force non-Muslims to convert to Islam.

In the second work of Ibn ᶜAqnin's, which perhaps reflects conditions at a different part of the century, the author speaks in one passage of his fellow Jews' having openly "manifested obedience of the gentiles out of fear," yet at the same time, having preserved "obedience of God" in their hearts.[34] In other passages of

[30] Maimonides, *Responsa*, ed. J. Blau, 2nd ed. (Jerusalem 1986) 4.33.

[31] A. Halkin, "*Le-Toledot ha-Shemad*," *Joshua Starr Memorial Volume* (New York 1953) 106–7. In his text, Halkin mistranslates the passage about children because he is sure that Ibn ᶜAqnin is speaking about converted Jews. But Halkin himself explains exactly what the passage means in note 52.

[32] Halkin, "*Le-Toledot ha-Shemad*" 106.

[33] Halkin, "*Le-Toledot ha-Shemad*" 104, note 34. Ibn ᶜAqnin speaks in the first person plural—"we," "us"—which, as Halkin observes, suggests that he was one of the sinners.

[34] Joseph Ibn ᶜAqnin, *Commentarius in canticum canticorum* (in Arabic and Hebrew), ed. A. Halkin (Jerusalem 1964) 360–61. The words "and accept their religion" in Halkin's translation are an interpretation and do not reflect the Arabic original.

the same composition, he congratulates his coreligionists for continuing, in all periods when they were persecuted for their religion (*shemadot*), to sanctify God's name, maintain their obedience of Him, and observe His commandments.[35] Jewish faith in God had been particularly striking in "the current persecution, for in it, as is well known, we persevere in studying the Law." The "apodictic sign" of Jewish devotion to God's Law was the "appearance in Fez of the great scholar, our master Moses ben Maimon."[36]

One further piece of testimony should be heard. This is a composition of unknown date which in most but not all manuscripts[37] is attributed to Maimonides and which today is generally, although probably in error, assumed to be a genuine work of his.[38] Its object is to refute an unnamed Jewish scholar who had excoriated those who buckled in the face of religious persecution (*shemad*) and accepted the Islamic faith.

According to the composition, the Muslim authorities "coerce [Jews] to acknowledge that man [that is, Muhammad], his apostlehood, and his being a true prophet" but require nothing "except a statement to the effect that one believes in that man." "They know full well that we do not believe the statement and a person mouths it only to save himself from the king by appeasing him and exalting his religion." While those who refuse to say the words risk being put to death, anyone who mouths them may, if he wishes, "fulfill all 613 commandments [of the Jewish Law] clandestinely, . . . and none will prevent him."[39]

Seeing that the formula "there is no god but Allah, and Muhammad is his apostle" is nothing less than the Muslim declaration of faith and that reciting the declaration is the pivotal step in converting to Islam, it sounds very much as if the author was being disingenuous and the Jews who acknowledged Muhammad's apostlehood were not just mumbling a few innocuous words. Indeed, as the author expands on what had happened, he calls his coreligionists the "religiously coerced" (*anusim*) and lets slip that they had to attend services in the mosque.[40] A few lines after asserting that Jews were permitted to observe their religious commandments privately without interference, he exhorts his readers to "fulfill the commandments *as far as possible*." Everyone should be as scrupulous as he can in observing whatever he can.[41] At least in the eyes of their persecutors, the persons about whom he is writing had, however they might deceive themselves, converted to

[35] Ibn ᶜAqnin, *Commentarius* 308–9, 312–13, 398–99.

[36] Ibn ᶜAqnin, *Commentarius* 398–99. Ibn ᶜAqnin signs off, pp. 500–501, with the hope that God will help him "purify himself from the impurity of the persecution."

[37] Maimonides (?), *Iggeret ha-Shemad*, in Shailat, *Letters and Essays of Moses Maimonides* (n. 4 above) 30, note 1. Partial English translation of the *Iggeret*: Kobler, *A Treasury of Jewish Letters* (n. 4 above) 179–82.

[38] See below, pp. 501-9.

[39] *Iggeret ha-Shemad* 30, 53; similarly on 41.

[40] *Iggeret ha-Shemad* 32.

[41] *Iggeret ha-Shemad* 54–55.

Islam, and the Muslim authorities were not so understanding regarding continued observance of Jewish religious practices as the author represented them.

Just where and when the religious persecution depicted in the composition took place is never stated. But at one point the author refers to "those who delude themselves and say that they will remain where they are until the Messiah comes to the land of the West, at which time they will leave and go to Jerusalem."[42] The composition therefore quite possibly describes—as scholars generally assume it does—coerced conversions to Islam at some stage of the Almohad persecution, conversions in which the victims did their best to preserve a clandestine Jewish life.

From Jewish writers, we have, in sum, more than one report of Jews' converting to Islam under Almohad coercion, Ibn Ezra's poem on the destruction of Jewish communities which makes no mention of conversion, and one or two reports that are ambiguous. The reports could relate to different periods of Almohad persecution and, in the case of the composition that defends those who mumbled a few words and continued to observe the commandments clandestinely, even to Muslim religious persecutions unconnected with the Almohads.

Muslim sources similarly speak of forced conversions of Jews and Christians. The historian Ibn al-Athīr writes that in 1160, when the Almohads conquered "Ifrīqiya," a term the meaning of which varies from context to context, but which usually means the area around Tunis, they offered the Jewish and Christian populations the choice "between Islam and death." It is perhaps significant that Ibn al-Athīr, despite the comprehensiveness of his history of North Africa, has not been found to mention other instances of forced conversions.[43]

Another Muslim historian, ᶜAbd al-Wāḥid b. ᶜAlī al-Marrākushī, born in Marrakesh in 1185 and writing in 1225, reports that from the rise of the Almohads until his day, the legal status of toleration that Jews and Christians had traditionally enjoyed under Muslim law—the *dhimma* status—had been abolished. "No church or synagogue is to be found in the entire Maghrib. Jews exhibit their Islam externally, recite the prayers in mosques, and have their children read the Quran, . . . although God alone knows what their hearts harbor and what occurs in their houses." Marrākushī also describes distinctive and singularly unpleasant dress that an Almohad leader at the end of the twelfth century decreed for "all Jews in the Maghrib" on the grounds that he was unsure of the genuineness of their acceptance of Islam: It consisted in "dark garments with extremely wide sleeves that reach almost to the feet, and, instead of turbans, heavy ugly caps like packsaddles, extending below their ears."[44] The chronicler does not say whether he means that Jews and Christians were forced to convert to Islam under threat of

[42] *Iggeret ha-Shemad* 57.

[43] Le Tourneau (n. 20 above) 59–60; Corcos, "*Yeḥasam shel Shalliṭe ha-al-Muwaḥadun*" (n. 28 above) 146–47.

[44] Cited by S. Munk, "Notice sur Joseph ben-Iehouda," *Journal asiatique* (1842) 39–42. Translation: Abū Muḥammad ᶜAbd al-Wāḥid al-Marrākushī, *Lo admirable en el resumen de las noticias del Maghrib*, trans. A. Huici Miranda (Tetuan 1955) 251–52.

death or whether they converted in order to avoid leaving Almohad lands. Nor does he mention that discriminating against converts in the manner he describes would have been contrary to Muslim law. In any event, a different Muslim historian, who wrote a century later, records the part of the story relating to the discriminatory dress with no hint that the decree was aimed at anyone but open and professing Jews.[45] A twentieth-century student of the period warns about Marrākushī's tendentiousness and inaccuracies.[46]

In the fourteenth century, after the Almohads had disappeared from the stage of history, yet another historian, Dhahabī, records the following anecdote: A certain Ibn Ḥamwiyya related that when he arrived in North Africa, "he asked Ibn ᶜAṭiyya, the secretary" of the Almohad rulers, why no Christians, Jews, synagogues, or churches were to be seen in the Maghrib. Ibn ᶜAṭiyya explained that after ᶜAbd al-Mu'min, the Almohad ruler, took Marrakesh in 1147, he invited the Jewish and Christian inhabitants to a theological discussion. When the talking was over, he offered them the choice between "Islam or death," although at the same time allowing them the option of disposing of their property and leaving the country; the choice would therefore not in fact have been between Islam and death, but between Islam and exile. "Most of the Jews dissimulated Islam and held on to their property, while the Christians, with the exception of a few who converted to Islam, moved to [non-Muslim] Spain." All "synagogues and cloisters" in the land were destroyed, and, Ibn Ḥamwiyya informed the questioner, "no polytheist [that is, Christian] or nonbeliever has publicly exhibited his disbelief" from that time forward until 1204, when "I left the Maghrib."[47] The story unfortunately has a weak link. Ibn Ḥamwiyya was born in 1175 or 1176, whereas Ibn ᶜAṭiyya, the supposed informant, fell into disgrace and was put to death by his Almohad masters eighteen years earlier, in 1158.[48]

We thus have a report, Ibn al-Athīr's, of compulsory conversion under pain of death, but it is limited to a single locality. Of the other reports in Muslim writers, one describes the alternatives as having been death, conversion, or exile. The second relates that Muslim territory had been cleansed of the Jews and Christians but does not tell just how the cleansing was achieved. Scholars studying the Almohad period have not uncovered a single official Almohad document that either decrees compulsory conversion to Islam or imposes a choice between exile and conversion.[49]

[45] Ibn ᶜIdhārī al-Marrākushī, *Al-Bayān al-Mughrib*, trans. A. Huici Miranda (Tetuan 1953) 1.204.

[46] E. Lévi-Provençal, *Documents inédits d'histoire almohade* (Paris 1928) iii. Fattal, *Le statut légal des non-Musulmans* (n. 21 above) 173, doubts Marrākushī's report.

[47] Munk, "Notice sur Joseph ben-Iehouda" 42–44. Dhahabī also quotes the report of al-Marrākushī which I give in the previous paragraph.

[48] Corcos, "*Yeḥasam shel Shalliṭe ha-al-Muwaḥadun*" 143. Ibid., 141, note, summarizes negative evaluations of Dhahabī's reliability.

[49] Abumalham, "La conversión según formularios notariales" (n. 21 above) 78; M. García-

There is finally the biographical dictionary of al-Qifṭī. It too speaks of Almohad efforts to force Jews to convert to Islam and it moreover reports that Maimonides himself had been one of those who complied. Qifṭī's report is of no small moment and it is my reason for treating the Almohad persecution at such length. If it is correct, the author of the most important medieval code of Jewish law and the most influential medieval Jewish philosopher, a man who left his imprint on all subsequent Jewish religious law and much subsequent Jewish thought, had once apostatized and lived as a Muslim.

Qifṭī's entry on Maimonides relates the following: ᶜAbd al-Mu'min, the Almohad ruler, set a date for the departure from his territories of all Jews and Christians who refused to convert to Islam; and he declared that anyone remaining after the announced date would forfeit life and property. Jews and Christians who had few ties departed, whereas those who were concerned about property and family "exhibited the external guise of Islam, while hiding their disbelief." "Moses the son of Maimon" chose the latter course. He publicly lived the life of a Muslim, reading the Quran and reciting Muslim prayers, until he was able to put his affairs (*aṭrāf*) in order. He then left Spain with his family, traveled to Egypt, and reassumed the identity of a Jew. At the end of Maimonides' life, a Muslim jurist from Spain by the name of Abū al-ᶜArab b. Maᶜīsha arrived in Egypt, recognized him, and accused him of having "accepted Islam in Spain." Maimonides' patron in the sultan's court rescued him—recidivism from Islam being punishable by death[50]—by declaring: "When a man is coerced, his acceptance of Islam is not legally binding."[51] It is to be observed that, as in Ibn Ḥamwiyya's report, the decree described by Qifṭī was a choice between conversion and exile, not conversion under pain of death. Maimonides is therefore represented as having accepted the Muslim faith not under the threat of the sword and in order to save his skin, but—notwithstanding the family's status in the community and its long history of religious leadership—to save his property as well as out of family considerations. Later he would himself write that anyone who lives in a land where he is prevented from observing the Jewish religion must abandon family and possessions and flee into the desert.[52]

There are grounds for questioning Qifṭī's reliability. A highly regarded French scholar has found him to have been not merely a plagiarist—a venial offense in the

---

Arenal, "Rapports entre groupes dans la péninsule ibérique," *Revue du monde musulman et de la Méditerraneé* 63–64 (1992) 95–96, called to my attention by D. Wasserstein of Tel Aviv University, who gave me the benefit of other valuable observations as well.

[50]Fattal, *Le statut légal des non-Musulmans*" (n. 21 above) 164–68. Abumalham, "La conversión según formularios notariales" (n. 21 above) 74, 76.

[51]Qifṭī, *Ta'rīkh al-Ḥukamā'*, ed. J. Lippert (Leipzig 1903) 317–19. English translation of the entry on Maimonides: B. Lewis, *Islam* (New York 1974) 2.189–92. On the validity of forced conversions to Islam, see above, p. 10.

[52]Maimonides, *Epistle to Yemen* (n. 24 above) 34; English translation [vii].

Middle Ages—but a slovenly one to boot.[53] In his story of Maimonides' conversion to Islam, Qifṭī seems to say that Maimonides moved directly from Spain to Egypt; in fact, as will appear, the family first spent time in North Africa. In other parts of Qifṭī's entry on Maimonides he records a date for Maimonides' death that is out of harmony with the date given by the medieval Hebrew sources and he shows himself to be completely confused about Maimonides' writings on the subject of resurrection of the dead.[54]

The conversion to Islam of a prominent religious judge and his family in Cordova would, one should expect, have left its mark. Maimonides had bitter personal enemies in Egypt as well as ideological foes throughout the Jewish world, and there were those who would have clapped their hands in glee at the opportunity of undercutting his reputation and besmirching his name. Yet no information about the conversion of the Maimon family or of the Abū al-ᶜArab b. Maᶜīsha accusation is known to have penetrated Jewish circles; no medieval Jewish writer ever hints at anything of the sort. Qifṭī, for his part, does not name his source for the story of Maimonides' conversion to Islam, an event that would have occurred more than half a century prior to the time he was writing. If members of Maimonides' family had known of Maimonides' apostasy, they would hardly have made it public, since disclosure could endanger their lives as well as his.[55] Even after Maimonides' death, such a disclosure would have placed his survivors in danger. It would also have caused acute embarrassment for the family within the Jewish community, and those were not days in which people rivaled one another in making distasteful secrets about themselves and their closest relatives public. Maimonides' devoted student Joseph ben Judah was an acquaintance of Qifṭī's—and had himself experienced the taste of Almohad rule[56]—but it is scarcely imaginable that he

[53]R. Blachère, "Une source de l'histoire des sciences chez les arabes," *Hespéris* 8 (1928) 359–61. Blachère adduces two instances where Qifṭī lifts articles on the same man out of two unacknowledged sources and where, since the subject's name was spelled differently in the two sources, he converts what are in fact articles on the same man into separate entries on two supposedly different men.

[54]Qifṭī, 319, gives 605 of the Hegira chronology as the year of Maimonides' death, and that corresponds to 1208–1209, whereas the best medieval Hebrew source gives 1204 as the year. He writes that Maimonides composed a treatise denying resurrection but withdrew it in the face of criticism, reserving it for the eyes of those who agreed with him. The statement is an inversion of what actually happened: Maimonides' remarks on resurrection elicited criticism, and as a consequence of the criticism he composed a treatise insisting that he did in fact believe in the resurrection of the body.

[55]Fattal, *Le statut légal des non-Musulmans* 169; M. Abumalham, "La conversión según formularios notariales" 74, 76.

[56]Joseph was born in Ceuta, North Africa, and Qifṭī, 392, writes that "when the Jews and Christians in those lands were forced to convert to Islam or go into exile, Joseph hid his religion" until he was able to flee to the East. There is an anachronism even here, since when Joseph was born, the Almohads already controlled Ceuta. At all events, Joseph would hardly have told his Muslim acquaintance that he had actually converted to Islam. Qifṭī's entry on Joseph ben Judah is

would betray his master. Moreover, if Joseph were the source for Qifṭī's information on Maimonides, the errors in the entry on Maimonides should have been avoided.

As for Abū al-^{c}Arab b. Ma^{c}īsha, a fourteenth-century Arabic historian has a different account. He portrays Abū al-^{c}Arab b. Ma^{c}īsha not as a legal scholar but as a theologian and a poet. And he relates that Ibn Ma^{c}īsha once aided a Jew named Abū Mūsā in the Maghrib and then, in 1189, attempted to denounce the same man in Egypt; the Jew Abū Mūsā was saved, when Ibn Ma^{c}īsha was murdered. The later account differs from Qifṭī's in regard to Ibn Ma^{c}īsha's profession and the name of the Jew whom he tried to denounce. Nor does it mention the motif of conversion to Islam, although that is perhaps implied. The fourteenth-century historian, as happens, commands no more credibility than Qifṭī does.[57]

Qifṭī's story could therefore be his own conjecture or reconstruction, growing out of reports reaching the East of Almohad policy toward Jews and Christians taken together with tales about Abū al-^{c}Arab b. Ma^{c}īsha, who turned up in Egypt and denounced Maimonides or someone with a similar name.

A more guarded version of the report that Maimonides converted to Islam is found in another Muslim historian, Ibn Abī Uṣaybi^{c}a, who was active in Egypt a generation after Qifṭī and who had the original version of Qifṭī's work before him. Ibn Abī ^{c}Uṣaybi^{c}a writes: "It has been said that Maimonides converted to Islam in the West [*maghrib*], that he learned the Quran by heart, and that he occupied himself with Muslim law."[58] If Ibn Abī ^{c}Uṣaybi^{c}a was using the term *maghrib* in the proper Arabic sense, his account conflicts with Qifṭī's; for in Arabic geographical parlance *maghrib* designates western North Africa, whereas Qifṭī reported that Maimonides converted to Islam not in North Africa but in Spain. Apart from that, the notion of Maimonides' having memorized the Quran and studied Muslim law lacks the ring of truth. Maimonides never reveals familiarity with either subject. When he once does have occasion to quote from the Quran, he represents what he quotes not as Quranic, but instead as something that "they," that

---

translated by Munk, "Notice sur Joseph ben-Iehouda" (n. 44 above) 14–18.

[57]The historian is Dhahabī, one of whose anachronisms was pointed out above, p. 16. I have relied on the summary in S. Munk, "Moses ben Maimon," *Archives israélites* 12 (1851) 329–30. Dhahabī writes that Ibn Ma^{c}īsha aided Abū Mūsā in the Maghrib when the latter's "blood was permitted," that is, when he was for some reason declared an outlaw; that Ibn Ma^{c}īsha was subsequently denounced, apparently for the aid he extended to the outlaw; that he fled to Egypt with the intent of denouncing Abū Mūsā there; but that he was murdered in Egypt in 1189. Maimonides left the Maghrib before 1168. If Ibn Ma^{c}īsha had to flee because he aided Maimonides and if he traveled to Egypt in order to seek vengeance, he should surely should have been able to complete the journey before 1189. Munk tried to harmonize Dhahabī's story with Qifṭī's by speculating that Ibn Ma^{c}īsha at first regarded Maimonides as a genuine Muslim and later decided to denounce Maimonides after he learned that he was living as a Jew in Egypt.

[58]Ibn Abī Uṣaibi^{c}a, *^{c}Uyūn al-Anbā'* (Beirut 1965) 582. Translated in A. Bar-Sela et al., "Moses Maimonides' Two Treatises on the Regimen of Health," *Transactions of the American Philosophical Society* n.s. 54.4 (1964) 3–4.

is, the Muslims, "literally say"; the quotation turns out to be a conflation of verses from two separate chapters of the Quran.[59] During the time in which he was supposedly memorizing the Islamic holy book and occupying himself with Islamic law, Maimonides was in fact busy studying medicine and astronomy, acquiring a breathtaking mastery of rabbinic literature, writing commentaries on more than half of the Babylonian Talmud, carefully observing rabbinic court procedures, and even serving as an apprentice rabbinic judge.

Maimonides' purported conversion to Islam has been debated by historians, some rejecting the story, others accepting it.[60] Corroborating evidence for the story has been drawn from the composition referred to earlier which is attributed to Maimonides in the majority of manuscripts, which maintains that acknowledging Muhammad's apostleship is just a matter of reciting a few words, and which apologizes for Jews of the time who uttered the words. The author of the composition identifies himself with those whom he defends, speaking of "our shame" and using such language as "we and our fathers have sinned to the Lord God."[61] He apparently had done what he rationalizes in others, undergoing a *pro forma* conversion to Islam in order to save himself while doing his best to observe the Jewish religious commandments privately. If the attribution of the composition to Maimonides is correct, his conversion to Islam would gain considerably in verisimilitude. But there exist enough works carrying Maimonides' name which cannot be his to teach us that the appearance of his name on a text does not create even a presumption of his authorship. His authorship of this particular composition is rendered questionable by internal considerations, which I shall discuss in a later chapter.[62]

The most formidable hurdle facing anyone who hesitates to accept Qifṭī's report is the information in Jewish and Muslim sources to the effect that the Almohads permitted no Jews and Christians to reside anywhere in their territories. As already seen, the reports regarding Almohad policy toward the Jews do not harmonize fully. Ibn Ezra's elegy as well as the passages interpolated into it described destruction but no systematic forced conversion, although a reworking of the elegy does record one such instance. Chinks, we have seen, can be detected in the credibility of the medieval Muslim writers who testify to the complete extirpation of Jewish and Christian life from North Africa. And no Almohad document decreeing the conversion of Jews and Christians to Islam has been uncovered.

Still more significantly, evidence can be assembled to show that whatever inimical policies the Almohads may have implemented regarding Jews and Christians were not as thoroughgoing and constant as some of the Jewish and

[59] Maimonides, *Epistle to Yemen* (n. 24 above) 44 and note 62; English translation [ix].

[60] For a partial bibliography, see D. Yellin and I. Abrahams, *Maimonides, His Life and Works*, 3rd ed. (New York 1972) 162, note 9; 175, note 9*.

[61] *Iggeret ha-Shemad*, in Shailat, *Letters and Essays of Moses Maimonides* (n. 4 above) 43.

[62] Below, p. 509.

Muslim writers who have been quoted would lead us to believe. One piece of evidence for the continuation of Jewish life in Almohad lands is simply the presence of the Maimon family in the city of Fez in the middle of the twelfth century. Fez lay close to the center of Almohad power. According to reports cited earlier, no fewer than 100,000 people were killed in the city during the Almohad conquest, and the Jewish community was destroyed. If Jews were not permitted to live in any Almohad area, it was madness for the Maimon family to choose Fez of all places for their residence and to carry their considerable library of scriptural and rabbinic works directly into the lions' den.[63] An alternative was, moreover, available not only to Fez, but to life under the Almohads, if the Maimon family was coming from Spain. According to a contemporary source, those who "feared the word of the Lord" crossed the border from Muslim to Christian Spain, albeit with difficulty, and were rescued there by Jewish relief agencies.[64]

The two sources for the Maimon family's presence in Fez are no less illuminating. The first is the remark by Joseph Ibn cAqnin that the "apodictic sign" of Jewish perseverance in studying the Law despite Muslim persecutions had been the "appearance in Fez of the great scholar, our master Moses ben Maimon."[65] Maimonides, in other words, appeared on the scene wrapped in the reputation of an expert in Jewish Law; he himself tells us that he had written commentaries on two-thirds of the tractates of the Babylonian Talmud before he reached the age of twenty-three and hence when still living in Spain or Morocco.

The second source for the family's presence in Fez is a long circular letter of "consolation" issued from that city in 1159–1160 and carrying the name of Maimon, the father. The letter may be taken as genuine; the very famous, like Maimon's son Moses, and not the lesser known, like Maimon himself, had their names attached to works that they did not write. But the letter would retain much of its significance for our purpose even if its author were someone else. It was written in Arabic, although probably in Hebrew characters, and it addresses Arabic-speaking Jews who clearly suffered under the oppression of their gentile rulers, who were demoralized, and whose level of religious observance had fallen.[66] No

[63]In *Responsa* (n. 30 above) §289, Maimonides speaks of the "codices" of the Talmud that he had in the "West." Ibn Danan (n. 15 above), 30, relates that the Maimon family moved to Fez in order to enable Moses Maimonides to study with a certain R. Joseph ha-Cohen; R. Joseph was later martyred when the authorities "demanded that he convert [to Islam] because they were jealous of him"; and the Maimon family then left Fez. As was seen earlier, Ibn Danan is an unreliable witness, and Maimonides never mentions this Joseph ha-Cohen. Note that even if the story of the Jewish scholar's martyrdom after 1160 is correct, it would indicate that Jewish life had been possible in Fez up to that time.

[64]Abraham Ibn Daud, *The Book of Tradition* (n. 23 above) Hebrew section 70–71; English section 97–98.

[65]Above, p. 14.

[66]Untitled Judeo-Arabic original, ed. L. Simmons, *Jewish Quarterly Review*, o.s. 2 (1890) (paginated separately following p. 334) 4–5. English translation: "The Letter of Consolation of Maimun ben Joseph," trans. L. Simmons, *Jewish Quarterly Review*, o.s. 2 (1890) 71; Hebrew

mention is made, however, of forced conversions. Maimon, if he be accepted as the author, assures his coreligionists that God had not forsaken His chosen people or forgotten His ancient promises, despite the punishment He was bringing down upon Israel for its sins.[67] Eventually, God would redeem His people and elevate them to everlasting glory.[68] In the meantime, readers of the letter were exhorted to keep faith, to study the Law and observe the religious commandments, whether in public or secretly,[69] and to be especially careful with the daily prayers prescribed by rabbinic law.[70] The letter is not of a sort that could have been signed by anyone pretending to be a Muslim in a fanatically Muslim country, nor one that could have been published in a land where professing the Jewish religion was a capital offense.

Persons identifiable as Jews continued to live in Fez after the Maimon family departed: A Muslim author writing twenty years later complained about the wealth possessed by Jewish merchants in Fez and the surrounding towns.[71] It may be pertinent as well that a letter forged in Maimonides' name and a fabricated account of his life assume the presence of a Jewish community in Fez in the second half of the twelfth century. Writers who wanted to sound credible could thus locate a Jewish community there during the period that concerns us.[72]

The presence of a religious Jewish life in the Almohad Empire is confirmed by Maimonides himself. He speaks of the custom of the Jews of the "West," or, a few lines later, of "Spain," to "wash" themselves before studying the Law and praying, if they had experienced a seminal emission; of Jews who visited from Christian lands and, "when they saw us washing ourselves after seminal emissions, would laugh at us and say"—not: how could you have abandoned your faith and converted to Islam, but—"'you have learned from Muslim [rules of] cleanli-

---

translation: R. Maimon ha-Dayyan, *Iggeret ha-Neḥama*, trans. B. Klar (Jerusalem 1945) 14–15.

[67]Letter of Consolation, Judeo-Arabic original 1–3; English translation 67–69; Hebrew translation 8–11.

[68]Letter of Consolation, Judeo-Arabic original 23–24; English translation 98–99; Hebrew translation 56–57.

[69]Letter of Consolation, Judeo-Arabic original 5; English translation 71–72; Hebrew translation 15–16.

[70]Letter of Consolation, Judeo-Arabic original 6–9; English translation 73–74, 76–77; Hebrew translation 18–19, 22–25. What Maimon says concerning prayer reveals something about conditions at the time. He stresses that pious Jews must recite the central prayer of the Jewish liturgy—that is, the prayer consisting of eighteen (more precisely, nineteen) blessings and recited in a standing position—three times a day, but that if a Jew cannot do so, he should be careful to recite it at least once daily. Persons who either do not know the entire prayer or who find themselves in a situation where reciting it would be dangerous should recite one of the accepted shorter versions. Those who do not know the shorter versions in Hebrew should recite the entire prayer in Arabic translation.

[71]Corcos, "*Yeḥasam shel Shalliṭe ha-al-Muwaḥadun*" (n. 28 above) 158.

[72]A. Neubauer, "Documents inédits," *Revue des études juives* 4 (1882) 174, 179; A. Marx, "The Correspondence Between the Rabbis of Southern France and Maimonides," *Hebrew Union College Annual* 3 (1926) 349.

ness'";[73] of liturgical prayers "composed among us in Spain" which he had "listened to,"[74] undoubtedly in a geographical location where the Spanish liturgy was followed; of a judicial procedure that he "witnessed many times" and performed himself when he served as a young rabbinic judge in the "West";[75] of a variety of legal procedures that he remembers being put into practice in rabbinic courts in the West;[76] of a defect that would often occur, "among us, in the wines of the West";[77] of multiple codices of a tractate of the Babylonian Talmud that he consulted "in the land of the West";[78] of phylacteries belonging to him when he lived in the "West" and of those belonging to a certain Moroccan Jewish scholar who lived about the same time in the "West."[79] Everything he characterizes as having witnessed himself may be presumed to reflect conditions after the Almohad conquest of Cordova, since he was only ten or eleven years old at the time of the conquest.[80]

[73]Maimonides, Letter to Pinḥas of Alexandria, in Shailat, *Letters and Essays of Moses Maimonides* (n. 4 above) 437.

[74]Maimonides, *Book of Commandments=Sefer ha-Miṣwot*, edited and translated into Hebrew by J. Kafah (Jerusalem 1971) introduction, 5. English translation: Maimonides, *The Commandments*, trans. C. Chavel (London 1967) 2. 365.

[75]Maimonides, Commentary on the Mishna, *Nedarim* 10:8, on the releasing of personal vows: "As I witnessed many times, and performed the release procedure myself in the presence of my fathers, . . . the release of vows being for us in the cities [or: lands] of the West [*bilād al-maghrib*] a daily occurrence, there being no heresy in our lands [i.e., no Karaites, who were skeptical about the efficacy of the legal tactic]." As Maimonides describes the procedure, it seems to have required one main judge and two subordinate judges, both of whom remained silent except to confirm the actions of the main judge. He appears to be alluding to his own service as a subordinate judge.

[76]Commentary on the Mishna, *Shebu*^{c}*ot* 6:7, regarding the formulation of an oath administered to a certain kind of litigant: "I saw my father, of blessed memory, administer the oath with this formula a number of times." *Responsa* §365, regarding a husband who tried to avoid financial obligations to his wife by announcing plans to immigrate to Palestine and demanding that his wife either accompany him or forfeit her marriage portion (see BT *Ketubbot* 110b): "The way I saw courts in the West [*ma*^{c}*arab*] deciding. . . ." (Maimonides recommends a procedure that differs from the one he saw in the West and that better protects the wife's interest.) *Mishneh Torah*: *H. Sanhedrin* 6.9, speaks of a judicial procedure that "was a daily occurrence in Spain." In *Responsa* §70, Maimonides makes a statement regarding "all the rabbinic courts in the East and West that I know of or have heard about." The last two of these instances could be reports of things that Maimonides had heard but not personally seen. Also possibly pertinent is *Mishneh Torah*: *H. Mamrim* 5.15, where Maimonides speaks of a procedure that he had "always seen" followed in rabbinic courts.

[77]Maimonides, Commentary on the Mishna, *Menaḥot* 8:6. I am taking for granted that, for ritual reasons, the Maimon family would never have drunk wine manufactured by non-Jews.

[78]Maimonides, *Responsa* (n. 30 above) §289, p. 543.

[79]Maimonides, *Responsa* §289.

[80]According to rabbinic law, an adult is, with exceptions, not considered a reliable witness regarding what he observed when still a minor. See BT *Ketubbot* 28a–b; Maimonides, *Mishneh Torah*: *H.* ^{c}*Edut* 14.2–3.

When Maimonides specifies "Spain"[81] as the location of what he observed, one might make the gratuitous conjecture that after the fall of Cordova, the Maimon family moved to the eastern sector of Muslim Spain which had not yet fallen under Almohad control; such references might, in other words, conceivably reflect conditions outside the Almohad sphere. But when he describes, in connection with issues of rabbinic law, what "is always the practice among us, in all the cities [or: in the entire land (*bilād*)] of Muslim Spain [*al-Andalus*], . . ."[82] he must have more in view than a corner of the country which had not yet fallen to the Almohads.

His references to Jewish practices that he had personally witnessed in the "West" (*maghrib, gharb, ma^c^arab*)[83] are more frequent than those to practices that he reports from "Spain." In Arabic parlance, as has been noted, the term *maghrib* means western North Africa. In Maimonides' usage, the Hebrew *ma^c^arab* and the Arabic *maghrib*—as distinct, I believe, from *gharb*, another Arabic word for West—can cover Spain as well as North Africa,[84] and consequently some of his

[81]See Commentary on the Mishna, *Pesaḥim* 2:2: "The custom among us in the Spanish peninsula is to eat" bread baked by a non-Jew. *Responsa* §299 speaks of "the common custom in the cities of Spain"; there, however, he could be referring to a custom that he knew only by report or through reading.

[82]*Responsa* §218, p. 387, regarding the sanctioning by rabbinic courts of the remarriage of women who had been twice widowed; see below, p. 39. In Maimonides, Commentary on the Mishna, *Baba Batra* 3:3, *bilād* plainly means "cities." *Mishneh Torah*: *H. Ḥanukka* 4.3, describes the manner in which candles are, or were, lit on the Hanukkah holiday, in "all our cities in Spain."

[83]Maimonides, *Responsa* §154: "All Torah scrolls in the West" are written according to a certain style, with the plain implication that Maimonides had seen such scrolls. *Responsa* §156, on permitting gentiles to bake bread for Jews on a Jewish festival: "That is what I saw [done by] all the scholars of the West who preceded me." *Responsa* §288, of a certain wedding custom: "This is the way it was done in our city in the West [*ma^c^arab*]; . . . Therefore the great scholars in our cities used to . . . . But as for what we [i.e., I] saw in Egypt . . . is plainly an error." *Responsa* §113, on a question of festival liturgy: "All the scholars of the West [*ma^c^arab*] followed this procedure." *Mishneh Torah*: *H. Shabbat* 29.14, regarding the types of wine that may be used in the blessing inaugurating the Sabbath: "This is the way we decide in the *entire* West." *H. Ḥobel* 8.11 speaks of legal procedures that were followed "at all times in the cities of the West." *H. Naḥalot* 6.12: The legal "custom in the West [*ma^c^arab*] is always" to disinherit Jews who convert to another religion. *H. Ḥobel* 3.6 speaks of legal decisions that were made "regularly among us in Spain." Some of these instances could be procedures that Maimonides heard about and did not himself witness. See also the passages cited by I. Friedlaender, *Arabisch-Deutsches Lexikon zum Sprachgebrauch des Maimonides* (Frankfurt 1902) xviii, note 1. Commentary on the Mishna, *Baba Batra* 10:1 and *^c^Uqṣin* 2:6, describe bits of realia "among us in the *maghrib*," and passages in the *Mishneh Torah* sometimes describe realia among "us in the *ma^c^arab*" which are not specifically Jewish.

[84]Maimonides, *Responsa* §294, p. 552 (*ma^c^arab*). S. Goitein, *Mediterranean Society* 1 (Berkeley 1967) 43, testifies to the broad sense of the term *maghrib*, and J. Blau, "At Our Place in al-Andalus," *Perspectives on Maimonides*, ed. J. Kraemer (Oxford 1991) 294, also makes a case for the broad sense of the term. In *Mishneh Torah*: *H. Tefilla* 11.5; *H. Ḥameṣ* 5.3, 7; *H. Issure Bi'a* 11.5, the Hebrew term *ma^c^arab* excludes Spain while covering, by implication, all of North

statements about conditions in the "West" could again conceivably have in view the small area of non-Almohad Muslim Spain. Others are free of any possible ambiguity. He writes, for example, that "in Spain and the West [*maᶜarab*] . . . we never" performed a certain procedure when examining the lungs of a slaughtered animal in order to determine whether it was ritually fit for consumption.[85] Again: A certain religious "practice among us"—here a private one—was "something well-known and commonly done in all of the West [*al-gharb*] and Spain."[86] By distinguishing the West from Spain, he shows that he is talking about western North Africa; he therefore must be describing Jewish religious behavior that he witnessed in Almohad territories. In writing to one questioner, he compares the legal issue before them with one faced "daily" by unlettered but pious Jewish merchants "in all the cities [or: the entire land (*bilād*)] of the West [*gharb*]": At inns, gentile wayfarers would deliberately drop non-kosher food into the Jewish merchants' pots. The legal decision at which Maimonides arrives is the practice followed, he says, by the unlettered "in the presence of all the scholars of the West [*maᶜarab*]."[87] His insistence on all the cities and all the scholars—that is to say, the rabbinic judges—of the West shows again that he is not talking exclusively about a non-Almohad corner of Spain. And even should one choose to stretch a point and suppose that each of the Jewish merchants he refers to was a crypto-Muslim, their consultation with rabbinic judges and the latter's decision were public Jewish acts.

Sijilmasa was a North African city where, when Maimonides was still a child, the Jewish community had reportedly been liquidated, with the inhabitants being offered the choice of converting to Islam or being put to death and the local rabbi leading those who capitulated.[88] Yet a letter of Maimonides' written around 1190 recalls a quarrel he once had with the rabbinic judge of Sijilmasa;[89] if Sijilmasa had a rabbinic judge, it must have had a Jewish community. On another occasion, Maimonides mentions that after his father's death, he received letters of condolence "from the end of the West [*maᶜarab*] and from Christian lands, a journey of several months."[90] We might perhaps again contemplate the gratuitous conjecture that the part of the West from which the messages came was a non-Almohad corner of Spain, although the expression "end of the West" hardly fits that hypothesis. But

---

Africa, including Egypt.

[85]*Mishneh Torah*: *H. Sheḥiṭa* 11.11.

[86]Maimonides, *Responsa* §185. He is explaining that the wearing of a woolen garment on top of a linen garment does not fall under the scriptural prohibition against wearing garments woven out of wool and linen; see Deuteronomy 22:11. Commentary on the Mishna, *ᶜUqṣin* 3:2, also distinguishes between *al-gharb* and Spain.

[87]Maimonides, *Responsa* §143.

[88]Above, p. 10.

[89]Letter to Joseph ben Judah, in Moses ben Maimon, *Epistulae*, ed. D. Baneth (Jerusalem 1946) 90.

[90]Letter to Japhet, in Shailat, *Letters and Essays of Moses Maimonides* (n. 4 above) 229.

when he states that his *Book of Commandments* had reached "the end of the West [*ma^c^arab*] and the cities of Christian Europe,"[91] the purport is clear. Since all of Muslim Spain was firmly under Almohad control by the time he composed the book, "the end of the West," even if taken to refer to Spain, can have only Almohad territory in view. The *Book of Commandments*, a Jewish book par excellence, thus circulated in Almohad territory. The circulation of Maimonides' rabbinic works in Almohad lands is also confirmed by Joseph Ibn ^c^Aqnin, who knew of all of Maimonides' main works and explicitly writes that Maimonides' code of rabbinic law had reached him in Morocco.[92]

It may be observed in passing that whatever Maimonides meant by the expression "end of the West"—whether Spain, Fez, or a location even further to the west—he is speaking of an area where he had once lived. For at a certain point he describes a form of magic that he had "seen in the furthest West [*maghrib*]"[93] and at another, to the manufacturing of a kind of container "to be found among us in the furthest West [*gharb*]."[94]

Correspondence received by Maimonides when he was living in Egypt further supplements the picture. A legal question sent to him for adjudication concerns a Jewish trader who had recently traveled to Tunis on business,[95] and another question concerns a Jewish trader who had traveled to "Tripoli in the West [*gharb*]" in either 1201 or 1202.[96] Both Tunis and Tripoli were under Almohad rule, yet Jews, we here find, were allowed to visit on business. Still another letter, written after 1177, is labeled in the manuscript as "one of the [legal] questions that the people of the West [*ma^c^arab*] addressed to Moses the son of Maimon."[97] At the time, the entire West, whether Muslim Spain or western North Africa, was in Almohad hands.

A final fragment that deserves a place in the mosaic we are fashioning is the comment of a certain Sheshet, the prince, a well-educated Jew who lived in Christian Spain and stepped forward at the beginning of the thirteenth century to defend Maimonides against criticisms of his code of Jewish law and attacks on his orthodoxy. Sheshet reports that he had himself heard a "scholar" in the retinue of the king of Marrakesh take pride in having studied "science [*ḥokma*] with "the Jewish scholar Abū ^c^Imrān ben ^c^Abd Allāh," that being one of the ways

[91] Maimonides, *Responsa* §447.

[92] Joseph Ibn ^c^Aqnin, *Commentarius in canticum canticorum* (n. 34 above) 142–43, 398–99.

[93] *Book of Commandments* (n. 74 above), neg. §31, p. 197.

[94] Commentary on the Mishna, (n. 16 above) *Kelim* 2:1; 6, pp. 55–56.

[95] Maimonides, *Responsa* §87, pp. 135–36.

[96] Maimonides, *Responsa* §88. The ship in which the man was traveling was impounded for political reasons, and his return had been delayed. The question addressed to Maimonides and his answer are translated by S. Goitein, *Mediterranean Society* 3 (Berkeley 1978) 66–68 .

[97] Maimonides, *Responsa* §271. The question refers to Maimonides' Code, which was finished in 1177 or 1178. The questioner in §162 refers to what he heard about the manner in which scrolls of the Law are produced in the West.

Maimonides' name was written in Arabic.[98] The report does not say whether the Muslim in question studied with Maimonides when the latter was still a young man living in Morocco or subsequently, after Maimonides had settled in Egypt. But it does establish that in the later years of the Almohad kingdom a Muslim in the royal court could not merely divulge but also take pride in having studied with a Jewish teacher, and that Maimonides was known unambiguously as a Jew.

We see, then, that after the accession of the Almohads, Jewish religious usages were practiced in various parts of their empire, rabbinic judges were active and ritual questions could be brought to them for adjudication, rabbinic studies could be pursued in Fez, a composition encouraging Jewish readers to be firm in their faith and fulfill their religious obligations could be disseminated from the same city, rabbinic books were imported and disseminated, local and foreign Jewish merchants engaged in trade, Jews living in Almohad lands were in correspondence with their brethren elsewhere, and difficult questions of rabbinic law could be sent from within the empire to an expert residing outside.

Statements about Christians' not being allowed to reside anywhere in Almohad territories have to be qualified as well, for Italian and French merchants are known to have traded in Almohad areas.[99] Foreign Christians at least could thus raise their heads among the Almohads.

There is, in sum, ample evidence from diverse sources that Jews as well as Christians—or at least foreign Christians—led an open Jewish or Christian life under the Almohads, although not necessarily without harassment. The Jewish and Muslim reports of ultimatums presented to Jews and Christians—Islam or death—and the portrayal of a land wholly cleansed of professing Jews and Christians consequently reflect local and temporal vicissitudes or are hyperbole. They do not permit an a priori inference about anyone's behavior. As for the only explicit source for Maimonides' conversion to Islam, namely, the reworking of Qifṭī's biographical dictionary[100]—a source that has Maimonides converting not to save his life but for the crasser motive of salvaging his property—it reveals itself to be an unreliable witness.

The foregoing by no means proves that Maimon and his son never uttered the formula whereby a person is transformed from a non-Muslim into a Muslim

[98] A. Marx, "Texts by and about Maimonides," *Jewish Quarterly Review* 25 (1935) 409, 417. In one spot, the writer treats Maimonides as still living, but elsewhere he, or a later copyist, places a tag after Maimonides' name indicating that he was no longer alive; see Marx, "Texts" 408.

[99] P. Boissonnade, "Les relations commercials de la France méridionale avec l'Afrique du Nord," *Bulletin de la section de géographie: Comité des travaux historiques et scientifiques* 44 (1929) 7–8; H. Krueger, "Genoese Trade with Northwest Africa," *Speculum* 8 (1933) 377–95 (brought to my attention by Corcos, "*Yeḥasam shel Shalliṭe ha-al-Muwaḥadun*" [n. 28 above] 149–51).

[100] A later Arabic legendary account of Maimonides' conversion to Islam is published by D. Margoliouth, "The Legend of the Apostasy of Maimonides," *Jewish Quarterly Review*, o.s. 13 (1901) 539–41. Margoliouth points out a blatant anachronism in the account.

according to Islamic law. It by no means proves that they never disguised themselves as Muslims when they found themselves in danger. But it does show that no credible arguments have been mustered for their having performed either of those two acts. Maimonides' conversion to Islam must therefore be viewed as unproved at best. Indeed, there is no evidence that the Maimon family was ever touched in any way by the Almohad religious persecutions.

Apart from the information that Maimonides was born in Cordova, that he was present in Fez, and that his father wrote a long circular letter from there in 1159–1160 when Maimonides was about twenty-two years old, little can be said about specific locations in which he spent the first three decades of his life. What is certain is only that he lived in both Spain and North Africa after he was old enough to act as a perceptive observer of rabbinic law and to have been accepted as a serious student of medicine. He has been seen to write confidently about rabbinic legal procedures and customs that he saw in both countries, and he also refers to masters of the art of medicine with whom he studied in both.[101]

Some time before 1167–1168, Maimonides put the West and its unpleasantness behind him, visited Palestine with his father and brother, and settled in Egypt. Whatever the reason may have been for the family's choosing Egypt as its new home, the consequence was the immediate ascendance of Maimonides' star. His life could easily have taken a different course had the family chosen a center of rabbinic scholarship, where he would have been one among several, rather than Egypt, where he was one of a kind.

That Maimonides had settled in Egypt by 1167–1168 is established by the passage quoted earlier from the conclusion of his Commentary on the Mishna;[102] that he could not have settled there much before 1164 is apparent from a letter written no earlier than Spring 1194, in which he speaks of having lived in Egypt for about thirty years;[103] and that he was a recognized figure in Egypt by 1169 appears from yet another document, written there in 1169, wherein he acts in a leading communal capacity.[104] The trip to Palestine is known from a letter that

[101]Regarding his medical education, see Maimonides, *On Asthma*, ed. and trans. G. Bos (Provo 2002,) chapter 13, §§33, 38; medieval Hebrew translation: Moshe ben Maimon, *On Hemorrhoids*, *On the Increase of Physical Vigor*, *On Asthma*, ed. S. Muntner (Jerusalem 1965). *Medical Aphorisms* (*Pirqe Moshe*), ed. S. Muntner (Jerusalem 1959) 8, §69; 22, §35; 24, §40. English translation, with same chapter divisions: *The Medical Aphorisms of Moses Maimonides*, trans. F. Rosner and S. Muntner, 2 vols. (New York 1970–1971). Munk, "Moses ben Maimon" (n. 57 above) 325–26.

[102]Above, p. 9.

[103]Maimonides, *Responsa* (n. 30 above) §233, deals with a string of quarrels between a man and his wife in Alexandria. A document arising out of the sad affair is dated Spring 1194. Maimonides afterwards wrote instructions about how the issue should be handled—instructions that were wholly ignored; see *Responsa*, p. 419—and in the course of doing so, mentions having "been in Egypt about thirty years"; see *Responsa*, p. 424.

[104]Below, p. 52.

Maimonides wrote years later to Japhet ben Elijah, a rabbinic judge in Acre who had extended hospitality to the Maimon family during its stay in the Holy Land. The letter says nothing about the visit beyond recalling, with a play on a verse in Psalms, that the three male members of the Maimon family and their host had "walked in the house of God [which may merely mean Palestine] in awe."[105] No mention is made of the female members of the family. It would certainly have been sensible to leave them in Egypt on the way to Palestine, since the crusaders controlled most of the Holy Land, and travel in the country was dangerous.

Maimonides' Commentary on the Mishna and his responsa, that is, his answers to questions of rabbinic law which were sent to him for adjudication, advice, or confirmation, occasionally mention objects and customs that he saw in Palestine.[106] But they disclose nothing about the visit—neither the itinerary Maimonides followed on his way from North Africa to Palestine and Egypt, the date and length of his stay in Palestine, nor his activities there.

Two further sources volunteer a few details. The fifteenth-century Saadia Ibn Danan writes that "Rabbi Maimon fled with his two sons to Alexandria, Egypt, and from there went up to Jerusalem."[107] The other report suggests 1165 as the date and implies that Maimonides took a different route, traveling not first to Alexandria, but directly from "the religious persecution" to "Acre."[108] The former itinerary

[105]Letter to Japhet, in Shailat, *Letters and Essays of Moses Maimonides* (n. 4 above) 230. I have translated the phrase from Psalms 55:15, quoted in the passage, following Maimonides, *Mishneh Torah*: *H. Bet ha-Beḥira* 7.5. In his *Epistle to Yemen* (n. 24 above) 2; English section [i], Maimonides speaks of the time when he "left the West" and visited God's "Holy Place."

[106]Commentary on the Mishna, *Soṭa* 2:4, *Bekorot* 4:4, *Para* 3:9; *Responsa* §320.

[107]Ibn Danan (n. 15 above) 30b.

[108]The source is a note attached to the commentary on tractate *Rosh ha-Shana* referred to above, pp. 6–7, the same commentary to which the note carrying the name of Maimonides' grandson David and giving the date of Maimonides' birth is attached. The manuscript containing the commentary and the two notes avers that the commentary itself was originally copied "from the hand of R. Moses, the light of the exile," and that the note we are now interested in was found "at the end of the book, in the hand of the rabbi and in his words." The note reads: "On Saturday night, the fourth day of the month of Iyyar, I embarked by sea, and on Saturday, the tenth of Iyyar, in the year and [*sic*] 25 of the creation chronology [that is, on the assumption that the events occurred in Maimonides' lifetime, Iyyar, 4925, i.e., Spring 1165], a wave arose, threatening to sink us, and there was great fury in the sea. I vowed to fast on those two days, to treat them as a full communal fast [that is, as a fast extending from sunset of one day to darkness of the next and involving restrictions beyond food and drink, in contrast to a personal fast, which extends from dawn to dark and is restricted to food and drink; see BT *Ta^{c}anit* 12b] together with my household and all those affiliated with me, and to command my children to do so forever. . . . On Saturday night, the third day of the month of Sivan, I disembarked in peace and we arrived at Acre. I had escaped the religious persecution and we had reached Palestine! I vowed that that day would be a day of joy and feasting . . . for me and my household forever. . . . On Tuesday, the fourth day of the month of Marḥeshvan, in the year 26 of the creation chronology [that is, on the assumption that the events occurred in Maimonides' lifetime, Marḥeshvan, 4926, i.e., the Fall of 1165] we left

would certainly have been more practical, since sea transportation from Morocco to Alexandria would be much easier to arrange than passage directly from Morocco to Acre, if the latter was at all available.[109] But it happens that neither of the two sources is reliable.[110] We must therefore make do with the unadorned fact of a stay in Palestine.

Acre to go up to Jerusalem, with the attendant danger. I entered the great holy house, and prayed in it on Thursday, the sixth day of the month of Marḥeshvan. On Sunday, the ninth day of the month, I left Jerusalem for Hebron to kiss the graves of my fathers [that is, the three patriarchs] in the cave. . . . I vowed that those two days, the sixth and ninth of Marḥeshvan, would be a holiday for me. . . . On Wednesday night [*sic*] and Tuesday, the twelfth day of Sivan, the Lord saw my affliction, and my brother arrived in peace." See *Jen Libanon* (n. 2 above) 1, which I corrected using Paris, Bibliothèque Nationale, Hebrew MS 336, 38b–39b. The passage is copied with small variants and without the last sentence, by E. Azkari, *Sefer Ḥaredim* (Jerusalem 1981) 253–54. Tz. Langermann was kind enough to examine microfilms of the other known manuscripts of the commentary on the tractate *Rosh ha-Shana* and he informed me that none of them has either the present note or the note written by Maimonides' grandson which was cited above, p. 7.

By stating that upon reaching Acre he escaped religious persecution, the writer implies that he came to Acre directly from a land—if Maimonides is the author, the land would be one of those ruled by the Almohads—where Jews were persecuted. The last sentence of the passage is obviously confused. But if we drop the words "Wednesday night and," the passage will say that the writer's brother arrived on Tuesday, the twelfth day of Sivan. In 1165, the twelfth day of Sivan fell on a Tuesday, whereas in 1166, it fell on a Saturday. Without the three offending words, the passage will accordingly say that the brother arrived nine days after the writer did, in the year 1165. Why the writer's brother would have traveled alone is unclear.

The preserved version of the note speaks of the years "25" and "26," and only the assumption that the events occurred in Maimonides' lifetime justifies fixing those years as 4925 and 4926. Two hundred years later, in 5125 and 5126 of the creation chronology, the days of the pertinent Jewish months fell on the same days of the week as in 4925 and 4926, and therefore the events of "25" and "26" could conceivably have occurred in 5125 and 5126, that is to say in 1365, instead. Other perpetrators would accordingly have to be credited with the religious persecution from which the author fled.

[109]Goitein, *Mediterranean Society* 1 (n. 84 above) 316–26, records a number of ship itineraries that he found in Geniza documents, and none describes a trip directly from Morocco to Acre.

[110]Ibn Danan's unreliability was pointed out above, p. 8. As for the second source, its credibility is impugned by the following considerations: The scribe who copied the note into the manuscript identifies the author as "R. Moses, the light of the exile," but the author of the note itself does not allude to his own identity. The manuscript states that the scribe copied both the note and the Commentary on *Rosh ha-Shana* from Maimonides' hand. Since the Commentary cannot be Maimonides'—see below, pp. 144–46—it follows that the note, which was in the same hand, also was not written by him. In the note, the writer says that he adopted certain days for himself and his offspring as "a full communal fast" in perpetuity. Maimonides, who was meticulous in his observance of talmudic prescriptions, but sometimes dismissive of posttalmudic ritual niceties, does not in his rabbinic code, *Mishneh Torah*: *H. Ta^{c}aniyyot* 1, recognize either personal fasts having the character of a communal fast, fasts accepted in perpetuity, or fasts that a person makes incumbent on his offspring. The note further states that the writer "entered the great

It can, nevertheless, be inferred that besides the trip to Palestine and to Egypt, Maimonides undertook other journeys between 1160 and 1167–1168. In the latter year, he completed his Commentary on the Mishna in Egypt, after laboring on it for seven years. He writes that completion of the Commentary was delayed and the work may contain errors because "there are mishna paragraphs for which I composed the commentary during the stages of a journey, and there are matters that I wrote down while on board ships [in the plural] on the high seas."[111] Authors bringing seven-year projects to a close do not cite a month or so at sea as an excuse for errors and for having failed to complete their work on time. Maimonides' travels during the period must therefore have included more than the trip to Palestine and then to Egypt.

When Maimonides reached Egypt, the country was still under the rule of the Shiite Fatimid dynasty that had seized power two centuries earlier, but the lamp of the Fatimids was rapidly going out. Two powerful and bellicose neighbors loomed to the northeast, the Crusader kingdom in Palestine and the Seljuk Turkic regime in Syria. Seljuk expeditionary forces visited Egypt several times in the 1160s, and in 1169 returned once more in response to Fatimid entreaties that they save the country from a Crusader invasion. The general in charge of the expeditionary force took along a nephew who had already accompanied him on previous occasions but who is reported to have joined the latest venture with reluctance; the nephew's name was Ṣalāḥ al-Dīn or Saladin. The Seljuks quickly accomplished the task for which they had been summoned and now they did not fold their tents and depart. Saladin's uncle died within a few months, and Saladin had himself inaugurated as the Fatimid vizier and de facto ruler. In 1171, when the last Fatimid monarch lay on his death bed, Saladin took formal control and restored Egypt to the Sunni Muslim fold.[112] He ruled until his death in 1193, spending half the time out of the country in military activity.

Maimon, Moses' father, died shortly after the family took leave of Japhet ben Elijah, the rabbinic judge of Acre, and prior to 1168.[113] Maimonides is reported to

---

holy house, and prayed in it," which appears to mean that he entered the temple premises. Maimonides would never have done so; see *Mishneh Torah*: *H. Bet ha-Beḥira* 7.7, and *H. Bi'at ha-Miqdash* 3.5. Some of the points made here were made by S. Eppenstein, "Moses ben Maimon," in *Moses ben Maimon*, ed. W. Bacher et al., 2 (Leipzig 1914) 24, note 1.

[111] Commentary on the Mishna, *Ṭohorot*, colophon.

[112] See A. Ehrenkreutz, *Saladin* (Albany 1972) 22–92.

[113] The most complete manuscript of the letter to Japhet ben Elijah, who was their host in Palestine, states that Maimon died a few months after the family parted from Japhet; see Maimonides' letter to Japhet in Shailat, *Letters and Essays of Moses Maimonides* (n. 4 above) 229. When Maimonides refers to his father in the Commentary on the Mishna, which was completed in 1167–1168, he employs a tag signifying that the father was no longer alive, but not the tag (see *Mishneh Torah*: *H. Mamrim* 6.5) signifying that his father had died within the previous twelve months. See the introduction to the Commentary 47 (where the tag is written as an addition or correction above the line); Commentary on *Shebu*ᶜ*ot* 6:7; Commentary on ᶜ*Eduyyot* 1:3, 4:7. A halakic responsum of Maimon's published by A. Freimann, "*Teshubot R.*

have stayed for a period in the city of Alexandria.[114] He settled, however, in Fustat, which was a short distance from the rulers' quarters in the new city of Cairo. The size of the Jewish population of Fustat-Cairo and of Egypt as a whole is uncertain, but in the modern conception it was not large. A Jewish traveler, Benjamin of Tudela, who passed through Egypt about the date when Maimonides arrived, states, according to one manuscript of his narrative, that the city had "around 7,000" Jews, while the reading in another—more problematic—manuscript of the narrative gives the smaller figure of 2,000.[115] The traveler does not say whether he meant to include all members of the community, only adult men, or perhaps only persons on the tax rolls. The fashion among historical demographers today is to set Jewish populations in medieval Islam at surprisingly low levels, and doubts have been expressed regarding even the smaller of the two figures offered by manuscripts of Benjamin of Tudela's account. Recent estimates—or, to be more precise, informed guesses, since the data on which they rest are very slim—set the Jewish population of Fustat-Cairo in Maimonides' time at from 1,500 to 4,000, and the total Jewish population of the country at from 10,000 to 20,000.[116]

The question how Maimonides supported himself can be answered only in part. Until 1177, he apparently did not have to concern himself about his livelihood. He relates that his brother David would "conduct business in the marketplace and earn money, while I sat in security."[117] Then tragedy struck. His brother drowned in the Indian Ocean when on a business trip, and one manuscript of the letter in which Maimonides refers to the accident indicates that it occurred approximately in

---

Maimon," *Tarbiz* 6 (1934–1935) 167, 174, answers a question that he had been asked concerning the city of Fustat and the response takes account of the city's topography. It would appear that Maimon was in Egypt when asked the question and when he answered, but there is no way of telling whether his presence there occurred before or after the trip to Palestine.

[114]Maimonides' opinion in *Responsa* §449, p. 729, appears to have been written in Alexandria. J. Faragi, a rabbi in Alexandria during the seventeenth century, asserts that Maimonides first lived in Alexandria before moving to Fustat; see Y. Kahana, *Meḥqarim be-Sifrut ha-Teshubot* (Jerusalem 1973) 37.

[115]Benjamin of Tudela, *Itinerary*, ed. and trans. M. Adler (London 1907), Hebrew Text 62; English translation 69–70.

[116]Arguments for the lower numbers are given by E. Ashtor, "Prolegomena to the Medieval History of Oriental Jewry," *Jewish Quarterly Review* 50 (1959) 57, 60; Ashtor, "The Number of Jews in Medieval Egypt," *Journal of Jewish Studies* 19 (1968) 12–13. D. Neustadt (Ayalon), "*Qawwim le-Toledot ha-Kalkala shel ha-Yehudim*," *Zion* 2 (1937) 221, sets the Jewish population of Egypt in the middle of the twelfth century at 20,000. N. Stillman, *The Jews of Arab Lands: A History and Source Book* (Philadelphia 1979) 48, arrives at a figure of 4,000 for the Jewish population—Rabbanite as well as Karaite—of Fustat.

[117]Letter to Japhet in Shailat, *Letters and Essays of Moses Maimonides* 230. Goitein discovered a letter from David Maimonides to his brother which was written when a business trip took David to the Sudanese coast of the Red Sea, and Goitein shows that the letter must have been written between 1169 and 1171. See Goitein, *Letters of Medieval Jewish Traders* (n. 6 above) 207–12.

1177.[118] There is additional evidence that from 1168, which was not long after Maimonides arrived in Egypt, until 1177 or 1178, he did not have the burden of earning his living. He worked during those years on his code of rabbinic law, and the task, he relates, occupied him "day and night" for the entire period;[119] the immensity of the enterprise and magnificence of the result show that the words are not hyperbolic. Maimonides later recalled that when his brother died he "had with him a large sum of money belonging to me, him, and others, and he left me with his widow and a small daughter."[120] From then on, Maimonides had the responsibility of supporting the family.

He served as a judge from the time that he arrived in Egypt but could not conceivably have accepted a regular salary for his rabbinic services. In his code of rabbinic law, he forbids any payment to judges apart from compensation for the exact amount of wages that they lose by temporarily leaving their usual occupation in order to attend to judicial proceedings. In this he follows a ruling of the Babylonian Talmud.[121] But uniquely among medieval rabbinic scholars, he goes further and construes rabbinic law as unequivocally prohibiting scholars from receiving any form of payment—apart from the aforementioned compensation to judges for lost wages—in exchange for their rabbinic knowledge. He viewed the prohibition as so fundamental, and its neglect on the part of his contemporaries so egregious, that he formulates it in his code with a burst of rhetoric, rather than in sober legal terms: Anyone who "undertakes to study the Law, to have no gainful employment, and to support himself through charity, profanes the divine name, shows contempt for the Torah, extinguishes the light of religion, brings evil upon himself, and removes his life from the world to come. For it is forbidden to derive any benefit from the words of the Law in this world." Whereupon he quotes a number of sayings from the classic rabbinic sources which reflect the same sentiment—sayings that, he laments, other commentators and codifiers "fling behind their backs" with the help of rationalizations.[122] Only the most brazen hypocrite could use language like that and still accept a regular salary for his own services as a rabbinic authority.

Notwithstanding his fulminations against scholars' being paid for their rabbinic scholarship, Maimonides does make the qualification that others are permitted, and indeed obliged, to assist a scholar by investing his money in business ventures,

[118]The manuscript of the letter to Japhet which was used by Shailat is dated in the first month of 1185 and states that the accident occurred "about eight years" earlier. The version of the letter in A. Lichtenberg, *Qobeṣ Teshubot ha-Rambam* (Leipzig 1859) 2.37b, has no date.

[119]Maimonides, *Responsa* (n. 30 above) 3.57.

[120]Letter to Japhet, in Shailat, *Letters and Essays of Moses Maimonides* 229–30.

[121]Maimonides, Commentary on the Mishna, *Bekorot* 4:6, and *Mishneh Torah*: *H. Sanhedrin* 23.5, following BT *Ketubbot* 105a.

[122]*Mishneh Torah*: *H. Talmud Torah* 3.10; Commentary on the Mishna, *Abot* 4:7. See also Commentary on the Mishna, *Nedarim* 4:3. Joseph Caro, *Kesef Mishneh, H. Talmud Torah* 3.10, is a rare instance where Caro categorically rejects Maimonides' legal opinion.

while the scholar stays home and studies.[123] He may accordingly have had businessmen help invest his funds after his brother died and in fact he is known to have had connections with Jewish merchants. In a letter to his former student Joseph ben Judah, he requests that Joseph, who was living in Syria, "make a reckoning" with a certain merchant when the latter arrives from India.[124] Another merchant, an Egyptian Jew, acknowledged on his deathbed that he owed Maimonides the sum of two and a half dinars and "also something else," for which Maimonides' word was to be accepted.[125] Whether the two merchants were conducting business for Maimonides' account can, of course, only be guessed. The approximate monthly salary of a workman in his day was from one and a half to two and a half dinars, while physicians serving royal patients would expect to receive a salary eight or more times as large.[126] The debt acknowledged by the Egyptian merchant on his deathbed was thus not especially large, but not negligible.

[123]Commentary on the Mishna, *Abot* 4:7; *Responsa* §325.

[124]Moses ben Maimon, *Epistulae* (n. 89 above) 70. What the manuscripts represent as a single letter is a rather long composition, extending some 2,000 words and touching on a number of disparate subjects. At the end it carries the date of Fall 1191. There is evidence indicating that it is not a single letter but is instead pieced together from at least two documents, whence it would follow that the date does not apply to all the parts. See: Z. Diesendruck, "On the Date of the Conclusion of the Moreh Nebukim," *Hebrew Union College Annual* 12–13 (1937–1938) 484–95 (evidence against the unity of the letter); Baneth, *Epistulae* 38–43 (a case for the letter's unity); A. Halkin, "*Sanegoreya* *ᶜal Sefer Mishneh Torah*," *Tarbiz* 25 (1956) 415–17, 422–23, a composition by a thirteenth-century writer which quotes from what it says Maimonides wrote to Joseph and which then introduces an additional quotation with the words: Maimonides "said to him in a different exchange of letters." The quotations that the writer reports come from two separate letters of Maimonides' are both found in the present composition, which the manuscripts and printed texts treat as a single letter.

J. Teicher, "Maimonides' Letter to Joseph ben Jehudah," *Journal of Jewish Studies* 1 (1948) 41, contended that the entire letter is spurious; but the details that it contains and the reference to it by the early thirteenth-century writer cited in the Halkin article testify to its essential authenticity. Teicher nevertheless does call attention to a genuine problem. The Arabic version of the letter, although not the two medieval Hebrew translations, has Maimonides say: In my Commentary on the Mishna, *Sanhedrin* 10:1, I clearly expounded the subject of resurrection, I enumerated those who have no place in the world to come, and I included among them the person who denies the resurrection of the dead. See *Epistulae* 66 (the Arabic text), and pp. 75 and 79 (the two Hebrew translations). In fact, Maimonides enumerated those who have no portion in the world to come and included among them the person who denies resurrection not in his Commentary on the Mishna but in his *Mishneh Torah*: *H. Teshuba* 3.6. The problematic passage in the Arabic version of the letter must therefore be regarded as an interpolation or a corruption. A small emendation will give: In the Commentary on the Mishna I clearly expounded the subject of resurrection; [elsewhere] I enumerated. . . ."

[125]S. Goitein, "The Moses Maimonides—Ibn Sanā' al-Mulk Circle," *Studies . . . in Honour of . . . David Ayalon* (Jerusalem 1986) 400, 405; *Mediterranean Society* 5 (n. 22 above) 445–47.

[126]E. Ashtor-Strauss, "Quelques indications sur les revenus dans l'orient musulman au haut moyen âge," *Journal of the Economic and Social History of the Orient* 2 (1959) 264–66,

The Arabic historian al-Qifṭi, by no means the most accurate of sources, reports that when Maimonides came to Egypt, he earned his living by trading in jewels and similar merchandise, that he taught science, that very soon after arriving in Egypt he was well-known as a physician but refused service with the Fatimid rulers, and that when the Fatimids were replaced by the Seljuks, the vizier al-Qāḍī al-Fāḍil became his patron and gave him an allowance.[127] Maimonides himself confirms that he had studied both the theory and practice of medicine before arriving in Egypt,[128] his intent presumably having been to prepare himself for the medical profession. Eventually, we know, he did develop a successful medical practice. But Qifṭī's indication that al-Fāḍil took Maimonides under his wing upon the accession of Saladin, in other words in the early 1170s, cannot stand.

First of all, Maimonides' labor "day and night" on his rabbinic code from 1167 to 1177 would not have been compatible with service as court physician; when he finally did receive such a position, he complained that it consumed a large portion of each day.[129] Second, around the year 1191, Maimonides wrote to Joseph ben Judah, who had seen his situation in Egypt and was now residing in Syria,[130] and he depicts his attendance as a physician on al-Fāḍil and others in Saladin's retinue as a recent, fortunate turn in his life. "I can inform you," he tells Joseph, "that I have achieved great fame in medicine among the nobles, such as the chief qāḍī, the emirs, and the house of the [vizier] al-Fāḍil, as well as other prominent people of the land, from whom one does not receive a penny."[131]

A medical composition of Maimonides' which was written in Egypt for a Muslim who suffered from a respiratory disorder suggests both that his medical skills were not fully recognized immediately upon his arrival in Egypt and that at the time when he wrote the composition, he was seeking employment as a physician. The composition is undated, but it is reasonable to assume that Maimonides wrote it no earlier than 1177 or 1178, when the intensive period of labor on his code of rabbinic law had come to a close. As we saw, it was when his brother died in approximately 1177 that the responsibility for supporting himself fell on him.

Maimonides already did have some medical experience at the time of writing the composition, for in it he mentions having treated an unnamed woman who likewise suffered from a respiratory condition and having followed her condition for at least three years after the treatment.[132] But a passage toward the end of the composition sounds very much like an oblique, and what to some tastes will be a rather gauche, application for employment. The passage stresses Maimonides' superiority to other medical practitioners while acknowledging that his medical skills fell short of

---

271–75.

[127] Qifṭī, *Ta'rīkh al-Ḥukamā* (n. 51 above) 318.

[128] Above, p. 28.

[129] See below, pp. 68–69.

[130] Moses ben Maimon, *Epistulae* (n. 89 above) 2.

[131] Moses ben Maimon, *Epistulae* 69.

[132] Maimonides, *On Asthma* (n. 101 above) chapter 12, §5.

perfection. Maimonides informs the addressee that he was not engaging in false modesty in making the acknowledgement, and stresses that he was not pursuing personal interest in all of this. He concludes by recommending his own medical counsel once again.

The passage begins by citing Hippocrates and Galen at length on the danger of engaging physicians who fall short of full competence and then continues: After you read what I have written so far, "you should not conclude that . . . I am the appropriate person for you to entrust with your body and soul. I call God as my witness that I fully realize that I am one of those who are not perfect in the art of medicine, who are terrified by it. . . . I, nonetheless, know myself better than others [know themselves] and can evaluate my knowledge and the knowledge of others better than someone can who is inferior to me in medical theory.

"I call God as my witness a second time, that the foregoing remarks were not made through humility. I am not imitating the style of erudite men who profess ignorance, although they are perfect [in knowledge], and who confess having accomplished little, although they are hard working. I am simply describing things as they are. I have made these comments lest you . . . fail to appreciate my counsel or suppose that it involves personal interest. I do not want you to take what I have said lightly and dismiss it."[133]

At all events, Maimonides clearly did serve members of the Muslim hierarchy as a physician from some point in the 1190s at the very latest. Such service presumably was remunerative, although, as Maimonides was seen to complain to his student Joseph, not every high-ranking patient took the trouble to pay for his medical care. It was common for Muslim rulers to have recourse to Jewish physicians,[134] and Maimonides' medical practice eventually penetrated into Saladin's court. Another of his letters, this one addressed to Samuel Ibn Tibbon and dated 1199, reports that he treated an unnamed "king [or: prince]" in Cairo as well as the endless ordinary people who came to his home in Fustat for treatment;[135] and a Muslim writer reports that Maimonides attended Saladin himself as a physician.[136] How much earlier than 1190 his practice of medicine started and when it became a significant source of his income remains in the realm of the unknown.

A supplementary source of income for Maimonides may have been the teaching of medicine. He is known to have had students in the subject;[137] a letter addressed

[133]*On Asthma*, chapter 13, §27.

[134]See M. Meyerhof, "The Medical Work of Maimonides" in *Essays on Maimonides*, ed. S. Baron (New York 1941) 270. S. Goitein, "The Medical Profession in the Light of the Cairo Geniza Documents," *Hebrew Union College Annual* 34 (1963) 179–80.

[135]Below, p. 69. It has been theorized that the letter as preserved is composite; see below, p. 70. If so, the date of 1199 may not apply to all of the parts.

[136]Below, p. 68.

[137]See the letter to Maimonides published and translated by J. Kraemer, "Six Unpublished Maimonides Letters from the Cairo Geniza," *Maimonidean Studies* 2 (1991) 73–80. Ibn Abī

to him by a wealthy man offered to pay generously to have Maimonides train the man's son in the medical art,[138] and in a letter to Joseph ben Judah, Maimonides proposes that Joseph turn to teaching medicine for his livelihood.[139]

The sole specific information we have regarding Maimonides' wife comes again from al-Qifṭī. He reports that Maimonides married the sister of a man named Abū Ma^cālī, who was a secretary in Saladin's court and who was in turn married to Maimonides' own sister.[140] There is ample evidence of a connection between the two men. A letter written to Maimonides by his brother David between 1169 and 1171 sends greetings to Bū ᶜAlī, plainly our Abū Maᶜālī, and to Bū Manṣūr;[141] Abū Maᶜālī' is known to have had a brother or half-brother named Abū Manṣūr.[142] A contemporary describes Abū ᶜAlī as "Rabbi [*rabbenu*] Moses' in-law [*ṣihr*]."[143] Maimonides writes to Joseph ben Judah that members of the Abū Maᶜālī family, whom Joseph knew from the period he had spent in Egypt, sent their greetings.[144] And a document from the Cairo Geniza sets the genealogies of the Maimonides and Abū Maᶜālī families side by side.[145]

Maimonides had a single son, Abraham, born, according to the best information, in 1186, when Maimonides was close to fifty years old.[146] A Muslim writer who met Abraham Maimonides when the latter was in his late forties describes him as a "tall, thin gentleman, pleasant company, well spoken, and an outstanding physician."[147] Scholars have speculated on the basis of one document or another that Maimonides had a daughter as well,[148] but the supposed evidence fails to support

---

Uṣaibiᶜa reports that his own father studied medicine with Maimonides; see Meyerhof, "The Medical Work of Maimonides" 270, note.

[138] See Kraemer, "Six Unpublished Maimonides Letters" 73–80. The fee is offered discreetly at the end. A different, undated letter written by a Jewish man who was apparently a newcomer in Fustat relates that he had met "Rabbi [*rabbenu*] Moses"—shown by another passage in the letter to be Maimonides—and discussed his desire to study medicine, that Rabbi Moses referred him to a different Jewish physician for instruction, and that when the man became ill, it was the other physician who diagnosed his malady and prescribed medication. See H. Isaacs, "An Encounter with Maimonides," in *Moses Maimonides, Physician, Scientist, and Philosopher*, ed. F. Rosner and S. Kottek (Northvale, N. J. 1993) 45, 47.

[139] Moses ben Maimon, *Epistulae* 68.

[140] Qifṭī, *Ta'rīkh al-Ḥukamā* (n. 51 above) 318.

[141] Letter from David Maimonides, in Goitein, *Letters of Medieval Jewish Traders* (n. 6 above) 211.

[142] Mann, *The Jews in Egypt and in Palestine* (n. 4 above) 2.319; Goitein, "Maimonides, Man of Action" (n. 16 above) 164.

[143] Isaacs, "An Encounter with Maimonides" 46, 48, and M. Friedman, "*Shene Ketabim Maimoniyyim*," in *Me'ah Sheᶜarim* (Twersky memorial volume) (Jerusalem 2001) 221.

[144] Moses ben Maimon, *Epistulae* (n. 89 above) 70–71.

[145] Mann, *The Jews in Egypt and Palestine* 2.319.

[146] The document published by Mann, *The Jews in Egypt and Palestine* 2.319, shows that Abraham was Maimonides' only son.

[147] Ibn Abī Uṣaibiᶜa, *ᶜUyūn al-Anbā* (n. 58 above) 583.

[148] For example, J. Münz, *Moses ben Maimon* (Frankfurt 1912) 321, and Freimann,

the conclusion. Descendants of Maimonides have not been traced beyond the beginning of the fifteenth century.[149]

Somewhat more is known of Maimonides' public activities in Egypt.

The Jewish community in Egypt, as in other Muslim countries, had its own judicial system, which applied rabbinic law to a full range of civil and religious matters—marriage, divorce, commercial relationships, religious observance—and which also tried to resolve the rare incidents of violence. No provisions had to be made for the ultimate violent crime, murder; murder was unknown in the Egyptian Jewish community.[150] The Jewish judges who staffed the courts may properly be called *rabbis*, since in Maimonides' world the term *rabbi* meant a rabbinic judge or rabbinic teacher.

Jews unwilling to be judged in a Jewish rabbinic court occasionally took their legal problems to Muslim courts,[151] which, being appointed by the country's ruler, were the closest that medieval Egypt had to a state judiciary. Communal pressure strongly discouraged such a step, however, and even when Muslim judges were appealed to, they did not always accept jurisdiction. The rabbinic courts had no police force upon which they could call to enforce their decisions,[152] yet they did have an effective tool at their disposal: the placing of recalcitrants under the ban (*ḥerem*). Within the closely knit communal framework, it was no small sanction. A solemn proclamation was made in the synagogues forbidding members of the community to conduct business with the person who had been placed under the ban, to eat or drink with him, to sit within four cubits of him, or to participate in his celebrations or mourning. The funeral of the person who died under the ban was to be treated as an occasion for joy, not grief; for a wicked man had been removed

---

"*Shalshelet ha-Yaḥas*" (n. 14 above) 22, on the basis of a letter to Joseph ben Judah in which Maimonides writes: "I have already informed you that the small girl [or: daughter (*bat*)] died, may God consider her death as an atonement. Do not grieve, my son, over the death of male or female." As Baneth observes in his edition of the letter, Maimonides' treatment of the child's death with so little personal involvement—to which we may add the incongruity of a father's consoling an outsider on his own personal loss—makes it highly unlikely that the child was Maimonides' daughter; see Moses ben Maimon, *Epistulae* 91, 94. S. Goitein, "*R. Ḥananeel ha-Dayyan ha-gadol*," *Tarbiz* 50 (1981) 376, 394, speculates about additional daughters of Maimonides' but offers no evidence.

[149] Freimann, "*Shalshelet ha-Yaḥas*" 27; P. Fenton, "Carmoly et le dernier des Maïmonide," *Revue des études juives* 148 (1989) 368–69, 373.

[150] See S. Goitein, *Mediterranean Society* 2 (Berkeley 1971) 330; *Mediterranean Society* 5 (n. 22 above) 305–6. Maimonides' responsa, as far as I could see, never deal with issues of criminal law.

[151] Examples in Goitein, *Mediterranean Society* 2.399–401. Maimonides, *Responsa* (n. 30 above) §349, reveals that it was even possible for a Jewish man and woman to have their marriage performed by Muslim authorities.

[152] Goitein, *Mediterranean Society* 2.379, gives examples of Jews who held minor positions in the national police.

from the scene.[153] Rabbinic courts thus had jurisdiction over a wide range of issues and wielded considerable power.

By the time Maimonides arrived in Egypt, in his twenties, he controlled all branches of rabbinic literature. He had not limited himself to the theory of the law, for he had, in the lands of his youth, carefully observed rabbinic judicial procedures as put into actual practice,[154] undoubtedly with the expectation of following his fathers in the judicial calling, and he had himself acted as a judge.[155] The level of rabbinic expertise in Egypt stood more than a few notches below that possessed by Maimonides, and when he stepped onto Egyptian soil in his late twenties, he was the most knowledgeable rabbinic legist in the land. Although he may have carried certification of his qualifications from the period he spent in Spain and Morocco, he is not known to have done so. Formal certification of judicial qualifications was not required in the medieval Jewish world.[156]

Very soon after his arrival, he started serving the Jewish community as a judge. He states at one juncture when dealing with legal stratagems for sidestepping a talmudic prohibition against a twice-widowed woman's marrying again—the talmudic scruple being that the death of two husbands had shown marriage to her to be dangerous:[157] "This is the way I have decided and acted in Egypt since arriving here."[158] His legal responsa indicate, moreover, that not long after arriving in Egypt, he functioned, formally or de facto, as chief judge of the rabbinic court in Fustat. He did not give up his judicial functions even when he had published the works that make him a towering figure in medieval intellectual history, even when he had become a physician of the vizier and then of the sultan and was overburdened by his medical practice, even when he suffered a lengthy illness followed by chronic fatigue during the last decade or so of his life. Two years before his death, he can still be seen unraveling knotty marital disputes and other matters.[159]

[153]This is the way Maimonides describes an actual excommunication in *Responsa* §349.

[154]Above, p. 23. In the letter to Pinḥas of Alexandria, in Shailat, *Letters and Essays of Moses Maimonides* (n. 4 above) 446, Maimonides writes that rabbinic judges trained—like himself—in Islamic countries were more adept in matters of litigation than those—like Pinḥas—who were trained in Christian countries, since Christian rulers did not allow Jewish courts to deal with such issues.

[155]Above, p. 23.

[156]Commentary on the Mishna, *Sanhedrin* 3:1; *Mishneh Torah*: *H. Sanhedrin* 6.9.

[157]BT *Yebamot* 64b.

[158]Maimonides, *Responsa* §218, p. 387.

[159]Maimonides, *Responsa* §233 is a question from Alexandria referring back to a divorce dispute that had been litigated in 1194 (see ibid., p. 423), and the question to Maimonides and his response are dated at least four years later (ibid., p. 420). §88 is a question from authorities in Alexandria, arising out of a marital agreement dated 1201 (ibid., p. 143) and containing a condition to be fulfilled one year after the execution of the document (ibid., p. 141). Since the time for fulfilling the condition had passed, the letter to Maimonides and his reply can be no earlier than 1202, two years before his death.

How Maimonides was appointed is unknown. When the Egyptian Jewish community had a single recognized leader, it was he who appointed local officials. Maimonides' legal opinion was that only the exilarch, the Jewish communal leader located in Iraq, had the power to invest rabbinic judges with full judicial authority anywhere in the world outside of Palestine.[160] In his own instance there is no information that any person of standing, domestic or foreign, initially appointed him as a judge, promoted him to the presidency of the Fustat court, and, if his formal jurisdiction ever extended beyond Fustat, as historians have speculated, invested him with the additional responsibility.

An allusion to some sort of judicial appointment is found in a letter preserved in several manuscripts, one of which dates the letter to 1185. Maimonides is answering a message from Japhet ben Elijah, the rabbinic judge who had been his host in Palestine, and he mentions that Japhet had written to congratulate him on his having received "authorization" (*harsha'a*),[161] which is a technical term for investiture of a judge. At the time, Maimonides had been serving for years as a rabbinic judge in Fustat, so that the appointment alluded to by Japhet ben Elijah must have gone beyond the initial judgeship. But exactly what the "authorization" was and whether Maimonides received it from within Egypt or from abroad is uncertain.

When rabbinic questions from the cities and towns of Egypt are answered by Maimonides in writing, he is generally the addressee. A few questions are, however, addressed to the Fustat court and answered by him.[162] There also are instances where questions are addressed to Maimonides but the answers are both signed by him and countersigned by colleagues;[163] and additional replies now carrying only his signature could originally have had countersignatures that subsequent copyists dropped. Where decisions are answered by Maimonides for the Fustat court and other judges countersign, he is apparently acting in the formal or de facto capacity of court president. One legal question was addressed to the court of an official of a nominally higher administrative status who bore the title of "prince [*nasi*] of the exiles of Israel." Maimonides writes the main opinion, his colleagues add concurring opinions, and the prince adds a *pro forma* concurrence to Maimonides' decision, half of which consists in flowery praise of Maimonides, while the other half spells out the prince's distinguished genealogy.[164] Here

160 Commentary on the Mishna, *Sanhedrin* 3:1; *Bekorot* 4:4. *Mishneh Torah*: *H. Sanhedrin* 4.14.

161 Letter to Japhet in Shailat, *Letters and Essays of Moses Maimonides* 230.

162 Maimonides, *Responsa* §393, addressed to his *bet din*, or court; §15, p. 23, to his "exalted *majlis*"; for the Hebrew equivalent of *majlis*, see n. 164 below. Both questions are in fact intended specifically for Maimonides. §16 is addressed to another judge and answered by Maimonides.

163 The opinion in *Responsa* §452, dated 1180, is countersigned by Maimonides' colleagues.

164 Maimonides, *Responsa* §373. The official is "Judah ben Josiah, the prince [*nasi*] of the exiles of Israel." The author of one of the concurring opinions, p. 655, states that the question had "come to the princely court [*be-moshab ha-nesi'ut*]." The same Judah ben Josiah also counter-

Maimonides was acting within a real, or quasi, administrative hierarchy that undoubtedly played a role, now murky, in the political jousting of the time.

Some of the issues treated in Maimonides' legal responsa are theoretical. In the preserved written responses involving actual cases, he and his court invariably enter the scene in a secondary capacity, after a case had already been brought before another court. It is hardly surprising that little written evidence has been preserved of his serving as a judge of first instance, since he and his court would try to avoid direct legal correspondence with plaintiffs or defendants. He must, nonetheless, have served as a judge at the primary level during periods of his life.

A number of times he writes that he had himself "acted" in a certain manner when faced with issues of the type for which his opinion was now solicited. When asked about the prohibition against a twice-widowed woman's remarrying, he informs his questioner that in cases of the sort, Jewish courts in Spain would circumvent the prohibition by closing their eyes and letting the woman remarry without formal permission. The courts would thereupon certify the *fait accompli.* "That," he goes on, "was the way the court of R. Isaac [Alfasi] acted. It is the way the court of his student R. Joseph ha-Levi [Ibn Migas] acted. . . . And it is the way that I [literally: we] have decided and have acted in Egypt since arriving here."[165] When asked about the circumstances under which a particular oath should be administered in civil disputes, he answers: These are "matters [adjudicated] before us daily, and we handle them by. . . ."[166] Two run-of-the-

---

signs *Responsa* §380, again as "the prince of the exiles of Israel." On the office, or quasi office, of *nasi*, see Mann, *The Jews in Egypt and Palestine* (n. 4 above) 1.172–76.

[165]Maimonides, *Responsa* §218. Maimonides often uses first-person plural forms when speaking of himself. In *Responsa* §15, he advises another court to handle a similar case in the same way. A note in Blau's edition of the *Responsa* points out that Ibn Migas' responsa prohibit a twice-widowed woman from marrying a third time, and Maimonides' rabbinic code, *Mishneh Torah: H. Issure Bi'a* 21.31, records the talmudic prohibition without comment. Both were, however, giving the formal rule and not offering tactics for sidestepping it. Today rabbinic courts generally follow the example of Maimonides' *Responsa* and do not enforce the prohibition.

[166]Maimonides, *Responsa* §428. Additional examples, not all of which are unambiguous (I have translated first-person plural pronouns as first-person singular, since Maimonides is plainly speaking about himself): *Responsa* §211, on allowing a man to manumit and marry his slave girl, even though they probably had forbidden sexual relations with one another and therefore should, according to the law, be separated permanently: "In cases of the sort, I have decided a number of times that the man should manumit and marry, and I acted in this way because. . . ." *Responsa* §220, on regulations regarding the wearing of four-cornered fringed garments on the Sabbath: "This is what I always do and the decision that I have always given." In *Responsa* §375, when asked whether a Jewish law court could go beyond the letter of the law in disposing of the possessions of a Jewish apostate, Maimonides responds: Authorities East and West "have decided" and "I myself [literally: we] always proceed, in the following way: When a man has committed apostasy and inherits something, . . . the wicked man is treated as if he were no longer alive" and the inheritance, instead of being given to him, is transferred to his "nonsinning sons" or to whoever else is the closest heir. *Responsa* §411, on agents assigned power of attorney who are negligent: "My procedure and that of my predecessors is . . . to remove the

mill documents are likewise known in which Maimonides performed tasks that local judges would handle as part of their daily duties. One is dated 1172, that is to say, not many years after his arrival in Egypt and during the time when he was busy writing his rabbinic code: Functionaries of the court record that they had followed Maimonides' instructions, made a detailed inventory—which is included—of the very modest possessions of a man who had just died, and were holding the property for the decedent's heir.[167] In the other document, the signatures of the witnesses on a power of attorney are followed by routine certification in Maimonides' hand.[168]

The actual cases that come up in Maimonides' responsa are typically matters that rabbinic figures in Egypt considered to be beyond their competence and for which they turned to Maimonides or his court for guidance. Sometimes, too, the judge who was first faced with an issue, or the judge's colleagues, would seek confirmation of an opinion tentatively prepared or a decision already issued—only to see, more often than not, the opinion and decision unceremoniously rejected by Maimonides. It has been suggested that on occasions such as these, where judges in the other Egyptian towns referred cases to Maimonides for guidance or review, he was acting in an official capacity, as supervising justice for rabbinic courts throughout Egypt.[169] The suggestion is not especially probable on its face, since

---

agent. . . ." Contrast *Responsa* §260, where Maimonides writes that he gave instructions on a certain liturgical matter "a number of times in answers to questions," that is, in writing. Goitein, "Maimonides, Man of Action" (n. 16 above) 166–67, states that he found no court document among the Geniza materials in which Maimonides signed as a judge of first instance, and he accordingly drew the conclusion that "Maimonides never served as judge."

[167]M. Friedman, "*R. Moshe ben Maimon be-Te*ᶜ*udot Mishpaṭiyyot min ha-Geniza*" *Shenaton ha-Mishpaṭ ha-Ivri* 14–15 (1988–1989) 184. English translation of the document: S. Goitein, *Mediterranean Society* 4 (Berkeley 1983) 335–38. The document is dated on one of the intermediate days of the Passover festival, and Maimonides' instruction (*amr*) to the court functionaries could simply have been a legal decision confirming that the matter fell within a category for which labor on the intermediate days of a festival is permitted. Because the document describes Maimonides as "the great rabbi," Goitein, 335–36, concludes that he was serving at the time as the "highest religious authority in the country," as an equivalent of the Muslim Grand Mufti; see below, n. 169. Friedman goes further and asserts that Maimonides was serving as head of the entire Egyptian Jewish community. The routine nature of the action to which Maimonides' name is attached speaks against such conjectures.

[168]Friedman, "*R. Moshe ben Maimon be-Te*ᶜ*udot Mishpaṭiyyot min ha-Geniza*" 177–81. As Friedman shows in his analysis of the document, Maimonides performed the task in an offhand way.

[169]Mann, *The Jews in Egypt and Palestine* 1.266–68, offers—with some hesitation—possible evidence for the existence, at various times, of an office of chief rabbinic judge for Egypt. Maimonides is often addressed as "the great rabbi," (*ha-rab ha-gadol*), and Goitein believes that the term means the "Jewish 'Grand Mufti,' whose legal opinions carried religious authority." See the reference to Goitein, *Mediterranean Society* 4 (n. 167 above), and Goitein, "Maimonides, Man of Action" (n. 16 above) 161. A document incorporated into Maimonides, *Responsa* §173 lends support to the contention that "great rabbi" was more than a rhetorical flourish but hardly

neither talmudic law nor Maimonides' codification of it makes provision for such an office. Judges in Egypt may have consulted with the Fustat court merely because of its status as *primus inter pares* within the Egyptian court system. They may have consulted with Maimonides in accordance with the obligation, laid down by the Babylonian Talmud and recorded in Maimonides' code of rabbinic law, that judges consult with a more accomplished judge regarding their cases, when one is to be found.[170]

In support of the suggestion that Maimonides did have jurisdiction extending beyond Fustat, the instances can be cited where he unceremoniously rejected the determinations of his correspondents[171] as well as those where officials in towns outside of Fustat refused to act before receiving instructions from the "head [or: chief]" (*ra'īs*), that is, Maimonides.[172] Once, the Alexandrian court wrote to Fustat for guidance before disqualifying a ritual slaughterer who had sinned; Maimonides responded confirming the disqualification, and a second Fustat judge countersigned and stated that he concurred in Maimonides' "legal opinion" (*fatwā*).[173]

On yet another occasion, we find him writing to a law court in a different town asking it to inform him whether a certain man and woman suspected of illicit sexual relations continue to meet so that he could pronounce a ban on them.[174] On still another, the Alexandrian court informed Maimonides that it had excommunicated a member of the priestly class and a divorcée who had been married by the gentile authorities, in violation of the scriptural prohibition against priests' marrying divorcées. Maimonides replied to the Alexandrians that he had supported their action by having the synagogues of Fustat and Cairo publicly excommunicate the sinful priest

---

bears out the conjecture that Maimonides was a Jewish grand mufti. In the document, an Alexandrian rabbinic court disqualifies a ritual slaughterer and to buttress its action cites a legal opinion issued by "Moses, the great rabbi in Israel . . . and Rabbi Isaac ben Sason"; see below. On the one hand, since Isaac ben Sason is not given the title, it seems to be reserved for Maimonides; on the other hand, if Maimonides were a grand mufti, no one else should have participated in his legal opinion. *Responsa* §16 incorporates a question sent to the same Isaac ben Sason; there Isaac is addressed with a string of honorific terms, from which "great rabbi" is again conspicuously absent. Maimonides calls his father "the great rabbi in Israel"; he calls R. Joseph Ibn Migas "the great rabbi"; a document regarding Maimonides calls his father "the great rabbi"; and another document attaches the tag "great rabbi in Israel" to both his father and great-grandfather See Mann, *The Jews in Egypt and Palestine* 2.317; I. Friedlaender, "Ein Gratulationsbrief an Maimonides," *Festschrift zu Hermann Cohens siebzigstem Geburtstage*" (Berlin 1912) 261; S. Assaf, "*Mi-Perusho shel ha-Rambam*," *Sinai* 6 (1940) 117; and Goitein, "Maimonides, Man of Action" 161. There is no reason to suppose that Joseph Ibn Migas, Maimonides' father, and Maimonides' great-grandfather had all been Jewish grand muftis in Muslim Spain.

[170]BT *Yebamot* 109b; Maimonides, *Mishneh Torah*: *H. Sanhedrin* 20.8.

[171]Examples: *Responsa* §§11, 39, 41, 47, 51, 96, 371, 381.

[172]Maimonides, *Responsa* §191; Friedman, "Social Realities in Egypt" (n. 17 above) 229. Similarly in *Responsa* §168, but without the term "head."

[173]Maimonides, *Responsa* §173.

[174]Maimonides, *Responsa* §352.

and his "harlot"[175] as well as any Jewish man or woman who might "conduct business with them, eat or drink with them, sit down within a radius of four cubits with them, or participate in their celebrations or their mourning." Should the two miscreants repent, they must return to the gentile authorities and be divorced, appear in a Jewish court and undergo the legally prescribed whipping, and then undertake by solemn oath in the presence of the sacred scroll of the Law never to repeat the sin. At that point, the Alexandrian court should remove its ban and, Maimonides requested, should also apprise him of the fact so that his court could remove its own ban. If the man and his wife remain recalcitrant, he would have the ban publicized throughout the Jewish communities of Egypt. For we "cannot be remiss in the face of an evil act of this magnitude, the lifting up of a hand in rebellion and the open repudiation of Moses, our teacher, and his perfect Torah."[176]

While instances such as the foregoing are certainly compatible with Maimonides' having held the official position of supervising judge for all Jewish courts in Egypt, they could merely reflect the preeminence of the Fustat court within the country or Maimonides' personal preeminence. And there are counterexamples.

In an undated incident, a party to a liturgical dispute that flared up in an Egyptian Jewish community requested a letter from Maimonides in support of his stand, and the man submitting the request explained: Respect for Maimonides was such that the other party in the dispute "may perhaps listen to . . . you."[177] Any power that Maimonides exercised here was solely of the moral sort.

In a letter written no earlier than 1179, Maimonides makes the following blunt comment to Pinḥas, a rabbinic judge in Alexandria, who had ignored Maimonides' guidance on a legal question: "The way I always deal with those who cling to their stupidity and are unwilling to change their minds is to keep silent and leave them to do as they please."[178] The letter contains a further telling statement. Maimonides explains to Pinḥas why he had had his judicial colleagues countersign an opinion that he issued on a separate legal matter. In it, Maimonides had rejected Pinḥas's view and, he observes, if he signed by himself, Pinḥas could have contended to the gentile officials that with Maimonides' expressing one opinion and Pinḥas's expressing another, there was no reason why the one should take precedence over the other.[179] Maimonides had his colleagues countersign in order to ensure that

[175]Maimonides is using the word in a rhetorical and not a technical sense. See *Mishneh Torah*: *H. Issure Bi'a* 18.2.

[176]Maimonides, *Responsa* §349. See Leviticus 21:7.

[177]Maimonides, *Responsa* §259, end of the query.

[178]Letter to Pinḥas of Alexandria, in Shailat, *Letters and Essays of Moses Maimonides* (n. 4 above) 447. The letter was written at least a year and a half after the completion of Maimonides' *Mishneh Torah* and hence no earlier than 1179.

[179]Letter to Pinḥas of Alexandria 447–48. The Muslim court may have been involved because the case involved an inheritance. Maimonides apologizes, perhaps ironically, for derogating from his own honor by having had his Fustat colleagues countersign the decision.

his, correct, opinion would prevail. When he left Pinḥas to cling to his stupidity and when he had his colleagues countersign a legal opinion to give it more weight than a decision solely in his name would carry, he could hardly have had the formal power simply to overturn the Alexandrian judge's decisions.

Instances can also be cited where Maimonides formulated his responses to legal questions as suggestions.[180] And as late as the mid-1190s, he could instruct the aforementioned Pinḥas of Alexandria how to handle a particular legal issue and nevertheless be informed subsequently that not "one thing was done" in accordance with his instructions.[181] In fine, there is evidence that even after Maimonides had become well established in Egypt, he did not hold the formal position of supervising judge for the entire country, and there is no solid evidence that he at any time held such a position.

Whatever his status, he felt no constraint to mince words. He allowed himself to write at different times—usually when names are not revealed but sometimes when they are—that one or another judge had propounded an "inanity," "a proposition too unsubstantial to undertake a refutation of it," "a muddle [*shibbush*]," "an enormous muddle," "a judgment . . . which in my view is a muddle and has no substance," "muddled talk," "bizarre imagining," a thesis "containing much error and a lack of reasoning." The usage insisted upon by a certain religious official was "a custom of ignoramuses." Of one unnamed judge Maimonides writes that he was "totally mistaken," of another that he was "an ignoramus," and of a third that he "understands nothing whatsoever."[182] In a nice bit of poetic justice, the most frequent derogatory label that Abraham ben David, the harshest critic of Maimonides' code of rabbinic law, would later affix to decisions in the code with which he disagreed was that they are a "muddle."[183]

Whether or not Maimonides' official responsibilities extended beyond the Fustat court, he initiated, or at least played the central role in, a number of actions that had ramifications reaching beyond that city and—although he appears to have been acting wholly in a judicial capacity—well beyond the conventional judicial sphere. The formal side of these efforts, if not always the substance, might evoke admiration in the most aggressive advocate of judicial activism.

One action, known from his son's rabbinic responsa, consisted in an "edict" (*taqqana*) accompanied by a "ban," which Maimonides, his colleague Isaac ben Sason, and "all the other rabbinic judges of the time" promulgated and pronounced. The edict prohibited any Jew in the towns of Egypt from performing marriages or administering divorces "without the order [*amr*] of the appointed officials

[180]For example, *Responsa* §§25, 393 (to Pinḥas of Alexandria).

[181]Maimonides, *Responsa* §233, pp. 419 and 423.

[182]Maimonides, *Responsa*, pp. 15, 61, 65, 85, 160, 256, 483, 634, 662, 680, 697, 707.

[183]A few from among the scores of instances: Abraham ben David's glosses on Maimonides, *Mishneh Torah*: *H. Shabbat* 17.35; 19.6; 21.27.

[*muqaddam*]" who were "commissioned . . . by the head [or: chief (*ra'īs*)] at the time."[184] Maimonides and his colleagues were placing control over marriages and divorces exclusively in the hands of the local appointee[185] who was commissioned by the central personage, the communal "head," charged with making local appointments. The edict could have served multiple purposes—the upholding of religious standards, the defense of the powers of the central Jewish communal organization, and the protection of local judges' authority and revenues.

That edict is undated. A series of events, one of which is dated, led Maimonides and his associates to assume a very different stance toward a person who was a "head" of the Egyptian Jewish community. The events swirled around a man named Abu Zikri.[186]

The initial glimpse of the matter comes from an undated question sent to Maimonides for a legal opinion. The questioners recount that Abu Zikri had recently risen to the position of "head" (*ra'īs*) within the Egyptian Jewish community and, in exercising his prerogative to appoint local officials, had demanded that local functionaries pay him a fee or be replaced. R. Peraḥia, the appointed official (*muqaddam*) and religious judge of the town of al-Maḥalla, either refused to pay the fee or was outbid. Members of the local community, including its leading figures, came to R. Peraḥia's support in the form of an "edict" (*taqqana*), a "covenant of the Lord," and an "oath." They undertook not to recognize the "authority [to perform religious functions]" (*reshut*) of anyone appointed for their town by Abu Zikri, not to include such an appointee in religious quorums, and not to pay Abu Zikri's appointee the local taxes pertaining to the office. Members of the community thereupon thought it would be wise to have Maimonides explain to them precisely what they had done. Maimonides' response dryly addresses only the legal side of the issue. He explains that the rabbinic legal category into which the action of the participating members of the community fell was that of a religious oath, that their action had the force of an oath for all those who signed it or assented to it orally, and that the sanctions attendant upon religious oaths therefore applied to

[184]Abraham Maimonides, *Responsa*, ed. A. Freimann and S. Goitein (Jerusalem 1937) 182–83, 189. The question was sent to Abraham no earlier than 1235.

[185]On the office and functions of a *muqqadam*, see Goitein, *Mediterranean Society* 2 (n. 150 above) 72–73; M. Cohen, *Jewish Self-Government in Medieval Egypt* (Princeton 1980) 204, 237. The precise connotation of the term is not, however, wholly clear.

[186]Maimonides mentions this Abu Zikri in a letter that he wrote to Pinḥas, the rabbinic judge in Alexandria, no earlier than 1179. He informs Pinḥas that Abu Zikri had paid "ninety dinars" to the government with the expectation of being appointed to a high office within the Egyptian Jewish community but had thus far received no "document from the king." He had only received permission to muster support from the community. In that he had failed, he had wasted his money, and he was now "fearful of the lowest member of the community and had no ally." See the letter to Pinḥas of Alexandria, in Shailat, *Letters and Essays of Moses Maimonides* 450. The events with which we are concerned here occurred at a juncture—whether after or before the letter to the Alexandrian judge is unclear, since Abu Zikri made more than one attempt to obtain high office—when he did succeed in purchasing the communal office that he coveted.

the signatories and to others who had assented, but not to anyone else. Several associate judges countersigned Maimonides' opinion, one of them the Isaac ben Sason, who has already been mentioned.[187]

A separate document followed which is dated 1187, was signed by Maimonides, and was countersigned by the same associate judges. A double-barreled action is here reported.

In the first part, "scrolls of the Law were taken out" of the ark and the "rabbis of Egypt" publicly pronounced an edict and a ban. The edict was directed at three Egyptian towns, one of them al-Maḥalla, the town just referred to; it named three judges responsible for the towns, the judge for al-Maḥalla being the same Peraḥia who was also just referred to; and it declared those three to be the only men authorized to perform marriages and execute divorces in the three towns. The accompanying ban was pronounced upon residents of the towns who used the services of a judge other than the three specified by name. In effect, the edict and ban adopted by members of the al-Maḥalla community, which Maimonides had determined had legal validity only as a self-imposed oath, were transformed by Maimonides and his colleagues into a judicial edict and ban. They were expanded to cover not merely the inhabitants of al-Maḥalla who had explicitly accepted them, but all of al-Maḥalla's inhabitants, as well as the inhabitants of two additional Egyptian towns. And the three judges were thereby protected from being removed by anyone, including, by implication, the "head" whose formal prerogative it was to appoint local officials.

The second part of the action described in the document signed by Maimonides and his associates consisted in a ban proclaimed against parties who bestowed "authority [to perform religious functions]" on a person lacking expertise in the areas of rabbinic marriage and divorce. In other words, it pronounced a ban upon anyone whatsoever—including, again, the head of the entire Egyptian Jewish community, the man ordinarily charged with making all local appointments—who appointed incompetents.[188] The action as a whole imposes strict limits on the privilege upheld by the judicial edict examined previously, the one known from Maimonides' son.[189] There Maimonides and the others insisted on the exclusive right of the personage called the "head" to appoint the officials responsible for marriage and divorce. Here they limit the right of anyone, plainly including the head, to replace at least three officials responsible for those functions; and they pronounce a ban upon anyone who might appoint incompetents anywhere in Egypt.

[187]Maimonides, *Responsa* §270, with the supplement in *Responsa* 4.8, and Goitein, "*Otograf*" (n. 7 above) 191–94. Maimonides' decision had BT *Shebu*ᶜ*ot* 36a in mind. A similar incident is recorded in a document discussed by D. Baneth, "*Te*ᶜ*udot min ha-Geniza*," *Sefer ha-Yobel le-kebod A. Marx* (New York 1950), Hebrew Part 87–89.

[188]Maimonides, *Responsa* §348. In *Mishneh Torah*: *H. Sanhedrin* 4.15, Maimonides extrapolates from BT *Sanhedrin* 7b and rules that an incompetent judge, even if he is duly appointed, lacks all authority.

[189]Above, p. 45.

We do not have to ask where responsibility for determining competence was henceforth to reside.

Ordinarily the Muslim government selected the head of the Jewish community, and a prime prerogative of the office was precisely the appointment of religious functionaries throughout the country. The information we have does not add up to a clear picture of the standing with the government enjoyed at the time by the head of the community. We therefore cannot tell whether Maimonides and his judicial associates—together with the Jews of al-Maḥalla—were taking the astonishing step of challenging not merely Jewish communal leadership, but the Egyptian government as well. It nonetheless is clear that Maimonides and his associates were assuming for themselves the right to review appointments made by the official Jewish leaders.

A third and very different kind of edict is dated by the manuscripts either in 1167 or 1176; if the former date is correct, Maimonides could have been in Egypt for only a very short time and was already mobilizing his colleagues to undertake a far-reaching religious reform. The edict was signed by Maimonides and countersigned by no fewer than nine additional judges and religious officials, and it expressly covered the entire country of Egypt.[190] It states that those drawing it up were new arrivals in Egypt who found the majority of Jewish married women there neglecting the rabbinic rules for purification after their menstrual periods. Instead of immersing themselves in a ritual bath, as rabbinic law requires, Jewish women commonly followed the way of the "heretics" (*minim*), that is, the Karaites, and only washed themselves.[191] It further states that the signatories had for several years publicly appealed to the Egyptian Jewish women to mend their ways and only then took action. Inasmuch as the initiative was undertaken primarily by judges, the sanctions were judicial. Jewish courts throughout Egypt were instructed not to allow widowed or divorced women to collect the monetary settlement due them upon dissolution of their marriages unless such women solemnly swore in court that they had observed the rabbinic purification rites before having sexual intercourse with their husbands. Courts were instructed to declare a ban on any Jewish man found to have knowingly had intercourse with a wife who flouted the rabbinic rites. And a ban was declared upon any Jewish court, present or future,

[190] A seventeenth-century Egyptian Jewish writer names Maimonides as the author of the edict and credits him with having saved the rabbinic Jewish community in Fustat-Cairo from being overwhelmed by the Karaite movement. See Kahana, *Meḥqarim be-Sifrut ha-Teshubot* (n. 114 above) 37.

[191] Karaite legists followed what they contended is the letter of Scripture—see, for example, Leviticus 15:13; 21—and instructed women to wash rather than immerse themselves in a ritual bath. Cf. the tenth-century Karaite, Y. Qirqisani, *K. al-Anwār*, ed. L. Nemoy 4 (New York 1942) 1052; and the fifteenth-century Karaite, E. Bashyaṣi, *Aderet Eliyahu* (Israel 1966) 241. In *Responsa* §263, Maimonides expressly states that Karaites are not heretics in the strict sense. The contents of the edict and Maimonides, *Responsa* §320, which refers to the edict, nonetheless show that the Karaite practice was at the heart of the issue.

that should disregard the edict.[192] When Maimonides refers to the matter on a later occasion, he writes that the ban extended to the "accursed" wives as well.[193]

A fourth edict is explicitly described as having been promulgated by Maimonides for the protection of Jewish women. It undertook "not to marry" a Jewish man from another country to a Jewish woman "in the entire land of Egypt" unless the man furnished proof that he had not left a wife behind in his homeland; and, further, not to allow immigrant Jewish men who had married women in Egypt to depart from the country unless they deposited a conditional bill of divorce for their wives. The bill of divorce would go into effect if the man failed to return to his wife within a specified time.[194]

There are, fifth, a question sent to Maimonides which refers to a "well-known edict" against a Jew's selling real estate to a gentile if the property had Jewish neighbors,[195] and, sixth, questions sent to him which appear to refer to a prohibition supported by a ban against a Jewish litigant's taking his dispute with another Jew to a gentile court.[196] Since Maimonides was in both cases asked about implementing the edicts, he may have had a part in promulgating them, but that is a surmise.

Of the six edicts here described, the texts of only the second, third, and, fourth have been preserved. Maimonides signed the fourth with the formula that he typically used for legal opinions: "thus wrote Moses" (*we-katab Moshe*). In the second, the edict following the al-Maḥalla incident, he signed: "thus wrote Moses son of Maimon, judge." In the third, he signed only his name; but since, as he later explained to a questioner, the core of the edict went back to mishnaic law,[197] and since it, like the others, was to be enforced through rabbinic courts, we are safe in

[192]Maimonides, *Responsa* §242; regarding the date, see p. 443, note 17, and I. Friedlaender, "Das arabische Original der anti-karäischen Verordnung des Maimonides," *Monatsschrift für Geschichte und Wissenschaft des Judentums* 53 (1909) 470. The edict is based on, but goes beyond, Mishna, *Ketubbot* 7:6.

[193]Maimonides, *Responsa* §320; Maimonides expressly states here that he and his colleagues were opposing purification procedures of Karaite origin. *Responsa* §189, where Maimonides explains how a delinquent wife was to be punished financially, does not, by contrast, speak of a ban pronounced against the wife.

[194]Maimonides, *Responsa* §347. Translated in Friedman, "Social Realities in Egypt" (n. 17 above) 234. To be precise, the departing husband was required to hand his wife a bill of divorce, but with the condition, should the two parties agree, that the divorce would not take effect unless he failed to return within a specified time, not to exceed three years.

[195]In *Responsa* §44, Maimonides' questioners write that the local court had prevented a litigant from selling property to a gentile when there were Jewish neighbors, "as we learned" from you. The questioner in *Responsa* §170 refers to the "well-known edict" against such sales. Goitein, *Mediterranean Society* 2 (n. 150 above) 292, records instances during the half century before Maimonides arrived in Egypt where persons transferring property stipulated expressly that the property could not be sold to non-Jews.

[196]Maimonides, *Responsa* §§26, 27, 408.

[197]Maimonides, *Responsa* §321 alluding to Mishna *Ketubbot* 7:6.

viewing Maimonides and the co-signatories as acting in the capacity of judges. The fifth is an extension of a talmudic prescription,[198] and it and the sixth are known through questions requesting that Maimonides explain the legal measures to be taken in enforcing them. Where the edicts have more than one signatory, Maimonides' name appears first. In edicts two through six, we can, in sum, be reasonably certain that Maimonides was acting in his judicial capacity.

Communal edicts were infrequent in twelfth-century Egypt, and the only known edicts of general applicability are, in fact, the ones just described.[199] The first four show Maimonides taking the lead and drawing his colleagues after him in the assumption of responsibilities that extend well beyond the day-to-day adjudication of legal disputes. Maimonides and the others act to enforce Jewish religious observance throughout the country, to defend the prerogatives of properly appointed judges, to uphold—on one occasion—the power of the head of the Egyptian Jewish community to appoint local officials, to seize for themselves—on another occasion—the right of reviewing such appointments, and to prevent Jewish husbands from abandoning their wives. Where sanctions were applied, they are of a sort that rabbinic courts would have at their disposal. Maimonides knew the political theories of Greek and Arabic philosophers, but the stance evidenced in the actions we have been examining drew its inspiration from an entirely different quarter. He and his colleagues were accepting for themselves the responsibility for religious observance and the public welfare with which the Babylonian Talmud had charged rabbinic courts and with which Maimonides himself charges them in his code of Jewish law.[200] The responsibility that the rabbinic courts in Egypt were

[198]It has its basis in BT *Baba Qamma* 114a, which does not prohibit sales to gentiles where there are Jewish neighbors but does allow the Jewish neighbors to have a ban pronounced against the seller if he does not undertake to compensate them for any loss they might suffer as a result of the sale. *Mishneh Torah*: *H. Shekenim* 12.7, codifies the talmudic rule.

[199]E. Ashtor, "*Qawwim li-Demuta shel ha-Qehilla ha-Yehudit be-Miṣrayim*, *Zion* 30 (1965) 130, 150.

[200]Following talmudic sources, Maimonides rules in Commentary on the Mishna, *Ketubbot* 4:6, and *Mishneh Torah*: *H. Mattenot ᶜAniyyim* 7.10, that a court may force a man to donate an appropriate amount to charity. *Mishneh Torah*: *H. Mila* 1.2 instructs courts to intervene and have a Jewish boy circumcised when the father neglects to see to the circumcision. *Mishneh Torah*: *H. Yom Ṭob* 6.21 places on them the responsibility for policing public areas to prevent the fraternizing of the sexes. *H. Yom Ṭob* 7.4 assigns them the responsibility for enforcing observance of the intermediate days of the festivals. *H. Geneba* 8.20 requires them to police weights, measures, and market prices, and *H. Gezela* 3.6 requires them to act against persons who habitually use others' property in improper ways that are not punishable by the letter of the law. *H. Ḥobel* 3.11 reserves for rabbinic courts the determination of the appropriate fine for a person who shames someone in public, and *H. Ḥobel* 7.14 reserves for them the determination of the fine for a person who snatches the fulfillment of a religious commandment away from someone else. *H. Roṣeaḥ* 2.4–5 allows a court to take action against murderers whom the rules of jurisprudence exempt from the death penalty; the court may go beyond the letter of the law and put such murderers to death, beat them to the verge of death, or incarcerate them for long periods of time. *H. Geneba* 1.10 charges courts with administering whippings to minors and slaves who

claiming for themselves was similar to that which Jewish religious authorities, especially those in Iraq, had claimed for centuries.[201]

Maimonides' scholarly standing enabled him to act in the political and social arenas independently of his judicial position. About the time that he arrived in Egypt—and apparently still during the reign of the last of the Fatimids, which in effect came to a close in 1169—a malefactor named Zuṭa gained the official leadership of the Jewish community. This Zuṭa may very well be identical with the Abu Zikri who was met in connection with the al-Maḥalla incident: Zuṭa's given name was Yaḥyā, while Zuṭa, which means "the small one," could be a disparaging nickname; and the common byname (*kunya*) of Yaḥyā in Arabic was precisely Abū Zikrī.[202] If Zuṭa/Yaḥyā and Abu Zikri are the same person, the affair at issue now was one of his earlier escapades.

The Hebrew composition, written in 1197, which tells the story does not do so in a clear fashion, and the pages of the preserved version may even be out of order. As the composition stands, it relates that Zuṭa took power on three different occasions: Some time before Maimonides arrived in Egypt, Zuṭa was able to have a popular leader of the Egyptian Jewish community, known as Samuel ha-Nagid, deposed and to replace him for sixty-six days. Samuel was soon restored to the office and he held it until the end of his life. After "the king of Egypt died and there arose a new king over Egypt"—probably the last of the Fatimids, who reigned from 1160 to 1171[203]—Zuṭa bought the leadership of the Jewish community for two hundred dinars a year. He "ruled for about four years," during which time he extorted money and wreaked general havoc. But "God . . . sent" Moses

---

steal or damage property (no known talmudic source). *H. She'ela* 6.4 gives the court the discretion to evaluate the plausibility of a depositor's claim against the person holding his deposit. *H. Malweh we-Loweh* 2.4 charges the court with deciding when it is, and when it is not, appropriate to require an oath (this is Maimonides' personal opinion regarding a certain posttalmudic form of oath). *H. Naḥalot* 10.7 gives the court the responsibility for intervening in order to protect orphans' interests. *H. Sanhedrin* 18.4–6, 24.4–10 rules that rabbinic courts may inflict a variety of punishments not prescribed by law. See the commentaries for the talmudic sources. H. Ben-Menachem, "*Yaḥas ha-Talmud ha-Yerushalmi we-ha-Babli le-Seṭiyyat ha-Shofet min ha-Din*," *Shenaton ha-Mishpaṭ ha-Ivri* 8 (1981) 113–32, documents the thesis that the Babylonian Talmud gave judges more discretion to act beyond the letter of the law than the Palestinian (Jerusalem) Talmud did.

[201]M. Havatselet, *Maimonides and the Geonites* (Jerusalem 1967) 123–24, quotes an idealized procedure that the Iraqi yeshivot expected to be followed in issuing edicts.

[202]Goitein, "*Otograf*" (n. 7 above) 192.

[203]It was probably the last of the Fatimids, because the historical account relating that God sent Maimonides to save the community indicates that Zuṭa was in office when Maimonides arrived in the country, and Maimonides did not arrive in Egypt until the second half of the 1160s. For another opinion, see J. Levinger, "Was Maimonides 'Rais al-Yahud?'" *Studies in Maimonides*, ed. I. Twersky (Cambridge, Mass. 1990) 88, note (which unnecessarily assumes that Zuṭa received his appointment immediately after the coronation of the new king).

Maimonides—which would appear to mean that Maimonides arrived in the country during Zuṭa's tenure in office—and Maimonides was able to have the miscreant removed.[204] A letter of Maimonides' written years after the event speaks of "informers" [*moserim*] who endangered his life during his first years in Egypt. These could have been Zuṭa and his supporters, who were acting to neutralize Maimonides or to take revenge by slandering him to the government.[205] Zuṭa's third tenure in office occurred later, extended two years, and ended when he became involved in a scandal.[206] If Zuṭa and Abu Zikri are indeed identical, his third period in office would have occurred at the time of the al-Maḥalla affair and hence belong to the period around 1187.

In 1169 and 1170, a few years after arriving in Egypt, Maimonides can also be seen taking the initiative in collecting substantial sums of money throughout the country for the redemption of Jewish prisoners who had been caught up in the crusader wars.[207] He had thus already stepped forward in a communal role. An

[204]A. Neubauer, "Egyptian Fragments," *Jewish Quarterly Review*, o.s. 8 (1896) 544–51; supplement in *Jewish Quarterly Review*, o.s. 11 (1899) 532; reedition with textual corrections in Z. Malachi, *Studies in Medieval Hebrew Literature* (in Hebrew) (Tel Aviv 1971) 42–51; D. Kaufmann, "The Egyptian Sutta-Megilla," *Jewish Quarterly Review*, o.s. 9 (1897) 170–72; D. Kaufmann, "Zur Biographie Maimūni's," *Monatsschrift für Geschichte und Wissenschaft des Judentums* 41 (1897) 460–64; Mann, *The Jews in Egypt and Palestine* (n. 4 above) 1.234–36.

[205]Maimonides, Letter to Japhet in Shailat, *Letters and Essays of Moses Maimonides* (n. 4 above) 229.

[206]Neubauer, "Egyptian Fragments" 549–50, which relates that Zuṭa's third rise to power occurred when Egypt was ruled by a "righteous king" who "did not take bribes"—most probably Saladin, who acceded to the rule of Egypt in 1171. With the aid of his son, Zuṭa now convinced the royal court that the Jewish community was plotting with enemies of the regime. The king allowed Zuṭa to "return to his position." Conditions remained thus for two years, until Zuṭa's son delivered three poor foreign Jews to the regime with the accusation that they were conspirators from abroad, and two of the men died in prison. That was the last straw. The community brought out "scrolls of the Law" and "declared a ban," a "curse, and a covenant," upon Zuṭa and his son (see above, p. 47). The upshot was that Rabbi Isaac—possibly Maimonides' colleague Isaac ben Sason—went to the royal court and convinced the authorities to remove Zuṭa. Zuṭa was then again excommunicated by the community. Why the account of the events does not mention Maimonides in connection with the later set of actions taken against Zuṭa is unexplained; but if the final deposing of Zuṭa-Abu Zikri was not achieved until the early 1190s, it could have taken place during the time when Maimonides suffered the lengthy illness that will be referred to presently.

[207]Three documents published, translated, and discussed by S. Goitein deal with the redemption of captives. One, signed by Maimonides and dated 1169, introduces an emissary whom Maimonides sent to collect money for redeeming captives, asks the inhabitants of an unnamed Egyptian town or towns to donate generously, and states that "we judges, elders, and scholars" are making extraordinary efforts in the cause. (Two earlier scholars read the date differently from Goitein, who edited the letter from printed facsimiles. The letter is found in the Jewish Theological Seminary, Elkan Adler Collection, and there the date of 1169 seems unmistakable.) A second document, dated 1170, is a letter to Maimonides accompanying a large donation, with Maimonides' acknowledgment of receipt of the donation on the back of the letter. The third

undated letter apparently addressed to him assumes that he regularly found funds for indigents to pay the government poll tax.[208] Toward the end of his life, in the year 1199, he writes that after morning prayers on the Sabbath, the Jewish community in Fustat would visit him and he would advise them regarding communal matters for the coming week.[209]

On the other side of the ledger, some of his efforts to introduce reforms in the areas of prayer and liturgy failed; the usages he tried to uproot were too stubbornly ingrained. In one notable instance, he issued a pronouncement that Jewish males who had experienced a seminal emission were allowed to pray without first washing themselves, but his lenient opinion occasioned fierce opposition, against which he had to defend himself.[210] His son, Abraham, writes that one of Maimonides' attempts to standardize liturgy in Egypt consisted in requiring the Palestinian congregation in Fustat to give up its three-year cycle of Sabbath Pentateuch readings and to accept the annual cycle instead. But "*shar al-ashrār,*" "the evildoer of all evildoers," commanded him to be silent, and the reform was stillborn.[211] *Shar al-ashrār* is an unmistakable pun on *sar ha-sarim*, "prince of princes," which was an honorific title of the leader of the Jewish community.[212] Clearly, a man who laid claim to the title "prince of princes" but was in reality the "evildoer of all evildoers" blocked Maimonides' efforts. There is reason to believe that Zuṭa, who, as we saw, laid claim to the leadership of the community, came from a family of Palestinian origin. He may therefore have been Maimonides'

---

document is truncated at the beginning and end, and therefore has neither a date nor a signature. It again introduces the emissary who is mentioned in the first document, appeals to Jewish communities to contribute generously to the fund for redeeming the Jewish captives, and states that the writer had written to two rabbinic judges in Palestine, authorizing them to negotiate with the captors. Goitein understands that all three documents are a response to the Crusaders' capture of Bilbays in 1168 and their imprisoning of much of the civilian population; Bilbays lay on the Egyptian side of the Palestine-Egypt border. See Goitein, "Maimonides, Man of Action" (n. 16 above) 155–60; S. Goitein, *Ha-Yishshub be-Ereṣ Yisrael be-Reshit ha-Islam* (Jerusalem 1980) 312–18. Maimonides, *Responsa* §452, dated 1180, is a legal treatment of monetary transactions growing out of the redemption of a captive. Shailat, *Letters and Essays of Moses Maimonides* 69, republishes fragments of letters written by Maimonides which also appeal for aid in what appear to be communal projects, but the preserved fragments do not reveal what the communal needs were.

[208]Goitein, *Mediterranean Society* 5 (n. 22 above) 371, reports that a letter written to Maimonides by a convert from Karaite to Rabbanite Judaism asks Maimonides to pay his poll tax "as you do for two hundred [or perhaps: for hundreds of] others."

[209]Letter to Samuel Ibn Tibbon, in Marx, "Texts by and about Maimonides" (n. 98 above) 377. The letter is dated 1199 but may, in its present form, be a composite. The 1199 date may therefore not apply to the entire letter as we have it.

[210]Letter to Pinḥas of Alexandria, in Shailat, *Letters and Essays of Moses Maimonides* 437.

[211] Mann, *Texts and Studies* (n. 12 above) 1.416.

[212]On the title "prince of princes" see Mann, *The Jews in Egypt and Palestine* (n. 4 above) 2.293; Goitein, *Mediterranean Society* 2.63.

nemesis on the present occasion.[213] The Palestinian communities continued to observe their ancient, triennial cycle of Pentateuch readings after Maimonides' death.[214]

Scholars have long speculated that Maimonides served not merely as chief judge of the Fustat court and perhaps as the supervising rabbinic judge for all of Egypt, but as the official leader of the entire Egyptian Jewish community.[215] The leaders of the Jewish community in Egypt were generally called *nagid*, or prince, which was an internal, Jewish title; at certain times they were called the "head of the Jews [*ra'īs al-Yahūd*]," which was a title bestowed by the Muslim rulers; and at times they enjoyed both titles.[216] In determining whether Maimonides ever held the office, we should first ask whether he is known to have borne either title.

In a couple of instances, he is called a *nagid*. A note from an unknown person has been preserved which congratulates Maimonides on his marriage to the "daughter of an upstanding family" and heaps compliments on him, one of them being: "prince [*nagid*] of the not widowed nation"; that is to say, he was the prince of the nation of Israel, which, in the words of the prophet, "is not widowed . . . of its God, the Lord of hosts."[217] Then, a rabbinic scholar newly arrived in

[213] If Zuṭa was also identical with Sar Shalom, the honorary head of the Palestinian Yeshivat Geon Ya^c^acob—see below, p. 60—he would be a most appropriate person to defend the Palestinian liturgy. The point was made by Levinger, "Was Maimonides 'Rais al-Yahud?'" (n. 203 above) 90. Abraham Maimonides' pun would now be double-barbed: *shar al-ashrār*, the evildoer of all evildoers, as a play both on *sar ha-sarim*, "prince of princes," and on Sar Shalom, the "prince of peace."

[214] Maimonides also encouraged the communities of Egypt to accept a significant departure from the talmudic form of prayer. According to the talmudic rite, the prayer commonly known as the *eighteen blessings* or the *standing prayer* is to be recited in the morning and afternoon liturgies silently by members of the congregation and then repeated aloud by the cantor for the sake of those who could not recite it themselves. In Maimonides' day, variations of the talmudic rite had developed. See *Responsa* §§256, pp. 470–71; Havatselet, *Maimonides and the Geonites* (n. 201 above) 172–74; G. Blidstein, "Maimonides' *Taqqanah* Concerning Public Prayer," *Maimonidean Studies* 3 (1992–1993) 14–17. Because decorum often deteriorated during the cantor's repetition, Maimonides recommended that on days when large numbers of worshipers were present in the synagogue, the silent individual recitation of the standing prayer and the subsequent recitation by the cantor should be collapsed into one. The cantor would recite the prayer aloud, those who could would at the same time recite it silently, and those who could not—there being few prayer books—would fulfill their obligation by listening attentively to the cantor. See *Responsa* §256 and the Blidstein article.

[215] Bibliography in D. Neustadt (Ayalon), "*Be-^c^Inyan Negiduto shel ha-Rambam*," *Zion* 11 (1945–1946) 147–48.

[216] Goitein, *Mediterranean Society* 2 (n. 150 above) 23; Cohen, *Jewish Self-Government* (n. 185 above) 14, 176.

[217] Note addressed to Maimonides, published by Friedman, "*Shene Ketabim Maimoniyyim*" (n. 143 above) 209; the verse is Jeremiah 51:5. Regarding the term *nagid*, see Friedman's comment on p. 211.

Alexandria who wished to introduce himself sent Maimonides a letter that is even more replete with compliments. As part of the gush of flattery, the writer applies to Maimonides the scriptural phrase "prince [*nagid*] and commander to the nations" and addresses him as *sar ha-sarim*, or prince of princes, an honorific that, as was just mentioned, likewise belonged to the leader of Egyptian Jewry.[218] Both letters are composed in a florid style; poems of a thirteenth-century Hebrew panegyrist in Baghdad have been discovered which praise different men as both *nagid* of God's nation and *prince of princes*, although those were not their official titles;[219] and no formal document attaches either term to Maimonides or for that matter calls anyone else in Egypt a *nagid* during the last four decades of the twelfth century.[220] There can be little doubt that the author of the congratulatory note and the scholar introducing himself to Maimonides did not intend the terms as titles. They were merely indulging in rhetoric when they addressed him as *nagid* and, in the one instance, as *sar ha-sarim.*

Maimonides is explicitly described as the "head of the Jews" by two Arabic writers, one of whom was, however, dependent on the other. The first of the two is al-Qifṭī, who, as has already been noted, was not a trustworthy witness. It may moreover be significant that Qifṭī's biographical dictionary attaches the title "head of the Jews" to Maimonides in its entry on Maimonides' student, not in its entry on Maimonides himself.[221] The second non-Jewish Arabic writer calling Maimonides the "head of the Jews" lived two generations after Qifṭī and copied the phrase from him.[222] Ibn Abī Uṣaybiᶜa, who spent time in Cairo, where he met Maimonides' son, and who drew from Qifṭī's work, uses a somewhat different expression. Earlier, Ibn Abī Uṣaybiᶜa was seen to have expressed himself more cautiously than Qifṭī on the question of Maimonides' conversion to Islam,[223] and his language is more cautious here as well. He describes Maimonides as "the head over them [that is, over the Jews] in the Land of Egypt,"[224] but does not deploy the formula *head of the Jews.* While none of these writers knew Maimonides personally, Ibn Sanā' al-Mulk, an Egyptian Muslim scholar who was Maimonides' younger contemporary and who did come into personal contact with him, calls him "the head [*ra'īs*] Abū ᶜImrān Mūsā al-Yahūdī" without further qualification.[225]

[218]Letter from Anatoli to Maimonides, in Lichtenberg, *Qobeṣ* (n. 118 above) 2.36b. The scriptural verse is Isaiah 55:4.

[219]Mann, *Texts and Studies* 1.267–68; 273, §9; 281, line 24.

[220]Mann, *The Jews in Egypt and Palestine* 1.236, 255; Goitein, *Mediterranean Society* 2.26.

[221]Qifṭī, *Ta'rīkh al-Ḥukamā* (n. 51 above) 392. As pointed out earlier, the book in its present form is the work of someone other than Qifṭī.

[222]Bar Hebraeus; see Neustadt, "*Be-ᶜinyan Negiduto shel ha-Rambam*" 147.

[223]Above, p. 19.

[224]Ibn Abī Uṣaibiᶜa, *ᶜUyūn al-Anbā* (n. 58 above) 582.

[225]F. Rosenthal, "Maimonides and a Discussion of Muslim Speculative Theology," *Jewish Tradition in the Diaspora* (Fischel Volume), ed. M. Caspi (Berkeley 1981) 110, and corrigenda.

An Arabic manuscript, preserved in Hebrew characters, of a work incorrectly attributed to Maimonides identifies the author of the work as "the head of the Israelite community, Mūsā ibn ᶜUbaydallāh, the Cordovan";[226] Mūsā ibn ᶜUbaydallāh was an Arabic version of Maimonides' name. It is uncertain whether the identification of Maimonides as the work's author and description of him as "head of the Israelite community" come from a Jewish or non-Jewish source and from when they date. However that may be, no known medieval Jewish writer uses the precise formula "head of the Jews" in reference to Maimonides, just as—with the rhetorical exceptions that have been quoted—none call him *nagid*.

Recent scholars have nonetheless read a letter addressed to Maimonides and the preserved fragment of a legal document (*shimmush*) regarding him, both undated, as alluding to the title. The latter document, which is truncated at both its beginning and end, speaks about Maimonides' "headship" (*riyāsa*), but the preserved fragment reveals neither what the document's purpose was nor what Maimonides headed.[227] The former is a grandiloquent composition congratulating Maimonides as well as the entire Jewish nation on God's having shed His grace on both by bringing about Maimonides' elevation to the "headship."[228] While plainly treating the event as something of considerable moment, it too fails to reveal what he was heading. If one should wish to speculate, Maimonides' headship in one or both instances could have been a medical distinction, for example, his appointment as a physician in the royal court. It could have been his position as head of the rabbinic court in Fustat. Or if Maimonides served as an official supervisory justice for rabbinic courts throughout the country, the distinction could have been the broader judicial position.

Besides the letter and legal document using the term *headship*, Jewish letters have been preserved which refer to Maimonides as the "head."[229] We have seen a

[226]I. Efros, *Maimonides' Treatise on Logic, Proceedings of the American Academy of Jewish Research* 8 (1938), Hebrew section 5. Regarding the authorship of the *Treatise on Logic*, see below, pp. 313-22.

[227]Goitein, "Maimonides, Man of Action" (n. 16 above) 161, 167. Goitein assumes that the document announces Maimonides' installation as the "head of the Jews" in 1171, although the text has no date and mentions no installation; the words "purpose" and "installation" in Goitein's translation are conjectural additions. Goitein further assumes that the letter adduced in the next note congratulates Maimonides upon his reinstatement in the office of head of the Jews some twenty years later, although there is again no date or indication of the distinction Maimonides had received.

[228]Friedlaender, "Ein Gratulationsbrief an Maimonides" (n. 169 above) 262–64.

[229](1) *Responsa* §191, and editor's note. (2) A letter replete with flattery which requests that Maimonides teach medicine to a young man. See Kraemer, "Six Unpublished Maimonides Letters" (n. 137 above) 75, line 18; 78. (3) An unpublished letter found in the Jewish Theological Seminary, New York, Elkan Adler collection. The letter is addressed to Maimonides, is dated 1198 or 1199, and contains a legal question for which the opinion of the "head" is needed. See Friedman, "Social Realities in Egypt" (n. 17 above) 229. The context, according to Friedman, indicates that Maimonides was being addressed as *head of the Jews*, but I have examined the letter

Muslim contemporary speaking of him in the same fashion, and a Persian Muslim who had little or no knowledge of Maimonides' personal history calls him *al-shaykh, al-ra'īs*, literally "the shaykh, the head."[230] These terms by themselves carry no significance at all. "Head" was a title accorded to physicians, and Avicenna, who was a renowned physician, was indeed known as *al-shaykh, al-ra'īs*, "the shaykh, the head."[231] Egyptian Jews were especially generous with honorific titles[232] and they lavished the title "head" on a variety of figures—on physicians,[233] and also on judges, local officials,[234] and rabbinic scholars.[235] An incident upon which Maimonides' opinion was requested demonstrates the point in the clearest possible fashion. A man whom the persons turning to Maimonides term both the "head" and the "appointed official [*muqaddam*]"[236] was delivering a lesson on the scriptural reading in a Cairo synagogue one Sabbath morning when an impatient congregant interrupted and asked in a loud voice: "How long do we have to listen to such balderdash?" Maimonides was asked to examine a copy of the lesson, determine whether it warranted the reaction, and instruct the questioners on the proper way of handling the matter.[237] The hapless gentleman whose insights into Scripture occasioned the outburst was obviously nothing more than a minor official within the Cairo community. He surely was not the head of all Egyptian Jewry.

---

and found no grounds for such a reading. (4) A letter dated 1202, which describes the removal of an anti-Semitic ruler of South Yemen and credits the "blessings" of the "head, Moses," presumably Maimonides, with having effected the change; Goitein, *Letters of Medieval Jewish Traders* (n. 6 above) 218.

[230]A. M. Tabrīzī, *Commentary on the Twenty-Five Premises from the Guide of the Perplexed* (Arabic and Persian), ed. M. Mohaghegh (Tehran 1981) 3.

[231]The medieval biography of Avicenna call him *al-shaykh, al-ra'īs*; see W. Gohlman, *The Life of Ibn Sina* (Albany 1974) 7–9. The title page of Avicenna's *Najāt* (Cairo 1938) gives him the same title.

[232]Maimonides, Commentary on the Mishna, *Bekorot* 4:4, scoffs at titles used in his time that had no substance. The weakness for titles, which permeated the culture, is documented by Goitein, *Mediterranean Society* 5 (n. 22 above) 260–70.

[233]Goitein, *Ha-Yishshub be-Ereṣ Yisrael* (n. 207 above) 326; *Mediterranean Society* 2 (n. 150 above) 246; 5.105–6.

[234]Mann, *The Jews in Egypt and Palestine* (n. 4 above) 1.258, 262. Cohen, *Jewish Self-Government* (n. 185 above) 166–68.

[235]Maimonides, Commentary on the Mishna, *Kil'ayim* 5:5 (end), refers to an unnamed "head of the heads of the Talmud" who could not explain the mishnaic paragraph.

[236]The questioner in *Responsa* §262, similarly speaks of an "appointed official [*muqaddam*]" who served as "head" of a certain city. In *Book of Commandments*, negative commandment #284, Maimonides refers to rabbinic judges as *appointed officials* (*muqaddam*).

[237]Maimonides, *Responsa* (n. 30 above) §110. Maimonides replied wryly that the lesson was of standard homiletic quality and the outburst therefore would appear to have been unjustified. But since the offender was known to be a religious and knowledgeable man, the authorities should either persuade the preacher to drop the matter or thoroughly investigate the incident's background in a judicial setting before considering sanctions.

In a word, documents that speak of Maimonides' "headship" may easily be read as referring to a medical or judicial office. Those that call him the "head" may merely recognize his medical, judicial, or scholarly standing.

Yet another term has been brought into play as evidence for Maimonides' having held the office of leader of the Egyptian Jewish community. Legal documents, such as marriage contracts, that were written in Egypt commonly contain the formula "by authority of" so-and-so, and documents have been found dated 1171 and 1172 in which the formula reads: by "the authority of our master Moses, the great rabbi in Israel."[238] The term *authority* in these contexts has a different meaning from the "authority" of local officials to perform specific judicial functions which was encountered earlier,[239] for the men whose authority is acknowledged in the documents we are now considering had no part in issuing them. There are instances where persons whose "authority" is recognized in Egyptian documents are known to have been the leaders of the entire Egyptian Jewish community.[240] From the documents representing themselves as written by the "authority" of Maimonides, it has accordingly been inferred that he held the office of leader of the entire Jewish community in 1171 and 1172[241]—although, as he once remarked, he was at the time occupied "day and night" in the composition of his rabbinic code and could not possibly have had the leisure to perform the duties expected of the communal head.

Maimonides and a writer of unknown date tell us what the authority referred to in such documents amounted to. It meant, in Maimonides' words, that no one was "to wed a woman or to write a legal document without inclusion of the name of so-and-so [the holder of the authority] or without . . . a prayer for his well-being. That is the purport of 'authority,' . . . and that is what people understand by it."[242] According to the other writer, holding "authority" meant that the formula "by authority of our teacher and rabbi [so-and-so]" was inscribed in "documents, such as deeds and contracts," it was recited at "betrothal feasts, marriage feasts, circumcision feasts, and the like," and it was recited at the opening of public

[238]Mann, *The Jews in Egypt and Palestine* 2.294; D. Kaufmann, "Zur Geschichte der Kethubba," *Monatsschrift für Geschichte und Wissenschaft des Judentums* 41 (1897) 215–16; Goitein, "*Ḥayye ha-Rambam*," *Perakim* 4 (1966) 31; M. Friedman, "*Meqorot Ḥadashim min ha-Geniza*," *Cathedra* 40 (1986) 74, note 36. The Egyptian Jewish custom of thus recognizing "authority" may echo the well-known Muslim custom of formally expressing allegiance to the caliph in Friday sermons.

[239]Above, pp. 46-47. The investing of communal figures with "authority" is referred to by Maimonides, *Responsa* §323; Commentary on the Mishna, *Bekorot* 4:4; Commentary on *Sanhedrin* 3:1; *Mishneh Torah*: *H. Sanhedrin* 6.2–4.

[240]Goitein, *Mediterranean Society* 2.21–22; Cohen, *Jewish Self-Government* (n. 185 above) 269.

[241]Kaufmann, "Zur Geschichte der Kethubba" 215-16; Goitein, "*Ḥayye ha-Rambam*" 31. By contrast, Mann, *The Jews in Egypt and Palestine* 1.266 and 268, conjectures that documents mentioning Maimonides' *authority* reflect his position as chief judge of all of Egypt.

[242]Maimonides, *Responsa* §329, p. 598.

prayers and sermons.[243] Holding authority in the time of Maimonides and the other writer was thus the privilege of having a formula inscribed in documents and a declaration made at social and communal events announcing to all and sundry—that one held authority. It was a hollow honorific.

The definition of authority just quoted from Maimonides is part of a legal decision that he sent to members of a provincial Egyptian community who had become disgusted by squabbling over the formula. The men in question pronounced a ban and, as in the case of a local ban that was discussed earlier, they wisely decided to ascertain what precisely they had wrought. The questioners described their ban as having forbidden "hearing [the declaration of the authority of] anyone in the world, not the exilarch nor the head of a yeshiva."[244] The language reveals two things. First, those who could be rendered homage by means of the empty formula included the heads of rabbinic academies and the exilarch; the latter was either the holder of the ever deteriorating office of that name in far off Baghdad or one of the descendants of the Iraqi exilarch family who had cropped up in Egypt and laid claim there to the ancestral title.[245] Secondly, the Egyptian Jewish community had no single recognized leader at the moment, no "head of the Jews"; for if it did, he would have to lead the list of those covered by a ban against proclaiming the authority of "anyone in the world." The attribution of the present legal opinion to Maimonides has been questioned,[246] but the inferences drawn here will not be affected if the opinion was written by another legal scholar living in roughly the same period.

Someone in Maimonides' day is in fact known to have held the title of head of a yeshiva—whether it was an actually functioning yeshiva is dubious—and to have enjoyed the distinction of the authority formula. Documents have been discovered which were issued in the years 1170, 1185, 1188, and 1195, under the "authority" of a certain Sar Shalom, the descendant of a scholarly family and holder of the designation "head of the [Palestinian] Yeshivat Geon Ya^{c}acob";[247] the title "head of Yeshivat Geon Ya^{c}acob" and titles of a similar sort current at the time in Iraq and

[243]Mann, *The Jews in Egypt and Palestine* 1.240; 2.303. The scholar in question, Yeḥiel ben Elyaqim, who is of unknown date, was asked whether the usage was improper from the viewpoint of rabbinic law. He answered that he saw no impropriety in it.

[244]Maimonides, *Responsa* §329, p. 596. Maimonides responded as he did above, p. 46, explaining that the ban had the force of a religious oath and was incumbent only on those who explicitly participated in it.

[245]Mann, *Texts and Studies* (n. 12 above) 1.230–42, outlines the history of the Babylonian exilarchs during Maimonides' lifetime. Goitein, *Mediterranean Society* 2.18, gives examples of pretenders to the title "exilarch" in Palestine and Egypt. Mann, *The Jews in Egypt and Palestine* 2.209, publishes part of a marriage document issued "by authority" of such a person.

[246]The responsum is problematic, because the ruling in *Responsa*, p. 597, line 4, imposes a condition for absolution from vows which Maimonides does not recognize in *Mishneh Torah*: *H. Shebu^{c}ot* 6.8. See Blau's note to *Responsa*, p. 596.

[247]Mann, *The Jews in Egypt and Palestine* 1.238, 2.294; Baneth, "*Te^{c}udot min ha-Geniza*" (n. 187 above) 87, 89.

Palestine happen to be cited by Maimonides in his Commentary on the Mishna as consummate examples of "mere fancy names" that lack all content.[248] Other examples of the "authority" formula's being connected with a head of a yeshiva are likewise known.[249]

There happens to be reason to suppose that the Sar Shalom who was the head of the Yeshiva also held the office of official leader of the Egyptian Jewish community during periods in his life, although not in 1195. The evidence consists in indications that he was identical with the Zuṭa who, as seen earlier, was reported to have held such an office for periods of sixty-six days, four years, and two years, and who, in turn, could have been identical with the troublemaker Abu Zikri. The three may have been one.

The case for identifying Zuṭa with Sar Shalom is stronger than that for identifying him with Abu Zikri. The historical composition tracing Zuṭa's career reports that he adopted the name Sar Shalom and that he laid claim to the leadership of the community because of his ancestry; Sar Shalom's father is known to have been a claimant to the leadership of the Egyptian community.[250] Zuṭa had scholarly pretensions and called himself a "head of a yeshiva"; Sar Shalom inherited the title of head of Yeshivat Geon Ya^{c}acob from his father and his brother, Nathaniel. This Nathaniel, who was Sar Shalom's predecessor as the head of the Yeshivat Geon Ya^{c}acob, also once served as leader of the Jewish community, and Zuṭa's second

[248]Commentary on the Mishna, *Bekorot* 4:4. If Sar Shalom was identical with Zuṭa—see immediately below—the disparagement was scarcely fortuitous.

[249]Goitein, *Mediterranean Society* 2 (n. 150 above) 20.

Goitein undertook to accommodate the documents pronouncing Sar Shalom's authority with his hypothesis that in Maimonides' case "authority" implied leadership of the entire Egyptian Jewish community. He posited a continuing struggle between Maimonides and Sar Shalom for the office of "head of the Jews," with Sar Shalom holding the distinction in 1170, losing it to Maimonides in 1171 and 1172, regaining it for twenty-five years, and then losing it once again to Maimonides. Goitein's theory is still more cumbersome, for he reports having found a document referring to a man named Saadia, which he read as indicating that this Saadia was the leader of Egyptian Jewry in 1169. Cf. Goitein, "*Ḥayye ha-Rambam*" 31. (Goitein does not identify the document in question, and I have not been able to locate it. In *Mediterranean Society* 2.528, note 47, he seems to suggest that a certain Bodleian Geniza fragment mentions Saadia, but I found no reference to Saadia in the Geniza fragment he cites.)

Hypotheses about the leadership of Egyptian Jewry in the second half of the twelfth century have to accommodate the following as well: (1) The report of the traveler Benjamin of Tudela, who visited Egypt in the 1160s and found there a man named Nathaniel, whom he called the "prince of princes" (*sar ha-sarim*) and described as "the head of the yeshiva and head of all the communities of Egypt." Cf. Benjamin of Tudela, *Itinerary* (n. 115 above), Hebrew Text 63, English translation 70–71; and Mann, *The Jews in Egypt and Palestine* 1.234–35, 2.292–94, who reasons convincingly that Nathaniel was Sar Shalom's older brother. (2) Zuṭa, very likely identical with Sar Shalom, who gained the leadership of the Jewish community for four years about the time that Maimonides arrived in Egypt, that is, soon after Nathaniel. (3) Abu Zikri, possibly identical with Zuṭa-Sar Shalom, who attained the distinction of "head" about 1187.

[250]Goitein, *Mediterranean Society* 2, 32, note 46.

term as community leader took place either immediately, or soon after his.[251] Noteworthy as well is the circumstance that Zuṭa's son participated in his father's claims to the leadership of the Jewish community, and in the thirteenth century, descendants of either Nathaniel or Sar Shalom showed a continued interest in the office of community leader: They filed complaints with government officials against a descendant of Maimonides' who then held the office.[252] Whoever Sar Shalom was, he was not a member of Maimonides' circle. He participated in none of the edicts promulgated by Maimonides and Maimonides' associates.

However the case may be, we have seen that while documents could be issued in Egypt under the "authority" of persons holding the title "head of the Jews," they could likewise be issued under the "authority" of persons who did not hold the title and were not recognized leaders of the Egyptian Jewish community.

The functions of the leader of the Egyptian Jewish community varied through the centuries, and one cannot be sure what they comprised at any given time. Where evidence is available, the primary functions are known to have been appointing judges and local officials, representing the needs of the Jewish community, including Karaites, to the Muslim government, and communicating the government's desires to the Jewish community. An incidental chore was resolving the miscellaneous problems of petitioners in distress.[253]

Maimonides can in no document be seen appointing judges or other officials.[254] He is never found communicating the demands of the government to the Jewish community or dealing directly with Karaites. The only known instance of his representing the needs of the community to the government were his efforts in removing Zuṭa from office shortly after he arrived in Egypt, and then he functioned not as the leader of the Jewish community, but as an agent working to depose the appointed leader. He did apparently arrange for payment of the poll tax of

[251]Mann, *The Jews in Egypt and Palestine* 1.234.

[252]Neubauer, "Egyptian Fragments" (n. 204 above) 547–48, and for the descendants of either Nathaniel or Sar Shalom, S. Goitein, "New Documents from the Cairo Geniza," *Homenaje a Millás-Vallicrosa* (Barcelona 1954) 1.709, 717–18. M. Ben-Sasson, "Maimonides in Egypt," *Maimonidean Studies* 22–23, identifies Zuṭa with the Sar Shalom who was the head of the Yeshivat Geon Ya^{c}acob, but I find other conjectures he makes to be farfetched. Mann, *The Jews in Egypt and Palestine* 1.235, rejects the identification of Zuṭa with Sar Shalom. If Zuṭa and Sar Shalom were indeed the same person, Goitein would be correct in conjecturing that Sar Shalom held the office of leader of the community (see n. 249 above), but incorrect in supposing that he held it for twenty-five years.

[253]Mann, *The Jews in Egypt and Palestine* 1.255–56; Goitein, *Mediterranean Society* 2.33–38; Benjamin of Tudela, *Itinerary* (n. 115 above), Hebrew Text 63, English translation 71; Cohen, *Jewish Self-Government* (n. 185 above) 199, 207, 232–36, 260, 278; R. Gotthiel, "An Eleventh-Century Document Concerning a Cairo Synagogue," *Jewish Quarterly Review*, o.s. 19 (1907) 527–38, published Muslim texts from a later period describing the office of "Head of the Jews" at the time.

[254]Maimonides could hardly have occupied the position of "head of the Jews" when he had to have other judges countersign an opinion in order to give it more weight; see above, pp. 43-45.

indigents,[255] yet that hardly proves that he held the office of head of the Jews. In one notable instance, he wrote a letter of introduction for a destitute stranger to present to an acquaintance, who may have been Maimonides' own father-in-law, requesting help in paying the stranger's poll tax; and the letter's tone casts Maimonides more in the role of a suppliant requesting a favor than of a person exercising power. Maimonides begins his appeal with the words: "Your servant Moses, who holds you in highest esteem, . . . requests your kindness in order to aid the bearer of this letter" by having "the poll tax collected for him there. . . ."[256] The documents relating to Maimonides' efforts on the behalf of Jewish captives similarly fail to show him acting as the administrative leader of the community; the only titles the documents attach to his name are rabbinic in character.[257] The incident of the captives occurred, moreover, too soon after his arrival in Egypt for him to have already risen to the leadership of the entire Jewish community. In fine, nothing whatsoever known of Maimonides' activities supports the hypothesis that he served as head of the Jews in Egypt.[258]

[255]Cf. above, p. 53.

[256]Letter from Maimonides in Shailat, *Letters and Essays of Moses Maimonides* (n. 4 above) 172–74. English translation: J. Kraemer, "Two Letters of Maimonides from the Cairo Genizah," *Maimonidean Studies* 1 (1990) 88–92.

[257]Above, p. 52. Goitein, *Ha-Yishshub be-Ereṣ Yisrael be-Reshit ha-Islam* (n. 207 above) 313, line 8; 317, lines 10, 13.

[258]In *Tarbiz* 32 (1962–1963) 185–88, and *Tarbiz* 34 (1964–1965) 232–36, Goitein published three letters that, he understood, show Maimonides administering charitable endowments and he surmised that Maimonides was doing so as the leader of the Egyptian Jewish community. The first of the letters, which is not complete, submits a request to the "Moses of the generation," undoubtedly Maimonides. The request refers to a charitable fund in Fustat to which the writer laid a claim, but the preserved segment breaks off before the petitioner's desires are spelled out. The second letter is written on the back of the first but has no apparent connection with it—the paper was reused for economy's sake—and Goitein identified the handwriting as Maimonides'. The writer sends a small sum of money as payment for clearing out an orchard, and he gives further obscure instructions about other persons who have claims regarding the property. There is no indication in what capacity, public or private, he was acting. The third letter, which is plainly addressed to Maimonides, although his name again does not appear in the preserved fragment, asks him to recognize the rights of the writer, who was afraid of losing an income from a charitable endowment. The writer hopes that Maimonides will deliver a favorable legal opinion to a third party, who is to make the final decision; see pp. 233–35, recto, lines 12–13, and verso, line 3.

Law courts had control over the disposition of charitable endowments. In *Responsa* §206, Maimonides decided that a court could dispense moneys from a charitable fund in whatever way it deemed appropriate unless the person who established the fund set the condition that the moneys might not at any time whatsoever be used for a purpose other than the one he had specified. Goitein, *Tarbiz* 32, 194, published the draft of a document presented to Maimonides and his fellow judges for certification; the document would have a sum of money paid to a certain individual out of a charitable fund, and it is taken for granted that the court had authority to approve the arrangement. Goitein also discovered other documents where officials other than the leader of the entire Egyptian Jewish community, including judges, administered charitable endowments. In *Mediterranean Society* 2.102, notes 33 and 34, and p. 103, he makes a token effort to harmonize

Four separate letters that Maimonides wrote between 1191 and 1199 are pertinent as well. They speak with pride of the reputation he had acquired as a physician and cite his time-consuming medical obligations as excuses for failing to respond promptly to inquiries or requests addressed to him and for not being able to meet with visitors.[259] Had he held the office of formal leader of the Jewish community in Egypt, it would have been natural for him to allude to the prestigious position and to cite its responsibilities in his apologies. His failure to do so is a further indication that he was not the official leader at the time. In one of the four letters, dated 1199 and addressed to Samuel Ibn Tibbon, Maimonides depicts his medical practice as placing such demands on his time that he could speak to members of the Fustat Jewish community only on the Sabbath: After Sabbath morning prayers, "all or most" of the members of the community would come to him, he would advise them regarding communal affairs for the following week, and they would then "read" with him "a little" until noon; that is to say, they would study religious texts. Later in the afternoon, some would return and again read with him.[260] That is hardly the way the leader of the entire Jewish community in Egypt would conduct official business.

The known sources applying to Maimonides titles distinctive to the leader of the Jewish community are, in sum: a pair of letters so replete with flattery and hyperbole that the term *nagid*, or prince, which they employ looks like mere rhetoric; al-Qifṭī's book, which expressly calls Maimonides the "head of the Jews," but which is not a trustworthy witness; an Arabic writer dependent on Qifṭī; and if "head of the Israelite community" is equivalent to "head of the Jews," an Arabic manuscript of a work erroneously attributed to Maimonides. All other documents that speak of his headship, that call him a head, or that refer to his authority, are compatible with his having held no office beyond his judicial or medical positions. Nor can Maimonides be seen at any time performing functions specifically pertaining to the office of head of the Jews. There is thus good reason to suspect that Qifṭī and the Arabic manuscript either were misinformed or used the phrase

---

these items with his hypothesis that the leader of the entire Egyptian community was the person who administered endowments. It is only a token effort, however. Therefore, even if the three letters which Goitein understood to show Maimonides administering charitable funds should do so, no inference may be drawn about his holding a position beyond that of judge of the Fustat court.

[259]Letter to Joseph ben Judah, in Moses ben Maimon, *Epistulae* (n. 89 above) 69; letter to Samuel Ibn Tibbon (dated 1199), in Marx, "Texts by and about Maimonides" (n. 98 above) 376–77; partial translation of letter to Ibn Tibbon in Kobler, *A Treasury of Jewish Letters* (n. 4 above) 211–13; letter to Jonathan of Lunel, in *Responsa* 3.56 (dated after 1199; see 3.43); letter to an unsophisticated person who asked Maimonides to teach him philosophy, written after the publication of the *Guide for the Perplexed*, and published in D. Baneth, "*Mi-Ḥalifat ha-Miktabim shel ha-Rambam*," *Sefer Zikkaron le-Asher Gulak uli-Shemuel Klein* (Gulak and Klein Memorial Volume) (Jerusalem 1942) 53, 55. The "burdens of the Gentiles," Maimonides here writes, left him no time to give the petitioner private lessons. English translation of the fourth of the letters: Kraemer, "Two Letters of Maimonides from the Cairo Genizah" 96–97.

[260]Letter to Samuel Ibn Tibbon, in Marx, "Texts by and about Maimonides" 377.

head of the Jews and *head of the Israelite community* as imprecise expressions of Maimonides' preeminence.

The supposition that Maimonides ever served as the appointed leader of the Egyptian Jewish community—at least until the last half decade of his life, a period for which no documents regarding his activities are preserved—is, therefore, highly questionable.[261] As far as can be determined, when he acted in the public arena, he did so in his capacity of president of the Fustat rabbinic court or by dint of his personal prestige. Indeed, no clear sustained picture can be obtained of the leadership of the Egyptian Jewish community in Maimonides' time. The only evidence in preserved and published documents that anyone at all held the position of "head of the Jews" during the last three decades of the twelfth century are the accounts of Zuṭa's and Abu Zikri's activities and the undated edict promulgated by Maimonides and his colleagues which reserves the right to appoint local officials for the "head"—on the assumption that the edict had in view persons holding the title "head of the Jews."[262] At the beginning of the thirteenth century, Maimonides' son Abraham did hold the formal title of the *nagid* of the Jewish community, and the title continued to be held by several generations of his descendants.[263]

A few more scraps of information can be gleaned about Maimonides' life and activities.

He gave instruction in a range of subjects. We saw a thirteenth-century Spanish Jew stating that he had personally heard a "scholar" in the retinue of the king of Marrakesh pride himself on having studied science [*ḥokma*] with "the Jewish scholar, Abū ᶜImrān ben ᶜAbd Allāh," that is, Maimonides.[264] It is not clear whether the studies took place when Maimonides was still a young man living in the West or, perhaps, after he had settled in Egypt. Al-Qifṭī also reports that, upon arriving in Egypt, Maimonides taught science.[265] When Joseph ben Judah appeared there as a complete stranger, Maimonides taught him mathematics, astronomy, and logic, starting at the elementary level, and he tells us that Joseph never reached the point where he considered him ready for instruction in metaphysics.[266] If Maimonides gave elementary lessons in science and philosophy to a man who turned up in Egypt as a stranger, it may be surmised that he did not

[261]The hypothesis that Maimonides served as head of the Jewish community is rejected by Mann, *The Jews in Egypt and Palestine* (n. 4 above) 1.255, 268; *Texts and Studies* (n. 12 above) 1.416–18; and E. Ashtor-Strauss, "Saladin and the Jews," *Hebrew Union College Annual* 27 (1956) 313–14.

[262]Sar Shalom at certain times had discretion over appointments. See Mann, *The Jews in Egypt* 1.237, 2.298–301. Some appointees negotiated directly with the government for their appointment; see Baneth *Teᶜudot min ha-Geniza*" (n. 187 above) 80, 90–93.

[263]Mann, *Texts and Studies* (n. 12 above) 1.418–27.

[264]Above, p. 26.

[265]Above, p. 35.

[266]*Guide for the Perplexed*, Dedicatory Preface; 2.24 (beginning).

have many advanced students in those subjects. He also taught medicine on an individual basis.[267]

If he ever conducted a formal school of any kind, it would, considering the times, undoubtedly have been an academy of rabbinic studies. In a letter written no earlier than 1179, he mentions that during the preceding year and a half he had taught the Babylonian Talmud, Alfasi's compendium of the Babylonian Talmud, and his own code of rabbinic law to different circles of students: Two or three of the students had studied subdivisions of Maimonides' code, two had studied tractates of the Babylonian Talmud in which they were interested, and the majority had studied Alfasi's compendium.[268] How many students there had been in all is not revealed nor is the framework in which Maimonides conducted the classes. The names of a few men who studied rabbinic texts with him are known,[269] and Geniza documents have been published in which unnamed persons record explanations of rabbinic passages that Maimonides had offered during what appear to have been classes or lectures.[270] Then there is an anecdote that a man writing after the death of Abraham Maimonides heard from him. It involves "students" who were receiving rabbinic instruction from Maimonides in his "house of study" (*bet midrash*), a term that could designate a part of Maimonides' domicile; a comment he once makes reveals that his house (*dār*) had an area large enough to accommodate what he calls "all the men of Fustat."[271] Since Maimonides' rabbinic code was among the texts discussed by Maimonides and the students at the session in question, the incident postdates the code's completion. The man who preserved the anecdote recounts that a visitor from Cairo happened to be present and at one

[267]Above, p.37.

[268]Letter to Pinḥas of Alexandria, in Shailat, *Letters and Essays of Moses Maimonides* (n. 4 above) 439. Maimonides states: "For about a year and a half, no one has studied my composition [that is, the *Mishneh Torah*] with me, except that two or three men studied a few of its Books. [Alternative translation: No one has studied my composition. Two or three men have studied sundry books.] Most of the students wanted to study" Alfasi's compendium of the Babylonian Talmud "and I taught them the entire work several times. Two asked to study Talmud and I taught them the tractates that they requested." Maimonides could hardly mean that he taught Alfasi's entire compendium several times in a year and a half.

[269]Mann, *The Jews in Egypt and Palestine* 2.316; I. Ta-Shma, "*Perush ha-Rambam la-Talmud,*" *Shenaton ha-Mishpaṭ Ha-Ivri* 14–15 (1988–1989) 300.

[270]M. Friedman, "*Reshimot Talmid be-Bet Midrash ha-Rambam,*" *Tarbiz* 62 (1992–1993). On 529, Friedman quotes one document that begins: "An explanation that we [or: I] heard from our Master and Rabbi, Moses, the great rabbi in Israel, on tractate *Baba Qamma.*" On 563 and 573, Friedman quotes from another document that reports: "A student said to our Master when the Book of Love [of the *Mishneh Torah*] was being studied with him: Why did our Master not" treat a certain liturgical issue in the *Mishneh Torah* in the same way that he treated an analogous issue. I could find nothing in either document to indicate the framework in which the classes or lectures took place. Friedman writes that he knows of other, unpublished Geniza documents in which Maimonides' explanations of talmudic passages are cited. The additional example he gives on pp. 576-77 again contains no indication that a class of any sort was involved.

[271]Moses ben Maimon, *Epistulae* (n. 89 above) 64.

point called Maimonides' attention to passages from the Talmud that he thought were pertinent—only to be dismissed somewhat curtly by Maimonides. It sounds as if the visitor had attended an open class, perhaps one of those that Maimonides is known to have held on the Sabbath.[272]

While it is certain, then, that Maimonides taught rabbinic texts in one format or another, the meager information does not justify conclusions about the venue in which he did so. The supposition of recent scholars that he conducted a formal rabbinic academy, although possible, goes well beyond the evidence.[273]

He is not reported ever to have preached a sermon or delivered a speech.

Writing in the early 1190s, Maimonides acknowledges that on a number of occasions in earlier years, he had engaged in angry polemics with various rabbinic scholars regarding matters of Jewish law. "I would," he writes, "please my friends and make my adversaries weep with my tongue and pen—wielding my tongue against those in the immediate vicinity and my pen against those who were at a distance." Although he gives us to understand that he had outgrown such behavior, he allowed himself, around the time he was writing those words, to be drawn into yet another nasty dispute, this one involving his former student Joseph ben Judah, who lived in both Syria and Iraq, and Samuel ben Eli, the principal of the rabbinic academy in Baghdad. While he was able to rein in his anger, he does not completely hide it.

A letter from him to Joseph discloses the following: Joseph had persuaded Maimonides to support the candidacy of someone for a communal office; Samuel had written to Maimonides that the person in question was a ne'er-do-well and did not deserve the appointment; and Maimonides had replied to Samuel that he would have refrained from acting in the matter if he had known of the controversy, but now it was too late to undo what had been done.[274] The particulars—who the candidate was, what the office was, whether it was a position in the Iraqi, the Syrian, or the Egyptian, Jewish community, whether Maimonides had merely endorsed the unidentified person's candidacy or had himself played a role in making the appointment—are all murky.[275] On one reading of Maimonides' letter, the position at issue was the exilarchy, the hereditary leadership of the Iraqi Jewish community, and Maimonides had lent his support to a candidate who gained the

[272]Halkin, "*Sanegoreya ᶜal Sefer Mishneh Torah*" (n. 124 above) 418, 424–25. The letter quoted above on p. 63, and the one published in Shailat, *Letters and Essays of Moses Maimonides* (n. 4 above) 562–63, show that Maimonides taught open classes on the Sabbath.

[273]S. Goitein, "*Temikatam shel Yehude Teman*," *Tarbiz* 31 (1961–1962) 369–70, summarizes a document directing that a very substantial sum of money be delivered to "R. Moses." Because of other names in the document, Goitein dates it to Maimonides' time. He surmises that the "R. Moses" in the document was Maimonides and, further, that the sum was intended for what he calls Maimonides' "yeshiva," but he offers no evidence apart from the size of the sum.

[274]Moses ben Maimon, *Epistulae* 60–61, 64–65.

[275]See Baneth's judicious analysis of the matter in *Epistulae* 80–85.

office over Samuel's opposition.[276] Whatever the merits of that reading, other passages in Maimonides' letter reveal that Joseph had indeed taken the part of a man holding the position of Iraqi exilarch in the man's struggle with Samuel,[277] and Maimonides, acceding to a request of Joseph's, had openly mustered support for the exilarch in Fustat.[278] Bolstering a known adversary of Samuel's would have been galling to the latter, and Maimonides surely understood as much when he acted as he did. At all events, Maimonides further informs Joseph that he had encouraged Samuel to bring the quarrel to a close and he appeals to Joseph to desist on his side.[279]

The tension between Maimonides and Samuel ben Eli ran deeper than disagreements about communal appointments. As will appear in a later chapter, Samuel had, with exquisite courtesy, criticized rulings on questions of rabbinic law issued by Maimonides[280] as well as Maimonides' stand on the dogma of resurrection of the dead.[281] Maimonides answered some of Samuel's criticisms of his halakic rulings in letters to other parties and he answered one criticism in a letter to Samuel himself. When writing to his adversary, Maimonides addresses him as "the great Gaon" and signs off with a prayer for the well-being of Samuel, his "sacred academy," and his "entire pure retinue." But his words exude sarcasm, and barely disguised contempt for Samuel peeks out between the *pro forma* civilities.[282] To others, Maimonides characterizes the distinguished principal of the Baghdadi academy as a run-of-the-mill homilist (*darshan*) and mediocre talmudist.[283] Maimonides' *Treatise on Resurrection* was written in response to Samuel's criticism of his position on resurrection and it too is disdainful of Samuel.

In later life, Maimonides' medical activities brought him fame and success. A letter of his written around 1190, which I have referred to, informs Joseph ben Judah that he was attending the chief *qāḍī*, that is, the chief Muslim religious judge, the vizier al-Fāḍil, and other members of the Muslim aristocracy as a physician, and that his medical expertise was greatly respected.[284] Medicine, Maimonides

[276]Moses ben Maimon, *Epistulae* 60. Baneth, *Epistulae* 83–85, argues against the hypothesis that Maimonides had furthered the appointment of a candidate for the exilarchy. To the considerations he offers, another may be added, namely, Maimonides' statement that he had not known of the appointment's controversial character. If the exilarchy itself was at issue, such a statement would be grossly disingenuous.

[277]Moses ben Maimon, *Epistulae* 62. Regarding Samuel's opposition to the recently appointed exilarch, see S. Assaf, "*Qobeṣ shel Iggerot R. Shemuel ben Eli*," *Tarbiz* 1.1, 126, and 1.2, 66–67.

[278]Moses ben Maimon, *Epistulae* 64.

[279]Moses ben Maimon, *Epistulae* 61, 64.

[280]Maimonides, *Responsa* (n. 30 above) §§308–10, 464.

[281]Below, pp. 515–20.

[282]Maimonides, *Responsa* §310.

[283]Moses ben Maimon, *Epistulae* 65–66; *Responsa* §300.

[284]Above, p. 35. From 1180 until Saladin's death, al-Fāḍil spent as much time away from

complains, consumed almost all of his time. He "always" spent the day with his patients in Cairo and upon returning home to Fustat, would "study what was pertinent [to his cases] in the medical literature. For you know how long and difficult the medical art is for one who is faithful and precise and wishes to say nothing without knowing a proof of what he says, without knowing where the proof is stated and what the reasoning underlying it is." Maimonides thereupon makes the following curious statement: "As for the common people, I am raised above them, and they can find no way to [reach] me."[285] He either means that he had removed himself from contact with the common crowd—and if that indeed is his meaning we shall see that he subsequently changed course and extended his medical practice to patients of all social strata—or else he means that he was now at last protected against his enemies.

The Muslim author Ibn Abī Uṣaybiᶜa, writing several decades after Maimonides' death, reports that Maimonides' patients included both Saladin and Saladin's oldest son, "King [or: Prince] al-Afḍal."[286] If the information is correct, the question arises why Maimonides did not mention his royal patients side by side with the chief *qāḍī* and the vizier al-Fāḍil in his letter to Joseph ben Judah. The answer could be that they were not currently under his care, that they only consulted with him by messenger and not in person, or that they only consulted with him infrequently; Saladin is known to have employed a number of physicians. Ibn Abī Uṣaybiᶜa further reports that Maimonides wrote a book entitled *Regimen of Health* for al-Afḍal.[287] The *Regimen of Health* is extant and contains the statement that Maimonides composed it at the bidding of the "royal master" al-Afḍal.[288] A channel through which Maimonides may have made contact with al-Afḍal is suggested by Qifṭī, who writes that Maimonides' brother-in-law was the secretary of the prince's mother.[289]

Ibn Abī Uṣaybiᶜa preserves an appreciation of Maimonides' medicine in the form of a poem composed by Ibn Sanā' al-Mulk, who was the scion of a prominent Muslim family and who knew Maimonides personally. The first line of the poem announces that whereas Galen's medicine treated only the body, Maimonides' treats

---

Egypt as he did at home. See A. Helbig, *Al-Qāḍī Al-Fāḍil* (Leipzig 1908) 24–30.

285 Moses ben Maimon, *Epistulae* 69–70. English translation of the letter: R. Weiss and C. Butterworth, *Ethical Writings of Maimonides* (New York 1975) 115–23. Maimonides speaks of his fame as a medical practitioner and the responsibilities it brought in the letter to Jonathan of Lunel, referred to above, n. 259.

286 Ibn Abī Uṣaibiᶜa, *ᶜUyūn al-Anbā* (n. 58 above) 582.

287 Ibn Abī Uṣaibiᶜa, *ᶜUyūn al-Anbā* 582.

288 Maimonides, *Fī Tadbīr aṣ-Ṣiḥḥat*, ed. and German trans. H. Kroner, *Janus* 27 (1923) 286; 28 (1924) 199. Medieval Hebrew translation: *Regimen sanitatis* (*Hanhagat ha-Beriut*), ed. S. Muntner (Jerusalem 1957) 27 (the medieval Hebrew translation loses Maimonides' reference to *al-Afḍal* in the opening lines of the composition). English translation: *The Regimen of Health*, trans. A. Bar Sela, et al., *Transactions of the American Philosophical Society*, n.s. 54.4 (1964) 16a.

289 Qiftī, *Ta'rīkh al-Ḥukamā* (n. 51 above) 318.

body and intellect, and the poem then declares that if the moon only had the good sense to place itself in Maimonides' hands, he would cure it of its periodic defects—its waning, which is followed by its total disappearance at the end of each month.[290] The fact that most of Maimonides' medical writings were commissioned by Muslims of high standing corroborates his fame as a physician within the Muslim community. The medical writings also confirm the assiduousness with which, as Maimonides wrote to Joseph ben Judah, he studied the medical literature.[291]

In the letter to Samuel Ibn Tibbon, which I have referred to a number of times, Maimonides outlines the course of his day in order to discourage Ibn Tibbon—who was to produce the classic translation of the *Guide for the Perplexed* into Hebrew—from making the difficult trip from southern France to Egypt in order to discuss philosophic issues with him. "Each day in the morning," Maimonides writes, he would travel the short distance from Fustat to Cairo and would there attend the "king [or: prince (*melek*=Arabic *malik*)]." When either the latter, one of his sons, one of his women, or a courtier was ill, "I spend all day in the palace." In the best event, "I return to Fustat in the afternoon, never earlier. When I arrive, overcome by hunger, I find my courtyard full of Jews and non-Jews of every class. . . . I dismount from my riding animal, wash my hands, go out, apologize" to the throng and ask them to "wait until I eat a light meal, [my sole meal] for the entire day.[292] Then I go out to attend to their medical needs and write prescriptions. They are not gone before nightfall and sometimes, I swear, until two hours or more hours after dark. I give them instructions lying prostrate from fatigue and when night falls, I am so weak that I can no longer talk."[293]

Here too a question arises, namely, the identity of the king, or perhaps prince, whom Maimonides was treating in 1199. Saladin died in 1193. Saladin's son ᶜAzīz, who succeeded his father as ruler of Egypt, died in 1198 and his ten-year-old heir did not yet have sons and women requiring medical attention. Prince al-Afḍal, who we have already seen was a patient of Maimonides', and who had been living in Syria, was appointed regent over the Egyptian territories on the death of ᶜAzīz. But al-Afḍal was soon back in Syria on military adventures and in early 1200 was deposed from the regency and banished from Egypt permanently.[294] Maimonides

[290]Ibn Abī Uṣaibiᶜa, *ᶜUyūn al-Anbā* 582, trans. Rosenthal, "Maimonides and a Discussion of Muslim Speculative Theology" (n. 225 above) 110 and corrigenda.

[291]See below, chapter 8.

[292]Maimonides' treatise *On Asthma* (n. 101 above), chapter 6, §§1, 4, states that people of strong constitution, but not the elderly and those recovering from an illness, may restrict themselves to a single full meal a day without damaging their health, although he advises them to eat something additional before going to sleep. Maimonides then indicates that that had been his own custom.

[293]Marx, "Texts by and about Maimonides" (n. 98 above) 376–77. Translation in Lewis, *Islam* (n. 51 above) 2.192.

[294]R. Humphreys, *From Saladin to the Mongols* (Albany 1977) 89–116.

could be describing a typical day in attending al-Afḍal and his retinue during the short time that the prince spent in Egypt as regent. Another possibility, as a scholar has argued on other grounds, is that what the manuscripts present as a single letter to Ibn Tibbon is in fact a pastiche, pieced together from different letters, written at different times.[295] In other words, the date 1199 may not cover the portion of the letter describing Maimonides' day, and the king, or prince, whom he treated could have been ᶜAzīz, al-Afḍal, or conceivably even Saladin.

At all events, it is clear that the chief *qāḍī* and Saladin's vizier were among Maimonides' actual patients, that he had royal patients as well, and that Prince al-Afḍal commissioned Maimonides to write a medical guide for him.[296]

The Ibn Sanā' al-Mulk who composed hyperbolic verses about Maimonides' medical skill tells of a gathering in which Maimonides debated a theological topic with both him and an additional Muslim luminary.[297] Maimonides thus moved in Muslim circles apart from his medical practice. A jaundiced portrayal of Maimonides comes from a different Muslim scholar, ᶜAbd al-Laṭīf al-Baghdādī, who visited Egypt from abroad a few years before 1193. Saladin's vizier al-Fāḍil, who was Maimonides' patron and medical patient, arranged for Ibn Sanā' al-Mulk to serve as the stranger's escort in Cairo. An object of the visit, ᶜAbd al-Laṭīf explains, was to meet three men, one of them being the very person with whom Ibn Sanā' al-Mulk and Maimonides debated the theological question, and a second, "the head [*ra'īs*], Moses son of Maimon." At ᶜAbd al-Laṭīf's request, Maimonides came to see him. The visitor found Maimonides to be a "consummately erudite [*fāḍil*] man, whose predominant quality was love of headship [*riyāsa*] and of service to the important men of the world."[298] *Love of headship* in the present context could mean Maimonides' satisfaction in his position as a court physician or simply ambition. ᶜAbd al-Laṭīf was a prickly individual, and his impressions of others must always be taken with a grain of salt.[299] Be that as it may, no one reading both Maimonides' correspondence with Jewish scholars and the medical works that he dedicated to the important men of the world, to Muslims of high standing, can help being struck by the contrast in tone. Maimonides' letters to

[295] I. Sonne, "*Iggeret ha-Rambam le-Shemuel ben Tibbon*," *Tarbiz* 10 (1939–1940) 137–40. S. Stern, "*Ḥalifat ha-Miktabim ben ha-Rambam we-Ḥakme Provinṣa*," *Zion* 16.1–2 (1951) 24–25, and Shailat, *Letters and Essays of Moses Maimonides* (n. 4 above) 517–19, offer fairly convincing refutations of Sonne's arguments.

[296] He asked Maimonides' advice concerning his medical problems on a subsequent occasion as well; see below, p. 464.

[297] Rosenthal, "Maimonides and a Discussion of Muslim Speculative Theology" 110. A further connection between Maimonides and Ibn Sanā' al-Mulk was discovered by S. Goitein, "The Moses Maimonides—Ibn Sanā' al-Mulk Circle" (n. 125 above) 400, 405: The wealthy merchant who acknowledged a debt to Maimonides on his deathbed (above p. 34) also instructed that the sum of one dinar, twelve dirhams be paid to Ibn Sanā' al-Mulk.

[298] ᶜAbd al-Laṭīf, quoted by Ibn Abī Uṣaibiᶜa, *ᶜUyūn al-Anbā* (n. 58 above) 687.

[299] S. Stern, "A Collection of Treatises by ᶜAbd al-Laṭīf al-Baghdādī," *Islamic Studies* 1 (1962) 57, 58, 64, 65.

Jewish scholars pulsate with self-confidence. The language and tone with which he addresses the Muslims who commissioned the medical works—men, after all, on whose whims not only his welfare but also that of his community depended—are respectful to the point, for the modern ear, of bordering on obsequiousness.[300]

He reveals a few piquant details about his personal habits. As just seen, he mentions that the only meal he would take during the day was a light meal in the afternoon.[301] The remark need not be understood to mean that he ate nothing else. In a medical treatise written a decade or more earlier, he notes that, at least at the time he was writing, he would have something to eat before retiring for the night. Going to sleep on an empty stomach, he explains, is unwise because it causes the stomach to become filled with unhealthy humors, and no one should leave his stomach in that state—unless, of course, he has thick, unmatured humors, which he wants the stomach to mature. From the medical rule that habits should not be changed radically,[302] Maimonides decided that it would be inadvisable for him to eat bread at bedtime, since such had not been his habit; when he experimented with bread at a late hour, he indeed confirmed that it damaged his digestion. He solved the problem by taking light, easily digested nourishment in the evening, namely, chicken soup, or the yolks of five or six cooked eggs seasoned with cane sugar and salt, or pistachio nuts and raisins, or raisins, almonds and sugar candy. He would drink sugar water or a honey drink and in the winter when it was cold, he would have wine, adjusting his intake in accordance with the weather.[303]

As will appear when we turn to Maimonides' medical writings, the theory that four humors in the human body—black bile, yellow bile, phlegm, and blood—hold the key to human health lay at the heart of his medical thinking. At one point in the medical treatise in which he describes his light evening repast, he recommends, on the authority of the second-century physician Galen, self-induced vomiting once or twice a month. The body is thereby cleansed of excess humors, particularly, of excess phlegm. Since some find vomiting difficult, Maimonides prescribes compounds that when ingested serve the same end. Either he was himself one of those who found self-induced vomiting difficult or he refrained from the procedure because the Babylonian Talmud disapproves of it.[304] As a substitute for vomiting,

[300] See below, pp. 460, 464, 467, 469.

[301] Above, p. 69.

[302] Maimonides quotes the rule in Galen's name in *Medical Aphorisms* (n. 101 above) 17, §23, as well as in *On Asthma* (n. 101 above), chapter 10, §1, and again without mention of Galen in *Regimen of Health* (n. 288 above), Arabic text 28.150–51; English translation 31. G. Bos, "Maimonides on the Preservation of Health," *Journal of the Royal Asiatic Society*, 3rd series, 4 (1994) 220, gives a reference to the rule in Galen and in an Egyptian medical writer prior to Maimonides.

[303] *On Asthma*, chapter 6, §4.

[304] See below, pp. 458, 463. Maimonides omits the prohibition against self-induced vomiting from his code of Jewish law, but to observe it supererogatorily would be in character for him.

he resorted to the medical properties of cane sugar. He would take a mixture of sugar and anise in the winter and in the summer would swallow the sugar with a little lemon juice. The simple alternative, taken every three or four days, worked like a charm. It enabled Maimonides to eliminate unwanted phlegm and keep his stomach "very clean."[305]

The same medical treatise relates yet another habit of Maimonides' which was motivated by medical considerations. He quotes Galen as having stated: "You should know that there is nothing as effective as sleep after a bath for maturing what needs to be matured [in the digestive system] and for dissolving noxious humors."[306] Maimonides writes that from the time he encountered Galen's statement, he would enter the bathhouse only after sunset and from the bath would go immediately to a fine deep sleep for the night. The result pleased him and he recommends it to his patient.

He believed that a healthy regimen protects a person against disease and he quotes Galen to the effect that no one who avoids improper digestion will fall ill.[307] When outlining a brief regimen of hygiene in his own name, he guarantees that those who observe it "will stay free of disease . . . until they die at an advanced age without ever needing a physician."[308] Unfortunately, his meticulousness in observing the precepts of Galenic medicine—keeping his digestion in good repair, dissolving or eliminating noxious humors—failed to protect him against protracted periods of illness.

After receiving news of his brother's death in 1177, he was for "about a year . . . bedridden with a case of serious boils, fever, and depression [*timhon lebab*]; I was on the verge of death." Whether the statement is to be taken literally must remain open, since accounts of lengthy physical disorders resulting from grief were something of a topos in his day.[309] The letter in which the statement appears is, incidentally, the one in which Maimonides reports having been the target of "informers" who tried to destroy him.[310] He refers to what could be the same lengthy illness when writing to Pinḥas of Alexandria. Pinḥas had addressed questions to Maimonides concerning the latter's code of Jewish law, which was completed in 1177 or 1178, and in his response Maimonides apologizes for not answering more promptly. The delay had been due to "illness," and several lines later Maimonides adds that he had been "sick, on the verge of death."[311]

[305] *On Asthma*, chapter 9, §15.

[306] *On Asthma*, chapter 10, §3.

[307] *On Asthma*, chapter 5, §5; *Regimen of Health* (n. 288 above), Arabic text, *Janus* 27.288; English translation 17.

[308] Maimonides, *Mishneh Torah*: *H. De*ᶜ*ot* 4.20.

[309] Goitein, *Mediterranean Society* 5 (n. 22 above) 243–45.

[310] Above, p. 52

[311] Letter to Pinḥas of Alexandria, in Shailat, *Letters* 436. In another letter to Pinḥas, *Responsa* §355, Maimonides writes that he would not be able to respond to trivial questions in the future "for I am harried by a number of matters, and my body is weak. . . . I have no free time at

Letters that he wrote in the last decade or so of his life tell of another long illness. One of them, which was addressed to a group of scholars in southern France in 1199 or later, states that then too he had been "ill for about a year" and even after recovering, had to spend "most of the day in bed."[312] In a subsequent missive to the same party Maimonides complains that it was still difficult for him even to write in his own hand, although he had nonetheless made the effort to do so out of respect for the addressees. He concludes, using scriptural phraseology: "I can no more go out and come in, I have become old and gray headed, not by reason of years, but by the nature of my body which is well acquainted with disease."[313] The passage in which Maimonides depicts his medical practice to Ibn Tibbon and states that he suffered from exhaustion at the end of each day[314] dates from more or less the same period.

Despite his physical weakness, he continued to answer rabbinic legal questions and work on his medical compositions. He died, according to the best information, in 1204, at the age of sixty-six or sixty-seven,[315] and his body was reportedly taken to Tiberias in Palestine for burial.[316] After his death he entered upon a new career in the world of folktale, and over the centuries scores of fantastic stories sprouted up concerning his birth, youth, education, death, and postmortal reappearance in dreams, his activities as a physician, judge, and miracle worker, his confrontations with, and victories over hostile gentiles, and more.[317]

Even without the fictional embellishments, his life was plainly eventful—born in Spain under the Almoravids, seeing his native country overrun by the Almohads at the age of ten or eleven, acquiring consummate rabbinic expertise as well as

---

all because of the weakness of my body and because of my own study in several areas." The same letter assumes that Pinḥas had not yet seen Maimonides' *Book of Commandments*, a work completed by 1170.

In an undated responsum to a rabbinic judge, *Responsa* §346 (end), Maimonides remarks: "I wrote these lines only because of my great affection toward you, although I am ill and harried day and night."

[312]The quotation is from Maimonides' letter to Jonathan of Lunel, in *Responsa* 3.56. The letter was written in 1199 or later; see Blau's comment in *Responsa* 3.43. A letter sent by Ibn Tibbon to Maimonides refers to a no longer extant response by the latter to a previous letter that Ibn Tibbon had sent, and in the no longer extant response, Maimonides informed Ibn Tibbon that he had suffered a long illness but had recovered. Ibn Tibbon began his correspondence with Maimonides after Maimonides completed his *Guide for the Perplexed* around 1190. Ibn Tibbon's letter is published in Lichtenberg, *Qobeṣ* (n. 118 above) 2. 26b.

[313]Maimonides, *Responsa* (n. 30 above) 4.34. In applying to himself Moses' words "I can no more go out and come in" (Deuteronomy 31:2), Maimonides may be alluding to the rabbinic exegesis of the verse: Moses was no longer able "to go out and come in in matters of the Law; Scripture here teaches you that the gates of wisdom had been shut fast for him"; see BT *Soṭa* 13b.

[314]Above, p. 69.

[315]See above, p. 7. Maimonides' nephew writes in the summer of 1205 that his uncle was no longer alive. See Kraemer, "Six Unpublished Maimonides Letters" (n. 138 above) 80, note.

[316]Above, p. 7.

[317]See Y. Avishur, *Shibḥe ha-Rambam* (Jerusalem 1998).

studying medicine and astronomy, at some point in his life studying philosophy, moving to Morocco, visiting Palestine, starting life anew in Egypt, quickly recognized there as the preeminent rabbinic legal authority in the land, constantly occupied thenceforth in judicial matters, wielding his judicial powers and prestige to introduce wide-ranging religious and communal reforms, suddenly having to assume responsibility for his own livelihood and that of his brother's widow and daughter, creating a medical practice and acquiring a reputation that brought him into the Sultan's court and perhaps made him the Sultan's personal physician. The rush of events was at least twice brought to a halt by lengthy illnesses, the second of which was succeeded by a period of infirmity. That Maimonides not only found time to put pen to paper, but was able to write the most significant code of Jewish law coming out of the Middle Ages, two further weighty rabbinic works, the most influential Jewish philosophic work composed in the Middle Ages, ten or eleven medical works, and a couple of minor compositions, is a marvel.

2

EDUCATION

> Maimonides used to say, and this is verbatim, "The forgetfulness that affects men did not affect me in my youth." Maimonides had to read a book just once and the contents were inscribed in his mind, he was master of it, and he was able to teach it to others. (From a Geniza fragment)

Maimonides' major writings fall into three main divisions—rabbinics, medicine, and philosophy. Medieval specialists in each of the three areas were expected to master a large body of material handed down from previous ages and channel their own originality into interpreting and reworking what they inherited. Little new was expected to be added to content. Maimonides, although he was a man of genius, was also a child of his time, and his genius expressed itself primarily in digesting what he had received from his predecessors and then recasting it in new configurations and new frameworks.

Once, in the course of expounding a rabbinic passage, he remarks that a person learns a subject best with the aid of a teacher, even if the teacher is not fully qualified; for whatever one learns from another "takes hold more firmly and is clearer" than what one learns by oneself.[1] The impression he nevertheless gives is that by far the larger part of the legacy he received from his predecessors and reworked in his own writings did not reach him through the medium of live instructors.

Rabbinics was the area in which his mastery was greatest and undoubtedly the area he mastered first. When recommending a course of study for others, he remarks that a student "should fill his belly with bread and meat," that is, acquire "knowledge of what is forbidden, permitted, and the like," before studying science

[1] Maimonides, Commentary on the Mishna (=*Mishna ᶜim Perush R. Moshe ben Maimon*, Arabic original and Hebrew trans. J. Kafah [Jerusalem 1963–1968]), *Abot* 1:6.

and philosophy.[2] As for himself, he calls rabbinics, in a flight of rhetoric, the "wife of my youth, with whose love I have been ravished from my early years."[3]

He must have had an elementary teacher who taught him how to read rabbinic texts when he was a boy; talmudic Aramaic, as he notes, was no longer spoken and was consequently not a language that one could understand without instruction.[4] Someone must also have initiated him into the labyrinths of talmudic dialectic. Yet, except for mentioning on a small number of occasions that he had received bits of information from his father, he names no teacher in rabbinics.

The items that he transmits in his father's name concern measurements, technical terms, and other details of rabbinic law. On two occasions, he relies on a tradition of his father's regarding the weight of silver required for coins used in religious ceremonies; he reports in one of the passages that his father got the tradition "from his masters," and in the second, "from his father, and the father from the grandfather."[5] On a different occasion, he reports the way his father "interpreted" a certain rabbinic measurement to him,[6] and on still another, a tradition of his father and father's teachers regarding the pronunciation of a mishnaic term.[7] His father was his source for the administering of a particular oath to plaintiffs in civil cases; Maimonides writes that he learned the proper formula for the oath by observing how his father would administer it when adjudicating legal disputes.[8] Regarding a blemish on the lungs of slaughtered animals, he mentions in the *Mishneh Torah*, his code of Jewish law, that his "father was one of those who disqualified [animals with such a blemish from consumption by Jews], but I am one of those who permit [their consumption]."[9] He does not take the trouble to deploy any of the polite phrases commonly resorted to by rabbinic writers when they disagree with their forebears or teachers.

That, as far as I have found, is the extent of rabbinic information reported by Maimonides in his father's name. It does not add up to very much, and nothing suggests that any of the information came to him in the course of formal instruction. The assertion, encountered in biographies of Maimonides, that he received his rabbinic education from his father is guesswork.

Maimonides further relates that he learned a certain court procedure from rabbinic judges in the West. He prescribes that a specific form be followed "as our legal

[2]Maimonides, *Mishneh Torah*: *H. Yesode ha-Torah* 4.13.

[3]Maimonides, *Responsa*, ed. J. Blau, 2nd ed. (Jerusalem 1986) 3.57.

[4]*Mishneh Torah*, introduction.

[5]Commentary on the Mishna, *ᶜEduyyot* 4:7; *Bekorot* 8:8.

[6]Commentary on the Mishna, *Kelim* 13:4. In an earlier passage, Commentary on *Shabbat* 13:4, Maimonides cites the same interpretation in the name of a "gaon," without mention of his father.

[7]Commentary on the Mishna, *ᶜEduyyot* 1:3.

[8]Commentary on the Mishna, *Shebuᶜot* 6:7. Maimonides writes that Maimon had learned how to administer the oath by watching his own teacher, Joseph Ibn Migas.

[9]Maimonides, *Mishneh Torah*: *H. Sheḥiṭa* 11.10.

scholars have handed down, . . . and as I witnessed many times and performed . . . myself in the presence of my fathers [*wālidīnā*; literally: our fathers], in accordance with the way that they, may they rest in peace, had done in the presence of their fathers and teachers . . . in the cities [or: lands] of the West."[10] The expression "my fathers" in the quotation could have the literal sense of Maimonides' actual father, grandfather, and forefathers but more likely has the same meaning as the expressions "legal scholars" and "teachers." In other words, Maimonides probably is talking about senior rabbinic authorities under whose tutelage he served as a fledgling judge. However the expression should be taken, the quotation and the report about the judicial oath that he watched his father administering to plaintiffs show that he absorbed elements of court procedure through observing judicial proceedings conducted by experienced rabbinic judges in Spain or North Africa and through acting himself under the supervision of his seniors. Court procedure, being a practical, rather than a theoretical subject, could be assimilated more easily by a would-be judge from real life than from books.

A number of passages in Maimonides' legal code record the legal opinions of men whom he calls his "masters." At one spot, he reports "the custom of my masters [*rabbotay*] and the rabbis of Spain" regarding a certain ritual on the Tabernacles festival: On the first night of the festival, they would enter the tabernacle (*sukka*), remain standing while reciting the kiddush prayer that inaugurates the holiday, recite the blessing: "Blessed art Thou O Lord . . . who hast . . . commanded us to sit in the tabernacle," and only then sit down.[11] A few of the passages give the positions of Maimonides' masters on miscellaneous laws of marriage and divorce.[12] But most of them, more than two dozen in all, report the "opinion" of his "masters" on issues pertaining to monetary disputes.[13]

[10]Commentary on the Mishna, *Nedarim* 10:8. See above, p. 22, note 75.

[11]Maimonides, *Mishneh Torah*: *H. Sukka* 6.12.

[12]*Mishneh Torah*: *H. Ishut* 2.7; 5.15 (his masters stated "things that should not be listened to"; *Maggid Mishneh, ad locum*, identifies the masters to whom Maimonides refers as Alfasi); 18.19 (agrees with his masters); *H. Gerushin* 9.31 (his masters took an "improbable" position because of an error in their texts; *Maggid Mishneh, ad locum* surmises that by his "masters," Maimonides here means Alfasi).

[13]*Mishneh Torah*: *H. Shebu^c^ot* 11.8 (identified by R. Nissim [on Alfasi], BT *Shebu^c^ot* 39a, as the position of Ibn Migas); 11.14 (some versions have "our masters" rather than "my masters"); *H. Mekira* 29:17; *H. Sheluḥin* 1.8; 6.4; 6.5 (see Alfasi, *Responsa* [Vienna 1794, and subsequent editions] §179); 9.3; *H. Sekirut* 2.3 (see Ibn Migas on BT *Shebu^c^ot* 42b); 2.7 (identified by *Maggid Mishneh* as the position of Ibn Migas); *H. Malweh we-Loweh* 1.6 (identified by *Maggid Mishneh* as the position of Alfasi), 2.2; 6.3; 6.7; 14.3 (identified by Rabad as position of Alfasi); 14.11; 14.13; 14.15 (a related opinion is identified by Ibn Migas, *Responsa* [Salonika 1791] §65, as the position of Alfasi); 23.16; 25.7 (identified as the position of Ibn Migas by Maimonides in *Responsa* §396; see Blau's note); 27.1; *H. Ṭo^c^en we-Niṭ^c^an* 1.4 (identified by *Haggahot Maimoniyyot* as Ibn Migas); 1.11 (see Alfasi, *Responsa* §92); 3.2; 3.7; 3.14; 5.8; 5.10 (see Ibn Migas on BT *Shebu^c^ot* 42a). In identifying the sources in Alfasi and Ibn Migas, I utilized the valuable *Mar'e Meqomot le-Sefer Mishneh Torah* (Brooklyn 1984).

Although Maimonides usually accepts the opinions that he cites in this fashion, he does not hesitate to demur.[14] Concerning one such opinion, for example, he allows himself to write that it leads to an "astonishing result, which reason cannot accept; in my view it is no more than the stuff of dreams."[15]

With a single exception, Maimonides does not disclose who the masters in question were. The exception is a passage where he refers to the legal opinion of persons whom he identifies as "my masters, R. Joseph ha-Levi [Ibn Migas] and his master [R. Isaac Alfasi]."[16] Alfasi was the author of a digest of the Babylonian Talmud which Maimonides and others of the time regarded as the most authoritative restatement of rabbinic law,[17] and Ibn Migas was Alfasi's most accomplished student and his successor as head of the talmudic academy in Lucena, Spain. Maimonides' father, who had been a student in Ibn Migas' academy, preserved records of the latter's lectures or unpublished writings, and Maimonides, who had access to the materials,[18] set Ibn Migas on an even higher pedestal than Alfasi.[19] Alfasi died before Maimonides was born, and Maimonides was only three or four years old when Ibn Migas died. He obviously did not study rabbinic texts with either. In calling them his masters he therefore can only mean that they were preeminent rabbinic jurisprudents of the previous generation in whose tradition he placed himself. The sole instance in which he identifies his "masters" thus does not have teachers with whom he actually studied in view.

A number of additional opinions that Maimonides cites from his masters, without identifying them further, have likewise been traced to either Alfasi or Joseph Ibn

[14]*Mishneh Torah*: *H. Shebu*ᶜ*ot* 11.14; *H. Mekira* 29:17; *H. Sheluḥin* 9.3; *H. Malweh we-Loweh* 27.1; *H. Ṭo*ᶜ*en we-Niṭ*ᶜ*an* 3.2; 3.7.

[15]Maimonides, *Mishneh Torah*: *H. Sheluḥin* 6.5. R. Joseph Ibn Migas also did not hesitate to criticize his teacher, R. Isaac Alfasi; see I. Ta-Shma, "*Yeṣirato ha-Sifrutit shel R. Yosef ha-Levi Ibn Migas*," *Kiryat Sefer* 46 (1970–1971) 144.

[16]Maimonides, *Mishneh Torah*: *H. She'ela* 5.6.

[17]Maimonides, Commentary on the Mishna, introduction, p. 47. Here Maimonides writes that he had doubts about fewer than ten of Alfasi's halakic decisions. In his *Responsa* (n. 3 above) §251, he writes that he differed from Alfasi about thirty times, relying in most instances on Ibn Migas. In the specific issue discussed in that responsum, however, he conjectures that the mistake was not Alfasi's at all, but a gloss from someone else's hand which was incorporated into Alfasi's text.

[18]Maimonides, *Responsa* §126; Commentary on the Mishna, introduction, p. 47.

[19]Maimonides expresses his respect for the two, and especially for Ibn Migas, in his Commentary on the Mishna, introduction, p. 47; he writes there that there was never a rabbinic scholar (*melek*) like Ibn Migas. He links Ibn Migas and Alfasi as twin authorities for decisions in *Responsa* §82, p. 127; §218, p. 387; §294; §310, p. 576 (together with other authorities, since the nature of this particular decision required maximum documentation). He cites Ibn Migas alone as an authority for his decision in §§257, 268, 269, 393, 396, 428. In his commentary on BT *Shabbat* 12b, he prefers Ibn Migas' interpretation of a talmudic passage to Alfasi's and on *Shabbat* 18b, he cites a practice that Ibn Migas learned from Alfasi. See S. Assaf, "*Mi-Perusho shel ha-Rambam*," *Sinai* 6 (1940) 115, 121.

Migas.[20] An eighteenth-century author of an invaluable work on rabbinic methodology goes as far as to assert that whenever Maimonides cites the opinions of his "masters," he means those two.[21] Notwithstanding the expert's judgment, it is conceivable that in some of the passages where Maimonides speaks of his masters, he means teachers with whom he actually studied and not Alfasi, Ibn Migas, or another representative of the jurisprudential tradition in which he placed himself. Alternatively, especially where the subject matter is civil law, he could be thinking of rabbinic judges who supervised his apprenticeship in the performance of judicial functions. Since convincing evidence cannot be mustered for any of the hypotheses, they all remain nothing more than that—hypotheses. A final piece of information may be mentioned for the sake of completeness: A fifteenth-century author furnishes the name of a rabbinic scholar with whom, he says, Maimonides studied when the family immigrated to North Africa. But the man's reports concerning Maimonides are riddled with errors, and as a consequence nothing that he writes about him can be relied on.[22]

Maimonides' remarks to the effect that he received a handful of rabbinic traditions from his father and was guided by his father and others in a pair of judicial procedures therefore exhaust what can be said with confidence about personal instruction he received in rabbinic matters. If he did have other teachers, his silence regarding them contrasts sharply with the explicit references to Alfasi and Ibn Migas found in his legal code and elsewhere. It strongly suggests that actual teachers did not play a major role in his rabbinic education. One of the charges hurled at Maimonides by Abraham ben David, the harshest critic of Maimonides' code of law, was precisely that he had not been trained by teachers who stood in the unbroken rabbinic tradition[23]—although whether the charge reflects actual information in R. Abraham's possession or merely an impression growing out of his examination of Maimonides' code is an additional item about which one can only speculate.

Still less can be said concerning persons with whom Maimonides studied philosophy. In contexts indicating that the subject matter was astronomy, a discipline affiliated with philosophy in the Middle Ages, he does speak of having "met the son" of the astronomer Ibn Aflaḥ of Seville, having read texts under the guidance of "a student" of the renowned Islamic philosopher Ibn Bājja (Avempace),

[20]See n. 13 above.

[21]Malachi ha-Kohen, *Yad Malachi* (Przemysl 1877) 2, rules regarding Maimonides, §32. Malachi ha-Kohen appears to make the statement without actually having checked to see that when Maimonides refers to his masters, he does indeed mean Alfasi and Ibn Migas.

[22]Saadia Ibn Danan, in a text published by S. Edelmann, *Ḥemda Genuza* (Königsberg 1856) 30b, relates that Maimon took his sons from Cordoba to Fez in order to allow Maimonides to study with a great scholar named R. Judah ha-Cohen; and a short time later, this Judah was killed by Muslims when he refused to convert to Islam. For Ibn Danan's lack of credibility, see above, p. 8.

[23]Below, p. 272.

and having talked with "students" of Ibn Bājja.[24] He refers to unnamed experts in astronomy from whom he learned how to make certain complicated astronomical calculations.[25] But neither he nor anyone else mentions a single teacher under whom he studied philosophy in the strict sense. Of his three main areas of expertise, the only one in which he expressly tells us that he received instruction from actual teachers is medicine. He names physicians under whose direction he studied the art of medicine in Spain and North Africa, and hence before reaching Egypt in his late twenties.[26]

Whether Maimonides was more or less self-taught in the areas of rabbinics and philosophy, as the evidence suggests, or whether he perchance received a thorough formal education from teachers who have fortuitously evaporated from the historical record, the only way to assess his training in rabbinics and philosophy, and for that matter in medicine as well, is to examine his writings and discover through them the works he read, studied, and utilized.

The languages that he was able to read were Hebrew, Arabic, and Jewish Aramaic. A pharmaceutical glossary he drew up lists terms in Arabic, Greek, Syriac, Persian, Spanish, and Berber,[27] but there is little likelihood that he could read any of those languages apart from Arabic. He misinterprets the rabbinic term *polmos/polemos*; he had no notion of the etymology of the medical term *melancholia*; and when a mishnaic passage makes a ruling regarding the "books of Homer" and the mishnaic text he used had a slightly corrupt reading, he was unable to penetrate to the true sense of the words and correct the obvious error.[28] He therefore could not have understood even simple Greek. The possibility of his having known Latin is more or less excluded by a fanciful etymology that his

[24]Maimonides, *Guide for the Perplexed* 2.9; 2.24, p. 52a.

[25]*Mishneh Torah*: *H. Qiddush ha-Ḥodesh* 11.3: "In regard to these principles, I have traditions from the mouth of scholars [*qabbalot mi-pi ha-ḥakamim*] and proofs not recorded in the books that are generally known."

[26]Above, p. 28.

[27]Below, p. 468.

[28]In Commentary on the Mishna, *Para* 8:9, Maimonides explains *polmos* as meaning *kingdom*. In *Medical Aphorisms* (*Pirqe Moshe*), ed. S. Muntner (Jerusalem 1959) 6.16, he represents Galen as having stated that in Greek, the word *melancholia* means "being terrified." English translation, with the same chapter numbers: *The Medical Aphorisms of Moses Maimonides*, trans. F. Rosner and S. Muntner, 2 vols. (New York 1970-1971). Mishna, *Yadayim* 4:6, speaks of the "books of Homeros," but the text of the Mishna that Maimonides used apparently had: "the books of Meros" or "of Merom" (*m* and *s* are easily confused in Hebrew manuscripts). In his Commentary on the Mishna, he accepts the corrupt reading and gives a farfetched interpretation of it. In Commentary on the Mishna, *Baba Batra* 8:6, he characterizes an obviously Greek term as a Hebrew-Aramaic "compound" word. In the commentary on *Menaḥot* 8:6, he reports that "one of the commentators" identified the term *heliaston* as Greek. In the commentary on *Para* 1:3, he gives an incorrect, popular etymology of a Greek word, but there the word is not a common one.

Commentary on the Mishna offers for the rabbinic Hebrew term *spaclaria/aspaclaria.* He explains it as a compound of two Hebrew words, wherease in actuality it is a transparent borrowing from the common Latin word *specularia*, window pane.[29]

Knowledge of Hebrew, Aramaic, and Arabic gave Maimonides access to everything of a rabbinic nature which might interest him; the great majority of rabbinic texts were written in Hebrew or Aramaic and the only exceptions that could be of interest to him were a handful of tenth- and eleventh century works in Arabic. He could also utilize the Arabic philosophic and medical literatures in their original languages. Like virtually all other students of philosophy and medicine in his milieu, he had access to Greek philosophic and medical works only in translation.

He is reputed to have had an extraordinary memory and to have retained everything he read. A medieval Jewish writer, referring specifically to Maimonides' rabbinic erudition, reports that he "used to say, and this is verbatim, 'The forgetfulness that affects men did not affect me in my youth.' He had to read a book just once and the contents were inscribed in his mind, he was master of it, and he was able to teach it to others."[30]

His knowledge of the classic rabbinic works was consummate. His rabbinic writings, his rabbinic responsa, and his *Guide for the Perplexed* draw confidently and creatively from the classic rabbinic canon, that is: the Mishna corpus; the appendix or parallel to the Mishna corpus known as the Tosefta; the compilations of halakic midrashic material relating to the books of the Pentateuch, namely, *Mekilta*—in both of its versions—*Sifra*, *Sifre*, and *Sifre Zuṭa*;[31] the entire

[29]Commentary on the Mishna, *Kelim* 30:2. Maimonides surmises that the term is compounded from the Hebrew words *safeq* and *re'iya* and hence means "doubtful vision." In Commentary on *Kelim* 26:3, he writes: It has "been said [*qīla*] that in . . . Roman," *sharwal/sharwul* means "insertion of the hand." The glossary style commentary on *Kelim* which is attributed to R. Hai and which Maimonides probably used had offered an explanation of what *sharwal/sharwul* means "in Greek."

[30]E. Mittwoch, "Ein Geniza-Fragment," *Zeitschrift der Deutschen Morgenländischen Gesellschaft* 57 (1903) 63, 65.

[31]For Maimonides' use of the midrashic literature, legal as well as nonlegal, see W. Bacher, *Die Bibelexegese Moses Maimûni's* (Budapest 1896) 36–37. On a number of occasions, Maimonides lists the rabbinic sources from which he drew, and when he does, the halakic midrashic compilations that he names are *Sifra* and *Sifre*; see J. Epstein, *Mekilta we-Sifre be-Sifre ha-Rambam, Tarbiz* 6 (1935) 344. As the terms are used today, *Sifra* designates the standard halakic midrashic compilation on Leviticus, and *Sifre*, the standard compilation on Numbers and Deuteronomy. Maimonides, however, must have employed the term *Sifre* more widely, so that it included a compilation on Exodus as well; see Epstein 344, 347–48. When he wrote his Commentary on the Mishna, he did not yet employ *Mekilta*, the standard compilation on Exodus; it apparently did not become available to him until after he reached Egypt. See Epstein 363. In later works, he does make broad use of both versions of the *Mekilta* and, in doing so, even names the *Mekilta* as the work he is citing, despite his having omitted mention of it when listing the sources for the very works in which he employs it; see Epstein 357–68, and M. Kasher, *Ha-Rambam we-ha-Mekilta de R. Shimᶜon b. Yoḥai* (Jerusalem 1979) 17–27, 49–168.

Babylonian Talmud; the more opaque Palestinian Talmud, a digest of which he at one point undertook;[32] and an array of nonlegal rabbinic works that he would have dated to the talmudic period.[33] He not only demonstrates a mastery of the classic rabbinic canon in his Commentary on the Mishna, which he completed at the age of thirty—although there he does not yet make use of the *Mekilta*, to which he apparently did not have access until he reached Egypt[34]—but in his introduction to the Commentary, he relates that before beginning the project at the age of twenty-three, he had written commentaries on two-thirds of the tractates of the Babylonian Talmud.[35] None but a most precocious scholar could control the texts to a point where he might compose respectable commentaries on two-thirds of the Babylonian Talmud by that age, and what appear to be preserved fragments of the youthful talmudic commentaries indicate that they were a fully competent work.[36]

The meticulousness with which he studied the classic rabbinic texts is reflected in the pains he took to elucidate them. He did the research necessary, for example, to identify the divers flora mentioned in the rabbinic texts[37] and to determine the precise value and current equivalents of rabbinic coins, weights, and measures.[38] His detailed explanations of aspects of animal physiology treated in rabbinic texts show that his knowledge of the subject went beyond the theoretical and that he had pored over the insides of slaughtered animals.[39] In order to establish accurate readings, at least for problematic passages, he would examine as many manuscripts of the Babylonian Talmud as he could find.[40] At one juncture, in a work completed when he was forty years old, he analyzes an issue of civil law where alternative readings of the text of the Babylonian Talmud affect the way in which the legal norm should be fixed. He writes: "Some copies of the Talmud read, . . . but it is an incorrect reading, and as a consequence, men who issued

---

Regarding Maimonides' use of *Sifre Zuṭa*, an alternate halakic compilation on Numbers, see Epstein 352, 368–71.

[32]For the terms *Mishna*, *Babylonian Talmud*, and *Palestinian Talmud*, see below, pp. 135–36, 138–39.

[33]An index to midrashic interpretations of Scripture which is attributed to Maimonides refers to forty-eight rabbinic and quasi-rabbinic midrashic works. See J. Fishman (Maimon), *Ḥayye ha-Rambam* (Jerusalem 1935) Part 2, iv–v; below, 301–2.

[34]See above, n. 31, and L. Finkelstein, "Maimonides and the Midrashim," *Jewish Quarterly Review* 25 (1935) 473–74.

[35]Commentary on the Mishna, introduction, p. 47; below, pp. 141–45.

[36]Below, p, 146.

[37]For example, Commentary on the Mishna, *Kil'ayim*, chapter 1; 5:8; *ᶜUqṣin* 3:5; *Mishneh Torah*: *H. Kele ha-Miqdash* 2.4.

[38]Examples: Commentary on the Mishna, *Pe'a* 8:5; *ᶜEduyyot* 1:2; *Menaḥot*, introduction (end); *Bekorot* 8:8. *Mishneh Torah*: *H. ᶜErubim* 1.12–13; *H. Bikkurim* 6.15, *H. Ṭoᶜen we-Niṭᶜan* 3.2.

[39]Commentary on the Mishna, *Ḥullin* 1:3; 2:1; 3. *Responsa* (n. 3 above) §§132, 252, 315.

[40]See Kasher, *Ha-Rambam we-ha-Mekilta* 172, to which add: Commentary on the Mishna, *Baba Batra* 10:9, with Kafah's note; introduction to the sixth order 6.31; *Kelim* 4:3.

decisions on the basis of those copies erred. I have examined the ancient versions, and found in them [the contrary reading]. . . . Here in Egypt I have had access to ancient volumes of the Talmud written [not on paper, but] on parchment, as the Talmud used to be written five hundred years ago. In the parchment editions I found two readings in regard to the issue under consideration, and both of them concur [on the critical point]."[41] In seeking out manuscripts of the Babylonian Talmud, Maimonides was by no means unique. Rabbinic experts regularly consulted and collated manuscripts in the Middle Ages.[42]

It is harder to assess his knowledge of posttalmudic rabbinic literature, which he, more than other medieval rabbinic scholars, relegated to a subordinate rank over against the rabbinic texts of the classic period.[43] Much of the difficulty comes from his habit of citing authorities anonymously, and the difficulty is compounded by the way he uses the term *geonim*. In strict usage, the *geonim* were the heads of the posttalmudic academies of Iraq through the middle of the eleventh century. Maimonides—partly, perhaps, as an expression of a policy of denying the Iraqi scholars the preeminent status that they claimed for themselves vis-à-vis the rest of the rabbinic world[44]—uses the term more broadly to designate rabbinic thinkers of the posttalmudic period in "Palestine, Iraq, Spain, and France."[45] As a consequence, when he cites *geonim* without further qualification, something he commonly does in his rabbinic writings, he could mean virtually any rabbinic writer who was active after the redacting of the Babylonian Talmud. It is therefore scarcely surprising that modern as well as medieval students of Maimonides are hard put to trace his posttalmudic references.[46] Even when a posttalmudic source can be identified, the question remains whether he drew from it directly or through an intermediary. At one point he expressly tells us that he was citing a responsum of an Iraqi gaon through what his father had told him.[47] In how many other instances his citations of *geonim* may have been mediated through others—such as Isaac Alfasi, Joseph Ibn Migas, or his father—is impossible to determine.

[41]Maimonides, *Mishneh Torah*: *H. Malweh we-Loweh*. 15.2.

[42]A few examples: Ch. Tchernowitz, *Toledoth ha-Poskim* 1 (New York 1946) 149–50, 156–57. E. Urbach, *Ba^{c}ale ha-Tosafot* (Jerusalem 1955) 247, 308, 528–29. J. Epstein, *Mabo le-Nussaḥ ha-Mishna* (Jerusalem 1964) 1099–1100, 1109, et passim.

[43]Maimonides, *Mishneh Torah*, introduction.

[44]Maimonides, *Responsa* §138; M. Havazelet, *Maimonides and the Geonites* (Hebrew) (Jerusalem 1967) 34–35.

[45]*Mishneh Torah*, introduction. In *Mishneh Torah*: *H. Malweh we-Loweh* 2.2, Maimonides calls the rabbinic scholars who followed directly upon the talmudic period the "early *geonim*." In *H. Ma'akalot Asurot* 11.10, and *Responsa* §269, he speaks of the "*geonim* of the West," and in *Responsa* §310, p. 576, he calls important Spanish rabbinic scholars *geonim*. A. Schwarz, "Das Verhältnis Maimuni's zu den Gaonen," *Moses ben Maimon*, ed. W. Bacher et al., 1 (Leipzig 1908) 332–409, enumerates 68 references to geonim in Maimonides' *Mishneh Torah*.

[46]Havazelet, *Maimonides and the Geonites* 39, observes that the full breadth of Maimonides' rabbinic sources cannot possibly be determined because they include lost works.

[47]Commentary on the Mishna, *Bekorot* 8:8.

Be that as it may, if we can rely on a statement made by Maimonides himself in 1176 or 1177, he had by then "studied all" posttalmudic rabbinic writings that he knew of, in addition to the classic rabbinic texts.[48] In instances where he does name his sources, he unrolls a solid array of posttalmudic Iraqi, Spanish, and North African rabbinic scholars, including a couple who would have remained unknown to posterity had he not happened to mention them. Rabbinic works and rabbinic authors whose names I have been able to find in Maimonides are: *Halakot Pesuqot*, *Halakot Gedolot*, *Halakot Qeṭu^{c}ot*, Aḥa of Shabḥa, Judah Gaon, Naṭronai Gaon, Samuel ben Ḥofni, Hai Gaon, Enoch the Sepharadi, Ḥefeṣ ben Yaṣliaḥ, Saadia Gaon, Ḥananeel ben Ḥushiel, Nissim ben Jacob, a certain Ibn Jasus or Ibn Jasum,[49] Isaac Ibn Ghayyaṭ, Isaac Alfasi, Isaac ben Baruk Albalia, Joseph Ibn Migas, a certain Moses of Cordova, and an unnamed Spanish author of a work on the Jewish calendar.[50] Recent scholars have uncovered in Maimonides echoes of the writings of *geonim* in the strict sense, that is to say, principals of the Iraqi rabbinic academies.[51] Despite his mentioning French *geonim*, he exhibits no knowledge of the talmudists of Central France and limited familiarity with talmudists of the southern part of that country.[52]

A responsum regarding phylacteries (*tefillin*), the pair of black leather boxes that Jewish men are instructed to bind on their arm and head each weekday, is—assuming with the generality of scholars that the responsum is genuine[53]—a good illustration of the care he could take in researching a rabbinic issue. At the same time, his own scrupulousness in observing religious rituals makes itself evident. While the classic rabbinic sources are unambiguous about the four paragraphs from the Pentateuch which are to be written on parchment, rolled up, and inserted in the phylacteries, the talmudic text specifying the order in which the four paragraphs are to be arranged inside the boxes is open to divergent interpretations.[54] Maimonides explains to his questioners his procedure in deciding which interpretation was correct and how the paragraphs should be arranged, both when he fixed the norm in

[48] *Mishneh Torah*, introduction.

[49] On this barely known figure, see S. Assaf, "*Qeta^c mi-ḥibburo shel Ibn al-Jasus (o al-Jasum)*," *Kiryat Sefer* 28 (1952–1953) 101.

[50] *Responsa* 3, index. Moses ben Maimon, *Epistulae*, ed. D. Baneth (Jerusalem 1946) 58. Commentary on the Mishna, introduction, pp. 46–47; *^{c}Arakim* 2:2. Havazelet, chapters. 2, 3, and 4. I. Twersky, *Introduction to the Code of Maimonides* (New Haven 1980) 51–55.

[51] S. Assaf, "*Sifre Rab Hai u-Teshubotaw ke-Maqor le-ha-Rambam*," *Sinai* 2 (1938) 522–26. Havazelet, *Maimonides and the Geonites*, chapters 2–6.

[52] *Mishneh Torah*: *H. Sheḥiṭa* 11.15 speaks of a custom regarding the consumption of meat from an animal with a certain blemish: "This custom was never followed in France or Spain and it was never heard of in the West."

[53] J. Kafah, "*She'elot Ḥakme Lunel u-Teshubot 'ha-Rambam,' Kelum Meqoriyyot Hen?*" *Sefer Zikkaron le-ha-Rab Yiṣḥaq Nissim* 2 (Jerusalem 1985) 243–45, argues that it is a forgery.

[54] BT *Menaḥot* 34b. Ancient phylacteries have been found in Palestine which do not reflect the rabbinic prescriptions regarding the passages to be inserted.

his legal code and when he fashioned phylacteries for his own use. He cites: the pertinent text in "all the old versions" of the Babylonian Talmud; four posttalmudic scholars, whom he names; "many *geonim*"; "all the people of the east and the earlier Palestinians"; and "trustworthy scholars who opened [and examined] the phylacteries of R. Hai" after Hai's death in order to ascertain the order in which the scriptural passages were arranged there.[55] R. Hai was particularly important because he was a man of unquestioned stature and reportedly had followed a different arrangement of the parchments from the one that Maimonides ultimately settled on. The present responsum goes into far more detail about sources than is usual for Maimonides. He was replying to a scholarly inquiry sent to him from abroad and wished to explain exactly how he arrived at a decision regarding a matter of great moment for the questioners and him. But if the procedure just described is not atypical, and if his asserted familiarity with posttalmudic rabbinic writings can be taken at its word, his control of the posttalmudic literature—with the exception of the works of the French rabbinists—was comparable to his control of the classic rabbinic sources.

His knowledge of the medical literature, and especially of the corpus of Galen's writings, also appears to have been solid. He tells us that he studied medicine before arriving in Egypt when he was in his twenties. His rabbinic writings do not, as far as I could discover, name any medical writer, but his Commentary on the Mishna, which he completed at the age of thirty, does contain a reference to the "chief" (*ra'īs*) physician,[56] by which he plainly means Galen. It likewise contains references to unidentified books on medicine,[57] veterinary medicine,[58] and anatomy.[59] Galen is the author whom Maimonides cites most often in his medical works, and the most comprehensive of his medical works calls Galen the greatest physician ever to have lived.[60] The work in question is arranged around a cadre of topics, and Maimonides culls from Galen's various writings, and reassembles under those topics, whatever he found to be pertinent to them. In the process, he quotes or paraphrases paragraphs from no less than ninety compositions authored by or attributed to Galen.[61] Many more compositions were credited to Galen in the Middle Ages: Medieval Arabic bibliographers record, between them, over 160 titles

[55]*Responsa* §289. The sentence about R. Hai should perhaps be translated: "trustworthy scholars" told me that "R. Hai's phylacteries were opened" and examined.

[56]*Shemona Peraqim* (=Commentary on Mishna, introduction to *Abot*), (n. 1 above) chapter 1, p. 373; English translation: Moses Maimonides, *Eight Chapters*, trans. J. Gorfinkle (New York 1912).

[57]Commentary on the Mishna, *ᶜUqṣin* 3:5. Maimonides also refers to "the physicians" and furnishes medical information in his Commentary on *Abot* 2:12; *Zebaḥim* 6:6; *Ḥullin* 3:5; *Bekorot* 7:5; 8:2.

[58]Commentary on the Mishna, *Ḥullin* 3:5.

[59]Commentary on the Mishna, *Nidda* 2:5; see also Commentary on *Ḥullin* 4:6.

[60]Maimonides, *Medical Aphorisms* (n. 28 above) 25, §59.

[61]Maimonides, *Medical Aphorisms*, appendix to Hebrew text, 400–12.

of compositions of a medical character attributed to him and understood to have been translated into Arabic.[62] Some of the titles are, however, doublets, some of the compositions were considered to be inauthentic by the Arabic bibliographers themselves, some were not available even to the medieval bibliographers and undoubtedly not to Maimonides, and some furnished nothing appropriate to Maimonides' purpose. He may, therefore, very well have consulted every medical composition that he regarded as genuinely Galenic, that might serve his purpose, and that was accessible to him.

Other writers on medicine whom he cites in his medical works are Hippocrates[63] and the following Arabic authors: Rāzī (Rhazes); Ḥunain ibn Iṣḥaq; Alfarabi; Avicenna, with a noteworthy failure to mention Avicenna's substantial, authoritative medical encyclopedia; Abū ᶜAlā' Ibn Zuhr; Abū Marwān Ibn Zuhr, who was the son of Abū ᶜAlā' and with whose own son Maimonides had been in contact before arriving in Egypt; Ibn Wāfid; Ibn Riḍwān; al-Tamīmī; and Ibn al-Tilmīdh.[64] In the introduction to his glossary of pharmaceutical terms Maimonides reports that he based the work on the books of five experts, namely Ibn Juljul, Ibn Wāfid, al-Ghāfiqī, Ibn Samajūn, and the Jewish Arabic writer Ibn Janāḥ.[65] Maimonides does not name all the known medical texts written by the authors whom he mentions, and most of the medical sources that he does name are either unpublished or lost. Medieval Arabic medicine is a field of study still in its infancy, and a precise assessment of his knowledge of the medical literature is therefore not yet on the horizon.

His control of the philosophical literature can be gauged more precisely.[66] Here two separate questions should be posed: How far had his study gone when he was writing his rabbinic works and how far did it go when he was writing his main philosophic work, the *Guide for the Perplexed*. We have to start by deciding, at least roughly, what we want the heading of philosophical literature to cover.

[62]F. Sezgin, *Geschichte des arabischen Schrifttums* 3 (Leiden 1970) 78–140.

[63]Besides occasionally citing Hippocrates, Maimonides wrote a commentary on the *Aphorisms of Hippocrates* (probably not an authentic work of Hippocrates). See below, pp. 438–43.

[64]See Maimonides, *Medical Aphorisms* xiii–xiv, and indexes to: Maimonides, *The Regimen of Health*, trans. A. Bar Sela et al., *Transactions of the American Philosophical Society*, n.s. 54.4 (1964); *On the Causes of Symptoms*, ed. J. Leibowitz and S. Marcus (Berkeley 1974); *Treatises on Poisons, Hemorrhoids, Cohabitation*, trans. F. Rosner (Haifa 1984). For the three generations of Ibn Zuhrs, see Maimonides, *Treatise On Asthma*, ed. and trans. G. Bos (Provo 2002) chapter 13, §38; medieval Hebrew translation: Moshe ben Maimon, *On Hemorrhoids, On the Increase of Physical Vigor, On Asthma*, ed. S. Muntner (Jerusalem 1965) 115–16. Extended sections of chapters 20 and 22 of Maimonides' *Medical Aphorisms* are drawn from Abū Marwān Ibn Zuhr and al-Tamīmī.

[65]Maimonides, *Explication des noms de drogues*, ed. and French trans. M. Meyerhof (Cairo 1940), Arabic text 3–4; French translation 4.

[66]Pines's introduction to his translation of the *Guide* provides a valuable survey of Maimonides' philosophic sources.

As Maimonides uses the term *philosophy*, the sciences of physics, chemistry, biology, and psychology are included, and astronomy is a closely allied discipline. His reading in all those areas is therefore pertinent to our purpose. He considered Greek philosophy prior to Aristotle, the philosophy of Aristotle himself, and the philosophies of post-Aristotelian Greek and Arabic thinkers standing in the Aristotelian tradition all to be deserving of the title of genuine philosophy.[67] By contrast, the lucubrations of the school of Islamic dialectical theology known as the *Kalam* did not qualify as philosophy as he uses the term[68]—this, even though the members of the school applied their dialectic to the same theoretical issues that occupied persons vouchsafed the label *philosopher* in the medieval Arabic world, and even though they and thinkers recognized as true philosophers engaged one another in written discourse through the centuries. Maimonides' opinion, held in common with other medieval Arabic Aristotelians, was that the Kalam thinkers failed to grasp the criteria whereby propositions regarding the universe can properly be judged true or false, and their failure to do so disqualified them from being classified as philosophers.[69] For their part, the Kalam thinkers were more than happy to eschew the badge.

If we sidestep for now the knotty question of precisely what does and does not constitute genuine philosophy and instead direct our attention to the fund of materials out of which Maimonides molded the propositions and reasoning making up what is commonly regarded as his philosophy, account must be taken of his knowledge of the Kalam. Notwithstanding his dismissive attitude toward the school, the Kalam served, at the very least, as a catalyst helping him to crystallize his stand on virtually every topic that we might want to call philosophic. I begin by considering his familiarity with Kalam thought at the time when he was writing his rabbinic works and then turn to the time when he wrote the *Guide for the Perplexed*.

As far as I could discover, the only one of Maimonides' rabbinic works that refers to the Kalam is his Commentary on the Mishna, which he completed at the age of thirty. The Commentary contains four passages that mention, and in each instance summarily reject, Kalam positions, and none of the passages goes beyond fundamental and notorious Kalam notions.

At one point, Maimonides writes: "I have heard . . . the Kalam thinkers maintain" that God is the direct and immediate cause of every event in the world.[70] The

[67] A. Marx, "Texts by and about Maimonides," *Jewish Quarterly Review* 25 (1934–1935) 379–80.

[68] Maimonides, *Guide for the Perplexed* 1.73 (10), distinguishes Kalam thinkers from philosophers.

[69] *Guide for the Perplexed* 1.73 (10, excursus). See Alfarabi, *Risāla fī al-ᶜAql*, ed. M. Bouyges (Beirut 1938) 7–8.

[70] *Shemona Peraqim*, chapter 8 (n. 56 above) p. 399. *Guide* 3.17 (3) identifies the thesis as a doctrine peculiar to the Asharite branch of Kalam.

words "I have heard" could be just a *façon de parler*, but they sound as if Maimonides was relying on something he happened to have heard rather than on a text he had studied by himself or under the direction of a teacher. In two more passages, he calls attention to defective Kalam reasoning. He speaks in one of them of "the enormous, reprehensible mistake" made by Kalam thinkers in supposing that "everything capable of being imagined has the possibility [of existing]."[71] They, in other words, supposed that no imaginable state of affairs—such as a flying elephant, to supply an example—can be excluded from the realm of possibility on empirical grounds or because of physical laws. In the other passage, Maimonides dismisses Kalam contentions in the general area of divine providence and retribution as "imagination and rhetoric resembling an argument" without being one.[72] Unfortunately he fails to tell us what the contentions were. The final reference to the Kalam in Maimonides' Commentary on the Mishna takes note of, and rejects, the Kalam proposition that ethical truths are discoverable by the human intellect. The ability of the human intellect to establish the truths of ethics was, in fact, a tenet of only one of the two main Kalam branches and not of the school as a whole.[73]

An additional scrap of information comes from the Muslim personage Ibn Sanā' al-Mulk, who describes a disputation that, he implies, was conducted before an audience.[74] The subject of the disputation was the "science of Kalam," and the participants were Ibn Sanā' al-Mulk himself, a second well-known Muslim scholar, and Maimonides. Nothing that the participants said is reported. The other Muslim scholar died at the end of 1186 or the beginning of 1187, and the event therefore took place by that date, when Maimonides was well along in writing the *Guide for the Perplexed.* Since Ibn Sanā' al-Mulk was born in 1155, it presumably did not take place before 1175, when Maimonides was still working on his law code.

That is as much as can be gathered regarding Maimonides' knowledge of the Kalam apart from what he discloses in his *Guide for the Perplexed.* It establishes that when he completed his Commentary on the Mishna at the age of thirty, he knew at least enough to write about the Kalam in a very general fashion and that a decade or more later he could dispute Kalam positions with well-placed Islamic contemporaries. Just how much further his knowledge may have gone at either stage remains uncertain.

Here and there, the *Guide for the Perplexed*, which Maimonides completed by 1191, when he was in his fifties, refers to Kalam opinions on one topic or

[71] *Shemona Peraqim*, chapter 1, p. 375. Both here and in *Guide for the Perplexed* 1.73 (10, excursus), Maimonides stresses the centrality of the principle for the Kalam.

[72] Commentary on the Mishna, *Berakot* 9:7. The terms *kalām* and *mutakallim* appear elsewhere in the section but there appear to have only the nontechnical sense of *speech* and *speaker*.

[73] *Shemona Peraqim*, chapter 6. It was the position of the Mutazilite branch.

[74] See above, p. 70.

another.[75] Most important, four full chapters of the work are devoted to the Kalam arguments for the creation of the world and the existence of God. In introducing the chapters, Maimonides tells us that he had studied the "books of the Kalam thinkers insofar as it was feasible" for him to do so.[76] He speaks about the "lengthy books and better-known compositions" of Kalam writers.[77] He categorizes certain principles of the Kalam as positions held unanimously, others as majority positions, and still others as minority positions.[78] And when he comes to the Kalam arguments for creation and the unity of God, he describes several of them as belonging to either "early" or "later" thinkers.[79] He was signaling unmistakably that he was knowledgeable on the subject.

The first of the four chapters devoted to Kalam arguments for creation and the existence of God lists and examines a set of theoretical principles on which, Maimonides submits, the atomistic and occasionalistic picture of the physical universe peculiar to the school rests. The remaining three chapters examine Kalam arguments for the creation of the world, call attention to the Kalam procedure of inferring the existence of God from creation, and then take up Kalam arguments for the unity and incorporeality of God. The four chapters give full rein to Maimonides' analytic and systematizing gifts. They are written so clearly and the Kalam positions are set forth with such confidence that more than one recent scholar employed them as a prime source for Kalam thought.[80]

Almost all the Kalam arguments that Maimonides records for the creation of the world, the unity of God, and the incorporeality of God can be traced to known Kalam sources.[81] In their case, Maimonides does accurately convey what divers Kalam texts had argued, although he never names a single thinker or work that he utilized. His presentation of the principles constituting the Kalam conception of the universe has, however, been shown in a recent meticulous study to be much less faithful to the sources, at least to the considerable body of Kalam texts available today. Maimonides characterizes as standard Kalam positions what were in

[75] *Guide for the Perplexed* 1.50 (thesis that God, although wholly one and simple in his essence, has essential attributes); 1.51 (question whether the Kalam atoms occupy space, and the sense in which man may be said to perform actions if the universe is completely controlled by divine omnipotence); 1.69 (beginning) (insistence on calling God an agent and not a cause);1.71, 95a (God's eternal speech, blurred in Pines's translation); 3.10 (thesis that the lack of a quality is itself a positive quality); 3.17 (3) and (4) (positions of the Asharite and Mutazilite branches of Kalam on the nature of divine providence).

[76] *Guide for the Perplexed* 1.71, p. 95b.

[77] *Guide for the Perplexed* 1.74 (beginning).

[78] *Guide for the Perplexed* 1.73 (5), (6), (7), (10), (11), (12).

[79] *Guide for the Perplexed* 1.74 (6); 1.75 (3), (5).

[80] M. Schwarz, "Who Were Maimonides' Mutakallimūn?" *Maimonidean Studies* 2 (1991) 160, note 1.

[81] Evidence regarding the arguments is provided in H. Davidson, *Proofs for Eternity, Creation, and the Existence of God in Medieval Islamic and Jewish Philosophy* (New York 1987), chapters 5 and 6.

actuality the views of small minorities of thinkers within the movement. Furthermore, the thinkers who held the positions that he labels as standard shift: In one instance, he may represent as standard the view of a particular circle of thinkers, and in another, what has been shown to be the view of a different circle altogether. Sometimes he records as the position of "most" Kalam thinkers or as a position that he "found they agree on" theses never even mentioned in known Kalam works.[82]

The reason why he misses the mark so badly in regard to the propositions embodying the Kalam picture of the physical universe can only be guessed, and no guess will be satisfactory. To suppose that he had access to few if any of the Kalam works available today but drew instead from an entirely different body of works will not do. The texts that have been preserved and are now available come from the more influential and better-known thinkers of both main branches of the school—the Asharites and the Mutazilites. From whom else would Maimonides have drawn? Perhaps, one may speculate, he once read a good deal of Kalam literature but was relying on his memory, which, when he sat down to write the *Guide for the Perplexed* in middle age, had become much more porous than it once was. Perhaps—and my own conjecture would tend in this direction—he reported in good part not what he had read but what he extrapolated that the principles of the Kalam thinkers must have been, given their proofs for creation and the existence of God. Medieval Arabic philosophers allowed themselves to recreate the thought of their predecessors in such a fashion. Or perhaps, if we allow ourselves to slide further down the slope of speculation, he relied on the products, now lost, of unknown and unreliable summarizers. Whatever the reason, he plainly did not take the care needed to attain precision and accuracy when expounding the principles of the Kalam school in his philosophic magnum opus, despite his assurances about having studied the "books of the Kalam thinkers insofar as it was feasible" for him to do so. That fact reveals something significant about Maimonides and should be kept in mind as we proceed.

Maimonides once remarks that while Kalam theology struck root among some Jewish thinkers outside of Spain, in Muslim Spain, the land of his birth, "all members of our nation . . . held fast to the doctrines of the philosophers and inclined toward their views, as long as their doctrines and views contradict no dogma [*qā^{c}ida*] of the Law."[83] Muslim Spain was indeed one of the areas in which Jews studied philosophy, but the numbers were very small. The notion that all the Jews living there were adherents of the philosophers—by which Maimonides undoubtedly means the Arabic Aristotelian school of philosophy—is hyperbole brought to a dizzying height. Still, Maimonides' own understanding of and attach-

[82]Schwarz, "Who Were Maimonides' Mutakallimūn?" 170–75, 176–81, 189–93; *Maimonidean Studies* 3 (1992–1993) 163, 169–72.

[83]*Guide for the Perplexed* 1.71, p. 94a.

ment to the Arabic Aristotelian picture of the universe is evident from early in his literary career.

As already noted, he names no teacher with whom he studied philosophy. Nor does he disclose when his study of the subect began or what form it took. His Commentary on the Mishna, which is his first preserved substantial work and which he completed at the age of thirty, nonetheless reveals that he had by then been initiated into the subject. The initiation could have occurred in conjunction with his medical studies, since serious students of medicine were required to be acquainted with science and philosophy.

The Commentary on the Mishna, which reproduces only a few generalities of the Kalam, and Maimonides' *Mishneh Torah*, his code of rabbinic law, which never alludes to the Kalam or its doctrines, both presuppose the main contours of medieval Arabic Aristotelianism. In both works, Maimonides avoids introducing the names of philosophers or, for that matter, of non-Jewish writers of any stripe. Nothing else could be expected. As a rule, his rabbinic works refrain from citing even Jewish authors by name. And adducing the theories of non-Jewish philosophers and preaching the philosophic ideal when expounding hallowed religious texts was audacious enough. Explicitly to name non-Jewish philosophic authorities in such contexts would have crossed the line into *lèse majesté*.

Arabic Aristotelian conceptions of God, the universe, and man peek out from scattered spots of the Commentary on the Mishna and are presented systematically in the opening chapters of the *Mishneh Torah*. Each, in its own fashion, thus teaches that God is a wholly incorporeal being and that His essence is unknowable.[84] They locate the world inhabited by man at the center of the physical universe and conceive of the celestial region as a series of transparent spheres—spherical shells—nested one within the other. The spheres are conscious, rational beings; the stars and planets are embedded in the surfaces of the spheres, and as the spheres rotate around the earth, they carry the stars and planets with them.[85] Both works envision a hierarchy of supernal incorporeal beings subordinate to God which parallels the hierarchy of celestial spheres and somehow governs it.[86] They repeat the basic concepts of Aristotelian physics,[87] Aristotle's theory of ethics,[88] and a theory of human intellect which was elaborated by followers of Aristotle out

[84]Commentary on the Mishna, *Berakot* 9:7; *Sanhedrin* 10:1, third principle; *Shemona Peraqim* (n. 56 above) chapter 8, p. 406. *Mishneh Torah*: *H. Yesode ha-Torah* 1.7, 11; 2.8.

[85]Commentary on the Mishna (n. 1 above) introduction, p. 45; *Sanhedrin* 10, introduction, p. 204; *Mishneh Torah*: *H. Yesode ha-Torah* 3.

[86]Commentary on the Mishna, *Sanhedrin* 10, introduction, p. 204; 10:1, first principle. *Mishneh Torah*: *H. Yesode ha-Torah* 2.3–8. See Aristotle, *Metaphysics* 12.1.1069a, 30–1069b, 2; 12.7.

[87]Commentary on the Mishna, introduction, p. 45; *Ma*ᶜ*aser Sheni* 1:5; *Ḥagiga* 2:1; *Shemona Peraqim*, chapter 8, p. 399; *Abot* 5:6. *Mishneh Torah*: *H. Yesode ha-Torah* 3.10–4.7.

[88]*Shemona Peraqim*, chapter 4; *Mishneh Torah*: *H. De*ᶜ*ot* 1.

of Aristotle's statements on the subject.[89] They endorse and propagate the philosophic ideal, which views the development of the human intellect as the goal of human life,[90] and they identify the developed human intellect as the element in man which survives the death of the body and attains immortality.[91] We have a good deal of philosophy here, an astonishing amount, considering that it is woven into rabbinic frameworks.

Maimonides' Commentary on the Mishna further cites with approval: "the philosopher," which in ordinary usage means Aristotle; "philosophers"; "the view of the philosophers"; "philosophers who are expert in philosophy"; "the discourse of expert philosophers," which agrees with the ancient rabbis on "all points"; the "early and later philosophers"; "the philosophy of Greece"; "first philosophy," that is, metaphysics; and "divine science," which again is metaphysics.[92] On one occasion, the only one in which I found a non-Jewish thinker cited by name in the Commentary, Maimonides quotes a "statement of Aristotle's" about friendship. It is an innocuous aphorism to the effect that a "friend is someone else who is you"; in other words, a friend is a person who acts toward you, and to whom you act, as if he and you were the same person.[93] The saying goes back to Aristotle's *Nicomachean Ethics*, but Maimonides' version differs in a significant respect from the form it took in the Arabic translation of that book.[94] There is evidence that the saying appeared in a medieval Arabic abridgment of the *Nicomachean Ethics*, now lost, in the form Maimonides gives. It is also quoted by several medieval Arabic writers in the form in which he gives it.[95] And general collections of aphorisms that circulated in Arabic record versions in Aristotle's name which, although not identical with Maimonides' version, are close.[96] Just how Maimonides came upon the saying cannot be determined from the data at hand, but we can be fairly

[89]Commentary on the Mishna, introduction, pp. 36–37, and *Abot* 3:20. *Mishneh Torah*: *H. Yesode ha-Torah* 4.7–9. In *Shemona Peraqim*, chapter 1, Maimonides outlines the medieval Arabic Aristotelian conception of soul.

[90]Commentary on the Mishna, introduction, pp. 42–43; *Mishneh Torah*: *H. Yesode ha-Torah* 4.8.

[91]Commentary on the Mishna, *Sanhedrin* 10, introduction, p. 205; *Abot* 4:22. *Mishneh Torah*: *H. Yesode ha-Torah* 4.9.

[92]Commentary on the Mishna, *Berakot* 9:7; *ᶜAboda Zara* 4:7; *Abot* 3:11; 5:13; *Sanhedrin* 10, introduction, p. 205; *Nidda* 3:2; *Shemona Peraqim*, chapter 1, p. 372; chapter 8, p. 405.

[93]Commentary on the Mishna, *Abot* 1:6.

[94]*Aristotelis Ethica Nicomachea* (medieval Arabic translation of the *Nicomachean Ethics*), ed. A. Badawi (Kuwait 1979) 314, paralleling Aristotle, *Nicomachean Ethics* 9.4, 1166a, 31–32: a "friend is someone else who is the same" (using the third person, not the second person). Averroes' Commentary on the *Nicomachean Ethics* repeats the saying in exactly those words.

[95]S. Harvey, "*Meqoran shel ha-Muba'ot min ha-Etika*," *Mi-Romi Lirushalayim* (Sermoneta Memorial Volume), ed. A. Ravitzky (Jerusalem 1998) note 45, supplemented by personal communications from Mr. Harvey.

[96]D. Gutas, *Greek Wisdom Literature in Arabic Translation* (New Haven 1975) 175, 405. The formulation on p. 405 is close to, although not identical with, Maimonides' version.

confident that he drew from a source different from the text of the *Nicomachean Ethics* itself.

A passage in the Commentary on the Mishna expresses approval for what the author of "the *Metaphysics*" had "said" regarding the inability of the human intellect to comprehend God's existence fully.[97] When mention is made of the author of the *Metaphysics*, Aristotle immediately comes to mind. But what Maimonides attributes to the unnamed author is not found in Aristotle and reflects, instead, conceptions of the Arabic Aristotelians.[98] Two passages in the Commentary draw from a work that they name as the *Problemata physica* (*al-Masā'il al-Ṭabīᶜiyya*). The references are to the Arabic translation of a pseudo-Aristotelian book carrying that title, and what Maimonides adduces is biological and physiological in character. One of the statements tells us that congenital deafness causes muteness, and the other that warm feet cause sleepiness;[99] Maimonides could have encountered both statements in the course of his medical education.

He finds within the ancient Mishna corpus itself allusions to a theory that, he states, is treated in "books written" on the subject of human intellect, and should there be any doubt about the standpoint from which the books in question treated the subject of intellect, he notes that a "very subtle philosophic conception" is involved.[100] The theory that he adumbrates and discovers within the bosom of the ancient Mishna was fashioned by post-Aristotelian philosophers out of remarks made by the genuine Aristotle. It is best known from works of the Greek philosopher Alexander of Aphrodisias and the Islamic philosopher Alfarabi.[101]

In an excursus to the Commentary on the Mishna, Maimonides copies extensively from an ethical work of Alfarabi's which was written in the spirit of Aristotle's ethics and at the center of which stands the Aristotelian theory of the middle way. That is the theory defining each human moral virtue as a psychological characteristic, or ingrained habit, lying midway between two vices. The virtue of bravery, for example, is the psychological characteristic or habit lying midway between the extreme characteristics of foolhardiness and cowardice, both of which

[97]*Shemona Peraqim*, chapter 8, p. 406: It is established in the *Metaphysics* that our intellects are unable to comprehend God's existence perfectly, the reason being the perfection of His existence and the deficiency of our intellects. And "he," that is, the author of the *Metaphysics*, had much to say on the topic.

[98]See, for example, Ghazali, *Maqāṣid al-Falāsifa* (a summary of Avicenna's philosophy) (Cairo n.d.) 180 (section on Metaphysics).

[99]Commentary on the Mishna, *Terumot* 1:2, possibly a reflection of pseudo Aristotle, *Problemata physica* 11.2. Commentary on the Mishna, *Yoma* 1:7, reflecting *Problemata physica* 8.2. Regarding the translation of the *Problemata physica* into Arabic, see F. Peters, *Aristoteles Arabus* (Leiden 1968) 66–67.

[100]Commentary on the Mishna, *Abot* 3:20.

[101]For Alexander, see H. Davidson, *Alfarabi, Avicenna, and Averroes, on Intellect* (New York 1992) 36. Alfarabi, *Risāla fī al-ᶜAql* (n. 69 above) 20; English translation: *Philosophy in the Middle Ages*, ed. A. Hyman and J. Walsh (New York 1967) 217. Maimonides cites Alfarabi's *Risāla* in the *Guide for the Perplexed.*

are defined as vices, and the virtue of generosity is the characteristic lying midway between the vices of prodigality and tightfistedness. Maimonides acknowledges in the excursus that he had borrowed here from non-Jewish philosophers and even copied verbatim from a "well-known book" by a non-Jewish author but he discreetly refrains from identifying the author and the name of the book.[102]

He liked to dress up his writing with anecdotes and homey analogies, and some of them can be traced to Muslim literature. At one juncture in the Commentary, he illustrates the extreme to which humility should reach—notwithstanding the theory of the middle way—through an anecdote that he read in "a book of ethics." A pious man, the anecdote goes, was traveling by sea in the poorest class of the boat when one of the wealthy passengers came down, saw him lying there dressed in rags, and felt such contempt for the man that he intentionally urinated on him. The pious man submitted to the humiliation with total equanimity and, he said, his ability to do so made that day the very happiest in his entire life.[103] The anecdote has a distinctive Ṣufi flavor to it and has parallels in Islamic Ṣufi texts prior to Maimonides.[104] The book of ethics in which he found it was plainly not philosophic in nature.

A few of the analogies employed by Maimonides in the Commentary on the Mishna have been traced by recent scholars to Islamic philosophic and theological works. The Islamic philosopher Avicenna, in the metaphysical part of his magnum opus, put forward the proposition that although members of the human species are unable to experience the intellectual pleasure enjoyed by God and other supernal beings, every intelligent person realizes that the pleasure of those beings is immeasurably superior to the physical pleasure experienced by—for example—"an ass in its belly and genital organs"; and Avicenna supported the proposition through the analogy of the impotent man who cannot enjoy the pleasure of sexual intercourse, the deaf man who cannot enjoy the pleasure of music, and the blind man (*akmah*) who cannot enjoy the pleasure of beautiful pictures, even though each of them realizes that the pleasures exist.[105] Ghazali, playing here the role of a

---

[102]H. Davidson, "Maimonides' *Shemonah Peraqim* and Alfarabi's *Fuṣūl al-Madanī*," *Proceedings of the American Academy for Jewish Research* 31 (1963) 33–34.

[103]Commentary on the Mishna, *Abot* 4:4.

[104]Hujwīrī (eleventh century), *Kashf al-Mahjūb*, trans. R, Nicholson (London 1936) 68, with the name of the Ṣufī personage who underwent the humiliation and described it as one of the two most successful experiences in his life; noted by A. Halkin, "Ibn ᶜAknin's 'Hygiene of the Soul,'" *Proceedings of the American Academy for Jewish Research* 14 (1944) 67, n. 1. An additional eleventh century instance of the anecdote is noted by R. Brague, "Maïmonide en français," *Revue de Métaphysique et Morale* 4 (1998) 589.

[105]Avicenna, *Shifā': Ilāhiyyāt*, ed. G. Anawati et al. (Cairo 1960) 424; French translation, with pagination of the Arabic given: *La Métaphysique du Shifā'*, 2 volumes, trans. G. Anawati (Paris 1978–1985); *Najāt* (Cairo 1938) 292. D. Schwartz, "Avicenna and Maimonides on Immortality," *Medieval and Modern Perspectives on Muslim-Jewish Relations*, ed. R. Nettler

theologian rather than a philosopher, although he was quite capable of playing the latter role as well, was concerned with a different thesis, namely, that persons who have never attained to knowledge of God, His attributes, and the kingdom of heaven are unable to appreciate how pleasurable such knowledge is. To support his thesis, Ghazali offered the analogy of a young boy who is not yet able to savor sexual pleasure and therefore prefers the pleasure of his "bat and ball" to sexual intercourse.[106]

Maimonides combines the two images to make a point that is closely related to, although not identical with Avicenna's. He writes: "Just as the blind man [*a^{c}mā*] cannot see colors, the deaf man cannot hear sounds, and the impotent man cannot experience the desire for sexual intercourse, . . . so the pleasures of the spiritual world are unknown in this physical world." Maimonides goes on: The opinion of "the Law as well as of metaphysical philosophers" is that the "angels"—that is, the supernal incorporeal beings subordinate to God—"the stars, and the celestial spheres," which were animate beings in Maimonides' view of things, derive unceasing, nonphysical pleasure from their intellectual concept of God. By the same token, when a man is fortunate enough to enter the state of incorporeal immortality, he no more wants to return to the pleasures of the physical world than a "great king" would want to leave his throne in order to "play ball again in the street, even though there undoubtedly was a time when he preferred such ball-playing to kingship." Maimonides would appear to have fastidiously avoided mention of the ass's belly and genitalia, although it is also possible that the analogy of the impotent man, the deaf man, and the blind man reached him in a version that lacked that earthy feature.[107]

The parallels with Avicenna and Ghazali are too distinctive to be accidental, but the analogies are so appealing that they could have circulated independently of the books in which they originated. Where Maimonides encountered them is therefore uncertain.

At the end of the Commentary on the Mishna, he informs his readers that during the time when he was composing the Commentary, he studied "other sciences,"[108] that is, sciences of non-Jewish provenance. As mentioned earlier, the Commentary refers to the science of medicine, veterinary medicine, and anatomy, as well as to the "chief" physician, which is an oblique reference to Galen.[109] It also mentions the *Almagest*, without naming the book's author, Ptolemy;[110] the *Almagest* was the most influential Greek astronomical work to reach the Middle Ages, and

---

(Luxembourg 1995) 188, calls attention to the parallel between this passage in Avicenna and what Maimonides says.

[106]A. Eran, "Al-Ghazali and Maimonides," *Jewish Studies Quarterly* 8 (2001) 148, 150, calls attention to the use of the analogy by Ghazali and Maimonides.

[107]Commentary on the Mishna, *Sanhedrin* 10, introduction, p. 204.

[108]Commentary on the Mishna (n. 1 above) 6.2, p. 738.

[109]Above, p. 85.

[110]Commentary on the Mishna, introduction, p. 37.

Maimonides once recalls having studied it with a pupil.[111] When the occasion arises, the Commentary on the Mishna draws from, or cites the authority of, mathematics[112] and geometry in particular,[113] physical science,[114] astronomy,[115] and optics.[116] One passage implies that Maimonides' study of mathematics and astronomy had extended over a period of years and predated his arrival in Egypt.[117] The majority of medieval rabbinists had little knowledge of mathematics and astronomy beyond what they learned from the classic rabbinic sources, and the general level was not high.[118] Maimonides, by contrast, studied both subjects from Arabic sources that drew from the Greek and he was well versed in both.

[111] *Guide for the Perplexed* 2.24, p. 51b.

[112] *Shemona Peraqim*, chapter 5 (the branches of mathematics).

[113] Commentary on the Mishna, introduction, p. 37 ("books of geometry" on the subject of "spherical shapes"); *Kil'ayim* 3:1; *^{c}Erubim* 1:5 (the "compositions" of expert geometers on the impossibility of determining the value of πι); *^{c}Erubim* 2:5 (the "surd" character of the diagonal of a square); *^{c}Erubim* 4:2 (an allusion to the theory behind the "astrolabe"); *Middot* 3:3 ("the geometers"); *Kelim* 18:2. Al-Qifṭī, not a wholly reliable witness, reports that Maimonides knew mathematics well, that he emended a certain Arabic work on geometry, the text of which was defective, and that he taught the text. Cf. Qifṭī, *Ta'rīkh al-Ḥukamā'*, ed. J. Lippert (Leipzig 1903) 317, 319. English translation: B. Lewis, *Islam* (New York 1974) 2.189, 191.

[114] Commentary on the Mishna, *^{c}Aboda Zara* 4:7, p. 357.

[115] Commentary on the Mishna, introduction, p. 37; *Rosh ha-Shana* 2:7; 2:9. Commentary on *Berakot* 1:1 cites the science of "mathematics" (*^{c}ilm al-ta^{c}ālīm*) as the source of information that is astronomical in character. In Maimonides' classification of the sciences, astronomy was a subcategory of mathematics.

[116] Commentary on the Mishna, *Sukka* 1:1; *Kelim* 30:2.

[117] Commentary on the Mishna, *Rosh ha-Shana* 2:7. Maimonides states that he had already conceived, and was planning to write, a treatise regarding the precise time of the appearance of the new moon, and that the treatise would be understood only by a person who had "prepared himself for many years in the propaedeutic sciences," that is, in mathematics and astronomy. If readers of the treatise would require years of preparatory study in order to understand it, Maimonides, the author, presumably spent years in preparation before writing it.

[118] The ancient rabbis were adept in arithmetic (see, e.g., Mishna, *Qinnim* 3:2) and had no trouble multiplying fractions, but the decimal notation of fractions was unknown to them. They used 3:1 as the ratio of the circumference of a circle to the diameter, that is, as πι. They had the closer approximation of one to seven-fifths as the ratio of the side of a square to the diagonal, hence of the leg of an isosceles right triangle to the hypotenuse; but they did not know the Pythagorean theorem. Regarding the ratio of 3:1 for the circumference of a circle, see Mishna *^{c}Erubim* 1:5; *Oholot* 12:6; PT *^{c}Erubim* 1:5; BT *Sukka* 7b; and the medieval commentaries of Rashi, Tosafot, R. Asher b. Jeḥiel, and Riṭba on the *Sukka* passage, and of R. Samson of Sens on the *Oholot* passage, all of which accept the ratio of 3:1. (Maimonides, on Mishna *^{c}Erubim* 1:5, assumes that the rabbis knew the ratio of 3:1 to be inexact; he writes that since the exact ratio cannot be determined, that is, since πι is an irrational number, the rabbis chose to employ the nearest whole number.) Tosafot, BT *^{c}Erubim* 14a, realizes that "mathematicians" do not accept the 3:1 ratio. Regarding the hypotenuse of an isosceles right triangle see BT *Sukka* 8a, and parallels. Tosafot on *Sukka* 8a–b, and Rashbam, Tosafot, Naḥmanides, and Riṭba on BT *Baba Batra* 102a reveal that they did not know the Pythagorean theorem. Tosafot on the *Sukka* passage

Although his *Mishneh Torah* conveys a good deal of basic philosophic information, it never uses the term *philosophy*. Maimonides does observe that "the Greek scientists wrote many books" on astronomy,[119] and it is fair to presume that one of the books he has in mind was the *Almagest*. In a section that offers highly detailed and technical astronomical calculations involving a good deal of practical trigonometry, he writes that "the ancient gentile scientists" differed greatly in their attempts to pinpoint the positions of the sun and moon in the heavens, yet "a small number of scientists" were eventually able to arrive at accurate results.[120] Students of the history of astronomy who have examined the astronomical calculations in Maimonides' *Mishneh Torah* have found that they employ data very close to those in tables prepared by the Arabic astronomer al-Battānī. It is accordingly likely that, side by side with the *Almagest*, he employed al-Battānī's tables in some form when working on the *Mishneh Torah*.[121] He further mentions astronomical information that he received from the "mouth" of astronomers and that went beyond anything found in commonly known books; he had the benefit of information communicated orally by teachers of astronomy in his day.[122]

Such is the evidence of Maimonides' study of philosophy and natural science which can be gleaned from his writings before he sat down to compose the *Guide for the Perplexed*.[123] He clearly found time for philosophy and science during the

---

nevertheless offers a good geometrical proof showing that the hypotenuse of an isosceles right triangle is in fact slightly more than seven-fifths of the leg, and Tosafot and Riṭba on *Baba Batra* 102a are able to correct a gross error made by Rashbam regarding the diagonal of a rectangle. R. Samson of Sens, in his commentary on Mishna *Kila'yim* 5:5, knows that "mathematicians" recognize what is in effect the Pythagorean theorem but he rejects it for all except isosceles right triangles because of a perceived conflict with the Mishna passage.

Meiri, an admirer of Maimonides, was familiar with non-Jewish science, and his commentary on the *Sukka* passage recognizes that the ratio of 3:1 for circles and the proportion of one to seven-fifths as the ratio of the leg of an isosceles right triangle to the hypotenuse are approximations.

For rabbinic astronomy see BT *Peṣaḥim* 94b. It is telling that the standard commentators on Maimonides' *Mishneh Torah* refrained from commenting on the astronomical chapters of *H. Qiddush ha-Ḥodesh*. In a gloss on *H. Qiddush ha-Ḥodesh* 7.7, R. Abraham b. David makes a sarcastic remark about Maimonides' self-satisfaction in his knowledge of astronomy, and then writes: "I am not an adept in astronomy, because my teachers also did not take the subject up, and therefore I have not checked what he [i.e., Maimonides] has written [here]."

119 *Mishneh Torah*: *H. Yesode ha-Torah* 3.5.

120 *Mishneh Torah*: *H. Qiddush ha-Ḥodesh* 11.1–3.

121 O. Neugebauer, "The Astronomy of Maimonides and Its Sources," *Hebrew Union College Annual* 22 (1949) 336–60. S. Gandz, "The Astronomy of Maimonides and Its Sources," *Archives internationales d'histoire des sciences* 29 (1950) 853–54, rejects the connection with al-Battānī because Maimonides speaks only about "Greek astronomical books" and he speculates that Maimonides must have used a translation of a lost set of Greek tables.

122 *Mishneh Torah*: *H. Qiddush ha-Ḥodesh* 11.3.

123 I leave aside the introduction to logic known as *Millot ha-Higgayon* which is commonly attributed to Maimonides. I consider it certain that Maimonides was not the author, and even if he were, there would be no way of determining a date for its composition.

period when he was working intensively on his comprehensive rabbinic compositions: He discloses familiarity with Arabic Aristotelian conceptions of God, man, and the universe. His Commentary on the Mishna makes a number of references to philosophy, the philosophers, the philosophic science of metaphysics, and sundry other sciences, but names Aristotle just once, citing only an innocuous aphorism from him. It mentions the *Problemata physica*, the author of a book of *Metaphysics*, and unnamed books on intellect. And it borrows a large amount of material from an ethical work of Alfarabi's.[124] Maimonides' *Mishneh Torah* consistently avoids mentioning any non-Jewish thinker or book by name and never uses the word *philosophy*. In one section, it does employ astronomical calculations that Maimonides acknowledges are dependent on Greek and Arabic astronomers.

By the age of forty he was thus familiar with the contours of medieval Arabic Aristotelian philosophy, he had studied other sciences, and he was well-versed in mathematics and astronomy. But, nothing that has been said demonstrates extensive philosophic study or any direct knowledge of Aristotle. He could have learned everything encountered so far from introductory handbooks of philosophy coming out of the Arabic Aristotelian school.

Maimonides' next major work was the *Guide for the Perplexed*. When Samuel Ibn Tibbon, who was preparing to translate it into Hebrew, wrote requesting clarification of a number of technical philosophic points, Maimonides responded in a confident tone, with the obvious implication that he knew whereof he spoke.[125] At one point in the *Guide*, he assures readers that he "had studied the books of the philosophers to the extent of my ability," just as he had studied Kalam works as far as he could.[126] The assurance is not overly encouraging when one recalls the gaps in his knowledge of the Kalam.

The *Guide for the Perplexed* does not hesitate to name the philosophers and philosophic works that Maimonides used, and the philosopher named most frequently is Aristotle. In the *Guide*, Maimonides styles Aristotle the "chief [*ra'īs*] of the philosophers."[127] In a letter to Samuel Ibn Tibbon, he expresses himself

[124]Maimonides' *Book of Commandments*, a prolegomenon to his rabbinic code, at one point quotes the "words" of "the students of the art of logic," and the quotation comes verbatim from Alfarabi's epitome of Aristotle's *De interpretatione*. What is involved is merely a peculiarity of Arabic grammatical terminology. See Maimonides, *Sefer ha-Miṣwot* (*Book of Commandments*), edited and translated into Hebrew by J. Kafah (Jerusalem 1971), rule 8, p. 26; English translation, with same divisions: Maimonides, *The Commandments*, trans. C. Chavel (London 1967); M. Küyel-Türker, *Fârâbi'nin Peri Hermeneias Muhtasari*, *Arastirma* 4 (1966) 46–47; English translation: *Al-Farabi's Commentary and Short Treatise on Aristotle's De interpretatione*, trans. F. Zimmermann (London 1981) 227.

[125]Letter to Ibn Tibbon, in I. Shailat, *Letters and Essays of Moses Maimonides* (in Hebrew) (Jerusalem 1987–1988) 545–49.

[126]*Guide for the Perplexed* 1.71, p. 95b.

[127]*Guide for the Perplexed* 1.5.

more strongly, characterizing "Aristotle's intellect" as the upper "limit of human intellect, with the exception of those upon whom the divine emanation has poured forth."[128] That is to say, Aristotle possessed the most highly developed human mind, except for the Hebrew prophets.

It is reasonably certain that Maimonides had, by this time, read at least some of Aristotle's works. Such might be inferred from one of his several letters to Ibn Tibbon. In it, Maimonides comments on the quality of translations of Aristotle into Arabic and recommends the handiwork of a particular translator,[129] thereby indicating that he was familiar with the translations he was judging. More specific evidence is furnished by citations of Aristotle's works in the *Guide* as well as in a few of Maimonides' other later writings.

He names five books in the *Guide* which he expressly identifies as works of Aristotle's: the *Physics*, *On the Heavens*, *Nicomachean Ethics*, *Rhetoric*, and *Metaphysics*. He quotes one or more passages from each of the first four while explicitly naming both the work from which he is quoting and Aristotle as the work's author. He states, for example, that Aristotle wrote such and such in the *Physics*, or *On the Heavens*, or the *Nicomachean Ethics*, or the *Rhetoric*, and what he represents as a quotation can be matched with a passage in the book named, although in the case of the *Rhetoric* what he says is to be found goes considerably beyond what is actually stated there.[130] We accordingly have evidence that he had direct knowledge of those four Aristotelian books, with the evidence being weakest in the case of the *Rhetoric*.

On one occasion in the *Guide*, Maimonides writes that he is quoting Aristotle but does not name any Aristotelian work; he records a brief statement that appears to

[128] Letter to Ibn Tibbon, edited in part by Marx, "Texts by and about Maimonides" (n. 67 above) 380. A similar statement is made by Maimonides' contemporary Averroes, Long Commentary on the *De anima*, ed. F. Crawford (Cambridge, Mass. 1953) 433.

[129] Letter to Ibn Tibbon, in Shailat, *Letters and Essays of Moses Maimonides* 532. The translations that Maimonides recommends are those of Isḥāq b. Ḥunayn.

[130] (1) *Guide for the Perplexed* 2.15, pp. 32a–32b, paraphrasing Aristotle, *Physics* 8.1.251b, 14, 16–19; cf. Isḥāq b. Ḥunayn's translation of the *Physics*, ed. A. Badawi (Cairo 1964–1965), with pagination of the Greek indicated. (2) *Guide* 3.43, quoting Aristotle, *Nicomachean Ethics* 8.9.1160a, 25–28, exactly; see the Arabic translation of the *Nicomachean Ethics* (n. 94 above) 293. (The Arabic translation of the *Nicomachean Ethics* used by Maimonides designates as Book 9 what editions today call Book 8.) (3) *Guide* 2.36, 79a, and 3.49, p. 117a, quoting a phrase from *Nicomachean Ethics* 3.10.1118b, 2 (the sense of touch is a source of shame, a statement that Maimonides repeats several more times). (4) *Guide* 2.15, p. 32b, quoting Aristotle, *De caelo* (*On the Heavens*) 1.10.279b, 4–12. See medieval Arabic translation: Aristotle, *De coelo et meteorologica*, ed. A. Badawi (Cairo 1961) 196. (5) *Guide* 3.49, p. 117a, where Maimonides writes that "you will find" a certain statement in Aristotle's *Rhetoric*, apparently referring to *Rhetoric* 1.11, 1370a, 18–25. See also: (6) *Guide* 2.20, where Maimonides writes that he is quoting a "statement" of Aristotle's but does not name the book; what he quotes comes from *Physics* 2.4.196a, 24–35. In (7) *Guide* 2.19, p. 42b, he quotes Aristotle's "statement" without naming the book, and the quotation matches Aristotle, *De caelo* 2.12.291b, 24–28. Medieval Arabic translation 269–70.

echo a sentence in Aristotle's *Metaphysics.*[131] On another occasion, he writes again that he is quoting Aristotle without naming any Aristotelian work, and the passage in question can be found, as he gives it, in Aristotle's *Topics.*[132] Since, however, he refers in the same context to Alfarabi's interpretation of the passage, and since the passage that he ostensibly quotes from Aristotle appears in Alfarabi's commentary on the *Topics,*[133] he may have taken the citation from Alfarabi and not directly from Aristotle. The conjecture grows in plausibility when we consider that the *Topics*, whether Aristotle's *Topics* or medieval reworkings of it, was part of the logical canon in Maimonides' time, and in his stated opinion, only Alfarabi should be resorted to for logic.[134]

On still another occasion, Maimonides interprets the biblical creation story as alluding to two strata of water vapor in the atmosphere surrounding the earth; he cites a rabbinic anecdote that—he understands—reflects the scriptural conception, and, in summarizing, he praises the rabbis for their ability to condense into a few words what was "demonstrated in the *Meteorology*."[135] He does not say that the *Meteorology* of Aristotle is the work he has in mind, and the two strata of water vapor supposedly alluded to in Scripture are not in fact found in Aristotle's *Meteorology*; that work speaks only of a single stratum.[136] The particular passage in the *Guide* is enigmatic, and one must be cautious about drawing conclusions from it.[137] All in all, it is doubtful whether Maimonides is referring to Aristotle's *Meteorology* or, at most, to a medieval Arabic reworking of the Aristotelian book.

[131] *Guide for the Perplexed* 2, introduction, proposition 25: "Aristotle's words" are: "matter does not move itself." That would appear to echo *Metaphysics* 12.6.1071b, 29–30. But the two preserved Arabic translations of the *Metaphysics* render the sentence differently from the way Maimonides gives it; see Averroes, *Tafsīr mā ba^{c}da al-Ṭabī^{c}a* (Long Commentary on the *Metaphysics*), ed. M. Bouyges (Beirut 1938–1952) 1564.

[132] *Guide for the Perplexed* 2.15, quoting *Topics* 1.11.104b, 14–17. Maimonides' quotation is very close to the Arabic text in *Organon Aristotelis in versione Arabica antiqua*, ed. A. Badawi (Cairo 1948–1952) 2.485.

[133] See the excerpt from Alfarabi's unpublished commentary on the *Topics* in G. Vajda, "A propos d'une citation non identifée d'al-Fārābī dans le *Guide des égarés*," *Journal asiatique* 253 (1965) 48. Alfarabi also refers to the passage in *K. al-Jam^{c} bayn al-Ḥakīmayn*, published in Alfarabi, *Philosophische Abhandlungen*, ed. F. Dieterici (Leiden 1890) 22; German translation, with pagination of the Arabic indicated: Alfarabi, *Philosophische Abhandlungen aus dem Arabischen übersetzt*, trans. F. Dieterici (Leiden 1892). Neither of Alfarabi's works says precisely what Maimonides reports Alfarabi said but he may be reading between the lines.

[134] Marx, "Texts by and about Maimonides" 379.

[135] *Guide for the Perplexed* 2.30, pp. 68b–69a.

[136] Aristotle, *Meteorology* 1.3, 340a, 32–34; 340b, 24–29; 4, 341b, 6–12.

[137] See Munk's note to his translation of *Guide for the Perplexed* 2.30, and S. Klein-Braslavy, *Perush ha-Rambam le-Sippur Beri'at ha-^{c}Olam* (Jerusalem 1987) 164–68. Among the many possibilities, Maimonides might be read as saying that Scripture distinguishes two strata of water vapor in the upper region, but the rabbinic anecdote refers only to one of them, and the existence of that one is what is demonstrated in the *Meteorology*.

At a number of junctures, Maimonides' *Guide* cites the views of Aristotle without actually quoting from him. Whenever the passages say something distinctive enough to indicate that Maimonides had a definite Aristotelian text in view, he refers, as far as I could ascertain, to the *Physics*, *On the Heavens*, or *Nicomachean Ethics*, three works that he quotes by name and from which he unambiguously draws.[138]

Maimonides' most comprehensive medical text, his *Medical Aphorisms*, contains two quotations from what it calls Aristotle's treatise *On Animals*. *On Animals* is a medieval term for a trilogy of Aristotelian biological works, known today by the titles of the books that it comprises—the *Historia animalium*, *Parts of the Animals*, and *Generation of Animals*. The first of the two quotations in the *Medical Aphorisms* turns out to be a passage from Aristotle's *Historia animalium*, and the second, which appears in a section of the *Medical Aphorisms* completed by Maimonides at the very end of his life and hence well after the *Guide for the Perplexed* had been written, comes from the *Generation of Animals*.[139] Neither quotation reproduces the Aristotelian original exactly, but both are fairly close. A separate composition, written by Maimonides shortly after he finished the *Guide*, has another reference to *On Animals*. There he reports that Aristotle's *On Animals* credited the gentleness of wild animals in Egypt to the abundance of food in the country; the comment is found in Aristotle's *Historia animalium*.[140] Furthermore, one of the general notions attributed to Aristotle in the *Guide for the*

Kafah, in his edition and translation of Maimonides' *Guide* (Jerusalem 1972) 2.384, reads the word that most translators understand to mean *Meteorology* as simply the Arabic word for *tradition*; Tz. Langermann, "*Ma^c^aseh ha-Raqi^c^a*," *Jerusalem Studies in Jewish Thought* 7 (1988) (Pines Festschrift) 473, follows him. The fatal weakness in Kafah's reading is that Maimonides would scarcely have spoken of something's being *demonstrated* in tradition.

[138](1) *Guide for the Perplexed* 1.5, referring to Aristotle, *De caelo* (*On the Heavens*) 2.12. (2) *Guide* 1.51, referring to Aristotle, *Physics* 6.1–2. (3) *Guide* 1.73 (3), referring to *Physics* 6.2. (4) *Guide* 2.1 (2), referring to *Physics* 8.5. (5) *Guide* 2.8, referring to *De caelo* 2.9. (6) *Guide* 2.14, several times; for sources in Aristotle, see Davidson, *Proofs for Eternity, Creation, and the Existence of God* (n. 81 above) 13, 16, 17, 24, 28. (7) *Guide* 2.19, p. 41b, referring to *De caelo* 2.5; 10; 12. (8) *Guide* 2.20, referring to *Physics* 2.4–5 (see above, n. 130 [6]). (9) *Guide* 2.40, p. 87a; and 3.8, p. 12b, referring to Aristotle, *Nicomachean Ethics* 3.10 (see above, n. 130 [3]). (10) *Guide* 3.10, referring to *Physics* 8.4. (11) *Guide* 3.49, p. 113a, where Maimonides makes reference to Book Nine (that is, Book Eight) of Aristotle's *Nicomachean Ethics*, and clearly has *Nicomachean Ethics* 8.1 in mind.

[139]Maimonides, *Medical Aphorisms* (n. 28 above) 9, §127, which says that it is quoting from "Part Nine of the Book *On Animals*" and is in fact quoting from *Historia animalium* 9 (7).12.588a, 3–5. *Medical Aphorisms* 25, §29, which says that it is quoting from "Part Eighteen of the Book *On Animals*" and is in fact quoting from *Generation of Animals* 4.1.765b, 18–28; medieval Arabic translation: Aristotle, *Generation of Animals, the Arabic Translation*, ed. J. Brugman and H. Lulofs (Leiden 1971) 139.

[140]Maimonides, *Treatise on Resurrection*, ed. J. Finkel, *Proceedings of the American Academy for Jewish Research* 9 (1939), Hebrew-Arabic section 23; Aristotle, *Historia animalium* 8 (9).1.608b, 29–35.

Perplexed is the proposition that each of an animal's limbs serves a specific purpose within the animal organism,[141] and that is the primary motif running through the *Parts of the Animals*, the third of the works making up Aristotle's biological trilogy. Maimonides thus may well have known and used all three parts of the trilogy, with the evidence for the *Generation of Animals* postdating the writing of the *Guide for the Perplexed* by more than a decade.

As was already mentioned, the *Metaphysics* is one of the Aristotelian works referred to by name in the *Guide for the Perplexed*, and a passage quoted in the *Guide* from Aristotle without any Aristotelian work's being named appears to come from his *Metaphysics*. Nevertheless, whenever Maimonides expressly states in the *Guide* that he is citing Aristotle's *Metaphysics* or intimates that he is doing so, what he records is not Aristotelian at all. The citations instead reflect positions taken by the Islamic philosopher Avicenna, especially in the metaphysical section of his primary philosophic work, a work that Maimonides never mentions.[142] The evidence is of a technical character, but it may be worthwhile to consider a couple of examples.

In Aristotle's physical scheme, four primary elements underlie all physical existence in the lower world inhabited by man, whereas the celestial spheres, planets, and stars are made of a different substance, proper to the upper region. Each of the four elements in the lower world is constituted through the adherence of the element's form—the form of fire, air, water, or earth—to a portion of the underlying matter of the world. The joining of the form of fire with matter results in the element fire, and so on. In the Arabic Middle Ages an added stage was introduced. Before matter can receive the form of an element, it must, so the thesis went, first possess what was called *corporeal form*. Corporeal form prepares matter for receiving the form of a full-fledged element; hence what receives the form of fire and the other elemental forms is now not the underlying matter of the world by itself, but matter as prepared by corporeal form. At one point in the *Guide for the Perplexed*, Maimonides makes an unmistakable reference to corporeal form, although without expressly using the term, and he introduces what he says with the words "Aristotle states . . . in the *Metaphysics*." He thus attributes the notion to Aristotle. The notion of corporeal form, which is alien to Aristotle, happens to have had Avicenna as its leading advocate.[143] Instead of citing the authority of Aristotle's *Metaphysics*, Maimonides should have cited the *Metaphysics* of Avicenna.

[141] *Guide for the Perplexed* 3.13, p. 23a.

[142] The analogy of the impotent, the deaf, and the blind man, which Maimonides incorporated into his Commentary on the Mishna—see above, p. 94—comes from the metaphysical section of this work of Avicenna's.

[143] *Guide for the Perplexed* 1.69; see commentaries of Narboni and Ephodi. H. Wolfson, *Crescas' Critique of Aristotle* (Cambridge, Mass. 1929) 580–85. Avicenna, *Shifā': Ilāhiyyāt* (n. 105 above) 64; *Najāt* (Cairo 1938) 203. Ghazali, *Maqāṣid al-Falāsifa* (n. 98 above) 93.

Another example: Before presenting his proofs of the existence of God, Maimonides lists twenty-five philosophic propositions that he planned to use in the proofs. He states that the twenty-five propositions were "demonstrated" by "Aristotle and the peripatetics [that is, philosophers of the Aristotelian school] coming after him" and, a few pages later, that they were "demonstrated" in either the "Book of the *Physics* and its commentaries" or the "Book of the *Metaphysics* and its commentary." Three of the twenty-five define and elaborate the metaphysical concepts *possibly existent by reason of itself* and *necessarily existent by reason of itself.* Those concepts are foreign to Aristotle and to every known work that can properly be called a peripatetic commentary on Aristotle's *Physics* or *Metaphysics.* They are instead Avicennan and play a prominent role in Avicenna's *Metaphysics*, particularly in his proof of the existence of God as a being necessarily existent by reason of itself.[144]

Additional instances can be cited of Maimonides' quoting Aristotle, the *Metaphysics*, or Aristotle's *Metaphysics*, where the propositions he adduces are in actuality metaphysical doctrines of Avicenna.[145] The conclusion has to be that he either read Aristotle's *Metaphysics* through heavily tinted spectacles furnished by Avicenna or treated Avicenna and his metaphysics—or whatever summary of

[144]*Guide for the Perplexed* 2, introduction, propositions 19, 20, and 21. For their role in Avicenna's *Metaphysics*, see Davidson, *Proofs for Eternity, Creation, and the Existence of God* (n. 81 above) 290–96.

[145]The first is minor, while the others are significant: (1) *Guide for the Perplexed* 2.19, p. 42b, reports that Aristotle's *Metaphysics* posited an incorporeal intelligence for each sphere, and *Guide* 2.4, p. 13b, reports that since Aristotle thought the number of spheres to be, on the best information, fifty, he set the number of incorporeal intelligences as, most likely, also fifty. Aristotle, *Metaphysics* 12.8, 1074a, 10–16, in fact set the number of celestial spheres and of intelligences not at fifty, but at fifty-five, or on another calculation at forty-seven. Avicenna, *Shifā': Ilāhiyyāt* 401, reports that Aristotle set the number at "approximately fifty, and something more." (Abraham Ibn Ezra knew the figure of fifty-five; see his commentary on Ecclesiastes 5:7.) (2) *Guide* 1.57: It "was made clear in the *Metaphysics*"—whose *Metaphysics* is not stated—that except in the case of the First Cause, unity is an accident in the being of what exists. The notion that both unity and existence have the status of *accidents* is foreign to Aristotle and was a notorious position of Avicenna's. See Avicenna, *Shifā': Ilāhiyyāt*, 109; Ghazali, *Maqāṣid al-Falāsifa* 101, 106, 219; Averroes, *Compendio de Metafísica*, ed. with Spanish trans. C. Quirós Rodríguez (Madrid 1919) 1, §§22, 39; German translation: *Die Epitome der Metaphysik des Averroes*, trans. S. Van den Bergh (Leiden 1924) 8, 17; and, specifically for *existence*, A. Goichon, *La distinction de l'essence et de l'existence d'après Ibn Sīnā* (Paris 1937) 142–43. (3) *Guide* 2.4 and 2.22 present and attribute to Aristotle an emanation theory, which Maimonides characterizes as "metaphysical," although he does not name any Aristotelian work. The theory, which is totally foreign to Aristotle, is in its general lines common to Alfarabi and Avicenna, and the criticism of it that Maimonides draws up echoes Ghazali, *Tahāfut al-Falāsifa*, chapter 3. Also to be noted is (4) *Shemona Peraqim*, chapter 8, p. 406, where Maimonides commends what the author of "the *Metaphysics*" had "said" and cites views that are not genuinely Aristotelian. See, further, H. Davidson, "Maimonides, Aristotle, and Avicenna," to appear in the R. Rashed Festschrift.

Avicenna's metaphysics he had recourse to[146]—as an acceptable substitute for the *Metaphysics* of Aristotle.

The most glaring omission in the list of Aristotelian works cited or utilized by Maimonides is the *De anima*, Aristotle's much studied and highly influential treatise on psychology and intellect. The *De anima* has a good deal to say about the manner in which the human intellect functions and the possibility of the intellect's attaining immortality; since those were central philosophic concerns of Maimonides', the book certainly should have interested him. It was moreover available in more than one medieval Arabic translation. Yet he never names or alludes to it in the *Guide for the Perplexed* or anywhere else. Another Aristotelian work that contains material bearing directly on Maimonides' philosophic concerns, yet which he never mentions, alludes to, or, as far as I could discover, draws upon in the *Guide* or elsewhere, is *On Generation and Destruction.*

Also pertinent is the collection of short Aristotelian compositions on psychological matters known as *Parva naturalia.* It is never mentioned or alluded to in the *Guide for the Perplexed.* Maimonides does mention the *De sensu* in a medical work and ostensibly quotes from it. The *De sensu* is one of the compositions making up the *Parva naturalia,* although in the Middle Ages the title *De sensu* was commonly extended to cover the collection as a whole; the whole collection was called *De sensu* rather than *Parva naturalia.* Maimonides' quotation would appear ultimately to go back to the following statement in Aristotle's *De sensu* in the narrow and original sense of the name: "It . . . pertains to the student of physics to know the first principles of health and disease. . . . Hence most students of nature . . . come in the end to issues of medicine, while *physicians who pursue their art more philosophically begin with matters of nature.*"[147] In Maimonides, the statement is transformed and reads: "Aristotle said in the *De sensu*: 'Most of those who die do so only because of the medicinal art, as a result of ignorance of nature on the part of the majority of physicians.'"[148] The supposed quotation is no longer a comparison of the

[146]Virtually everything of a metaphysical character attributed by Maimonides to Aristotle but actually deriving from Avicenna can be found in Ghazali's summary of Avicenna's philosophy, the *Maqāṣid al-Falāsifa.* There are, moreover, striking similarities between what Maimonides writes, for example, in *Guide for the Perplexed* 2.4, and Ghazali's *Maqāṣid al-Falāsifa* 209–21.

[147]Aristotle, *Parva naturalia*: *De sensu* 1.436a, 17–436b, 1.

[148]Maimonides, *Fī Tadbīr aṣ-Ṣiḥḥat* (*Regimen of Health*), ed. H. Kroner in *Janus* 27-29 (1923–1925) 296; English translation (n. 64 above) 21a. The passage also comes up in Maimonides, *On Asthma* (n. 64 above), chapter 13, §§20–21, where he writes: "Aristotle made the following statement in one of his famous works: 'First we should study nature, for instance, [the phenomena of] health and disease, for most physicians erred in this area with the result that the medicinal art and medical treatment become the cause of human death' . . . . In another translation of the passage, I found the statement as follows: 'Most of those who die do so because of the medicinal art.'"

curricula of students of physics and medicine. Instead, the concern has shifted to deficiencies in the education of the majority of physicians, and Aristotle's thought has been twisted to such an extent that the core is only faintly discernible. There can be little doubt that Maimonides is borrowing from an author who commented on the damage done by inadequately educated physicians and who supported the point through reference to Aristotle's *De sensu*. Maimonides failed to realize that what Aristotle wrote had been adapted to another purpose and that he was quoting the adaptation and not the *De sensu* itself.

The absence of the *Parva naturalia* from the Aristotelian works that Maimonides cites or can be seen to draw from in the *Guide* is noteworthy. Segments of it helped inspire the Arabic-Aristotelian theory of prophecy, and that theory underlies Maimonides' understanding of the prophetic phenomenon.

By contrast, little can be concluded from the absence from the *Guide* of any work of logic apart from the passage in the *Topics* which was referred to earlier. Maimonides may have studied Aristotle's logic but not have found any of the issues with which the *Guide* deals to require a reference to it. Besides, he characterizes Alfarabi as the only source to which one should resort for logic and may well have felt that Alfarabi was so satisfactory a substitute that Aristotle's logical works could be safely ignored.

Finally, a page from the pseudo-Aristotelian work *Liber de plantis* has been discovered which carries Maimonides' signature.[149] He must therefore have possessed, and presumably have read, that work.

In sum, Maimonides displays a familiarity with Aristotle's *Physics*, *On the Heavens*, *Nicomachean Ethics*, *Rhetoric*, and two of Aristotle's biological works. There is a suggestion of his having read the third of the biological works and possible evidence of his having studied and used the *Topics*. It is doubtful whether the *Meteorology* that he refers to is Aristotle's book of that name. What he calls Aristotle's *Metaphysics* is Avicenna's metaphysical philosophy, which he confused with Aristotle's, or at best Aristotle's metaphysics as refracted through an Avicennan prism. He discloses no familiarity with other works of Aristotle, even those having immediate bearing on his interests such as the *De anima* and *On Generation and Destruction*. He does not mention the *Parva naturalia* in the *Guide for the Perplexed* and when he cites it in a medical work, he does so in a manner revealing that he was not utilizing the *Parva naturalia* itself but was, unknowingly, quoting a medical writer who cited the Aristotelian work for his own purposes.

Arguments from silence are proverbially inconclusive. It is conceivable that Maimonides did know the genuine *Metaphysics* of Aristotle as well as the *De anima*, *On Generation and Destruction*, *Parva naturalia*, and additional Aristotelian works, yet when working out his philosophical system perversely read

[149] S. Hopkins, "A New Autograph Fragment of Maimonides' *Hilkhot ha-Yerushalmi*," *Journal of Semitic Studies* 28 (1983) 275.

the *Metaphysics* through Avicennan spectacles and wholly ignored everything in the other works which was pertinent to his concerns. Such a hypothesis is neither plausible nor flattering to Maimonides. The conclusion that the evidence strongly suggests, with all due reservations about arguments from silence, is that the Aristotle whom Maimonides praises as the greatest natural human intellect to have seen the light of day was known to him only in a truncated and distorted guise.[150]

When the gaps in Maimonides' knowledge of Aristotle are compared with the thoroughness of his rabbinic studies in particular, but also with his study of Galen, the contrast is striking. He demonstrates complete mastery of the fundamental rabbinic texts—the Mishna corpus, the Babylonian and Palestinian Talmuds, and other texts belonging to the classic rabbinic canon. The fundamental medical texts were, in his view, the Galen corpus, and when composing his main medical work, he was sufficiently motivated to have obtained, studied, excerpted, and summarized ninety of Galen's compositions; he may well have examined others as well, possibly all the compositions of Galen accessible to him. The fundamental philosophic texts were those making up the Aristotelian corpus. Here it was a dozen, not a hundred works that were at issue, yet as far as the evidence goes, Maimonides failed to invest the effort and time needed to obtain and study the works in the corpus. Some of the gaps in his knowledge of Aristotle could of course have been related to the nonaccessibility of books in Fustat. Even if so, he did not make the effort to import from abroad all the Aristotelian works translated into Arabic which could be acquired by persons who were sufficiently motivated and had the contacts that he had.

From the practical standpoint, the contrast is understandable. Rabbinics was the area in which Maimonides cut his teeth. He approached philosophy only later—but that was also true of medicine. Rabbinics and medicine were his vocations, albeit a nonremunerative one in the case of the former, whereas he could only pursue his philosophic interests during free time. Further, when he wrote his main rabbinic works, he had no distractions and was able to devote himself almost exclusively to his rabbinic studies. During the time that he wrote his main philosophic work, the *Guide for the Perplexed*, he was, as far as we know, earning his living as a physician and spending his evening hours with medical texts that shed light on his cases. Inquiries regarding questions of rabbinic law continued to be addressed to him, and he felt the obligation to reply. He may simply not have had the leisure for a comprehensive study of the Aristotelian corpus.

Yet, when considered from the standpoint of Maimonides' stated ideology, the contrast between his thoroughness in studying the rabbinic sources and Galen and

[150]Pines writes in the introduction to his translation of the *Guide*, lxi: "There is no reason to doubt that Maimonides was acquainted with all the writings of Aristotle known in Moslem Spain, i.e., practically the whole *Corpus Aristotelicum*. . . . It is, moreover, abundantly clear that, from an early age, Maimonides had lived with these texts and that they formed a notable part of his intellectual makeup." He offers no evidence to support the sweeping assertions.

the lack of thoroughness in his study of Aristotle is hard to fathom. He repeatedly insists that the well-being of the human body is not an end in itself and has a rationale solely insofar as the body serves the soul. The role of medicine in a correctly structured human life, while "very large," as he puts it, is consequently of an instrumental, not ultimate, character: Medicine has the task of fashioning the human body into a tool that will serve the soul, the lower faculties of the soul are to serve the intellectual faculty, and intellect is the component in man that concerns itself with the true goal of human life.[151] Maimonides was, moreover, convinced that the contents of science and philosophy are integral to the rabbinic worldview and that rabbinic religion not only permits but mandates the study of philosophy. He was certain—bizarre though it may sound to us—that a highly valued, and no less highly obscure, subject of nonlegal scriptural and rabbinic study called the "account of the chariot" is identical with the philosophic science of metaphysics.[152] A page or two after identifying the account of the chariot as the science of metaphysics, he quotes a talmudic statement to the effect that the legal give and take of experts in rabbinic dialectic is "a small thing," while the account of the chariot is a "major thing";[153] he is saying in so many words that the ancient rabbis themselves rated metaphysics as of greater value than rabbinic dialectic. Although philosophy demands a large investment in time, Maimonides stresses that time cannot be put to more profitable use. When treating the subject of God's attributes, he recommends spending years, when necessary, to master a single science, should the science teach one how to construe just a single divine attribute properly. For nothing deserves the expenditure of human time more than knowledge of God and anything contributing to such knowledge.[154]

If Maimonides had acted in harmony with what he preached, he would have stinted on his other studies in order to reserve maximum time for philosophy and science. He would have limited his medical practice to what would earn him enough for his basic needs and to what the Muslim rulers demanded of him. He would have acquired all the available works of the greatest philosopher to have lived, invested a maximum of energy and time in mastering those works, and gone on to other works of science and philosophy that contribute to an understanding of Aristotle and to knowledge of God. But he did not do so. In the chapters that follow, we shall encounter other inconsistencies and paradoxes in Maimonides' life.

Aristotle is difficult in the original, and even more so in medieval Arabic translation. When writing to Samuel Ibn Tibbon, who was about to undertake a

[151] *Shemona Peraqim*, chapter 5. *Mishneh Torah*: *H. De^cot* 3.3. *Guide for the Perplexed* 3.27; 54.

[152] Commentary on the Mishna, *Ḥagiga* 2:1. *Mishneh Torah*: *H. Yesode ha-Torah* 2.11; 4.11. *Guide for the Perplexed*, Introduction, p. 3b.

[153] *Mishneh Torah*: *H. Yesode ha-Torah* 4.13, quoting BT *Sukka* 28a.

[154] *Guide for the Perplexed* 1.59, p. 72b. See below, pp. 362–63.

translation of the *Guide for the Perplexed* into Hebrew, Maimonides accordingly advises him to "read the books of Aristotle only in their interpretations, [namely] the interpretation of Alexander [of Aphrodisias], the interpretation of Themistius, or the commentary of Averroes."[155] The Arabic original of the letter is lost, and we must make do with a pair of medieval Hebrew translations from the Arabic. Consequently, the Arabic terms behind the Hebrew words that I have rendered as "interpretation" (*perush*) and "commentary" (*be'ur*), Maimonides' intent in differentiating between the two, and the phrase "only *in* their interpretations" are puzzles. By writing that Aristotle should be read *in* the interpretations of his works, he could mean that commentaries and paraphrases of Aristotle's works are a legitimate substitute for the Aristotelian works themselves; but that is no more than a guess. The prescription that Aristotle must, at the very least, be read in conjunction with the three named commentators is, nevertheless, unambiguous. We likewise saw Maimonides alluding to the indispensability of commentaries on Aristotle in the *Guide for the Perplexed* itself. The twenty-five philosophic principles that he planned to use for his proofs of the existence of God are, he wrote, demonstrated either in the "Book of the *Physics* and its commentaries" or in the "Book of the *Metaphysics* and its commentary."[156]

A number of Greek commentaries on Aristotle circulated in Arabic translation, most notably those of Alexander of Aphrodisias and Themistius. Among them were Alexander's commentaries on Aristotle's *Physics* and *Metaphysics*, and Themistius' paraphrases of Aristotle's *Physics*, *On the Heavens*, and Book 12 of the *Metaphysics*.[157] The *Physics*, *On the Heavens*, and *Metaphysics* were three of the works of Aristotle that Maimonides referred to by name. The Arabic translation literature, moreover, offered Maimonides three possible substitutes for Aristotle's *De anima*, a book that, we saw, is glaringly absent from Maimonides' writings: There existed an Arabic translation of Alexander's reworking of Aristotle's *De anima*, a translation of a composition on intellect written largely in an Aristotelian spirit and carrying Alexander's name, although it may not be a genuine work of his, and a translation of Themistius' Paraphrase of the *De*

[155]Marx, "Texts by and about Maimonides" (n. 67 above) 378–79.

[156]*Guide for the Perplexed* 2, introduction.

[157]M. Steinschneider, *Die arabischen Uebersetzungen aus dem Griechischen* (Graz 1960), pp. (89), (92), (93), (105). Peters, *Aristoteles Arabus* (n. 99 above) 34. Alexander's commentary on Aristotle's *Metaphysics*: J. Freudenthal, *Die durch Averroes erhaltenen Fragmente Alexanders zur Metaphysik des Aristotles* (Berlin 1885). The medieval Hebrew version of Themistius' Paraphrase of Aristotle's *De caelo*, translated from the medieval Arabic version: *Commentaria in Aristotelem Graeca* 5.4, ed. S. Landauer (Berlin 1902). (Maimonides' quotations from Aristotle's *De caelo* betray no echoes of Themistius' paraphrase; it is therefore not likely that he used the paraphrase as a substitution for the Aristotelian text itself.) The medieval Hebrew version of Themistius' Paraphrase of *Metaphysics* 12, also translated from the Arabic: *Commentaria in Aristotelem Graeca* 5.5, ed. S. Landauer (Berlin 1903).

anima.[158] All of the commentaries, paraphrases, and reworkings of Aristotle's writings just mentioned were used by Averroes, who was Maimonides' contemporary and fellow countryman.[159] Maimonides cites none of them in the *Guide for the Perplexed* or in any other of his works.

The *Guide* does contain a passage that originates, as far as is known, in Alexander's commentary on Aristotle's *Metaphysics*,[160] but Maimonides could have learned of it from other sources.[161] In his Commentary on the Mishna, Maimonides was seen to refer to books written on the subject of intellect, and what he adduces from those books could be derived either from Alexander's paraphrase of the *De anima*, from the *De intellectu* attributed to Alexander, or from Alfarabi.[162] Otherwise neither in the *Guide* nor anywhere else does Maimonides ever record interpretations of Aristotle distinctive enough to be connected to Alexander, Themistius, or any other Greek commentator on Aristotle.

As for Averroes' commentaries on Aristotle, the third set of commentaries that Maimonides recommended to Ibn Tibbon, they reached Maimonides when he was already well advanced in writing the *Guide* or after he had completed the task. He informs a former student of his that after receiving them, he had read some, but had not had time to read them all, and he had found them to be a fine exposition of Aristotle.[163] Averroes composed his commentaries in three cycles, known as the

[158]Steinschneider, *Die arabischen Uebersetzungen aus dem Griechischen*, p. (134). Arabic translation of Alexander (?), *De intellectu: Texte arabe du περι νου d'Alexandre d'Aphrodise*, ed. J. Finnegan (Beirut 1956), and *Commentaires sur Aristote perdus en grec*, ed. A. Badawi (Beirut 1968) 31–42. Arabic translation of Themistius' Paraphrase of the *De anima*: *An Arabic Translation of Themistius Commentary on Aristoteles 'De anima'*, ed. M. Lyons (Columbia, S.C. 1973).

[159]Averroes' Long Commentary on the *Physics* 8, comm. 42, refers to the interpretation of Alexander and Themistius on a certain passage. Alexander's commentary on the *Physics* has not been published, but the interpretation of the passage ascribed by Averroes to Themistius can be found in Themistius, Paraphrase of the *Physics*, *Commentaria in Aristotelem Graeca* 5.2, ed. H. Schenkl (Berlin 1900) 221. Averroes' Long Commentary on the *De caelo* 1, comm. 69, cites Themistius' Paraphrase of the *De caelo*; the source is found in *Commentaria in Aristotelem Graeca* 5.4, ed. S. Landauer (Berlin 1902), medieval Hebrew translation of Themistius' Paraphrase of the *De caelo* 27–28; Latin translation 42. For Averroes' use of Alexander's commentary on the *Metaphysics* and of Themistius' Paraphrase of *Metaphysics* 12, see Bouyges' index to his edition of Averroes' Long Commentary on the *Metaphysics* (n. 131 above) 3, p. (26). For Averroes' use of the works of Alexander and Themistius relating to the *De anima*, see Davidson, *Alfarabi, Avicenna, and Averroes, on Intellect* (n. 101 above) 282, 293, 326.

[160]See Munk's translation of the *Guide* 2.1, p. 38, note, which points out that Maimonides' second proof of the existence of God echoes the development of a thought of Aristotle's in Alexander's commentary on Aristotle's *Metaphysics*.

[161]Davidson, *Proofs for Eternity, Creation, and the Existence of God* (n. 81 above) 277. One of the sources is the work attributed to Alexander which is referred to below in n. 166.

[162]N. 101 above.

[163]In a letter to Joseph ben Judah, Maimonides writes that he had recently received "everything Averroes wrote on the books of Aristotle" with the exception of the *Parva naturalia*; see Moses

Epitomes, Middle Commentaries, and Long Commentaries. The Middle Commentaries cover the same ground as the Epitomes but in a different format, and the Long Commentaries go back again to four of Aristotle's most important works and expound them in still another, more exhaustive format. What Maimonides says about the commentaries of Averroes in the letter to his former student does not reveal the cycle to which the commentaries he saw may have belonged. Although Maimonides returned and made corrections of his rabbinic works after having completed them, there is no evidence of his having done the same for the *Guide for the Perplexed.* At all events, he did not make any corrections based on what he learned from Averroes' commentaries on Aristotle. Averroes is never mentioned in the *Guide*, Maimonides never quotes Aristotle through the medium of Averroes' commentaries as medieval Jewish philosophers would henceforth do, and nothing of a philosophic character that he writes in the *Guide* or elsewhere can be traced to Averroes.

There is, then, no evidence whatsoever that when writing the *Guide for the Perplexed*, Maimonides used the commentaries with which, he subsequently told Ibn Tibbon, Aristotle should be read, namely, the commentaries of Alexander, Themistius, and Averroes.[164]

Maimonides does quote Alexander of Aphrodisias a half dozen times in the *Guide* and in two instances names the work from which he quotes. Neither work is a commentary on Aristotle and neither can be matched with writings of Alexander known from the Greek. One of the two may, perhaps, be a genuine composition of Alexander's which has been lost in the original.[165] The other, although attributed to Alexander in the Arabic translation literature, is, at least in the form in which the medieval Arabs preserved it, almost surely not an authentic work of his.[166] Maimonides quotes Themistius only once, with no hint of the composition from which he is borrowing. He merely credits Themistius with a bland piece of sententiousness to the effect that "what exists does not conform to [men's] opinions; rather correct opinions conform to what exists."[167]

The rest of Greek philosophy has left only the most superficial traces in Maimonides' writings. The letter to Ibn Tibbon in which Maimonides recommends the commentaries of Alexander, Themistius, and Averroes evaluates a number of

---

ben Maimon, *Epistulae* (n. 50 above) 70. From page 67 of the same letter, it is clear that Maimonides had at the time completed at least the first of the three parts of the *Guide*.

[164]Pines writes in the introduction to his translation of the *Guide* lxiv: "It may be taken as certain that Maimonides made extensive use" of Alexander's commentaries. He offers no grounds for his certainty.

[165]*Treatise on Governance* (*Maqāla fī al-Tadbīr*), cited in *Guide* 3.16.

[166]*On the Principles of the Universe* (*Fī Mabādī' al-Kull*), published by A. Badawi, *Arisṭū ᶜinda al-ᶜArab* (Cairo 1947) 253–77, cited in *Guide* 2.3. Maimonides quotes from the same work in *Guide* 1.31, but there he writes only that he is quoting Alexander without naming the work of Alexander's to which he is referring.

[167]*Guide for the Perplexed* 1.71.

other philosophers. Maimonides is there dismissive of Plato.[168] In the *Guide for the Perplexed*, he mentions Plato a few times and here his tone is respectful. One of the references, however, only partly reflects what Plato actually said: Maimonides attributes to Plato the position that the heavens are "generated-destructible," whereas Plato held only that the heavens are generated, not that they are subject to destruction.[169] Another reference represents itself as a direct quotation from Plato. In Maimonides' words: "Plato states: 'God looks at the world of intellects, whereupon existence emanates from Him.'" The emanation, or flowing out, of existence from the First Cause of the universe is a pivotal neoplatonic conception, and the proposition that emanation occurs as a consequence of God's looking at the world of intellects also has an unmistakably neoplatonic flavor to it. Both theses are foreign to the genuine Plato, although the neoplatonists read their theories back into their great predecessor, who lived centuries earlier. Wherever Maimonides may have found the notion of God's looking at the world of intellects and of the resultant emanation of existence, he was mistaken in supposing that he was quoting from Plato himself.[170]

The name of Plotinus, the central figure in Greek neoplatonism, never appears in Maimonides. That is hardly surprising, since the name barely penetrated medieval Arabic literature.[171] Nevertheless paraphrases and elaborations of parts of Plotinus' *Enneads* did circulate in Arabic without the author's name, and Maimonides should have been able to acquire copies if he wished to. The paraphrases played a significant role in the Arabic Middle Ages, since they transmitted Plotinus' fruitful conception that the universe emanates from the First Cause through a series of stages. A scheme of emanation through stages lies at the heart of Maimonides' picture of the universe, and therefore a reference or allusion to the paraphrases of the *Enneads* available in Arabic might have been expected.[172] None is detectable in the *Guide for the Perplexed* or, as far as I could discover, elsewhere in Maimonides. The scheme of emanation with which he worked was known to him solely from the Arabic Aristotelian school of philosophy.

In the *Guide*, Maimonides mentions Epicurus several times but provides no information beyond the general and obvious. He tells us, for example, that Epicurus was an atomist, that he did not recognize the existence of God, and that he rejected divine providence. Since nothing written by Epicurus is known to have been translated into Arabic, we can be sure that Maimonides acquired his scanty information through a secondary channel.[173] At one point in the *Guide*,

[168] Marx, "Texts by and about Maimonides" 380.

[169] *Guide for the Perplexed* 2.13 (2), as well as 2.25.

[170] *Guide for the Perplexed* 2.6.

[171] F. Rosenthal, "Plotinus in Islam," reprinted in his *Greek Philosophy in the Arab World* (Brookfield, Ver. 1990) item iv.

[172] Alfarabi and Avicenna refer to the paraphrases.

[173] *Guide for the Perplexed* 1.73 (1): Epicurus believed in a fixed number of atoms. 2.13: As Alexander reported, Epicurus did not recognize a God who governs the world, but instead

Maimonides identifies John Philoponus as a link between Christian antiphilosophic theology and the Kalam movement in Islam;[174] nothing he says indicates that he had ever seen anything written by Philoponus. In his letter to Ibn Tibbon, he warns Ibn Tibbon about a couple of works falsely attributed to Aristotle[175] and briefly mentions and makes short shrift of a few real and mythical "early" Greek philosophers, namely, "Empedocles, Pythagoras, Hermes, and Porphyry."[176] None of the names comes up elsewhere in Maimonides.

Maimonides cites Galen five times in the *Guide for the Perplexed*, and in doing so names two works of his that stand on the borderline between philosophy and medicine.[177] Maimonides' medical writings, which frequently cite the medical works of Galen, mention three additional philosophical or semi-philosophical compositions of his;[178] some of the references are highly critical, for while Maimonides had unbounded respect for Galen the physician, he considered Galen a very mediocre philosopher.

The astronomer Ptolemy is mentioned several times in the *Guide*, each time in connection with astronomical issues.[179] Maimonides refers once to the tenth book of Euclid,[180] in a tone indicating that he was familiar with Euclid's geometry; in one of his medical writings, he moreover displays knowledge of an Arabic commentary on Euclid.[181] He also refers in the *Guide* to a geometrical theorem on the phenomenon of asymptotes, which, he writes, is found in "the second book of

---

believed that the processes of generation and destruction occur by the chance joining of atoms. 2.32: Since Epicurus did not believe in the existence of God, he did not believe in prophecy. 3.17: Since Epicurus held that the world is not governed by a First Cause and things come about by the chance joining of atoms, he completely rejected providence.

[174]*Guide for the Perplexed* 1.71.

[175]Marx, "Texts by and about Maimonides" 378: the *Book of the Apple* and the *Book of the Golden House.*

[176]Marx, "Texts by and about Maimonides" 380. By Empedocles, Maimonides undoubtedly means the neoplatonic material that went under that philosopher's name in his day. Hermes was a mythical figure, but writings attributed to the "threefold-great Hermes" circulated in Greek and Arabic. One of the books of Porphyry's that Maimonides is referring to could have been an Arabic treatise on soul which carried Porphyry's name. The historical Porphyry lived well after Aristotle.

[177]*Guide for the Perplexed* 1.73 (end): *De naturalibus facultatibus* (*On the natural faculties*). 3.12; 32: *De usu partium* (*The Usefulness of the Parts of the Body*).

[178]Maimonides, *Perush le-Firqe Abukraṭ* (medieval Hebrew translation of the Arabic text of the Commentary on *The Aphorisms of Hippocrates*), ed. S. Muntner (Jerusalem 1961) introduction, p. 4: Galen's Commentary on Plato's *Laws*; 1.1, p. 10: Commentary on Plato's *Timaeus*; English translation: Commentary on the Aphorisms of Hippocrates, trans F. Rosner (Haifa 1987) 11, 18. *Medical Aphorisms* (n. 28 above) 25, §51, et passim: Commentary on Plato's *Timaeus*; 25, §59: *De demonstratione.*

[179]*Guide for the Perplexed* 2.9; 11; 24 (where Maimonides also refers to the *Almagest*).

[180]*Guide for the Perplexed* 1.73 (3).

[181]The Arabic commentator is al-Nayrīzī. See G. Freudenthal, "Maimonides' *Guide of the Perplexed* and the Transmission of the Mathematical Tract 'On Two Asymptotic Lines,'" *Vivarium* 26 (1988) 115, note.

Conic Sections," that is, Book Two of a work of that name written by the Greek mathematician Appolonius of Perga.[182] An Arabic composition has come to light which consists of glosses on Appolonius' *Conic Sections*, and the manuscript identifies Maimonides as the author of the glosses.[183] The attribution must be regarded as uncertain, however; for so many items with Maimonides' name are clearly not his that the appearance of his name in a manuscript is insufficient by itself to establish his authorship.[184]

Such are Maimonides' citations from the philosophic and nonmedical scientific works of Greek writers apart from Aristotle. Despite Maimonides' declaration that he studied the philosophic literature to the extent of his ability and despite his virtual assertion that he used commentaries of "the peripatetics" on Aristotle's *Physics* and *Metaphysics*, there is no credible evidence of his ever having studied any Greek philosophy except for Aristotle and the two works attributed to Alexander.

To return again to the letter postdating the *Guide for the Perplexed* in which Maimonides evaluated previous philosophers for Ibn Tibbon: he there offers brief assessments of the four leading figures of the Arabic Aristotelian school, Alfarabi, Ibn Bājja (Avempace), Avicenna, and Averroes. In the Arabic world, Alfarabi had the reputation of being the "second teacher," that is, the thinker who was second only to Aristotle in instructing mankind. Maimonides, in the same spirit, describes Alfarabi as "a great man," praises his books as flawless, and states that the only logical treatises one should consult are Alfarabi's. He specifically recommends a book of Alfarabi's called the *Principles of Existent Beings*. The book in question—better known under the title of *al-Siyāsa al-Madaniyya*, or *Political Government*—opens by sketching the structure of the universe very much as Maimonides was to do, whereupon it turns to political theory. Ibn Bājja, Maimonides' letter to Ibn Tibbon continues, "was likewise a great philosopher" and his compositions are "correct." Maimonides rates Avicenna's writings as inferior to Alfarabi's, although he grants that they have "value" and are worthy of study. It is perhaps not pure coincidence that Averroes, a contemporary of Maimonides' and a fellow citizen of Cordova, also considered Avicenna to be inferior to Alfarabi; the two Cordovans may have been echoing an evaluation of Avicenna that was current among intellectuals in the city. As for Averroes, Maimonides was already seen to list him among the commentators with whom Aristotle should be read.[185]

[182]*Guide for the Perplexed* 1.73 (10, excursus). See Appolonius of Perga, *Treatise on Conic Sections*, edited in modern notation, T. Heath (New York 1896) 53.

[183]Tz. Langermann, "The Mathematical Writings of Maimonides," *Jewish Quarterly Review* 75 (1984) 57–59.

[184]Freudenthal, "Maimonides' *Guide of the Perplexed* and the Transmission of the Mathematical Tract 'On Two Asymptotic Lines'" 115, note, gives specific reasons for doubting the attribution.

[185]Marx, "Texts by and about Maimonides" 378–80. The letter also mentions a few other Arabic thinkers, whom Maimonides dismisses out of hand.

Alfarabi is the Arabic philosopher cited most frequently in Maimonides' writings, and to the extent that Maimonides was conscious of his sources, Alfarabi was undoubtedly the Arabic philosopher who had the strongest impact on his thought. As was noted earlier, Maimonides' Commentary on the Mishna quotes at length from an ethical work of Alfarabi's, without mentioning the author's name or the title of his composition, and it may allude to a book of his on the subject of the human intellect.[186] Maimonides' *Book of Commandments* also quotes from a logical work of Alfarabi's without giving the author's name.[187] In the *Guide for the Perplexed*, Maimonides refers to Alfarabi a half dozen times, naming four of his philosophic works,[188] and possible echoes of Alfarabi's logic have been discerned in passages of the *Guide* where he is not named.[189] Alfarabi makes one more appearance in the final chapter of Maimonides' most comprehensive medical composition. In three places there, Maimonides cites Alfarabi and, in doing so, names two further philosophic works of Alfarabi's; he says explicitly that he is quoting directly from at least one of them. The books in question have been preserved and published, but I was not able to identify the pertinent passages, and we must therefore allow for the possibility that a mistake of some sort has crept in.[190] All in all, there is good evidence, apart from the letter to Ibn Tibbon, that Maimonides knew, and at various times used, a half dozen of Alfarabi's philosophic compositions and weaker evidence that he used others as well.

Maimonides refers to Ibn Bājja five times in the *Guide for the Perplexed* and cites two of his works.[191] In addition, the distinction between four kinds of

[186]Above, pp. 93–94.

[187]Alfarabi's epitome of Aristotle's *De interpretatione* (n. 124 above).

[188]*Guide for the Perplexed* 1.73 (10); 1.74 (7) (Alfarabi's *On Changing Beings*); 2.15, p. 33b; 2.18, p. 37b (Alfarabi's *Risāla fī al-^{c}Aql*, from which Maimonides quotes Alfarabi's "words"); 2.19, p. 43b (Alfarabi's Glosses on the *Physics*, from which Maimonides quotes Alfarabi's "words"); 3.18, pp. 38b–39a (Alfarabi's introduction to his Commentary on Aristotle's *Nicomachean Ethics*).

[189]Munk's translation of the *Guide* 1.193, note, and 1.197, note. The medieval Arabic compendium of logic known by the Hebrew name of *Millot ha-Higgayon* and mistakenly taken to be a work of Maimonides' is to a large extent based on Alfarabi's logic.

[190]Maimonides, *Medical Aphorisms* (n. 28 above) 25, §58, is an ostensible quotation or paraphrase from Alfarabi, *Book of Letters* (*K. al-Ḥurūf*), yet nothing in the edited text of Alfarabi's *Book of Letters* fits what Maimonides purports to cite from him. At best, Maimonides is paraphrasing Alfarabi, *Book of Letters* (*K. al-Ḥurūf*), ed. M. Mahdi (Beirut 1969) 135–39, but Mahdi, in his introduction to the text, p. 39, conjectures that Maimonides is in fact quoting from Galen and not Alfarabi. *Medical Aphorisms* 25, §§59–60 quotes two passages from Alfarabi's Long Commentary on the *Prior Analytics*, and both passages sign off with the words: "end of quotation from Alfarabi." I was not able to identify either passage in the available text of Alfarabi's Commentary on the *Prior Analytics.*

[191]*Guide for the Perplexed* 1.74 (7); 2.9; 2.24, p. 51b (a discourse of his on astronomy); 2.24, p. 53b; 3.29, p. 62b (Commentary on the *Physics*, also referred to in Maimonides' Letter to Ibn Tibbon, in Shailat, *Letters and Essays of Moses Maimonides* [n. 125 above] 546).

human perfection—the possession of property, physical health, ethical perfection, and intellectual perfection—around which the final chapter of the *Guide* is built, has been traced to Ibn Bājja.[192] Avicenna's name never appears in the *Guide*.[193] Nevertheless, and despite Maimonides' judging him inferior to Alfarabi, he contributed considerably to the formation of Maimonides' philosophic thinking: What Maimonides calls Aristotle's *Metaphysics* is, we saw, not Aristotelian but Avicennan, and Maimonides' picture of the structure of the universe, while it draws from both Alfarabi and Avicenna, owes more to the latter than to the former,[194] although Maimonides was unconscious of the debt. As noted earlier, Averroes, whose commentaries on Aristotle reached Maimonides when he was well along in writing the *Guide* or had already completed it, plays no discernible role in Maimonides' thought.

He was very likely familiar with the Islamic philosopher Ghazali. Ghazali was a protean and versatile figure, who decked himself out at various times as a Kalam thinker, a mystic, a philosopher in the Arabic Aristotelian mode, and to complete the gamut, as a critic of philosophy on its own terms. We saw that an image found in a theological work of his makes an appearance in Maimonides' Commentary on the Mishna.[195] When Ghazali assumed the guise of critic of philosophy, he developed a subtle refutation of Avicenna's position on the eternity of the world, and Maimonides, without mentioning Ghazali, reworks strands of reasoning directly traceable to Ghazali's refutation of Avicenna in his own proofs for the creation of the world. Maimonides moreover acknowledges that his proofs for creation adapt what he identifies as Kalam motifs, refined and raised to a salubrious philosophic level; that may be an oblique acknowledgement of his debt to Ghazali.[196] An additional work of Ghazali's, an excellent and very readable summary of Avicenna's philosophy, could have served as one of the sources from which Maimonides acquired his knowledge of the Arabic Aristotelian picture of the universe and, more specifically, of Avicenna's metaphysics.[197]

A passage in the *Guide for the Perplexed* suggests that Maimonides also may have been familiar with the Islamic philosopher Ibn Ṭufail. Ibn Ṭufail wrote a philosophic novel, constructed on the premise that a highly intelligent boy grows up on a desert island without ever seeing another human being. It was one more literary motif that caught Maimonides' fancy. In the course of his arguments for creation, he contends that certain physical phenomena may be possible yet seem

[192] A. Altmann, "Maimonides' 'Four Perfections,'" *Israel Oriental Studies* 2 (1972) 15–23.

[193] Maimonides cites him elsewhere as a medical authority; see, n. 86 above. In his *Treatise on Resurrection*, Maimonides refers to a work of Avicenna's on the hereafter, but what he says about it indicates that he did not himself see it; see below, p. 528, n. 194.

[194] See Davidson, *Alfarabi, Avicenna, and Averroes on Intellect* (n. 101 above) 197–207.

[195] Above, p. 95.

[196] H. Davidson, "Maimonides' Secret Position on Creation," in *Studies in Medieval Jewish History and Literature*, ed. I. Twersky (Cambridge, Mass. 1979) 28–34.

[197] See n. 146 above.

impossible to those who have never experienced them. To illustrate the point, he asks us to imagine a highly intelligent boy who is brought up on a desert island without ever seeing a woman or female animal: When the boy is told that each human initially spends a gestation period of nine months completely enclosed within the womb of a female member of the species and then exits naturally through a passageway in the woman's body, he is of course incredulous.[198] The theme of growing up in isolation on a desert island almost surely goes back to Ibn Ṭufail's novel. It is so attractive, however, that it could easily have been utilized by more than one writer and therefore may have come to Maimonides' attention independently of Ibn Ṭufail.

In his letter to Ibn Tibbon, Maimonides names a philosophic composition—now lost—of the great physician and Islamic heretic Ibn Zakarriyā Rāzī and he dismisses it as worthless.[199] In the *Guide* he refers to the same book and comments: Among its other "enormous inanities and stupidities," it purveys the false notion that evil is more prevalent in the universe than good.[200] He also cites a few Arabic scientific works.[201]

The medieval Jewish philosophers did not impress him. The letter to Ibn Tibbon offers, presumably at Ibn Tibbon's request, Maimonides' opinion of two Jewish philosophers. One is Isaac Israeli, a man who had in several works, including a *Book of Definitions*, espoused a scheme of the emanation of the universe from the First Cause which was an unsophisticated version of Plotinus' neoplatonic scheme. In his reply to Ibn Tibbon, Maimonides expresses the uncharitable judgment that "the *Book of Definitions* and *Book of Elements* composed by Isaac Israeli" are "wholly inanities, wind, and vanity; for Isaac Israeli was . . . only a physician."[202] Since Maimonides himself was convinced that the universe emanates from the First Cause, or God, through a series of stages, his objection must have been not to emanationism as such, but solely to Israeli's simplistic version. The other Jewish philosopher evaluated by Maimonides for Ibn Tibbon was Joseph Ibn Ṣaddiq, who had been a rabbinic judge in Cordova, Spain, when Maimonides was a child. Maimonides informs Ibn Tibbon that he had never seen Ibn Ṣaddiq's theological work but he "knew" the man and his qualities. The comment is ambiguous, perhaps deliberately so, out of respect for Ibn Ṣaddiq's rabbinic

[198] *Guide for the Perplexed* 2.17. Ibn Ṭufail, *Ḥayy ibn Yaqẓān*; English translation: L. Goodman, *Ibn Tufayl's Hayy Ibn Yaqzān* (New York 1972).

[199] Marx, "Texts by and about Maimonides" (n. 67 above) 378. The name of the work is *Ilāhiyyāt*, that is, *Divine Matters*, or *Metaphysics*.

[200] *Guide for the Perplexed* 3.12, p. 18a. In his *Treatise on Resurrection*, Maimonides mentions, but shows no familiarity with, the *K. al-Mu*[c]*tabar*, a philosophic work by the twelfth-century Abū al-Barakāt; see below, p. 528, n. 194..

[201] *Guide for the Perplexed* 1.73 (3): the Banū Shākir, *Book of Ingenious Devices. Guide* 2.9: Ibn Aflaḥ, a work on astronomy. *Guide* 2.24 and 3.14: Thābit Ibn Qurra, a work on astronomy. *Guide* 2.24: al-Qabiṣi, a treatise on the distances between the celestial spheres.

[202] Marx, "Texts by and about Maimonides" 378.

standing. It is most likely dismissive, although it has been read by some as approbation.[203]

A fragment of Saadia's theological work, *Beliefs and Opinions*, has been discovered with a faint signature on the title page which a scholar who examined the fragment identified as being in Maimonides' hand.[204] If the identification of the signature is correct and the copy of *Beliefs and Opinions* did belong to Maimonides, he may be presumed to have read it. At a certain juncture, he speaks of arguments for the existence and unity of God which were borrowed from the Kalam by "one [or: some] of the *geonim*," and the *gaon*, or one of the *geonim*, in question could very well have been Saadia.[205] Maimonides also refers to Saadia by name in contexts where philosophy and Saadia's philosophic activity are not involved.[206]

Apart from these remarks, Maimonides mentions no Jewish philosopher in any context. It is reasonable to suppose that he perused medieval Jewish works of a philosophic character which came his way, and scholars have called attention to passages in his works which might possibly be echoes of Judah Hallevi, Abraham Ibn Ezra, and Abraham Ibn Daud.[207] The evidence is very far from conclusive, and even should every one of the conjectures hit the mark, the medieval Islamic philosophers plainly had much more to offer Maimonides than the Jewish philosophers did.

Note should finally be taken of other directions in which Maimonides' studies and reading ran. He was a careful student of the Hebrew Bible. A less serious motive for his biblical interests would have been stylistic. When still young, he learned to write the flowery Hebrew that was a mark of culture among educated Spanish Jews and consisted in weaving fragments culled from throughout the Bible

[203] Marx, "Texts by and about Maimonides" 379. D. Kaufmann, *Geschichte der Attributenlehre* (Gotha 1877) 336–37, reads Maimonides' evaluation as approbation. S. Stroumsa, "*He*ᶜ*ara* ᶜ*al yaḥaso shel ha-Rambam le-R. Yosef ibn Ṣaddiq*," *Jerusalem Studies in Jewish Thought* 9 (1990) 37–38, makes what appears to me to be the more plausible case for the opposite interpretation.

[204] A. Scheiber, "Autograph Manuscripts of Maimonides," *Acta Orientalia Academiae Scientiarum Hungaricae* 33 (1979) 188.

[205] *Guide for the Perplexed* 1.71, p. 94a

[206] See the index to Maimonides, *Responsa*; Moses Maimonides, *Epistle to Yemen*, ed. A. Halkin with English trans. B. Cohen (New York 1952) 64; English translation [xii].

[207] Regarding all of these philosophers, see Kaufmann, *Geschichte der Attributenlehre*, index, s. v. Maimuni. Regarding Hallevi, see Pines, introduction to his translation of the *Guide* cxxxiii; H. Kreisel, "Judah Halevi's Influence on Maimonides," *Maimonidean Studies* 2 (1991) 108–21. Regarding Abraham Ibn Ezra, see Bacher, *Die Bibelexegese Moses Maimûni's* (n. 31 above) 172; Saadia, *Sefer ha-Miṣwot*, ed. Y. Perla (Warsaw 1914) 1.15–16 (an overstatement of Ibn Ezra's influence on Maimonides' *Book of Commandments*); I. Twersky, "Did R. Abraham Ibn Ezra Influence Maimonides?" (in Hebrew), in *Rabbi Abraham Ibn Ezra*, ed. I. Twersky and J. Harris (Cambridge, Mass. 1993) 25–40.

into rhyming prose.[208] He also knew how to compose Hebrew poetry in the Spanish metrical mode, a genre in which the use of recherché biblical phraseology was obligatory.[209] His more serious motive for studying the Bible was religious and theological. The inspired nature of the Hebrew Bible was beyond doubt for him, and even when writing unadorned Hebrew or Arabic prose, he scarcely completed a page—exception being made for his medical writings, which were intended for a non-Jewish readership—without buttressing one or more points with biblical quotations. When quoting, he often interprets and at times he expresses open pleasure with his innovative and illuminating interpretations.[210] The quotations are drawn from every book of the Old Testament and they number in the thousands. Although he never produced a commentary on the Bible as such, anthologists have accordingly been able to collect and organize his interpretations of individual verses into de facto Bible commentaries.

As ancillaries to his reading of the Hebrew Bible, he studied the traditional Jewish Aramaic translations of the biblical books. He believed that the Aramaic translation of the Pentateuch—Targum Onkelos—stood in the direct line of tradition originating in God's revelation to Moses;[211] he treats it as a repository of inestimable philological and theological lore, and it carried much more weight for him than all the medieval Jewish philosophers and theologians together. In particular, he appreciates the pains that Targum Onkelos takes in interpreting away anthropomorphic descriptions of God in the Pentateuch,[212] conjuring away anthropomorphisms being among Maimonides' own highest exegetic and theological priorities.[213] He read up on Hebrew grammar, a subject that had come into its own in the Middle Ages, and cites three medieval Hebrew grammarians by name while giving indications of having drawn from additional grammarians, lexicographers, and Bible commentators.[214] When he takes pride in the fact that his younger brother, who had been his own student, had excelled in knowledge of Hebrew grammar,[215] he incidentally reveals the value that he himself attached to the subject.

[208]Examples: Commentary on the Mishna, introduction (n. 1 above) p. 1; *Epistle to Yemen* 1; *Epistulae* (n. 50 above) 12–16; *Responsa* (n. 3 above) 3.55–56; Shailat, *Letters and Essays of Moses Maimonides* [n. 125 above) 468–70.

[209]Commentary on the Mishna, prefatory poem.

[210]For example, Maimonides, *Book of Commandments*, negative commandment #355.

[211]*Shemona Peraqim* (n. 56 above) chapter 7, p. 395; *Guide for the Perplexed* 2.33, p. 76a.

[212]Bacher, *Bibelexegese Moses Maimûni's* (n. 31 above) 37–44.

[213]Bacher, *Bibelexegese Moses Maimûni's* 19–22.

[214]Bacher, *Bibelexegese Moses Maimûni's* 171 (references to passages where Maimonides names Ibn Janāḥ, Moses Ibn Gikatilla, and Ibn Bal^c^am); 168 (fairly clear echoes of Ḥayyūj); 171–72 (possible echoes of Saadia's translation of the Bible, Saadia's Bible commentary, and Ibn Ezra's commentary on the Bible). Maimonides, Commentary on the Mishna, *Terumot* 1:1: "modern lexicographers," identified by Kafah, *ad locum*, as Menahem ben Saruq. Further conjectures in Bacher vi–vii, 173–74.

[215]Letter to Japhet ben Elijah, in Shailat, *Letter and Essays of Moses Maimonides* 230.

He reports that he had read through a small library of compositions representing themselves as ancient works of star worship and magic. They helped him to rationalize some of the opaque biblical rituals: He interpreted them as Scripture's counterweights and correctives to the ceremonies of ancient star worshipers, that is, as divinely ordained tactics for weaning the Israelites away from idolatry.[216] History and Arabic poetry are two genres that he rejected because they "contain neither science nor practical" value and are a "mere waste of time."[217] He condemns the writing or reading of lascivious stories and poems in the Arabic mode, and even the writing and reciting of wine songs. Activity of the sort is, in his judgment, a misuse of time and, worse, a perverted utilization of the precious gifts—soul and intellect—with which God has endowed man. They are therefore a sin toward God.[218] Quotations from Arabic belletristic literature nevertheless occasionally infiltrate his writings.[219]

Summary. In Maimonides' youth, rabbinics was his chief area of study. Such could be surmised a priori from the milieu in which he was raised, and he offers rhetorical confirmation when he describes rabbinic studies as the wife with whose love he had been ravished from his early years. The fact that he could compose a competent Commentary on two-thirds of the Babylonian Talmud by the age of twenty-three testifies to an early mastery of the classic rabbinic literature. His consummate control of that literature then manifests itself in his Commentary on the Mishna, which he began at the age of twenty-three and completed seven years later. The Commentary on the Mishna at the same time shows him to have had the entire Hebrew Bible at his fingertips.

His control of posttalmudic rabbinic literature is harder to gauge than his knowledge of texts from the classic period. He assures us, however, that his mastery of rabbinic literature included the posttalmudic no less than the classic stratum, and he cites a good array of posttalmudic rabbinic writers. Except for a few details that he quotes in his father's name and a couple of judicial procedures

[216]Commentary on the Mishna, *ᶜAboda Zara* 3:3 (a conversation that Maimonides had with a person trained in astral magic); 4:7; *Mishneh Torah*: *H. ᶜAbodat Kokabim* 1.1; *Guide for the Perplexed* 3.29.

In the *Epistle Against Astrology*, a work attributed to Maimonides but of questionable authenticity, Maimonides says, or is made to say, that astrology was the first subject he studied, that he had studied the subject intensely, and that he believed he had read every work available in Arabic on the subject of idolatrous religion. See A. Marx, "The Correspondence between the Rabbis of Southern France and Maimonides about Astrology," *Hebrew Union College Annual* 3 (1926) 351, §8.

[217]Commentary on the Mishna, *Sanhedrin* 10, introduction, p. 210.

[218]*Guide for the Perplexed* 3.8, p. 14a. Commentary on the Mishna, *Abot* 1:16, p. 419, adds that writing lascivious poems in the holy language makes the sin all the more serious. *Responsa* §224 uncompromisingly states the rabbinic prohibition against singing and music.

[219]See Commentary on the Mishna, *Abot* 1:3; 6. *Guide for the Perplexed* 3.39 (end), alludes to pre-Islamic Arabic poetry.

that he reports having learned from his father and other judges in the West, nothing is known of teachers from whom he may have received instruction in rabbinics.

He does give the names of teachers with whom he studied medicine when still living in the West. To the extent that his writings on medicine can be dated, they stem from the last period of his life, a period in which he developed a successful medical practice. They disclose that he had by then studied a number of medical writers and paid special attention to Galen, whom he considered to be the greatest of all physicians. His most ambitious medical work, which he did not complete until the year of his death, cites ninety of Galen's works.

He mentions having studied "sciences" during the time when he worked on his Commentary on the Mishna and he refers to men with whom he studied astronomical texts, apparently before arriving in Egypt. A passage in the Commentary on the Mishna assures us that he possessed particular expertise in the science of astronomy, and a section of his code of law, completed a decade later when he was forty, demonstrates a highly sophisticated control of astronomical theory.

While Maimonides never mentions any teacher with whom he studied philosophy in the strict sense, his Commentary on the Mishna and code of Jewish law reveal a familiarity with the Arabic Aristotelian picture of the universe, which he was convinced is substantially identical with the picture of the universe of the Bible and ancient rabbis. The Commentary makes a number of references to the "philosopher," "philosophers," and "philosophy." It explicitly quotes Aristotle once; although what it adduces derives ultimately from Aristotle, Maimonides' source appears to have been one of the collections of aphorisms circulating in Arabic at the time and not Aristotle himself. The Commentary contains a reference to philosophic "books written" on the subject of intellect and it quotes extensively from an ethical work of Alfarabi's without naming Alfarabi as its source.

By the age of thirty, he thus knew the Hebrew Bible backward and forward. He had attained a mastery of the vast sea of classic rabbinic texts, knowledge of posttalmudic rabbinic literature, and expertise in astronomy, and he had studied medicine. He had a familiarity with the philosophic and scientific worldview of the Arabic Aristotelians, but virtually all of his philosophic information could have been acquired from handbooks of philosophy coming out of the Arabic Aristotelian school. There is no evidence at this juncture of his life of his having studied philosophy in any depth or of his having ever opened a single book of Aristotle's. The breadth and variety of his learning were nonetheless extraordinary. His attainments become prodigious when it is remembered that, although he did not have to concern himself with his livelihood, the peregrinations undertaken by the family had been constant distractions, and, since well before the age of twenty-three, he had spent considerable time on his own literary efforts.

His training in philosophy naturally is displayed to its fullest in the *Guide for the Perplexed*, which he completed in his early fifties. Aristotle was for him the greatest human mind apart from the Israelite prophets, and he assures readers of the *Guide* that he had "studied the books of the philosophers to the extent" of his ability. One might therefore expect—as I in fact did before carefully examining the evidence—that his knowledge of Aristotle would parallel his knowledge of the fundamental texts in the areas of rabbinics and medicine. The *Guide* discloses that he utilized four of Aristotle's works and suggests that he may have read a few more. But it reveals no familiarity with key works of Aristotle's from which he could have profited, and what it says about Aristotle's *Metaphysics* is a distortion. In a letter, Maimonides advised Samuel Ibn Tibbon to study Aristotle in conjunction with the commentaries of Alexander and Themistius. Although he does quote from two works attributed to Alexander in the Arabic Middle Ages, he reveals no evidence of having used the commentaries of either Alexander or Themistius on Aristotle. Nor is there evidence of his having read the works of any other Greek philosopher.

As for philosophers closer to Maimonides in time, his knowledge of the Kalam literature, which he himself would not classify as genuinely philosophical, likewise betrays significant gaps—this, notwithstanding his assurance that he had studied the "books of the Kalam thinkers insofar as it was feasible" for him to do so. He read and used a number of Alfarabi's works as well as a few of Ibn Bājja's. Avicenna's influence on him was considerable, but he was not conscious of it because of his failure to distinguish Avicenna's views from Aristotle's. He apparently borrowed from a major work of Ghazali's. Averroes' writings did not come to his notice until after his own philosophic views had crystallized and his *Guide for the Perplexed* had been substantially, or wholly, written. The medieval Jewish philosophers offered him little of interest.

Of the three main areas in which he wrote, rabbinics was plainly the one in which his scholarly preparation was most thorough, and philosophy—surprisingly—the one in which it was the least.

3

Rabbinic Works I

> Go over and over what I have written here and contemplate it well. If you let yourself suppose that you have gotten to the heart of it in one or ten readings, then, God knows, you have been led into an absurdity. (Commentary on the Mishna, completed when Maimonides was thirty years old, *Sanhedrin* 10, introduction)
>
> The full value . . . can be truly understood only by someone who has agonized days and sleepless nights over one of the halakot [belonging to the present subject] . . . without attaining to a single reliable principle, who goes on to read the present introduction and the commentary that follows, and who thereupon finds everything he struggled over set out according to the underlying principles. What has been accomplished here will then be appreciated. (Commentary on the Mishna, introduction to the sixth Order)

At a certain juncture in the *Guide for the Perplexed*, Maimonides follows the Islamic philosopher Avicenna in stating that when a human intellect thinks a thought, the man's role in the process is limited to preparing his intellect for receiving it. The thought itself comes to the human mind from without, as an emanation continually made available—constantly broadcast, as it were—by a supernal being called the active intellect. Maimonides then adds, perhaps on his own, that the amount of emanation received by an individual from the active intellect may suffice solely to perfect the recipient with a given thought or set of thoughts and make him a man of intelligence. Sometimes, however, a person prepares himself to the degree that the amount of emanation exceeds what he needs for his own use and reaches the level at which it "inescapably leads him to compose books and teach," thereby imparting perfection to others as well.[1] Maimonides is talking about thoughts of a scientific and philosophic character but on at least one occasion he extends the notion to further types of knowledge. When discussing some of his innovative interpretations of Scripture, he writes that he was unable to keep his discoveries to himself, because God's universe is so constructed that someone who "attains to a perfection" is led to "emanate it upon others."[2] From what we have learned about Maimonides, we can hardly be surprised to see him including himself among those whose measure of emanation is such that they cannot help sharing the knowledge to which they have attained.

Whether or not it was truly thanks to an especially large measure of emanation that he received from the supernal regions, Maimonides was led, if not driven, from a young age and until the end of his life, to put his thoughts on paper for the edification of his compatriots. His first area of literary activity was rabbinics. He composed commentaries on two-thirds of the tractates of the Babylonian Talmud before the age of twenty-three and, according to the best information, completed the last of his monumental rabbinic works in 1178, when he was forty years old. He did return at later dates to correct what he had written and he mentions additional projects in the rabbinic area which he started. But there is no evidence of his having brought any substantial rabbinic composition to completion after 1178. In 1199, five years before his death, he lamented that ill health and the press of his responsibilities prevented him from completing various rabbinic projects that he had begun.[3] While his rabbinic interests never ceased—his letters and legal responsa testify to that—his book-length compositions in the area of rabbinics therefore belong, as far as is known, to the first half of his mature life.

A few concepts should be clarified before we turn to Maimonides himself. The most basic is *Oral Torah*, also often translated as *Oral Law*.

In the first instance, the term *Torah* designates the five books of Moses, the Pentateuch, although it could be employed with the meaning of all the books of the Hebrew Bible. Rabbinic Judaism's defining doctrine is that there is not one Torah but two, that side by side with the Written Torah, or Written Law, and specifically the five books of Moses, an Oral Torah likewise exists. The latter supplements the Written Torah by filling in details of items that appear, yet are not fully spelled out, in it and by supplying matters that are absent from it. The recognition of a second

[1] Maimonides, *Guide for the Perplexed* 2.36–37.

[2] *Guide for the Perplexed* 2.29 (end), with reference to the previously quoted statement, but without the distinction between persons who receive only enough emanation for their own needs and those who receive an excess.

[3] Maimonides, *Responsa*, ed. J. Blau, 2nd ed. (Jerusalem 1986) 4.33.

Torah paralleling and supplementing the written one is explicit or tacit in all rabbinic sources preserved from the classic period—that being the designation I shall use for the period in which the Mishna corpus and Talmud compilations were produced. The preserved sources go on to presuppose something much more far-reaching, namely, that the Oral, like the Written, Torah goes back to the biblical Moses, that God presented Moses with both.

Maimonides subscribes to the rabbinic doctrine without reservation. God, he affirms, revealed to Moses each commandment recorded in Scripture together with the interpretation (*tafsīr=perush*) of the scriptural text containing the commandment;[4] the interpretation supplies details that are not explicit in the text. As an illustration, he adduces the requirement that Jews "dwell in booths seven days" during the autumnal Tabernacles festival. The requirement is explicit in Scripture and is therefore a commandment of the Written Torah. "Particulars and details" of the commandment, such as the minimum size of the booths, the materials to be used in thatching them, and the categories of persons who are required to dwell in them during the festival week are not explicit in Scripture but were taught by God to Moses. Those particulars and details were, Maimonides writes, then transmitted by Moses to the nation of Israel and they make up the Oral Torah.[5]

Maimonides traces the transmission of the Oral Torah through forty stages, first from Moses to Joshua, and then step by step down to the generation of rabbinists who, as he views rabbinic history, brought the classic rabbinic period to a close in the fifth Christian century. One link in the chain of tradition is bound to catch a reader's eye. Ahijah the Shilonite, in Maimonides' account, participated in the exodus of the Israelites from Egypt, attended Moses' lectures while still a youth, but did not formally receive the Oral Torah from Moses. He was blessed with extraordinary longevity and received the Oral Torah centuries later from King David and David's rabbinic court. Ahijah then transmitted it to the prophet Elijah, who in turn handed it on to the next link in the chain.[6] Maimonides has here elaborated, and gone considerably beyond, remarks in the Palestinian and Babylonian Talmuds. The two Talmuds speak of Ahijah's longevity and connection with Elijah, but not of his place in the transmission of the Oral Torah.[7] Maimonides

[4]To be precise, he sometimes writes that God gave Moses the interpretation of the verse and sometimes, the interpretation of the commandment.

[5]Maimonides, Commentary on the Mishna (=*Mishna* ᶜ*im Perush R. Moshe ben Maimon*), Arabic original and Hebrew trans. J. Kafah (Jerusalem 1963–1968) 1, pp. 1–3; English translation from a Hebrew translation of the original: *Maimonides' Introduction to his Commentary on the Mishnah*, trans F. Rosner (Northvale, N. J. 1995). Maimonides, *Mishneh Torah*, introduction. The commandment to dwell in booths is found in Leviticus 23:42.

[6]Maimonides, *Mishneh Torah*, introduction.

[7]See BT *Baba Batra* 121b; PT ᶜ*Erubin* 5:1. The connection of Ahijah with David is absent from the two talmudic passages. J. Levinger, "ᶜ*Al Torah she-be*ᶜ*al pe be-Haguto shel ha-Rambam*," *Tarbiz* 37 (1968) 291, supposes that Maimonides (a) did not believe what he wrote and (b) was merely inventing legitimacy for rabbinic tradition during the period from Joshua to David.

either had an additional source not identifiable today or drew the added and startling inference himself.

The term *Oral Torah*, it should be noted, was sometimes used in rabbinic circles more comprehensively to include not only what was believed to have been communicated by God to Moses and passed on by him to his successors, but also the innovations of those successors, that is to say, the legislation of the ancient rabbis. Maimonides, if I understood correctly, occasionally employs the term in the latter, broader sense.[8] But when he expresses himself carefully, he defines Oral Torah as what has been "learned from tradition," that is, the "details and interpretations" of the Written Torah which were received by Moses "at Sinai"; and again: "the transmitted interpretation . . . from the mouth of God." Legal and ritual innovations that were "introduced after the giving of the Law [to Moses], that were ratified by prophets and [rabbinic] scholars, and that were accepted by all of Israel," must, he stresses, be "accepted and observed" by the entire nation. They nonetheless are not, for Maimonides, part of the strict sense of Oral Torah.[9]

It is helpful to distinguish two types of subject matter that occupied the ancient rabbis. On the one hand, the rabbis dealt with legal and ritual subjects, generally known as *halaka*, and on the other, with nonlegal, nonritual subjects, generally known as *aggada*,[10] or, in the form of the word that Maimonides preferred, *haggada*.[11] *Halaka*, in the dichotomy, is a collective term comprising the interpretations believed to have been given by God to Moses and to constitute the Oral Torah in Maimonides' usage of the term.[12] It also comprises regulations coming from the hands of the rabbis themselves.[13] Thus the details regarding the booths dwelt in during the Tabernacles festival which are believed to have been communicated by God to Moses are halaka. And the rabbinic innovation that Jews living at a distance from the Land of Israel must dwell in booths for eight days, and not merely the seven mandated by Scripture,[14] is halaka as well. Each item of halaka, each law or ritual, is called *a halaka*, and the plural of the word is *halakot*.

This second part of Levinger's supposition is ruled out by Maimonides' making Ahijah a link in the chain of tradition only after David.

[8]See *Mishneh Torah*, Introduction (end); *H. Talmud Torah* 1.12.

[9]Maimonides, *Mishneh Torah*, ed. J. Cohen and M. Katzenelenbogen (Jerusalem 1964) 1, 65; Commentary on the Mishna, *Sanhedrin* 10:1, eighth principle, taken together with *Mishneh Torah*: *H. Teshuba* 3.8. *Mishneh Torah*: *H. Mamrim* 1.2.

[10]See BT *Soṭa* 40a; BT *Baba Qamma* 60b.

[11]*Mishneh Torah*: *H. Melakim* 12.2; W. Bacher, *Die Bibelexegese Moses Maimûni's* (Budapest 1896) 34–35. In the cited instances, Maimonides uses the plural: *haggadot*.

[12]In *Mishneh Torah*: *H. Mamrim* 1.4; *H. Abel* 1.1, Maimonides may not be using the term precisely in the sense that I give.

[13]See Maimonides, Commentary on the Mishna, introduction (n. 5 above), p. 19, for an additional, intermediate category of "halaka."

[14]BT *Sukka* 47a.

Aggada is a collective term for the myriad miscellaneous items of rabbinic lore which are nonlegal in character. It includes observations about God and man, nonbinding ethical and practical advice, historical information, anecdotes about the heroes and villains of Jewish history, rabbinic science, popular medicine, folk beliefs that a modern reader would classify as superstition, dream interpretation, and more. To illustrate again: The regulations regarding prayer transmitted by the Oral Torah in Maimonides' narrow sense of the term together with regulations for prayer instituted by the rabbis would all be halaka. Nonbinding rabbinic lore concerning prayer, such as its efficacy, is aggada.[15]

The line between halaka and aggada is not always easy to draw. Instructions found in the authoritative rabbinic sources—some of the rabbinic thoughts on prayer, for example[16]—do not always present themselves unambiguously as binding rules, and hence halaka, or as nonbinding advice, and hence aggada. The existence of a gray area between the two sectors does not, however, detract from the value of the dichotomy.

Maimonides exhibits considerable interest in the aggada of the ancient rabbis. Aggada (*derashot*), he once writes, contains all the "divine [or: metaphysical] matters and [all] the truths . . . that men of science have opined and on which the philosophers have spent ages."[17] His scheme of the history of the world and of the Israelite nation relies heavily on aggada.[18] He writes of a few items of aggada that they are known through "tradition" or as "transmitted interpretation,"[19] which could mean that they go back to the biblical Moses. Nevertheless, when he states that "the details, particulars, and interpretations of each and every commandment—this is [the] Oral Torah" given to Moses and "handed down from one law court to another," he is plainly restricting Oral Torah to halaka;[20] the details, particulars, and interpretations of the commandments, like the commandments themselves, are legal and ritual in character. Similarly, when he identifies the legal and ritual regulations that the ancient Sanhedrin "learned through tradition" as the "Oral Torah," he is including halaka alone.[21] For Maimonides, Oral Law therefore comprises only halaka and not aggada.[22]

[15]BT *Berakot* 10a; 32b; *Baba Batra* 25b; et passim.

[16]*Berakot* 5b; 29b; 31a; et passim.

[17]Commentary on Mishna, introduction p. 35. Although Maimonides speaks about the *derashot* in the Babylonian Talmud, he plainly has in mind what is commonly called *aggada*.

[18]See W. Bacher, "Die Agada in Maimuni's Werken," in *Moses ben Maimon*, ed. W. Bacher et al., 2 (Leipzig 1914) 135–36, 144–49.

[19]Cf. Bacher, *Die Bibelexegese Moses Maimûni's* (n. 11 above) 28, note 1; 37, note 3.

[20]Maimonides, *Mishneh Torah*, ed. J. Cohen and M. Katzenelenbogen, 65.

[21]Maimonides, *Mishneh Torah*: *H. Mamrim* 1.2. Here Maimonides expressly excludes from the category of Oral Law even rabbinic clarification of the commandments when it is arrived at through the exercise of rabbinic logic and has not been transmitted by Mosaic tradition.

[22]*Leviticus Rabba* 22.1 includes *haggada* among the subjects given to Moses at Sinai but it is a consciously paradoxical passage, for it also includes among the things given to Moses: "even what a seasoned student will say in the presence of his teacher." Maimonides, *Mishneh Torah*:

From the classic period into the Middle Ages and beyond, halaka was the principle subject of Jewish education. Rabbinic virtuosi in the generations and centuries preceding and following Maimonides, have occupied themselves primarily with halaka. It should scarcely be surprising that he too concerns himself primarily with halaka in his rabbinic works.

For an understanding of classic and subsequent rabbinic thought and literature, account must be taken of an additional dichotomy, a dichotomy of method.

In one mode of their activity, the ancient rabbis searched the biblical text for signposts that, they were certain, had been intentionally embedded there by the divine source of Scripture and they followed them to propositions lying below the surface of the text. The rabbis might, for instance, search the biblical verses commanding the Israelites to dwell in booths on the Tabernacles festival for signposts pointing to details about the booths which are not explicit. Thus, Scripture says: "Thou shalt make for thee the festival of tabernacles seven days, when thou gatherest in from thy threshing-floor and from thy winepress." The Babylonian Talmud explains that the juxtaposition of the term "tabernacles" with the gathering in "from" the threshing-floor and winepress points to something not made explicit in the biblical text, a piece of Oral Law or a halaka, namely, the manner in which roofs for the booths dwelt in during the holiday must be fashioned. The tabernacles, or booths, must be thatched with materials such as those that are removed *from* what is processed in the threshing-floor and winepress. They must be thatched with agricultural waste products, materials that have grown out of the ground and been harvested but are not edible. Maimonides paraphrases the Talmud's explanation: The scriptural verse furnishes an "allusion" to the materials with which the Tabernacles booth must be thatched, and "tradition" informs us that "Scripture is talking [here] about the waste products of the threshing-floor and winepress. That is to say, the tabernacle is to be made using them and what is similar to them."[23]

The method of searching out what is latent in Scripture was not limited to halaka. Signposts in the biblical text could be followed to propositions of a nonhalakic, that is, aggadic, character as well. To illustrate again—now with an example not found in Maimonides—the rabbis might follow signposts embedded in the story of Abraham's readiness to sacrifice his son Isaac and thereby uncover details that are not expressed in the text. Scripture relates that Abraham "took in his hand the fire and the knife" as he prepared to perform the sacrifice, but it employs a rare word for knife—*ma'akelet*. The word *ma'akelet* is derived from the Hebrew and

---

Seder Tefillot kol ha-Shana, nusaḥ ha-qaddish, can be read, but need not be read, as placing aggada within the category of Oral Law.

[23]Deuteronomy 16:13; BT *Sukka* 12a; Maimonides, Commentary on the Mishna, *Sukka* 1:4. Put more technically and precisely, the booths must be thatched with that which (a) grows out of the ground and (b) also belongs to the class of objects incapable of contracting ritual impurity.

Semitic root that signifies "eating." The unusual choice of the word, which for the rabbinic interpreter of Scripture could scarcely be accidental, indicates to him that everything the people of Israel *eat* during their history, every benefit they enjoy, comes to them through the merit of Abraham's readiness to sacrifice his son and Isaac's readiness to be sacrificed.[24]

That is one method employed by the rabbis in their scholarly activity. They searched Scripture for signposts that were planted there by the divine author and that lead to propositions that lie below the surface. The second method consisted in formulating brief statements of a halakic or aggadic character without reference to the biblical text. In this mode, the rabbis could set down details of the obligation to dwell in booths during the Tabernacles festival or details of the Abraham story in brief statements fit for memorization without citing Scripture. They could state flatly, without reference to Scripture, that the booths must be thatched with materials having the character of agricultural waste products[25] or that throughout its history the Jewish nation draws upon the merit of Abraham and Isaac.[26]

The two modes of rabbinic study and teaching are the methods of *midrash* and *mishna* respectively. As the examples indicate, they are not mutually exclusive. Any given item, whether of halaka or aggada, is amenable to both methods. The rules for thatching the festival booths and the Jewish nation's drawing on the merits of its forefathers Abraham and Isaac might be formulated and transmitted both as a decoding of the divine text and as brief statements standing independently of Scripture.

Little imagination is needed in order to wonder whether the propositions that the ancient rabbis believed they were extracting from Scripture with the aid of signs implanted in the text are indeed present there or whether the practitioners of the midrashic method were reading things in. Medieval Jewish Bible commentators were conscious of the issue. Maimonides, for his part, never addresses it systematically. He never, in fact, seems to use the term *midrash* in the sense of a particular method of interpreting Scripture—although he regularly employs forms of the verb *lidrosh*, which is derived from the same linguistic root (*d-r-sh*) and has the meaning: "to interpret midrashically,"[27] and he also uses the noun *midrash* in the sense, well attested in posttalmudic literature, of a collection of scriptural interpretations arrived at through the method, in other words, a collection of midrashic interpretations of Scripture.[28] Notwithstanding the reservations,

[24]Genesis 22:6; *Genesis Rabba* §56.3.

[25]Mishna *Sukka* 1:4; Maimonides, *Mishneh Torah*: *H. Sukka* 5.1.

[26]PT *Ta*ᶜ*anit* 2:4; *Pesiqta Rabbati* 40. (Both passages are embedded in midrashic material but are not themselves midrashic.)

[27]Maimonides, *Book of Commandments* (*Sefer ha-Miṣwot*), ed. and Hebrew trans. J. Kafah (Jerusalem 1971), introduction, rule 9, p. 34. English translation: Maimonides, *The Commandments*, trans. C. Chavel (London 1967) 2.399.

[28]See Bacher, *Die Bibelexegese Moses Maimûni's* (n. 11 above) 35–36.

Maimonides provides us with a number of comments that make it possible to delineate his attitude toward the midrashic method.

He writes in the introduction to his Commentary on the Mishna that the "interpretations" of scriptural commandments which were received by Moses from God and handed down by him orally to subsequent generations can be corroborated from the biblical text. For the "wisdom of the revealed word" has brought about that, "in addition to being transmitted" orally, "those interpretations can be derived from Scripture through the several forms of dialectical reasoning and through links [*isnād*], hints [*talwīḥ*], and allusions [*ishāra*], occurring in the scriptural text."[29] By the forms of dialectical reasoning, Maimonides means the thirteen well-known canons of rabbinic dialectic.[30] It is not they, but the links, hints, and allusions that interest us here. Maimonides has already told us that interpretations received by Moses and constituting the Oral Torah clarify what is dictated or prohibited by verses in Scripture which contain divine commandments. He is now saying that paralleling their oral transmission, the interpretations received by Moses can also be derived from links, hints, and allusions embedded in the text of Scripture itself.

The terms *hint* and *allusion* are transparent enough. An irregular or unexpected feature in a biblical verse hints at, or alludes to, what is not immediately apparent. A notion of what Maimonides means by a *link* is furnished when he writes of a category of ritual impurity nowhere explicitly mentioned in Scripture that it is "a tradition linked to" a certain verse in the Pentateuch.[31]

Link, *hint*, and *allusion* are very likely not three independent phenomena for him. On one occasion, he states that a certain talmudic inference is drawn "by way of hint and allusion" from Scripture "as you understand those terms from what I explained in the introduction" to the Commentary on the Mishna.[32] Here the terms *hint* and *allusion* appear to be synonymous. On another occasion, he writes with reference to conclusions drawn in one of the ancient rabbinic midrashic compilations: "These are links and hints whereby the scriptural text hints" at what is known through tradition;[33] link and hint now appear to be two sides of the same

[29]Commentary on the Mishna (n. 5 above) , introduction, pp. 17, 19. Most of the passages quoted from Maimonides here and in the following few notes are recorded by Bacher, *Die Bibelexegese Moses Maimûni's* 27–33. At one critical point, I have followed Bacher 28 and corrected Kafah's translation.

[30]See Maimonides, *Book of Commandments*, rule 2, p. 12; English translation 2.373. The thirteen canons are listed in *Sifra*, introduction.

[31]Commentary on the Mishna, *Ṭohorot* 1:1. A few additional instances where Maimonides writes that items of Oral Law going back to Moses are corroborated by linkages in Scripture: Commentary on the Mishna, *Terumot* 1:7 (a particular ritual regulation "is linked" to a scriptural verse); *Ma*ᶜ*aserot* 1:1 (a certain ritual rule "is linked to" a verse); *Ḥalla* 1:1 ("a linkage" of a ritual rule to a certain scriptural verse); *Zebaḥim* 13:3 (regulations that "are tradition, but linked to" scriptural verses); *Miqwa'ot* 2:7 (a certain principle known by "tradition . . . is linked" to and derived from a certain verse); *Nidda* 5:3; *Makshirim* 6:6.

[32]Commentary on the Mishna, *Ḥullin* 11:1.

[33]Commentary on the Mishna, *Nega*ᶜ*im* 6:1.

coin. His thinking, I would suggest, was that the Mosaic tradition, which comprises interpretations of the scriptural commandments, is *linked* to the text of Scripture through *hints* and *allusions* present in the text. At all events, formulas to the effect that the content of the oral Mosaic tradition is linked to, alluded to, or hinted at in Scripture are frequent in Maimonides.[34]

It is, moreover, a fundamental "principle" (*aṣl*) for him that "no dispute whatsoever" took place among the ancient rabbis regarding "the interpretations transmitted from Moses." "We find no dispute occurring among the rabbis [*ḥakamim*] [regarding such interpretations] at any time from Moses" to the redaction of the Babylonian Talmud. To suppose that differences of opinion regarding the laws (*aḥkām*) "transmitted from Moses" could have arisen through "error . . . or forgetfulness" on the part of the transmitters would, "God knows, be shameful and reprehensible, . . . incorrect, in conflict with [rabbinic] principles, and disparaging of the men through whom the Law has been transmitted. It is baseless." Whenever the classic sources report disputes regarding religious laws and rituals—and the rabbinic sources are notoriously replete with such disputes—that fact by itself is sufficient to establish that the laws and rituals in question are not part of the Mosaic tradition.

Maimonides offers several illustrations. Scripture instructs the Israelites to take the "fruit of goodly trees" in their hands on the Tabernacles festival together with a palm branch, willow branches, and "boughs of thick trees"; and the Babylonian Talmud has a discussion in which it disproves the hypothesis that the fruit of goodly trees is a peppercorn and another in which it disproves the hypotheses that the boughs of thick trees are branches of olive, chestnut, or oleander.[35] Maimonides nonetheless insists: No member of the ancient rabbinic community ever doubted that by the fruit of goodly trees Scripture meant a citron and that by the boughs of thick trees it meant myrtle branches. Again, although Scripture mandates "an eye for an eye," no member of the rabbinic community ever imagined that a person who blinds the eye of another was to be punished by having his own eye taken out; no one ever doubted that the expression "an eye for an eye" signifies monetary restitution. Since those interpretations of the pertinent biblical texts are part of the oral tradition going back to Moses, differences of opinion can never have occurred in connection with them.[36]

[34]See the previous two notes. A few more instances: Commentary on the Mishna, *Menaḥot* 5:5: "transmitted by tradition and linked [*musnad*] to [scriptural] verses"; *Keritot* 2:2: a "tradition" with a "linkage [*ta^calluq*] . . . to a verse"; *Menaḥot* 10:4: "many hints [*talwīḥ*] in the [biblical] text," but in fact a "tradition"; *^cUqṣin* 1:1: "Tradition informs us that the intent of the allusion is, ..." With a somewhat different thrust, Commentary on the Mishna, *Nega^cim* 13:1 (end) speaks of: "linkages that call attention to these legal regulations transmitted by tradition."

[35]BT *Sukka* 32b; 35a. The biblical verse is Leviticus 23:40.

[36]Commentary on the Mishna, introduction, pp. 16–17, 20. In *Guide for the Perplexed* 3.41, Maimonides represents the straightforward meaning of the biblical command as being

Maimonides does recognize that disputes might take place among the ancient rabbis concerning "the allusion to the transmitted interpretation which occurs in the verse." In other words, once the rabbis possessed an interpretation transmitted from the time of Moses informing them precisely what a given scriptural verse commanded, they might disagree about the allusion or hint in Scripture that corroborates the interpretation. One of the ancient rabbis could conclude that the allusion identifying the citron and nothing else as the fruit to be taken on the Tabernacles festival is found in a certain feature of the biblical text, while others might conclude that another feature supplies the allusion. One rabbi could find the allusion to the monetary restitution that must be made for blinding a person's eye in a certain feature of Scripture, while others might find it in other features.[37] But that the fruit is a citron and that monetary restitution is the mandated punishment for blinding a person's eye was never in dispute.

Although Maimonides does not employ the term *midrash* in any of the passages I have cited, details of a scriptural commandment which are derived from a hint or allusion present in the biblical text would be nothing other than items of halaka which are derived midrashically. He, therefore, recognizes that at least some midrashic inferences from Scripture genuinely reflect Scripture's intent.

The ancient rabbis themselves took note of instances where midrashists ostensibly discovered signposts in Scripture which led to halakic propositions latent there but in actuality were using Scripture as a peg on which to hang their own creations.[38] Maimonides naturally is aware of such instances[39] and he offers the following example. In the Book of Deuteronomy, Moses commands the Israelites: "Observe, therefore, and do them [that is, God's statutes], for this is your wisdom and understanding in the sight of the nations. . . ." The Babylonian Talmud reports that one of the ancient rabbis reasoned as follows: What does Scripture

---

literally an eye for an eye, and various attempts have been made to remove the apparent disharmony between that statement and what he writes here.

Although Maimonides insists here that differences of opinion cannot be brought about through forgetfulness on the part of the transmitters of Mosaic tradition, he makes much of a talmudic dictum to the effect that halakot may be completely forgotten; see below, p. 168.

[37]Commentary on the Mishna, introduction, p 17, with reference to Exodus 21:24; Leviticus 23:40; BT *Sukka* 35a; BT *Baba Qamma* 83b–84a; and parallels.

[38]W. Bacher, *Die bibel- und traditionsexegetische Terminologie der Amoräer* (Leipzig 1905) (reprinted as Part Two of *Die exegetische Terminologie der jüdischen Traditionsliteratur* [Darmstadt 1965]) 13.

[39]Commentary on the Mishna, introduction, p. 18 (*asmakta*). If I read Kafah's translation of the Commentary on the Mishna correctly, he unnecessarily understands Maimonides as saying that the *linkages* cited in notes 31 and 34 were created by the rabbis themselves.

On a few occasions Maimonides does make the curious statement that one or another regulation instituted by the rabbis has its hint (*talwīḥ*; *remez*) in Scripture. See Commentary on the Mishna (n. 5 above), introduction to the sixth order, p. 19 (a certain regulation instituted by the rabbis has a *talwīḥ* in the "text" of Scripture). *Mishneh Torah*: *H. Abot ha-Ṭum'ot* 6.1; 12.7 (a *remez* in the Torah). I assume that, as often happened, he was simply not being precise.

mean by the "wisdom and understanding" that is present to "the sight of the nations"? Must it not be the calculation of something that everyone in the world can see; and that being so, must it not be the mathematical and astronomical "calculation of the seasons of the year and [the courses of] the constellations"? Whereupon the rabbi in question concluded that "it is a divine commandment for man to calculate the seasons of the year and [the courses of] the constellations." Maimonides characterizes inferences of the sort, where phrases are torn out of context and conclusions drawn that are wholly unrelated to the obvious meaning of the scriptural text, as conscious "homiletic exegesis" (*derash*). The rabbis advancing them never expected them to be taken as genuine reflections of Scripture's intent.[40]

In short, Maimonides recognizes instances where the ancient rabbis derived Oral Torah interpretations from Scripture through hints and the like that are, through the wisdom of the revealed word, embedded in the biblical text. He also recognizes instances where the rabbis consciously read their own legal innovations into Scripture. I could find no clear-cut criteria in Maimonides for deciding which midrashic interpretations are linked to, and derived from, hints embedded in Scripture and which ostensible derivations from Scripture are the creation of the rabbis and merely hung on the text by them.[41]

To a certain extent, Maimonides has said nothing unusual. All talmudic and posttalmudic rabbinic literature presupposes that the ancient rabbis were carriers of the Mosaic tradition, it assumes that the rabbis extracted laws and rituals from Scripture by following signs in the biblical text to what lies below the surface, and it recognizes that they sometimes hung their own legislation on the text of Scripture. What is peculiar to Maimonides over against the mainstream of medieval rabbinists is the relative weight that he places on the rabbis' role as carriers of the Mosaic tradition. As he saw things, when the ancient rabbis corroborated interpretations of Scripture by deriving them from allusions and hints embedded in the text—in effect, through midrashic exegesis—they were able to do so only because Mosaic tradition told them what legal regulations to look for. If the tradition in the possession of the rabbis had not guided them by informing them precisely what the

[40] *Book of Commandments*, rule 2, 13–14; English translation 2.375. The biblical and rabbinic passages are Deuteronomy 4:6, and BT *Shabbat* 75a.

[41] There are negative criteria. As we have seen, when a difference of opinion is recorded regarding a halaka, the halaka is not, for Maimonides, an interpretation transmitted from Moses; Scripture would consequently not contain hints and allusions from which the halaka can be derived, and any ostensible midrashic derivation of such a halaka would not reflect Scripture's meaning. This is only a negative criterion because Maimonides recognizes that sometimes no difference of opinion is recorded concerning halakot that are *not* transmitted from Moses; see Commentary on the Mishna, introduction p. 4. Maimonides, *Book of Commandments*, rule 2, p. 14, also cites a well-known talmudic statement to the effect that "Scripture never loses its straightforward sense" (BT *Shabbat* 63a, and parallels), and he maintains that to be a genuine exposition of the biblical text, an exegesis must be related to the straightforward sense of the text; English translation 2.375. But he recognizes exceptions; see Commentary on the Mishna, introduction p. 6; *Book of Commandments*, rule 9, 33; English translation 2.398.

correct interpretation of a given scriptural commandment was, they could never have been sure that they had discovered Scripture's intent through their own perspicacity.[42] In searching for the allusion to the Oral Law halaka in Scripture, they might moreover disagree. When they did, there is no way of ascertaining which of them had been successful, which had identified the allusion correctly. Since the details of the commandment were known before the midrashic process began, no one is the worse for the uncertainty.

So much for halaka. We have seen that the midrashic method was also deployed by rabbis of the classic period for nonlegal, that is to say, aggadic ends. Since interpretations of Scripture making up the Oral Torah do not include aggada for Maimonides, it should follow that aggada is not covered by his statements about the hints and allusions actually embedded in the biblical text. And he, indeed, points out that exegeses of an aggadic character (*derashot*) do not reflect Scripture's intent.

He outlines a pair of errors that he had encountered regarding exegeses of the sort which are recorded in the classic rabbinic sources. The occasion is a discussion of Scripture's purpose in instructing Israelite men to take in their hands, on the Tabernacles holiday: a citron, a palm branch, three myrtle branches, and two willow branches. The classic midrashic compilations offer a number of homiletic rationales for the taking of just the four species. They explain that the citron represents Abraham, the palm branch represents Isaac, the myrtle branches represent Jacob, and the willow branches, Joseph. Alternatively, the citron, palm branch, myrtle branches, and willow branches, represent the four matriarchs, Sarah, Rebecca, Leah, and Rachel. Again: The four represent the Sanhedrin, the generality of rabbinic scholars, the three rows of scholars who sat before the Sanhedrin when it conducted its business, and the two scribes who recorded the proceedings. And so on.[43] Maimonides had found persons who took aggadic exegeses to be a genuine exposition of the biblical text and accorded them the same impeccable authority that appertains to the "laws handed down by tradition." He had found other, equally misguided persons who dismissed such exegeses with derision because they could not possibly reflect the intent of Scripture. In truth, Maimonides writes, anyone of intelligence will understand that aggadic interpretations make no pretense of conveying Scripture's meaning. They are

[42]Maimonides almost surely had in mind BT *Sanhedrin* 88a, where greater weight is put on tradition than on rabbinic dialectical reasoning. The discussion in BT *Sanhedrin* 88a–b was of cardinal importance for him: He copies sections from it in *Mishneh Torah*: *H. Mamrim* 1.4 and 4.1, he draws from it in a number of paragraphs of *H. Sanhedrin*, and he interprets a statement from it in Commentary on the Mishna, introduction p. 20. A position similar to Maimonides' was taken by R. Hai, according to a passage quoted by Z. Karl, "*Ha-Rambam ke-Mefaresh ha-Torah*," *Tarbiz* 6 (1935) 405, note 2. See also the position expressed by Ibn Ezra in his short commentary on Exodus 21:8.

[43]*Leviticus Rabba* 30:9–12; *Pesiqta de-Rav Kahana* 27:9.

"clever poetic locutions" that the midrashist "linked" to a biblical verse as a kind of "poetic trope."[44]

That observation is found in Maimonides' *Guide for the Perplexed*, his main philosophic work. One of his rabbinic works makes the same point with the help of a different illustration: The Book of Deuteronomy states that God's word "is not in heaven, . . . neither is it beyond the sea," and a midrashic comment in the Babylonian Talmud sees therein the truth that "the Torah is not found among the conceited and haughty nor among those [merchants] who travel to distant lands." Here, Maimonides writes, rabbinic exegesis has obviously read something into Scripture; the rabbis "linked" their moral lesson "to the verse by way of a clever locution."[45] Both his rabbinic works and his *Guide for the Perplexed* also occasionally describe nonlegal midrashic interpretations of Scripture as having been advanced "by way of homily" (*derash*), with the unmistakable intimation that the interpretations have no genuine basis in the biblical text.[46]

Maimonides nevertheless treats at least some midrashic interpretations of an aggadic sort as genuine interpretations of Scripture.[47] The most significant instance revolves around the biblical promise that by obeying God's commandment "it will be well with thee and thou wilt prolong thy days." The Babylonian Talmud explains the promise as the twofold assurance that it will "be well with thee in the world that is entirely good," and thou wilt "prolong thy days in the world that is entirely long"; the man who obeys God will gain his reward in the world to

[44]*Guide for the Perplexed* 3.43, pp. 96b–97a. In *Guide* 2.24, p. 54a, Maimonides gives his own interpretation of Psalms 115:16—"The heavens are the heavens of the Lord, But the earth hath He given to the children of men"—using the method of "clever poetic locution."

The two unacceptable approaches to aggadic midrashic interpretations of Scripture distinguished here parallel the two unacceptable approaches to rabbinic aggada outlined by Maimonides in the Commentary on the Mishna, *Sanhedrin* 10, introduction, pp. 200–202.

[45]Commentary on the Mishna, *Abot* 2:6, with reference to Deuteronomy 30:12–13, and to BT ᶜ*Erubin* 55a. Maimonides must have liked this particular clever poetic locution, since he repeats the verse and the rabbinic explanation of it in *Mishneh Torah*: *H. Talmud Torah* 3.8, now without indicating that the interpretation does not reflect Scripture's genuine intent. Another example of a "clever locution" is given by Maimonides in his commentary on ᶜ*Uqṣin* 3:12.

[46]Bacher, *Die Bibelexegese Moses Maimûni's* (n. 11 above) 30–31.

[47]See p. 126 above. In connection with the rabbis' use of Scripture to predict future events, Maimonides writes: "There are verses in the Torah, the intent of which is one thing, but which contain an *allusion* [*ishāra*] to something else." He offers two instances where the ancient midrashists found an allusion to a future event in the numerical value of the letters of a word in Scripture and he adds that "there are many examples." Here he is recognizing that nonliteral interpretations of a nonhalakic character do reflect the genuine intent of Scripture. See Moses Maimonides, *Epistle to Yemen*, ed. A. Halkin with English trans. B. Cohen (New York 1952) 82; English translation xv. In his *Treatise on Resurrection*, ed. J. Finkel, *Proceedings of the American Academy for Jewish Research* 9 (1939), Hebrew-Arabic section 27, Maimonides concedes that the Pentateuch could possibly contain "hints and allusions" (*talwīḥ, ishāra*) to the dogma of resurrection; he does not, however, hide his opinion that such in fact is not the case and that no such hints and allusions are present in Scripture.

come.[48] In this instance, Maimonides does not label the midrashic reading of Scripture as a clever poetic locution but describes it instead as a "transmitted interpretation" and, again, as an interpretation known by the rabbis "through tradition," with the suggestion that it correctly reflects Scripture's intent. He was so taken by the midrashic reading that he cites it in one work after another as a proof-text for the immortality of the human soul, or intellect.[49] I could again discover no sufficient criterion in Maimonides' writings for differentiating between aggadic midrashic interpretations of Scripture that are merely clever locutions and the infrequent, more privileged instances of transmitted interpretations that carry the cachet of tradition.[50]

To recapitulate, Maimonides joined mainstream medieval rabbinists in recognizing that much midrashic exegesis in the realm of halaka is grounded in hints and allusions present in the scriptural text. In his opinion, however, such exegesis is known to reflect Scripture's intent only because Mosaic tradition told the rabbis what to look for. The exegesis is moreover never definitive, since one of the ancient rabbis could find the hint of the transmitted halaka in one feature of Scripture and another rabbi could find it in another. Maimonides calls attention as well to halakic midrashic exegesis that the rabbis realized has no basis in the biblical text. As for midrashic exegesis of an aggadic nature, he makes the general statement that it comprises poetic locutions and was not put forward as representing the genuine intent of the biblical verses to which the rabbis linked them. In a few instances, he nonetheless labels midrashic exegesis of an aggadic sort as consisting in transmitted interpretations, by which he apparently means that it does capture Scripture's intent. In subordinating halakic midrashic exegesis to the tradition transmitted by Moses to the rabbis and in characterizing aggadic exegesis in general as a man-made literary trope, he unquestionably delimited the significance of the midrashic method more narrowly than the mainstream did.

Dicta formulated in the mishnaic mode—statements standing independent of the text of Scripture—won out as the preferred vehicle for transmitting halaka. Precisely when halakic collections in the mishnaic form were first made is a

[48]BT *Qiddushin* 39b, and BT *Ḥullin*, 142a, in connection with the commandment to let the mother bird go before one takes her young from the nest; see Deuteronomy 22:7. The talmudic passages explicitly speak of "resurrection of the dead," but Maimonides understands the promise to be immortality of the human intellect.

[49]Commentary on the Mishna, *Sanhedrin* 10, introduction, p. 205 ("it has come to us by tradition through the rabbis. . . ."); *Mishneh Torah*: *H. Teshuba* 8.1 ("they [the rabbis] learned through tradition. . . ."); *Guide for the Perplexed* 1.42 (a "transmitted interpretation"); 3.27; *Treatise on Resurrection*, Hebrew-Arabic section 7.

[50]In *Guide for the Perplexed* 3:43, he gives one sign of poetic locutions: Sometimes the rabbis said: Do not read the scriptural text as it stands, but change the vocalization and read it as if said. . . . In those instances, the rabbis did not pretend to convey the genuine meaning of the scriptural verse.

debatable and oft-debated question. At the very least, there is convincing evidence that prior to the oldest surviving collection, other collections existed which have not survived.[51] Around the beginning of the third Christian century a comprehensive compilation of material primarily of a halakic character and primarily taking the guise of brief statements without reference to Scripture was composed in Hebrew. The proviso that the compilation is *primarily* halakic must be made because it includes a small proportion of aggada. The further proviso that the material is set forth *primarily* without reference to Scripture is also needed, because sentences formulated in the midrashic mode are occasionally included.

A scholar known as Judah the Prince is credited by the rabbinic sources with the compiling of the surviving collection of statements of halaka, and it is consequently known as his Mishna. The term *mishna* has a number of senses. It is the rabbinic method of formulating and transmitting brief statements without reference to Scripture. Any individual statement formulated by use of the method is called a *mishna*. So are the collections of mishna statements of a halakic character, including those made by rabbis preceding Judah the Prince. And the term perhaps has other meanings as well.[52] But once Judah's compilation appeared on the scene, it came to be known as the mishna par excellence. When one spoke subsequently, and when one speaks today, of *the mishna* without qualification, Judah the Prince's compilation is meant. In what follows, I capitalize the word Mishna when referring to his compilation.

While Oral Torah is by definition unwritten and more than one ancient rabbinic source insisted strongly on its being kept that way, the oral material was eventually written down. Whether Judah the Prince's Mishna compilation—which, is in good part Oral Torah even in Maimonides' restricted usage of the term—was put into writing from the very beginning is one of the long-debated questions, and evidence can be marshaled on both sides.[53] The opinion prevalent among medieval Spanish Jews was that Judah himself put his Mishna in writing,[54] and Maimonides follows the Spanish opinion.

He believes that in the early generations, a "prophet" or "president of a court" would "write for himself a protocol of the traditions he received from his masters but in public would give instruction orally. Similarly, each [student] would, to the

[51] See *Abot de-Rabbenu Natan*, standard version, chapter 18; H. Albeck, *Mabo la-Mishna* (Jerusalem 1959) 83–85.

[52] W. Bacher, *Die älteste Terminologie der jüdischen Schriftauslegung* (Leipzig 1899) (reprinted as Part One of *Die exegetische Terminologie der jüdischen Traditionsliteratur* [Darmstadt 1965]) 122–23; Albeck, *Mabo la-Mishna* 3–4.

[53] See BT *Temura* 14b, in particular, and J. Epstein, *Mabo le-Nusaḥ ha-Mishna* (Jerusalem 1964) 692–702. For scholars who line up on each side of the oral versus written issue, see H. Strack, *Introduction to the Talmud and Midrash*, revised edition (Edinburgh 1991) 35–49.

[54] For the division on the issue between medieval French rabbinic scholarship, on the one side, and medieval Spanish rabbinic scholarship, on the other, see S. Assaf, *Tequfat ha-Geonim we-Sifrutah* (Jerusalem 1955) 152.

extent of his ability, write down whatever interpretations of the Law and whatever halakot he received orally as well as new regulations."[55] He would make a written record of halakic items taken from the Mosaic tradition as well as of regulations introduced after the time of Moses, but only for his personal use. Judah the Prince took a new tack. He "composed . . . a mishna book" in which he set down "all the traditions, all the laws, and all the explanations and interpretative comments [*perushim*]," his intent being to create a book for the use of the entire scholarly community. "Everyone" henceforth made written copies of Judah's composition.[56] Maimonides' view, then, is that with Judah's compilation, halaka took the form of a comprehensive and uniform book.

Judah the Prince's Mishna was originally organized into sixty tractates, but a subsequent subdivision of two of the tractates expanded the number to sixty-three. Each of the sixty-three has its own primary topic, and in all but one instance, the topics are halakic;[57] the exception is the tractate *Abot*, commonly known in English as the *Ethics of the Fathers*, the subject matter of which is ideological and ethical, and hence aggadic. Either at the original redaction or soon thereafter, the tractates were grouped under six rubrics, called "Orders." These comprise: (1) agricultural ritual laws, with tractates on: tithes for the Levites and poor, produce reserved for the priest, additional types of produce reserved for the poor, first fruits, the leaving of fields fallow on the sabbatical year, and the like; (2) laws of the Appointed Days, comprising tractates on the Sabbath, festivals, and other special days; (3) what were called laws pertaining to women, with tractates on betrothal, marriage, divorce, and associated matters; (4) torts and civil law; (5) regulations governing the Temple sacrifices; and (6) the laws of ritual impurity. Although the rubrics are broad, they were not sufficient to cover all the halakic subjects of concern to the ancient rabbis. Accommodation was, however, made. Thus, the tractate on liturgy is set at the head of the entire corpus because of its religious importance. It thereby gets subsumed into the Order of Agricultural Law. The tractate on vows is placed in the Order of Women, because the scriptural discussion of vows deals particularly with those made by daughters and wives. The tractate on idolatry is placed in the Order of Torts, presumably because idolatry was a crime as well as a sin and hence fell under the jurisdiction of the court system. The *Ethics of the Fathers* is also placed in the Order of Torts, for reasons that can only be guessed.

Then there are topics that were not large enough to justify an entire tractate of their own. They received niches within one or another of the given tractates, even though we might not always think that they belong logically to the tractate to which

[55]The beginning of *Guide for the Perplexed* 1:71 does not contradict what Maimonides is saying here. See M. Schwarz's Hebrew translation of the *Guide*.

[56]*Mishneh Torah*, introduction. There are echoes of R. Sherira's famous letter here; see Albeck, *Mabo la-Mishna* 66. In *Responsa* (n. 3 above) §442, Maimonides similarly speaks of Judah the Prince as having "written" his Mishna.

[57]There are, however, two tractates, *Tamid* and *Middot*, that stand on the border between halaka and aggada.

they are assigned. Prime examples are the phylacteries worn by Jewish men and the fringes (*ṣiṣit*) to be tied to the corners of garments. Both topics find their place in the tractate that has as its formal subject the bringing of meal offerings in the Holy Temple.

Half of the tractates in the Order of Torts and Civil Law and the nonritual parts of the tractates on marriage and divorce treat issues of a character likely to engage the attention of a secular legal system. The rest of the Mishna corpus, and it is obviously the larger part, treats subjects of a religious and ritual character which a secular legal system would not regard as its responsibility.

The Jerusalem Temple, which was the venue for sacrifice, was destroyed over a century before the redacting of the Mishna, and the sacrificial rituals thereupon ceased being practiced. As the rabbis saw things, many of the agricultural and impurity regulations also lost their mandatory character with the destruction of the Temple. Of the agricultural laws that continued to be observed, the larger part was tied to Palestine and contiguous areas; they consequently did not apply to Jews living elsewhere. Some of the laws within the rubric of civil and criminal law were also understood to be operative only in Palestine, and a number of these went out of practice even in Palestine when the Temple was destroyed. At the time when Judah the Prince's Mishna was compiled, considerable portions of it therefore dealt with matters that were no longer in effect at all. And for Jews living at a distance from Palestine, over half the legislation in the Mishna had no practical application. Those parts of the Mishna were only of theoretical interest, to be studied for study's sake. The hope, of course, always glowed bright that God would soon redirect the course of history, the Jerusalem Temple would be rebuilt, the exiles ingathered, and the entire halaka again practiced in full.

Judah the Prince's Mishna, whether written down as Maimonides believed or transmitted orally as others have understood, quickly gained canonic status. It was recognized throughout the Jewish world as the authoritative repository of halaka. And it became the curriculum for study not solely in the schools of Palestine, where rabbinic activity had hitherto been centered, but also in schools within the area known by the Jews as Babylonia and roughly corresponding to today's Iraq. Some—certainly not all—of the protocols of the postmishnaic schools in the two geographical areas were preserved, snowballing as they passed from generation to generation, and they were eventually redacted into two vast compilations. According to Jewish tradition, which Maimonides repeats, one of the compilations, the Palestinian or Jerusalem Talmud, was produced by Palestinian scholars living a generation or so after Judah the Prince, and the other, the Babylonian Talmud, by the fifth generation of postmishnaic rabbinic scholars in Iraq.[58] The two Talmuds

[58]*Mishneh Torah*, introduction. Maimonides adds that the Babylonian Talmud was redacted "about a century" after the Palestinian, which would place it in the fourth century. Some scholars today set the date later.

are composed in Aramaic with a good admixture of Hebrew, in contrast to the Mishna, which is almost entirely in Hebrew.

Both Talmuds are arranged in the form of section-by-section analyses of the Mishna. But they do far more than analyze. Mishna paragraphs serve as jumping-off points for discussions that range far afield in divers directions. The two Talmuds explain statements in the Mishna, extract subsurface meanings from it—the term *talmud* having originally been synonymous with *midrash*—adduce related halakic material purportedly belonging to the mishnaic period which failed to enter the authoritative Mishna, take up new halakic issues, record a large amount of midrashic interpretation of Scripture, weave in substantial amounts of aggada, and subject all the grist entering their mills to subtle dialectical examination. Theses that are endorsed or are proposed hypothetically are scrutinized for possible internal inconsistencies. They are measured against other authoritative theses, whether scriptural or rabbinic, and possible contradictions are brought to light. When a thesis is challenged, the challenge is in turn subjected to the same intense scrutiny, and when a contradiction is resolved, the resolution may undergo scrutiny as well. Both Talmuds organize their material largely by association of ideas, and digressions abound.

Presumably because so much of the Mishna no longer had any bearing on everyday life, the redactors of the Babylonian Talmud arranged the protocols at their disposal around only thirty-seven of the sixty-three Mishna tractates. The Babylonian Talmud does have tractates for most of the Mishna tractates dealing with sacrifices, despite the sacrifices' not having been performed for centuries. But it has just a single tractate for the Order of Agricultural Law, the one built around the Mishna tractate dealing with liturgy and hence the single tractate in the Order of Agricultural Law which has nothing to do with agriculture. The Babylonian Talmud also has only a single tractate for the Order of Ritual Impurity, one constructed around the Mishna tractate dealing with menstrual impurity. The subject matter was of immediate, daily significance since the Book of Leviticus forbids sexual relations during and immediately after a woman's menstrual period, quite apart from the existence of a Temple in Jerusalem. Material that the redactors of the Babylonian Talmud had at their disposal and wanted to preserve regarding topics to which they did not devote full tractates—notably in the areas of agricultural and impurity law—was tucked into the thirty-seven tractates that the Babylonian Talmud does comprise; rabbinic redactors were adept at finding niches. The Palestinian Talmud as it exists today has thirty-nine tractates, although Maimonides seems to report that he knew, or knew of, tractates of the Palestinian Talmud for all mishnaic tractates belonging to the first five Orders.[59] That would

[59]Commentary on the Mishna, introduction, p. 46. Y. Brody, "*Le-Pesiqat ha-Rambam ᶜal pi ha-Talmud ha-Yerushalmi*," *Maimonidean Studies* 4 (2000) 10, suggests an interpretation of the passage which would remove the indication that Maimonides knew of tractates of the Palestinian Talmud matching all the mishnaic tractates in the first five Orders.

imply fifty-one tractates in all. While both Talmuds are organized into fewer tractates than the Mishna, they are far lengthier. The Babylonian Talmud is, moreover, three times as long as the Palestinian.

The two Talmuds won recognition as canonic repositories of halaka and also of aggada, at a level second to Judah the Prince's Mishna. Together with the Mishna, they became the authoritative guides for Jewish behavior and belief, indeed for Jewish life. Of the two, the Babylonian Talmud, in its final redaction, established itself as the ultimate arbiter for law and ritual throughout the Jewish world. It prevailed over the Palestinian Talmud because it is edited with more polish and because it had the backing of the Iraqi schools, which were the foci of rabbinic activity and authority during the centuries immediately after its redaction.

We may now consider Maimonides' rabbinic writings.

Talmudic Commentaries. Students of both the Palestinian and Babylonian Talmuds encounter formidable hurdles. On the purely technical level, the absence of vocalization in the manuscripts and the printed texts makes them difficult merely to read. For persons not versed in Aramaic, the language can be a stumbling block. There is a wide range of topics with innumerable intricate details. The discussion constantly shuttles from thesis to refutation of the thesis to refutation of the refutation, but the texts have no punctuation to show the reader where matters stand at any given moment. And the serpentine chains of reasoning are never made wholly explicit. To meet the obvious need, rabbinic scholars in Iraq, who were followed by scholars in other sectors of the Jewish world, began to provide students of the Babylonian Talmud with aids. In Iraq these took the guise of glossaries of difficult words, the exposition of puzzling passages that Jews living in other countries asked the leaders of the Iraqi schools to elucidate, and full-fledged commentaries on entire tractates.[60] Most of the early commentaries have not been preserved and are known today through citations or fragments that survived by chance.

A little over a century before Maimonides, a North African rabbinic scholar, R. Ḥananeel ben Ḥushiel, composed a commentary on two-thirds of the tractates of the Babylonian Talmud, and other commentaries on tractates of the Babylonian Talmud came out of North Africa. There was commentarial activity in Spain as well, and R. Joseph Ibn Migas, the teacher of Maimonides' father, is known to have composed commentaries on at least two complete tractates of the Babylonian Talmud; the two commentaries have been preserved and published.[61] The need to furnish students of the Babylonian Talmud with written aids was also recognized in

[60]Assaf, *Tequfat ha-Geonim we-Sifrutah* (n. 54 above) 138–44. S. Baron, *Social and Religious History of the Jews* 6 (New York 1958) 41–43.

[61]*Ḥiddushe ha-Riy Migas ᶜal Masseket Shebuᶜot* and *Ḥiddushe ha-Riy Migas le-Masseket Baba Batra*, both of which have appeared in several editions. The attribution to Ibn Migas is confirmed by Naḥmanides' quotations from both commentaries in Ibn Migas' name.

Central France and in Germany, areas with which Maimonides was not in touch, and endeavors there culminated in the marvelous running commentary on almost the entire Babylonian Talmud produced in the eleventh century by the French scholar Rashi. Rashi's masterpiece is probably the best expository commentary on any book done by a member of any of the three monotheistic religions in the Middle Ages. But it never reached Maimonides.

Maimonides writes that he was cognizant of no commentary on the entire Babylonian Talmud.[62] He does take note of the commentaries of Ibn Migas on the two tractates[63] and speaks as well of posttalmudic scholars "who commented on individual halakot, those who commented on individual chapters [of the Babylonian Talmud] which were considered difficult, and those who commented on tractates or [entire] Orders."[64] The language is so unspecific that there is no way of determining how far the commentaries at his disposal match what has survived today.

Before his twenty-third birthday, he too put his hand to interpreting the Babylonian Talmud. He composed what he calls "interpretative comments [*perushin*][65] on three Orders [of the Babylonian Talmud], namely, [the Orders dealing with] holy days, women, and torts, with the exception of four tractates for which" he still intended to "write something" when time would permit. In addition, he "wrote" on a tractate that had been assigned to the Order of sacrificial law although the subject of the tractate is not sacrifices. The tractate in question—*Ḥullin*—has the Jewish dietary laws, among other things, as its subject, and Maimonides explains that he included it among the tractates on which he commented because of its importance for daily life.[66] He had, in short, produced commentaries on two-thirds of the tractates of the Babylonian Talmud, his focus being on tractates with everyday relevance. Those were the tractates on which R. Ḥananeel ben Ḥushiel had also focused.

Since Maimonides wrote his talmudic commentaries before the age of twenty-three, he did the work in either Spain or Morocco and hence under the unfriendly eyes of the Almohad rulers. It is reasonable to assume that he consulted whatever earlier commentaries were available to him, and there is in fact evidence of his having used the commentaries of R. Ḥananeel.[67] When he describes the project, however, the only sources that he mentions using are Joseph Ibn Migas' talmudic

[62]Commentary on the Mishna (n. 5 above) p. 46.

[63]Maimonides, *Responsa* (n. 3 above) §251.

[64]*Mishneh Torah*, introduction.

[65]I translate *perushin* as "interpretative comments" rather than "commentaries" because of the way Maimonides uses the term (a) in Commentary on the Mishna, *Menaḥot* 5:5, where he contrasts the style of his Commentary with the method of *perushin*, and (b) in *Epistulae*, ed. D. Baneth (Jerusalem 1946) 56, where he speaks somewhat disparagingly of *perushin*.

[66]Commentary on the Mishna, introduction, p. 47.

[67]Regarding his use of R. Ḥananeel, see Maimonides, *Responsa* §251; S. Assaf, "*Mi-Perusho shel ha-Rambam*," *Sinai* 6 (1940) 109, 115, 116, 119.

commentaries and "notes" that his father and others had preserved from Ibn Migas.[68]

Obtaining a clear picture of Maimonides' talmudic commentaries is complicated by a remark that he made at least ten years after the statements cited so far. On the later occasion he writes, according to an ungainly Hebrew translation from the original Arabic—the original having been lost—that he had not yet found time "to provide explanations for my commentary on difficult halakot throughout the [Babylonian] Talmud."[69] The language, notwithstanding its awkwardness, indicates that his plan at the later date was to interpret difficult halakic passages not merely in three of the Orders, but in the entire Babylonian Talmud; and he had not yet been able to bring the wider project to completion and perhaps not even to start.

An additional circumstance clouds things further. A medieval Jewish author writes that Maimonides "commented on three Orders of the Babylonian Talmud as is the rule among all commentators," but the commentaries had not been disseminated widely. The medieval author himself had seen "two or three tractates" from among the commentaries in question and he testifies that Maimonides had "composed them in Arabic."[70] The writer would appear to be referring to Maimonides' original cycle of commentaries, which focused on the three Orders of the Babylonian Talmud most widely studied and not on the Babylonian Talmud as a whole. Yet when Maimonides' own son quotes "word for word and letter for letter" from Maimonides' commentary on a tractate belonging to one of those three Orders, what he quotes is in Hebrew.[71] It is conceivable of course that Maimonides composed some of the commentaries in the first cycle in Hebrew and some in Arabic, or that he did the two cycles of commentaries in different languages and Maimonides' son was quoting from the later cycle while the other writer was referring to the earlier. The bottom line, however, is that it can only be guessed whether Maimonides' plan for a commentary on difficult halakot throughout the Babylonian Talmud was an expansion and refinement of the commentaries that he finished before the age of twenty-three or a different project altogether, whether he pursued one of the two projects exclusively or primarily in Arabic and the other in Hebrew, and what progress, if any, he made in composing the later cycle of commentaries.[72]

[68] Maimonides, Commentary on the Mishna, introduction, p. 47.

[69] *Responsa* §251. See below, pp. 295–96.

[70] M. Zacks, *Ḥiddushe ha-Rambam la-Talmud* (Jerusalem 1963) introduction, 13. I. Ta-Shma, "*Perush ha-Rambam la-Talmud*," *Shenaton ha-Mishpat ha-Ivri* 14–15 (1988–1989) 302, note 9, suggests that the medieval scholar saw only students' reports of Maimonides' written and oral commentaries.

[71] Abraham Maimonides, *Responsa*, ed. A. Freimann and S. Goitein (Jerusalem 1937) §3, pp. 10–11.

[72] Assaf, "*Mi-Perusho shel ha-Rambam*" 103, supposes that there was in fact only one cycle of commentaries, which Maimonides hoped to revise. Zacks, *Ḥiddushe ha-Rambam la-Talmud*, introduction, 15–16, argues for two distinct cycles. See further, below, pp. 295–96.

Brief quotations from about ten of Maimonides' commentaries, or what have a fair probability of being his authentic commentaries, on the Babylonian Talmud have been uncovered in medieval rabbinic authors.[73] The quotations are in Hebrew, and what is quoted looks in every instance as if it was originally written in that language. The fragments come, with a single very doubtful exception,[74] from commentaries on the three Orders of the Babylonian Talmud on which, Maimonides informs us, he initially focused his attention. They could therefore be quotations from the commentaries he composed before the age of twenty-three; if they are, they lend support to the supposition that that cycle was composed in Hebrew. Most of the preserved quotations are found in the writings of persons who saw the commentaries in Egypt, and as just seen, a medieval Jewish writer reports that Maimonides' talmudic commentaries were not widely disseminated. The suggestion has accordingly been made that Maimonides was not yet satisfied with them, that he did not want them to be disseminated in the form he had so far managed to give them, and that only master copies kept in Fustat could be consulted.[75]

In the sole instance where more than isolated fragments have survived, extended sections are preserved from a commentary that makes a strong, although not conclusive, claim to belong to Maimonides.[76] The tractate of the Babylonian Talmud commented on is the one dealing with the Sabbath laws; it is hence a tractate belonging to the Order of Appointed Days, one of the three Orders covered in Maimonides' initial plan. The language is Hebrew, or to be more precise, the mélange of Hebrew and talmudic Aramaic which was commonly employed by posttalmudic rabbinists, and the sections of the commentary which have been preserved definitely do not look like a translation from the Arabic. The commentary

[73]Zacks records quotations or fragments from what he believed to be twelve of Maimonides' talmudic commentaries, but he acknowledges that in a few instances, the attribution to Maimonides is uncertain. In fact, the attribution to Maimonides is uncertain in more instances than Zacks admits.

[74]The doubtful exception is a citation from what Zacks, *Ḥiddushe ha-Rambam la-Talmud* 2, takes to be Maimonides' commentary on the Talmud, *Berakot*; *Berakot* is a tractate belonging to the agricultural order. The medieval authors—Tosafot and R. Mordecai ben Hillel—who preserve the citation do not, however, state that they are quoting from a talmudic commentary of Maimonides'. They are more likely drawing from Maimonides' code of rabbinic law. See Zacks, p. 2, note 3.

[75]Ta-Shma, "*Perush ha-Rambam la-Talmud,*" 300–1, 305, note 17. The fragment from the commentary on BT *Megilla* attributed to Maimonides which has been preserved takes a much more fundamentalist attitude toward aggada—specifically to the aggadic tradition that the Written Torah was composed in its entirety 2,000 years before God created the world—than his Commentary on the Mishna or *Mishneh Torah*. That might tend to support Ta-Shma's guess that Maimonides did not want to publish the commentaries before revising them because he did not consider them to be a mature piece of work.

[76]Published by Assaf, "*Mi-Perusho shel ha-Rambam*" (n. 67 above), and republished by Zacks, *Ḥiddushe ha-Rambam la-Talmud*. Assaf 115, note 35, and 123, note 114, gives the grounds for identifying Maimonides as the commentary's author.

does not expound the talmudic tractate on the Sabbath line by line or even paragraph by paragraph, yet it also does not restrict itself to particularly difficult sections.[77] It takes up one or more passages from virtually every page of the tractate, provides the subject matter's background, and spells out the passage's reasoning in a straightforward fashion. Such had been the procedure followed by others including R. Joseph Ibn Migas,[78] and Ibn Migas is himself cited a number of times, always in a tone of highest respect. If the commentary is an authentic work of Maimonides' and if his two cycles of talmudic commentaries were distinct in conception and execution, the present commentary would appear to belong to the first cycle—notwithstanding, again, the statement of the medieval writer who had seen commentaries seemingly from the same cycle which were written in Arabic.[79]

In addition to the extended portion of the commentary on the *Sabbath* tractate, a commentary on the entire talmudic tractate *Rosh ha-Shana*, the Jewish New Year, has been preserved which the manuscripts label as a composition of Maimonides' and which several medieval writers cite as his.[80] But Maimonides could not have been the author; for astronomical matters that come up in the mishnaic and talmudic tractate *Rosh ha-Shana* receive explanations in the commentary which could not have come from his hands.

As the physical universe was conceptualized by the medieval Arabic astronomers who carried weight with Maimonides, nine main celestial spheres rotate around the earth. The seven wandering stars, or planets, recognized in the Middle Ages—the five visible planets together with the sun and the moon, which were also classified as planets in the Middle Ages—were understood to be embedded in the seven innermost spheres. The eighth sphere contains the fixed stars, that is, the stars located beyond our solar system; the outermost sphere contains no planet or star; and the rotations of the spheres give rise to the apparent motions of the planets and stars around the earth. Maimonides acquired a mastery of astronomy in his youth, while still living in the countries of the West, and when he speaks of the celestial spheres, the nine-sphere system is the one he recognizes.[81]

The commentary on the tractate *Rosh ha-Shana* which is attributed to Maimonides assumes a different system. Instead of the nine standard spheres, it posits ten; and it manages to do so by distributing the fixed stars, those lying beyond our solar system, between two separate spheres.[82] Maimonides would

[77]Assaf, "*Mi-Perusho shel ha-Rambam*" 109.

[78]See Ibn Migas's commentary on *Baba Batra*; I. Ta-Shma, "*Yeṣirato ha-Sifrutit shel R. Yosef ha-Levi Ibn Migas*," *Kiryat Sefer* 46 (1970–1971) 143.

[79]Zacks, *Ḥiddushe ha-Rambam la-Talmud* 28, note 269, has, however, offered arguments, including the language consideration, for assigning it instead to the second cycle of Maimonides' commentaries.

[80]E. Kupfer, "*Hashlama le-Ferush Rabbenu Moshe ben Maimon*," *Sinai* 55 (1964) 231.

[81]See Maimonides, *Mishneh Torah*: *H. Yesode ha-Torah* 3.1.

[82]The commentary on BT *Rosh ha-Shana* 20b locates some of the fixed stars in an eighth celestial sphere and some in a ninth. See *Jen Libanon* 9. Ibn Ezra's commentary on Psalms 8:4

have rejected the extra sphere as otiose and would have had no reason to endorse such a scheme.[83]

There is a still stronger consideration, which was noted more than a century ago. The commentary on the talmudic tractate *Rosh ha-Shana* attributed to Maimonides interprets a pair of knotty mishnaic and talmudic passages to mean that under certain circumstances a new moon can be sighted just twelve hours after the waning moon of the previous month could still be seen.[84] Sheer beginners in astronomy know that a new moon cannot appear so soon after the moon of the previous month was visible.[85] It is hard to imagine Maimonides' entertaining such a possibility even in his youth. Still more to the point, when Maimonides—in his Commentary on the Mishna—touches on the relevant mishnaic and talmudic passages, he expressly warns against heeding "ignoramuses" who put forth the very interpretation offered by the commentary on the tractate *Rosh ha-Shana* which the manuscripts tell us he composed. Only "a totally common man, who has no more grasp of the celestial spheres than an ox or an ass" could, Maimonides writes in his Commentary on the Mishna, imagine that a new moon might be sighted no more than twelve hours after the waning moon of the previous month was visible.[86] Not merely would

---

speaks of ten levels between God and the lower region, but as Ibn Ezra, Shorter Commentary on Exodus 23:20 explains, only nine are celestial spheres. The highest of the ten, "the throne of glory," is a collective term for the incorporeal movers of the spheres, identified by Ibn Ezra with the angels.

[83]In the *Guide for the Perplexed*, Maimonides expresses himself more skeptically about man's ability to understand the heavens than he does in the *Mishneh Torah*. In *Guide* 2.11, he states that the accepted astronomical scheme, in which all the stars beyond our solar system are located in a single sphere, is to be preferred because it is more economical; but he concedes that each star could conceivably have its own sphere, with the movements of all the stellar spheres synchronized in order to maintain the relative positions of the stars to one another. He does not contemplate the distribution of the fixed stars between two separate spheres.

[84]*Jen Libanon* 18, on BT *Rosh ha-Shana* 25a: *pe^c amim she-ba be-arukka, pe^c amim she-ba bi-qeṣara.*

[85]R. Zeraḥia ha-Levi, a talmudic commentator who lived in southern France about the time of Maimonides, knew of astronomers who made fun of the rabbinic sources for having accepted the possibility of the new moon's being sighted after twelve hours. Zeraḥia had enough astronomical knowledge to realize that such was impossible and he interprets Mishna, *Rosh ha-Shana* 2:9, exactly as Maimonides does in order to obviate the implication. See Zeraḥia ha-Levi, *Sefer ha-Ma'or, Rosh ha-Shana* 25a.

[86]Maimonides, Commentary on the Mishna, *Rosh ha-Shana* 2:9, and see his *Mishneh Torah*: *H. Qiddush ha-Ḥodesh* 1.3; 2.6. The impossibility of Maimonides' having offered the interpretation that a new moon could be sighted twelve hours after the old moon had been seen, and accordingly the impossibility of his being the author of the commentary in question, was pointed out by H. Slonimski, "*Mazkir Nishkaḥot*," *Ha-Ṣefira* (1880) 391, as well as by Ṣ. Jaffe, note to H. Graetz, *Geschichte der Juden*, Hebrew trans. S. Rabbinowicz 4 (Warsaw 1894) 467. Slonimski added other considerations that argue against the attribution of the commentary to Maimonides. S. Assaf, "*Mi-Perusho shel ha-Rambam*" (n. 67 above) 107, 108, note 24, and M. Kasher, *Maimonides and the Mekhilta* (in Hebrew) (New York 1943) 162–63, also recognize that Maimonides cannot be the author. S. Lieberman, *Hilkhoth ha-Yerushalmi of Rabbi Moses*

Maimonides not have endorsed the view that he now dismisses with scorn; it is inconceivable that he would ever have placed himself in the class of ignoramuses, totally common men who have no more grasp of things than an ox or an ass. He must accordingly be ruled out as the author of the commentary in question.

Historians have uncovered three citations in medieval works, and a fourth passage in the eighteenth-century bibliophile and rabbinic scholar Ḥ. Azulai, which the authors of the respective works represent as quotations from Maimonides' commentary on the tractate *Rosh ha-Shana* but which are not found in the preserved commentary on *Rosh ha-Shana* incorrectly carrying his name.[87] They may belong to Maimonides' authentic commentary on the tractate.

We are left, then, with isolated quotations that represent themselves as coming from Maimonides' talmudic commentaries and with extended sections from what may well be his commentary on the Sabbath tractate.

The preserved comments invariably shed helpful light on the texts forming their subject. They are by no means unique, however, and a fair number of medieval rabbinists were capable of composing comments on the Babylonian Talmud of similar caliber. What is striking is the precociousness of Maimonides' achievement. He informs us that he had composed commentaries on two-thirds of the tractates in the Babylonian Talmud by the age of twenty-three. He thereby accomplished as much as anyone known to him had done during a lifetime. And if the preserved quotations and the extended section indeed belong to the initial cycle of Maimonides' talmudic commentaries, his youthful work was of mature, albeit not exceptional, quality.

Commentary on the Mishna. The challenges faced by students entering on Judah the Prince's Mishna corpus are different from those faced by students of the Babylonian Talmud. Students of the Babylonian Talmud, once it had been put into writing, need help just to read the Aramaic properly, and virtually everyone has to be guided through the intricacies of the dialectical reasoning. By contrast, most of the Mishna is not, considered at the level of the words, difficult to read for someone with a Hebrew education; and the mishna paragraphs are typically formulated in short crisp sentences, with only occasional instances of dialectical reasoning in the talmudic vein.[88] There are nonetheless hurdles enough. The Mishna comprises

---

ben Maimon (New York 1947) 12, responded to Slonimski by observing that Maimonides often corrected what he had previously written. But while it is true that Maimonides could change his mind, he never would brand an interpretation he had himself once accepted and subsequently rejected as the view of an ignoramus and of a totally common man no better than an ox or an ass.

[87]Zacks, *Ḥiddushe ha-Rambam la-Talmud* 98–100; Ta-Shma, "*Perush ha-Rambam la-Talmud*" (n. 70 above) 304 (quoting Azulai, who reported that Maimonides commonly cited Ibn Migas in his—genuine—commentary on the tractate *Rosh ha-Shana*, which is precisely what one would expect).

[88]Instances of dialectical reasoning in the Mishna are listed by Z. Frankel, *Darke ha-Mishna*, revised edition (Tel Aviv 1959) 300–302.

some ten thousand brief statements of law[89] which embrace a broad spectrum of subjects, ranging from the quotidian to the recherché. Reference is made to physical objects no longer familiar in medieval times, not to speak of ours—flora, human and animal physiological abnormalities, agricultural and artisans' tools, household implements, architectural artifacts, coins, weights, measures, and the like. The rationale for the myriad statements of law is almost never made explicit, and their very terseness often renders them obscure. Differences of opinion are frequently recorded on legal issues, and the rationale for the differences is usually left unstated.

From the time that the Palestinian and Babylonian Talmuds were redacted, they served as a kind of commentary on the Mishna, their initial function being, after all, to explore the Mishna paragraphs around which they are constructed. Since the Mishna was commonly studied in conjunction with the talmudic, and particularly the Babylonian Talmud's, elaboration of it, rather than in isolation, the need for an independent commentary on the Mishna was not felt as acutely as the need for talmudic commentaries. A commentary on the Mishna would be needed, first, by persons who wished to study tractates of the Mishna for which no talmudic accompaniment, or, as things generally turned out in practice, no Babylonian talmudic accompaniment, had been compiled. Secondly, it would be needed by persons who wished to study even the tractates for which a talmudic elucidation did exist but who did not wish to consult it; there is evidence of the existence of such circles in the Middle Ages. The posttalmudic Iraqi schools, which did commentatorial work on the Babylonian Talmud, also produced commentaries on sections of the Mishna. Inasmuch as the demand was smaller, these commentaries were fewer in number[90] and time has taken no less a toll of them than of the early talmudic commentaries. A commentary on the entire Mishna was composed about a half century before Maimonides[91] but it is an uneven work, in large part no more than a glossary, and it has gaps.

At the age of twenty-three Maimonides began a new project, a Commentary on the entire Mishna corpus. He completed it seven years later, in the Hebrew year corresponding to the last third of 1167 and first two thirds of 1168, and subsequently returned repeatedly to correct both style and content.[92] In a letter

89The Mishna corpus is conventionally divided into about 3,800 paragraphs, and the paragraphs generally contain more than one statement of law.

90See Albeck, *Mabo la-Mishna* (n. 51 above) 237–38.

91*Encyclopaedia Judaica*, art. Nathan ben Abraham II.

92D. Sassoon, *Descriptive Catalogue of the Hebrew and Samaritan Manuscripts in the Sassoon Library* (London 1932) 92–93; Maimonides, *Responsa* (n. 3 above) §217: I have corrected "about ten points, in each of which I had followed the opinion of one of the *geonim*, of blessed memory, but subsequently realized the error." Commentary on the Mishna (n. 5 above), editor's introduction 15–16. Lieberman, *Hilkhoth ha-Yerushalmi of Rabbi Moses ben Maimon* 6–12. An especially illuminating instance is found in Maimonides' introduction to the sixth order of the Mishna, pp. 20–21, where his earlier opinion had been that the ritual impurity emanating

written more than two decades after he completed the Commentary, he acknowledges that the original version needed corrections in places and he remarks: "I make no claim to having reached my final perfection from the very start or to having never erred. On the contrary, whenever it becomes clear to me that things are different from what I wrote, I always retract my opinion." He takes advantage of the same occasion to place blame for mistakes in the initial version on his having followed interpretations offered by prior, highly regarded posttalmudic rabbinic scholars.[93]

When Maimonides began writing the Commentary on the Mishna, he and members of his family lived under the Almohads; during the period in which he worked on it, he visited Palestine with his father and younger brother; and by the time he completed it, he had settled in Egypt. His journeys during the period must also have included more than a trip to Palestine and thence to Egypt; for he apologizes for any shortcomings on the grounds that "there are mishna paragraphs for which I composed the commentary during the stages of a journey, and there are matters that I wrote down while on board ships [in the plural] on the high seas."[94] Two sea journeys within the Mediterranean basin are hardly an adequate excuse for possible shortcomings in a seven-year literary enterprise.

Although the Palestinian and Babylonian Talmuds look at first blush like a kind of commentary on the Mishna, their reliability as guides for interpreting the Mishna text can be questioned. A number of protocols recorded in the two Talmuds are attributed to rabbis active immediately after the compiling of the Mishna and likely to have had direct knowledge of the original meaning of the text; but the protocols passed through other hands before the final redactions were done. Furthermore, the men whose outlook animates the two talmudic compilations harbored a distinct point of view. The term *talmud*, as already mentioned, was originally synonymous with the term *midrash*, and the men of the Talmud were true to the etymology. They viewed the Mishna as midrashists viewed Scripture and searched for signposts deliberately embedded in the Mishna text which lead to subsurface meanings; superfluities in the text are, for example, often taken as allusions to things that the Mishna chose to intimate but leave unsaid. Again, when the men responsible for the two Talmuds—and especially the Babylonian—perceived internal discrepancies within a Mishna paragraph, between one Mishna paragraph and another, or between a Mishna paragraph and statements in other sources that they took to be authoritative, they did their best to harmonize the discrepancies away, sometimes by even emending the texts.

---

from a dead bird was instituted by the rabbis (*mi-dibere soferim*, *de-rabbanan*), but where he went back and decided that such impurity had instead the sanction of the *Torah*; see the editor's note to the passage and also the parallel passage in Maimonides, Commentary on the Mishna, *Para*, to which the editor refers. The section should disabuse all those who suppose that Maimonides was not serious about what he was doing.

[93]Moses ben Maimon, *Epistulae* (n. 65 above) 58.

[94]Above, p. 31.

Anyone approaching the Mishna without prepossession may accordingly ask whether interpretations of the Mishna in the two Talmuds do go back to rabbis who were in immediate contact with the freshly minted Mishna, whether superfluities and other irregularities in the Mishna text were in truth consciously planted there by the redactor—or redactors—as signposts pointing to latent meanings, and whether the talmudic harmonizations and the emendations of the text accurately reflect the Mishna's intent.

Maimonides was fully conscious of the talmudic approach to the Mishna. He "saw the Talmud doing to the Mishna what no one could ever gain access to through logical reasoning. It . . . tells you that a given mishna [paragraph] is constructed in such and such a fashion, or that words are missing in a given mishna [paragraph] and it should be construed in such and such a fashion, or that a mishna [paragraph] represents the view of a particular rabbi [rather than the majority view] and his rationale was such and such. The Talmud, moreover, adds words to the Mishna, deletes words, and clarifies the reasoning behind them." He is unequivocal about the extent to which such constructions placed on the Mishna should be credited. Far from resisting interpretations that construe the Mishna text as saying something different from what it appears to say, his "aim" was "to interpret the Mishna as the [Babylonian] Talmud does, to restrict myself to the interpretations that are normative, and to omit any interpretation rejected in the Talmud."[95] Instances have been uncovered in which Maimonides' Commentary on the Mishna strays from its stated aim and interprets a mishnaic phrase or sentence differently from the way the Babylonian Talmud does. The instances are extremely few in number, and, significantly, always occur in contexts where the divergence has no apparent bearing on the halakic norm.[96]

Maimonides tells readers that his Commentary on the Mishna "contains four immense utilities." It performs four functions.

(1) No one, he submits, can possibly remember everything that the "Talmud" says about each Mishna paragraph. Even the most accomplished rabbinic student would, when encountering a Mishna passage, have to review the parallel talmudic discussion and then peruse the rest of the Babylonian—and also the Jerusalem—Talmud if he wanted to be sure that he had overlooked nothing pertinent. Maimonides promises that his Commentary will do the work for all who

[95]Commentary on the Mishna, introduction, pp. 47–48.

[96]Commentary of *Tosefot Yom Ṭob* on Mishna, *Nazir* 5:5; A. Geiger, *Nachgelassene Schriften* 3 (Berlin 1876) 58, and note 35; Frankel, *Darke ha- Mishna* 343–44; Albeck, *Mabo la-Mishna* 244. I. Weiss, "*Toledot . . . Moshe ben Maimon*," *Bet Talmud* 1 (1881) 168, note 10, cites a few passages from the Commentary where he believes that Maimonides' departure from the talmudic interpretation does affect the halakic norm. G. Blidstein, "Where Do We Stand in the Study of Maimonidean Halakhah?" *Studies in Maimonides*, ed. I Twersky (Cambridge, Mass. 1990) 16–17, calls attention to Weiss's tendentiousness. Frankel, *Darke ha- Mishna* 339, points out that Saadia Gaon had also justified interpreting Mishna paragraphs in a manner different from the way the Babylonian Talmud interpreted them.

study the Mishna. It will expound each paragraph against the background of everything relevant that is to be found anywhere in the "Talmud." (2) The Mishna typically records multiple opinions on a given halakic issue, and even when it employs one of the devices at its disposal to indicate which opinion should be followed, the Babylonian or Palestinian talmudic compilation may state or indicate a different norm on one ground or another. Maimonides' Commentary draws upon the entire talmudic literature to determine the halakic norm for each issue treated in the Mishna. (3) Beginners in rabbinic studies will be able to use his Commentary as an "introduction" to the "entire Talmud." (4) His Commentary will place at the fingertips of accomplished scholars matters that they have already learned. The foregoing objects will be achieved in "concise language, although without leaving the reader in doubt. For our composition does not intend to instruct inanimate stones; we are instructing only those who are able to understand."[97] Maimonides evidently did not lack self-assurance. At the age of thirty, he was confident that he had sufficient mastery of the vast talmudic literature to bring everything pertinent in it to bear on the Mishna and he was certain that his juridical judgment was equal to the task of determining the correct halakic norm for every issue treated there. Repeatedly within the Commentary he digresses to extol his achievement[98] and his success in clarifying mishnaic passages that preeminent scholars preceding him had failed to fathom.[99]

The fourth function that Maimonides expected his Commentary to perform overlaps the first. There is also a potential tension in his undertaking to serve the needs of beginners and of the educated at the same time—and, moreover, to do so concisely. The Commentary, it happens, sometimes explains words that could trouble only a beginner, particularly in the first Order of the Mishna,[100] while leaving matters unexplained throughout which even persons versed in rabbinic matters could well need to have clarified; such occurs especially where opinions considered by Maimonides to be nonnormative are involved.[101] Of the four functions, the one that he executed most consistently is the second. From beginning to end, and whether or not the issue at hand had practical application in his day, he is careful to state the halakic norm as he understood it to be indicated by the Mishna itself or by the talmudic compilations. On occasion, he is not satisfied

[97]Commentary on the Mishna, introduction, p. 48.

[98]For example, Commentary on the Mishna, *Yoma* 2:1; 3:8; *Kelim* 10:1 (end); below, pp. 153, 159.

[99]Commentary on the Mishna, *Shebi*^{c}*it* 10:5, first version (in a later version of the Commentary, Maimonides accepted the interpretation that he originally rejected out of hand; see *Responsa* §217); *Baba Batra* 2:4; ^{c}*Aboda Zara* 5:8; *Nega*^{c}*im* 1:4; introduction to the order of *Ṭohorot* p. 34.

[100]Examples: Commentary on the Mishna, *Berakot* 6:1, 3, 7; *Pe'a* 5:3; 8:7; *Terumot* 2:2; *Ma*^{c}*aser Sheni* 4:1.

[101]Examples in Frankel, *Darke ha- Mishna* (n. 88 above) 345–46. A few additional examples: *Menaḥot* 5:1; *Qinnim* 3:4; *Kelim* 8:9; *Nega*^{c}*im* 3:6.

with marking the halakic position to be followed in matters treated in the mishna paragraph he is dealing with and he goes on to determine the norm in matters related to those in the paragraph but not taken up by it.[102] He was descended from a line of rabbinic judges, and determining halakic norms, even in areas that no longer had practical application, was a primary concern of his in all his rabbinic writings.

The Mishna style of exposition pays much more attention to particular legal situations than to general rules, to clarifying how each of the innumerable cases it limns should be adjudicated rather than to enunciating principles covering them. General rules looked so anomalous to the postmishnaic generations that when the Mishna happens to offer one side by side with the particulars it treats, the redactors of the Babylonian Talmud and posttalmudic rabbinists tend to view the rule as a superfluity requiring explanation, as a signal through which the Mishna alludes to something beyond what it makes explicit. They commonly search for what more is alluded to, what further situations and norms are intimated by the Mishna's having taken the trouble to add the rule.[103] Maimonides, who had a strong penchant for abstracting and systematizing, sets himself apart. The value of general rules lies for him in their clarification of the specific cases, not in an intimation of additional ones, and his Commentary regularly seeks to bring to light the broad rule or rules that cover the regulations set down in a given mishna.

To take an example: Scripture prohibits slaughtering "a cow or ewe . . . and its young both in one day," and the Oral Torah understands Scripture to be prohibiting the slaughtering of both the mother and its offspring on the same day, without regard to the order in which the two are killed. In one of its many dichotomies, the Oral Law further distinguishes between animals that have been dedicated for sacrifice in the Temple and those that have not. Slaughtering either type in the location unauthorized for it—slaughtering a nondedicated animal within the Temple premises or a dedicated animal outside of those premises—constitutes a sin. And, according to the Oral Law, meat from a nondedicated animal slaughtered within the Temple premises and the parts of a dedicated animal that was slaughtered outside can neither be consumed nor placed on the altar.

With these Oral Law presuppositions—as well as additional, more technical presuppositions that I have not gone into—at the back of its mind, but without mentioning any of them, a certain paragraph in the Mishna takes up various possible situations and their halakic ramifications. For instance, one member of a mother–offspring pair might be a dedicated animal and the other nondedicated, and first the former and then the latter might be slaughtered outside the Temple premises on the same day. Slaughtering the first would involve the sin of slaughtering a dedicated animal in the unauthorized location, and the animal would be disqualified

[102]Examples in Frankel, *Darke ha- Mishna* 346.

[103]*Tosefot Yom Ṭob*, commentary on Mishna, *Megilla* 4:2, and *Qinnim* 3:3, feels the need to point out that the Mishna occasionally states a general rule *without* thereby alluding to something in addition to what it makes explicit.

from being offered on the altar. Slaughtering the second would involve the sin of slaughtering the second member of a mother–offspring pair on the day on which the first member had already been slaughtered; but, despite the sin, the animal would not be disqualified from human consumption. Alternatively, both the mother and its offspring might be nondedicated, one of the pair might be slaughtered outside the Temple premises, and the second, slaughtered later in the day within those premises. The slaughtering of the first would involve no sin, and the animal would be flawless and qualified for consumption. The slaughtering of the second would involve a double sin, the sin of slaughtering a nondedicated animal in the unauthorized location and the sin of slaughtering the second half of a mother–offspring pair on the same day as the first half; because of the first of the two sins, the latter animal would be disqualified from human consumption. Proceeding step by step in similar fashion, the mishna paragraph lists twelve possible situations. Maimonides, in his Commentary, observes that in actuality four further situations are conceivable, but the Mishna omits them. Then he sets down four general halakic "principles" that cover all sixteen situations and shows how each of the situations is to be adjudicated in accordance with those principles.[104] I have not counted the rules that Maimonides' Commentary cites from the Mishna and other rabbinic sources, but the total easily runs into the hundreds.

Maimonides also had a penchant for general introductions. Here and there throughout his Commentary, he offers prefatory remarks designed to place a mishna paragraph or subject in its proper framework,[105] and on eight occasions the prefatory remarks expand into formal introductions. These are not all cut from the same cloth. Five of them restrict themselves to matters of the ritual and legal sort which constitute the sum and substance of the Mishna. The others venture into areas of ideology and are designed to supplement the legal side of the Jewish religion with its spiritual, ethical, and intellectual side.

The former are introductions to the Mishna tractate dealing with animal sacrifices; to the tractate dealing with meal offerings brought in the Temple; to that dealing with the sacrifices brought by the high judicial court or the high priest as atonement for certain types of judicial errors; to the entire sixth Order of the Mishna, the Order comprising the tractates dealing with ritual impurity; and—the shortest of the five—to the tractate treating ritual impurity contracted specifically by human hands. The introductions either provide readers with classification schemes for conceptualizing the subjects—classifications of the different forms of animal or meal offerings, of the different forms of impurity—or they outline the rules by which the subjects are governed. As will be observed, the introductions of the present sort all fall within the abstruse areas of sacrificial and impurity law. With

[104]Commentary on the Mishna, *Ḥullin* 5:1. The prohibition against slaughtering a cow or ewe and its young both in one day is stated in Leviticus 22:28.

[105]Examples in Frankel, *Darke ha- Mishna* 341.

the exception of part of the introduction to the tractate on the impurity of hands,[106] none of the subjects had practical application in Maimonides' day. His aim was to help students master the purely theoretical side of the Law.

The introduction to the Order of the Mishna dealing with ritual impurity is especially noteworthy. The subject is one of the most difficult in rabbinic law: Impurity is something intangible and unfamiliar, and the intricate distinctions and regulations governing it are much more complex than the better-known regulations governing such matters as activities permitted and forbidden on the Sabbath or foodstuffs that are permitted and forbidden—kosher and nonkosher. Maimonides characterizes impurity law as "replete with doubts and fathomless" and he notes that even leading rabbinic figures of the classic period "stood in trembling" before segments of it. He disparages what "great teachers" of the posttalmudic period had written on the topic as "long in words, light in usefulness." And he observes ruefully: "If you go to heads of today's rabbinic academies . . . you will find, . . . as a consequence of our many sins," that they fail to understand even relatively clear and straightforward aspects of the subject.[107]

The best means of approaching the subject, the thirty-year-old Maimonides announces without pretense of false modesty, is through his introduction to the sixth Order of the Mishna taken together with his commentary on the tractates belonging to the Order. Only someone who has "agonized days and sleepless nights" over the statements on impurity law scattered through the rabbinic corpus and then turned to Maimonides' introduction will appreciate "what has been accomplished here."[108] Readers who wish to master impurity law are advised in particular to memorize three things "thoroughly, until it is all fluent on your tongue without your having to make any effort to remember it. . . . Reading it even a thousand times without memorizing will be insufficient; it must be as fluent on your tongue as the 'Hear O Israel' prayer." The three things to be memorized are: the principles laid down in Maimonides' introduction to the Order of impurities; the "text" of Chapter One of the first mishnaic tractate in the Order, a chapter that the redactor of the Mishna designed as an introduction not merely to the tractate but to the Order as a whole; and the "text" of Maimonides' commentary on the same chapter.[109] He would subsequently assert in his *Book of Commandments* that his commentary on the sixth Order of the Mishna allows persons desiring to understand "anything within the area of impurity and purity" to dispense with the "study of any other book."[110]

While the self-congratulation may go against the grain, Maimonides' introduction to the Order of impurity law does disperse the clouds and present the subject with

[106] According to rabbinic law, bread must not be eaten with impure hands.

[107] Commentary on the Mishna, introduction to the sixth order, pp. 33–34, 37.

[108] Commentary on the Mishna, introduction to the sixth order, p. 37.

[109] Commentary on the Mishna, introduction to the sixth order, pp. 32–33.

[110] *Book of Commandments* (n. 27 above), positive commandment #108.

exemplary clarity. He meticulously identifies the classes of objects in which ritual impurity originates, the classes of objects to which it may be transmitted, the levels of impurity to which the different classes are susceptible, the levels of impurity that they can transmit to other objects, and the processes whereby the transmission takes place. He supports his definitions and descriptions with proof-texts from a panoply of rabbinic sources—this in contrast to the procedure he would follow in his code of Jewish law, where he would systematically avoid citing the rabbinic texts on which he bases his legal opinions. As his Commentary progresses within the Order from paragraph to paragraph and chapter to chapter, his comments illuminate their obscurities as well.

Maimonides' general introductions of the other sort, those that are concerned with ideology and theology, are introductions to the entire Mishna; to the tractate *Abot*—commonly known as the *The Ethics of the Fathers*, and the only tractate of the Mishna which is wholly nonhalakic, and hence aggadic, in content; and to a few statements on Jewish dogma and particularly on the dogma of resurrection which appear in the tractate *Sanhedrin.*

The introduction to the entire Mishna has as its primary theme the concept of Oral Torah. Maimonides affirms unqualifiedly that Moses received an Oral Torah from God at Sinai together with the Written Torah. He then traces the transmission of the twin Torahs from Sinai down to the redaction of Judah the Prince's Mishna, classifies legal items in the rabbinic sources in accordance with their differing Mosaic and post-Mosaic provenances, outlines the structure of the Mishna, pursues the transmission of Jewish law from the composition of the Mishna down to the redaction of the Babylonian Talmud, sets forth what—he understands—the redactors of the Babylonian Talmud sought to accomplish in their compilation, offers a brief sketch of posttalmudic halakic literature, lays out the goals of his own Commentary, and concludes with biographical information on the rabbis whose names appear in the Mishna. The mere enumeration reveals that he is less sharply focused here than he was in the introductory sections previously considered, where the Mishna and Talmuds supply the raw material and he systematizes it. Not only that. He allows himself digressions within the sundry main topics, departing, as he says at a certain spot, "far from the aim I am pursuing."[111] One of the digressions treats the distinction between true and false prophets, the subcategories of each, and crieria for determining whether someone belongs to one or the other group,[112] another, the obligation that Jews have to obey true prophets,[113] a third, the ancient rabbis' reasons for not teaching metaphysical philosophy openly and instead disguising their profound metaphysical thoughts in bits of aggada whose outward garb stands in "total opposition to reason,"[114] a fourth, the purposes served by the

[111]Commentary on the Mishna, introduction, p. 45.
[112]Commentary on the Mishna, introduction, pp. 4–14.
[113]Commentary on the Mishna, introduction, p. 13.
[114]Commentary on the Mishna, introduction, pp. 35–39.

various species of beings making up the natural world inhabited by man,[115] a fifth, the object of human life,[116] and there are more.

The Mishna tractate *Abot*—commonly known in Hebrew as *Pirqe Abot* and in English as the *Ethics of the Fathers*—is essentially a catena of brief pieces of ethical advice and exhortation for members of the rabbinic community. Maimonides, however, places a broader and more philosophical slant on it. "The tractate's aim," in his words, is to encourage man to perfect himself through "ethical and rational virtues."[117] He accordingly felt the need to furnish readers with an introduction to the tractate in order to supply what he considers to be the requisite background for understanding and attaining the virtues in question. His sources, as he explicitly acknowledges, are not only the rabbis, but also the works of ancient and recent non-Jewish philosophers, although he discreetly avoids mentioning the philosophers' names.[118]

The background needed by students of the mishnaic tractate *Abot* turns out to be the conception of soul of the Arabic Aristotelian philosophers and the Aristotelian theory of the ethical middle way, the theory in which each human ethical virtue is defined as an intermediate psychological characteristic cultivated by the human subject in his soul; where facing danger is concerned, the virtue of bravery is thus the psychological characteristic lying midway between the extremes of cowardice, on the one hand, and rashness, on the other, both of which are vices. Ancillary matters come up here too—for example, human free will[119] and the question whether, and when, overcoming one's inclinations and forcing oneself to be virtuous is superior to possessing effortless, inborn virtue.[120] And Maimonides again allows himself the characteristic brief digressions, a few of which he signals by observing "we have departed from the subject of the chapter"[121] or "now I shall return to my subject."[122] The digressions treat such miscellaneous matters as the qualifications for prophecy,[123] Moses' vision of God,[124] the sense borne by the term "possibility" in Kalam thought,[125] and the efficacy of music in dispelling melancholia.[126]

[115]Commentary on the Mishna, introduction, pp. 39–41.

[116]Commentary on the Mishna, introduction, pp. 41–45.

[117]Commentary on the Mishna, *Abot* 5:2.

[118]*Shemona Peraqim* (=Commentary on the Mishna [n. 5 above], introduction to *Abot*) chapter 1, p. 372. English translation: Moses Maimonides, *Eight Chapters*, ed. and trans. J. Gorfinkle (New York 1912).

[119]*Shemona Peraqim*, chapter 8.

[120]*Shemona Peraqim*, chapter 6, p. 391.

[121]*Shemona Peraqim*, chapter 4, p. 387.

[122]*Shemona Peraqim*, chapter 1, p. 374; chapter 4, p. 384; chapter 5, p. 387.

[123]*Shemona Peraqim*, chapter 7, pp. 393–94.

[124]*Shemona Peraqim*, chapter 7, p. 395.

[125]*Shemona Peraqim*, chapter 1, p. 375.

[126]*Shemona Peraqim*, chapter 5, p. 388.

Besides playing its role within the Commentary on the Mishna, Maimonides' introduction to the tractate *Abot* acquired a life of its own. It circulated as a separate work and in that form has retained popularity until today. Since it happens to be divided into eight chapters, the title it carries when standing alone is simply *Eight Chapters*.

Finally there is Maimonides' introduction to the statements on dogma found in the tenth chapter of the mishnaic tractate *Sanhedrin*. His primary theme is human eudaemonia (*sa^c^āda*), true human well-being and happiness.[127] "Eudaemonia and the ultimate goal" of human existence consist, in his words, in the "permanence of the soul through the permanence of its object of knowledge and through its becoming identical therewith, as expert philosophers have stated, using arguments [*ṭuruq*] too long to expound here."[128] The sentence is far from translucent and would scarcely be comprehensible to readers possessing only a rabbinic education; I shall return to it. In the course of his introduction to the present chapter of *Sanhedrin*, Maimonides makes a point similar to a point made in one of the digressions in his introduction to the entire Mishna: He attributes a hidden wisdom to the aggadic sector of classic rabbinic literature, even when the garb in which the rabbis robed their truths might strike readers as outlandish. And he discusses the various eschatological locales and events recognized by the rabbis, namely, paradise, hell, resurrection of the body, and the messianic age.

He concludes by enumerating what he represents as the thirteen "principles and foundations of our Law" (*sharī^c^a*). They begin with the existence, unity, and incorporeality of God, and the proposition that God alone is eternal; then they go on to such doctrines as the phenomenon of prophecy, the uniqueness of the prophecy of Moses, the divine origin of the Written and Oral Torahs, God's knowledge of events in the world, divine providence, reward and punishment for one's behavior during this life, and the resurrection of the dead.[129] Most startling is the obligation to "know" that the human species is capable of bringing forth prophets. As Maimonides explains briefly but unambiguously, the principle in question consists in *knowing* that persons of "superior natural qualities" may develop their intellect to the level where it "makes contact" with the supernal incorporeal being called the "active intellect," whereupon they receive an "emanation" from the active intellect; "these are the prophets, and this is prophecy and what it means." In a rabbinic venue and with no apparent qualms, Maimonides is mandating that every good Jew conceptualize prophecy as it was conceptualized by the Arabic Aristotelian school of philosophy.[130] He in effect informs readers, the naive no less than the sophisticated, that when Scripture describes God as speaking to Isaiah, Jeremiah,

[127]English translation of the introduction: J. Abelson, "Maimonides on the Jewish Creed," reprinted in J. Dienstag, *Eschatology in Maimonidean Thought* (New York 1983) 131–61.

[128]Commentary on the Mishna, *Sanhedrin* 10, introduction, p. 205.

[129]Commentary on the Mishna, *Sanhedrin* 10:1, pp. 210–17.

[130]Commentary on the Mishna, *Sanhedrin* 10:1, sixth principle.

Ezekiel, and the other prophets with the exception of Moses, they did not receive a message from God Himself. They were men of superior intellectual attainments who, thanks to their personal qualities and initiative, received an emanation from an incorporeal being subordinate to God in the hierarchy of existence.

Maimonides undoubtedly attached significance to what he calls the thirteen "principles and foundations of our Law"; he writes that Jews who hold firmly to them belong to the nation of Israel and must be accepted with love and brotherhood, whereas those who do not are heretics, separate themselves from the nation, and must be hated and destroyed.[131] It is not at all certain, however, that he meant to promulgate a formal creed for the Jewish religion.

The expression "principles and foundations of the Law" sounds more momentous than it is. Maimonides had a weakness for both principles and lists, and in his Commentary on the Mishna and elsewhere, he constantly identifies one thing or another as a principle (*aṣl*) and lists principles of one sort or another. To cite only a very small sample, we find the "three . . . principles" governing culpability for transferring objects from private to public, or public to private, premises on the Sabbath; the "four principles" underlying the laws of the levirate marriage (*yibbum*); the "four principles" governing implementation of the scriptural prohibition against slaughtering "a cow or ewe . . . and its young both in one day"; and the "many principles" involved in preparing the ashes of the red heifer.[132]

Of the thirteen principles in the present list, twelve reappear in Maimonides' *Mishneh Torah* but they do so in a different guise. Maimonides is there concerned with the *denial* of the existence of God, of His unity, of His incorporeality, and of the other tenets, not their affirmation, and the point he makes is that denial of those doctrines are some of the sins—he enumerates a total of twenty-four—which cause a person to lose his portion in the world to come.[133] Most of the thirteen principles

[131]Commentary on the Mishna, *Sanhedrin* 10:1, p. 217.

[132]Commentary on the Mishna, *Shabbat* 1:1; *Yebamot* 1:1; *Ḥullin* 5:1; *Para* 4:4. A few additional examples taken from the Commentary on the Mishna: *Nidda* 4:4: the "principles" needed for understanding the status of a woman whose menstrual period coincides with the beginning of her birth contractions; *Sanhedrin* 7:3: the "many principles" involved in judging sexual crimes; *Makkot* 3:1: "the many principles" involved in punishment through whipping; introduction to *Horayot*, p. 468: "principles" needed for an understanding of the subject of sacrifices that have to be brought by judges who err in judgment; *Baba Qamma* 2:1: a "principle" regarding damage caused by an animal; *Baba Meṣiᶜa* 8:2: "principles" we follow in matters of litigation; *Para* 5:4: the "principle" that every vessel to be used in the temple service must be immersed in a ritual bath even if it is not known to be impure; *Miqwa'ot* 2:1: the "principle" that once a person or object becomes ritually impure, he or it is presumed to be in that state until one knows with certainty that the impurity was removed, as by immersion in a ritual bath. Many more examples can be cited.

[133]*Mishneh Torah*: *H. Teshuba* 3.6–8. Maimonides seems to have overlooked the eleventh of the thirteen principles: reward and punishment for one's behavior during this life.

appear one more time in Maimonides' *Guide for the Perplexed.* But in the *Guide*, they are not labeled as principles and they again do not take the shape of a creed.[134]

Whatever his intent may have been, his thirteen principles of the Law, like his *Eight Chapters*, acquired a sturdy independent life of their own. They became by far the best-known Jewish creed, and every author since Maimonides who has dealt with Jewish dogma has taken his list of principles into account. It was the catalyst for a new literary genre, which consisted of attempts by a series of Jewish thinkers to delineate the formal dogmas of the religion.[135] Editions of the thirteen principles in Latin translation which were published during the sixteenth century taught non-Jews what—in Maimonides' judgment—Jewish belief comprises.[136] The principles were recast over ninety times in poetic guise[137] and they gained a place for themselves in the Jewish liturgy.

The most popular of the poems based on Maimonides' thirteen principles of the Jewish faith is the fourteenth-century *Yigdal*; *y-g*, the first two consonants in the first word in the poem, form the Hebrew numeral "thirteen."[138] *Yigdal* is printed in almost all versions of the traditional Jewish prayer book in use today and it is recited or sung by various Jewish communities at one spot or another in their prayer services. Most of the traditional prayer books in current use also incorporate the nub of Maimonides' thirteen principles a second time in the form of a credo, which they place at the end of the daily morning service.[139] There are two main versions. In prayer books of Jewish communities with roots in the Near Eastern countries, the so-called Sephardic communities, the credo opens with the single declaration "I believe fully in the thirteen principles of the holy Torah" and then lists the principles one after another, each in a brief clause. In prayer books of the Ashkenazic communities, the credo consists of thirteen separate declarations, each beginning afresh with the words "I believe fully that . . ."; a statement of the principle then follows, and the principles are developed in slightly more detail than in the other

[134]*Guide for the Perplexed* 1:35; A. Hyman, "Maimonides' Thirteen Principles," *Jewish Medieval and Renaissance Studies*, ed. A. Altmann (Cambridge, Mass. 1967) 135.

[135]See M. Kellner, *Dogma in Medieval Jewish Thought* (Oxford 1986). The medieval debates regarding the dogmas of the Jewish faith continued into the nineteenth century. See M. Sofer (Ḥatam Sofer), *Responsa, Yoreh De^{c}a* §356.

[136]M. Steinschneider, *Catalogus librorum hebraeorum in Bibliotheca Bodleiana* (Berlin 1852–1860) columns 1888–89.

[137]A. Marx, "A List of Poems on the Articles of the Creed," *Jewish Quarterly Review* 9 (1918–1919) 305–36; I. Davidson, *Thesaurus of Mediaeval Hebrew Poetry* (New York 1924–1933) 4.493.

[138]The poem was probably composed by a late thirteenth-century Italian Jew. See Davidson, *Thesaurus of Mediaeval Hebrew Poetry* 2.266.

[139]Neither the poem nor the credo appears in the Lurianic prayer book, in prayer books of the Ḥabad movement, which take the Lurianic rite as their model, or in the prayer book based on the practices of R. Elijah of Vilna. The omission of the poem and credo from these prayer books was undoubtedly not accidental. Copies of the Roman-rite prayer book and of current Yemenite prayer books which I examined do not have the credo but do have the *Yigdal* poem.

version.[140] As part of the condensation of Maimonides' language, everything overtly philosophical is, in both instances, edited out. Although the "I believe fully . . . " credos are printed in prayer books, they, unlike the *Yigdal* poem, have not become part of the formal liturgy of either the Sephardic or Ashkenazic rite. Individuals who choose to recite them do so to themselves after their daily prayers.

What has happened is noteworthy. While a few of the traditional Jewish prayer books that have appeared in print since the invention of movable type were designed by leading rabbinic scholars, and a few were sponsored by religious organizations, there has never been a central authority or commission that established rules for the content of traditional prayer books. When deciding what to include—which prayers, the exact wording of the prayers, and the like— publishers have generally followed the guidelines set by the law codes, particularly the *Shulḥan ᶜAruk.* But those guidelines are concerned primarily with the basic structure of the liturgy and give only passing attention to details. They do not prescribe such things as credos. On occasion, publishers of prayer books consulted with rabbinic authorities. They naturally tried to meet the needs and wants of the communities to which they marketed their products and to a considerable extent they simply copied from one another. Ultimately, however, book publishers are autonomous businesspeople who make their own decisions. It was they and not the community of scholars who, consciously or not, took upon themselves to settle a theological issue of no little import, the centuries-long debate concerning Jewish dogma which was largely engendered precisely by Maimonides. The businessmen through their commercial products, the prayer books, have decided that the Jewish religion does indeed have a credo. And they have awarded Maimonides the palm, elevating him into the final authority on questions of doctrine and enshrining his thirteen principles—stripped of their philosophical accoutrements—as dogmas of the Jewish religion.

Although Maimonides may not have intended to draw up a formal creed for the Jewish religion, he would hardly have been surprised. His treatment of the hereafter and other issues of dogma concludes with the acknowledgment that he had "spoken at very great length and departed from the basic purpose of my composition," which after all is a Commentary on the Mishna. "I did so," he explains, "because I saw it to be useful in [the area of] belief. . . . Read over and over what I have written here and contemplate it well. If you let yourself suppose that you have gotten to the heart of it in one or ten readings, then, God knows, you have been led into an absurdity." "I did not write it haphazardly, but after . . . investigating correct and incorrect opinions, distilling out which of them should be believed, and seeking support through arguments and proofs relative to each point."[141]

[140]The credo takes the same form in European prayer books of the original, German-Polish type (*nusaḥ ashkenaz*) and those of the Ḥasidic (*nusaḥ sefarad*) type.

[141]Commentary on the Mishna, *Sanhedrin* 10:1, p. 217.

Mishna is predominantly legal and ritual in character, but Maimonides promises, early on in his Commentary, that "whenever a whiff of a statement relating to belief comes up, I shall offer some explanation. For the exposition of a principle [of belief] is preferable to anything else that I might expound."[142] As just seen, at the three junctures where he found that the Mishna permitted, he incorporated disquisitions on the ideology of the Oral Torah, the nature of the human soul, human ethical virtue, human eudaemonia and the afterlife, the principles of the Jewish faith, and similar topics. As opportunities arise, he offers observations on the human intellect,[143] human free will,[144] and miracles.[145] He lays bare the errors of idolatry,[146] astrology,[147] divination,[148] the belief in "talismans,"[149] and reliance on amulets,[150] and he inveighs against a materialistic[151] or a hedonistic life.[152] He rationalizes away apparent superstitions harbored by the rabbis. When, for instance, the Mishna mentions the "evil eye," Maimonides explains that the term means uncontrolled desire for physical possessions.[153] He does not construe the "evil spirit" spoken of by the Mishna as a malevolent, independently existent agent lying in wait for man in the world surrounding him but instead internalizes it as either a type of human "melancholia"[154] or an injury to the human power of judgment.[155]

In the course of his Commentary, he encounters a paragraph of the Mishna which refers to an ancient midrashic exposition of two sections of the Bible, the sections known as "the account of the chariot" and "the account of creation." The account of creation is the creation story in the Book of Genesis, and the account of

[142]Commentary on the Mishna, *Berakot* 9:7.

[143]Commentary on the Mishna, introduction, p. 37; *Abot* 3:20.

[144]Commentary on the Mishna, *Abot* 3:18.

[145]Commentary on the Mishna, *Abot* 5:5: Miracles that would take place in the future were preprogramed into nature during the process of creation.

[146]Commentary on the Mishna, introduction, pp. 5–6; *ᶜAboda Zara* 4:7.

[147]Commentary on the Mishna, *ᶜAboda Zara* 4:7

[148]Commentary on the Mishna, *Sanhedrin* 7:7.

[149]Commentary on the Mishna, *Pesaḥim* 4:10; *ᶜAboda Zara* 3:1; 3:3; 4:7.

[150]Commentary on the Mishna, *Soṭa* 7:4. Mishna *Shabbat* 6:2 sets rules for the use of amulets on the Sabbath, and Maimonides' Commentary on the Mishna explains the passage without commenting on the efficacy of amulets.

[151]Commentary on the Mishna, introduction, p. 44; *Abot* 4:22.

[152]Commentary on the Mishna, introduction, p. 42.

[153]Commentary on the Mishna, *Abot* 2:12, 14.

[154]Commentary on the Mishna, *Shabbat* 2.5

[155]Commentary on the Mishna, *ᶜErubim* 4:1. See also Commentary on *Ohalot* 11:7, where Maimonides tries to rationalize a questionable assumption of the rabbis' regarding the canine digestive process. He did not, however, transcend some commonly accepted beliefs of his day: For example, he recognizes the spontaneous generation of rodents and writes that although the phenomenon is "inexplicable," he had heard reports of it by persons who witnessed it; see Commentary on the Mishna, *Ḥullin* 9:6.

the chariot—which was touched on in the previous chapter[156]—is the vision beheld by the prophet Ezekiel; the Book of Ezekiel recounts that the prophet saw a vehicle—the chariot—on which "the appearance of the likeness of the glory of the Lord" floated or was seated.[157] The Mishna discloses nothing about the midrashic exposition of the two except that it is highly sensitive and to be shared only with select students, and the exposition of the account of the chariot must be protected by an even thicker cloak of secrecy than the exposition of the account of creation. Other rabbinic sources of the classic period add little. An absence of data rarely precludes speculation, and there has been no lack of conjecture regarding the content of the rabbinic exposition of the two accounts.

When Maimonides comments on the mishnaic paragraph in which the subject comes up, he ventures his own reconstruction. He identifies the account of creation with "physical science" and the account of the chariot with "metaphysical science";[158] the two critical scriptural passages contain the nub of two of the main branches of philosophy, and the rabbis' midrashic interpretation of the two scriptural accounts expand on that nub. Why did the rabbis insist that what they say about physics and metaphysics be kept secret, while imposing no similar restriction on the mathematical sciences, the third main branch? The reason, Maimonides submits, is that persons who enter upon the study of physics and metaphysics without sufficient preparation will fall into "idiocy and dementia," or, alternatively, they will "turn their backs" on the truth, or, again, their "beliefs will become confused."[159] He was so taken with his discovery of the identity of the two accounts that he repeats it in his code of Jewish law and then again in the *Guide for the Perplexed.*[160]

He goes further. He avers that the midrashic elaboration of the scriptural accounts of creation and the chariot comprise the "principles" (*uṣūl*) underlying the "substance [*gufe*] of the Torah."[161] Not only, then, did the ancient rabbis recognize the sciences of physics and metaphysics and expound them to select individuals; their exposition of those sciences are the principles upon which the legal

[156]Above, p. 107.

[157]Ezekiel 1.

[158]Maimonides does not even identify the account of creation and account of the chariot as sections of Scripture which present the sciences of physics and metaphysics in allegorical garb. He identifies them flatly and with no further ado as physics and metaphysics, telling us, it would seem, that the rabbis taught philosophy straightforwardly and not through a midrashic interpretation of Scripture. Similarly in his *Mishneh Torah.* In the *Guide for the Perplexed,* he does call the creation story in Genesis the *account of creation,* and Ezekiel's vision the *account of the chariot,* and he proceeds to interpret the former as a *figurative* version of the science of physics and the latter as a *figurative* version of the science of metaphysics.

[159]Commentary on the Mishna, *Ḥagiga* 2:1, taken together with Commentary on the Mishna, introduction, p. 35.

[160]*Mishneh Torah*: *H. Yesode ha-Torah* 2.11; 4.10–11. *Guide for the Perplexed,* introduction.

[161]Commentary on the Mishna, *Ḥagiga* 2:1.

and ritual regulations forming the substance of the divine Torah rest. The thesis, which will strike the modern reader as wildly anachronistic, may have a certain theological plausibility, but it was unheard of in rabbinic circles. Once Maimonides adopted it, he had a justification for weaving science and philosophy into his Commentary on the oldest preserved repository of the Oral Torah, the Mishna.

In the previous chapter, we saw that in the Commentary, he cites with approval: the "philosopher," that is to say, Aristotle, "philosophers who are expert in philosophy," the "early and later philosophers," "the philosophy of Greece," and "first philosophy," that is, metaphysics.[162] I found only a single passage in the Commentary on the Mishna which expresses a reservation about anything philosophical. The passage warns against a mistake made by "many" of those whom Maimonides significantly calls "philosophizers," rather than philosophers, concerning an issue in theoretical psychology. He neglects to tell us what the mistake was.[163]

The Commentary on the Mishna presupposes the structure of the physical universe as envisaged by the medieval Arabic Aristotelian philosophers. It thus pictures the corporal universe as geocentric, and the celestial segment of the universe as a series of transparent spheres nested within one another. The stars and planets are borne by the spheres, and the rotation of the spheres around the earth gives rise to the motion of the stars and planets. Physical objects in the lower world are all composed of the four basic Aristotelian elements—fire, air, water, and earth.[164] These notions were not controversial in the Middle Ages and although one would not expect to encounter them in a Commentary on the Mishna, they do not stand out.

Maimonides takes as granted that God is an incorporeal being, that God's essence is unknowable, and that God does not possess attributes. A healthy measure of creativity is required in order to uncover the incorporeality of God in either Scripture or the classic rabbinic texts; Maimonides, nevertheless, not merely accepts it but incorporates it into his thirteen articles of the Jewish faith.[165] Once having embraced divine incorporeality, he is inevitably led to interpret away rabbinic descriptions of God which carry physical implications. For instance, the Mishna records Rabbi Akiba's position that tanneries, which were proverbially

[162]Above, p. 92.

[163]*Shemona Peraqim*, chapter 1, p. 374. For the contrast between the philosophizer and the genuine philosopher, see A. Goichon, *Lexique de la langue philosophique d' Ibn Sīnā* (Paris 1938) 282. In Commentary on the Mishna, *Rosh ha-Shana* 2:7, Maimonides refers to a subject about which even "philosophers disagree"; the issue, however, concerns astronomy.

[164]Commentary on the Mishna, introduction, p. 45; *Ma^caser Sheni* 1:5; *Sanhedrin* 10, introduction, p. 204; *^cAboda Zara* 4:7, p. 358.

[165]In Commentary on the Mishna, *Sanhedrin* 10:1, third principle, Maimonides makes the incorporeality of God an article of the Jewish faith. Commentary on the Mishna, *Berakot* 9:7, states the unknowability of God. *Shemona Peraqim*, chapter 8, pp. 405–6, states the unknowability of God and God's freedom from attributes.

malodorous, must not be located to the west of a city, and the Babylonian Talmud explains Akiba's rationale as being that God's "Presence" resides in the west. Now, if God is incorporeal, He obviously does not occupy space and therefore cannot reside either in the west or at any other spot on the compass. Maimonides accordingly stretches the meaning of the mishnaic and talmudic passages. He interprets Rabbi Akiba's intent as being not that God or His Presence actually dwells in the west, but that the most sacred part of the Holy Temple, and hence the site toward which Jews face during prayer, stood on the Temple's western side. Rabbi Akiba's opinion that tanneries must be not be placed to the west of a city reflects that circumstance.[166]

Maimonides has been seen to embrace the Arabic Aristotelian proposition that not God, but an incorporeal being subordinate to God and known as the "active intellect," is the fount of the prophecy enjoyed by the biblical prophets. He not only endorses the proposition—with the reservation that Moses, the greatest of the prophets, differed from the others in receiving his prophecy directly from God; he builds another of his thirteen principles of the Jewish faith around it.

When he touches on two of the ultimate puzzles, the purpose of the world's existence and the purpose of the existence of the human species, he cites philosophers side by side with the prophets of Israel. Prophets and philosophers alike, he asserts in his introduction to the Commentary on the Mishna, agreed that everything in the lower world inhabited by man is directed toward a single goal, toward bringing forth men who excel in "knowledge and practice" (*ᶜilm* and *ᶜamal*). Lest readers imagine that the knowledge spoken of here is of a legal and ritual nature, he immediately adds that by the knowledge men must acquire, he "means" the "conceiving of the true essences [of things] . . . and the knowledge [*idrāk*] of everything a man can know." Should a laggard remain who is still too slow to grasp what Maimonides is saying, he makes things even clearer on the next page, where he writes: "The goal of the human species is the conceiving of intelligible thoughts" and that goal is attained by persons who are "students of science and philosophize."[167] Nor is the "practice" recommended by philosophers and prophets merely the observance of the religious commandments. By practice, Maimonides means "balance in natural matters, . . . [that is,] taking from them only what contributes to the maintenance of the body and the improvement of one's qualities [*khulq*],"[168] in other words, a general avoidance of physical indulgence looking forward to moral perfection.

As already seen, he understood that the Mishna tractate *Abot* has the aim of encouraging men to perfect themselves through the acquisition of ethical and

[166]Commentary on the Mishna *Baba Batra* 2:9, with reference to BT *Baba Batra* 25a. The Commentary on the Mishna also interprets away anthropomorphic language in *Ḥagiga* 2:1 and *Sanhedrin* 6:7.

[167]Commentary on Mishna, introduction, pp. 42–43.

[168]Commentary on Mishna, introduction, p. 42.

intellectual virtue. In his introduction to his commentary on that tractate, he goes still further and characterizes the commandments of the holy Torah not as ends in themselves but as means whose end is the acquisition of ethical virtue: "The Torah prohibits what it prohibits and commands what it commands solely" in order to inculcate correctly balanced psychological characteristics—to inculcate virtue as Aristotelian ethical philosophy defined it.[169]

Human eudaemonia, Maimonides wrote in a sentence quoted earlier, consists in the "permanence of the soul through the permanence of its object of knowledge and through its becoming identical therewith, as expert philosophers" have established.[170] To penetrate the opaque phrases, one must be familiar with what lies behind them. Maimonides is assuming the following propositions, which were common currency among the medieval Arabic Aristotelians: Objects in the physical world have a material and a formal side, the latter being not the external shape of an object, but the internal principle, or essence, making it what it is; the form of a cat, for example, is its felinity. When a human intellect has as the object of its thought something that possesses a material and a formal side—as when a man has the thought of a tree, a cat, or the like—the human soul separates, or abstracts, the formal from the material side, and the intellect takes hold of the formal side. In every act of thinking, the human intellect becomes identical with its thought: When the intellect has something belonging to the physical world as the object of its thought, it becomes identical with the form abstracted from the thing in question; during the time that it thinks the thought of a tree or a cat, the intellect is identical with the form abstracted from the tree or cat. It is possible, however, for the human intellect to have as the object of its thought not only beings within the physical world, but beings belonging to the incorporeal, imperishable realm as well. Since incorporeal beings possess no material side, their forms do not have to be abstracted from a material substratum. Consequently, when a human intellect succeeds in having a being of that sort as the object of its thought, what it takes hold of is the incorporeal being in its entirety.

From the foregoing, not inconsiderable body of unstated premises, Maimonides draws the crowning inference that he states flatly in his Commentary on the Mishna: A human intellect that succeeds in having as the object of its thought a being belonging to the incorporeal realm—hence a being imperishable by its very nature—becomes identical with the imperishable object of its thought and thereby equally imperishable and immortal. Human well-being and immortality, Maimonides tells his readers, consist in thinking such a thought, in the intellect's having an incorporeal being as the direct object of its thought.[171] A Commentary on the Mishna was scarcely the place to offer an inkling of the manner in which the

[169] *Shemona Peraqim*, chapter 4 , p. 384.

[170] Above, p. 156.

[171] See Commentary on the Mishna, *Abot* 3:20; *Guide for the Perplexed* 1:68; H. Davidson, *Alfarabi, Avicenna, and Averroes, on Intellect* (New York 1992) 36.

human intellect might accomplish the extraordinary feat, and Maimonides says nothing more on the subject.

What he has incorporated into his Commentary on the Mishna, the primary text of the Oral Torah, is astonishing: a concept of the deity borrowed from Arabic Aristotelian metaphysics, an explanation of the phenomenon of prophecy drawn from the Arabic Aristotelian school, the purpose of life as viewed by that same school of philosophy, conceptions of the virtuous man, human eudaemonia, and human immortality drawn from Arabic Aristotelian ethics and psychology. While—as is hardly surprising—he does not enter into details, he makes no attempt whatsoever to disguise what he is about.

Accomplished medieval rabbinists of all stripes scrupulously treated the rabbinic world of thought as self-contained.[172] The cabalists among them, for example, carefully compartmentalized their areas of interest and kept their rabbinic works free of their theosophic beliefs. Maimonides is unusual in welcoming a foreign ideology into a rabbinic context and he does so out of the conviction that the ideology is not foreign at all. A modern observer may view him as performing acrobatics in order to graft a philosophic system of thought on to religious texts, but he saw things differently. Nothing he writes in the Commentary on the Mishna or elsewhere ever suggests that he thought of himself as forcing extraneous beliefs on the traditional texts. He perceived himself instead as eliciting the foundation on which the "substance of the Law" rests, as restoring to their native rabbinic framework "the truths that men of science have opined and on which the philosophers have wasted ages."

Maimonides composed his Commentary on the Mishna in Judeo-Arabic, a stratum of the postclassical Arabic language which medieval Jews almost always wrote in Hebrew characters and which employs a greater or lesser sprinkling of Hebrew words and phrases, largely depending on the subject matter.[173] Works on secular subjects would use less Hebrew, and rabbinic works, such as Maimonides' Commentary on the Mishna, more. During Maimonides' lifetime, the havoc wreaked by the Almohads on the Jewish communities of Morocco and Arabic Spain and the coincidental decline of the Iraqi academies shifted the center of gravity of rabbinic studies from Jewish communities that read Arabic to those that did not. As a consequence, from the thirteenth century onward, the majority of rabbinic students who might interest themselves in a commentary on the Mishna no longer could read Maimonides' Commentary in its original language. To render the Commentary accessible to them, a translation into Hebrew was needed.

[172]A partial exception is Ḥefeṣ ben Yaṣliaḥ, who buttressed the commandments of believing in God and in the unity of God with quasi-philosophic arguments. See Ḥefeṣ ben Yaṣliaḥ, *A Volume of the Book of Precepts*, ed. B. Halper (Philadelphia 1915) 31–40.

[173]J. Blau, *The Emergence and Linguistic Background of Judaeo-Arabic*, 2nd ed. (Jerusalem 1981) 25, 34, 44–46, 215, 226–27. A precise definition of Judeo-Arabic and, for that matter, of classical Arabic is not easy.

Maimonides remarks on one occasion that he wanted to translate the Commentary himself[174] but he never did. It was instead translated into Hebrew piecemeal by a number of men, most of whom did their work around the turn of the fourteenth century, well over a century after the Commentary was written. The translators were not always sufficiently adept in the subject and in the language of the Arabic text, and the translations are therefore sometimes flawed, particularly in the case of the Order of ritual impurity, where Maimonides is especially helpful.[175]

He stopped seven or eight times in the Commentary to praise his accomplishment and, setting aside questions of taste, the praise is in place.[176] His is the oldest known full-fledged commentary on the entire Mishna. Virtually all of classic rabbinic literature is at his fingertips: the Mishna itself, the appendix to the Mishna known as the *Tosefta*, the two Talmuds, the compilations of halakic midrashic material.[177] He brings to bear whatever he needs, effortlessly and wherever necessary. His judgment is excellent. Yet although the Commentary is a most impressive piece of work, it, like every other human artifact, is not perfect. While Maimonides' explanations are unexcelled at their best, he fails at times to treat matters that require comment, and his explanations occasionally miss the mark.

He went back more than once and made corrections.[178] The medieval Hebrew translations were, however, generally done from the early version and usually do not reflect the revisions. The translations themselves, as just mentioned, are sometimes flawed. Whether for any of these reasons or by mere chance, medieval rabbinists made only limited use of the Commentary,[179] and it did not in the end prevail as the standard tool for studying the Mishna.

Three and a half centuries after Maimonides, an Italian rabbi, Obadia Bertinoro, composed a new commentary on the entire Mishna. Bertinoro wrote in Hebrew, with the heavy admixture of Aramaic words and phrases which is typical of posttalmudic rabbinic writing. Although his language is not pure, his exposition of the mishnaic text is limpid. He had the commentatorial gift, to a greater degree than Maimonides, of saying enough but not too much. Like Maimonides, he read the Mishna through the spectacles of the Babylonian and Palestinian Talmuds, and especially the former—nothing else could be expected—and he followed Maimonides' example in addressing relative beginners and advanced scholars at the same time. He followed Maimonides' example in an additional way as well, in consistently enunciating what the halakic norm is. By contrast, general rules and

[174]Letter to Joseph Ibn Jabir, in I. Shailat, *Letters and Essays of Moses Maimonides* (in Hebrew) (Jerusalem 1987–1988) 409.

[175]Frankel, *Darke ha- Mishna* (n. 88 above) 352.

[176]See below, pp. 548–49.

[177]For these terms, see above, pp. 136, 138–39; below, p. 169. One classic rabbinic work that Maimonides did not use when composing the Commentary is *Mekilta*.

[178]See S. Hopkins, *Maimonides's Commentary on Tractate Shabbat* (Jerusalem 2001) xxi–xxiii.

[179]Frankel, *Darke ha- Mishna* 351.

introductions, of which Maimonides was so fond, held no appeal for him. And while he consulted Maimonides' Commentary throughout and frequently accepted Maimonides' interpretations of problematic passages, he relied more on sources other than Maimonides.[180] Since Bertinoro's time, additional valuable complete or partial commentaries on the Mishna have appeared, all of which consult Maimonides' Commentary, although, again, without necessarily accepting its interpretations.[181] By today, a small library of commentaries and glosses on the Mishna is available. It will scarcely be surprising that neither Bertinoro's commentary nor the others dream of incorporating philosophic theses into their exegesis of the sacred Mishna text.

There are instances where an explanation that Bertinoro gives on one passage is inconsistent with the explanation he gives on another.[182] When a Mishna paragraph can be understood in different ways, he does not always choose the interpretation that later writers would view as most plausible. And the quality of his commentary on the sixth Order of the Mishna falls below that of his commentary on the other Orders. As a consequence, commentaries on the Mishna subsequent to his occasionally outstrip it in one respect or another. Nevertheless, the overall excellence and attractiveness of his work made it, for centuries, the standard commentary on the Mishna. Needs and preferences change, and in recent decades, a commentary composed by an Israeli scholar, P. Kehati, has won a large following. Kehati still reads the Mishna through the spectacles of the two Talmuds, but he makes good use of the commentators who came after Bertinoro. Modern-minded students find his language, which is pure Hebrew, to be more accessible than the mélange of Hebrew and Aramaic employed by Bertinoro, and editions of his commentary are accompanied by a vocalized text of the Mishna,[183] which adds to its attractiveness for many. While Bertinoro still remains the standard commentary among students of a traditional bent, Kehati's has become the accepted commentary among the more modern. Maimonides' Commentary, although regularly reprinted and recently retranslated into Hebrew, has been relegated to secondary status. His introduction to the tractate *Abot*, which is known as the *Eight Chapters*, and abbreviated versions of his list of thirteen principles of faith continue to circulate independently of the whole.

[180]Particularly, Rashi's commentary on the Babylonian Talmud. See *Tosefot Yom Ṭob*, introduction; Albeck, *Mabo la-Mishna* (n. 51 above) 250.

[181]Regarding commentaries on the Mishna, see Frankel, *Darke ha- Mishna* 336–64; Albeck, *Mabo la-Mishna* 237–53.

[182]*Tosefot Yom Ṭob*, introduction. Random examples, most of which I identified through the medium of *Tosefot Yom Ṭob*: Bertinoro's explanations of *Berakot* 3:3, and ᶜ*Erubin* 10:1; of *Rosh ha-Shana* 4:1 and 4:2; of *Pesaḥim* 3:1, and *Ḥalla* 1:2; of *Menaḥot* 12:4, and *Miqwa'ot* 3:1; of *Kelim* 3:2 (oil is less viscous than water and wine!), and *Makshirin* 3:2; of *Kelim* 9:2, and *Ohalot* 5:3; of *Kelim* 18:7, and *Ohalot* 1:2; of *Kelim* 19:3 (a), and 3 (b); of *Kelim* 29:2 (a) and 29:2 (b); Bertinoro's setting of the norm in *Beṣa* 5:2, and ᶜ*Arakin* 8:6.

[183]The Mishna text accompanying his commentary is not, however, a critical edition.

The Book of Commandments. Judah the Prince's Mishna corpus recognizes a distinction between laws and rituals that carry the sanction of the "Torah" and others that carry the lesser sanction of "the rabbis."[184] In the Babylonian Talmud, the contrast between the two levels is ubiquitous, and as the distinction is drawn there, the higher level, the category of "Torah," includes both what is explicit in the Written Torah as well as the interpretation and supplementation provided by oral tradition.[185] The line is drawn between the laws and rituals of the Written Torah together with their Oral Torah enhancement, on the one hand, and laws and rituals instituted by the rabbis, on the other.

The Babylonian Talmud introduces a further notion, namely, that exactly 613 commandments were communicated to Moses. The pivotal passage in the Babylonian Talmud credits the notion to a certain R. Simlai, a Palestinian rabbi who was active about the end of the third and the beginning of the fourth century, a man whose reported expertise lay in aggada, not halaka, and consequently someone who stood outside the circle of rabbinic figures wielding authority in the ritual and legal sphere. R. Simlai, according to the key passage, "taught [*darash*]: 613 commandments were stated to Moses, 365 negative commandments, paralleling the number of days of the solar year, and 248 positive commandments, paralleling the number of discrete segments [*evarim*] in [the body of] a human being."[186] Negative commandments are those prohibiting something, typically taking the form "thou shalt not." Positive commandments are those dictating something, typically taking the form "thou shalt."

The statement recorded in the name of R. Simlai leaves a good deal open. The intent could be that all of the 613 commandments stated to Moses are explicit in the Written Torah but it could also be that some are known only through the Oral Torah enhancement. The statement does not even indicate whether the 613 were all preserved and handed down to posterity. The Babylonian Talmud itself asserts that hundreds or even thousands of "halakot" and dialectical inferences were lost when Moses died. When the matter is considered entirely from the rabbinic standpoint, it would therefore be quite possible that some of the commandments given to Moses were forgotten and lost forever at his death or later.[187]

[184]Mishna, *Yadayim* 3:2. Other instances: Mishna, *Shebi*ᶜ*it* 10:3; *Yebamot* 2:4; *Gittin* 4:2–9; *Ṭohorot* 4:11; *Tebul Yom* 4:6.

[185]See the passages cited by Bacher, *Die bibel- und traditionsexegetische Terminologie der Amoräer* (n. 38 above) 2.

[186]BT *Makkot* 23b. For variants, cf. Maimonides, *Sefer ha-Miṣvoth*, ed. Ch. Heller, 2nd ed. (Jerusalem 1946) 5, note 1.

[187]BT *Temura* 15b–16a. Maimonides quotes the passage for a different purpose in his *Book of Commandments* (n. 27 above), rule 2, p. 15. He reasons that since the dialectical inferences made by Moses numbered in the thousands, they could not be what the Babylonian Talmud has in mind when it speaks of 613 commandments given to Moses. The point he wants to make is that a regulation validated only by being deduced from Scripture through the canons of rabbinic dialectic does not qualify for inclusion in the 613.

The dictum ascribed to R. Simlai looks, indeed, as if he, or the tradition transmitted in his name, did not reach the figure empirically and a posteriori, so to speak, that he—or it—did not painstakingly seek out all the commandments communicated to Moses, count them, and discover that the number came to exactly 613. The figure looks as if it was fixed a priori, by adding the days of the solar year to the number of segments of the human body.[188] The object of the dictum would accordingly be hortative. Every Jew, the preacher would be exhorting his listeners, must observe God's prohibitions each day of the year. Every Jew must mobilize each part of his body in fulfilling God's positive commands.[189]

The pivotal passage, as already said, appears in the Babylonian Talmud. No mention of, or allusion to, 613 commandments received by Moses is found in the Mishna. The number is not mentioned or alluded to in other preserved rabbinic compositions belonging to the same stratum of rabbinic literature as the Mishna and dating from roughly the same period—the corpus of mishnaic material known as the *Tosefta* and the compilations of midrashic material of a halakic character which represent themselves as the work of rabbis who lived in the period up to the publication of Judah the Prince's Mishna.[190] The Palestinian Talmud knows nothing of the notion.[191] Three other passages within the Babylonian Talmud do refer to a total of 613 commandments, all in nonhalakic contexts, and each time, the number is treated as something commonly known and accepted.[192] References to 613 commandments appear as well in compilations of midrashic material which are contemporaneous with, or later than, the Babylonian Talmud.[193] Neither the Babylonian Talmud nor the midrashic compilations that speak of 613 commandments ever list them or suggest what, exactly, they comprise.

Centuries later, in the Middle Ages, a question would be posed from the standpoint of rabbinic jurisprudence. It would be asked whether the opinion of the Palestinian rabbi who set the number of Mosaic commandments at 613 should be taken as normative. His could be a minority opinion, whereas the majority or

[188]Mishna, *Oholot* 1:8, distinguishes 248 segments of the human body.

[189]BT *Makkot* 23b–24a cites a midrashic argument in the name of another rabbi in order to corroborate the number 613.

[190]Printed editions of *Mekilta*: *Ba-Ḥodesh-Yitro* §5 have the number 613, but that is apparently an interpolation, since the manuscripts do not have it. See *Mechilta d'Rabbi Ismael*, ed. H. Horovitz (Jerusalem 1960) 222. Printed editions of *Sifre*: *Deuteronomy* §76, speak of "365 negative commandments of the Torah," but the best sources have instead: "300 positive commandments." See *Sifre on Deuteronomy*, ed. L. Finkelstein (Berlin 1939) 141, and note.

[191]The Palestinian Talmud, *Ta^{c}anit* 4.8 (5), has a version of the passage that appears in BT *Yebamot* 62a and *Shabbat* 87a (see next note), but whereas the version in the two Babylonian Talmud tractates gives 613 as the number of the commandments, the version in the Palestinian Talmud gives no number. That strongly suggests that the number was not originally part of the passage and was added by the redactors of the Babylonian Talmud.

[192]BT *Shabbat* 87a; *Yebamot* 47b; 62a (identical with *Shabbat* 87a); *Nedarim* 25a; *Shebu^{c}ot* 29a (virtually identical with *Nedarim* 25a).

[193]See *Yefe ^{c}Enayim* on BT *Makkot* 23b; A. Rabinowitz, *Taryag* (Jerusalem 1967) 40.

consensus, and hence authoritative, position could be that the commandments enjoying Mosaic sanction add up to a different number. Or perhaps they are not reducible to any definitive number at all.[194]

If Maimonides had thought that a difference of opinion obtained within the classic rabbinic sources regarding the number of Mosaic commandments, he would have had to rule out the possibility of ascertaining what the normative position is. For when he encounters differences of opinion among the ancient rabbis regarding matters of belief, he departs from his practice of determining which among the diverse recorded positions on an issue is authoritative. In his words: "Where differences occur between the rabbis regarding opinions involving no action, the halakic norm cannot be affirmed to be in accordance with the opinion of so-and-so" over against the opinion of those who disagree.[195] In effect, he is saying, the rules that evolved in talmudic and posttalmudic times for deciding between opposing positions recorded in the classic rabbinic texts are designed for legal and ritual matters. Inasmuch as the exact number of the laws and rituals given to Moses is not itself a ritual or legal issue, if a difference of rabbinic opinion obtained regarding the number, Maimonides' guideline would preclude the possibility of determining which opinion is normative and which is not.

Despite the questions that might be raised, the notion of exactly 613 commandments' having been given to Moses struck root in rabbinic circles. It consequently became inevitable that efforts would be made to determine precisely what they are. What is generally considered to be the oldest attempt to identify them is made in the preface to *Sefer Halakot Gedolot*, a comprehensive and influential code of rabbinic law, which Maimonides and historians today ascribe to a little-known ninth-century rabbinist named Simeon Kayyara.[196] The preface enumerates concisely and without elaboration 613 commandments that, in its formulation, "Israel"—rather than Moses—"received on Mount Sinai."[197] Other rabbinic writers as well as authors of liturgical poetry followed with their

[194]Naḥmanides, Critique of Maimonides, *Sefer ha-Miṣwot*, first rule; S. Duran, *Zohar ha-Raqi*ᶜ*a* (Vilna 1879) 117; English translation of the Duran passage: E. Urbach, *The Sages* (Jerusalem 1979) 1.343–44. As we shall see, multiple obligations can sometimes be construed as a single commandment

[195]Commentary on the Mishna, *Shevu*ᶜ*ot* 1:4. Similarly in Commentary on *Soṭa* 3:3, and *Sanhedrin* 10:3.

[196]Maimonides mentions Simeon Kayyara in *Book of Commandments* (n. 27 above) rule 10, 43, in a manner showing that he takes him to be the author of *Halakot Gedolot*. It has been argued that the commandments were enumerated in liturgical pieces preceding *Halakot Gedolot*; see M. Guttmann, *Beḥinat ha-Miṣwot* (Breslau 1928) 9–10. The argument is strongest in the case of the liturgical composition beginning with the words *Atta hinḥalta Torah le-*ᶜ*ammeka*.

[197]*Sefer Halakhot Gedolot*, ed. E. and N. Hildesheimer (Jerusalem 1971–1987) 3, appendix, 112, and the alternate version, *Sefer Halakot Gedolot*, ed. A. Traub (Warsaw 1875), introduction, 6. At an earlier point, the version published by Traub, introduction, p. 4, quotes R. Simlai's statement in a different form. The matter is discussed in the Hildesheimer edition, 3, appendix, note 324.

enumerations. Scholars in medieval and modern times have found the list in *Halakot Gedolot* to be fraught with problems, and some of the problems have a bearing on our subject.

The preface to *Sefer Halakot Gedolot* does not divide the commandments into the two categories, 365 negative commands and 248 positive commands, which the seminal statement reported by the Babylonian Talmud in the name of R. Simlai would require. Instead, it muddies the picture by introducing additional categories. It starts by distinguishing six types of capital punishment, treating each as a category in its own right, and classifying under them 71 sins and crimes that, by divine Law, entail a death penalty of one type or another. It goes on to enumerate 277 negative and 200 positive divine commandments. And it arrives at the figure 613 with the help of still another category, which it calls the 65 "scriptural sections of statutes and ordinances for which the community is responsible," in other words, sections of the Pentateuch containing commandments incumbent on the community rather than on the individual.[198] Some of the "scriptural sections" in this last category contain subheadings. One section, for instance, comprises the regulations for establishing a high court (the Great Sanhedrin), for establishing intermediate courts, for judging cases in which the punishment is monetary in character, for judging cases in which the punishment is a whipping, and for judging cases in which the punishment is the death penalty. Those look like not one, but multiple commandments, and the enumerating of sections for which the community is responsible therefore looks like a device for squeezing extra commandments into a nominal enumeration of 613.

The problematic nature of the scheme is compounded when items crop up more than once. Sometimes what seems to be the same item occurs more than once within the very same category,[199] and sometimes an item appearing in one category reappears in a second. Thus a half dozen transgressions that are included under one or another of the types of capital punishment reappear in the category of negative commandments: "Desecration" of the Sabbath is listed among the sins punishable by death through stoning, while the divine prohibition against doing "any manner of work" on the Sabbath is listed separately in the category of negative commandments; murder is listed among sins punishable by beheading and again as a negative commandment; and so on.[200] Then, eighteen items from the earlier categories reappear in the list of scriptural sections for which the community is responsible.[201] Commentators on *Halakot Gedolot* have long taken up the challenge of showing why the apparent doublets are not doublets at all but represent

[198] *Sefer Halakhot Gedolot*, ed. E. and N. Hildesheimer, 3, appendix, 25–112.

[199] *Sefer Halakhot Gedolot*, ed. E. and N. Hildesheimer, 3, appendix, notes 126, 231, 267, 446, 468.

[200] *Sefer Halakhot Gedolot*, ed. E. and N. Hildesheimer, 3, appendix, notes 47, 52, 61, 62, 63, 225, 360.

[201] *Sefer Halakhot Gedolot*, ed. E. and N. Hildesheimer, 3, appendix, notes 408, 424, 434, 442, 453, 454, 456, 466, 469, 470, 473, 476, 477, 478, 481, 482, 483, 486.

distinct items. The classifying of "desecration" of the Sabbath among sins punishable through stoning side by side with the listing of a negative commandment prohibiting "any manner of work" on the Sabbath has been resolved as follows: The desecration punishable by stoning comprehends most forms of labor on the Sabbath, whereas the negative commandment prohibiting "any manner of work" is concerned with labor not punishable by death, such as driving an animal on the Sabbath.[202] While that particular explanation may work after a fashion, many of the attempts to interpret away doublets—such as the murder doublet—stretch ingenuity beyond the breaking point.[203]

There is yet a further problem. The Babylonian Talmud had characterized the commandments in question as laws "stated to Moses," and *Halakot Gedolot* described them as commandments that "Israel received on Mount Sinai." Yet the list contains items that are clearly post-Mosaic.[204] In the two most blatant instances, *Halakot Gedolot* includes within its enumeration of positive commandments received at Sinai the reading of the Esther scroll on the Purim holiday and the lighting of candles on the Hanukkah holiday.[205] The Purim holiday commemorates events that are dated a millennium after the revelation at Sinai. The Hanukkah holiday commemorates events that took place still later. How could ceremonies attached to those two holidays be commandments stated to Moses, in the language of the Babylonian Talmud, or given to Israel at Sinai, in the language of *Halakot Gedolot*?

When we turn to Maimonides, we find him accepting without a second thought that, as he puts it: "613 commandments were stated to Moses at Sinai, 365 paralleling the days of the solar year, and 248 paralleling the segments in [the body of] a human being." Again: "The totality of commandments that are contained in the Book of the Torah and that God ordered us to observe is 613." The dictum is reported by Maimonides not as the opinion of an individual rabbi but as a "text of the Talmud" and a doctrine that "they," that is, the rabbis of the Babylonian Talmud in general, espoused.[206] We saw earlier that legal traditions transmitted from the time of Moses and making up the Oral Torah are, so Maimonides understands, characterized by the absence of any recorded difference of opinion concerning them in the classic rabbinic texts. Perhaps the handful of references to 613 commandments in the Babylonian Talmud, with no suggestion of a dissenting opinion, convinced him that here too he was in the presence of an ancient and authoritative tradition.

[202]*Sefer Halakhot Gedolot*, ed. E. and N. Hildesheimer, 3, appendix, note 47.

[203]See the notes in Hildesheimer's edition which I have cited above.

[204]*Sefer Halakhot Gedolot*, ed. E. and N. Hildesheimer, 3, appendix, note 324.

[205]*Sefer Halakhot Gedolot*, ed. E. and N. Hildesheimer, 3, appendix, notes 378, 420.

[206]Maimonides, *Book of Commandments* (n. 27 above), introduction, p. 7; rule 1, p. 9. *Mishneh Torah*, introduction.

Maimonides' *Book of Commandments* is the composition that he devoted to the enumeration of the 613 commandments. In the introduction, he writes that he was drawn to the subject after completing what he calls his "well-known" Commentary on the Mishna. As his next major work, he contemplated a comprehensive code of Jewish law, and he wanted to ensure that he would overlook nothing pertinent, neither legal and ritual obligations prescribed by the Torah nor obligations instituted by the rabbis. To that end, he needed an exhaustive list of the commandments given to Moses and carrying the sanction of the Torah.

As he considered possible ways of proceeding, the "grief" from which he "had already suffered for years" was reawakened. He was familiar with the influential list of commandments in the introduction to *Sefer Halakot Gedolot* and also with the enumeration, only small portions of which survive today, done subsequently by a scholar named Ḥefeṣ ben Yaṣliaḥ. He had "listened to" numerous Spanish liturgical compositions that enumerate the Mosaic commandments. All those endeavors, he laments, were not merely inadequate. They contained mistakes "the enormous odiousness of which I cannot describe." The more he reflected on the errors that had been made and the way in which "one [writer on the subject] would follow another without thinking, the greater our misfortune appeared to" him. He saw his predecessors' failure to handle the issue properly as a fulfillment of the doleful biblical prophecy: "And the vision of all this is become unto you as the words of a writing that is sealed, which men deliver to one that is learned, saying 'Read this, I pray thee,' and he saith 'I cannot, for it is sealed.'"[207] Maimonides plainly regarded the correct enumeration of the 613 commandments as a weighty matter.

At first, he thought that he might merely draw up a concise list of the 613 commandments as a preface to his code of Jewish law much like, he might have added, the preface to *Sefer Halakot Gedolot*. But the calamitous situation prevented him from furnishing "the correct enumeration . . . without elaboration and proof." If he did, the first person to examine it would dismiss it out of hand as erroneous, "the evidence of its erroneousness" being Maimonides' departure from "what so-and-so and so-and-so had said. For that is the mentality of most of the better class of people today. The correctness of a statement is judged not by its content, but by the extent to which it agrees with some predecessor's statement, without any effort's being made to judge the earlier statement. And [if that is how things stand with the better class] how much more so with common people."

Before undertaking his code of Jewish law, Maimonides accordingly decided to make a detour and compose a comprehensive work on the 613 commandments. He would begin by establishing rules (*uṣūl*) for what the list of commandments given to Moses at Sinai must and must not contain and then he would give the actual enumeration of positive and negative commandments. He would justify the

[207]*Book of Commandments*, introduction, pp. 1, 4–5. The scriptural verse cited by Maimonides is Isaiah 29:11.

positions that he took "through the texts of the Torah and through the statements of the rabbis in interpreting them."[208]

Maimonides thus tells us that after the Commentary on the Mishna, his next large literary project was to be a code of Jewish law, and he wrote his *Book of Commandments* as a prolegomenon to it. A statement he makes on a subsequent occasion repeats that the *Book of Commandments* was written before the law code.[209] The Commentary on the Mishna was completed in 1167–1168, and Maimonides indicates that he began work on the code either immediately, or very soon, afterwards.[210] Virtually no time is thus left for the composition of the *Book of Commandments*. And yet a good deal of thought and labor went into it.

A possible explanation would be that he wrote the *Book of Commandments* while already engaged in the preliminary stages of his code of law, and the two overlapped. Another possibility would be that, despite what he said, he thought out the *Book of Commandments* and prepared material for it while still working on his Commentary on the Mishna. At a certain juncture in the Commentary, he makes a remark that can be translated as either: The matter under consideration here "*will be* explained [*yubayyan*] in my book on the enumeration of the commandments"; or: the matter under consideration "*is* explained. . . ."[211] Maimonides is referring to one of the general rules that he in fact spells out in the introduction to the *Book of Commandments* and on which his enumeration of the commandments rests. If the second of the two possible renderings of the sentence reflects his meaning, the sentence would most likely be an addition that he made to the Commentary on the Mishna after the work was complete.[212] If, however, it is the first rendering that captures his meaning—and that is the way the remark has been understood by translators of the *Book of Commandments*—he already had a conception of the book when still writing the Commentary on the Mishna. It may also be pertinent that when the Commentary on the Mishna classifies the varieties of ritual impurity, Maimonides invests considerable energy in distinguishing between impurity regulations carrying the sanction of the Torah and those instituted by the rabbis. The distinction between what is legislated by the Torah and what by the rabbis lies at the heart of the *Book of Commandments*. At that stage in the composition of the Commentary on the Mishna, he was, therefore, in effect doing spade-work for the other book.

Whatever the case may be, he was about thirty years old when he started writing the *Book of Commandments* and he apparently completed it with dispatch. There

[208] *Book of Commandments*, introduction, pp. 4, 6–7.

[209] Maimonides, *Responsa* (n. 3 above) §447.

[210] Below, p. 206.

[211] Commentary on the Mishna, *Ḥullin* 1:5.

[212] Commentary on the Mishna, *Menaḥot* 4:1, has the remark ". . . as I have demonstrated in my book on the enumeration of the commandments." Those words, according to the editor's apparatus to the *Menaḥot* 4:1 passage, are absent in the original version of the Commentary and belong to a later revision.

is evidence that he went back and made corrections after completing it,[213] as he is known to have done to his Commentary on the Mishna.

Maimonides' fondness for general rules finds ample expression in the introduction to his *Book of Commandments*, where he formulates fourteen rules for determining what should and should not be included in the enumeration of 613 Mosaic commandments.[214] We have seen him say that he based the *Book of Commandments* on "the texts of the Torah" and "the statements of the rabbis in interpreting them." In justifying his fourteen rules he does indeed draw upon the Pentateuch and the classic rabbinic works,[215] particularly upon the implications of the key passage which affirms, in the version he had, that 613 commandments were communicated to Moses at Sinai.[216] He relies equally, however, on something that he does not mention—on what we would call ordinary common sense. At one spot, for instance, he contends: It is not "possible for anyone of intelligence to say" that each of the seven occasions where Scripture prohibits consuming animal blood constitutes a separate commandment;[217] it does not stand to reason that Scripture would be imposing a distinct and separate commandment every time it happens to repeat the same prohibition.

Maimonides' fourteen rules serve in actuality as criteria not so much for identifying what should be included in the list of 613 commandments given to Moses as for determining what should be excluded; almost all of the rules are designed for the latter purpose. Ten have *Sefer Halakot Gedolot* as at least a partial target, each of the ten criticizing the earlier work for having included inappropriate items.[218]

A few more rays of light are shed on Maimonides' procedure by a letter that he wrote at least a decade after he completed the *Book of Commandments*. There he states that virtually every commandment he identified as one of those given to Moses is "explicit [*meforash*] in the Torah," and in the "three or four" exceptions, a regulation not explicit in the Pentateuch is expressly designated as a commandment

[213]*Book of Commandments*, negative commandment #179, p. 266, note 88; Kafah's introduction to his edition of *Book of Commandments* 11–12; Maimonides, *Sefer ha-Miṣvoth*, ed. Heller (n. 186 above), editor's introduction, p. 18.

[214]Saadia, *Sefer ha-Miṣwot*, ed. Y. Perla (Warsaw 1914)) 1.15–16, attempts to trace some of Maimonides' rules back to Abraham Ibn Ezra's *Yesod Mora* but he overstates the case for Ibn Ezra's influence on Maimonides. Ibn Ezra makes dozens of ill-organized remarks on the different characters of different kinds of commandments, and, at most, a few of those remarks may be echoed in Maimonides' rules.

[215]For example, rule 11.

[216]Rule 3.

[217]See *Book of Commandments*, rule 9, p. 34. Rules 7, 10, and 12 are also based on common-sense considerations.

[218]Rules 1, 2, 3, 4, 5, 7, 8, 10 (where Maimonides explicitly names Simeon Kayyara, the author of *Halakot Gedolot*, as the target of his criticism), 12, 14.

"of the Torah" by the transmitters of the oral tradition.[219] If the sentence is combined with what we saw previously, the implication will be that Maimonides searched out everything commanded by the Pentateuch and the rabbis, whereupon he brought his fourteen rules into play in order to determine which items in the Written Torah and rabbinic literature pass the test and qualify for inclusion among the privileged 613. The elimination of the inappropriate items produced exactly the desired number of 248 positive and 365 negative commandments. And of these, the vast majority turned out to be commandments enunciated in the Written Torah.

The first of Maimonides' fourteen rules asserts that the 613 commandments can include no laws and rituals enacted after the time of Moses. So much, he writes, should have gone without saying, and articulating a rule to the effect should have been otiose. Since the commandments are defined as having been stated to Moses at Sinai, they plainly contain nothing of post-Mosaic provenance. Only because *Sefer Halakot Gedolot* and writers following in its wake had been blind to the obvious and incorporated post-Mosaic legislation in their lists was it necessary to promulgate a rule excluding everything post-Mosaic.[220]

Maimonides' second rule explains how he identified the three or four instances where regulations not explicit in Scripture nevertheless qualify for enumeration in the select list. He writes: When "there is no verse" in Scripture explicitly prescribing a certain law or ritual, yet "the transmitters" of the tradition going back to Moses deduce the law or ritual from what Scripture says using their canons of dialectical reasoning, and when they moreover mark the regulation as "part of the body of the Torah" (*guf Torah*) or as "from the Torah," then the regulation "must be enumerated" among the 613. By contrast, when the transmitters of the tradition fail to mark a regulation lacking a verse in Scripture as being *from* the Torah, it is "rabbinic" in status (*mi-de-rabbanan*) and is not to be enumerated—this, even if they should derive it from Scripture by the use of one or another of their hermeneutic tools.[221] What is decisive in every instance is therefore the presence or absence of an explicit statement by the ancient rabbis to the effect that a given regulation is "from" the Torah or "part" of the Torah. Regulations that are not marked lack the sanction of the Torah.

The position that Maimonides takes here stirred up a small tempest in rabbinic circles. The chief critic of the *Book of Commandments* rejected the proposition that commandments derived by the ancient rabbis from Scripture through their canons of dialectical reasoning or through some other hermeneutic tool, such as the discovery of signposts in the text of Scripture, lay no claim to reflecting Scripture's

[219] *Responsa* §355. When he enumerates the commandments in the *Book of Commandments*, Maimonides writes that negative commandments #76, #135, #194, and #336 have no explicit biblical verse and are known to be commandments only through Mosaic tradition, supported either by the dialectic device of *gezera shawa* or by a hint embedded in the biblical text.

[220] *Book of Commandments*, rule 1.

[221] *Book of Commandments*, rule 2, pp. 12–13; English translation 2.373–74.

intent except when the classic rabbinic texts expressly mark them as such.[222] As that critic put it, the proposition should be inverted. The presumption should always be that what the rabbis infer from Scripture is genuinely present there, and rabbinic inferences from Scripture hence identify commandments with Mosaic status unless the rabbis expressly label them as *not* doing so.[223] Maimonides had no lack of defenders, and they countered, in good rabbinic style, with a subtle distinction. They explained that although regulations deduced by the ancient rabbis but not marked as part of the Torah are characterized by Maimonides as "rabbinic" in status, he was not—paradoxical though it might sound—denying that such regulations reflect the intent of the Written Torah. He was only saying that despite reflecting Scripture's intent, they do not qualify for enumeration among the critical 613 commandments.[224]

In additional rules, Maimonides asserts that when a positive and a negative commandment cover the same ground, both are to be counted, the positive one—for instance, the obligation to rest on the Sabbath—being enumerated with the positive commandments, and the negative one—the prohibition against working on the Sabbath—with the negative commandments.[225] He posits that unspecific scriptural exhortations to obey God, such as the biblical injunction "be not stiff-necked," do not belong in the list.[226] When a command has components, such as instructions for the several steps in performing a given sacrifice, the subordinate instructions are not to be counted as distinct commandments side by side with the overall command.[227] Thus the regulations governing the slaughtering of a sacrificial animal, receiving its blood in a bowl, carrying the blood to the altar, putting it in designated places there, burning portions of the animal on top of the

[222]Naḥmanides, Critique of Maimonides, *Book of Commandments*, rule 2; Saadia, *Sefer ha-Miṣwot*, ed. Perla (n. 214 above) 1.18–20; Rabinowitz, *Taryag* (n. 193 above) 26–28.

[223]Naḥmanides, Critique of Maimonides, *Book of Commandments*, rule 2.

[224]Duran, *Zohar ha-Raqiᶜa* (n. 194 above) 14–15; I. de Leon, *Megillat Esther*, on Maimonides, *Book of Commandments*, rule 2; Malachi ha-Kohen, *Yad Malachi* (Przemisl 1877) 2, rules regarding Maimonides, §7. Maimonides, Commentary on the Mishna, *Kelim* 17:12, and *Mishneh Torah*: *H. Ishut* 1.2–3, can be read as giving credence to their interpretation.

[225]*Book of Commandments*, rule 6.

[226]*Book of Commandments*, rule 4. See *Sefer Halakhot Gedolot*, ed. E. and N. Hildesheimer, 3, appendix, note 204. The verse is Deuteronomy 10:16.

[227]*Book of Commandments*, rule 10; see *Sefer Halakhot Gedolot*, ed. E. and N. Hildesheimer, 3, appendix, note 432. Rule 11, which apparently is not directed specifically against *Halakot Gedolot*. Rule 12, with undisguised criticism of *Sefer Halakot Gedolot*, although not by name; see *Sefer Halakhot Gedolot*, 3, appendix, notes 411, 454.

Rule 10 addresses the preparations that Scripture requires for the performance of a commandment, such as baking showbread to place in the Temple; Maimonides insists that the placing of the showbread is the commandment. Rule 11 is concerned with separate objects that together form a single commandment, such as the holding of a citron, a palm branch, branches of willow, and branches of myrtle on the Tabernalces holiday. Rule 12 is concerned with the details of performing a commandment, such as the steps in offering a sacrifice; Maimonides' position is that each type of sacrifice as a whole, not the steps in offering it, constitutes a commandment.

altar, and so on, are not separate commandments but components making up a single whole. When Scripture gives alternative instructions for handling a given issue—as when it prescribes different death penalties for different classes of adulteresses—the alternative instructions are, similarly, not to be enumerated as distinct and separate commandments.[228] Regulations with temporary applicability, such as those in force only as long as the Israelites wandered through the wilderness and had not yet entered the Promised Land, are likewise to be excluded.[229] Commandments extending over a number of days, as the requirement that Jewish men dwell in booths during the seven days of the Tabernacles festival, are to be counted only once.[230] With the help of two of his fourteen rules, Maimonides does away with the extra categories—the categories of death penalties and the category of scriptural sections incumbent on the community—that *Sefer Halakot Gedolot* added to the original talmudic dichotomy of positive and negative commandments.[231] In a further rule, he again makes established tradition the ultimate criterion: When Scripture repeats itself and dictates or prohibits the same act in a number of passages, the presumption must be that only a single formal commandment is involved. But there is an exception. Should the Mosaic tradition transmitted by the rabbis state or imply that the repetitions delineate more than one commandment, then more than one must be enumerated.[232] For whatever the rabbinic "interpreters" who "transmit" the Mosaic tradition report must be taken as "the truth," and that is the case even if the "straightforward sense" of Scripture points in another direction.[233] The Mosaic tradition entrusted to the ancient rabbis is once more the decisive factor.

After expounding his rules for determining which laws and rituals should or, in most of the instances, should not be included among the 613 commandments given to Moses at Sinai, Maimonides lists first the 248 positive and then the 365 negative commandments that, in his judgment, qualify. On one occasion, he indicated that he arranged the commandments in the *Book of Commandments* in accordance with a plan.[234] He usually does group related items together within the lists of positive and of negative commandments. Positive commandments relating to the festivals, the justice system, the Holy Temple, sacrifices, and so on form blocks, as do negative commandments having to do with the festivals, forbidden food stuffs, forbidden sexual relations, the nazirite, and other topics. Maimonides also carefully chose the commandments with which the lists of positive and negative

[228] *Book of Commandments*, rule 7. See *Sefer Halakhot Gedolot*, ed. E. and N. Hildesheimer, 3, appendix, note 7.

[229] *Book of Commandments*, rule 3.

[230] *Book of Commandments*, rule 13.

[231] *Book of Commandments*, rules 7 and 14.

[232] *Book of Commandments*, rule 9.

[233] *Book of Commandments*, rule 9, p. 33. See above, pp. 124, 130–31.

[234] Maimonides, *Responsa* (n. 3 above) §447.

commandments open, as well as the commandments with which his entire enumeration closes. Otherwise, it is hard to unearth any overall plan that he may have had in view.[235]

The first item in the positive list is the obligation to "believe that a cause exists which produces all existent things, as embodied in God's saying [at the beginning of the Decalogue]: 'I am the Lord your God'"[236]—in other words, the obligation to believe in the existence of God. The commandments that follow are the obligations to believe in God's unity, to love God, to fear Him, and to worship Him. The first item in Maimonides' list of negative commandments is the prohibition against "believing that divinity pertains to any other being, as embodied in God's saying [in the second of the Ten Commandments] . . . 'thou shalt have no other gods before Me,'"[237] and it is followed by commandments prohibiting various types of idolatry. Each list thus begins with fundamentals of religious belief.

The final three commandments in the *Book of Commandments*, the 611th, 612th, and 613th, are instructions to the king not to "multiply horses to himself," not to "multiply wives to himself," and not to "greatly multiply to himself silver and gold." Scripture explains that the first of the three is designed to prevent anyone who occupies the office of king from sending his people back to Egypt, where the best horses are raised, and that the second has the purpose of ensuring that the king's heart will not turn away from the Lord. Maimonides understands that the last of the three is likewise designed to ensure that the king's heart will not turn away from God.[238] The three commandments are scarcely distinctive in themselves, but Maimonides places them at the very end because they provide a transition to the thought with which he wished to conclude the book.

He takes note of a rabbinic tradition according to which King Solomon sinned by undertaking to observe the intent of the three commandments without observing the commandments themselves.[239] Solomon multiplied horses, being confident that he could do so without sending his subjects back to Egypt, and he multiplied wives and silver, being confident that he would remain true to the Lord. The example of Solomon, who was the wisest of men, reveals—Maimonides writes—why God has kept the specific purposes of most of His commandments hidden from mankind: When someone knows the purpose of a commandment, he may be tempted like Solomon to concern himself only with the intent and make light of the commandment itself. Whereupon Maimonides signs off with the declaration toward which he had been maneuvering for a couple of pages, namely, that although Scripture has a solid rationale for not disclosing the purposes of the divine

[235]An attempt to discover Maimonides' plan is made by A. Hillvitz, "*Seder ha-Miṣwot be-Minyano shel ha-Rambam,*" *Sinai* 10 (1946) 258–67.

[236]Exodus 20:2 and Deuteronomy 5.6. Regarding the term "believe," see below, pp. 234–35.

[237]Exodus 20:3 and Deuteronomy 5.7.

[238]Deuteronomy 17:16–17. See *Book of Commandments*, negative commandment #365.

[239]BT *Sanhedrin* 21b.

commandments, not a single commandment is arbitrary. God framed each of them to serve a specific purpose.[240]

As he lists the positive and then the negative commandments, Maimonides ordinarily devotes a short paragraph to each, but he occasionally writes a page or more. He starts by setting forth the commandment. For instance, negative commandment 172 is the prohibition against eating the flesh of an unclean animal, such as the camel, the pig, and the hare; commandments 173 and 174 are the prohibitions against eating the flesh of an unclean fish or an unclean fowl; commandment 175 is the prohibition against eating "winged swarming things," that is, flying insects; and commandment 184, the prohibition against consuming an animal's blood. With the very few exceptions to which he has been seen to refer, he adduces a verse from the Pentateuch where the commandment is found—for example, "Ye shall eat no manner of blood." In the case of the exceptions, he cites rabbinic sources to prove that although the commandment is not explicit in Scripture, it is marked by the rabbis as one of the 613 communicated to Moses.

After recording the commandment and the proof-text, Maimonides may mention a few of the Written and Oral Torah instructions for fulfilling it; on a later occasion, he would remark that since his object in the *Book of Commandments* was to convey the essence of the commandments and not their details, the instructions he gives for fulfilling the commandments are not always wholly in accord with accepted halakic norms.[241] Where failing to observe a commandment entails a punishment, he tells what the punishment is. He thus writes that eating a quantity the size of an olive of the flesh of an unclean animal, unclean fish, or unclean fowl is punishable by a whipping. He does not specify the kind of blood that is covered by the Mosaic prohibition—according to the classic rabbinic sources Mosaic law prohibits only the blood of animals and fowl—perhaps because he did not want to go into the rabbinic regulations concerning the consuming of the blood of fish, locusts, crawling things, and human beings, which have different halakic statuses from one another. Nor does he define the minimum amount of blood which entails culpability, perhaps because he was unsure at this stage of his studies whether to classify blood as a forbidden food and define the minimum quantity as the size of an olive, or to classify blood as a forbidden beverage and define the minimum quantity somewhat larger. He does, however, state the punishment: Deliberately consuming blood that is prohibited by the Mosaic commandment is punishable by having one's soul cut off by God, that being a more severe punishment than undergoing a whipping at the hands of a human court. Consuming blood inadvertently must be atoned for through the sacrifice of a sin-offering.[242]

[240]*Book of Commandments*, negative commnadment #365.

[241]*Responsa* §310, p. 574. Cf. B. Benedikt, *Ha-Rambam le-lo Seṭiyya min ha-Talmud* (collected articles) (Jerusalem 1985) 126–27.

[242]In *Mishneh Torah*: *H. Ma'akalot Asurot* 6.1, Maimonides treats blood as a food and accordingly defines the minimum quantiy entailing culpability as the size of an olive. See the marginal note in the Frankel edition of the *Mishneh Torah* for a different rabbinic opinion.

When he finds it necessary, Maimonides notes that a commandment has restricted applicability—to an institution, such as the law courts, rather than to individuals; to Israelite males and not to females; to a subgroup within the nation, such as the priestly class, rather than to the population as a whole; solely to persons living in Palestine; or exclusively to periods in history when a Holy Temple stands in Jerusalem.[243] He usually concludes by directing readers to tractates of the Babylonian Talmud where more information concerning the commandment can be found

In a few curious instances, he notes that the Babylonian Talmud records a difference of opinion between the rabbis concerning a given regulation and he shows how one of the recorded opinions entails that the regulation should be enumerated among the 613, while another entails that it should not. Then he gives his reason for preferring one of the opinions over the other—or others—and enumerating or rejecting the commandment, as the case might be. For example: Scripture mandates that men who, for one reason or another, fail to sacrifice the Paschal lamb at the appointed time must compensate by performing the sacrifice exactly a month later. Maimonides observes that the Babylonian Talmud records a difference of opinion between certain rabbis regarding the legal status of the substitute sacrifice, the implication of one opinion being that bringing the substitute Paschal lamb constitutes a commandment in its own right, whereas the implication of another opinion is that the substitute is merely a continuation of the general obligation to sacrifice a Paschal lamb. He determines that the "halaka" is in accordance with the view implying that it is indeed an independent commandment and he therefore includes it as a separate commandment in his enumeration of positive commandments.[244]

We might well suppose that the inclusion of a commandment among the critical 613 would be part of the commandment's interpretation which, as Maimonides told us earlier,[245] was communicated by God to Moses and handed on to later generations. But if such information is part of the transmitted interpretation, the rabbis should never have expressed differences of opinion regarding it, because of another principle set down by Maimonides: He insisted that differences of opinion never occur among the rabbis regarding the Mosaic oral tradition.[246] There seems to be an inconsistency here, and I do not see how it should be resolved.

[243]Maimonides distinguishes commandments of this last sort, which cannot be observed at all times but remain in effect, from commandments that were in effect for a certain period of time, such as the period when the Israelites were in the desert, and then were never in effect again.

[244]*Book of Commandments*, positive commandment #57. Other unambiguous instances: negative commandment #333; introduction, rule 9.

[245]Above, p. 124.

[246]A passage in Maimonides' Commentary on the Mishna and another in his *Book of Commandments* suggest that the requirement that no difference of rabbinic opinion can occur regarding the Mosaic tradition (above, p. 130) applies to each commandment as a whole but not to the commandment's details. J. Levinger, *Darke ha-Maḥshaba ha-Hilkatit shel ha-Rambam*

When Maimonides later wrote that all but three or four items in his list of 613 commandments are "explicit" in the Pentateuch, he used the term *explicit* with a good deal of elasticity. Some of the scriptural proof-texts he cites for supposedly explicit positive commandments do not command anything at all, and some of his texts for explicit negative commandments are scriptural verses that prohibit nothing as they stand and, at best, imply a prohibition. An example of the former is the very first commandment, the obligation to believe in the existence of God. Maimonides' proof-text is the opening statement in the Decalogue: "I am the Lord your God,"[247] but those words form a declarative sentence and do not command either what Maimonides says they do or anything else. He is relying on a talmudic passage that characterizes the opening of what we in English call the Ten Commandments—in Hebrew they are called the ten words, or ten statements[248]—as one of the 613 commandments given to Moses.[249] As an example of the second sort, scriptural verses that at best imply a prohibition, we may take a regulation concerning the "second tithe," the one-tenth portion of harvest produce which, by the Oral Torah understanding of Scripture, is not presented to the Levite but is eaten by the owners themselves in Jerusalem. In his list of negative commandments, Maimonides records the "prohibition against eating the second tithe when in mourning for a dead relative." His proof-text is the scriptural requirement that all Israelites solemnly declare once every three years: "I have not eaten thereof [that is, of the second tithe] in my mourning."[250] The negative commandment turns out to be not an explicit scriptural prohibition but rather an implication of the solemn declaration that Israelites are periodically required to make.

Once Maimonides was satisfied that he had identified a scriptural verse containing a commandment, he invariably read the verse, and construed the commandment, in accordance with the Oral Torah. Some of the constructions he is thereby led to place on scriptural commandments would never occur to anyone not steeped in the rabbinic sources. Scripture, for example, instructs Israelites to "remember the Sabbath day to keep it holy." Maimonides, in his list of positive commandments, writes that Scripture there "commands us to say certain things at the outset and end of the Sabbath day [that is, to recite a *kiddush* prayer at the outset and a *habdala* prayer at the end], in which we proclaim the day's greatness, its exaltedness, and the difference between it and the preceding and following days of

---

(Jerusalem 1965) 63–65, cites writers who take that to be the solution to the problem, but he himself cuts the knot in a different way, by maintaining that Maimonides was being disingenuous in insisting that no differences of opinion occur among the rabbis regarding the Mosaic tradition.

[247]Exodus 20:2.

[248]Exodus 34:28.

[249]*Book of Commandments*, positive commandment #1. Maimonides is relying on BT *Makkot* 24a. Other examples: positive commandments #9, #95, #149, #197.

[250]*Book of Commandments*, negative commandment #151. See Deuteronomy 26:14. Other examples: negative commandments #150, #152, #183. Maimonides justifies instances of this sort in rule 8 (end).

the week."[251] Scripture dictates: "Ye shall not eat with the blood." Maimonides understands that the commandment embodies—among other things—a prohibition against a young man's engaging in gluttony.[252] Scripture states: When two men quarrel "and the wife of the one draweth near to deliver her husband out of the hand of him that smiteth him, and she putteth forth her hand and taketh him by his private parts, then thou shalt cut off her hand; thine eye shall have no pity." At first look, it appears as if divine law is imposing a grotesquely disproportionate punishment on the woman. But in Maimonides' list of commandments, the verse serves as the proof-text for a pair of eminently reasonable positive and negative prescriptions: First, when a person's life is threatened—as when the woman described in Scripture endangers a man's life by taking hold of vulnerable organs—bystanders are commanded to rescue the person even if, in the process of doing so, they have to maim or kill the attacker.[253] Secondly, it is prohibited to have pity on someone who threatens the life of another and refrain from rescuing the victim.[254] In these instances and others of a similar character, Maimonides anchors commandments in scriptural texts that indeed take the form of commands. But he relies completely on the Oral Torah interpretations transmitted by the rabbis when determining what Scripture is commanding.

Even scriptural verses that might seem crystal clear and unproblematic are read through Oral Torah spectacles in Maimonides' *Book of Commandments*. The Decalogue dictates: "Thou shalt not steal." Nothing, one might suppose, could be more straightforward. Yet when Maimonides records the prohibition in his list of negative commandments, he follows the Oral Torah and defines the act of stealing prohibited by the Decalogue as the stealing of a member of the Israelite nation, in other words, as kidnapping a Jewish person.[255] The Book of Deuteronomy mandates: "Fathers shall not be put to death for the children, neither shall children be put to death for the fathers; every man shall be put to death for his own sin." In later books of the Bible itself, the verse is quoted and understood in its obvious sense, as a prohibition against punishing children for their fathers' sins, and vice versa. Maimonides, however, reads the first half of the verse as a commandment concerning the validity of witnesses: Scripture is prohibiting judges from accepting the testimony of fathers regarding their sons, and of sons regarding their fathers.[256] In all of the examples I have given in the present paragraph and the

[251] *Book of Commandments*, positive commandment #155; the verse is Exodus 20:8.

[252] *Book of Commandments*, negative commandment #195; the verse is Leviticus 19:26. See *Book of Commandments*, introduction, rule 9, p. 37, for other prohibitions that, according to the rabbis and Maimonides, are embodied in the same verse.

[253] *Book of Commandments*, positive commandment #247; the verse is Deuteronomy 25:12.

[254] *Book of Commandments*, negative commandment #293.

[255] *Book of Commandments*, negative commandment #243. The verse is Exodus 20:13.

[256] *Book of Commandments*, negative commandment #287. The verses are Deuteronomy 24:16, 2 Kings 14:6, and 2 Chronicles 25:4. Negative commandment #355 is another good example of the point made here.

previous one, Maimonides supports his delineation of what a given commandment embodies by citing appropriate rabbinic sources; in one instance, he expressly writes that he is following the "transmitted interpretation."[257] He is again taking for granted that what the rabbinic sources say regarding the commandments is a part of the Mosaic tradition entrusted to the rabbis and reflects Scripture's true intent.[258]

In sum, Maimonides acknowledges that in three or four instances he had no explicit scriptural basis for the commandments he registers; these receive their certification solely from the rabbinic oral tradition. In other instances, the scriptural verses that he cites as the basis for a commandment either command nothing at all or merely imply a command. In still other instances, the proof-texts he cites from Scripture do plainly command something, but only a person steeped in rabbinic law could understand the scriptural prescriptions as Maimonides does. Even when the scriptural verse he cites is an unambiguous command, Maimonides, without apology, pours the Oral Torah elaboration into the commandment. Once he was sure that a commandment is one of the 613 communicated to Moses, he assumes, with no further ado, that the rabbinic interpretation and elaboration of the commandment are validated by a tradition going back to Moses.

It should be evident by now that his treatment of the 613 commandments is animated throughout by an implicit trust in what he believed to be an unbroken and unerring tradition in the possession of the ancient rabbis. He learned a good part of that tradition from the texts that have, since talmudic times, been recognized as authoritative repositories of the Oral Torah, namely, the Mishna, the Babylonian as well as the Jerusalem Talmud, and the appendix—or parallel—to the Mishna known as the Tosefta. He also draws extensively from what are known as the halakic midrashic compilations, that is, collections of midrashic exegesis of the Pentateuch which date roughly from the mishnaic period and focus primarily on legal matters. These midrashic compilations stand apart, on the one hand, from the Mishna and the Tosefta, which are of the same approximate period and focus on the same legal subjects but do not formulate what they have to say in the midrashic mode. On the other hand, they stand apart from what are known as the aggadic midrashic compilations, which date several centuries later and concern themselves exclusively with nonlegal matters. He draws from the two versions of *Mekilta*, which are compilations of halakic midrashic interpretations on the book of Exodus; from *Sifra*, a halakic compilation on Leviticus; from *Sifre Zuṭa*, a compilation on Numbers; and from *Sifre*, a compilation on both Numbers and Deuteronomy.[259]

[257]*Book of Commandments*, negative commandment #287. The same expression is used in negative commenadment #76, to justify its inclusion among the 613 privileged commandments.

[258]Further examples in Ch. Tchernowitz, *Toledoth ha-Poskim* 1 (New York 1946) 206. What Maimonides says here does not seem to harmonize with what he says about homiletic exegesis, above p. 132. Naḥmanides, Critique of Maimonides, *Book of Commandments*, rule 2, points out problems of a similar sort in Maimonides' stance toward rabbinic tradition.

[259]M. Peritz, "Das Buch der Gesetze," *Moses ben Maimon*, ed. W. Bacher et al., 1 (Leipzig 1908) 471–72. Some of the passages that Maimonides cites from what he calls *Mekilta* relate to

The halakic midrashic compilations were not usually recognized as authoritative for establishing halakic norms. For the purpose of defining the 613 commandments, Maimonides nonetheless treats them as fully authoritative repositories of the Mosaic tradition, comparable in authority to the Mishna, the Tosefta, and the two Talmuds.

He was pleased with his accomplishment, just as he was pleased with his other major works. A decade or more after he completed the *Book of Commandments*, someone who apparently did not know of it wrote asking him why he had, in his code of Jewish law, classified certain commandments as he did. In responding, Maimonides calls his correspondent's attention to the *Book of Commandments* and describes his methodological introduction to the book as "fourteen chapters containing important rules and numerous principles, which are like mountains upon which everything depends." The rules contain what "a person should take firm hold of in enumerating the commandments . . . in order not to enumerate them as many did who lacked reliable criteria. . . . Copies of the book have reached Iraq, the end of the West, and the cities of Christian Europe. If a copy is available to you, every doubt that you might have [regarding the 613 commandments] will evaporate. I am sorry that I wrote the book in Arabic, for everyone needs to read it. I am waiting for the opportunity to translate it—with God's help—into Hebrew."[260] In another letter, likewise written a decade or more after the completion of the *Book of Commandments*, Maimonides similarly praises his introduction to the book as containing "important rules, . . . which a person must know, whereupon he will clearly see the error of everyone, from the author of *Halakot Gedolot* until today, who enumerated the commandments except for me."[261]

Just a very few allusions to philosophic and scientific matters can be uncovered in the *Book of Commandments*[262] and they fade into insignificance when compared with the substantial philosophical and scientific veins running through Maimonides' two other major rabbinic works, his Commentary on the Mishna and his code of Jewish law. The *Book of Commandments* nonetheless opens an invaluable window of its own into his mind and innermost convictions. His

---

verses in the book of Numbers, and not to verses in Exodus; see Peritz, p. 472, note 1. Those passages come from what is more commonly known as *Sifre Zuṭa*.

[260]*Responsa* §447. Since Maimonides' correspondent is writing after Maimonides' *Mishneh Torah* was published, at least a decade had passed since he completed the *Book of Commandments*. Maimonides also expresses his desire to translate the *Book of Commandments* into Hebrew in a letter to Joseph Ibn Jabir, in Shailat, *Letters and Essays of Moses Maimonides* (n. 174 above) 409.

[261]*Responsa* §355, written after the *Mishneh Torah*.

[262]*Book of Commandments*, rule 8, quotes from a logical work of the Arabic philosopher Alfarabi; (see above, p. 98, n. 124). Positive commandment #1 describes God with language that philosophers used for the first cause of the universe. Negative commandment #31 refers to the philosophic theory of imaginative prophecy; see *Guide* 2.37. In negative commandment #179 (end), Maimonides remarks: "Natural science" teaches that wasps, ants, and the like are not born of male and female parents but are generated spontaneously.

Commentary on the Mishna and legal code affirm without reservation that God presented a Written and Oral Torah to Moses and that the rabbis are the repositories of the Oral Torah. Yet readings of Maimonides are afoot today, particularly among scholars who focus on his philosophy, which assert or entail that such affirmations are disingenuous, that Maimonides did not believe in the possibility of God's intervening in the course of history and selecting a specific human being to be the recipient of a unique prophetic message. Scholars construing Maimonides in such a manner cannot have read the *Book of Commandments* with care. Only the most ill-attuned of tin ears could listen to his words—his fervid indignation at the "enormous odiousness" of his predecessors' treatment of the 613 commandments that "were stated to Moses at Sinai" and that "God ordered us to observe"; the pains he takes to formulate comprehensive rules for identifying the commandments received by Moses;[263] his undisguised satisfaction with the rules; his meticulousness in determining what precisely the 613 commandments are; his reliance on the unerring tradition communicated by God to Moses and handed on by the latter, when he had to decide whether or not to include a commandment in the list—without realizing that he was in earnest.[264] He was clearly convinced that precisely 613 privileged commandments had been given by God to Moses, that the ancient rabbis were in possession of an unbroken tradition going back to Moses' unique prophecy, and that his own methodology and enumeration of the commandments had repaired a disgraceful rent in Jewish religious belief. I shall come back to the topic in a later chapter.

The *Book of Commandments*, like Maimonides' Commentary on the Mishna, is written in Judeo-Arabic. With the shift of the center of gravity of rabbinic studies to Jewish communities that read only Hebrew, the need for a Hebrew translation was felt, just as the need was felt for a translation of the Commentary on the Mishna. Maimonides said that he regretted having written the book in Arabic and was waiting for the opportunity to translate it into Hebrew. If the opportunity ever presented itself, he let it slip through his fingers, and the *Book of Commandments* had to be translated by others.

In the century after his death no less than three Hebrew translations were made.[265] Unfortunately, the state of international communication was so poor that

[263]In formulating his ninth rule and having it take account of the pertinent rabbinic texts, he has to invent a bizarre, unknown kind of insect. See *Book of Commandments*, negative commandment #179, and R. Abraham ben David's caustic comment on *Mishneh Torah*: *Ma'akalot Asurot* 2.23.

[264]Levinger, "*ᶜAl Torah she-be ᶜal pe be-Haguto shel ha-Rambam*" (n. 7 above), points out problematic passages in the *Guide for the Perplexed* and argues, pp. 289–90, that Maimonides did not truly believe in the Mosaic origin of rabbinic tradition. Levinger does not take into consideration how critical it was for Maimonides, as seen in his *Book of Commandments* and elsewhere, to determine the precise level of sanction that various commandments carry.

[265]Maimonides, *Sefer ha-Miṣvoth*, ed. Heller (n. 186 above), editor's introduction, pp. 2, 8.

despite the multiple translations, the book did not reach some European Jewish scholars whose admiration for Maimonides was such that they would have pored over anything he wrote about the scriptural commandments had it been available to them.[266] Wherever the book did reach, Maimonides' fourteen rules for identifying the 613 commandments given to Moses and his actual enumeration of the commandments created the framework for study of the issue. Even the chief critic of the *Book of Commandments* praises it, in scriptural phraseology, as a "book that giveth goodly words," and as "dearer than all precious vessels."[267] If Maimonides expected, however, that his *Book of Commandments* would foreclose further speculation, he was unrealistic. The very opposite occurred. His *Book of Commandments* became the catalyst for a new, multifaceted genre of rabbinic literature.

Critiques appeared, most notable that drawn up by Moses Naḥmanides, to which I have referred several times. Naḥmanides was a thirteenth-century rabbinist who equaled Maimonides in breadth of rabbinic knowledge and who possessed one of the sharpest minds in the Jewish Middle Ages; it was he who characterized the *Book of Commandments* as dearer than all precious vessels. Naḥmanides writes that he undertook his critique with the object of defending the honor of *Sefer Halakot Gedolot* against Maimonides' withering attack. But he raises questions unrelated to *Halakot Gedolot* and makes substitutions for about fifty of the commandments that Maimonides enumerated.

By the nature of things, Naḥmanides' critique elicited heated rebuttals from Maimonides' partisans. Authors also came forward who redid the job, drawing up new enumerations of the commandments, which diverged to a greater or lesser extent—although never radically—from Maimonides' list. Commentaries were written on Maimonides' enumeration and on the enumerations of those who differed from him. Compositions appeared that combined a list of the commandments with an exposition of the purposes for which—the proponents thought—God ordained them. Writers exercised their ingenuity through inventing new arrangements of the commandments as enumerated by either Maimonides or someone else. The commandments were, for instance, rearranged in accordance with the weekly synagogue readings from the Pentateuch, or were shown to be all subsumable under the Ten Commandments, or, in one bizarre and deservedly anonymous effort, were all subsumed under the three consonants of the Hebrew name *Moshe*, the Hebrew form of *Moses*. Still other compositions recast the 613 commandments in poetic form. A few even had non-Jews as their authors.[268] The total number of books and commentaries on the subject of the 613 commandments

[266]Maimonides, *Sefer ha-Miṣvoth*, ed. Heller, editor's introduction, p. 2.

[267]Naḥmanides, Critique of Maimonides, *Sefer ha-Miṣwot*, introduction. At the end of his critique of Maimonides' second rule, Naḥmanides writes that the book is "most sweet, yea altogether lovely," with the exception of the second rule.

[268]See A. Jellinek, *Quntres Taryag* (Vienna 1878). Item 51 in his list is the work that subsumes the commandments under the consonants of the name "Moses."

which appeared subsequent to Maimonides' *Book of Commandments* now well exceeds a hundred.[269] His *Book of Commandments* nevertheless remains the foremost text on the subject, and although the second of his fourteen rules for identifying the commandments given by God to Moses aroused controversy, no one, as far as I know, has ever developed an alternative set of criteria for determining what should, and should not, be included.

The notion that there are precisely 613 commandments of the Law has established itself firmly in traditional Jewish circles. The very number 613 and its Hebrew representation, *taryag*, have become common currency, and no child completes a year or two of traditional Jewish education without being exposed to it. Nevertheless, and despite the gallons of ink and reams of paper expended on the subject, the genre remains a secondary one in the rabbinic literary constellation. It rests, after all, on nothing more than an, admittedly fruitful, aggadic remark in the Babylonian Talmud.

[269] Jellinek, *Quntres Taryag*, lists 144 works written on the subject of the 613 commandments, over 100 of them subsequent to Maimonides. Further works on the subject have been written since Jellinek.

4

Rabbinic Works II

> In the deciding of halakic norms for the entire Talmud and for all laws of the Torah, no one has preceded me since the time of Judah the Prince and his holy collaborators [who compiled the Mishna corpus]. (Letter to Pinḥas of Alexandria, regarding the *Mishneh Torah*)
>
> In the time to come . . . all Israel will use only my composition, and every other will undoubtedly be disregarded. (Letter to Joseph ben Judah, regarding the *Mishneh Torah*)

The Mishneh Torah, Maimonides' Code of Jewish Law. Halaka, the legal and ritual side of rabbinic literature, makes up over 95 percent of the subject matter of Judah the Prince's Mishna corpus. The Palestinian Talmud and, even more, the Babylonian Talmud cast a broader net, but as long as they perform their primary task of expanding upon the Mishna, halaka is their subject matter as well. The halakic system contemplated by these works is designed to govern every aspect of human life, secular as well as religious, communal as well as individual. It stretches out its wings to embrace commercial activity, civil and criminal liability, agriculture, sexual behavior, marriage, divorce, contractual arrangements between husband and wife, inheritances, education, the structure of the courts, trial procedure, oaths and vows, permitted and forbidden food stuffs, Sabbath and festival observance, prayer, the Holy Temple and its rites, the removal of every whiff of idolatry from Jewish life, ritual impurity, sanctions to be imposed on those who fail to obey the regulations, and more. If the commandments given to Moses numbered 613, the halakic regulations in the Mishna and two Talmuds are more than ten times as numerous.

In their halakic statements, the Mishna and two Talmuds almost always look at hypothetical and representative specific cases; to take a much cited example, instead of establishing a general principle for adjudicating conflicting claims over property, they prescribe the measures to be taken should two persons appear in court holding, and laying claim to, the same garment. The occasional general rules appearing in the Mishna seemed so anomalous that when they do occur, the Babylonian Talmud often expresses wonder that the redactor of the Mishna took the trouble to include them and then asks what the redactor intended to add to the specifics by supplying the rules.

Although the Mishna has halaka as its subject matter and although it contemplates a system of regulations that would govern virtually every aspect of human activity, one cannot say without qualification that its object is to state halakic norms, to tell people what to do and what to refrain from doing under various circumstances. To make such an assertion about the two Talmuds, to say without qualification that their object is to furnish norms, would be still more misleading. The three corpuses do at times delineate exactly which business practices, foods, sexual relations, religious acts, and the like are permitted, which are mandatory, and which forbidden, and how to redress missteps. But they plainly have something further in view.

Certain rabbis of the Mishna period erected so intricate a network of provisos around three particular scriptural commandments that, according to the classic rabbinic sources themselves, the commandments in question could not possibly have been practiced. The rabbis who heaped up the provisos are understood to have believed that the three commandments, as promulgated by Scripture and developed by the Oral Law, were never meant to be put into effect; they were there solely in order that a student might "study and receive reward therefor."[1] At times, the Mishna prescribes unambiguously what should or should not be done under specified conditions, but the conditions are such that no human being could possibly determine whether they had been fulfilled.[2] Regulations of the sort are also perforce theoretical. The Mishna spells out details for other procedures that, it says, went out of practice centuries earlier and would never be reinstituted. By the time the Mishna was redacted, these too had become purely theoretical.[3]

The Mishna is moreover notorious for recording disagreements, for reporting that Rabbi X stated A and Rabbi Y stated not-A. It does have a few devices for disclosing which of the differing opinions represents the norm. On occasion, it expressly labels one as the *halaka*, that is, as authoritative. More often, it indicates the same indirectly by labeling an opinion as the view of the majority—or, in its terminology, the view of the "sages"—rather than that of an individually named

[1]BT *Sanhedrin* 71a, and parallels in the Tosefta and Palestinian Talmud. The commandments are: Leviticus 14:34–53 (the leprous house); Deuteronomy 13:13–18 (the idolatrous city); Deuteronomy 21:18–21 (the rebellious son). Maimonides records the rabbinic regulations governing all three in his code.

[2]For example: Mishna, *Ḥullin* 2:1; *Oholot* 3:1–5; 4:3–4; 13:5; *Miqwa'ot* 7:6; *Nidda* 2:5; *Zabim* 1:6.

[3]Mishna, *Soṭa* 9:9.

rabbi.[4] It nonetheless also frequently records the differing opinions of two or more individual rabbis on a given issue without marking any as the view of the majority. If its aim were to establish what should and should not be done and nothing else, why, one cannot help asking, does it report demurring opinions alongside those that it recommends? And why does it repeatedly record disagreements on a given issue without disclosing which view it deems correct? The Mishna corpus itself poses the first of the two questions and offers answers.[5] It does not address the second.

The two Talmuds also sometimes label one or another of the opposing opinions recorded in a given Mishna paragraph or that they cite from other sources as *the halaka*.[6] They, further, offer rules for deciding which of the opposing opinions they cite is authoritative in a number of the instances where neither they nor the Mishna marks any as such. Thus they state criteria for determining when anonymous—as distinct from majority—opinions in the Mishna are, and when they are not, to be considered normative.[7] They provide a few rules for deciding which individual opinion should be followed in instances where Mishna paragraphs record neither a majority nor an anonymous ruling but only the divergent positions of individual rabbis. They do so by assigning greater weight to certain rabbis over against others.[8] The Babylonian Talmud tells us, for instance, that when differences between R. Akiba or R. Judah the Prince and other individuals are reported, Akiba's view or Judah the Prince's view takes precedence over the others.[9]

The two Talmuds thereby set the norm for some of the issues that the Mishna left undetermined and furnish criteria for ascertaining it on others. But they take back at least as much as they give: They do not hesitate to raise doubts about rulings that the Mishna had, in one way or another, indicated are authoritative.[10] And they bring up hundreds of additional possible situations, which the Mishna,

[4]Mishna, *ᶜEduyyot* 1:5, states the rule that the majority opinion is authoritative.

[5]Mishna, *ᶜEduyyot* 1:4–6. Three answers are given: The recording of rejected opinions of great scholars reveals their willingness to be corrected. The recording of minority opinions provides future rabbinic courts with additional options, should they need them in emergencies. If someone reports that he knows a tradition which diverges from the accepted norm stated in the Mishna, the newly reported tradition can be identified as one of the minority, and hence rejected, opinions recorded in the Mishna.

[6]For the Palestinian Talmud see M. Kosovsky, *Concordance to the Talmud Yerushalmi* (Jerusalem 1979–), entry *halaka.* For the Babylonian Talmud, see Ch. Kasovsky, *Thesaurus Talmudis* (Jerusalem 1954–1982), entries *halaka, hilketa.*

[7]PT *Taᶜanit* 2:13; BT *Yebamot* 42b.

[8]S. Assaf, *Tequfat ha-Geonim we-sifrutah* (Jerusalem 1955) 148.

[9]BT *ᶜErubim* 46b. For other rules in the Babylonian and Palestinian Talmuds, see Samson of Chinon, *Sefer Keritut* (Jerusalem 1965) 4.3; J. Ḥagiz, excerpts from *ᶜEṣ Ḥayyim*, printed in the introduction to the Romm editions of the Mishna.

[10]BT *Baba Batra* 130b, expresses reservations as to whether all opinions marked as *halaka* in a talmudic context are binding. BT *Nidda* 7b states that even opinions that are explicitly labeled as *halaka* in the Mishna are not necessarily to be accepted as normative.

notwithstanding its exhaustiveness, fails to address; and after spinning a dialectical web around them, they more often than not neglect to state what the authoritative position is.

These traits, which are familiar to all students of rabbinic literature, can hardly be inadvertent. They reveal that creating a body of material for study was at least as important for the Mishna and two Talmuds as prescribing the halaka to be followed in each instance. And in that respect the rabbinic texts have been eminently successful. Through the centuries, they, and particularly the Babylonian Talmud, have served as the subject matter of higher education for hundreds of thousands of Jewish students. Hundreds of thousands of working men have, through the centuries, spent their leisure time studying the Mishna and Babylonian Talmud, and outdated though such study might appear to modern eyes, the number of persons engaged in it at all levels has expanded steadily and substantially during recent decades. The other side of the coin is that anyone desiring to know what he is expected to do or not to do in a particular situation may be left in the dark. Maimonides' Commentary on the Mishna undertook to supply the lack insofar as the Mishna corpus is concerned.[11] He drew upon the resources available to him and, for virtually every paragraph in the Mishna, stated which opinion was, in his judgment, normative.

Not only do the Mishna and two Talmuds repeatedly fail to state or indicate which position should be followed on a given issue; there are additional stumbling blocks to using them as a guide in legal and ritual matters. Topics can crop up in unexpected places. To take a few well–known instances: Regulations governing the wearing of phylacteries and instructions for knotting fringes on the corners of garments are incorporated into the mishnaic tractate whose announced subject is the bringing of meal offerings in the Temple. The means whereby different categories of property can be legally conveyed from one party to another are treated in the mishnaic tractate devoted to betrothal of a bride. The distinction between different levels of impurity associated with genital discharges is taken up in the tractate whose subject is the Purim holiday. Even when the Mishna and two Talmuds do not stray from their formal topic, they barely ever organize their material in what a reader today would consider a logical fashion. And topics are occasionally treated in the Mishna, and typically treated in the Talmud corpuses, in more than one location; the several treatments sometimes agree with each other, sometimes complement each other, and sometimes conflict. Unless a person has the entire mishnaic and talmudic literature at his fingertips, he can never be sure that he has taken into account everything pertinent to a given halakic issue, and when the texts conflict, he will easily find himself in a quandary. Maimonides mentioned considerations of the sort when listing the functions that he intended his Commentary on the Mishna to serve.[12]

[11] Above, p. 50.

[12] See above, pp. 149–50.

The state of affairs cried out for a new rabbinic genre, for compositions that would take account of everything pertinent in the Mishna and two Talmuds, apply established criteria, determine norms for the myriad cases touched upon in those works, and present their findings in a format that could be navigated with ease. In a word, the situation cried out for law codes based on the pertinent rabbinic sources and organized logically.[13]

Though the need should have been obvious from the moment that the Babylonian Talmud underwent redaction, it was apparently not acted on immediately. The earliest known rabbinic law code appeared in eighth-century Iraq. By Maimonides' day, a number of codes were in circulation; he refers to some by name and reveals knowledge of others. For our purpose it will be helpful to consider two types of code which had appeared by his time.

The first comprises codes of a comprehensive character. These state norms for a wide spectrum of subjects, although with the consistent exclusion of that—notably Temple ritual and most of the impurity laws—which was no longer practiced in their day. The initial crop of such works carry the term *Halakot* in their titles, thereby announcing their character—they are comprehensive collections of halakot. Maimonides names five. Posttalmudic authorities, he writes, "produced compositions on the subject of halakic norms in Arabic and Hebrew, such as *Halakot Gedolot*, *Halakot Qeṭuᶜot*, *Halakot Pesuqot*, the *Halakot* [better known as the *She'iltot*] of R. Aḥa of Shabḥa, and more. But the *Halakot* produced by the great rabbi, our master Isaac [Alfasi], renders all the others dispensable."[14] Maimonides must here be using the term "Hebrew" in a loose sense that includes Aramaic. Four of the five books he names were written not in Hebrew but in Aramaic, and that was the language most commonly used in codes of the present type.[15]

The code from the Iraqi region which attained the widest circulation was the ninth-century *Sefer Halakot Gedolot*, a work we met earlier in connection with the issue of the 613 commandments received by Moses at Sinai.[16] The title literally means: *Book of Large Halakot*; it can be translated more idiomatically as *A Comprehensive Collection of Halakot*. *Sefer Halakot Gedolot* undertakes to rule on all issues treated in the Mishna corpus and Babylonian Talmud which still had practical bearing in its day. It does so by copying out and lightly paraphrasing halakic portions of the Mishna and Babylonian Talmud, omitting the dialectical give and take as well as almost all nonlegal, or aggadic, material, and then marking the opinion to be followed in each instance either expressly or—by recording the one it prefers and omitting demurring opinions—indirectly. Although *Halakot Gedolot*

[13]These are codes in the sense of corpuses that undertake to record the law, as distinct from codes in the sense of corpuses that undertake to legislate and create law. See M. Elon, *Jewish Law* (Philadelphia 1994) 3.1144–47, for the distinction.

[14]Maimonides, Commentary on the Mishna (=*Mishna ᶜim Perush R. Moshe ben Maimon*), ed. J. Kafah (Jerusalem 1963–1968), introduction, pp. 46–47.

[15]See S. Baron, *Social and Religious History of the Jews* 6 (Philadelphia 1958) 78–87.

[16]Above, p. 170.

presents its materials more or less in the order in which they appear in the Babylonian Talmud, the author allows himself a degree of freedom: He creates new headings. When general material on a given subject comes at a late stage of a tractate of the Mishna or the Babylonian Talmud, he does not hesitate to move it forward to the beginning, so that readers will encounter the general before the particular. Where the Babylonian Talmud takes a subject up in more than one tractate, he often gathers all the material together in a single place. He incorporates a few rulings from the Tosefta—the appendix to the Mishna—and the Palestinian Talmud. And he takes account of posttalmudic halakic developments. *Halakot Gedolot* nevertheless advances only a moderate distance beyond the classic sources in the direction of a logical arrangement that would enable users not entirely at home in the Babylonian Talmud to find what they seek.

The code that Maimonides was just seen to laud most warmly was the *Halakot* of the eleventh-century R. Isaac, whose family came from the city Fez in Morocco and who is therefore commonly known as Alfasi.[17] Alfasi spent the larger part of his long life in North Africa but in his seventies crossed the Mediterranean Sea to Muslim Spain, where he assumed the presidency of an already existing rabbinic academy at Lucena. His successor in the Lucena academy was Joseph Ibn Migas, the man under whom Maimonides' father studied and whom Maimonides regarded as an incomparable talmudic scholar.

His *Halakot* followed the pattern set by previous *Halakot* in covering a wide spectrum of subjects while at the same time limiting itself to those that still had practical application, and it can be seen as perfecting the procedure of *Sefer Halakot Gedolot*. Alfasi went through the Mishna and the Babylonian Talmud and copied out their contents while leaving aside what was no longer practiced, most of the dialectical give and take, and almost everything of a nonhalakic character. He too did not hesitate to shift material from one place to another—from other sections of the tractate at hand, from other tractates, from the Palestinian Talmud—in order that everything pertinent would be brought to bear on the particular issue he was treating; but the basic structure of the Babylonian Talmud remained. When his presentation did not itself make the opinion he accepted obvious, he generally marked it explicitly, although on occasion he recorded differing opinions without expressly saying which he accepted. And he took account of posttalmudic legal developments. Alfasi deftly restitched all the components into a smooth-flowing whole, his own comments and transitions being written in an Aramaic with a distinct, posttalmudic flavor.[18] In essence, his *Halakot* is an epitome of the parts of the Babylonian Talmud that still had practical application. With all its elegance and authority, it too lacks the logical arrangement that would enable users to find what they need with ease.

[17]He himself apparently was not born in Fez. See B. Benedikt, "*He^carot le-Toledot ha-Rif*," *Kiryat Sefer* 27 (1951) 119–20.

[18]Printed editions also include a few Arabic excursuses.

In the context where Maimonides writes that Alfasi's work rendered other collections of *halakot* dispensable, he adds that he disagreed with Alfasi's opinion on fewer than ten issues.[19] On a later occasion, he remarks that his disagreements with Alfasi extended, at the time, to about thirty items;[20] scholars have, nonetheless, uncovered a larger number of disagreements. A letter that Maimonides wrote after completing his own code names the rabbinic texts apart from his code which he was reading with students, and the only ones named are the Babylonian Talmud and Alfasi's *Halakot*.[21] Notwithstanding his respect for Alfasi, he does not hesitate to tell the same correspondent that his own code outstrips Alfasi's.[22]

An additional code of the same type, *Halakot Qeṣubot*, has features that deserve to be mentioned. *Halakot Qeṣubot*, which may be identical with the work that Maimonides calls *Halakot Qeṭu*ᶜ*ot*,[23] differs from other exemplars of its kind inasmuch as it is written in Hebrew, rather than in Aramaic. In that respect, it was not strictly unique, for another of the comprehensive codes circulated in both the Aramaic original and a Hebrew translation.[24] But it differs in a couple of further noteworthy respects as well: Unlike the remaining members of the type, it recasts the talmudic material it draws upon in its own words, a feature that goes hand in hand with its reproducing in Hebrew what the Babylonian Talmud expressed in Aramaic. And it systematically avoids citing the classic rabbinic sources to support its rulings.[25]

Such are the comprehensive codes. The second type of code which is pertinent for our purpose comprises dozens of compositions produced by three *geonim*, or provosts, of the Iraqi rabbinic academies in the tenth century, namely, Saadia Gaon,[26] Samuel ben Ḥofni,[27] and Hai Gaon.[28] Most codes of this type have been lost and are known only by name, but some have survived in whole or in part. All apparently were written in Arabic. The ones that have survived wholly or in part as well as the titles of those that have not reveal several significant departures from the *Halakot* format. Each limits itself to a single, carefully circumscribed legal or ritual

[19] Commentary on the Mishna, introduction, p. 47.

[20] Maimonides, *Responsa*, ed. J. Blau, 2nd ed. (Jerusalem 1986) §251.

[21] Letter to Pinḥas of Alexandria, in I. Shailat, *Letters and Essays of Moses Maimonides* (in Hebrew) (Jerusalem 1987–1988) 439.

[22] Shailat, *Letters and Essays of Moses Maimonides* 444.

[23] Above, p. 193. N. Danzig, *Introduction to Halakhot Pesuqot* (in Hebrew) (New York 1993) 54–56, thinks that *Halakot Qetu*ᶜ*ot* is identical with *Halakot Pesuqot* and that Maimonides is therefore recording a doublet.

[24] *Hilkot Re'u* was a Hebrew translation of *Halakot Pesuqot.*

[25] *Halachot Kezuboth* (*Halakot Qeṣubot*), ed. M. Margulies (Jerusalem 1942).

[26] Saadia, *Traité des successions* (*Sefer ha-Yerushot*), ed. J. Müller (Paris 1897). L. Ginzberg, *Geonica* (New York 1909) 1.165–66.

[27] S. Assaf, "*Shelosha Sefarim Niftaḥim li-Rab Shemu'el ben Ḥofni*," in *Zikkaron li-Nishmat R. A. Y. Kuk*, ed. J Fishman (Maimon) (Jerusalem 1945) 117–59; S. Abramson, "*Mi-Sifre Rab Shemu'el ben Ḥofni*," *Tarbiz* 17 (1946) 138–64.

[28] R. Hai Gaon, *Meqqaḥ u-Memkar* (Vienna 1800); *Mishpete Shebu*ᶜ*ot* (Jerusalem n.d.).

subject. The codifiers, as far as can be judged from the preserved examples, ignored the arrangement that their subject matter had taken in the Mishna and the Babylonian Talmud and replaced it with a topical arrangement of their own. In almost all cases, the codifier supports the norms that he sets down through citations from the Mishna and Babylonian Talmud, but in one instance, Saadia's digest of inheritance law, a different procedure is followed in that respect too. Like *Halakot Qeṣubot*, Saadia's inheritance code—at least in the preserved version—presents its rulings without reference to the mishnaic or talmudic sources from which he drew.[29]

When Maimonides came on the scene, a variety of forms thus awaited him: comprehensive codes, which, however, restricted themselves to laws and rituals still practiced in posttalmudic times; narrow codes, focused on specific, carefully circumscribed subjects; codes in which the authors remained faithful to the arrangement that the pertinent material had in the classic rabbinic sources, and others whose authors ignored the original arrangement and devised their own topical schemes; codes that support their rulings by citing sources in the classic rabbinic texts, and one or two that present their rulings without doing so; the use by the codifiers of the Aramaic and Arabic languages, as well as, in at least one instance, of Hebrew. From these precedents, Maimonides fashioned something unprecedented.

His law code is comprehensive in conception, but to a greater extent than that of any of his predecessors, for he did not restrict himself to regulations in actual practice in his day. He undertook, as he writes in the introduction, to record every regulation of the Oral Torah, whether found in the Mishna corpus, the Babylonian and Jerusalem Talmuds, the Tosefta, or the classic compilations of halakic midrashic material, so that "the entire Oral Torah" would be accessible to "all readers."[30] Even more, his code would encapsulate "the entire Oral Torah, together with the positive ordinances, customs, and negative ordinances, enacted from the time of Moses until the compilation of the Talmud."[31] It would, in other words, comprise the details and interpretations of the Written Torah which were communicated by God to Moses and which alone constitute Oral Torah in Maimonides' sense of the term; and in addition, rabbinic innovations from subsequent periods—the observance of the Purim and Hanukkah holidays, the

[29]S. Abramson, "*Ha-Geniza she-be-Tok ha-Geniza*," *Proceedings of the Rabbinical Assembly of America* 15 (1951) 228, found fragments of a manuscript of the work in which the talmudic sources are cited. A fragment of a different specialized code of Saadia's published by S. Schechter, *Saadyana* (Cambridge 1903) 40–41, also cites proof-texts from the rabbinic sources.

[30]Maimonides, *Mishneh Torah*, introduction. Maimonides' statements on the scope of his code and his motives for composing it, cited in this and the following paragraph, are translated and discussed in I. Twersky, *Introduction to the Code of Maimonides* (New Haven 1980) 24–47.

[31]*Mishneh Torah*, introduction. It will be noted that Maimonides here uses the term *Oral Law* in the sense of the Mosaic tradition, to the exclusion of the subsequent contributions of the rabbis.

divers ordinances enacted by the rabbis for one purpose or another, and so on—which are not Oral Torah in his usage.[32] He scrupulously records items that were no longer in practice and, as he states, were never expected to be put into practice again.[33] A few years after completing the project, he wrote to an acquaintance that "in the deciding of halakic norms for the entire Talmud and for all laws of the Torah, no one has preceded me since the time of Judah the Prince and his holy collaborators [who compiled the Mishna corpus]."[34]

Maimonides' design, then, was to determine halakic norms for the entire spectrum of rabbinic law, both in areas that still did, and those that did not, have practical application in his day. His code was to be comprehensive in another respect as well. In contrast to his predecessors, who based their codes on the Mishna corpus and Babylonian Talmud with sparing use of the Palestinian Talmud, he undertook to extract the halakic norms stated or implied not only in the Mishna corpus and two Talmuds, but also in the other classical rabbinic writings.[35] It should nonetheless be stressed that whenever the Mishna corpus and Babylonian Talmud treat a legal issue, they retain their primacy for him and only very seldom, if indeed ever, does he diverge from them.[36]

To reflect its character, Maimonides named his work the *Mishneh Torah.* The term, much like the Greek *deuteronomy*, means "second Law" or "reiteration of the Law," and both the Hebrew and Greek terms, *mishneh torah* and *deuteronomy*, derive from a phrase in the fifth book of the Pentateuch, the book that we in fact know as Deuteronomy.[37] *Mishneh Torah* was itself one of the old rabbinic names for that book of the Pentateuch and it was the name that Maimonides himself ordinarily used.[38] When the two terms—*Mishneh Torah* and Deuteronomy—are employed as names for the biblical book, they embody the notion that the fifth book of the Pentateuch is a second Law, or the reiteration of the first four books. Maimonides explains that he chose *Mishneh Torah* as the title of his code because "a man may first read the Written Law and then read the present work. He will learn from it the entire Oral Law, and he will not need any further work besides the two."[39] In other words, Maimonides' *Mishneh Torah* is a second Law not so

[32]See above, p. 125.

[33]For example, *Mishneh Torah*: *H. Roṣe'aḥ* 9.12, and *H. Soṭa* 3.19, following Mishna *Soṭa* 9:9.

[34]Letter to Pinḥas of Alexandria, in Shailat, *Letters and Essays of Moses Maimonides* (n. 21 above) 439–40.

[35]See Twersky, *Introduction to the Code of Maimonides* 10, note 12.

[36]See below, pp. 218–19.

[37]Deuteronomy 17:18: "He [the king] shall write him a *copy of this law* [*mishneh torah*]. . . ."

[38]*Book of Commandments*, negative commandment #175; *Mishneh Torah*: *H. Tefilla* 13.2; 7; *H. Ma'akalot Asurot* 1.14; *H. ᶜAbadim* 1.1; *Guide for the Perplexed* 2.34, p. 76a. Maimonides also, less frequently, called Deuteronomy *Eleh ha-Debarim*; see *H. Ḥagiga* 3.3.

[39]*Mishneh Torah*, introduction.

much in the sense of a reprise as in the sense of a complement. It is designed to serve as a full and sufficient complement of the Written Torah.

The specialized codes composed by the three tenth-century provosts of the Iraqi academies set aside the arrangement that the limited material falling within their ken had in the Mishna and two Talmuds. Maimonides follows their example in his comprehensive code. He dismantles the ancient rabbinic edifices and rearranges the bricks out of which they were constructed in a new logical structure. On one occasion he writes of his *Mishneh Torah*: It "assembles [*meqqabeṣ*] all the regulations promulgated on a given subject . . . so that the halakot relating to the subject would not be separated and scattered in a variety of places."[40] On another occasion, he declaims more colorfully that he "brought together things which were separated and scattered, between the hills and mountains; I beckoned to them, 'one of a city and two of a family.'"[41] He rearranged the regulations scattered through the classic rabbinic sources so that everything belonging together would be placed under the appropriate heading.

Both the comprehensive and the specialized law codes omitted most or all of the dialectical reasoning that forms the connective tissue of the two Talmuds. Maimonides, in a similar spirit, undertakes systematically to omit the dialectical give and take, or, as he puts it, all raising of "difficulties" and "resolving" them.[42] He does so, according to his introduction to the code, in order that readers would find everything "clear and ready at hand,"[43] in other words, for purposes of presentation and pedagogy. But his motive was deeper. In a letter to Joseph ben Judah he encourages Joseph to base his rabbinic studies on the *Mishneh Torah* and Alfasi's epitome of the Babylonian Talmud. Whenever Joseph discovers a discrepancy between the two, he should turn to the talmudic sources and seek the reason for it. He should not, however, "waste time" studying "interpretative comments" (*perushim*), such as those written for the purpose of unraveling the dialectic intricacies (*ta*ᶜ*qīd*) in the Talmud; for Maimonides' *Mishneh Torah* has exempted students of the Law from expending their time and energy in that sort of activity.[44]

A statement along the same lines but more radical is transmitted by an unidentified author who lived a generation or two after Maimonides and had contact with his son. The man in question has left a short piece, written in a highly partisan tone, in praise of Maimonides' *Mishneh Torah* and he quotes from letters that, he reports, Maimonides wrote regarding the book. One of them, addressed again to Joseph ben Judah, is preserved in another source, and its authenticity therefore has

[40]Letter to Pinḥas of Alexandria, in Shailat, *Letters and Essays of Moses Maimonides* 444.

[41]*Responsa* 3.57. The biblical phrase is from Jeremiah 3.14.

[42]*Mishneh Torah*, introduction: *qushya* and *peruq*.

[43]*Mishneh Torah*, introduction. In the Letter to Pinḥas of Alexandria, in Shailat, *Letters and Essays of Moses Maimonides* 440, Maimonides explains that he omitted the talmudic dialectic because he was writing a "composition" (or "compilation") rather than a "commentary."

[44]Moses ben Maimon, *Epistulae*, ed. D. Baneth (Jerusalem 1946) 69.

independent corroboration. The letter of interest here, which is also quoted in Maimonides' name, is not otherwise known. The author of the partisan piece is the only warrant for its authenticity.

Maimonides, he tells us, wrote in this other letter that the "primary purpose" of the classic rabbinic texts was to make known "what a man is obliged to do and from what he is obliged to refrain." The "give and take" that is ubiquitous in the two Talmuds and makes its appearance to a much lesser extent in other classic rabbinic texts occurs, by contrast, only "incidentally." It was resorted to when a "statement" (*kalām*)—which might mean either a passage of the Bible or a rabbinic opinion—gave rise to multiple interpretations, and rabbis belonging to a subsequent generation disagreed about what the correct interpretation is. In cases of the sort, different rabbis might deploy dialectical reasoning in support of their differing interpretations of the statement. Their reasoning serves only to establish which of the interpretations is correct; it is a means to an end and not an end in itself. The letter attributed to Maimonides moreover observes: Rabbinic studies have unfortunately come on bad times, and the true intent of the classic literature has been forgotten. Scholars were now taking as their "object . . . the waste of time" of studying talmudic argumentation for its own sake, "as if the purpose and object [in studying the classic rabbinic texts] were nothing other than an exercise in dialectic."[45] Not only, then, were posttalmudic commentaries that endeavor to decipher the intricacies of the talmudic dialectic a waste of time. Studying the talmudic argumentation for its own sake was no less so.[46]

Maimonides' position in the two letters, if we accept the one by the unidentified author as authentic, is that talmudic dialectic was only a means for discovering what Jews are obliged to do and refrain from doing. Once the obligations became known to the rabbis and once they have been made known to the student of rabbinic literature, the argumentation no longer serves a purpose. As a consequence, now that Maimonides has deciphered the reasoning and established the halakic norm in each and every instance for readers of the *Mishneh Torah*, students need study only the result; they are exempt from retracing the argumentation leading up to it. These statements by Maimonides do not harmonize well with a paragraph in the *Mishneh Torah*, based in turn on a passage in the Babylonian Talmud, which recommends spending a third or more of one's study day in drawing talmudic analogies and inferences.[47] And they represent a highly unconventional stand within the rabbinic

[45] A. Halkin, "*Sanegorya al Sefer Mishneh Torah*," *Tarbiz* 25 (1956) 417, 423.

[46] Maimonides may be saying the same in *Epistulae* 69.

[47] *Mishneh Torah*: *H. Talmud Torah* 1.11–12. Maimonides goes on to say that after a person masters the first two areas of Jewish study, namely, Scripture and Oral Law—Oral Law being the Mosaic tradition as recorded in the Mishna corpus and elsewhere—he should devote even more than a third of one's time to drawing talmudic analogies and inferences. The passage is problematic, however, since the segment of Jewish study consisting in talmudic analogies and inferences includes, according to Maimonides, the study of science and philosophy.

community. The prevailing view in rabbinic circles from the redaction of the Mishna corpus until today has been that immersing oneself in the dialectic argumentation of the ancient rabbis, rethinking and reliving it for its own sake, has incomparable religious value. During the years that Maimonides composed his code, students in the rabbinic schools of central France were not only immersing themselves in the argumentation of the Babylonian Talmud; they were fashioning subtle tools for propelling dialectical reasoning in the talmudic mode to new heights.

Although he consistently omits the dialectic argumentation that is characteristic of the Babylonian and Palestinian Talmuds, Maimonides does allow himself to incorporate midrashic rationales for a considerable number of regulations in the *Mishneh Torah*[48]—this despite his insistence that the authenticity of the Oral Torah is grounded in the tradition going back to Moses, and the midrashic and dialectic reasoning supporting that tradition is secondary.[49] To take an illustration: In the section on mourning, he is not satisfied with stating that a person in mourning for a close relative is not permitted to cut his hair, wash his clothes, wash his body, or anoint himself with oil. After recording those prohibitions, he continues: "And whence do we know that it is forbidden for the mourner to cut his hair? The children of Aaron [the priest] were commanded [after close relatives had just died]: 'Let not the hair of your head go loose.' By implication, cutting hair is forbidden to all who are *not* priestly mourners; *they* must let it grow loose."[50] "And whence do we know that it is forbidden for the mourner to wash his clothes, to wash his body, and to anoint himself? As is written [in the case of a woman who was commissioned to act out the role of a mourner]: 'Feign thyself to be a mourner, and put on mourning apparel [which is assumed to mean clothes that have not been washed], and anoint not thyself with oil.' As for washing the body, it is included in anointing; for washing precedes anointing, as is written [in the case of yet another biblical figure, and in a context wholly unrelated to mourning:] 'Wash thyself and anoint thee.'"[51]

It is to be noted that when deciding halakic norms, Maimonides gave preference to what emerges "straightforwardly" from the Babylonian and Palestinian Talmuds over the implications of the dialectical reasoning recorded in the two Talmuds; see below, p. 219.

[48]Examples are given by Ch. Tchernowitz, *Toledoth ha-Poskim* 1 (New York 1946) 202–6. Tchernowitz supposes that Maimonides entered into such explanations in order to refute the ideology of the Karaites.

[49]Above, pp. 129–33.

[50]*Mishneh Torah*: *H. Abel* 5.1–2, based on BT *Mo*ᶜ*ed Qaṭan* 14b. The scriptural verse is Leviticus 10:6. The Babylonian Talmud and Maimonides are interpreting the verse midrashically, since the prohibition against priests' letting their hair grow in a state of mourning does not logically entail a prohibition against other mourners' cutting theirs.

[51]*Mishneh Torah*: *H. Abel* 5.3, based on BT *Mo*ᶜ*ed Qaṭan* 15a–b. The scriptural verses are 2 Samuel 14.2 and Ruth 3:3. Unless Maimonides had an additional source that can no longer be identified, he has thoroughly reworked the material.

Besides incorporating a number of midrashic rationales from the rabbinic sources, Maimonides often finds the midrashic rationales important enough to rework them, as he does, for example, in connection with the mourning regulations just quoted.[52] He sometimes goes as far as to generate interpretations of Scripture of his own which, from our vantage point at least, are midrashic in nature,[53] although it always remains possible that he regarded some of them as straightforward interpretations of Scripture and hence not midrashic at all. It is hard to determine whether he introduces midrashic reasoning where he does haphazardly, merely because a notion or catena of notions happens to have caught his fancy, or whether he does so with a definite plan. If he did have an object in view when introducing such reasoning in certain places but not in others, no one has yet been able to unearth it.

In what became a highly controversial feature of the *Mishneh Torah*, Maimonides follows the model of *Halakot Qeṣubot* and the preserved version of Saadia's code of inheritance law and offers his rulings without citing the rabbinic sources on which they are based.[54] The introduction to the *Mishneh Torah* names the rabbinic works—the Mishna corpus, the Tosefta, the Babylonian and Palestinian Talmuds, the halakic midrashic compilations—from which he drew. But once having listed his sources summarily, Maimonides sets down his rulings from the beginning to the end of the *Mishneh Torah* without indicating the source in the classic rabbinic literature—the Mishna, Tosefta, or Talmud, the tractate, the chapter, the view of which ancient rabbi—that led him in each instance to rule as he did.

[52]He almost always touches up the style of what he quotes in order to fit it smoothly into the framework of the *Mishneh Torah*. The passage cited in the previous note is one example of his reworking midrashic material. Another example: *Mishneh Torah*: *H. Sanhedrin* 2:7, where he lists the qualifications for serving as a rabbinic judge which, he writes, are "explicit in the Written Torah." Some of the qualifications are indeed explicit in the scriptural texts that he cites, but others emerge only after the verses are interpreted midrashically by the rabbis. And then Maimonides reworks the rabbinic sources; see the commentary *Leḥem Mishna, ad locum*. An example from a nonhalakic context: In *H. Melakim* 11.1, Maimonides—in all seriousness, as far as one can tell—incorporates a midrashic interpretation of the prophecy of the non-Israelite prophet Balaam; see Numbers 24:17–18. In his midrashic reading, Balaam predicts the advent of two messiahs: (1) King David, "who "saved Israel from the hands of its enemies" and (2) a descendant of David, who will be the future Messiah. The only known parallel or source for Maimonides' interpretation is the late and derivative midrashic work *Midrash Aggada*; see reference in the Frankel edition of the *Mishneh Torah*. Many more examples of his reworking midrashic material can be cited.

[53]Malachi ha-Kohen, *Yad Malachi* (Przemysl 1877) 2, rules regarding Maimonides, §4; I. Weiss, "*Toledot ha-Rab Rabbenu Moshe ben Maimon*," *Bet Talmud* 1 (1881) 231, note 34; Tchernowitz, *Toledoth ha-Poskim* 206; Benedikt, *Asuppat Ma'amarim* (Jerusalem 1994) 163–64, 167, 173–74, 179–80, with the qualification that Benedikt, 173, believes that in the examples he cites Maimonides did have sources in the classic rabbinic texts.

[54]For rabbinic scholars who criticized Maimonides for failing to cite his sources, see Twersky, *Introduction to the Code of Maimonides* (n. 30 above) 103–5.

In sum, Maimonides envisaged the most comprehensive posttalmudic code of Jewish law ever undertaken, a code that proposes to incorporate each and every regulation of the Oral Torah as well as post-Mosaic innovations. He puts aside the arrangement of the legal and ritual regulations in the classic rabbinic texts in favor of a new arrangement of his own. He wholly excludes the dialectic argumentation of the two Talmuds and states elsewhere that talmudic argumentation is a means to an end and not an end in itself. And he mentions his sources summarily in the introduction and then makes no further reference to the rabbinic texts from which he drew.

Maimonides, as we saw, wrote his two previous preserved rabbinic works, the Commentary on the Mishna and his *Book of Commandments*, in Arabic. The *Mishneh Torah*, by contrast, is written in Hebrew, a choice for which he again had a precedent. The form of Hebrew that he uses is the language of the Mishna. He explains that he decided not to compose the *Mishneh Torah* in biblical Hebrew, because the biblical idiom is ill suited for Oral Torah material, and not to compose it in Aramaic, because Aramaic was no longer well understood in his day.[55] As for his reason for preferring Hebrew to Arabic, he once writes that Hebrew opened rabbinic works to a wider readership, and he expresses a desire to translate his Commentary on the Mishna and *Book of Commandments* from Arabic into that language.[56] He had become convinced that Hebrew would henceforth be the appropriate medium for rabbinic writing.

Where the *Mishneh Torah* records rulings that were already formulated in mishnaic Hebrew, Maimonides copies out and touches up his sources. Where he draws from the Aramaic parts of the two Talmuds, he translates into a fluent, natural-sounding simulation of the mishnaic language,[57] although here and there Arabic usages infiltrate his Hebrew.[58] At times, especially when his focus shifts to nonlegal matters, he allows himself a flourish in the more rhetorical biblical style.[59] The result pleased him. After a man who had difficulty with the Hebrew of the *Mishneh Torah* wrote, asking Maimonides to translate the book into Arabic, Maimonides replied that it would lose its charm if he did. He may, however, have

[55]Maimonides, *Book of Commandments* (*Sefer ha-Miṣwot*), edited and translated into Hebrew by J. Kafah (Jerusalem 1971), introduction, p. 2.

[56]Above, pp. 166, 185.

[57]Maimonides' innovations to the mishnaic idiom, some due to the influence of Arabic, are listed by W. Bacher, "Zum sprachlichen Charakter des Mischne Thora," *Moses ben Maimon*, ed. W. Bacher et al., 2 (Leipzig 1914) 280–91. A few examples of Maimonides' retaining technical legal terms in their Aramaic form, rather than translating them into Hebrew, are given by I. Sideman, "*Signon Mishneh Torah*," *Sinai* 7 (1943) 111.

[58]For example: *yesh sham*, "there exists," in *Mishneh Torah*: *H. Yesode ha-Torah* 1.1, and frequently; *qarob min*, "close to," in *H. Qiddush ha-Ḥodesh* 1.2; *ᶜad she-* in the strong Arabic sense (=*ḥattā*) of "with the result that," in *H. Shebuᶜot* 9.14, *H. Zekiyya u-Mattana* 6:17, *H. ᶜEdut* 10.1; *ḥazar*, "become," in *H. Pesule ha-Muqdashin* 19.6.

[59]Cf. Bacher, "Zum sprachlichen Charakter des Mischne Thora," 291–94.

overestimated the transparency of his language. He advised the same man to acquire a basic knowledge of Hebrew and assured him that once he acquainted himself with the language of one of the fourteen books of the *Mishneh Torah* he would find that he could understand the whole; for the Hebrew "is very easy to understand and very quickly mastered."[60] In actuality, seasoned scholars to this day toil over statements in the *Mishneh Torah*, attempting to fathom Maimonides' meaning.

I have described the *Mishneh Torah* as a *code* of rabbinic law. That is the common description and it is apt, since although the *Mishneh Torah* covers areas of halaka that were not applicable in Maimonides' day, it is designed as a law code. Maimonides states that his object was to instruct people in their religious and legal obligations,[61] he sometimes expressly presents his rulings as guidelines for judges making everyday legal decisions,[62] and he prides himself on having decided "halakic norms for the entire Talmud."[63] Rabbinic scholars coming after him have viewed the *Mishneh Torah* as a code of law and employed it as such. It is nonetheless to be noted that Maimonides does not himself call it a code of law, and for that matter, no term with the precise meaning of *law code* exists in mishnaic or medieval Hebrew. Both in the introduction to the *Mishneh Torah* and in subsequent works, he calls it, in Hebrew, a *ḥibbur* and, in Arabic, a *ta'alīf*, that is, a "composition" or, in another possible understanding of the Hebrew and Arabic terms, a "compilation."[64] Although he named it the *Mishneh Torah*, he often prefers to speak of it as his "large composition [or: compilation]"[65] or "large composition of religious law."[66] It is a composition because in it he undertakes "to put together" [*leḥabber*]—or, on the alternative translation, it is a compilation because in it he undertakes "to compile"—all regulations regarding "the permitted and prohibited, the ritually impure and pure." Again, it is a composition—or compilation—inasmuch as it "assembles" (*meqqabeṣ*) the entire Oral Torah together with post-Mosaic innovations.[67]

In the introduction to the *Mishneh Torah*, Maimonides remarks that he was writing in the Hebrew year corresponding to the final third of 1176 and the first

[60]Letter to Joseph Ibn Jabir, in Shailat, *Letters and Essays of Moses Maimonides* (n. 21 above) 404, 409.

[61]Below, p. 208.

[62]A few examples: *Mishneh Torah*: *H. Qeri'at Shema*^{c} 3.11; *H. Ishut* 6.14; 10.16; 14.14; *Nedarim* 9.13; *H. Malweh we-Loweh* 15.2.

[63]Above, p. 107.

[64]*Mishneh Torah*, introduction. Letter to Pinḥas of Alexandria, in Shailat, *Letters and Essays of Moses Maimonides* 440.

[65]Maimonides, *Treatise on Resurrection*, ed. J. Finkel, *Proceedings of the American Academy for Jewish Research* 9 (1939), Hebrew-Arabic section, 4.

[66]*Guide for the Perplexed*, introduction, p. 6a; 2.10, p. 22b; 2.32, p. 73b; 3.29, p. 63b.

[67]*Mishneh Torah*, introduction.

two-thirds of 1177.[68] A packet of responsa has been preserved in which he answers thirty-two questions sent to him by scholars in Tyre, and in seven of the responsa he informs his questioners that the issue they raised either "is," or "was," or "will be" made clear to them in his "large composition" or, alternatively, in his "large composition comprising all rulings of the religious law"; as just seen, he liked to call the *Mishneh Torah* his large composition. When he refers in the packet of responsa to the sections of his large composition which discuss the issues raised, he designates them by the names that the pertinent sections have in the *Mishneh Torah* as we know it today.[69] When he writes there in one place that certain matters "are made clear at the beginning of my large composition" and refers in another to what "I explained at the end of my large composition," the subjects are discussed in the *Mishneh Torah* in the locations where he says they are.[70] His tone and language assume that the recipients of the responsa had not yet seen the composition, which is plainly the *Mishneh Torah*, but imply that they would soon receive a copy.

The last responsum in the packet, the one containing the reference to the "beginning of my large composition," has a note appended to it. Here Maimonides mentions that he had answered all the questions sent to him from Tyre, signs his name, and gives May 1177, as the date.[71] It is conceivable, of course, that someone other than Maimonides put together the packet of responsa as we have it and this other person placed Maimonides' note where it is; it is, in other words, conceivable that some of the questions in the packet were sent to him from Tyre after May 1177, and the responsa imparting the impression that the *Mishneh Torah* had been completed belong to that later date. If we take things on their face, however, the *Mishneh Torah* was more or less ready for scribes in May 1177, and a copy could soon be dispatched to Tyre.[72] The introduction to the *Mishneh Torah*, in which Maimonides says that he was writing in the Hebrew year corresponding to the final third of 1176 and first two-thirds of 1177, would have been composed about the time that he completed the entire work.

[68] *Mishneh Torah*, ed. J. Cohen and M. Katzenelenbogen (Jerusalem 1964), introduction, 13; see apparatus.

[69] *Responsa* (n. 20 above) §121: "Halakot of Repentance of my large composition." §129: "Halakot of Heave Offerings [for the priests]," and "Halakot of Tithes."

[70] *Responsa* §§148, 150; Shailat, *Letters and Essays of Moses Maimonides* 195–96.

[71] *Responsa* 1.286.

[72] Another possibility is suggested by *Responsa* §433, where Maimonides remarks that a "first edition" of the *Mishneh Torah* was disseminated "in fascicles out of order" and that he later went back and made additions. The reference to fascicles of a first edition suggests that after completing a provisional version of the entire book, he allowed scribes to transcribe parts; persons who were impatient would thereby be permitted to see sections of particular interest to them without waiting for the polished version. The reference to fascicles might also mean that he issued the book piecemeal before finishing the whole. In either case, the version referred to in the packet of responsa dated May 1177 may have been provisional, and Maimonides may have still needed a year or more to bring the *Mishneh Torah* to completion.

Another passage in the *Mishneh Torah* gives evidence of a later date for its completion. There Maimonides reports that he was writing not in 1176–1177, but in the following Hebrew year, the year corresponding to the last third of 1177 and first two-thirds of 1178.[73] He was thus working on the *Mishneh Torah* four months or more after May 1177. Furthermore, he illustrates points in the chapters coming immediately after the one with the 1177–1178 date by employing specific dates from the spring of 1178.[74] Those passages suggest that he was still working on the *Mishneh Torah* a full year after May 1177.

It happens that the chapters in which all the references to dates subsequent to May 1177 occur belong to a highly technical discussion involving complex astronomical and trigonometric calculations, and the chapters have signs of being a digression within the wider context in which they are found. A scholar who dealt with the problem has theorized that Maimonides completed the body of the *Mishneh Torah* by the spring of 1177. He later went back, according to the suggestion, and added the technical chapters in which he says that he was writing in the year corresponding to the last third of 1177 and first two-thirds of 1178, and in which he illustrates points with dates from the spring of 1178.[75]

There is evidence from an entirely different quarter that Maimonides could not have brought the *Mishneh Torah*, or at least the main body of it, to completion any later than 1177 or, perhaps, early 1178. He tells of having "labored day and night for about ten continuous years in assembling [*qibbuṣ*] this composition."[76] In approximately 1177, his brother David drowned on a business trip, and, we saw, Maimonides wrote that the blow left him bedridden for a year. When he got up from his sickbed, he was responsible for his livelihood, for supporting his brother's widow and daughter, and for debts that his brother had left. Even allowing for hyperbole in the statement about being bedridden for an entire year, the ten continuous years in which he worked day and night on the *Mishneh Torah* could not have extended beyond the day that news arrived of his brother's death.[77]

If we may conclude that the decade in which he labored on the *Mishneh Torah* day and night ended in 1177 or 1178, when Maimonides was thirty-nine or forty

[73]*Mishneh Torah*: *H. Qiddush ha-Ḥodesh* 11.16. In 9.7, Maimonides is writing in the year 1170; pointed out by S. Gandz, "Date of the Composition of Maimonides' Code," *Proceedings of the American Academy for Jewish Research* 17 (1948) 3.

[74]Pointed out by Gandz, "Date of the Composition of Maimonides' Code" 4.

[75]Gandz, "Date of the Composition of Maimonides' Code" 3–4. A fourteenth-century Karaite author states that Maimonides wrote his code in 1178; see Gandz 6–7. The report in H. Graetz, *Geschichte der Juden*, 4th ed. (Leipzig n.d.) 6.288, note 1, that Salomon Munk saw a manuscript in which the completion of the *Mishneh Torah* is dated to 1180, has never been corroborated.

[76]*Responsa* 3.57. Elsewhere too, Maimonides describes the composition of the *Mishneh Torah* as an *assembling* of material; see above, pp. 198, 203. Shailat, *Letters and Essays of Moses Maimonides*, 202, is therefore in error when he infers from the term *assembling* in the present letter that Maimonides is not talking about the final version of the book.

[77]The point is made by Shailat, *Letters and Essays of Moses Maimonides* 199.

years old, we get 1167 or 1168 as the approximate date at which he began. The last third of 1167 and first two-thirds of 1168 were the year in which he completed his Commentary on the Mishna. We are left with a scenario in which he started work on the *Mishneh Torah* less than a year after finishing the Commentary on the Mishna. In between the two, he managed to write the *Book of Commandments* as well.

His achievement was prodigious. He completed the *Book of Commandments* in a matter of months, and the *Mishneh Torah* in about ten years. He wanted the *Mishneh Torah* to be exhaustive and to embrace every legal or ritual item in the rabbinic sources, whether or not it was still practiced. Even assuming that at the age of thirty he already controlled the vast body of classic texts, he had, in order to accomplish the task he set for himself, to comb through them for everything relating to the issues to be included. He likewise had to comb through Alfasi's *Halakot* and the other codes of rabbinic law for whatever bearing they might have on the same issues. An accretion of customary law and ritual had deposited itself on the laws and rituals embodied in the classic rabbinic sources, and the customs of different localities often diverged. Codes of Jewish law, when they appeared, began recording posttalmudic, customary practice. Maimonides' attitude to posttalmudic custom was by no means uncritical, and he does not hesitate to reject customs that he judges to be in conflict with the talmudic halaka.[78] But he recognized that custom had inextricably infiltrated Jewish law and ritual. He therefore had to take posttalmudic custom, universal as well as local, into account as he prepared the raw material for his code.[79]

For each of the myriad issues treated in the *Mishneh Torah*, it was necessary, then, to collate whatever was pertinent in the nooks and crannies of the entire body of ancient and posttalmudic material. Maimonides thereupon had to analyze all the pertinent bits and pieces and determine which opinion was authoritative. After he settled upon the building blocks out of which he would construct the code, he had to put them into a uniform language. Many items were already formulated in mishnaic Hebrew, so that he could merely have copied them. Yet even these are often touched up and polished as they pass under his pen, so that they emerge clearer and more precise in the *Mishneh Torah* than they had been in the original.[80]

[78]Examples: *Mishneh Torah*: *H. Tefilla* 7.9 (rejects the custom of reciting as a block and set prayer in the synagogue, various blessings that the rabbis had prescribed for recitation separately when certain specific events take place, such as the blessing to be recited when the cock crows in the morning); *H. Issure Bi'a* 11.14 (rejects a custom that extended the period of time a menstruating woman is required to refrain from sexual relations); *H. Issure Bi'a* 11.15 (rejects a custom that extended the period of time a woman must refrain from sexual relations after childbirth, branding it as an influence of the Karaites and "heresy"). *Responsa* §299.

[79]On custom in the *Mishneh Torah*, see Weiss, "*Toledot*" (n. 52 above) 230; Twersky, *Introduction to the Code of Maimonides* (n. 24 above) 124–33.

[80]Apt examples are given in Tchernowitz, *Toledoth ha-Poskim* 1 (n. 48 above) 260–66. On Maimonides' stylistic gifts see also Elon, *Jewish Law* (n. 13 above) 3.1208–10. Where the

Items written in Aramaic had to be translated into the idiom that he had chosen. He had to determine where each of the thousands of rulings should be placed within the framework that he had devised. The *Mishneh Torah*, as we shall see, contains more than just halaka, and the nonhalakic parts also had to be thought out, formulated, and assigned to their appropriate places.

Maimonides is reputed to have had a phenomenal memory, and he placed strong reliance on it when preparing his first draft. Once, in response to an inquiry submitted by a circle of readers who were baffled by a certain legal decision, he affords a glimpse into his procedure. He informs his questioners that when preparing the original version of the code he spent "several days" on the particular matter they raised. He goes on: In the "first, immature draft [of the code], which I composed relying on my memory and which I did not copy" for distribution, I determined the norm "as it appears" to be indicated in the best-known treatment of the issue in the Babylonian Talmud and as the questioners thought it should be decided. But "when I copied [my draft into a final version] and carefully examined what is relevant to each and every issue in the [classic rabbinic] books," I changed my mind and determined that the correct ruling is the one now recorded in the *Mishneh Torah*.[81]

After he had produced his final version, Maimonides had the additional mechanical chore of putting it into a shape that would be readable by the scribe or scribes who were going to transcribe it.[82] He undoubtedly recycled the work he did on his Commentary on the Mishna for the *Book of Commandments* and then reused the work he did on both in the *Mishneh Torah*. Completing the latter during a span of some ten years was nonetheless an extraordinary feat. Historians have supposed that he held one or another communal or professional office during the decade in which he wrote the *Mishneh Torah*. He did continue to make judicial decisions when called upon during that period, but he could not possibly have performed any time-consuming function. He could not, to be specific, have conducted a medical practice or have held the position of leader of the entire Egyptian Jewish community.[83]

Babylonian Talmud clarified the mishnaic formulation, Maimonides incorporates the talmudic clarification into his citation of the mishnaic law or ritual.

[81]*Responsa* §345, one of the responsa sent to the scholars of Lunel. J. Kafah, "*She'elot Ḥakme Lunel u-Teshubot 'ha-Rambam,' Kelum Meqoriyyot Hen?*" *Sefer Zikkaron le-ha-Rab Yiṣḥaq Nissim* 2 (Jerusalem 1985) 235–52, rejects the authenticity of the entire series of Lunel responsa.

[82]Fragments of a draft of the code which are written in Maimonides' own hand have been discovered, and they contain corrections and insertions that only the author could have deciphered and prepared for the scribes. It is unclear whether the fragments belong to a first or final draft. See M. Lutzki, Appendix to *Mishneh Torah* 5 (New York: Shulsinger Bros. 1947); E. Hurvitz, "Additional Newly Discovered Handwritten Pages from Rabbi Moshe ben Maimon" (in Hebrew), *Hadorom* 38 (1974) 9, 14–22.

[83]See above, p. 56.

On a number of occasions, Maimonides discusses his motives for undertaking the *Mishneh Torah.* In the introduction to the book itself he bewails the decline of rabbinic competence in his day and observes that few were any longer able to understand the geonic literature, not to speak of the classic rabbinic texts; he seems not to have heard of the efflorescence of rabbinic studies in central France. To meet the needs of the day, he composed the *Mishneh Torah,* wherein he "assembles the entire Oral Torah, together with the positive ordinances, customs, and negative ordinances" posterior to the Oral Torah, so that every law, every commandment, everything ordained by scholars and prophets, would be clear "to the small and to the great." "No one will ever require a further composition for any Jewish law."[84] The words "to the small and to the great" would appear to mean that Maimonides wrote the code to serve both. If, however, what he writes here is to be harmonized with statements to be quoted in the following paragraph, his meaning will have to be slightly different. It will have to be that his purpose was to make the laws and commandments as clear to the small as they are to the great, who are capable of understanding on their own.

In the introduction to his *Book of Commandments,* the work designed as a prolegomenon to the *Mishneh Torah,* Maimonides expressly brings out the code's practical function. The projected code would comprise all Jewish legal and religious obligations. With its publication, a person "would not need any further book after the Torah for learning what his obligations are according to the religious law [*shari*ᶜ*a*], be they obligations carrying the sanction of the Torah [*de-orayta*] or the sanction of the rabbis [*mi-de-rabbanan*]."[85] A letter sent by Maimonides to Pinḥas of Alexandria after the *Mishneh Torah* had entered circulation points again to its practical legal function and identifies the nonexpert as the person whom Maimonides intended to serve. He writes that he composed it just as he "stated expressly in the introduction to the composition," that is, "solely . . . for those incapable of plumbing the profundities of the Talmud and discovering there what is prohibited and what, permitted."[86] A letter to a different party says the same. In composing the code, he writes now, his object had been "solely to clear paths and remove impediments for students, in order that they not feel disheartened by the magnitude of the dialectic reasoning, with the result that mistakes would be made in fixing the halaka."[87] Apart from the possible discrepancy between the introduction to the *Mishneh Torah,* which would appear to say that the *Mishneh Torah* was intended to serve small and great, and the two letters, which say that it was intended only for the nonexpert, the variations between the statements examined thus far are

[84] *Mishneh Torah,* introduction.

[85] Maimonides, *Book of Commandments* (n. 55 above), introduction, p. 3.

[86] Letter to Pinḥas of Alexandria, in Shailat, *Letters and Essays of Moses Maimonides* (n. 21 above) 439.

[87] *Responsa* 3.57.

negligible. The gist is that Maimonides composed the *Mishneh Torah* to provide the Jewish world, and nonexperts in particular, with a complete conspectus of Jewish law.

Maimonides puts things very differently when writing to his student Joseph ben Judah in the 1190s and after he had been hurt by criticism of the *Mishneh Torah*. He tells Joseph: "As God knows, I wrote the present composition in the first instance only for myself, in order to dispense with investigation and searching [the rabbinic sources] for whatever I might need [on any occasion], as well as for my old age [when I shall find it difficult to search through the classic sources]. And for the sake of God as well, for I have, by God, been very jealous for the Lord God of Israel. I saw a nation lacking a comprehensive composition in the true sense and lacking sound, authenticated opinions, and I therefore did what I did solely for God. That is one point." There is a "second point": When composing the code, he realized that it "would undoubtedly fall into the hands of an evil, jealous man, who would denigrate its virtues . . . , of an unlettered ignoramus, who would have no conception of what had been accomplished in it. . . , of a deluded, confused tyro, who would have problems with passages . . . , and of a blockheaded, dull-witted pietist, who would contest the principles of proper belief which the book contains; and [I realized that] those persons would be the majority." Yet he had consoled himself in the expectation that the book would also "undoubtedly come into the hands of the 'remnant whom the Lord calleth,' men of justice, judgment, and healthy mind, who would appreciate what I have accomplished," men such as Joseph himself and similarly minded scholars in the south of France who had written to Maimonides praising the *Mishneh Torah*.[88]

If the statements in the letter to Joseph ben Judah be taken at face value, Maimonides did not after all compose the *Mishneh Torah* for "the small," for "students," "solely . . . for those incapable of plumbing the profundities of the Talmud." He wrote it as a reference resource for himself[89] and for the greater glory of God, so that the Jewish nation would possess a comprehensive composition, regardless of whether anyone other than he would ever open it. Only secondarily did he hope that the book might also serve the handful of rabbinic scholars enlightened enough to appreciate it.

The thoughts expressed in the letter to Joseph create the unbelievable scenario of a brilliant savant's working ten years on a monumental work primarily for his own use. A short time before he wrote to Joseph, Maimonides had the occasion to draw a distinction between persons who study exclusively for their own edification and those who feel driven to instruct others, and he made the apposite remark: "A person who knows something does not compose [books] for himself, to teach

[88]Moses ben Maimon, *Epistulae* (n. 44 above) 50–52.

[89]Twersky, *Introduction to the Code of Maimonides* (n. 30 above) 74–75, points out that the notion of writing a book only for oneself is to be found in Baḥya Ibn Paquda and, after Maimonides, it became something of a topos.

himself what he already knows."[90] What is still more curious, Maimonides' declaration that he composed the code in the first instance for himself and secondarily for the small "remnant whom the Lord calleth," is contradicted by a statement he makes just a few lines further on in the very same letter to Joseph, at least as it has been preserved. In the later statement he foresees a time when his code would gain universal acceptance, and other rabbinic compositions—he does not make clear whether he means only posttalmudic compositions or the classic rabbinic texts as well—would fall into desuetude. His code would serve not only himself and a handful of others but all of Israel.

The descriptions of Maimonides' motives in the introduction to the *Mishneh Torah* and in the other passages of a similar vein undoubtedly reflect his genuine intent: He wrote it as a summing-up of rabbinic law for the education of those interested in the law and for nonexperts in particular. The letter to Joseph ben Judah does bring out a significant feature of the *Mishneh Torah* not mentioned in any of the other places, namely, that the book is concerned with both law and correct belief. Otherwise, the sentiments expressed by Maimonides to Joseph are obviously a reaction to criticism emanating from the rabbinic authorities in Baghdad, especially to their censure of passages in the *Mishneh Torah* which deal with Jewish belief. Maimonides more than once insisted that criticism, even when nasty, did not trouble him in the least. He makes a statement to that effect in the letter to Joseph from which I have been quoting.[91] Similarly, when writing to the principal of the rabbinic academy in Baghdad—one of his critics—he tells the man, with more than a soupçon of superciliousness, that whereas most human beings become upset when objections are made to what they say or write, "God be He praised has freed me from that."[92] On a rational level he knew that it was ridiculous to be annoyed by the yelping of mediocrities for whom he had no respect. And yet he was human and subject to everyday human emotions to a greater extent, perhaps, than he realized. When the *Mishneh Torah* elicited criticism of a kind that he was unprepared for, he was stung to the quick despite himself, as his characterization of the critics—evil and envious men, unlettered ignoramuses, deluded tyros, blockheaded pietists—makes sufficiently clear. He decided in a heated moment that the code's true purpose would be to serve him as a reference resource, to glorify God, and incidentally also to guide the select few who could appreciate its value. The explanation of his motives in the letter to Joseph, while revealing little about Maimonides' object in writing the *Mishneh Torah*, says much about Maimonides the man. It reveals that his overtowering intellectual gifts did not immunize him against the emotions to which lesser mortals are prey.

Maimonides' remark about the Jewish nation's lacking a "comprehensive composition in the true sense" and its lacking sound precise opinions is an apparent

[90] *Guide for the Perplexed* 2.37.

[91] Moses ben Maimon, *Epistulae* 50.

[92] *Responsa* §310, p. 572, and 4.21.

allusion to comprehensive Muslim religious works that circulated at the time. The prime example was Ghazali's *Reviving of the Religious Sciences*, which summarizes Muslims' legal and ritual obligations while also treating Islamic beliefs. The first part of Ghazali's work happens to carry the title "Book of Knowledge"—or "Book of Science"—which is precisely the title that Maimonides chose for the first of the fourteen Books of the Mishneh Torah.[93] In content, the *Mishneh Torah* is nonetheless very different from Ghazali's work.

Maimonides' *Book of Commandments*, his prolegomenon to the *Mishneh Torah*, tells us that in looking ahead, he wanted to be certain that the projected work would take account of all 613 positive and negative commandments which were "stated to Moses at Sinai" and are "contained in the Book of the Torah." That was his motive for composing the preliminary work. The introduction to the *Mishneh Torah* makes clear that his chief concern now would be not with the Mosaic commandments themselves but with the Oral Torah interpretations of them and with ordinances instituted by post-Mosaic authorities—that is to say, not so much with commandments (*miṣwot*) as with halakot. Maimonides nevertheless puts his enumeration of the commandments to full use. As part of his introduction to the *Mishneh Torah*, he repeats the entire list of 613 commandments that he arrived at in the previous work. Prior to each of the sections of the *Mishneh Torah*, he lists the divine commandments relating to the section. When he finds it feasible, he begins a section by once again recording the pertinent Mosaic commandments; and as he proceeds, he tries to find a place within the section for any scriptural commandments that he did not manage to work into the opening lines. The details of the commandments given in the *Book of Commandments* sometimes differ from the details he now sets forth in the *Mishneh Torah*,[94] and Maimonides later explained that the former work was concerned primarily with identifying the nub of the commandments, whereas the *Mishneh Torah* spells out the details with precision.[95]

In the *Book of Commandments*, Maimonides also looked ahead to the projected code's structure. He asked himself whether he should "divide [it] as the Mishna is divided . . . or differently," by reorganizing Jewish law "in accordance with what reflection judges to be most appropriate, and easiest, for study." With implied criticism of Judah the Prince's Mishna, where items belonging to widely disparate subjects are sometimes threaded together in a single tractate through analogy and the association of ideas, he settled on a nonmishnaic scheme. He decided that the "best division," the one most suited for helping students understand and remember what

[93]There were additional medieval Islamic works that either were entitled "Book of Knowledge" or contained sections entitled "Book of Knowledge." See F. Rosenthal, *Knowledge Triumphant* (Leiden 1970) 70–96.

[94]B. Benedikt, *Ha-Rambam le-lo Seṭiyya min ha-Talmud* (collected articles) (Jerusalem 1985) 114–26.

[95]*Responsa* §310, p. 574; cf. Benedikt, *Ha-Rambam le-lo Seṭiyya min ha-Talmud* 126–27.

they study, would replace the sixty tractates of the Mishna with sections of "halakot," each of which would be devoted exclusively to a specific subject. The code would have "[a section on] the halakot of the tabernacle [in which Jewish men dwell during the festival of Tabernacles], [one on] the halakot of the palm branch [held by Jewish men on each day of the Tabernacles festival], [one on] the halakot of the parchment scroll affixed to the doorposts of Jewish residences [*mezuza*], and [one on] the halakot of fringes [that Scripture and the rabbis require to be tied to the corners of garments]." Each section would then be subdivided into "chapters," and the chapters further subdivided into paragraphs, each of which would be called an individual "halaka."[96]

There were precedents for the form "halakot of such-and such." *Sefer Halakot Gedolot* generally was faithful to the mishnaic division into tractates when presenting its rulings and it continued to use the tractates' names. But it supplemented its division into tractates with ancillary headings that it called "the halakot of such-and-such." A number of the designations used by Maimonides— including "the halakot of the palm branch," "the halakot of the parchment scroll affixed to the door post," and "the halakot of fringes"—had indeed already appeared in *Halakot Gedolot*. Nor was that work original here. The earliest known posttalmudic code, which scholarly consensus today dates a century earlier than *Halakot Gedolot*, used headings of the same sort.[97] In calling each individual paragraph a *halaka*, Maimonides had a still more ancient precedent, for that had been a term used to designate a paragraph of the Mishna corpus.[98]

The plan for the structure of the *Mishneh Torah* which Maimonides outlines in the *Book of Commandments* envisages, then, sections of halakot which are divided into chapters, these latter then being subdivided into paragraphs. A briefer outline of the structure of the book that he gives in the introduction to the *Mishneh Torah* itself envisages a similar structure.[99] Both fail to mention one further level of organization.

The Mishna corpus was divided at its highest level into six overall rubrics called Orders, each with a one-word title, and the sixty, or sixty-three, tractates were arranged under those six Orders.[100] Maimonides, for his part, divides his *Mishneh*

[96]*Book of Commandments* (n. 55 above), introduction, p. 3. As the *Mishneh Torah* finally took shape, Maimonides did not leave the halakot of the tabernacle, the halakot of the palm branch, and the halakot of the scroll affixed to the doorpost, as independent sections. In order to avoid sections that would be unattractively short, he combined the first two with a third subject to form the single section of "halakot of the ram's horn, the tabernacle, and the palm branch," and he joined the third with related topics to form another single section.

[97]Jehudai Gaon, *Sefer Halachot Pesuqut* (Jerusalem 1971). *Halakot Qeṣubot* (n. 25 above) has headings of a similar sort.

[98]Maimonides, Commentary on the Mishna (n. 14 above), introduction, p. 25; J. Epstein, *Mabo le-Nusaḥ ha-Mishna*, 2nd ed. (Jerusalem 1964) 1,000.

[99]*Mishneh Torah*, introduction (end).

[100]Above, p. 137.

Torah at the highest level into fourteen rubrics, which he calls *Books.* Each of them carries a title of the form "Book of X," where X is always a single word, as were the names of the mishnaic Orders. Three of Maimonides' Books have exactly the same names as Orders of the Mishna, and the names of two others are variations on names of two of the remaining three.[101] His fourteen Books are plainly his substitute for the six Orders of the Mishna, and the new division again embodies an implied criticism: It suggests that the six-fold mishnaic division was inadequate and that his division into fourteen Books captures the breadth and variegated character of Jewish law better than the mishnaic Orders did.[102] Maimonides does not appear to have regarded the division into fourteen Books as essential to his plan, since he does not mention it when describing the projected structure of the code in the *Book of Commandments*—he may not even have decided on it yet—or when outlining the structure at the beginning of the code itself.

He expands the six Orders of the Mishna into fourteen Books in two ways: by analyzing mishnaic Orders into their components and by introducing wholly original headings. He thus breaks down the mishnaic Order of Torts into four separate Books of the *Mishneh Torah.*[103] And he creates new headings for subjects that had been tucked away here and there throughout the Mishna and Talmud corpuses: He organizes regulations scattered throughout the Mishna and two Talmuds which govern liturgical and related matters under what he calls the "Book of Love." He creates another main heading, which he entitles the "Book of Holiness," for regulations concerning forbidden sexual relations and forbidden foods, they too being items that were scattered through the ancient texts. The names of the mishnaic Orders had each delimited a realm in which things were to be done or avoided—for example, Agriculture, Festivals, Holy-things—and most of the names that Maimonides chooses for the fourteen Books of the *Mishneh Torah*

[101]Maimonides' Books of "Women," "Seeds," i.e., agricultural law, and "Torts" repeat names of Orders of the Mishna corpus. His Book of "Times" takes its name, with a slight variation, from the Mishna Order of "Appointed-time"; both deal with the festivals and other special days. His book of "Purity" takes its name from the Mishna Order of "Purities"; both deal with laws of ritual impurity. Maimonides chose not to use the name of the remaining Order of the Mishna, "Holy-things," that is, sacrificial law, for his own Book of sacrificial law and used the title "Holiness" for a Book devoted to something completely different; see immediately below.

[102]A list of the fourteen Books and their contents is given by Twersky, *Introduction to the Code of Maimonides* (n. 30 above) 260–72.

[103]He divides the larger portion of the material in the Order of Torts into four Books of the *Mishneh Torah*, namely the Books of "Torts," "Contracts," "Civil litigation," and "Judges," this last dealing with the rabbinic court system. The contents of the Order of Torts was still not exhausted. The subject matter of one tractate in the Order, the tractate of Oaths, became the opening subject in the Book of Asseverations, or Solemn Declarations, that is, the Book of the *Mishneh Torah* dealing with commitments men take upon themselves through solemn declarations. And most of the material from two more tractates of the Order of Torts, the tractates dealing with idolatry and ethics, is incorporated into still another Book of the *Mishneh Torah*, the Book of "Knowledge," or "Science."

do the same. The names "Love" and "Holiness," by contrast, reflect not a realm of activity governed by legislation, but the legislation's purpose. Maimonides entitles the rubric devoted to liturgy the "Book of Love" because "we are commanded to observe these commandments in order to love God and keep Him constantly in mind"; the liturgical acts prescribed in the Book are not to be performed mechanically and as matters of routine, but rather with the object of awakening love of God within oneself. He calls the other rubric the Book of "Holiness" because "through the prohibited sexual relations and food restrictions, God made us holy and separated us from the gentiles."[104] Here it is the divine purpose in instituting the sexual and dietary restrictions that the name brings to the fore: God's object was to sanctify His chosen people and protect them against the allurements of the gentile nations. A more weighty instance of Maimonides' creating a Book of the *Mishneh Torah* where nothing analogous was found in the structure of the ancient Mishna is the first of the fourteen Books, which will be taken up later in the present chapter.

The fourteen-fold initial division of the *Mishneh Torah* gave rise to a popular nickname for the work. Until recent times, written Hebrew represented numerals solely by letters of the alphabet; today, it generally employs Arabic numerals. The Hebrew letters signifying the numeral fourteen are *y-d*. Hebrew *yd*, vocalized *yad*, means *hand*, and Scripture once speaks of *ha-yad ha-ḥazaqa*—"the mighty hand"—that the biblical Moses "wrought in the sight of all Israel."[105] Not many decades after Maimonides' death, an unknown medieval admirer saw that the biblical metaphor, with its echo of the numeral fourteen, would serve as a perfect designation for the literary masterpiece that the latter-day Moses, Moses Maimonides, had also wrought in the sight of all Israel.[106] The pendulum has swung back, but for centuries, Maimonides' code was more commonly known as *ha-Yad ha-Ḥazaqa* than as *Mishneh Torah*, the title that Maimonides himself chose and that has recently returned to fashion.[107]

Under the fourteen Books, Maimonides subsumes the eighty-three sections, each of which is called the "Halakot" of a given subject. Just as he ignores the overall classification scheme of Judah the Prince's Mishna, so too does he disregard, within each of the sections of Halakot, the sequence in which rulings had been

[104] *Mishneh Torah*, ed. Cohen and Katzenelenbogen (n. 68 above), 66–67.

[105] Deuteronomy 34:12.

[106] For early instances of use of the nickname *ha-yad ha-ḥazaqa* for the *Mishneh Torah*, see B. Cohen, "Classification of the Law in the Mishneh Torah," *Jewish Quarterly Review* 25 (1935) 529, note 41.

[107] Twersky, *Introduction to the Code of Maimonides* 105, suggests that the nickname was preferred over the original title as a silent reproach to Maimonides' audaciousness in calling his code a "repetition of the Law." Twersky, "R. Joseph Ashkenazi," *Salo Baron Jubilee Volume* (Jerusalem 1974) 3.189–90, quotes a passage from the fifteenth-century Solomon Duran which in fact defends Maimonides against the charge of impropriety in giving the name "repetition of the Law" to his code.

presented within the individual tractates of the Mishna and two Talmuds. Thus in contrast to the Mishna, which often goes out of its way to take up peripheral matters precisely at the beginning of a tractate while leaving the heart of the subject for later,[108] he almost invariably opens a section with something basic. He often, although not always, begins or, having concluded, summarizes a subject by laying out all the underlying general rules.[109] The general rules covering the particulars are not, however, allowed to displace the gamut of specific hypothetical cases that the Mishna, two Talmuds, and other classic sources spelled out in minute detail. Whatever general rules Maimonides offers stand side by side with the full array of mishnaic and talmudic case law.

For example, the tractate of the Mishna dealing with the Sabbath had started by tacitly taking for granted one of the many Sabbath prohibitions, the prohibition against transferring objects from public to private, or private to public premises. What the tractate treats at the outset is the circumstance, which a modern reader might consider trivial but which was plainly noteworthy for the redactor of the Mishna, that that particular transgression can be looked at from different points of view; and when it is, two variations of the act are distinguishable, each of which is divisible into two further variations, and each of the latter into two more. Maimonides' Section of Halakot of the Sabbath opens very differently. He systematically collects, sets forth, and explicates all the rules scattered through the Mishna and Babylonian Talmud, in the Sabbath tractate and elsewhere, for determining when committing one of the acts prohibited on the Sabbath renders the perpetrator guilty of a crime involving a punishment and when the perpetrator is assumed to have acted inadvertently and is accordingly exempt from punishment. He thereupon takes up additional general matters, such as the abrogation of the Sabbath prohibitions whenever human life is threatened and the propriety of employing gentiles to perform labor on the Sabbath. From the general he turns to the specific, starting with the Sabbath eve. He discusses the preparations for the Sabbath that may, that may not, and that must be made on Friday and then proceeds to the thirty-nine categories of labor forbidden on the holy day itself. With the thirty-nine categories of labor as a cadre, he records the divers specific cases spelled out in the rabbinic sources.

The eighty-three sections of halakot in the *Mishneh Torah* are divided into a total of 982 chapters, and these, in turn, are subdivided into the paragraphs each of which is again called a *halaka*. In our editions of the *Mishneh Torah*, the paragraphs are numbered, but those numbers first appear in sixteenth-century printed editions. Preserved fragments of Maimonides' draft which are written in

[108]Examples: Mishna *Shibi*ᶜ*it* 7:1–2; *Bikkurim* 1:3; 3:1–6; *Shabbat* 7:1–3; *Yebamot* 6:1; *Giṭṭin* 9:2.

[109]Examples: *Mishneh Torah*: *H. Sefer Torah* 10.1; *H. Berakot* 1.1–4; *H. Shabbat* 1; *H. Gerushin* 1.1; *H. Bikkurim* 1; *H. Naḥalot* 1.1–3; *H.* ᶜ*Edut* 9.1.

his own hand[110] as well as fragments from early copies that were made by others[111] mark the paragraphs without numbering them. The paragraph divisions in the preserved fragments also occasionally differ from the divisions in the standard editions today, and a different division can affect meaning.[112] The number of paragraphs in a chapter ranges from as few as two to as many as forty, and there are 14,900 in all.[113] Not every paragraph contains a halakic ruling, for the *Mishneh Torah* embraces subjects besides law and ritual—philosophy, theology, science, religious history, ethics, hygiene, and more. Many, however, contain multiple rulings, and on a rough estimate, the *Mishneh Torah* comprises over 15,000.

They cover the familiar and the arcane, daily situations as well as situations that could have occurred only in days of old, and even then no more than once in a lifetime. We find rulings governing commercial behavior as conducted throughout the Jewish world in Maimonides' time, as well as the practice of agriculture in Palestine during periods when a Holy Temple is standing; civil and criminal liability, whether falling within the jurisdiction of rabbinic courts in all places at all times, within the exclusive jurisdiction of judges who received their ordination from already ordained judges in Palestine before the chain of ordination was severed almost a thousand years prior to Maimonides' birth, or solely within the jurisdiction of the Great Sanhedrin of seventy-one judges which can operate only on the premises of the Holy Temple and only when a Temple is standing; everyday court procedure, as well as actions to be taken against senior scholars of the Law who challenge decisions of the Great Sanhedrin at times when the Sanhedrin is operative; prayer, its accessories, and festival observance, as well as Temple rites that had fallen into desuetude 1,100 years earlier and were not expected to be practiced again until the coming of the Messiah; everyday food preparation in accordance with Jewish dietary regulations, and the preparation of the ashes of a red heifer employed in ancient purification rites; marriage and divorce, as well as the trial by ordeal conducted by a priest in the Temple for a married woman whose behavior occasioned a strong suspicion of adultery; the procedure for circumcising male infants at all times and all places, as well as obsolete procedures for trying a boy who had reached the age of puberty, was not yet more than three months beyond that age, and had been accused by both parents in high court of the capital

[110]Lutzki, Appendix to the Shulsinger edition of the *Mishneh Torah* 5 (n. 82 above); Hurvitz, "Additional Newly Discovered Handwritten Pages from Rabbi Moshe ben Maimon" (n. 82 above) 14–22, 34–38.

[111]See E. Roth, "*Qeta^cim mi-Mishneh Torah le-ha-Rambam*," *Genizah Publications in Memory of . . . David Kaufmann* (in Hebrew) (Budapest 1949) 63.

[112]The Frankel edition of the *Mishneh Torah* tries to restore the original paragraph markings on the basis of Yemenite manuscripts.

[113]S. Neuhausen, *Bible Quotations in the Code of Maimonides* (in Hebrew) (Baltimore 1941) 104 and English preface.

crime of having twice stolen money from them in order to buy meat and wine, which he then gorged and guzzled outside of his parents' house.[114]

As a matter of course, Maimonides records the laws of writing Torah scrolls and of fashioning phylacteries. But he also offers practical advice for designing a Torah scroll with symmetrical dimensions[115] and for molding a single piece of leather into a square box for phylacteries.[116] Since, he writes, he had found "a terrible confusion in all the scrolls that I have examined," he lists from an ancient Torah scroll the places where scribes copying the Torah are required to begin full or partial paragraphs.[117] He gives the laws of prayer as a matter of course and in addition sketches the entire daily liturgy, the liturgy for the Sabbath and festival days,[118] and that for the Passover eve, the *haggada*.[119] These are merely a sample. The code, as already said, has eighty-three sections, and each is dedicated to its own quotidian or arcane topic.

Where the classic rabbinic sources report differences of opinion on an issue, Maimonides had to decide which opinion to follow. As noted earlier, a handful of rules for determining what the halakic norm is can be found in the classic rabbinic texts. Additional rules are found in the writings of posttalmudic Iraqi rabbinic scholars.[120] And two or three books devoted entirely to the methodology of determining halakic norms and presumably reflecting what had become accepted in posttalmudic rabbinic circles were composed in the Iraqi milieu.[121] Although no one could dream of composing a law code without rules for handling differences of opinion, rabbinic law codes themselves refer to them, at best, only in passing.

[114]This is the Oral Law understanding of the law of the rebellious son, Deuteronomy 21:18–21. I have given only some of the limitations that the Oral Law places on the scriptural law; it in fact circumscribes the law of the rebellious son still further. See Mishna, *Sanhedrin* 8, *Mishneh Torah*: *H. Mamrim* 7, and above, n. 1.

[115]*Mishneh Torah*: *H. Sefer Torah* 9.1–7. In a symmetrical Torah scroll, the girth and the height are equal; see BT *Baba Batra* 14a.

[116]*Mishneh Torah*: *H. Tefillin* 3.2–4.

[117]*Mishneh Torah*: *H. Sefer Torah* 8.4. The scroll Maimonides follows in his instructions and that he followed when writing his own Torah scroll was a copy of the entire Old Testament which had been corrected by Ben Asher, kept in Jerusalem as a model for writing Torah scrolls, and subsequently brought to Egypt.

[118]*Mishneh Torah*, appendix to the Book of Love. More fully in D. Goldschmidt, "*Seder ha-Tefilla shel ha-Rambam*," *Yedi^{c}ot ha-Makon le-Ḥeker ha-Shira ha-^{c}Ibrit* 7 (1958) 185–213.

[119]*Mishneh Torah*: *H. Ḥameṣ u-Maṣṣa*, appendix.

[120]S. Assaf, *Darke ha-Talmud u-Kelale ha-Hora'a* (Jerusalem 1927). Mishnaic, talmudic, and posttalmudic rules—not limited to those of the Iraqi *geonim*—for setting halakic norms are recorded by Malachi ha-Kohen, *Yad Malachi* (n. 53 above) 1, letters *he* and *resh*.

[121]*Seder Tannaim we-Amoraim*, ed. K. Kahan (Kahana) (Frankfurt 1935) Hebrew section 12–28. Assaf, *Tequfat ha-Geonim we-Sifrutah* (n. 8 above) 148–49. Baron, *Social and Religious History of the Jews* 6 (n. 15 above) 30–31.

Notwithstanding his penchant for systematization, Maimonides, does not, in either his Commentary on the Mishna or his *Mishneh Torah*, discuss the criteria he employed when making his rulings. In his *Book of Commandments* he does touch on the subject here and there, and the criteria he cites are standard and accepted ones.[122] After the *Mishneh Torah* was published, he was questioned by scholars in southern France and elsewhere about some of the rulings he made, and in his replies, he cites standard and accepted criteria to justify having ruled as he did.[123] When we can observe him actually deciding which of several conflicting opinions on a given issue he should certify as authoritative, we can almost always see him following criteria that are known from the classic rabbinic sources or that had evolved and been generally accepted after the redaction of the Babylonian Talmud.[124]

One of the basic principles in his time was that when an issue is addressed by the Mishna corpus as interpreted in the Babylonian Talmud or by the Babylonian Talmud on its own, those two authorities take precedence over all other sources.[125] In a responsum Maimonides takes the principle for granted.[126] He also subscribed to it by implication in the introduction to his Commentary on the Mishna when he undertook to interpret the Mishna as the "Talmud," that is, the Babylonian Talmud, does,[127] and again in the introduction to the *Mishneh Torah*, where he states that

[122]*Book of Commandments*, rule 9 (end), et passim.

[123]For example, *Responsa* §§297, 299, 303, 308, 317, 326, 334, 340, 344, 464.

[124]Maimonides was so committed to the accepted criteria for determining halakic norms in preference to any other consideration that he sometimes follows accepted criteria when setting the norm on an issue discussed in one passage of the Mishna or Babylonian Talmud, then follows the same or other criteria when setting the norm on a related issue discussed in another mishnaic or talmudic passage, and as a result lays down two rulings that are inconsistent. See, for example, the ruling in *Mishneh Torah*: *H. Shofar* 2.4, to the effect that a person must have proper intent in order to fulfill the commandment of listening to the ram's horn on the New Year's holiday, and the apparently incompatible ruling in *Mishneh Torah*: *H. Ḥameṣ u-Maṣṣa* 6.3, to the effect that a person need not have proper intent in order to fulfill the commandment of eating unleavened bread on Passover. Other examples: *Mishneh Torah*: *H. Ishut* 9.2, and *H. Mekira* 22.12 (spelled out in *Maggid Mishna* on the former passage); *H. ᶜAbodat Kokabim* 5:11, and *H. Sanhedrin* 18.2; *H. Maᶜaser Sheni* 11.17, and *H. Bikkurim* 4.3 (relying on the Palestinian Talmud). The phenomenon is pointed out by J. Levinger, *Darke ha-Maḥshaba ha-Hilkatit shel ha-Rambam* (Jerusalem 1965) 166–77. G. Blidstein, "Where Do We Stand in the Study of Maimonidean Halakhah?" *Studies in Maimonides*, ed. I. Twersky (Cambridge, Mass. 1990) 10, believes that the phenomenon has been overstated and submits that Maimonides often does try to keep his rulings in different areas consistent with one another.

[125]Sources are given by Y. Brody, "*Le-Pesiqat ha-Rambam ᶜal pi ha-Talmud ha-Yerushalmi*," *Maimonidean Studies* 4 (2000) 2–3. The principle that the Tosefta and Palestinian Talmud become authoritative where the Mishna and Babylonian Talmud do not take a stand on a halakic issue is found in *geonic* literature. See Assaf, *Darke ha-Talmud u-Kelale ha-Hora'a* §§59, 67.

[126]*Responsa* §299.

[127]Above, p. 149.

all Jews have the obligation to observe every regulation promulgated by the Babylonian Talmud.[128]

A letter of his to Pinḥas of Alexandria after publication of the *Mishneh Torah* avers that the "Talmud has decided every halaka either specifically," by stating that such-and-such is the halaka, or "in a general way, by [providing] the criteria through which halakot are to be decided." The majority of rulings in the *Mishneh Torah* accordingly either emerge "straightforwardly from the Babylonian or Palestinian Talmud" (*talmud ᶜaruk . . . be-ferush ba-Babli o ba-Yerushalmi*), or else come from the classic midrashic compilations, or are "a straightforward passage in the Mishna," or are a passage in the Tosefta. In other words, the norms he records in the *Mishneh Torah* are articulated explicitly in one of those sources or can easily be inferred from them with the aid of established criteria.[129] Maimonides does not bother to mention that whenever the Babylonian Talmud addresses an issue, it takes precedence and overrides the Tosefta and the other rabbinic sources; that went without saying. Scholars have thought that they find instances where Maimonides decides matters in accordance with the Tosefta, with the Palestinian Talmud, or with the halakic midrashic compilations, even when those sources conflict with the Mishna and Babylonian Talmud. The evidence that has been adduced is questionable and if such ever happened, it was very rare.[130]

[128]When he wrote to Pinḥas of Alexandria that his rulings in the *Mishneh Torah* reflect halakic norms stated straightforwardly in the Mishna, two Talmuds, and other rabbinic sources, he would accordingly have meant that he relied on the other sources when they do not conflict with the Babylonian Talmud.

[129]Letter to Pinḥas of Alexandria, in Shailat, *Letters and Essays of Moses Maimonides* (n. 21 above) 442–43. Benedikt, *Ha-Rambam le-lo Seṭiyya min ha-Talmud* (n. 94 above) 15, points out that the expression *talmud ᶜaruk* in the sense in which Maimonides uses it is found in BT *Shebuᶜot* 40b. Maimonides, *Responsa* §345, where Maimonides explains that he ruled on the basis of a straightforward talmudic statement (*talmud ᶜaruk*) rather than on the basis of a proposition put forward hypothetically in the course of the dialectic give and take, is taken by Benedikt, pp. 13, 82, 109, 144, as a general key to understanding rulings of Maimonides' which have been perceived to be in opposition to the established criteria for determining halakic norms. Benedikt, p. 255, cites a notion in Alfasi which is similar to Maimonides'.

[130]On Maimonides' treating the Tosefta as an authority equal to the Mishna corpus, see: R. Abraham ben David, gloss on *Mishneh Torah*: *H. Para Adumma* 6.7 (which, by contrast, is explained by the commentary *Kesef Mishneh* as an instance where the Tosefta complements the Mishna and does not conflict with it); *Kesef Mishneh* on *Mishneh Torah*: *H. Abot ha-Ṭum'ot* 17.4; Benedikt, *Ha-Rambam le-lo Seṭiyya min ha-Talmud* 143. Weiss, "*Toledot*" (n. 53 above) 232, note 36, cites a small number of instances where he reads Maimonides as relying on the halakic midrashic compilations over against the Babylonian Talmud when setting a norm; in each of the examples, Maimonides could, however, have understood that the alternative source did not conflict with the Babylonian Talmud, but rather complemented it. Malachi ha-Kohen, *Yad Malachi* 2, rules regarding Maimonides, §9, doubts whether there is more than a single instance of Maimonides' giving precedence to a halakic midrashic compilation over the Babylonian Talmud. He incidentally endorses a rule to the effect that the halakic midrashic compilations are never to be recognized as authoritative even when not in conflict with the Babylonian Talmud. Maimonides

Maimonides' letter to Pinḥas continues: There remain a small number of places where rulings in the *Mishneh Torah* do not emerge directly from the classic sources. In cases of the sort, his procedure was to label the pertinent ruling with the qualification: the "*geonim* ruled," "it is an enactment of the later rabbis," or a similar tag; or by saying: "the matter appears to me as follows" or "from here you can infer that the matter is such-and-such."[131] A hundred or so times, particularly in areas of law that still had practical application in Maimonides' day, the *Mishneh Torah* does cite what it identifies as decisions or enactments of *geonim*[132] and of men whom Maimonides calls his "masters." They are either instances where talmudic passages lend themselves to different interpretations and the *geonim* and Maimonides' masters had decided in accordance with one of the possible interpretations as against the others, or instances where posttalmudic authorities had enacted new regulations to meet a perceived need. About 170 times, Maimonides qualifies a ruling by noting that he was expressing his own opinion. These almost invariably relate to interstices of law and ritual where the classic sources are silent or where they speak but the criteria for determining the halakic norm fail to reveal

---

plainly did not recognize such a rule; see above, p. 198, and Letter to Pinḥas of Alexandria, in Shailat, *Letters and Essays of Moses Maimonides* 443. Kasher, *Maimonides and the Mekhilta* (in Hebrew) (New York 1943), lists 100 passages in the *Mishneh Torah* where he finds Maimonides following the *Mekilta* of R. Shimᶜon, and item #46 in his list is the only one where I could see Maimonides apparently laying down a ruling in opposition to the Mishna and Babylonian Talmud. See also Maimonides, *Responsa* §326, where he rejects a position taken in the halakic midrashic compilation *Sifre* on the grounds that it is not reflected in either of the two Talmuds or in the Tosefta.

When Maimonides seems to make a ruling in accordance with the Palestinian Talmud over against the Babylonian, he again may have understood that the former merely complements the latter. In *Responsa* §299, he recommends a ruling in the Palestinian Talmud precisely on those grounds. Tchernowitz, *Toledoth ha-Poskim* 1.220, lists over a dozen passages in the *Mishneh Torah* where he supposes that Maimonides "decides [an issue] in accordance with the Palestinian Talmud and against the Babylonian," but as far as I could see, all the items on the list could have been understood by Maimonides as instances where the Palestinian Talmud complemented, and did not conflict with the Babylonian. There is also the possibility that Maimonides preferred the Palestinian Talmud over the Babylonian when the former sets forth a ruling straightforwardly, while the contrary ruling is only implied by the dialectic give and take in the latter. See Benedikt, *Ha-Rambam le-lo Seṭiyya min ha-Talmud* 84. Still another hypothesis is that where the Palestinian Talmud contains a tractate devoted to subject X and the Babylonian Talmud does not, then Maimonides gave preference to the Palestinian Talmud as against the Babylonian even when a tractate of the latter devoted to a different subject happens, incidentally, to take up an issue falling within the scope of X; see Brody, "*Le-Pesiqat ha-Rambam ᶜal pi ha-Talmud ha-Yerushalmi*" (n. 125 above) 9.

[131] Letter to Pinḥas, in Shailat, *Letters and Essays of Moses Maimonides* 443.

[132] See A. Schwarz, "Das Verhältnis Maimuni's zu den Gaonen," *Moses ben Maimon*, ed. W. Bacher et al., 1 (Leipzig 1908) 332–409. Levinger, *Darke ha-Maḥshaba ha-Hilkatit shel ha-Rambam* (n. 124 above) 220–25, lists forty-eight instances where Maimonides cites a posttalmudic opinion and expresses his own judgment as to whether the opinion in question is or is not authoritative.

exactly what it is.[133] Sometimes when Maimonides labels an opinion as his own, he passes judgment on the correctness of positions held by men whom he identifies as the *geonim* or his teachers.

The distilling of halakic norms out of the classic rabbinic sources and the Babylonian Talmud in particular was, in actuality, considerably more complex than Maimonides acknowledged when writing to Pinḥas of Alexandria. The Babylonian Talmud often discusses an issue in several places and handles it differently each time. Maimonides then had the problem of deciding which treatment of the issue was authoritative.[134] The wording of the Babylonian Talmud is often open to differing interpretations; obviously, by construing a passage in a certain fashion rather than another, Maimonides might arrive at a different ruling from rabbinists who read the passage differently.[135] At times, the established criteria are insufficient for determining which of the opinions in the Babylonian Talmud should be followed; when deciding on those, Maimonides had to rely on secondary considerations, and the secondary considerations to which he had recourse might not be recognized as binding by other medieval rabbinists.[136] For whatever reason, the *Mishneh Torah* contains rulings, quite apart from the ones that Maimonides expressly labeled as coming from the *geonim*, his masters, or himself, which diverge from the way the majority of posttalmudic scholars thought the halakic norm should be set.[137] On one occasion he concedes that although—he was confident—a certain ruling stated in the *Mishneh Torah* was correct, a ruling contrary to his was also legitimate.[138] He once expressly admits that he had made a mistake and writes that he would emend the *Mishneh Torah* in accordance with his questioners' objection.[139] There is evidence of his having made additional corrections as well.[140]

[133]See Levinger, *Darke ha-Maḥshaba ha-Hilkatit shel ha-Rambam*, third appendix.

[134]See Malachi ha-Kohen, *Yad Malachi* 1, letter *he* §§150, 193, 233; Benedikt, *Ha-Rambam le-lo Seṭiyya min ha-Talmud* 90–93, 99.

[135]Examples in H. Gross, "R. Abraham b. David aus Posquières," *Monatsschrift für Geschichte und Wissenschaft des Judentums* 23 (1874) 80–81. Joseph Ibn Migas, for whom Maimonides expressed unbounded admiration, constantly records alternative interpretations in his talmudic commentaries. See I. Ta-Shma, "*Yeṣirato ha-Sifrutit shel R. Yosef ha-Levi Ibn Migas*," *Kiryat Sefer* 46 (1970–1971) 143–45.

[136]See Malachi ha-Kohen, *Yad Malachi* 2, rules regarding Maimonides, §13; Gross, "R. Abraham b. David aus Posquières" 78; Benedikt, *Ha-Rambam le-lo Seṭiyya min ha-Talmud* (n. 94 above) 107–9.

[137]Examples: Benedikt, *Ha-Rambam le-lo Seṭiyya min ha-Talmu* 11, 194–95, et passim. Benedikt, *Asuppat Ma'amarim* (n. 53 above) 163–64. In the former work, pp. 69–85, Benedikt maintains that in fact there are no such instances.

[138]Responsa (n. 20 above) §300 (one of the responsa sent to Lunel, the authenticity of which is rejected by Kafah, "*She'elot Ḥakme Lunel u-Teshubot 'ha-Rambam*,'" [n. 81 above]).

[139]*Responsa* §287, another of the Lunel responsa.

[140]*Responsa* §433. *Kesef Mishneh* on *Mishneh Torah*: *H. Ishut* 1.2; 3.20, to be read together with Maimonides, Commentary on the Mishna (n. 14 above), *Qiddushin* 1:1, note 15.

The *Mishneh Torah* has been searched from beginning to end for places where nonhalakic considerations—Maimonides' rationalism, his philosophic or medical beliefs—led him to set down rulings that run counter to what is indicated by the classic rabbinic sources and particularly the Babylonian Talmud. If Maimonides ever did rule in such a manner, he would have broken faith with his readers, for he undertook to reflect, faithfully, the content and intent of the rabbinic sources. As far as I know, not one clear-cut instance has ever been uncovered.[141]

Here and there, he does leave out items that appear in the Mishna or the Babylonian Talmud, that are of a sort a comprehensive code of Jewish law might well contain, and that are recorded in other codes. While some may simply have been overlooked—no human being can undertake to collect and organize 15,000 scattered items without missing a few—Maimonides' personal beliefs also very likely played a role. The omissions nevertheless do not necessarily conflict with his undertaking. In two of his responsa, he points out that legally binding regulations promulgated by the rabbis must be distinguished from what is merely rabbinic advice.[142] He could easily have justified the omission of some items to himself on the grounds that they were not legally binding and hence fall outside the orbit of a code of law.

Consider his omission of the regulation that persons praying without a quorum should not use the Aramaic language. The Babylonian Talmud's reason for the

---

Kesef Mishneh on *Mishneh Torah*: *H. Lulab* 7.7. Kafah's introduction to the *Book of Commandments* (n. 55 above) 15–16. J. Kafah, "*Qer'iat Shema*^{c} *u-Tefilla bi-Meqom Ṭum'a*," *Sefer Yobel le . . . Yosef . . . Soloveitchik* (Jerusalem 1984) 593. B. Benedikt, Review of Tchernowitz, *Toledoth ha-Poskim*. *Kiryat Sefer* 25 (1949) 169 points out that Alfasi made extensive corrections to his *Halakot*.

[141]Levinger, *Darke ha-Maḥshaba ha-Hilkatit shel ha-Rambam* (n. 124 above) 181, examines the relevant material meticulously and concludes that Maimonides can never be seen to set a norm in open opposition to the classic rabbinic sources. Weiss, "*Toledot*" (n. 52 above) 229–30, asserts that in a number of instances Maimonides' personal convictions slant his decisions in the *Mishneh Torah*, but he identifies only one possible genuine instance, namely, *H. Sheḥiṭa* 8.23. Maimonides there prohibits consumption of meat from an animal that suffers from a certain defect—a missing upper jaw—although the classic rabbinic sources do not mention the defect. Weiss contends that Maimonides, because of his medical studies, regarded the defect as fatal, and accordingly ruled that meat from an animal suffering from it may not be eaten. In *Responsa* §315, Maimonides does cite considerations from medical science in justifying his ruling; but he justifies it as well on the grounds that the Mishna corpus represents a related defect—loss of the lower jaw; see Mishna *Ḥullin* 3:2—as not disqualifying animals from human consumption. By specifying that the less serious defect does *not* disqualify an animal, the Mishna—so Maimonides argues—implies that the more damaging defect does. Nor was Maimonides the first to disqualify animals with the defect; Saadia Gaon had already done so. See J. Brumer, "*Minyan ha-Gidim ha-Asurim le-R. Saadia Gaon*," *Proceedings of the American Academy for Jewish Research* 30 (1962) Hebrew section 7, pointed out by Twersky, *Introduction to the Code of Maimonides* (n. 30 above) 56, note 89.

[142]Maimonides, *Responsa* §§218, 395.

regulation is that the ministering angels and not God are in charge of prayers recited without a quorum, and angels do not understand Aramaic;[143] Maimonides did not believe that God has ministering angels who mediate prayers addressed to Him. The *Mishneh Torah* further omits the talmudic instruction to pour water on each hand three times every morning in order to remove the evil spirit that settles on human hands during sleep[144] and their instruction not to greet a stranger on the street at night because the stranger might be a demon.[145] Maimonides certainly did not believe that an evil spirit settles on a person's hands and can be removed only by washing them in the prescribed fashion[146] or—although rabbinic authors coming after him found it hard to conceive of his having taken so radical a step[147]—that a person may encounter a demon when walking abroad at night. We can assume that his rationalism and aversion to superstition played a role in his omission of these rabbinic dicta. Then he leaves out the rabbinic prohibition against eating meat and fish together because the combination can cause leprosy,[148] the rabbinic injunction to take salt whenever one eats food and to drink water whenever one drinks another beverage because failure to do so may lead to halitosis or

[143]BT *Shabbat* 12b; *Soṭa* 33a. Mishna *Soṭa* 7:1 includes prayer in a list of seven recitations—grace after meals, the "Hear O Israel" passage, and so on—that may be made in any language. Maimonides in his Commentary on the Mishna, *Soṭa* 7:1, writes that a person should "try" to use Hebrew when praying without a quorum, but he avoids any mention of the ministering angels. The rules about making the other six recitations in any language are recorded at appropriate spots in the *Mishneh Torah*, but Maimonides for some reason omits the rule about praying in a language other than Hebrew.

[144]BT *Shabbat* 109a.

[145]BT *Megilla* 3a.

[146]Mishna, *Bekorot* 7:5, records a regulation concerning a man who is affected by a sickly (*qiṣrit*) spirit, which Maimonides, Commentary on the Mishna, explains as a predominance of black bile, or melancholia, in the system. In *Mishneh Torah*: *H. Bi'at ha-Miqdash* 8.16, he recasts that mishnaic regulation in his own language as referring to a person in whom "an evil spirit has struck terror." Mishna, *Giṭṭin* 7:1, records a regulation concerning a man who is affected by *qurdiaqos* (καρδιακός). The Babylonian Talmud glosses *qurdiaqos* as the name of a certain "spirit," but Maimonides, Commentary on the Mishna, explains it as a form of epilepsy resulting from foreign material's filling the lobes of the brain. In *Mishneh Torah*: *H. Gerushin* 2.14, he recasts this regulation too as referring to a person in whom "an evil spirit has struck terror," whereupon he explicitly labels the condition as a "disease." He can safely be read as using the expression "evil spirit" as the designation of a disease in *H. Bi'at ha-Miqdash* 8.16 as well. In *Mishneh Torah*: *H. Berakot* 6:16, he records a regulation from BT *Ḥullin* 105a–b, which prohibits spilling the water with which one washes one's hands at the end of a meal on the ground. According to the Babylonian Talmud, the reason for the prohibition is that an "evil spirit" settles on such water. Maimonides omits the reason; Alfasi also had done so in his code. For instances where Maimonides gives a rational explanation to the term "evil spirit" when it appears in the Mishna, see above, p. 160.

[147]M. Shapiro, "Maimonidean Halakah and Superstition," *Maimonidean Studies* 4 (2000) 71–72, lists traditional rabbinic scholars who refused to recognize that Maimonides might have rejected the existence of the evil spirit and demons.

[148]BT *Pesaḥim* 76b. The *Shulḥan ᶜAruk* records the prohibition.

croup,[149] as well as additional instructions of a similar nature.[150] He was very likely swayed in those instances by the circumstance that the system of medicine in which he was trained did not recognize the dangers; in his medical writings, he in fact specifically warns *against* drinking water during meals because water interferes with digestion.[151] Yet, whatever his motives, the items mentioned and others of a similar nature may be viewed as nonbinding advice.[152] Maimonides could therefore have justified the omissions to himself on that ground.

Sometimes he records a ruling but explains it differently from the way the classic rabbinic sources did.[153] Once when asked about a passage in the *Mishneh Torah* where his explication of a halakic ruling differed from the explication given by the classic texts, he replied that he had made the change deliberately. For his "intent throughout the entire composition was to explain the legal regulations in the most plausible fashion or in accordance with the most common situations."[154] He is saying that in order better to serve the readership he foresaw, he allowed himself to

[149]BT *Berakot* 40a. The *Shulḥan* ^c^*Aruk* records this prohibition too.

[150]To take one more example: BT *Baba Batra* 126b states: There is a tradition that "the saliva of a man's firstborn cures eye disease"; as a consequence, should a father announce that the saliva of one of his sons cures eye disease, he thereby indirectly testifies that that son is his firstborn. Alfasi, *ad locum*, records the passage from the Babylonian Talmud. Maimonides, *Mishneh Torah*: *H. Naḥalot* 2.16, omits mention of saliva and eye disease and instead formulates a general rule: A father's statement about a particular son implying that he considers him to be his firstborn constitutes evidence that the son is indeed the man's firstborn. The *Ṭur* and *Shulḥan* ^c^*Aruk* lay down a general rule modeled on Maimonides' rule but then illustrate it by citing the talmudic example of a father's announcement concerning his son's saliva.

[151]Below, p. 462.

[152]The following is instructive: BT *Baba Qamma* 82a attributes ten ordinances to the biblical Ezra, one of which is the instruction to "eat garlic on the eve of the Sabbath"; the rationale was that garlic increases the supply of semen in the male, and Friday night is the time when a man usually has sexual intercourse with his wife. Alfasi records the Ezra ordinances in his code, including the one about garlic. Maimonides incorporates the other nine ordinances in the *Mishneh Torah* but omits the one concerning garlic. In his Commentary on the Mishna, *Nedarim* 8:4, he reveals his thinking when he notes that in times past, it was a Jewish "custom" to eat garlic on the Sabbath eve, because the geographic location and general diet of the population were such that garlic "aided" sexual intercourse. He, in other words, understood the eating of garlic to have been a custom bound to circumstances that no longer obtain.

Maimonides was not alone in failing to accept the binding character of rabbinic medicine. See B. Lewin, *Oṣar ha-Geonim*, *Giṭṭin* (Jerusalem 1941) 152; Tosafot, *Mo*^c^*ed Qaṭan* 11a; Tosafot, *Yoma* 77b.

[153]See Malachi ha-Kohen, *Yad Malachi* (n. 53 above) 2, rules regarding Maimonides, §4; Ḥ. Madini, *Sede Ḥemed* 6, *kelale ha-poseqim* §5.2; Benedikt, *Ha-Rambam le-lo Seṭiyya min ha-Talmud* (n. 94 above) 47–58. Levinger, *Darke ha-Maḥshaba ha-Hilkatit shel ha-Rambam* (n. 125 above) 92–113, lists and discusses a number of instances and, p. 185, makes the radical, and in my judgment highly tendentious, assertion that although Maimonides accepted the legislation of the ancient rabbis, he disassociated himself, "intellectually and emotionally," from the explanations given by the rabbis for their legislation.

[154]*Responsa* §252.

substitute a simplified explanation for the more complicated or convoluted one found in the sources.[155] A few of the instances where his explanation diverges from the one stated or implied in the classic sources were, we may conjecture, motivated by uneasiness with the ruling itself: He could not bring himself to leave out the ruling because of his undertaking to make his code complete but did allow himself to alter the reason for it.

Take for example, his ruling, based on his reading of a passage in the Babylonian Talmud, that it is "permitted to recite incantations over a [scorpion or snake] bite, even on the Sabbath." The plain intent of the passage was that incantations work. Maimonides, however, qualifies his ruling with the comment that an incantation is permitted solely "to put the victim's mind to rest and fortify his spirit, since his life is in danger, despite the incantation's having no effect at all."[156] Again, both the Babylonian and Palestinian Talmuds prohibit keeping food under one's bed, the former giving as the reason that "an evil spirit settles" on such food, whereas the latter offers no reason. Maimonides records the prohibition using language that shows he is quoting from the Palestinian, and not the Babylonian, Talmud. He ignores the explanation given by the Babylonian Talmud and explains the prohibition on natural grounds: One must not keep food under a bed because of the danger that "something harmful may fall in" when the food is out of sight.[157]

[155]Maimonides' simplification of the explanations that the rabbis gave for their regulations does not harmonize with his remark, in the letter to Joseph ben Judah, that his primary object in composing the *Mishneh Torah* was to provide himself with a reference work. *Mishneh Torah*: *H. Qiddush ha-Ḥodesh* 7.7 is an instance where he did not simplify but, on the contrary, substituted a technical scientific explanation for a straightforward explanation found in the rabbinic sources.

[156]*Mishneh Torah*: *H. ᶜAbodat Kokabim* 11.11. A notorious comment of R. Elijah of Vilna on *Shulḥan ᶜAruk*, *Yoreh Deᶜa* 179:6, criticizes Maimonides for having followed "accursed philosophy" in his statement about incantations' having no effect at all and adds that other rabbinic figures "hit Maimonides over the skull" for making the radical statement. Someone in the Romm publishing establishment edited out the word "accursed" in the magnificent Romm edition of the *Shulḥan ᶜAruk*; see. J. Dienstag, "*Ha-im Hitnagged ha-Gera le-Mishnato ha-Pilosophit shel ha-Rambam*," *Talpioth* 4 (1949) 253, 255.

The pertinent talmudic passage, BT *Sanhedrin* 101a, permits reciting incantations over scorpions and snakes themselves, but Maimonides reads the passage as permitting incantation over scorpion and snake *bites*. *H. ᶜAbodat Kokabim* 11.4–5 deals with rabbinic rulings concerning various forms of divination, and there too Maimonides reads the underlying rabbinic passages in a manner that he could feel comfortable with and sets down his rulings accordingly.

[157]BT *Pesaḥim* 112a; PT *Terumot* 8:5 (where the prohibition is called a concern of the "people," as distinct from scholars, which nevertheless should be observed); *Mishneh Torah*: *H. Roṣe'aḥ* 12:5. Prior to Maimonides, Alfasi, on BT *ᶜAboda Zara*, chapter 2, had also quoted the prohibition from the Palestinian, rather than from the Babylonian, Talmud but he gave no reason why food may not be kept under the bed. Maimonides would have justified his explanation by pointing out that the prohibition against keeping food under the bed is accompanied in the Palestinian Talmud by other prohibitions based—as he read the text—on hygienic and not

The following appears in the *Mishneh Torah*: When someone rents a piece of agricultural land and his crop fails because of blight, and when, moreover, most of the crops sowed by others in the area that year also fail because of blight, the renter can require the owner to refund the rental price. If it happens, however, that not only do most of the crops in the area suffer from blight but all crops sowed by the renter in the same year, whether there or elsewhere, are blighted, he cannot sue for a refund. "Since all his fields were blighted," the crop failure in the rented land "was due to the renter."[158] We are left wondering how the renter can be held responsible for blight. A look at the source clarifies matters: The Babylonian Talmud tells us that since all the renter's crops failed, the failure must have been due to his bad luck and he therefore has no legal claim against the owner of the land.[159] Maimonides would have been uncomfortable with the notion that a litigant's bad luck affects his legal standing and still more uncomfortable with the astrological penumbra surrounding the notion of good and bad luck. He therefore omits the explanation given by the Babylonian Talmud and leaves us with a riddle.

What is noteworthy here is not that Maimonides fails to repeat the Babylonian Talmud's explanation but that he records the ruling, despite any reservations he may have had about it. The ruling is stated unambiguously in the Babylonian Talmud, it is of a legal character, and he would have betrayed his undertaking if he omitted it.

There are other places where Maimonides includes items with which he must have felt uncomfortable. To take one more example, he records, albeit in summary fashion, regulations from the Mishna corpus and Babylonian Talmud which permit the wearing of written amulets outside the house on the Sabbath if it has been proven that they heal the sick, while prohibiting the wearing of amulets that are unproven.[160] Elsewhere he expresses an unambiguous opposition to the use of written amulets.[161] Since a full account of the Sabbath laws required inclusion of the rules concerning the wearing of amulets when a person moves from private to

---

preternatural considerations. Other instances of his omitting instructions from the classic rabbinic sources which involve demons, an evil spirit, the evil eye, and the like, or of his altering the rabbinic explanations of such instructions, are given by Shapiro, "Maimonidean Halakhah and Superstition" (n. 147 above) 75–94.

[158]*Mishneh Torah*: *H. Sekirut* 8:5.

[159]BT *Baba Meṣiᶜa* 106a.

[160]*Mishneh Torah*: *H. Shabbat* 19.14, summarizing Mishna *Shabbat* 6:2 and BT *Shabbat* 61a–b. Maimonides omits many of the casuistic details regarding written amulets which the Babylonian Talmud furnishes and which Alfasi's code records. In *Mishneh Torah*: *H. Shabbat* 19.13, he summarizes even more drastically. He does not list the amulets that Mishna *Shabbat* 6.10, and BT *Shabbat* 67a, allow to be worn outside the house on the Sabbath and that Alfasi also listed, namely: a locust's egg, a wolf's tooth, a nail from a crucified man. Instead, he restricts himself to the rationale for the regulation, as stated in BT *Shabbat* 67a, and simply rules that "anything" the "physicians say is efficacious" may be worn outside of the house on the Sabbath.

[161]He rejects amulets in Commentary on the Mishna, *Soṭa* 7:4, and in *Guide for the Perplexed* 1.61. See also the quotations immediately above concerning incantations.

public premises or vice versa, or when he walks the distance of four cubits in a public area, Maimonides felt that he had to record those regulations.[162]

There are even instances where he incorporates explanations from the rabbinic sources which ran counter to his scientific convictions, although he could easily have ignored them, his motive for incorporating them being the lesson they teach. Thus in the concluding paragraph of his section on the scriptural "plague of leprosy" (*ṣara^c^at*),[163] he reworks what the ancient texts had said about the cause of the affliction as follows: It is unnatural for the plague of leprosy to appear in inanimate objects such as houses and garments. Its appearance in the walls of houses in Palestine, as assumed by Scripture, was consequently a miracle, a miraculous divine punishment for the Israelite owners' having committed the sin of speaking evil of other persons. If an owner of an affected house should fail to learn from the initial infection and continue to speak ill of others, the plague would miraculously attach itself to his clothing. If he still failed to heed the silent admonition and persisted in his evil ways, divine retribution would transfer the plague to the man's very body. Such is the seriousness of the sin of speaking evil of another.[164] The description of the miraculous etiology and spread of leprosy was scarcely in harmony with Maimonides' medical understanding or his rationalist outlook. But the moral lesson taught by the rabbis in connection with leprosy was well worth including. He would later write in his main philosophic work that Scripture itself propagates unscientific beliefs in order to accomplish its ends. For instance, in order to persuade men to behave honestly and responsibly, Scripture encourages them to accept the unscientific proposition that God becomes "very angry" at malefactors.[165]

At one point in the *Mishneh Torah*, Maimonides insists that where scientific knowledge is concerned, "it makes no difference who the author is, whether

[162]Other instances where Maimonides included rabbinic instructions that ran counter to his personal outlook: *H. Tefilla* 9.7, read in the light of *Guide for the Perplexed* 3.48; *H. Tefilla* as explicated by Shapiro, "Maimonidean Halakhah and Superstition" 103.

[163]Leviticus 13.

[164]*Mishneh Torah*: *H. Tum'at Ṣara^c^ot* 16.10; Maimonides expresses the same notion in his Commentary on the Mishna, *Nega^c^im* 12.5. The connection between the disease of "leprosy" and the sin of slander goes back to the biblical story of Miriam; see Numbers 12:1, 10, and Deuteronomy 24:8–9. It is common in the classic rabbinic sources; see Tosefta, *Nega^c^im* 6.7; BT *^c^Arakin* 15b; 16b; *Leviticus Rabba* 16:1–6; 17:4.

A similar instance is *Mishneh Torah*: *H. Issure Bi'a* 19.17, which follows BT *Qiddushin* 70a; 71b: Quarrelsome families and persons who go about stigmatizing others as being of illegitimate birth are themselves likely to be of illegitimate birth; persons who stigmatize others as belonging to the caste of nonemancipated slaves and hence as not full-fledged Jews are themselves likely to be of the caste of nonemancipated slaves.

[165]Maimonides, *Guide for the Perplexed* 3.28: In addition to the "true beliefs" taught by the Law, the Law also calls upon man to accept "certain beliefs, credence in which is necessary for the health of society, such as our belief that God becomes very angry with those who disobey Him."

prophets or gentiles framed the proofs. For when the reason for something is set forth clearly and its truth is known through faultless proofs, we do not rely on the author, but on the proof . . . and the reason" that he furnishes.[166] Maimonides nonetheless understood that law and ritual are not science and he lays down the significant principle that when the science of his day conflicts with rabbinic laws and rituals, science has to defer.

The context is the physical defects in an animal that, according to the dietary laws, render meat ritually unfit for consumption. The meat is unfit because, the ancient rabbis understood, the defects in question are fatal and animals affected by them cannot survive for a year; the meat therefore falls under the biblical prohibition against eating the flesh of a "torn" (*ṭerefa*) animal.[167] After recording all the conditions identified by the rabbis which place animals in the category of the "torn" and render their flesh unfit for consumption, Maimonides states: "The foregoing defects are not to be added to. A ruminant of one of the domesticated species, a ruminant of one of the nondomesticated species, or a fowl, suffering from any defect other than those enumerated by the authorities of the classic rabbinic period and agreed upon by Jewish courts *is* able to survive, even if we learn from medical considerations that it cannot. By contrast, when it appears from current medical considerations that any of the defects the rabbis enumerated and declared to be fatal are not fatal, so that the animal could survive, you must rely on what the rabbis enumerated [and treat the defects as fatal]. For it is written: 'According to the Law which they shall teach thee, . . . thou shalt do.'"[168] Maimonides is articulating something of a positivistic stance. He started with the talmudic premise that eating the flesh of animals suffering from fatal conditions falls under the biblical prohibition against eating the flesh of "torn" animals. Echoing a statement in the Babylonian Talmud, he further recognized that the general categories of fatal defects are "a halaka given to Moses at Sinai."[169] From that point on, he is now saying, Scripture invested the ancient rabbis with the authority to spell out specifically which physical conditions are fatal and which are not. What the rabbis determined to be a fatal defect, and established practice ratified as such, overrides other considerations including the findings of veterinary science.[170]

[166]*Mishneh Torah*: *H. Qiddush ha-Ḥodesh* 17.24, Frankel edition. Maimonides further writes: The methods of calculating the positions of the sun and the moon in the heavens which are found in books composed by the "scientists of Greece" were found as well in the "books composed by Israelite scientists from the tribe of Issachar in the days of the prophets." Unfortunately, however, the Israelite treatises, unlike the gentile writings, have "not come down to us."

[167]See Exodus 22:30.

[168]*Mishneh Torah*: *H. Sheḥiṭa* 10.12–13, reflecting BT *Ḥullin* 54a. The verse is Deuteronomy 17.11, and Maimonides is interpreting it midrashically.

[169]*Mishneh Torah*: *H. Sheḥiṭa* 5.2, following BT *Ḥullin* 43a.

[170]As happens, Maimonides does add one defect to the rabbinic list of defects disqualifying animals from consumption. When he was asked about it, he justified his addition on medical

To summarize: In codifying rabbinic law and ritual, Maimonides allows his personal views only very limited latitude, and they do not lead him to make rulings in opposition to what the classic rabbinic sources indicate the halakic norm should be. He does omit a handful of rabbinic regulations that he undoubtedly felt uneasy about but—at least as far as I could discover—all are items that can be viewed as advice offered by the rabbis and not as legally binding. In a few instances, he records rulings as the rabbinic sources gave them, while adjusting or simply leaving out the rabbinic explanations. At the same time, he could include explanations from the classic rabbinic texts which were not in accord with his personal outlook, for the reason that they teach a moral lesson. When he establishes a policy for dealing with clashes between current science and rabbinic halaka, he states unequivocally that halaka overrides science.

The *Mishneh Torah* certainly does not display what one would want to call a liberalizing spirit. Take, for instance, Maimonides' rulings regarding "heretics, that is to say, worshipers of false deities"; regarding "those who commit sins solely as an act of rebellion against the religious law, even who merely eat nonkosher meat or wear garments woven of wool and linen solely out of a spirit of rebellion"; and regarding those "who deny the Torah and the [phenomenon of] prophecy." Partly relying on the Babylonian Talmud and partly supplementing it, Maimonides states that "it was [in days of old] a divine commandment [or: good deed, *miṣwa*] to kill such persons. If one could do so with a sword in public, one would do it; otherwise, one would act by subterfuge and bring about their death in that fashion."[171] On the basis of passages in the Babylonian Talmud, he holds that when circumstances warrant, a law court should on its own administer a whipping and, if necessary, even the death penalty to malefactors, although the formal law does not prescribe such a punishment for the misdeeds committed.[172] In a similar vein, but now going beyond anything expressed in the rabbinic sources, he recommends that law courts administer a beating to minors who are in the habit of stealing or of damaging property.[173] The Mishna and Babylonian Talmud state that a man who has lived with his wife for ten years without bearing children is not allowed to continue to live with her while refraining from remarrying, for he must obey the scriptural commandment to be fruitful and multiply; and a secondary talmudic discussion of the subject states that the man is forced to divorce his wife even "with whips," if necessary.[174] Maimonides records the strict position in the *Mishneh Torah*: The man in question "is forced and beaten with a whip" until he

grounds as well as on the grounds that the additional defect was in fact implied in the Mishna. See n. 141 above.

[171] *Mishneh Torah*: *H. Roṣe'aḥ* 4.10.

[172] *Mishneh Torah*: *H. Sanhedrin* 24.4–5, following BT *Sanhedrin* 46a, *Qiddushin* 81a, and Alfasi on both.

[173] *Mishneh Torah*: *H. Geneba* 1.10.

[174] Mishna *Yebamot* 6:6; BT *Yebamot* 64a; BT *Ketubbot* 77a..

acquiesces.[175] And in a singularly distasteful ruling, Maimonides decides that a husband can force a recalcitrant wife "even with a whip" to perform the household chores that rabbinic law has laid down as her wifely obligations.[176] The classic rabbinic sources nowise support the ruling, and Maimonides' most acerbic critic, a man of staunchly conservative attitudes, reacted as one cannot help hoping that Jewish judges faced with the situation always would. He dismisses Maimonides' ruling curtly with the comment: "I have never heard of chastising wives with a whip."[177]

Students of the *Mishneh Torah* have been able to point to words or phrases that reveal the care and effort Maimonides lavished on inconspicuous details of his masterpiece—much as the workmanship in a well-built house expresses itself in meticulous attention to minute details on the part of the architect and artisans. Nevertheless, the codifying side of the *Mishneh Torah* is not perfect. Scholars have been puzzled by lapses in the work's organization.[178] There are rulings that appear to run counter to the principles for deciding halaka which Maimonides accepted.[179] Inconsistencies have been found, that is to say, instances where a ruling made at one spot in the *Mishneh Torah* contradicts or appears to contradict a ruling made at another spot.[180] Maimonides' terminology is sometimes

[175]*Mishneh Torah*: *H. Ishut* 15.7, following Alfasi on BT *Yebamot* 64a. *Shulḥan* *ᶜAruk*, *Eben ha-ᶜEzer* 154:10; 21, repeats the ruling while expressing hesitation about the use of whips, and R. M. Isserles' glosses on the *Shulḥan Aruk* state that the ruling is no longer observed.

[176]*Mishneh Torah*: *H. Ishut* 21.10.

[177]Abraham ben David, gloss on *H. Ishut* 21.10. Naḥmanides, according to *Maggid Mishna* on *H. Ishut* 21.10, and R. Solomon Adret, in his novellae on BT *Ketubbot* 63a, appear to rule as Maimonides did.

Further strict rulings: *Mishneh Torah*: *H. Issure Bi'a* 4.14–16 (a wife must examine herself after sexual relations with her husband to be sure that she did not menstruate during intercourse); *Ma'akalot Asurot* 6.10; 12; 17 (strict rules for removing blood from meat); *H. Shebu ᶜot* 12.7 (a child is to be punished physically if he makes a vow that he is incapable of keeping).

[178]B. Ziemlich, "Plan und Anlage des Mischne Thora," *Moses ben Maimon*, ed. W. Bacher et al., 1 (n. 132 above) 273; Tchernowitz, *Toledoth ha-Poskim* 1 (n. 48 above) 210–13, who makes the point that Maimonides sometimes did not free himself from the order of topics in the Mishna corpus and Babylonian Talmud; Twersky, *Introduction to the Code of Maimonides* (n. 30 above) 290–95.

[179]Above, p. 219.

[180]Benedikt, *Ha-Rambam le-lo Seṭiyya min ha-Talmud* (n. 94 above) 20–24, 37; Twersky, *Introduction to the Code of Maimonides* 313–17 (In Twersky's second example, the reference "*Yibbum* iv, 5" should be corrected to "*Yibbum* iv, 35.") Benedikt contends that there are in fact no actual contradictions; although his explanation that Maimonides was careful to give precise details only in his primary treatment of a subject and sometimes treated a subject in a general and imprecise fashion in other contexts works well for some of his examples, it is not adequate in the case of the contradictions he discusses on pp. 20, 21–22, and 37. One of these instances is explained by R. Elijah of Vilna (quoted by Benedikt) as simply a change of mind on Maimonides' part. A second is similarly solved by Kafah, *Book of Commandments* (n. 55 above), editor's

ambiguous.[181] A surprising feature is the occasions on which, rather than polishing and clarifying the rulings that he records, he simply repeats statements or phrases verbatim from the classic sources which even persons conversant with rabbinic Hebrew and familiar with the lineaments of rabbinic law will not understand without help. The number of passages in the *Mishneh Torah* whose wording requires further clarification is, of course, a function of each reader's rabbinic expertise. But there are scores of passages that readers fully adept in rabbinic law will fail to understand unless they happen to remember the precise context in the classic sources from which Maimonides draws and often unless they have the context deciphered for them.[182] One of the chief commentators on the *Mishneh Torah* accounted for these passages by recalling that Maimonides undertook, after all, to *compile* and not to comment; he accordingly was required only to "copy" what the classic texts had stated and not to "explain" it.[183] The apologia surely misses the mark. Maimonides promised his readers, and the nonexpert in particular, that the *Mishneh Torah* would encapsulate the entire Oral Torah and that to learn the Oral Torah, they would need no additional rabbinic text.

He was perhaps so eager to finish his immense project that he neglected, as writers often do, to go back a tedious final time and submit his code to one more editing.

The Mishneh Torah: Its Nonlegal Side.[184] We are familiar with Maimonides' fondness for introductions; he does not stint on them in the *Mishneh Torah.* A general introduction to the entire code summarizes the rabbinic doctrine of an Oral Torah going back to Moses, a topic that Maimonides treated much more fully in the introduction to his Commentary on the Mishna. It then states his object in composing the *Mishneh Torah*, repeats his enumeration of the 613 commandments given to Moses at Sinai, and furnishes a table of contents. Within the body of the

---

introduction, p. 15, on the basis of manuscript evidence, as a correction by Maimonides after the *Mishneh Torah* was published; the correction, Kafah proposes, was introduced into one of the now contradictory passages but not into the other.

[181]Examples: The term *ḥokma* can mean wisdom (passim), prudence (*Mishneh Torah*: *H. ᶜAbadim* 9.8), science (*H. Qiddush ha-Ḥodesh* 17.24), and philosophy (*H. Teshuba* 5.5). *Deᶜa* can mean knowledge, intellect, and psychological characteristic. *Nefesh* sometimes means soul, sometimes rational soul, and sometimes the human intellect in a state of actuality. For *deᶜa* and *nefesh*, see the pertinent entries in D. Baneth, "*La-Ṭerminologeya ha-Pilosophit shel ha-Rambam*," *Tarbiz* 6 (1935) 254–84.

[182]A few of the many examples: *Mishneh Torah*: *H. Ma'akalot Asurot* 11.24; *H. Tum'at Met* 16.5; 22.6; *H. Para Adumma* 8.5; 12.6; *H. Kelim* 10; 11; 20.12, 14–16; et passim; *H. Malweh we-Loweh* 27.15.

[183]*Kesef Mishneh*, on *Mishneh Torah*: *H. Tum'at ha-Met* 12.8. Similarly, on *Mishneh Torah*: *H. Tum'at ha-Met* 16.5 (end), and *H. Tum'at Ṣarᶜat* 4.9.

[184]The general point made in the following pages is made by Twersky, *Introduction to the Code of Maimonides* (n. 30 above), and "Some Non-Halakic Aspects of the *Mishneh Torah*," *Jewish Medieval and Renaissance Studies*, ed. A. Altmann (Cambridge, Mass. 1967).

code, he begins the section of Halakot of Prayer with a few sentences on prerabbinic forms of prayer and the historical factors that led the rabbis to institute a fixed liturgy.[185] The section on setting the first day of the lunar month begins with a description of the rabbinic lunar calendar.[186] Maimonides opens his treatment of the Hanukkah holiday with an account of the historical events that the holiday commemorates.[187] A one-paragraph introduction to the Halakot of Marriage describes the manner in which—Maimonides believed—marriages were effected before the Israelites received the Torah.[188] The section on the construction of the Holy Temple in Jerusalem begins with an account of central venues of divine worship through Israelite history, which is then accompanied by a list of the appurtenances that, according to halaka, are indispensable in any central location of divine service.[189] He opens the section on enforcing obedience to the rabbinic authorities with the rationale for requiring such obedience.[190]

The foregoing are largely reworkings of material drawn from the classic rabbinic texts. The most comprehensive introduction in the *Mishneh Torah* is the first of the fourteen Books, which comes immediately after the general introduction. It is another of the rubrics created by Maimonides which have no parallel in the division of the Mishna into six Orders.

Maimonides entitles it "The Book of Knowledge" (*Sefer ha-Madda*ᶜ), and it comprises, in his words, "all the commandments that make up the foundation of the religion of Moses and that a person must know at the outset."[191] In its structure, the Book of Knowledge looks like the other thirteen Books of the *Mishneh Torah.* It is divided into five sections of Halakot, and they, like all the other sections of the *Mishneh Torah*, are divided into chapters and then into individual halakot. Each of the sections takes pertinent divine commandments as its cadre, about seventy-five commandments coming into play in all. Around the commandments, Maimonides arranges regulations from the halakic side of the classic rabbinic sources as well as—to a greater extent than elsewhere in the code—ethical instruction from the aggadic side. Material of the sort would fit comfortably into any work of rabbinic law. Some of the chapters and paragraphs, however, put forth statements that are atypical of rabbinic codes and of rabbinic writing in general. These chapters and paragraphs articulate Maimonides' conception of the Jewish religion and, more broadly, of man's place in the universe, and they are integral to Maimonides' plan.[192]

185 *Mishneh Torah*: *H. Tefilla* 1.1–7.

186 *Mishneh Torah*: *H. Qiddush ha-Ḥodesh* 1.1–4.

187 *Mishneh Torah*: *H. Megilla wa-Ḥanukka* 3.1–2.

188 *Mishneh Torah*: *H. Ishut* 1.1.

189 *Mishneh Torah*: *H. Bet ha-Beḥira* 1.1 –6.

190 *Mishneh Torah*: *H. Mamrim* 1.

191 *Mishneh Torah*, introduction, list of contents of the fourteen Books.

192 Ḥefeṣ ben Yaṣliaḥ, an Iraqi rabbinic scholar of the ninth or tenth century, did something similar in his magnum rabbinic opus, but that is not a code; see n. 196 below.

Each of the sections in the Book of Knowledge makes its contribution to the picture. One of them opens with a précis of the Aristotelian theory of human ethical virtue. It is the theory, already met in Maimonides' Commentary on the Mishna, that every human ethical virtue is a psychological characteristic located midway between two undesirable, extreme characteristics; the virtue of generosity, for example, is the psychological characteristic located midway between miserliness and profligacy, both of which are vices. The same section also furnishes a regimen of diet and hygiene for helping man attain and maintain physical health.[193] Maimonides' reason for including it is that every person has the obligation "to direct his heart and all his actions exclusively to knowledge of God." Everyone should accordingly render "his body healthy and strong in order that his rational soul will be equipped for knowing God, inasmuch as it is impossible to understand and study the sciences [*ḥokmot*] when hungry or ill. . . . He who follows this path during his entire life worships [*ᶜobed*] God at all times, even when conducting business, even when engaged in sexual intercourse; for his intent is . . . that his body be healthy so as to worship God. Even . . . if he goes to sleep with a conscious purpose, in order that his mind and body rest and that he not fall ill and be prevented from worshiping God, . . . his sleep is worship [*ᶜaboda*] of God, be He blessed." Human life must, in a word, be structured; every aspect of it, including a person's physical state, should serve the goal, and the goal is "knowing God."[194] Since knowing God is, moreover, true worship of God, whatever promotes such knowledge, including eating healthy foods and observing good sleep habits, can be considered a part of divine worship. The context being a code of Jewish religious law, Maimonides does not disclose that the theory of ethical virtue which he outlines goes back to Aristotle and came to him through the Muslim philosopher Alfarabi, and that the section on hygiene is drawn entirely from Galenic medicine.

In another of the sections in the Book of Knowledge, he finds a spot for his understanding of the human afterlife. In another, he offers his theological reading of history. Still another has as its subject the divine commandments to study the Holy Law and show respect for the men who teach it; in the course of presenting the branches and details of those commandments, Maimonides finds an opportunity to slip in the statement that philosophy was an integral part of the religious studies of the ancient rabbis.[195]

Of all the sections of the Book of Knowledge, the most significant for our purpose is the first, which caries the title "Halakot of the Foundations of the Torah." Maimonides' placing it at the very beginning of the *Mishneh Torah* seems, in fact, to be his justification for calling the Book containing it the "Book of Knowledge." The subject of knowledge dominates the initial chapters of the

[193]*Mishneh Torah*: *H. Deᶜot* 4.
[194]*Mishneh Torah*: *H. Deᶜot* 3.2–3.
[195]See below, pp. 237–38, 241–42, 244.

Halakot of the Foundations of the Torah, but makes only a minor appearance in the remaining four sections of halakot in the Book.

As already noted, the *Mishneh Torah* is built around Maimonides' list of the 613 commandments communicated by God to Moses at Sinai. The Halakot of the Foundations of the Torah starts with an exposition of what Maimonides took to be the first two divine commandments.

In his *Book of Commandments* he had placed at the head of his list of positive commandments the obligation to "believe that a cause exists which produces all existent things," that is to say, to believe in the existence of God; the second commandment in his list was the obligation to believe God's unity. The biblical verses in which Maimonides discovered the two obligations were the opening sentence of the Decalogue, "I am the Lord thy God," and the verse that had become a virtual declaration of the Jewish faith, "Hear O Israel, the Lord our God, the Lord is one."[196] By enumerating belief in God's existence and unity as the first and second commandments, he signaled that the Jewish religion, despite its undeniable emphasis on ritual acts, is grounded in belief.

The *Mishneh Torah* makes a critical change in the formulation. Maimonides begins the Halakot of the Foundations of the Torah and hence the Book of Knowledge and the body of the entire *Mishneh Torah* with the declaration: The "most basic foundation [of the Torah and religion] and the pillar of the sciences is to know that there exists a First Being, which brings every other being into existence." A few lines further on, he identifies the first of the positive commandments given to Moses as that very obligation, the obligation to "know" the existence of a First Being. He identifies the second positive divine commandment as the obligation to "know" that the First Being is one. The scriptural verses in which he uncovers the two commands are those that he cited in the *Book of Commandments*—"I am the Lord thy God" and "Hear O Israel . . . the Lord is one."[197] The initial positive commandments of the *Book of Commandments* thus

[196]Maimonides, *Sefer ha-Miṣwot*, positive commandments #1, #2; Exodus 20:2; Deuteronomy 5:6; 6:4. He had precedents. Ḥefeṣ ben Yaṣliaḥ produced a work on the subject of the 613 commandments of the Written Law, and the first two commandments in his list were precisely the commands to believe the existence and unity of God. See Ḥefeṣ ben Yaṣliaḥ, *A Volume of the Book of Precepts*, ed. B. Halper (Philadelphia 1915) 31, 34, 35, 38–39. Ḥefeṣ even offered a quasi-philosophic argument for the existence of God. And in explicating the unity of God he wrote that anthropomorphic descriptions of God in Scripture merely "liken God to the language of men" and are not intended to be taken literally; compare the expression "in conformity with the language of men" used by Maimonides in connection with anthropomorphisms, below p. 239. second precedent is Ibn Ezra, who in his Commentary to Exodus 20:2, construes the first of the Ten Commandments as the injunction to "believe . . . without doubt that the God denoted by the tetragrammaton is the sole God" and who then proceeds to explain that the highest level of belief is to "know God" by inference from the universe He produced. See, further, my article in the Joseph Dan Festschrift.

[197]*Mishneh Torah*: *H. Tesode ha-Torah* 1.1; 6–7. The first negative commandment of the Law, which Maimonides finds in the second of the Ten Commandments—"thou shalt have no

reappear in the *Mishneh Torah* as injunctions not merely to believe but to know. The Book of *Knowledge* has opened, appropriately enough, with the mandate to acquire *knowledge*, and Maimonides tells us that knowledge is the foundation on which the entire Jewish religion rests.

Later, in his *Guide for the Perplexed*, he would analyze the notion of belief, distinguish different levels, and conclude in effect that belief at its acme coalesces with knowledge.[198] The *Book of Commandments*, which formulated the first two positive divine commandments as injunctions to *believe* the existence and unity of God, can accordingly be read as enjoining belief not at any level, but at the level that is tantamount to knowledge. Maimonides can be read in retrospect as taking the same position in the *Book of Commandments* as in the *Mishneh Torah* and intimating there too that the first two commandments of the Written Law are injunctions to *know* the existence and unity of God.

He once remarks that because of the readership he foresaw for the *Mishneh Torah*, he cast what he wrote about the nature of God in a narrative guise and did not accompany his assertions with proofs.[199] In fact, the Halakot of the Foundations of the Law does sketch, albeit in barest outline, a proof of the existence of God and a proof of God's unity. The proofs provide readers with a starting point for knowing, and not just accepting at some lesser level of belief, the pair of propositions embodied in the first two positive commandments that he enumerates.

The proof for the existence of God sketched in the Halakot of the Foundations of the Law is a simplified version of Aristotle's demonstration of the existence of a First Mover of the celestial spheres. All Maimonides says is that "the celestial sphere rotates continually, and it is impossible for it to move without a mover," whence it follows that a First Being, or "God," "moves the sphere with an infinite power."[200] In other words, the unceasing motion of the celestial sphere makes it possible to infer the existence of a being of infinite power who keeps the sphere constantly in motion, and that infinitely powerful being is what is known as God. To simplify matters, Maimonides has for now put aside the significant detail that

---

other gods before Me"—is formulated in his *Book of Commandments* as the "prohibition against *believing* that divinity pertains to anyone but God." In *Mishneh Torah*: *H. Yesode ha-Torah* 1.6, he formulates it as the prohibition against "harboring the thought" (*ma^{c}aleh ^{c}al da^{c}ato*) that "another god exists" in addition to God.

[198]Maimonides, *Guide for the Perplexed* 1.50. Maimonides reasons that when "no alternative to a belief is in any manner possible and the mind can find no way of rejecting the belief or conceiving the possibility of the alternative," then the belief is "certain." If no alternative to a belief is possible, and the mind determines that such is the case, the mind can be said to know the proposition. Belief at its acme, belief that is certain, hence coalesces with knowledge. A similar notion is found in Baḥya, *Ḥobot ha-Lebabot* 1.2.

[199]Maimonides, *Treatise on Resurrection* (n. 65 above), Hebrew-Arabic section, 4.

[200]*Mishneh Torah*: *H. Yesode ha-Torah* 1.5. Maimonides is simplifying because of the readers whom he is addressing.

there are a number of celestial spheres and that for all of them to be kept rotating, each with its own motion, additional, subordinate movers must be assumed to exist as well.

His proof for God's unity is an extension of the foregoing. The reasoning is subtle, and Maimonides again provides merely the kernel. Fleshed out a little more fully than he gives it in the *Mishneh Torah*, the reasoning goes: Since the celestial sphere rotates around the earth without ceasing, the cause maintaining it in motion must, as just seen, be infinite in power. Only incorporeal beings possess infinite power, whence it follows that the cause responsible for the rotation of the sphere is incorporeal. It is from this point that the subtlety enters.

An old philosophical axiom states that a plurality of beings identical in their essence can be distinguished from one another and enumerated only when they are present in matter. To take an illustration—mine and not Maimonides'—multiple members of the elephant species can be distinguished from each other solely because elephants are made of matter; thanks to their material side, the elephant standing here is distinguishable from the one standing there.[201] If a multiplicity of beings identical in essence is conceivable only insofar as they are present in matter, when beings do not exist in matter, there can be no more than one exemplar of each type. The being whose nature it is to be the mover of the celestial sphere has been seen to be incorporeal and not to exist in matter. Consequently, no more than a single exemplar of the type can exist. There can be only one mover of the sphere.[202]

Maimonides does not say in so many words that a person must comprehend and be convinced by these or alternative demonstrations of the existence and unity of a First Being in order properly to fulfill the two initial commandments given by God. Nor does he spell out the demonstrations in sufficient detail for persons unfamiliar with them to understand exactly what he is driving at. Still, if the two commandments mandate knowledge and not an inferior level of belief, fulfilling them properly will be contingent on comprehending and being convinced by a rational proof; for how might a person genuinely *know* propositions about beings

[201]Put more technically: Matter is the principle of individuation.

[202]*Mishneh Torah*: *H. Yesode ha-Torah* 1.7; 2.5. As I interpret what Maimonides writes in *Mishneh Torah* 2.5, the incorporeal intelligences are differentiated from one another by reason of being different in essence. *Guide for the Perplexed* 2, introduction, proposition 16, gives another explanation of the way in which they are differentiated, and it is possible to read *Mishneh Torah* 2.5 as saying what Maimonides writes there.

Aristotle proved the existence of a First Mover in both his *Physics* and *Metaphysics*, but he established the unity of the First Mover differently in the two works. In *Metaphysics*, 12.8.1074a, 33–37, he inferred the First Mover's unity from its incorporeality, whereas in *Physics* 8, he established the First Mover's unity through a different train of reasoning. Above, in chapter 2, I pointed out that when Maimonides wrote the *Guide for the Perplexed*, he was familiar with Aristotle's *Physics* and quotes from it, but that he on no occasion shows evidence of having read Aristotle's *Metaphysics*.

beyond the reach of sense perception except through rational demonstration? Maimonides is hence intimating to readers of the *Mishneh Torah* that to observe the first two positive commandments of the Torah properly they must learn philosophic demonstrations for the existence and unity of God. Not only that. The first two commandments have, for Maimonides, a privileged status within the list of 613, since the propositions they embody are the bedrock on which the Torah and Jewish religion rest. To attain a firm grasp of the most fundamental stratum of the Torah, one must study philosophy.

The Aristotelian proof of the existence of an incorporeal mover of the heavens comes up again later in the Book of Knowledge, in the Halakot of Pagan Worship. There Maimonides treats the various scriptural commandments and rabbinic regulations that not merely forbid worshiping gods other than the true God but also distance Jews from any whiff of polytheistic and idolatrous practice. Before entering into the legal particulars, he recreates the historical events that, he was persuaded, brought about mankind's unfortunate descent into polytheism. He is relying in part, as he tells us, on compositions that medieval star worshipers circulated in his day regarding their beliefs[203] and he also incorporates motifs from rabbinic aggada. In his re-creation of history, worship of the stars originated in the generation of the biblical Enosh.[204] People at the time started sacrificing to the stars and bowing down to them on the mistaken supposition that God would want homage paid to the ministers on high whom He employs in governing the world. Further deterioration in human understanding led to the worshiping of man-made images as a medium for paying homage to the stars, and mankind eventually descended to its nadir by wholly forgetting that behind the stars there stands a single incorporeal God.

The turning point came when the patriarch Abraham appeared on the scene. Without benefit of human instruction, Abraham discovered the existence of the God who lies beyond the heavens through what was—although Maimonides naturally does not label it as such—an anticipation of Aristotle's proof of the existence of a

[203]He could have used the information regarding the Ṣabians recorded by Shahrastānī; see S. Pines, "Shiᶜīte Terms and Conceptions in Judah Hallevi's *Kuzari*," *Jerusalem Studies in Arabic and Islam* 2 (1980) 196–97. The Ṣabian position is in fact more nuanced than Maimonides' account of the beliefs of the early pagans.

[204]The verb used in Genesis 4:26 is ambiguous and the verse can therefore be read in three different ways, one of which says something positive about mankind in the days of Enosh, while the other two say something negative. The verse can be read as stating that in the days of Enosh, (1) mankind *began* to pray in God's name or (2) mankind either (a) *profaned* God's name or (b) *began* to apply God's name to false deities. Targum Onkelos on Genesis 4:26 has been preserved in two versions, one of which apparently takes position (1) while the other takes position (2-a). Targum "Jonathan" takes position (2-b). *Genesis Rabba* and Rashi take position (2-a). Ibn Ezra takes position (1). David Qimḥi, in his Commentary on Genesis 4:26, outlines the three possibilities

Maimonides read the verse in accordance with either (2-a) or (2-b). Interpretation (1) would appear to be the most natural reading of the verse.

First Mover of the celestial spheres. Abraham realized that the sun, moon, and stars are embedded in a transparent sphere that continually rotates around the earth. He reasoned to himself that the celestial sphere, being a finite physical body, does not possess the power needed to maintain itself in motion indefinitely; whence he concluded that a being beyond the sphere, a transcendent God, must exist who is responsible for the unceasing circular motion and "who created everything." Abraham thereupon taught the belief in a single supernal cause of the universe to all who would listen.[205] He did what, Maimonides understood, every Jew must do to fulfill the initial commandments of the Law and he went on to teach others to do the same.

To return to the Halakot of the Foundations of the Torah: As Maimonides elaborates on the commandment to know the unity of God, he focuses less on that attribute than on another, shifting his attention to God's incorporeality, which, we just saw, served as an intermediate step in the demonstration of God's unity. It is easy to surmise the reason. The declaration that God is one is ready at hand in Scripture, most notably in the "Hear O Israel" verse, and Maimonides could safely presume that none of his Jewish readers would be tempted to recognize a multiplicity of deities. The incorporeality of God and its implications were, by contrast, not at all obvious in Scripture and they were not universally accepted. Yet divine incorporeality was no less a cornerstone of the Jewish religion for Maimonides than divine unity.

In order that the incorporeality of God, like God's existence and unity, might stand on two legs, he wanted scriptural, and not merely philosophic, testimony for it too. He therefore quotes biblical verses that, he writes, make God's incorporeality "clear" (or: "explicit"; *meforash*).[206] The verses are: "The Lord your God, He is God in heaven above and on earth beneath";[207] "for ye saw no manner of form

[205]*Mishneh Torah*: *H. ᶜAbodat Kokabim* 1. I have expanded the reasoning slightly. Maimonides is putting a philosophic twist on the tradition in *Midrash ha-Gadol*: *Genesis*, ed. M. Margulies (Jerusalem 1947) 204–5, and *Bet ha-Midrasch*, ed. A. Jellinek (Leipzig 1853) 2.118, according to which Abraham discovered the true God through observing the rising and setting of the celestial bodies. The tradition is picked up in Quran 6:76–79, and the Quranic passage then led Muslim thinkers to the notion, paralleling what Maimonides writes here, that Abraham formulated a proof of the existence of God from the movements of the heavens. See Averroes, *Tahāfut al-Tahāfut* 10, §6; English translation: Averroes, *Tahafut al-Tahafut*, trans. S. Van den Bergh (London 1954) 251. The theme of Abraham's teaching proofs of the existence of God to mankind comes up again in *Guide for the Perplexed* 2.39.

[206]*Mishneh Torah*: *H. Yesode ha-Torah* 1.8.

[207]Joshua 2:11. Maimonides reasons that a body cannot be in two places at the same time. By locating God in two places, in both heaven and earth, Scripture therefore informs us here that God is not a body. The Babylonian Talmud, *Sukka* 5a, contains the statement that God never descends from the heaven to the earth, but what if anything that statement might have played in Maimonides' thought can only be guessed. In fact, he was certain that God does not exist in place at all. H. Wolfson, "Maimonides on the Unity and Incorporeality of God," reprinted in his *Studies*

on the day that the Lord spoke unto you";[208] and "to whom then will ye liken Me that I should be equal?"[209]

Maimonides has indulged here in more than a modicum of exaggeration. Scripture undoubtedly affirms that man cannot have a visual perception of God; the second of the verses just quoted can perhaps be read as implying as much. Scripture undoubtedly anathematizes graphic representation of God.[210] But neither the three verses cited by Maimonides nor any other verse in the Hebrew Bible makes it clear or explicit that God is incorporeal, and if Scripture is read without prepossession, no biblical verse even hints at such a notion. Similarly, the classic rabbinic texts will be combed in vain for a hint of the incorporeality of God. Divine incorporeality is a philosophic doctrine and it entered Jewish thought in the train of philosophy. It was so central for Maimonides that he nonetheless grasped at straws in seeking scriptural support.

However that may be, if God is an incorporeal being, He has no physical qualities. It follows that when inerrant, divine Scripture uses physical language in describing God, the descriptions do not carry their obvious sense. Maimonides accordingly writes, in the Halakot of the Foundations of the Law, that whenever Scripture depicts God in physical terms, it merely "speaks in conformity with the language of men," with no intent of being taken literally. Physical descriptions of God in Scripture are to be read as metaphors—allegories—that, whatever they wish to say about God, do not entail corporeality. And not only must descriptions involving obvious physical parts or qualities, such as the attribution to God of hands, a head, movement, and speech, be interpreted allegorically. God is equally free of psychological qualities, such as anger and joy, since they too are rooted in the physical. Psychological qualities ascribed to God in Scripture must be interpreted away as well.[211]

The incorporeality of God was a subject to which Maimonides was drawn repeatedly. He included it in the list of thirteen principles of faith which he incorporated into his Commentary on the Mishna, placing it right after the existence and unity of God.[212] In the Halakot of the Foundations of the Torah, we have seen him intertwine the incorporeality of God with the commandment to know God's unity. Elsewhere in the Book of Knowledge, he brands those who affirm "that there exists one ruler of the world but He is a body and has a shape" as heretics and he denies them a place in the afterlife.[213] When he reminisced years later about his accomplishments in his rabbinic writings, he singled out having

---

in the History of Philosophy and Religion 2 (Cambridge, Mass. 1977) 437, tries to recreate the philosophic filter through which Maimonides read this verse and the next.

[208]Deuteronomy 4:15.

[209]Isaiah 40:25.

[210]For example, Exodus 20:4; Deuteronomy 4:12; 15–18.

[211]*Mishneh Torah*: *H. Yesode ha-Torah* 1.9; 11–12.

[212]Commentary on the Mishna, *Sanhedrin*, 10:1, third principle.

[213]*Mishneh Torah*: *H. Teshuba* 3.6–7.

taught the incorporeality of God to persons who were "thought to be sages in Israel" but were unsure whether or not God is a body, and to others who, still more scandalously, "claimed to be sages in Israel" yet actually believed that God is a corporeal being. In an inversion of Maimonides' position, these latter spurious sages branded anyone who rejected the corporeality of God as a heretic, whereas, in truth, their corrupt belief rendered them, in the intemperate language that Maimonides sometimes allowed himself, "the most ignorant of mankind and more immersed in error than animals. Their brains are filled with old wives' tales and the worthless imaginings of women and children."[214] We shall see that the first motive Maimonides gives for writing his *Guide for the Perplexed* was the necessity of teaching the "perplexed" how the anthropomorphic descriptions of God in Scripture can be harmonized with God's incorporeality.

He was not the first Jewish thinker to insist on the incorporeality of God. Medieval Jewish philosophers had done so from the start, regardless of the school of philosophy with which they aligned themselves. Nor was the allegorizing away of psychological as well as physical descriptions of God in Scripture, nor again the application of the rule that "Scripture speaks in conformity with the language of men" to physical descriptions of God in Scripture, original with Maimonides.[215] But by including divine incorporeality among the principles of the Jewish faith in the Commentary on the Mishna and by insisting on it so strongly in the *Mishneh Torah*, he became the tenet's champion. The incorporeality of God was the primary legacy bequeathed by medieval Jewish philosophy to the Jewish religion, and Maimonides was the man who did most to ingrain it in the hearts of the faithful. Prayer books that enshrine his thirteen principles in the guise of a poem and a second time as a formal credo[216] continue his work. They have convinced

[214]Maimonides, *Treatise on Resurrection*, (n. 65 above), Hebrew-Arabic section, 3.

[215]The rejection of both physical and psychological anthropomorphisms is already found in Saadia, *Book of Beliefs and Opinions*, Part 2, introduction. As Maimonides knew, the rule that "Scripture speaks in conformity with the language [*ki-leshon*] of men" had an entirely different, technical sense in ancient rabbinic hermeneutics; it meant, in opposition, to R. Akiba's exegetic method, that superfluous language in Scripture serving a rhetorical function need not have midrashic significance. See W. Bacher, *Die älteste Terminologie der jüdischen Schriftauslegung* (Leipzig 1899) (reprinted as Part One of *Die exegetische Terminologie der jüdischen Traditionsliteratur* [Darmstadt 1965]) 98. Writers prior to Maimonides had already altered the original sense of the rule and made it mean that anthropomorphic descriptions of God in Scripture are not to be taken literally. See W. Bacher, *Die Bibelexegese der jüdischen Religionsphilosophen des Mittelalters vor Maimūni* (Budapest 1892) 72; W. Bacher, *Die Bibelexegese Moses Maimūni's* (Budapest 1896) 19; and R. Hai Gaon, in *Oṣar ha-Geonim*, ed. B. Lewin, *Berakot* (Haifa 1928) 1 (*Responsa*), 131. The rule is repeatedly deployed in its new, theological sense by Abraham Ibn Ezra in his Bible Commentary. The medieval Hebrew translation of the lost Arabic text of Ḥefeṣ ben Yaṣliaḥ's book on the commandments lays down a similar rule. Ḥefeṣ maintains that anthropomorphic descriptions of God in Scripture "liken God to the language of men" and are not to be taken literally. See n. 196 above.

[216]Above, pp. 158–59.

innumerable worshipers through the centuries that the incorporeality of God is indeed an integral constituent of the Jewish faith.

I have been examining Maimonides' exposition of the first two positive commandments in his list of 613: the injunctions to know the existence of God and to know God's unity. From them, the Halakot of the Foundations of the Law turns to the commandments to love God and to stand in awe of Him. Love of God, as Maimonides explicates it, arises out of admiration of what God has fashioned, and awe before God arises out of a person's realization of his own insignificance within the total economy of the divine handiwork. It follows that only persons who have an understanding of what God has fashioned will be able to fulfill those two commandments properly.

To provide readers with the requisite tools for gaining that understanding, Maimonides sketches a picture of God's universe, which meant for him the universe as it was conceived by the medieval Arabic Aristotelian philosophers. He describes the panoply of celestial spheres that carry the stars and planets around the earth; the supernal incorporeal beings that are the First Mover's agents in maintaining the celestial spheres in constant motion and that are called *angels* in religious parlance; and the lower world in which man dwells and that is ultimately analyzable into four physical elements: earth, water, air, and fire. He defines matter and form as the terms were used in Aristotelian philosophy. He endorses the philosophic theory according to which the forms of natural objects in our lower world come from outside the physical world, emanated from the last link in the hierarchy of supernal incorporeal beings subordinate to God—from a being known to the philosophers as the *active intellect.* In a few sentences, he limns the theory of human intellect current among the Arabic Aristotelians and informs his readers that the part of man which gains immortality is the "intelligible thought" (*de*ᶜ*a, da*ᶜ*at*) constituting man's true "form."[217] In connection with an additional scriptural commandment, the commandment to "heed a prophet who speaks in God's name," he echoes still another notion borrowed from the Arabic Aristotelian school of philosophy. Prophecy, he explains, comes to human beings worthy of it not directly from God but through the mediation of the same active intellect from whom the forms of natural objects emanate.[218]

Maimonides takes up human immortality more fully in a later section, still within the Book of Knowledge. There he follows the rabbinic sources and states that with specified exceptions, "all Israel have a portion in the world to come, even though they may have sinned," and further that "the pious from among the gentiles likewise

[217] *Mishneh Torah*: *H. Yesode ha-Torah*, 2–4. In 2.7, Maimonides lists ten names of angels, and *ishim*, his name for the tenth, is the term he uses in the *Mishneh Torah* for the active intellect of medieval Arabic Aristotelianism. If there were any doubt, *H. Yesode ha-Torah* 4.6, makes clear that *ishim* is identical with the *active intellect*.

[218] *Mishneh Torah*: *H. Yesode ha-Torah* 7.1.

have a portion in the world to come."[219] The exceptions are persons who harbor certain incorrect beliefs or commit certain misdeeds and fail to repent. Most of the noxious beliefs and deeds—there are twenty-four in all—are drawn by Maimonides from the rabbinic sources, while a few are his extrapolations out of the sources.[220] They are disparate in character. Among the persons who forfeit their portion in the world to come are those who "assert that there is no God and the world has no governor, or that the world does have a governor but there are two or more," who deny God's authorship of the entire Written Torah, who reject the Oral Torah, who deny the resurrection of the dead, who engage in slander, or who undergo a surgical procedure to hide their circumcision. We have seen that a person also loses his portion in the world to come if he affirms "that there exists one ruler of the world but He is a body and has a shape,"[221] that is, if he harbors the erroneous belief that God is a corporeal being.

As for what the world to come is, Maimonides writes: In the world to come, as the rabbis conceived it, "there is no body or corporeality; only the souls of the righteous, [existing] without a body, like the ministering angels." The happy future state is consequently beyond the grasp of the "soul [*neshama*] that stands in need of a body," in other words, the subrational levels of the human soul. It is reserved exclusively for "the form of the [rational] soul [*nefesh*], that is to say, for [human] intellectual thought [*de*^{c}*a*]" of God and of the supernal incorporeal beings subject to Him.[222]

Form was a common philosophic appellation for human intellect that has passed from a state of potentiality to the state of actual thought.[223] Maimonides is saying that what survives the death of the human body and lives on forever is the intellectual faculty within the soul when that faculty has passed to actuality and become identical with thought of God and of supernal incorporeal beings subordinate to God in the hierarchy of being; we met the notion earlier in his Commentary on the Mishna.[224] Such, he moreover submits, was what the ancient rabbis meant when they spoke of the "world to come." He never tells us how all Israel can have a portion in the world to come—which would seem to mean that the

[219]*Mishneh Torah*: *H. Teshuba* 3.5. See Mishna, *Sanhedrin* 10:1. On the issue whether pious gentiles have a portion in the world to come, Tosefta *Sanhedrin* 13:2 and BT *Sanhedrin* 105a record opposing opinions. Maimonides had rabbinic grounds, as well as his own ideological reasons, for following the opinion that they do. See his Commentary on the Mishna, *Sanhedrin* 10:2, and the commentary of *Kesef Mishneh* to *Mishneh Torah*: *H. Teshuba* 3.5.

[220]He includes *denial* of twelve of the thirteen principles of faith listed in his Commentary on the Mishna among the twenty-four. See above, p. 157.

[221]*Mishneh Torah*: *H. Teshuba* 3.6–8.

[222]*Mishneh Torah*: *H .Yesode ha-Torah* 4:8–9; *H. Teshuba* 8:2–3.

[223]Maimonides, *Eight Chapters* 1 (end); H. Davidson, *Alfarabi, Avicenna, and Averroes, on Intellect* (New York 1992) 20, 54, 326.

[224]Above, p. 164. Maimonides is speaking loosely when stating that the human intellect can possess thought of God Himself; he did not believe that it can have thought of God's essence.

uneducated as well as the educated do—if immortality is a matter of developing one's intellect to the level where it becomes identical with a thought of supernal incorporeal beings;[225] nor how, if immortality is a function exclusively of intellectual development, such things as denying resurrection or disguising one's circumcision can cause one to forfeit it.[226]

The truth is that the classic rabbinic texts gave little attention to the survival of human souls, which they presupposed, and no attention to the survival of actualized human intellects, which they never dreamed of. The variety of immortality that they insisted upon most strongly was the future restoration of souls to resurrected human bodies, and resurrection of the body was one of a handful of beliefs that may properly be called rabbinic dogmas.[227] It is fairly certain that, contrary to what Maimonides writes, the classic rabbinic sources understood the expression "world to come" as a designation for the state of existence which ensues when God restores dead bodies to life at the time of resurrection.[228] Yet Maimonides' discussion of immortality in the *Mishneh Torah* makes no mention of resurrection of the dead apart from making the statement that denying resurrection causes one to lose one's portion in the world to come—which for him means to lose the immortality of one's intellect. Not surprisingly, some of his contemporaries suspected that he did not in his heart of hearts accept the dogma of resurrection. Maimonides responded heatedly that he had been maligned by the critics and he composed a small treatise in which he defended his orthodoxy on the issue. I discuss the treatise in a later chapter.[229]

It is obvious that Maimonides has incorporated a good deal of philosophy into the Book of Knowledge, the first of the fourteen Books of the *Mishneh Torah*. His rationale—or, for those who choose to read him more cynically, his

[225]Perhaps Maimonides understood that all who have been blessed with the resources of the Written and Oral Torah possess the requisite means for developing their intellects; hence a portion in the world to come awaits them, although it is up to them whether or not they gain it. See also Commentary on the Mishna, *Makkot* 3:17, where Maimonides writes: "It is a principle of belief in the Law that when someone performs one of the 613 commandments *as it should be performed*, allowing no ulterior consideration whatsoever to enter into his observance and doing the commandment . . . wholly *out of love, as I have explained* to you [in the Commentary on the Mishna, *Sanhedrin* 10, introduction, p. 199], such a man merits the life of the world to come through that [single] commandment. . . . ." Regarding love of God, see p. 241 above and p. 246 below.

[226]It is clear, however, why believing God to be a corporeal being entails a loss of immortality. If a human intellect becomes imperishable and immortal by having God or another being belonging to the incorporeal realm as the object of its thought, anyone who imagines that God and the incorporeal beings subordinate to Him are corporeal does not possess the required thought.

[227]Mishna, *Sanhedrin* 10:1.

[228]BT *Sanhedrin* 90a; *Genesis Rabba* 14:5, and parallels.

[229]See below, pp. 510–36.

rationalization—for doing so was that philosophy provides the necessary means for fulfilling the initial commandments of God's Law. He also finds support for what he has done in the classic rabbinic sources themselves.

As mentioned in the previous chapter, the Mishna corpus knows of an esoteric elaboration of "the account of the chariot," that is to say, of Ezekiel's chariot vision, and an esoteric elaboration of "the account of creation," that is, of the creation story in Genesis. Maimonides was confident that he had penetrated the haze surrounding the accounts of creation and the chariot; in his Commentary on the Mishna, he stated flatly that the former is nothing other than "physical science," and the latter, "metaphysical science."[230] In the *Mishneh Torah*, he draws upon his discovery to give a rabbinic justification for including philosophy in a rabbinic code of law. The chapters devoted to the nature of God and the other supernal incorporeal beings conclude with the statement: "What I have said on this subject . . . is like a drop in the ocean in comparison with what must be expounded. . . . The exposition of all the principles [touched upon here] . . . is called the account of the chariot."[231] He concludes his philosophic picture of the physical universe in a similar vein: "What I have said on the present subject is like a drop in a bucket. They are profound matters, but not as profound [as the account of the chariot]. The exposition" of what has been discussed here "is called the account of creation."[232] The philosophic sciences of metaphysics and physics, which he outlined in order to provide readers with the means for acquiring knowledge of God's existence, unity, and incorporeality, for loving and standing in awe of God, were, he is telling us, fully known to the rabbis. They just did not call them metaphysics and physics but used other names instead.

Maimonides goes further. When expounding the scriptural commandment to study the Written and Oral Torah, he includes the ruling, or piece of advice, based on a passage in the Babylonian Talmud, that students of the Law should allocate their time between three areas of religious study—the Written Torah, the Oral Torah, and *gemara*; gemara is defined by him as the deployment of the talmudic method for the purpose of extracting inferences from the Oral Torah transmitted by Moses.[233] So far, his counsel would be endorsed as unexceptionable even in the most conservative rabbinic circles. Then he makes—obliquely but unambiguously—the extraordinary statement that the area of study known as gemara includes philosophy.[234] The ancient rabbis themselves thus regarded philosophy as integral to the study of the Law, and latter-day rabbinists hence have the obligation to do as

[230]Above, p. 161.

[231]*Mishneh Torah*: *H. Yesode ha-Torah* 2.11.

[232]*Mishneh Torah*: *H. Yesode ha-Torah* 4.10.

[233]BT *Qiddushin* 30a. Where Maimonides writes *gemara*, the passage has *talmud* in the printed editions of the Babylonian Talmud.

[234]*Mishneh Torah*: *H. Talmud Torah* 1.11–12, understood in the light of *H. Yesode ha-Torah* 4.13.

their forebears did and accord philosophy a place specifically in their own *rabbinic* curriculum.

And he goes still further; for he makes a point of quoting a passage from the Babylonian Talmud which ranks the account of the chariot as superior to dialectic argumentation.[235] The implication is obvious. He is saying that the rabbis not only valued the science of metaphysics and not only accorded it a place in their rabbinic curriculum. They ranked study of metaphysics higher than immersing oneself in the dialectic argumentation that serves as the connective tissue of the Babylonian and Palestinian Talmuds. Philosophic metaphysics was for the rabbis themselves talmudic study at its highest level.

Maimonides had no intention of throwing the gates of philosophy open and inviting all and sundry to enter. The classic texts, together with their avoidance of disclosing what the account of creation comprises, warned that it was too sensitive a topic to be communicated to more than one person at a time. When Maimonides concludes his description of the physical universe, which is the subject matter of the science of physics and hence—on his reading—of the rabbinic account of creation, he repeats the admonition not to teach the subject "publicly," the reason being that not everyone has the ability to understand it correctly.[236] The rabbis warned that the account of the chariot was even more sensitive and was to be communicated solely in the form of "subject headings" and solely to a person of impeccable cognitive qualifications who can "understand by himself."[237] When Maimonides concludes his brief discourse on God and the other supernal beings, which is the subject matter of metaphysics and hence of the account of the chariot, he repeats the old rabbinic admonition to teach the doctrine to only "one man, with the proviso that the man is wise and understands by himself. . . . For these things are extremely profound and not every human mind is able to tolerate them."[238] When, morevoer, he cites the passage from the Babylonian Talmud which ranked the account of the chariot, and hence metaphysics, as superior to talmudic dialectic, he adds the condition that "knowing what is permitted and forbidden and the like . . . should nonetheless precede in time. For those things settle man's mind at the outset. They are the great beneficence that God emanated to make human life in this world possible and thereby [create the conditions enabling mankind] to attain the world to come. And they are something that everyone, young and old, male and female, intelligent and unintelligent, can comprehend."[239]

Maimonides, in sum, encourages everyone to learn philosophic proofs whereby the existence and unity of God can be known; he turns the philosophic truth that

[235]*Mishneh Torah*: *H. Yesode ha-Torah* 4.13, quoting BT *Sukka* 28a. Twersky, *Introduction to the Code of Maimonides* (n. 30 above) 494–95, shows how other rabbinists interpreted the passage in *Sukka* 28a, so as not to belittle the value of talmudic dialectic.

[236]*Mishneh Torah*: *H. Yesode ha-Torah* 4.10–11.

[237]*Mishna*, *Ḥagiga* 2:1; BT *Ḥagiga* 13a.

[238]*Mishneh Torah*: *H. Yesode ha-Torah* 2.12.

[239]*Mishneh Torah*: *H. Yesode ha-Torah* 4.13.

God is an incorporeal being into a principle of the Jewish religion; he provides readers with a philosophic picture of the universe in order to help them fulfill the commandments of loving God and standing in awe of Him; and he reads metaphysics and physics into Scripture and rabbinic aggada, makes those two philosophic sciences integral parts of the rabbinic curriculum, and declares that metaphysics is rabbinic study at the highest level. He insists, however, that learning one's day-to-day religious duties precedes metaphysics and that whatever goes beyond a basic outline of physics and metaphysics must be restricted to the intellectual elite. The yoking of the need to impart basic philosophic information to all with the restriction of advanced philosophic study to the elite was a motif that would also run through his main philosophic work, the *Guide for the Perplexed.*

The Book of Knowledge concludes with an exhortation: "A person loves God only through the knowledge he has of Him. Love is proportional to knowledge—little, if the knowledge is little, and great, if the knowledge is great. Man must therefore devote himself to understanding and comprehending the sciences [*ḥokmot*] and disciplines that inform him about his Maker, to the extent, of course, that a human being is able to understand and know."[240] Devoting oneself to knowledge and science in order to love God—that is the note Maimonides wanted to reverberate in the minds of those who came away from his comprehensive introduction to the *Mishneh Torah.*

It is tempting to reflect with a knowing smile: How ingenious and disingenuous of our author to disseminate a considerable dose of philosophy under the cloak of a rabbinic code of law, to camouflage his motive for incorporating the philosophic elements into his code as a desire to help readers fulfill the initial divine commandments communicated to Moses at Sinai, and then to crown the legerdemain with a preposterous interpretation of the biblical and rabbinic account of the chariot and account of creation. But cynicism is often a variety of naiveté, and in the present instance the cynical reading is almost surely a naive reading. Maimonides' industriousness and decade-long labor in collating bits and pieces from every corner of the rabbinic canon to construct a consummate code of Jewish law do not bespeak disingenuousness. Anachronistic though it may strike a

[240]*Mishneh Torah*: *H. Teshuba* 10.6. Maimonides knew that he was here going against the grain of conservative readers, and an ambiguity in the Hebrew term *ḥokma* helped him to cloak some of what he is saying. In Scripture, *ḥokma* means "wisdom," both man's and God's. Maimonides, in the *Mishneh Torah*, sometimes uses the term in that sense as when he speaks of God's *ḥokma*, God's wisdom; see *Mishneh Torah*: *H. Yesode ha-Torah* 2.2, 4.12. But he also uses the term in the sense of "science," as when he speaks of the *ḥokma*, the "science," of astronomy and geometry on which the "wise men [or: scientists] of Greek wrote numerous books"; see *Mishneh Torah*: *H. Qiddush ha-Ḥodesh* 17.24. Because of the term's ambiguity, the appeal to readers to study *science* can be read, by those who choose to do so, as an unfocused appeal to acquire *wisdom.* In *Guide* 3.54, Maimonides states that *ḥokma* in the strict sense of the term as used by Scripture is the discipline whereby the theoretical content of the Torah "may be *demonstrated*."

modern reader, he was, it is reasonably safe to say, convinced that philosophy and the Law once formed a single, broad unified domain in rabbinic Judaism, and he saw himself as the restorer of the primeval unity.[241] A similar attitude led him to incorporate into the *Mishneh Torah* the segment to be considered next.

In Maimonides' time, philosophy and science were not delimited in the way that they are today and they were not mutually exclusive. We have seen Maimonides call metaphysics a *science*, whereas few in our day would characterize it as such. The sketch of physical science which he incorporates into the Halakot of the Foundations of the Law was regarded by him as part and parcel of *philosophy*, and in his day it undoubtedly was. Today, physics has of course moved out of the discipline of philosophy and makes its home in what has become the distinct and separate realm of natural science.

In addition to everything else that it contains, the *Mishneh Torah* has a series of chapters that qualify unambiguously as natural science in today's usage of the term. These are the chapters referred to earlier in which Maimonides says that he was writing in the Hebrew year corresponding to the last third of 1177 and first two-thirds of 1178 and which show signs of having been inserted into the *Mishneh Torah* after it was more or less complete.[242] They belong to the section of the Halakot of Sanctifying the Month, that is to say, the halakot of setting the first day of lunar months.

As is well known, rabbinic Judaism employs a calendar of twelve lunar months which keeps pace with the solar year by the intercalation of a thirteenth month every few years, as needed. Days are counted from nightfall of one evening to nightfall of the next, and months accordingly also begin at nightfall. During the period of the Mishna and two Talmuds, a new month was declared when a new moon was first seen in the western sky shortly after sunset, that being the time of day when the initial sighting is possible.[243] In about half the instances, a new moon appears—if weather conditions allow—twenty-nine days following the previous new moon, and in about half, thirty days following it. About half the lunar months therefore had twenty-nine days and about half, thirty.

The classic rabbinic sources depict the following procedure for determining whether a month is to have the smaller or larger number of days: If two adult male witnesses testify before the properly authorized court in Palestine that they descried a new moon after sunset of the twenty-ninth day of the outgoing month,[244] the twenty-ninth day is reckoned as the last day of the month. The thirtieth day, which begins at nightfall, starts the new month. In the absence of such testimony, the

[241] In the same vein, see Twersky, *Introduction to the Code of Maimonides* 215, 228.

[242] Above, p. 205.

[243] See Y. Levinger, "*Ḥizzuy ha-Re'iyya shel ha-Yareaḥ he-Ḥadash,*" *Teḥumin* 14 (1994) 477–78, for a more exact statement.

[244] To be more precise, if several thirty-day months followed one another in a row, a new moon might be sighted earlier than the evening following the twenty-ninth day.

thirtieth day is assigned to the outgoing month, and the new month starts on the thirty-first. The decision whether or not to add a thirteenth month to a given lunar year in order to bring it into line with the solar year would be made ad hoc. At a date that cannot be ascertained with any confidence—Maimonides' opinion is that the change occurred before the redaction of the Babylonian Talmud[245]—the setting of the beginning of the month on the basis of eyewitness testimony was abandoned, and a fixed, perpetual rabbinic calendar was instituted. The fixed calendar had, with minor exceptions, alternating twenty-nine- and thirty-day months and it established in perpetuity exactly which lunar years would receive the extra, thirteenth month.

In his section on setting the first day of lunar months, Maimonides spells out the ancient procedure for determining the initial day of the month through eyewitness testimony. Then he outlines the working of the calendar that replaced the eyewitness system and that was, perhaps after some development, operative in his time and is still operative today. He explains when, according to the fixed calendar, new months begin,[246] which months have twenty-nine and which thirty days, which years receive a thirteenth month, and related matters. Finally, in a third segment, he takes up the subject of concern to us here.

On average, the interval between one appearance of a new moon and the next is slightly more than twenty-nine and a half days, but the actual intervals vary from month to month. There are a number of reasons, the first being the velocities of the moon and the sun. As the moon rotates around the earth each month and the sun performs its annual apparent rotation around the earth, a new moon can become visible each time that the moon catches up with the sun—or, put more technically, when it reaches the same astronomical *longitude* as the sun and the two are in *conjunction*—and then advances a certain additional distance beyond the sun. Neither the velocity of the moon nor the apparent velocity of the sun is uniform, however, and the amount of time that the moon needs to reach the required position therefore varies. Other factors also come into play, such as: (a) The altitude of the moon above the horizon at sunset of the twenty-ninth day; the moon's altitude

[245]*Mishneh Torah*: *H. Qiddush ha-Ḥodesh* 5.3. For the argument that the process leading to the fixed calendar in its present form extended over centuries, see S. Stern, *Calendar and Community* (Oxford 2001) 180–206, 253–56.

[246]In setting the first days of the months of a given year, the fixed calendar takes its departure not from the days on which a new moon can be sighted but from the days on which the moon, in its rotation around the earth, reaches the same longitude as the sun, and the moon and sun are in *conjunction*. To be more precise: The fixed calendar works from the *mean* conjunctions of the moon with the sun, that is, the times when the two are on average in conjunction. As a consequence, the first days of months and hence the days on which holidays occur according to the fixed calendar do not always coincide with what they would be if the first day of each month were determined through eyewitness testimony; they can be either earlier or later. The mean conjunction of moon and sun is called *molad* in Hebrew. (In fact, the Hebrew term *molad* can be used in slightly different senses; see Levinger, "*Ḥizzuy ha-Re'iyya shel ha-Yareaḥ he-Ḥadash*," 476–77.)

varies throughout the year, and the greater it is on the critical day, the more likely that the moon will be sighted. (b) The moment of sunset; in order for the new moon to be visible, the sun must set and drop a certain distance below the horizon while the moon is still above the horizon. In short, a new moon can become visible in any given month either earlier or later than the twenty-nine and a half day average might lead one to expect, and the divergences are due to a number of factors. A recent historian has described determining "in advance the visibility of the new crescent" as "one of the most difficult problems of ancient and medieval astronomy."[247]

In his Commentary on the Mishna, Maimonides states that calculating the day on which the new moon might be sighted in Palestine in any given month is not easy but can be done. God, he writes, communicated the method to Moses at Sinai; philosophers and gentile scientists, by contrast, had not been able to agree on the correct way of making the calculation. The issue had only theoretical significance in Maimonides' time, since the perpetual calendar was firmly entrenched and no one foresaw a return to the eyewitness system before the coming of the Messiah. He nonetheless speaks, in the Commentary on the Mishna, of a plan for a "separate composition" on the issue. With the aid of "clear proofs" that only persons ignorant of astronomy could reject, he would show how to make the calculation. Because the subject is so technical, only a person who had "prepared himself for many years in the propaedeutic sciences," that is to say, in mathematics and astronomy, would be able to comprehend the projected composition. Anyone lacking the requisite training would find himself at a loss. Resorting to the language of Scripture, Maimonides remarks in his elitist fashion that for such a person, the composition would be "a price in the hand of a fool."[248] At the time when he worked on the Commentary on the Mishna, most of which he wrote before reaching Egypt and which he completed shortly after settling there, he was thus not merely confident that he had the requisite training to calculate the day on which a new moon might be sighted; he was confident that he could expound the scientific underpinning as well. The knowledge of astronomy that he would employ in the projected composition had presumably been acquired when he was still living in the West.

Eventually, Maimonides carried out a version of the project not as a separate and independent composition but as part of the *Mishneh Torah*. The rationale for putting a series of technical astronomical calculations into a rabbinic code was found by him in the Babylonian and Palestinian Talmuds.

Passages in the two Talmuds suggest that in the days when the beginning of a new month was fixed on the basis of eyewitness testimony, the rabbinic authorities would use their knowledge of the moon's cycle to check the witnesses'

[247] O. Neugebauer in *The Code of Maimonides*, Book Three, Treatise Eight, trans. S. Gandz (New Haven 1956) 113.

[248] Commentary on the Mishna, *Rosh ha-Shana* 2.7.

credibility.[249] In the *Mishneh Torah*, Maimonides interprets the passages, somewhat unnaturally, to mean that the rabbinic authorities in ancient Palestine were capable of making "calculations as astronomers, who know the positions and movements of the stars and planets, do." They would "explore the situation meticulously until they could ascertain whether or not the moon might be sighted at the expected time, that is, on the evening following the twenty-ninth day."[250] They would calculate the exact spot reached by the moon in the lunar cycle just ending, the exact spot reached by the sun, the altitude of the moon at the moment when the witnesses reported having sighted the new moon, and so on. Through their computation, they would judge whether or not it was physically possible for a person in Palestine to see the new moon when the eyewitnesses reported having made the sighting, and only if they concluded that the new moon could have been seen would they give credence to the witnesses' testimony.

The assumption that the rabbis of the classic period possessed so high a level of astronomical knowledge goes well beyond the textual evidence;[251] in its anachronism it resembles Maimonides' supposition that the rabbis knew the sciences of physics and metaphysics. He may have been encouraged in the assumption by the circumstance that medieval Muslim courts, which set the first day of lunar months through eyewitness testimony much as the ancient rabbinic courts had done, did rely on sophisticated astronomical computations to check the eyewitness testimony presented to them.[252] Once Maimonides made the assumption and interpreted the rabbinic sources as meaning that rabbinic courts would determine the possibility of viewing the new moon, he had a rationale for including the method for making the determination in his comprehensive code of Jewish law. It should hardly be surprising that no other rabbinic code before or since has ever done anything of the sort.

After the opening segment of the Halakot of Sanctifying the Month, which gives the procedure whereby the beginning of the month is set through eyewitness testimony, and the second segment, which outlines the fixed rabbinic calendar, Maimonides explains in the third segment how to calculate the possibility of the moon's being sighted on the evening after the twenty-ninth day of any outgoing month. As it stands, the segment is complicated enough, but his original plan must have been more ambitious. His Commentary on the Mishna warned that only

[249]BT *Rosh ha-Shana* 20b, 25a, and parallels in the Palestinian Talmud.

[250]*Mishneh Torah*: *H. Qiddush ha-Ḥodesh* 1.6. Similarly in 6.1. In 2.4, and also in Commentary on the Mishna, *Rosh ha-Shana* 2:7, Maimonides takes Mishna *Rosh ha-Shana* 2:7 to mean that the court would examine the eyewitnesses in order to be sure not only that their testimonies were consistent with each other but also that they were consistent with the court's astronomical calculations.

[251]In *Guide for the Perplexed* 2.8 and 3.14, Maimonides acknowledges that the rabbis' knowledge of the structure of the heavens was not perfect.

[252]F. Bruin, "The First Visibility of the Lunar Crescent," *Vistas in Astronomy* 21 (1977) 332.

persons who had studied mathematics and astronomy for years would be able to understand the projected composition. The *Mishneh Torah*, by contrast, does not address solely those who are highly trained in mathematics and astronomy. Maimonides now presumes that "everyone who . . . is eager about scientific subjects . . . will desire to know the method whereby they [that is, the ancient law court] made the calculations for ascertaining whether or not the new moon is visible" at the expected time.[253] The Commentary on the Mishna stated that the planned composition would support its instructions with "clear proofs"; the *Mishneh Torah* offers no proofs and suggests to readers who wish to appreciate the "reason for all these calculations" that they consult works of astronomy.[254] To serve the readers for whom the *Mishneh Torah* was intended, Maimonides begins with a clarification of elementary astronomical concepts that anyone who had studied astronomy for weeks, not to speak of years, would have found superfluous.[255] And in the tables for making the calculations, he sometimes simplifies and gives approximations instead of exact figures; for, he writes, he did not want to throw the reader who "is unfamiliar with the matter . . . into a panic through a multitude of calculations that do not contribute" to the object at hand, namely, the possibility of "sighting the moon."[256] The composition on the visibility of the moon as originally planned would apparently have furnished the mathematical and astronomical grounds for each stage in the computation and would have supplied more precise astronomical tables.

In a preface to his treatment of the subject in the *Mishneh Torah*, Maimonides writes, much as he did in his Commentary on the Mishna, that "the early gentile" astronomers and mathematicians differed greatly regarding the correct way of making the determination, and even scientists of stature went astray. In more recent times, he goes on, a few astronomers discovered the correct method; if he was being consistent, he would have to mean that they rediscovered what God had taught Moses and what the ancient rabbis had known. Maimonides represents himself as especially qualified for dealing with the subject, because he was in possession of "traditions from the mouth of scholars" (*qabbalot mi-pi ha-ḥakamim*) as well as astronomical "proofs not recorded in the books that are generally known." He is presumably alluding to his studies with Islamic astronomers before coming to Egypt.[257] "For all these reasons," he found it "appropriate to explain the method of doing the calculation" so that everyone who wished to approach the problem would have the means at his disposal.[258]

He further forewarns readers competent in astronomy that the lack of precision in some of his tables and figures was not due to carelessness and oversight on his

[253] *Mishneh Torah*: *H. Qiddush ha-Ḥodesh* 11.1.
[254] *Mishneh Torah*: *H. Qiddush ha-Ḥodesh* 17.24.
[255] *Mishneh Torah*: *H. Qiddush ha-Ḥodesh* 11.7–15.
[256] *Mishneh Torah*: *H. Qiddush ha-Ḥodesh* 11.6.
[257] See above, pp. 79–80.
[258] *Mishneh Torah*: *H. Qiddush ha-Ḥodesh* 11.2–3.

part; here he has in mind the approximations that he resorted to in order to avoid throwing readers into panic.[259] Despite the qualification, the process is highly complex. Maimonides begins by showing how to make a rough determination of the moon's location on the evening following the twenty-ninth day of the outgoing month by using the average length of the lunar cycle. He shows how to build on the initial rough result and refine it through corrective formulas, based on astronomical tables, until the moon's exact position on the critical day is known. He explains how to pinpoint the location reached by the sun in its annual apparent rotation around the earth and to calculate where the moon stands vis-à-vis the sun. He provides formulas for ascertaining the altitude of the moon above the horizon. After further refinements and corrections, he shows how to reduce the findings to straightforward criteria for deciding whether or not the new moon might be sighted at the critical moment.[260]

The astronomical tables to be used in making the calculations were not compiled by Maimonides, and he did not develop the intricate formulas himself. Ultimately, the formulas and calculations go back to Ptolemy. Many of them have been found to be closely related to those of the Arabic astronomer al-Battānī, who lived two and a half centuries before Maimonides,[261] although al-Battānī is not the source of all the steps in Maimonides' account.[262] Maimonides also had the benefit of oral instruction from the scientists with whom he studied. Nevertheless and despite not being the author of the formulas and astronomical tables, he was fully adept in applying them and he shows himself to be in total control of the astronomy of his day. He was, moreover, able to adapt the calculations that he drew from his sources, whatever they were, to the latitude and longitude of Palestine.[263] We find in him a scholar who had the intelligence and memory, and had invested the time and energy, needed for mastering the vast sea of classic rabbinic literature by the age of twenty-three, who had managed to study medicine during the same period, who had acquired a knowledge of philosophy, and who now reveals himself to have possessed an impressive level of expertise in the intricacies of medieval astronomy. He was not an ordinary man.

The philosophic and medical material in Book One of the *Mishneh Torah* and the astronomical segment in the halakot of setting the first day of the lunar month constitute the strictly philosophic and scientific side of the work. The nonhalakic elements are still not exhausted, however. Where it seemed appropriate,

[259] *Mishneh Torah*: *H. Qiddush ha-Ḥodesh* 11.5.

[260] For the technicalities, see Neugebauer's Astronomical Commentary in *The Code of Maimonides*, Book Three, Treatise Eight, trans. S. Gandz.

[261] O. Neugebauer, "The Astronomy of Maimonides," *Hebrew Union College Annual* 22 (1949) 337–49. *The Code of Maimonides*, Book Three, Treatise Eight, trans. S. Gandz, xlvi; index, *sub voce* al-Battānī.

[262] Tz. Langermann, "*Sugyot astronomiyyot*," *Da^cat* 37 (1996) 109–11.

[263] See Neugebauer's remarks in *The Code of Maimonides*, Book Three, Treatise Eight, 147.

Maimonides injects bits of edifying advice of one kind or another. The edifying comments are scattered throughout the *Mishneh Torah*, but he found certain spots to be especially well adapted for them.

Tractates of the Mishna corpus sometimes sign off in their final paragraph on a nonlegal note that stands in contrast with the sober legal tone of the body of the tractate. Other rabbinic compositions of the classic period also sometimes conclude sections on a fresh note.[264] Maimonides was naturally familiar with the rabbinic device[265] and he employs it as an additional structural touch in the *Mishneh Torah*. Each of the fourteen Books concludes with an observation of a nonlegal character, and some of the sections of halakot do so as well. Maimonides can even arrange the contents of a Book or a section in such a way that the legal subject taken up last provides a suitable transition to the thought with which he wished to close.[266] His concluding comments have a different emphasis from those in the classic rabbinic texts. There the comments occasionally moralize in the spirit of the rabbinic worldview but more typically celebrate the divine Law and persons dedicated to it or else extend comfort to Israel in its hours of gloom. In Maimonides, they serve as an ethical and spiritual accompaniment to the ritual and legal particulars making up the body of the code.[267]

A number of the nonlegal comments coming at the end of Books and sections of the *Mishneh Torah* or scattered elsewhere through the work simply repeat sentiments found in the rabbinic sources. At the end of one section of Halakot, Maimonides, for instance, expresses harsh disapproval of those who take charity without needing it, disapproval of those who decline charity although they thereby endanger their very lives, and warm approval of persons who by scrimping can avoid taking charity; all three sentiments are drawn from the rabbinic sources.[268] In other comments, ethical motifs borrowed from the rabbinic aggada are refracted through Maimonides' personal religious perspective. Still others have no known rabbinic source and appear to be wholly his. The illustrations offered in the following pages are all instances where, as far as I could discover, Maimonides does more than merely copy from an earlier source.

[264]Notably, *Leviticus Rabba*.

[265]Maimonides, Commentary on the Mishna, *Yadayim* 4:8, calls attention to the effort of the redactor of the Mishna to conclude the tractate on a favorable note and avoid concluding it on a negative note.

[266]Examples: *Mishneh Torah*: *H. ᶜAbadim* 9.8, and *H. Shemiṭa we-Yobel* 13.13, discussed below, p. 257.

[267]Maimonides also gives practical advice. For example, *H. ᶜArakin wa-Ḥaramin* 8.13, which is the end of a Book: A man should not donate more than he can afford to the Holy Temple, for he will thereby impoverish himself and require the aid of others. *H. Naḥalot* 6.13, which is not the conclusion of either a Book or a section: A man should not favor one son over another even in small things in order to avoid arousing the kind of jealousy and competition that Jacob created between Joseph and his brothers. In both instances, Maimonides is drawing from rabbinic sources.

[268]*Mishneh Torah*: *H. Mattenot ᶜAniyyim* 10.19 (the final paragraph in the section).

In one of his comments, Maimonides warns trustees responsible for the property of an orphan that they must keep their account books "scrupulously" even in circumstances where the law exempts them from presenting an accounting before a human court. For the ultimate accounting must be made before the father of orphans Himself, before God.[269] Another comment addresses the institution of slavery. Slavery is sanctioned by both Scripture and rabbinic Judaism, and Maimonides had no qualms about it. But he advises Jewish owners of non-Jewish slaves not to insist on their strict legal rights and not to work their slaves "with rigor." The master should, for ethical reasons as well as out of prudence, behave with mercy and justice toward his slaves. He should refrain from oppressing and humiliating them in word or act, be generous with food and drink, and heed their complaints. Masters of slaves and indeed all Israel must constantly keep in mind that cruelty and impudence are qualities of "the uncircumcised gentiles" and not of "the seed of Abraham, our father."[270]

A number of the nonlegal comments relate to the divine commandments, which, we have seen, serve as the skeleton around which the *Mishneh Torah* is constructed. Thus, in one passage, Maimonides exhorts readers to fulfill the commandments solemnly and with respect, not offhandedly. For respect is thereby accorded not to the commandments themselves but to Him "who enjoined them, who rescued us from groping in the darkness, and who bestowed them . . . as a light to guide [man] in the ways of righteousness."[271] Elsewhere, Maimonides repeats a familiar notion that fulfilling the commandments with a feeling of joy is an essential element in service to God and he includes the proviso that—as Scripture had taught—part of the joy in observing the religious festivals lies in feeding the stranger, the orphan, the widow, and others who are needy. To which he adds: If a person feasts with his own family while closing his door to those who are poor and bitter of soul, he engages in the "joy of his belly" and not in the "joy of a commandment." Whoever behaves in such fashion brings shame upon himself, as the prophet said: "I will spread dung upon your faces, even the dung of your *festivals*."[272] He further remarks—as a reaction, we may surmise, to demeanor

[269] *Mishneh Torah*: *H. Naḥalot* 11.12 (the final paragraph in the Book).

[270] *Mishneh Torah*: *H. ᶜAbadim* 9.8 (uncensored version; the final paragraph in the Book). One may speculate that Maimonides attributed cruelty only to *uncircumcised* gentiles, thereby excluding Muslims, as a form of self-censorship.

[271] *Mishneh Torah*: *H. Sheḥiṭa* 14.16 (the final paragraph in the Book). In 14.15, Maimonides ends the legal portion of *H. Sheḥiṭa* with an item that provides a smooth transition to the remark with which he signs off in 14.16.

[272] *Mishneh Torah*: *H. Yom Ṭob* 6.18; he makes a similar point in *H. Ḥagiga* 2.14. I have translated the biblical verse, Malachi 2:3, as Maimonides' midrashic reading requires. The classic rabbinic texts interpreted the verse differently, and Maimonides' interpretation is apparently original with him; see BT Shabbat 151b; Leviticus 18.1; and parallels. The *Zohar* took a liking to Maimonides' interpretation, plays with it, and in one passage weaves it together with the old rabbinic interpretation; see *Zohar* 2.88b; 199b; 3.104a.

he had observed around him—that whoever worships God with conceit or pride is both sinful and stupid.[273]

He calls attention to an old distinction between "ordinances" (*mishpaṭ*), which are scriptural commandments whose reasons and purposes are transparent, and "statutes" (*ḥoq*, *ḥuqqa*), which are scriptural commandments having no discernible purpose.[274] The classic rabbinic sources record two opinions about the latter. According to one opinion, they are wholly arbitrary and aim at nothing beyond instilling blind obedience to God; according to the other, they too have specific purposes and reasons, which are, however, fathomable only to a select few.[275] The first of the two opinions is more prominent in the classic rabbinic texts. But medieval Jewish rationalists prior to Maimonides had already been attracted to the position that no scriptural commandment, whether or not its reason and purpose are apparent, is merely an exercise in obedience, that each was instituted with a specific object in view.[276]

Against this background, Maimonides draws a distinction between "the ordinances," that is, the "commandments for which the reason is clear and the value of performing them . . . known, such as the prohibition against robbery and murder"; and "the statutes," which are the "commandments whose reason is not known, . . . such as the prohibition against eating pork or meat cooked with milk."[277] Commandments of the latter sort, his wording indicates, do not lack reasons; their reason and purpose are simply not known. In the same spirit, he writes elsewhere in the *Mishneh Torah* that "although the statutes of the Torah are all divine decrees, . . . you should examine them carefully and assign them reasons to the extent of your ability."[278]

The principle that each and every divine commandment was instituted for a specific purpose was close to his heart. Before composing the *Mishneh Torah*, he wrote in his *Book of Commandments*: "There is not a single commandment that does not have a reason, although most of the reasons are beyond the comprehension of the minds of the ordinary person."[279] Later, in the *Guide for the Perplexed*, he would repeat that position[280] and then go on to expound the

[273]*Mishneh Torah*: *H. Lulab* 8.15 (the last paragraph in the section).

[274]*Pesikta de-Rav Kahana*, ed. B. Mandelbaum (New York 1962) 54–55, 71–72, 74; BT *Yoma* 67b; E. Urbach, *Ḥazal* (Jerusalem 1971) 329–31.

[275]Urbach, *Ḥazal* 333–34.

[276]Saadia, *Book of Beliefs and Opinions* 3, §§1–2 (with nuances); A. Ibn Ezra, *Yesod Mora* 8; Ibn Ezra, Commentary on Psalms 78:5.

[277]*Mishneh Torah*: *H. Me^cila* 8.8 (the last paragraph of the Book of Temple Service) making use of *Sifra* on Leviticus 18:4. Maimonides creates a homiletic link between the ritual and legal material in *H. Me^cila*, the Halakot regarding illegal personal use of Temple property, and his comment.

[278]*Mishneh Torah*: *H. Temura* 4.13 (the last paragraph of the Book).

[279]*Book of Commandments*, negative #365.

[280]*Guide for the Perplexed* 3.26; 31.

purposes served by a large number of apparently arbitrary scriptural commandments, while furnishing guidelines for discovering the rationales of the rest.[281] Here in the *Mishneh Torah* he is not systematic in addressing the purposes of the seemingly arbitrary commandments. In most instances he records commandments of the sort with no explanation at all, and in some he labels a commandment as a divine statute or decree and leaves it at that.[282] But he does offer explanations for a few.

For instance, the rule that Jewish law courts do not accept self-incriminating statements in criminal cases is, he writes, a divine "decree," whereupon he explains the rationale: A person making self-incriminating statements may do so because of suicidal tendencies, and self-incrimination is therefore not allowed into evidence.[283] The blowing of the ram's horn on the New Year's holiday is another "decree." It nonetheless contains a "hint"—and here Maimonides becomes rhetorical. The ram's horn exhorts us: "Awaken from your sleep ye who sleep, and arouse yourselves from your slumber ye who slumber; search your deeds, repent, and remember your Creator."[284] He construes certain obscure prohibitions in the scriptural Book of Leviticus—against marring the corners of one's beard, making cuts in one's flesh to remember the dead, and tattooing the body—as reactions to idolatrous practices. Since idolatrous religions prescribed such actions, the Written Torah prohibits them as part of its war against idolatry.[285] The notion that many of the divine decrees were intended as tactics in the battle against idolatry would later be put to extensive use in his *Guide for the Perplexed.*

Other comments in the *Mishneh Torah* focus on the possession of material goods. In an artistic touch that I have not mentioned so far, Maimonides places a scriptural verse as a motto at the head of each of the fourteen Books. As the motto for the Book of Acquisition (*Qinyan*), the Book dealing with contracts and the various legal modes of acquiring property, Maimonides chooses the biblical verse: "The beginning of wisdom is: acquire wisdom; yea with all thy acquiring [*qinyan*], acquire understanding."[286] The intimation is unmistakable. While the Book of Acquisition will expound the legalities involved in the acquisition of physical property, the truly worthwhile human acquisitions are wisdom and understanding. A section of the same Book is the Halakot of the Conveyance of Gifts. After setting forth the legal niceties relating to gifts, Maimonides shifts in the section's

[281] *Guide for the Perplexed* 3.35–49.

[282] *Mishneh Torah*: *H. Tefilla* 9.7 (a commandment that is assigned a purpose in *Guide for the Perplexed* 3:48); *H. ᶜEdut* 13.15; 18.3.

[283] *Mishneh Torah*: *H. Sanhedrin* 18.6. *H. Mamrim* 7.11 is another instance where Maimonides assigns a reason to a commandment that is a "decree"; see Ibn Abi Zimra's commentary *ad locum.*

[284] *Mishneh Torah*: *H. Teshuba* 3.4. *H. Miqwa'ot* 11:12 (final paragraph in the Book) is another instance where Maimonides finds a "hint" in one of the divine decrees.

[285] *Mishneh Torah*: *H. ᶜAbodat Kokabim* 12.7; 11; 13. See Leviticus 19:27–28.

[286] Proverbs 4:7.

concluding paragraph into his nonlegal, edifying mode. He notes that persons who are truly pious and scrupulous in their behavior do not themselves need the rules. For they "do not accept gifts from human beings; they trust in God, blessed be He, and not in liberal men."[287]

The disparagement of material possessions is linked by Maimonides with his intellectualization of the Jewish religion. He makes the point in unexpected contexts. For example: Scripture assigns responsibility for the Temple service to the Levites and to the priests, who were a segment of the tribe of Levi, and for that reason permits them only limited land holdings in Palestine, while compensating them with certain perquisites. As he nears the conclusion of the Book of the *Mishneh Torah* containing the laws that govern the perquisites of priests and Levites, Maimonides steers the discussion around to the restrictions on Levites' holding land in Palestine. He signs off: The reason why the tribe of Levi did not receive a defined territory was that they were "separated for worshiping God, serving Him, and instructing the people in His straight ways and righteous statutes." "Nor is it solely the tribe of Levi. Every person . . . whose intelligence leads him to separate himself . . . in order to serve and worship God, [that is,] to *know* Him, . . . and who casts off the yoke of the sundry [monetary] calculations that men are concerned with, . . . God will be his portion and inheritance for ever and ever. God will also supply him with his needs in this life, as He supplied the needs of the priests and Levites."[288]

Scripture, as the rabbis understood it, commands that a small parchment scroll (the *mezuza*), on which two passages from Scripture are written, be affixed to the doorposts of Israelite dwellings, and the required passages begin with the familiar verse: "Hear O Israel, the Lord our God, the Lord is one." Maimonides explains the purpose of the commandment: Whenever a person passes by a scroll affixed to a doorpost, he "encounters God's unity," which is inscribed in it, recalls his love of God, awakens from his spiritual slumber, shakes off his concerns about the vanities of this world, realizes that nothing but knowledge of God is permanent—in other words, the immortal component in man is human intellect at the stage where it possesses knowledge of God—and is led to conduct himself in an upstanding fashion.[289] By custom, one of God's names was in Maimonides' day, and still is today, written on the back of the parchment attached to the doorpost. Maimonides is not enthusiastic about the practice but concedes that it does "no harm" since the addition is made on the outside of the scroll. But he goes on with a fierceness that has no basis in the rabbinic sources: Persons who add the names of angels, names of God, or an apotropaic verse from the Bible to the inside of the scroll, the side

[287]*Mishneh Torah*: *H. Zekiyya u-Mattana* 12.16. As a proof-text, Maimonides cites Proverbs 15:27: "He that hateth gifts shall live"; he is building on anecdotes in the Babylonian Talmud about rabbinic figures who refused to accept gifts on the grounds that "he that hateth gifts shall live"; see BT *Megilla* 28a, and parallels.

[288]*Mishneh Torah*: *H. Shemiṭa we-Yobel* 13.12–13.

[289]*Mishneh Torah*: *H. Mezuza* 6.13.

where the scriptural verses are written, commit a sin so grievous that they lose their portion in the world to come. Such "fools" turn a sacred artifact representing God's unity and the love and worship of God into an "amulet for their own [material] benefit," a magical charm for protecting their houses and other wretched material goods.[290]

Related to the scroll affixed to the doorpost are the phylacteries, which Jewish males bind on their upper arm and above their forehead every weekday. As the Oral Law interprets Scripture, the phylacteries contain parchment scrolls on which four passages from the Pentateuch are written, two of the four being identical with the passages inscribed on the doorpost parchments. In his section on the Halakot of Phylacteries, Maimonides submits that wearing them makes a man "modest, God-fearing," and resistant to "laughter and idle talk." Such a man "does not contemplate evil thoughts, but instead turns his mind exclusively to truth and justice," that is, to the pursuit of knowledge and morality. Maimonides accordingly advises readers to wear them on their arm and above their forehead through the entire day and not only during morning prayers, as was the usual practice in his time and remains so in ours.[291] The parchment scroll attached to the doorpost, the phylacteries bound to one's person, and the fringes that Scripture prescribes be tied to the corners of one's garment,[292] are—Maimonides writes in a rationalistic interpretation of a passage in the Babylonian Talmud—the angels surrounding man and protecting him from sin, as was promised by the Psalmist when he declaimed: "The angel of the Lord encampeth round about them that fear Him, and delivereth them."[293] Maimonides did not believe in personal angels.

The threads are episodic and disjointed, but when combined they coalesce into a broad motif—the moral, spiritual, and intellectual spirit that should quicken the flesh and bones of halakic life. Maimonides exhorts readers: Fulfill the commandments of the Law solemnly and respectfully. It is sinful and foolish to perform them with conceit or pride. Seek out the purposes of the commandments of the Written Torah, even of those that appear to be arbitrary decrees. Do not close your doors to the poor on the festivals, for he who does so engages in the joy of his belly, not the joy of the festival. Refuse gifts from a human hand and trust solely in God. When you encounter the parchment scrolls containing the "Hear O Israel" passage which are attached to the doorposts of your dwellings, they will recall to

[290]*Mishneh Torah*: *H. Mezuza* 5.4; see below, pp. 286–87. Maimonides expresses a similar sentiment in *H. ᶜAbodat Kokabim* 11.12.

[291]See *Mishneh Torah*: *H. Tefillin* 4.25. On the practice of wearing phylacteries specifically during morning prayers, see *Mishneh Torah*: *H. Tefillin* 4.26.

[292]Numbers 15:37–41; Deuteronomy 6: 8–9.

[293]*Mishneh Torah*: *H. Mezuza* 6.13, where Maimonides gives a rationalist twist to BT *Menaḥot* 43b, which in turn is based on Psalms 34:8. By contrast, Rashi explains in his interpretation of the talmudic passage that actual angels come and protect the man who performs the commandments in question from sin. R. Samuel Edels (Meharsha) explains that God creates angels ad hoc to protect the man from sin.

you the love of God. Put your efforts into acquiring wisdom and not physical goods.

The pursuit of knowledge, particularly knowledge of God, is the most pervasive nonhalakic theme in the *Mishneh Torah.* Maimonides takes the theme up one more time when he discusses the messianic age, and what he wanted to say was important enough for him to do so twice, once early in the *Mishneh Torah* and then climactically at the end. The last two chapters of the fourteenth and final Book of the *Mishneh Torah* have the Messiah and the messianic age as their subject, and the final paragraphs of the Book, and hence the closing paragraphs of the code, state: "The sages and prophets were not desirous of the messianic time in order to rule the world, or to lord it over the gentiles, . . . nor in order to eat, drink and be merry, but rather in order to have leisure for the Law and its science [or: its wisdom; *ḥokma*]." Whereupon the *Mishneh Torah* concludes by proclaiming: In the days of the Messiah "the entire world will have only one concern, to know God. They will therefore be wise [or: scientists] to a high degree and know profound, hidden things. And they will acquire knowledge of their creator, to the extent that a human being is able to do so, as is written: 'For the earth shall be full of the knowledge of the Lord, as the waters cover the sea.'"[294]

That is the final lesson that Maimonides wanted to plant in the consciousness of everyone who completes the study of the *Mishneh Torah*: When human history reaches its goal, the earth will be full of the knowledge of the Lord.

Resumé. Considered separately, the features and components of Maimonides' *Mishneh Torah* disclose little that is original. Nevertheless, and notwithstanding minor flaws, the *Mishneh Torah* is one of the two preeminent literary achievements of the Jewish Middle Ages, the other being Rashi's commentary on the Babylonian Talmud. Its originality lies primarily in the overall conception and in execution.

Comprehensive codes had been composed previously, certain codifiers had rearranged the legal and ritual material at their disposal in new topical systems of their own, all codifiers had at the very minimum compressed the talmudic dialectic and some had cut it away completely, and two codes had recorded their rulings without citing the classic rabbinic sources for support. Maimonides envisaged a code of rabbinic law in the tradition of the comprehensive codes, but one that would pursue comprehensiveness further than had been done before. His innovation here consisted in carrying comprehensiveness to its logical conclusion: The *Mishneh Torah* would use as its cadre all 613 commandments given to Moses. It would

[294]*Mishneh Torah*: *H. Melakim* 12:4–5 (following the reading of most of the manuscripts and the Frankel edition). The scriptural verse is Isaiah 11:9. The other passage dealing with the messianic age is *H. Teshuba* 9.2.

Additional examples of nonhalakic, edifying comments in the *Mishneh Torah* are given by Twersky, *Introduction to the Code of Maimonides* (n. 30 above) 421–30. Additional examples of Maimonides' making a case for knowledge and science in the *Mishneh Torah* are given by. Twersky, "Some Non-Halakic Aspects of the *Mishneh Torah*" (n. 184 above).

draw into its embrace all the elaborations of the commandments which were handed down from Moses' time and all the regulations promulgated by the ancient rabbis. The entire body of Jewish law, parts still practiced as well as parts that no longer were, would be put at the disposal of small and great. With precedents for each step, Maimonides then replaced the organization of the legal and ritual regulations in the classic rabbinic texts with a topical arrangement of his own, wholly excluded the dialectic give and take of the Babylonian and Jerusalem Talmuds, and after naming his rabbinic sources in summary fashion in an introduction, dispensed with any further reference to them.

In his new arrangement and partly in his own words, he sets out Jewish ritual and law in its vast detail—civil and criminal law, agricultural and commercial law, personal status, Sabbath and festival laws and rituals, liturgy, dietary regulations, Temple ritual, purity and impurity regulations, and the rest. The great majority of items are drawn from the classic sources; a relatively small number are identified by him as the opinions and enactments of posttalmudic authorities, and a similarly small number are identified as his own inferences from his sources. When he identifies the criteria he applied in determining what the norm is in one instance or another, he cites those that were generally recognized in rabbinic circles in his day—although there are occasional rulings in the *Mishneh Torah* which, in the judgment of commentators, do not sit well with the criteria that he says he followed. He remained faithful to his undertaking even when he may not have felt comfortable with a given ruling because of his philosophic or scientific views. In rare instances, he omits an item with which, we may surmise, he felt uneasy; but he could with plausibility have considered the omitted items to be pieces of advice offered by the ancient rabbis and not legally binding. In a few instances, he drops the explanation that the classic texts gave for a regulation and substitutes an explanation more in accordance with his personal views or else gives no explanation at all. No one, as far as I have seen, has been able to uncover an instance where Maimonides deliberately decided an issue in opposition to what the rabbinic sources indicate the halakic norm to be

Ninety-five percent or more of the contents of the *Mishneh Torah* is legal and ritual in character, and almost all readers perceive and use it as a code of law. But Maimonides envisaged something more encompassing than the most complete of legal codes. As he wrote to his student Joseph ben Judah, he "saw a nation lacking a comprehensive [legal] composition in the true sense and lacking sound, authenticated opinions," and he undertook to supply both deficiencies.[295] He would set forth not merely the entire gamut of law and ritual, but the doctrinal underpinning as well. The portion of the *Mishneh Torah* devoted to nonlegal matters, though far smaller quantitatively, was, from the author's point of view, not secondary in importance. "The exposition of a principle" of the Jewish faith, he once wrote, "is preferable to anything else that I might expound."

[295] Above, p. 209.

Above all, Maimonides teaches that scriptural and rabbinic law stands on a foundation of knowledge. It can scarcely be fortuitous that the initial Book of the *Mishneh Torah* is entitled the Book of Knowledge, that the first sentence of the body of the *Mishneh Torah* makes knowledge of the existence of God the pillar on which the Law rests, that the first subject taken up is the commandments to *know* the existence and the unity of God, that the concluding paragraph of Book One of the *Mishneh Torah* appeals to man to devote himself to the sciences informing him about his Maker, that the final lines of the entire *Mishneh Torah* portray the messianic age as a time looked forward to solely because ideal conditions for pursuing knowledge will then obtain, that Maimonides' closing words are the verse from the prophet Isaiah's eschatological vision which foresees: "The earth shall be full of the knowledge of the Lord." The first Book of the *Mishneh Torah* and the *Mishneh Torah* as a whole are designed so that they open and conclude with the motif of knowledge of God.

In one of its many facets, the *Mishneh Torah* delineates a program for the ideal human life. The ideal life is structured, with all human activity directed to a single goal, and that goal again is knowledge of God, which at the same time is true worship of God. Such knowledge is the key to human immortality; for, Maimonides teaches, what survives the death of the body is the human intellect when it has passed to a state of actuality and reached the stage where it possesses knowledge of God and the other supernal incorporeal beings.

It is in particular philosophic and scientific knowledge of God that Maimonides is talking about. On his reading, Abraham, the father of the Israelite and Jewish people, framed a philosophic proof of the existence of God more than a millennium before Aristotle—whose name never appears in the *Mishneh Torah*—cast the same proof in the mold familiar to students of Greek philosophy. Fulfillment of the commandments to *know* the existence and the unity of God is contingent on learning philosophical proofs for the two tenets and being convinced by the proofs. The subsequent Written Torah commandments to love and stand in awe of God can be fulfilled properly, on Maimonides' exegesis, only through knowledge of God's handiwork, and he is thereby led to provide readers with a brief picture of the universe as conceived by the Arabic Aristotelians. The ancient rabbis were not merely acquainted with philosophic physics and metaphysics under other names; they made the study of philosophy a component of the rabbinic curriculum itself, albeit a component to be put fully at the disposal only of those capable of assimilating it safely. Maimonides quotes a passage in the Babylonian Talmud which ranks the account of the chariot higher than the dialectic give and take of the two Talmuds. Since the account of the chariot is, on Maimonides' reading, nothing other than the philosophic science of metaphysics, the rabbis themselves were ranking the science of metaphysics above talmudic dialectic.

The metaphysics and physics that Maimonides incorporates into the *Mishneh Torah* were commonplaces and disclose no special expertise. Although the astronomical segment explaining how the visibility of the moon can be determined was certainly not commonplace, it likewise was not original with him. He was not the first medieval Jewish thinker to maintain that the study of philosophy and science is mandated by Scripture.[296] It was nonetheless he who invited the ostensibly alien doctrines into the inner sanctum of rabbinic Judaism, into a code of Jewish law, and who then insisted that he was merely bringing to light the age-old rabbinic worldview and not in fact innovating. Formulas commonly bruited about as characterizations of medieval philosophy have led more than one writer to portray Maimonides as engaged in a harmonization of science and philosophy with Scripture and the words of the rabbis. Such a portrayal reflects the perspective of a modern observer standing outside and looking in but fails to do justice to what Maimonides says he was doing and, we can be reasonably sure, saw himself as doing. In his perspective, science and philosophy are not disciplines distinct from the scriptural and rabbinic worldview which can nonetheless be brought into harmony with it. They are themselves integral to the worldview of Scripture and the ancient rabbis.

About the time that Maimonides completed the *Mishneh Torah*, his life underwent a wrenching change with the death of his brother. When he finally drew himself together, he found himeself the family breadwinner and he never again was able to devote himself wholly to his studies. He is not known to have completed any additional substantial project in the rabbinic area, and although his literary labors by no means ceased, his next large work, the *Guide for the Perplexed*, does not display the same intensity and thoroughness as the *Mishneh Torah.*

[296]Maimonides' Muslim contemporary Averroes similarly maintained that "revelation" (or: "the religious law"; *shar*^{c}) requires man to examine the universe rationally, and hence philosophically. See Averroes, *On the Harmony of Religion and Philosophy*, trans. G. Hourani (London 1961) 44–45. Averroes, however, was less willing than Maimonides to teach the masses basic philosophic truths, such as the incorporeality of God.

5

Rabbinic Works III

> The "ark of God," which contains "the tables of the covenant, the breastplate of judgment, and the Urim and Thummim." (Aaron ben Meshullam's characterization of Maimonides' *Mishneh Torah*)
>
> An "error," "darkness and not light," "confused, botched, and muddled," "an opinion pulled out of his belly," "vanity and breaking of the spirit," "rootless and feeble." (Abraham ben David's characterization of rulings in Maimonides' *Mishneh Torah*)

The Reception of the Mishneh Torah. As the *Mishneh Torah* was disseminated through the Jewish world, it evoked diverse reactions. The bits of edifying advice were unexceptionable and generated little comment: Who, after all, would challenge, or feel the need to gloss, Maimonides' exhortations to share the joy of the festivals with the indigent, handle the property of orphans scrupulously, treat physical acquisitions as of little value, refuse gifts from human hands, and behave humanely to slaves? The varying reactions were elicited by the halakic side of the *Mishneh Torah* and by passages embodying Maimonides' rationalist and philosophic views.

Schematization inevitably entails simplification. It is nonetheless illuminating, at the price of sacrificing nuances and ignoring gray areas, to distinguish three main approaches in what is actually a gamut of reactions to the *Mishneh Torah*: A handful of readers extolled the legal and ritual as well as the philosophic and rationalist sides of the work and embraced both wholeheartedly and without reservation. Another relatively small band probed only for weakness. Some of the members of this group were more comprehensive in their critiques, and some less so, some were driven by undisguised animus, while others did their work in a neutral key and without heat, but all had in common a focus on purported errors.

There were, thirdly, a far larger number of scholars who expressed admiration for the legal and ritual side of the *Mishneh Torah*, devoted themselves to exploring the marvels of that side of the work in ever greater depth, with only occasional demurrals here and there, and who either ignored the philosophic elements, placed a construction on them which brought them into agreement with what they deemed to be Jewish orthodoxy, or bemoaned the sad spectacle of such a giant's having succumbed to the blandishments of alien doctrines.

a. To persons of a rationalist bent, Maimonides became a virtual patron saint. A certain Sheshet ben Isaac, who represents himself as a member of the Jewish aristocracy of Zaragosa in Aragon—he calls himself a *nasi*, a "prince," and attaches the title *nasi* to the names of his father and grandfather[1]—is an exemplar. Meir Abulafia, a Spanish rabbinic scholar who was active early in the thirteenth century, had written a critique of the *Mishneh Torah* which rejected some of Maimonides' legal rulings but objected in particular to his statements concerning the afterlife.[2] In defense of Maimonides, Sheshet sings the praises of both the philosophic and legal sides of the *Mishneh Torah.* If, Sheshet writes, Abulafia had taken the trouble to study the "wisdom [or: science] and ethical exhortations" in "the Halakot of the Foundations of the Law" and "Halakot of Repentance"—the latter being the section containing Maimonides' main treatment of the afterlife—he would have "seen that Maimonides demonstrates everything he says." As for the legal rulings in the *Mishneh Torah*, "one must not budge to the right or the left" from them.[3] Sheshet recalls an incident from a time when he happened to have been in Castile and heard a rabbinic judge disparage the legal side of the *Mishneh Torah.* "What does Maimonides know that we don't know," the unnamed judge remonstrated. "And seeing that Maimonides does not cite proofs from the talmudic sages for what he writes, who will listen to him?" Sheshet relates that he spoke up, berated the judge, and silenced him. He further reports that when the *Mishneh Torah* arrived in Castile, its congenial language and new "appealing arrangement of the commandments" attracted men for whom rabbinic texts had been closed books. Nonscholars began to study the work and they acquired a solid knowledge of rabbinic law. As rabbinic judges, including the one whom Sheshet squelched, saw their monopoly over rabbinic law seep away, they became jealous, and "their anger burned." Therein, writes Sheshet, in nothing more than base jealousy, lay the motive for rabbinic opposition to the *Mishneh Torah.*[4]

Criticism of the *Mishneh Torah* by the same Meir Abulafia who moved Sheshet to leap to Maimonides' defense led Aaron ben Meshullam, a rabbinic scholar in Lunel, in the south of France, to praise the code even more extravagantly. In

[1] A. Marx, "Texts by and about Maimonides," *Jewish Quarterly Review* 25 (1935) 428.

[2] See below, pp. 277–78.

[3] Marx, "Texts by and about Maimonides" 417.

[4] Marx, "Texts by and about Maimonides" 427.

responding to Abulafia, Aaron ben Meshullam lauds the *Mishneh Torah* as the greatest work to have seen the light of day since the redaction of the Babylonian Talmud. It is, in his words, the "ark of God," which contains "the tables of the covenant, the breastplate of judgment, and the Urim and Thummim."[5] The list of medieval Jewish writers who embraced the *Mishneh Torah* without reservation includes, understandably, Maimonides' son, Abraham, who was not strictly a rationalist,[6] and Joseph ben Judah.[7] Others are the littérateur and translator Judah al-Ḥarizi,[8] an exilarch named David ben Daniel,[9] Yedaiah Bedersi,[10] and Tanḥum ben Joseph of Jerusalem.[11]

b. At the opposite end of the spectrum stood the critics. Maimonides wrote to his former student, Joseph ben Judah, that he had expected the *Mishneh Torah* to be the target of criticism;[12] and opposition and criticism were not slow in coming. In the same letter to Joseph, he refers to mediocrities in Fustat who through self-conceit and jealousy refused to study or even look at his "large composition." They wanted to avoid having it said that Maimonides had taught them anything.[13] Who the mediocrities were and whether they may have had additional, more respectable motives than those Maimonides ascribes to them is not known. Something is, however, known about three critiques of the *Mishneh Torah* which came to Maimonides' attention.

[5]*K. al-Rasā'il*, ed. J. Brill (Paris 1871) 38. For information regarding Aaron ben Meshullam, see I. Twersky, *Rabad of Posquières* (Cambridge, Mass. 1962) 252.

[6]On halakic matters, see Abraham Maimonides, *Responsa*, ed. A. Freimann and S. Goitein (Jerusalem 1937), index, pp. 220–21. On theological matters, see Abraham Maimonides, *Milḥamot ha-Shem*, ed. R. Margaliyot (Jerusalem 1953) 52–54, 59–75.

[7]Joseph expressed outrage over Samuel ben Eli's critique of legal and doctrinal parts of the *Mishneh Torah*. He asked Maimonides' permission for opening a rabbinic academy in which the *Mishneh Torah* would be a central subject of study. See Moses ben Maimon, *Epistulae*, ed. D. Baneth (Jerusalem 1946) 54–55, 65, 79.

[8]J. al-Ḥarizi, *Taḥkemoni* (Tel Aviv 1952) chapter 46, pp. 348–49, expresses blanket admiration of the *Mishneh Torah*, without explicitly mentioning the nonlegal parts. Al-Ḥarizi was so committed to Maimonides' philosophy that he translated the *Guide for the Perplexed* into Hebrew.

[9]Document published in *Ginse Nistaroth* 3 (1872) 119.

[10]Yedaiah ha-Bedersi, *Ketab ha-Hitnaṣṣelut*, in Solomon Adret, *Responsa*, standard editions, 1, §418. Bedersi enthusiastically embraces Maimonides "books" in general and is primarily interested in their doctrinal, not their halakic, side.

[11]W. Bacher, *Aus dem Wörterbuche Tanchum Jeruschalmi's* (Budapest 1903) 23–24; Hebrew section 5.

Shem Ṭob Falaquera, *S. ha-Mebbaqesh* (Warsaw 1924) 102, and Joseph Ibn Kaspi, in *Hebrew Ethical Wills* (Philadelphia 1926) 137, both recommend Alfasi's epitome of the Babylonian Talmud and Maimonides' *Mishneh Torah* as the sole posttalmudic rabbinic books that need to be studied

[12]Above, p. 209.

[13]Moses ben Maimon, *Epistulae* 53–54.

Pinḥas ben Meshullam was a rabbinic judge in the Egyptian city of Alexandria with whom Maimonides had a difficult and shifting relationship. Maimonides could treat his Alexandrian colleague with hauteur.[14] Pinḥas for his part usually wrote to Maimonides deferentially,[15] yet he could also address Maimonides as an equal. As the two remained locked in their awkward minuet, Maimonides repeatedly found reason to vent annoyance with his Alexandrian colleague, although there were times as well when he made an effort to placate Pinḥas for actual or perceived slights.[16]

Pinḥas sent Maimonides his objections to the method employed in the *Mishneh Torah*. What he wrote is lost, but from Maimonides' reply we learn the following: Pinḥas suggested that Maimonides wanted study of the *Mishneh Torah* to replace the study of Talmud. The introduction to the *Mishneh Torah*[17] and letters of Maimonides'[18] lend plausibility to the contention, but Maimonides' reply to Pinḥas denies it outright and indignantly. Pinḥas further criticized Maimonides for recording his rulings without giving the names of the individual rabbis to whom the rulings are ascribed in the classic rabbinic sources.[19] Maimonides answers that the names attached to rabbinic regulations in the rabbinic sources are of no significance, because the regulations did not originate with the men named; authoritative rabbinic laws and rituals are part of the tradition ultimately going back to Moses. A third objection of Pinḥas' is identical with one raised by the rabbinic judge in Castile whom Sheshet berated and it would continue to echo through the centuries.[20] Pinḥas complained that some of the rulings in the *Mishneh Torah* are hard to fathom because Maimonides did not explain why he decided as he did. Maimonides here responds that a small proportion of rulings in the *Mishneh Torah* are labeled by him as emanating from posttalmudic scholars—the *geonim*—or as his own inferences from the ancient or *geonic* sources. In those instances, readers have been told who the authors of the rulings are and will have to judge whether the inferences drawn are correct or not.[21] In the remaining instances, and they are by

[14]See above, pp. 44–45.

[15]Maimonides, *Responsa*, ed. J. Blau, 2nd ed. (Jerusalem 1986) §393. Pinḥas writes to Maimonides: "I, the least of your students" present before you the opinion I issued on a certain issue, "so that you might inform me whether my decision is correct or not."

[16]See below, p. 548.

[17]See above, p. 208.

[18]See above, pp. 198, 210.

[19]The same criticism is raised by Abraham ben David; see below, p. 273. It would also be raised by Samson ben Abraham of Sens in *K. al-Rasā'il* (n. 5 above) 131–32, Ḥ. Crescas, *Or ha-Shem* (Vienna 1859) 2a.

[20]Abraham ben David (see below, p. 273); Moses of Coucy, *Sefer Miṣwot Gadol* (Venice 1547) introduction 3a; Asher ben Jehiel, *Responsa* (reprinted Jerusalem 1965) §31.9; Isaac ben Sheshet, *Responsa* (reprinted New York 1954) §44; Crescas, *Or ha-Shem* 2a; S. Luria, *Yam shel Shelomo*, introduction to *Baba Qamma*.

[21]Maimonides himself stated the following rule regarding rulings of the *geonim* on legal issues that the ancient rabbinic texts do not address: If "we find no clear proof" for what they say, we

far the majority, Maimonides simply records halakic norms that emerge straightforwardly (*talmud ᶜaruk . . . be-ferush*) from the Mishna corpus, the two Talmuds, and the other ancient rabbinic sources. Since these are plainly marked as normative by the ancient sources, they need no further proof.

Maimonides is telling Pinḥas and, in effect, others who would raise the same objection, that in the great majority of cases, the ancient authorities make the halakic norm unambiguously clear and there can consequently be no dispute concerning it. In truth, as observed in the previous chapter, determining what the authoritative rabbinic sources intend as the halakic norm was much more complex than Maimonides admits. The history of rabbinic legal thought reveals that codifiers and commentators frequently fail to agree on the interpretation of mishnaic and talmudic texts. When they do agree on the meaning of a text, they may differ regarding the criteria to be used in determining the norm that the text intends to set. Even when they concur on the applicable criteria, they are capable of applying them differently. And a halakic issue may be addressed in more than one passage of the Mishna and Talmud, and the several passages may handle the issue differently. Time after time, codifiers and commentators have therefore disagreed on halakic norms.[22]

Maimonides does concede to Pinḥas that the *Mishneh Torah* has a shortcoming, albeit a shortcoming flowing from the work's strength. Although he is satisfied that the majority of laws and rituals recorded in the *Mishneh Torah* emerge immediately from the classical rabbinic texts and do not require proofs, he admits that it is sometimes difficult to rediscover the text from which a given ruling flows; for much of the code's artistry lies in its assembling bits and pieces from every corner of the classic rabbinic canon and rearranging them in a new scheme. He recalls an occasion when a rabbinic judge visited him and asked to see the source from which he had derived a certain ruling; Maimonides could not for the life of him remember from where he had drawn the ruling until after the visitor left.

That, he writes, is the point that Pinḥas should have made, rather than complaining about an absence of proofs. He was sorry now that he had not accompanied the *Mishneh Torah* with a handbook recording his sources wherever they are not obvious, listing, for example, the sources of everything in his section on the Sabbath which is not drawn from the Sabbath tractates of the Mishna and Babylonian Talmud. When he would find the time, he tells Pinḥas, he hoped to return and supply the lack by composing such a handbook.[23] He never did return and compose it, and the enterprise of unearthing Maimonides' sources has kept commentators occupied from the time the *Mishneh Torah* was published until today.

---

should neither reject their ruling nor accept it, but hold it in abeyance until proof is forthcoming. *Responsa* §310, p. 576; similarly in §138.

[22]Above, p. 221.

[23]Letter to Pinḥas of Alexandria, in I. Shailat, *Letters and Essays of Moses Maimonides* (in Hebrew) (Jerusalem 1987–1988) 438–45. Translation: I. Twersky, *Introduction to the Code of Maimonides* (New Haven 1980) 32–37.

A second critic of the *Mishneh Torah* who came to Maimonides' attention was Samuel ben Eli, the principal of the rabbinic academy in Baghdad, and a person with whom Maimonides had an even more tense relationship than with Pinḥas. When writing to Joseph ben Judah, Maimonides speaks of Samuel as a person who does not "know anything." He hesitated to answer letters sent to him by Samuel for the convoluted reason that should he answer, etiquette would require him to express himself respectfully, and Samuel would then undoubtedly exhibit Maimonides' language as evidence of the latter's recognition of Samuel's worth. Regarding one of Samuel's compositions, Maimonides remarks that even allowing for the man's ignorance, he was still astonished at the foolishness and nonsense he found there.[24]

In a different letter to Joseph, Maimonides takes up Samuel's critique of three rulings recorded in the *Mishneh Torah* which relate to permissible and forbidden activities on the Sabbath. Maimonides explains why the criticisms, which had been sent to him by an unnamed intermediary, do not hold water.[25] Elsewhere, he characterizes the criticisms as superficial[26]—this, although each of them is perfectly cogent within the framework of posttalmudic rabbinic discourse and each would be raised independently by subsequent critics and commentators of the *Mishneh Torah*.[27]

A separate Sabbath issue deserves being mentioned here, even though it touches on the *Mishneh Torah* only marginally. A member of the Baghdad community had written to Maimonides soliciting his opinion on the question whether a Jew is permitted to travel by boat on a river on the Sabbath, and Maimonides had replied with a formal halakic responsum explaining why such travel is permissible.[28] Samuel then stepped in with his own letter to Maimonides. He addresses Maimonides with exquisite courtesy—he had a stronger sense of *noblesse oblige* than Maimonides did; he remarks that the responsum sent to the Baghdadi Jew had been shown to him as Maimonides undoubtedly realized it would be; and he sets forth his reasons for rejecting Maimonides' ruling.[29] This time, Maimonides not only responded; he wrote a lengthy surrejoinder designed to demonstrate that his position was correct and Samuel's objections, unfounded. The surrejoinder deploys perfunctory civilities but in between them it seethes with disdain for Samuel and his rabbinic reasoning. The final paragraph lays bare an underlying cause of Maimonides' antipathy. Maimonides reports that he had received a copy of the treatise in which Samuel—"may God keep watch" over him—criticized Maimonides' treatment of the human afterlife in the *Mishneh Torah*. And he

[24]Moses ben Maimon, *Epistulae* (n. 7 above), 59–60, 65.

[25]Maimonides, *Responsa* (n. 15 above) §464.

[26]*Responsa* §300.

[27]See A. Freimann, "*Teshubat ha-Rambam le-R. Joseph ha-Ma*ᶜ*arabi*," *Sefer ha-Yobel . . . muggash le-Dr. Binyamin Menashe Levin*" (Jerusalem 1940) 29–33.

[28]*Responsa* §308.

[29]*Responsa* §309.

informs Samuel that he had composed a treatise of his own in order to clear himself of the "evil name being sent forth" about him.[30]

It seems that Jews in Yemen had understood the *Mishneh Torah* as intimating that the classic rabbinic statements concerning a future resurrection of human bodies are all allegories and had asked Samuel whether Maimonides represented the ancient rabbis' position correctly. Samuel's piece on resurrection does not refer to Maimonides by name, but it was public knowledge that the *Mishneh Torah* was the target. Maimonides response, known as the *Treatise on Resurrection*, will be discussed in a later chapter.

The remaining critique of the *Mishneh Torah* that came to Maimonides' attention was from southern France. It was the tip of a larger iceberg, and that tip, which Maimonides saw, was the very opposite of unfriendly. In the 1190s he received a series of questions regarding halakic decisions in the *Mishneh Torah*, of which twenty-four—assuming that they and Maimonides' replies are all genuine[31]—are known. The sender was R. Jonathan of Lunel, who was acting as spokesman for a circle of rabbinic scholars in the area. Jonathan's introductory letter gushes forth such a profusion of bombastic compliments in rhymed prose that a modern reader might easily see them as parody.[32] In the course of his letter, Jonathan mentions that news of Maimonides' philosophic work, the *Guide for the Perplexed*, had reached the people of Lunel, and he asks Maimonides to "satisfy" their hunger by sending a copy.[33] Such a request could hardly help pleasing the author.

Maimonides answers Jonathan most graciously and in a tone contrasting sharply with that of his responses to Pinḥas of Alexandria and Samuel ben Eli. He thanks the questioners for the care with which they had studied the *Mishneh Torah*, praises their rabbinic acumen, tells them that with the deterioration of rabbinic scholarship, they were the last hope for the future of rabbinic studies, acknowledges that "forgetfulness is ubiquitous, especially among the elderly," and encourages his questioners to "examine and scrutinize" everything he wrote.[34] As for the twenty-four questions regarding rulings in the *Mishneh Torah*, Maimonides explains why most of the criticisms had missed the mark. He does not, however, hesitate to concede in one instance: "The matter is certainly just as you said. I have copied the correction into my text [of the *Mishneh Torah*], for I erred, . . . and you should correct your text as well."[35] In a second instance, he explains why his interpretation of the pertinent talmudic passage is more plausible than that of his

[30]*Responsa* §310. Below, pp. 524–33.

[31]J. Kafah, "*She'elot Ḥakme Lunel u-Teshubot 'ha-Rambam,' Kelum Meqoriyyot Hen?*" *Sefer Zikkaron le-ha-Rab Yiṣḥaq Nissim* 2 (Jerusalem 1985) 235–52, rejects the authenticity of this entire collection of responsa. Even if Kafah were right regarding the responsa, it is virtually certain that Jonathan's cover letter and Maimonides' reply to it are genuine.

[32]See *Responsa* 3.49–54.

[33]*Responsa* 3.52.

[34]See *Responsa* 3.56–57.

[35]*Responsa* §287.

questioners, yet recognizes that the alterative interpretation has cogency "and if someone demurs on the issue, let him demur."[36] In four instances, he finds that the questioners employed an erroneous text of the *Mishneh Torah*, either because a scribe had copied incorrectly[37] or because the copy they received had been made from fascicles of the draft, which did not yet reflect the final revision.[38] By admitting at least one incorrect decision and by recognizing the cogency of his correspondents' demurral on another, Maimonides tacitly refutes his own assertion that laws and rituals in the *Mishneh Torah* which are not labeled there as emanating from posttalmudic scholars all emerge straightforwardly from the classic rabbinic sources.

The reverential tone in which Jonathan and his circle expressed themselves when writing to Maimonides was not mere etiquette. Lunel became a bastion of fealty to the *Mishneh Torah*. Aaron ben Meshullam, the man who described the *Mishneh Torah* as the ark of God, was answering an attack on Maimonides which had been sent to the aforementioned Jonathan of Lunel and he informed his correspondent that the *Mishneh Torah* had already become the standard code for deciding halakic questions in Lunel.[39]

These have been the critiques of the *Mishneh Torah* that Maimonides was cognizant of. Southern France, which produced the twenty-four questions of the men of Lunel, also produced the two most thoroughgoing critiques of the *Mishneh Torah*, neither of which, we can be fairly certain, ever came to Maimonides' attention.

Moses ha-Kohen was a scholar living in the general area of Lunel, and perhaps in Lunel itself. The years in which he was active are uncertain. Some notion of the date is furnished, however, by the circumstance that he knew of Maimonides' reply, written in the 1190s, to at least one of the questions raised by Jonathan's circle,[40] and by the further circumstance that he quotes one or more glosses on the *Mishneh Torah* from the author to be discussed immediately below, a man who was Maimonides' older contemporary and did not live beyond the twelfth century.

[36]*Responsa* §300, a criticism also raised by Samuel ben Eli, according to Maimonides' letter to Joseph ben Judah, *Responsa* §464.

[37]*Responsa* §§302, 316, 354.

[38]*Responsa* §433.

[39]*K. al-Rasā'il* (n. 5 above) 38.

[40]*Hassagot ha-Remak*, ed. S. Atlas (Jerusalem 1969) 1.43, refers to Maimonides' reply to the question raised by the scholars of Lunel regarding *Mishneh Torah*: *H. Berakot* 8.11. The question and Maimonides' reply are found in Maimonides, *Responsa* §298. R. Moses bluntly characterizes the justification that Maimonides gives there for his ruling in *H. Berakot* 8.11 as "nothing."

Atlas edited Moses ha-Kohen's comments on the first three of the fourteen Books of the *Mishneh Torah* from Bodleian Hebrew MS Opp. Add 4to 44 (=Neubauer #617). The description of the manuscript in Neubauer's catalogue indicates that it contains the glosses on the remaining Books of the *Mishneh Torah* as well.

Moses ha-Kohen's comments on the *Mishneh Torah* run into the hundreds.[41] He treats Maimonides neither deferentially nor discourteously, often speaking of him as "this master [or: rabbi; Hebrew: *rab*]"[42] but sometimes in a phrase that has a more respectful sound to it for the rabbinic ear, as "the master, R. Moses."[43] Although the preserved comments cover the entire *Mishneh Torah*, including Book One, the Book of Knowledge, none grapples with the methodological matters that troubled other critics and none touches on Maimonides' philosophic or rationalist views; they concern themselves exclusively with Maimonides' halakic rulings. R. Moses proceeds in an unemotional, businesslike fashion, occasionally, even expressing approval.[44] Usually, he points out, *sine ira et studio*, instances where Maimonides had, in his judgment, erred or omitted an essential qualification,[45] where his community followed a different custom,[46] or simply where the scholarly tradition in which he had been trained arrived at an alternative result on the basis of the same classic rabbinic sources.[47]

The best-known critic of the *Mishneh Torah* was R. Abraham ben David (Rabad) of Posquières, again in southern France, a scholar of the very highest rabbinic credentials and a man who equaled, if he did not surpass, Maimonides in self-assurance.[48] He was Maimonides' senior by a few years and apparently drew up his glosses before Moses ha-Kohen undertook the task, since Moses ha-Kohen quotes one or more of them.[49] There is an apparent connection, which has never been adequately clarified, between Abraham ben David and the scholars of Lunel who sent the twenty-four questions to Maimonides, for over half of their preserved questions have parallels in his glosses.[50] Like Moses ha-Kohen, R. Abraham takes up hundreds of individual paragraphs of the *Mishneh Torah*. His stature and

[41]The number of comments on the first three of the fourteen Books of the *Mishneh Torah* exceeds a hundred. Atlas's preface to *Hassagot ha-Remak* quotes Hebrew writers who speak of "hundreds and thousands" of glosses of R. Moses' on the entire *Mishneh Torah*.

[42]*Hassagot ha-Remak* 1.21; 26, et passim; perhaps as a reaction to R. Abraham ben David's habit of referring to Maimonides disdainfully as "this author," "this compiler," or "this man."

[43]*Hassagot ha-Remak* 1.97.

[44]Examples: *Hassagot ha-Remak* 1.24; 68; 71.

[45]Examples: *Hassagot ha-Remak* 1.22; 25; 28; 31; 71.

[46]Examples: *Hassagot ha-Remak* 1.24; 25; 46; 2.6.

[47]Examples: *Hassagot ha-Remak* 25; 48; 76; 80.

[48]Regarding R. Abraham ben David's preeminence as a rabbinist, see Twersky, *Rabad of Posquières* (n. 5 above) 51–54.

[49]*Hassagot ha-Remak* 2.6 quotes "R. Abraham" and repeats the wording of the latter's gloss to *Mishneh Torah*: *H. ᶜErubim* 1.16. A comment of his in *Hassagot ha-Remak* 1.39 appears to echo Abraham ben David's gloss on *Mishneh Torah*: *H. Berakot* 1.19, but does not mention Abraham ben David by name. On 1.47 and 59, Moses cites interpretations of "Rabad," which was R. Abraham ben David's acronym, and on 1.75, he cites an interpretation that he ascribes to "Rabad" and, in the next sentence, to "the master, R. Abraham." I was not able to find these last three passages in the works of Abraham ben David.

[50]Maimonides, *Responsa* (n. 15 above) 3.43.

pyrotechnic literary style have shunted the comments of R. Moses to the periphery of the world of rabbinic scholarship, although those comments are no less cogent and although—or could it be partly because?—they are articulated more clearly and are easier reading.[51]

In contrast to Moses ha-Kohen, Abraham ben David was motivated by an animosity, which he makes no effort to hide. The very manner in which he refers to the target of his critique exudes disparagement, for he avoids ever mentioning Maimonides' name, speaking of him instead as "this author," "this compiler," or even "this man." A couple of times he calls Maimonides "this scholar" (or: "this wise man"; *ẓe he-ḥakam*), but in both instances the words sound sarcastic. Only once does he slip and speak of Maimonides in terms that would satisfy the requirements of rabbinic etiquette, as "the rabbi-author" (*ha-rab ha-meḥabber*).[52] He concludes his criticism of one ruling in the *Mishneh Torah* by remarking: "To summarize, talmudic study is intended solely for persons who have a reliable tradition [*qabbala*] or the ability to use rabbinic dialectic correctly."[53] The unmistakable intimation is that Maimonides qualified on neither score: He never received adequate instruction in halaka from teachers standing in the chain of posttalmudic rabbinic tradition and he did not know how to apply rabbinic dialectic and derive correct halakic conclusions from the texts. He was entirely unequipped for the codifying task that he undertook.

Historians like to call attention to a passage in which R. Abraham acknowledges Maimonides' accomplishment by characterizing the *Mishneh Torah* as a "sizable piece of work." But at least as striking as the acknowledgment is the grudging tone in which it is made. At issue is a complicated question of agricultural ritual law on which Maimonides had brought his knowledge of medieval geometry to bear. Before entering into the specifics of Maimonides' ruling, R. Abraham writes: "What he says here has no source in the [Babylonian] Talmud or the Tosefta, and logic [*sekel*] does not support it. . . . By the life of my head, had he not accomplished a sizable piece of work by *collecting* the statements of the [Babylonian] Talmud, the Palestinian Talmud, and the Tosefta, I would *collect* against him a gathering of the nation, together with its elders and its scholars. For he [constantly] alters the language and terminology of the rabbinic sources and twists the rabbinic discussions in new directions. . . ."[54] We can only imagine what the nation, its elders, and its scholars would have been expected to do when Abraham ben David marshaled them against Maimonides.

Abraham ben David casts his net more broadly than Moses ha-Kohen: While most of his comments focus on legal matters, the methodology of the *Mishneh*

[51] Joseph Caro takes account of Moses ha-Kohen's glosses throughout *Kesef Mishneh*, his commentary on the *Mishneh Torah*, but he is a notable exception.

[52] References are given by Ch. Tchernowitz, *Toledoth ha-Poskim* 1 (New York 1946) 272–73.

[53] Abraham ben David, gloss on *Mishneh Torah*: *H. Shemiṭa we-Yobel* 9.8.

[54] Abraham ben David, gloss on *Mishneh Torah*: *H. Kela'im* 6.2.

Torah and Maimonides' rationalist and philosophic views also fall under his critical eye.

In the introduction to the *Mishneh Torah*, Maimonides submitted that "a man may read the Written Torah and then read this work, from which he will learn the entire Oral Torah. Besides the two, he will not need any further work." R. Abraham seizes upon the opportunity and, in a gloss, registers his rejection of the entire enterprise from the outset. Maimonides, he writes, "thought that he was improving matters but he did not, for he departed from the method of all previous authors. They cited a proof for what they said and gave the names of those from whom they drew"; as a consequence, rabbinic judges would know at once which source had been used and what the basis for every ruling was and they could judge for themselves whether the codifier had ruled correctly. Abraham ben David's statement is not wholly accurate, for Maimonides did have precedents for recording rulings without furnishing the reasons for them or the sources from which they are drawn.[55] Be that as it may, the glossator continues with an allusion to what he was just seen to identify as the twin pillars of rabbinic adjudication. He writes, when faced with Maimonides' rulings: "I do not know why I should abandon the scholarly tradition in which I stand [*qabbalati*] or the proof that I have mustered [in support of my position], in favor of this author's composition [*ḥibbur*]. If the person disagreeing with me is greater than I, well and good, but if I am greater than he, why should I give up my opinion in favor of his?" Furthermore, in instances where the posttalmudic rabbinic scholars differ, "this author selects the opinion of one and records it in his composition. But why should I rely on his decision . . . without knowing who the scholar holding the other opinion was and whether the other opinion holds water? It was only because 'a surpassing spirit was in him,'" only because of an overweening self-conceit, that Maimonides created his newfangled kind of code.[56]

Maimonides explained to Pinḥas of Alexandria why he did not give reasons for his rulings in the *Mishneh Torah*. Rulings based on his own judgment or the judgment of one of the posttalmudic scholars are, he said, all clearly labeled as such in the *Mishneh Torah*, and the remainder flow directly from the rabbinic sources. Abraham ben David almost surely did not see the letter, but what his reaction would have been if he did can easily be surmised. He would have responded, first, that by marking some of the rulings in the *Mishneh Torah* as his own or as the opinions of posttalmudic rabbinic scholars, Maimonides accomplished nothing, since he failed to apprise readers of opposing opinions, and secondly, that the halakic norm often does not emerge unambiguously from the classic rabbinic texts and one must therefore always explain how a text is being interpreted.

[55] Above, pp. 195–96.

[56] Abraham ben David, gloss on *Mishneh Torah*, introduction. The quotation is from Daniel 6:4. For glosses on the Introduction, Book One, and Book Two, of the *Mishneh Torah*, I used *Hassagot ha-Rabad*, ed. B. Naor (Jerusalem 1985).

Among the passages of a philosophic and rationalist character in the *Mishneh Torah* to which Abraham ben David takes exception is the paragraph in the Halakot of Repentance where Maimonides brands persons who believe that God is a body and has a shape as heretics and where he condemns such persons to the loss of their portion in the world to come. R. Abraham censures Maimonides not for construing the deity as an incorporeal being, but for branding those who believe otherwise as heretics. "Why," he asks, does Maimonides "call a person of the sort a heretic? Great and good scholars held that opinion because of what they found in Scripture and, even more, because of what they found in rabbinic aggadot that confuse the mind."[57] If the version of the gloss preserved in the printed editions of the *Mishneh Torah* is correct, the censure was more pointed. The standard printed version has Abraham ben David say: "Great scholars *who are better than he* held that opinion because of what they found in Scripture. . . ."

The expression "rabbinic aggadot that confuse the mind" does not suggest someone who took a fundamentalist stance toward the ancient rabbinic sources. Abraham ben David nevertheless could, when in a different frame of mind, upbraid Maimonides for interpreting rabbinic aggada nonliterally. One of his glosses is occasioned by the passage where Maimonides wrote that in "the world to come there is no body or corporeality; only the souls of the righteous, [existing] without a body, like the ministering angels."[58] R. Abraham, undoubtedly on the basis of a sentence in the Babylonian Talmud,[59] understood the *world to come* as the era that will follow upon the future restoration of souls to bodies at the time of resurrection. Maimonides' construal of the *world to come* as something nonphysical accordingly leads the glossator to suspect that Maimonides rejected the rabbinic belief. He comments on the passage: "This man's words are, in my view, close to [those of] a person who denies the resurrection of bodies. . . . By the life of my head, that was not the rabbis' opinion"; whereupon he quotes statements from the rabbinic aggada to prove that the ancient rabbis believed in a literal resurrection of the dead.[60] Additional instances can be cited where he criticizes Maimonides for not accepting the literal sense of statements in the classic aggada[61] and for incorporating sentiments of a philosophic and scientific nature into the *Mishneh Torah*.[62]

[57] Abraham ben David, gloss on *Mishneh Torah*: *H. Teshuba* 3.7.

[58] Above, p. 242.

[59] Below, p. 510.

[60] Abraham ben David, gloss on *Mishneh Torah*: *H. Teshuba* 8.2.

[61] Abraham ben David, glosses on *Mishneh Torah*: *H. Teshuba* 8.4; *H. Melakim* 12.1 (as quoted in *Hassagot ha-Rabad*, ed. B. Naor, p. 64, note).

[62] Abraham ben David, glosses on *Mishneh Torah*: *H. Yesode ha-Torah* 1.10, on Moses' request to see God's glory; *H. Teshuba* 5.5, which attacks Maimonides for setting forth the difficulty in combining belief in God's foreknowledge with belief in human free will and then not offering a solution; *H. Qiddush ha-Ḥodesh* 7.7, which begins with the sarcastic remark: "this author greatly prides and congratulates himself on his knowledge of the present science [i.e.,

As already said, the bulk of Abraham ben David's critique is directed against the halakic side of Maimonides' code.

A very small number of his glosses demonstrate his fairness by expressing approval of one or another of Maimonides' legal or ritual rulings.[63] A few others point out what he takes to be errors committed by the copyists or slips of the pen on Maimonides' part;[64] despite dismissing Maimonides as incompetent in talmudic reasoning, and the *Mishneh Torah* as riddled with errors, R. Abraham realized that his adversary could not consciously have committed some of the elementary mistakes he found in the copy of the *Mishneh Torah* which reached him. Still other glosses call attention to alternative ways of interpreting the rabbinic sources upon which Maimonides relied,[65] to customs of the French Jewish communities which diverged from those recorded in the *Mishneh Torah*,[66] or simply to variant readings in the talmudic texts which lead to conclusions different from those drawn by Maimonides.[67]

But what lends Abraham ben David's work its distinctive flavor are the slashing criticisms in which R. Abraham dismisses a halakic decision of Maimonides' as a "lack of understanding,"[68] an "error,"[69] "falsehood,"[70] "vanity and breaking of the spirit,"[71] a "muddle,"[72] "darkness and not light,"[73] "confused, botched, and muddled,"[74] "rootless and feeble,"[75] "an opinion out of his belly,"[76] and the

---

astronomy] and thinks that he reached its summit"; *H. ᶜAbodat Kokabim* 1.3, an oblique criticism of Maimonides' position that the biblical Abraham learned of the existence of God through a philosophic proof.

[63]Examples in Tchernowitz, *Toledoth ha-Poskim* 1 (n. 52 above) 279 (Tchernowitz finds "about ten" instances); Twersky, *Rabad of Posquières* (n. 5 above) 194–95.

[64]Examples in Twersky, *Rabad of Posquières* 147.

[65]Examples in H. Gross, "R. Abraham b. David aus Posquières," *Monatsschrift für Geschichte und Wissenschaft des Judentums* 23 (1874) 80, 83; Twersky, *Rabad of Posquières* 152. Tchernowitz, *Toledoth ha-Poskim* 1.291–94, tries to reduce many of these differences in interpretation of the rabbinic texts to ideological differences between Maimonides and Abraham ben David, but the thesis is highly questionable.

[66]Twersky, *Rabad of Posquières* 167.

[67]Examples in Gross, "R. Abraham ben David aus Posquières" 81; Twersky, *Rabad of Posquières* 150.

[68]Gloss on *Mishneh Torah*: *H. Ishut* 12.9; *H. Abot ha-Ṭum'ot* 1.17.

[69]Gloss on *Mishneh Torah*: *H. Nizqe Mamon* 2.5; 9; et passim.

[70]Gloss on *Mishneh Torah*: *H. Ma'akalot Asurot* 1.2.

[71]Glosses on *Mishneh Torah*: *H. Ishut* 23.2; *Shemiṭa we-Yobel* 4.6; *Bet ha-Beḥira* 4.5. The phrase is from Ecclesiastes 1:14, and 4:16, which I have translated following Rashi's interpretation, on the supposition that Abraham ben David most likely understood it in that way.

[72]Gloss on *Mishneh Torah*: *H. Shabbat* 17.35; 19.6; 21.27; *H. Megilla*1.14; and dozens of other glosses.

[73]Gloss on *Mishneh Torah*: *H. Abot ha-Ṭum'ot* 20.9.

[74]Gloss on *Mishneh Torah*: *H. Maᶜaser Sheni* 1.5.

[75]Gloss on *Mishneh Torah*: *H. Bi'at Miqdash* 1.7.

[76]Gloss on *Mishneh Torah*: *H. Kelim* 12.13.

like;[77] where he complains that Maimonides appended an incorrect qualification to a rabbinic ruling and "in the multitude of words there wanteth not transgression"[78] or that Maimonides committed precisely the opposite error and "failed to furnish a qualification when he should have explained";[79] where he declares that the "wind should carry away" what Maimonides wrote on a certain subject[80] or that Maimonides should "go out and teach [it] to little boys";[81] where he imagines a future time when he would "merit" celebrating the Passover festival in Jerusalem with Maimonides waiting on the table and serving a Paschal lamb prepared according to a certain ruling in the *Mishneh Torah*, whereupon he would "slam the meat down on the ground" in front of Maimonides in order to dramatize that preparation of meat in accordance with the latter's opinion renders it ritually impermissible.[82] R. Abraham typically completes his invective by contending that Maimonides wholly misunderstood the Babylonian Talmud, that norms recorded in *Mishneh Torah* have absolutely no basis in the rabbinic sources, or that rabbinic texts point to norms diametrically opposed to those laid down by Maimonides.

A later author of a valuable work on rabbinic methodology was able to read Abraham ben David's glosses—with the remarks to the effect that Maimonides had not received proper instruction in rabbinic matters, that he did not know how to apply rabbinic dialectic, that his rulings were falsehoods, muddles, and so on—and still intone solemnly: "R. Abraham ben David did not wish to detract from Maimonides' honor; God forbid that holy scholars such as he" would behave in that fashion. By demurring on certain legal matters, he wanted to make sure that no one would follow Maimonides blindly and thereby fall victim to opinions expressed in the *Guide for the Perplexed*.[83] With all due respect to the later author, Abraham ben David's object, when viewed objectively, was to demolish Maimonides completely. He wanted to guarantee that the *Mishneh Torah* would never become either an authoritative law code for the Jewish nation or, worse, the substitute for the classic Oral Law sources which, the glossator understood, Maimonides intended it to be. And he did not hide his dislike for his adversary.

Events did not turn out quite as R. Abraham hoped they would. The *Mishneh Torah* never displaced the classic Oral Law sources—and Maimonides, we saw, insisted to Pinḥas of Alexandria that such had not been his intent. Nor did it, in the

[77]Further examples: Tchernowitz, *Toledoth ha-Poskim* 1.272–73; Twersky, *Rabad of Posquières* 163–64.

[78]Gloss on *Mishneh Torah*: *H. Sheḥiṭa* 11.5, quoting Proverbs 10:19. R. Abraham may have been hinting at the second half of the verse as well: "But he that refraineth his lips is wise."

[79]Gloss on *Mishneh Torah*: *H. Ṭum'at Ṣara^c^at* 4.5.

[80]Gloss on *Mishneh Torah*: *H. Mamrim* 2.9.

[81]Gloss on *Mishneh Torah*: *H. Ishut* 22.19.

[82]Gloss to *Mishneh Torah*: *H. Qorban Pesaḥ* 10.11.

[83]Malachi ha-Kohen, *Yad Malachi* 2, rules regarding Maimonides, §43, repeated in *Kelale ha-Rambam* and *Kelale ha-Rabad*, which are printed at the beginning of standard editions of the *Mishneh Torah*.

long run, become the standard code for the entire Jewish nation, although there were periods when it was recognized as the standard in much of the Jewish world. The *Mishneh Torah* nonetheless has for centuries enjoyed enormous authority in rabbinic circles, and by a caprice of history, Abraham ben David's critique contributed to that outcome. On almost every point on which he attacked Maimonides, commentators stepped forward and defended Maimonides' position, albeit at times through farfetched ratiocinations. When the smoke cleared on the field of battle, the *Mishneh Torah* remained erect, not infallible perhaps, yet only slightly scarred. By virtue of withstanding the onslaught of one of the sharpest of rabbinic minds and sharpest of rabbinic pens, it demonstrated its steel, and its authority only grew. In traditional rabbinic academies today—the yeshivot—the *Mishneh Torah* is often the most intensely studied text after the Babylonian Talmud. Through another of history's caprices, R. Abraham ben David has come to be remembered best not for any of his other erudite and subtle writings, but as an accessory of the very code that he tried so hard to destroy. For centuries, he has been known primarily as the glossator on the *Mishneh Torah.*

Abraham ben David's comprehensive critique of the *Mishneh Torah* was followed soon after by the critique of Moses ha-Kohen, which was already described. Sections have been preserved of a general critique of the *Mishneh Torah* by a certain R. Meshullam, an accomplished rabbinic scholar who also lived in southern France and who was active in the first half of the thirteenth century; the preserved passages, all of which deal with halaka, are modulated in the balanced tone struck by Moses ha-Kohen.[84] And through the ages commentators continued to call attention to problematic rulings in the *Mishneh Torah.* But criticism of the legal side of the *Mishneh Torah* reached its climax with Abraham ben David and Moses ha-Kohen.

On the doctrinal front, the worst was to come. Abraham ben David, as just seen, accused Maimonides of, apparently, rejecting the rabbinic doctrine of resurrection of the dead. The same accusation was made in a guarded and polite fashion by Samuel ben Eli, the principal of the rabbinic academy in Baghdad. It continued to be made, and the voices grew louder and louder. The Spanish scholar Meir Abulafia raised questions about a few of the halakic decisions in the *Mishneh Torah* but was much more perturbed by Maimonides' statement that in "the world to come there is no body or corporeality; only the souls of the righteous, [existing] without a body, like the ministering angels." He too assumed that when the rabbis spoke of the *world to come* they meant the state of the world after human souls are restored to their bodies and he too read Maimonides as denying that a future resurrection will take place. Abulafia attempted to organize a public repudiation of Maimonides' departure from orthodox doctrine, sending his concerns first to

[84]Glosses of R. Meshullam, published in J. Lubetski (Lubetsky), *Bidke Bathim* (Paris 1896) 31–44.

Jonathan of Lunel and then, after being rebuffed there, to a rabbinic scholar in central France.[85] Abulafia's efforts were fruitless. But the opposition of other thirteenth-century figures to the theological views stated in both Maimonides' *Mishneh Torah* and his *Guide for the Perplexed* bore fruit that ripened into an ugly brouhaha.

The epicenter was once again southern France. Although many of the events are obscure, it is known that in the first third of the thirteenth century, a certain Solomon ben Abraham of Montpellier lashed out at rationalists around him who went to extremes in allegorizing Scripture and who, he wrote, "mocked the words of our rabbis." As Solomon later represented his position, he had the highest admiration for Maimonides and was only criticizing readers of Maimonides who misunderstood what he had written. Solomon's opponents report, however, that he expressly accused Maimonides of writing "heretical books."[86] One of his allies likewise agrees that Solomon had attacked Maimonides' orthodoxy,[87] although a different person sympathetic to Solomon complains that that was simply a slanderous report spread abroad by the opponents.[88] Wherever the truth may lie, the rationalist camp rallied to Maimonides' defense and accused Solomon ben Abraham of defaming a great man.[89] To mobilize support for his antirationalist stance, Solomon turned to rabbinic scholars in central France, where he foresaw a sympathetic hearing. The authorities to whom he turned examined Maimonides' writings, believed that they found "profanation of God" there, and promulgated "decrees" and "curses."[90] Specifically, they placed "everyone who reads the *Guide for the Perplexed* and the Book of Knowledge [of the *Mishneh Torah*] under the ban."[91]

[85]*K. al-Rasā'il* (n. 5 above) 1–4, 13–15. Abulafia's critique of Maimonides' halakic rulings are found in *K. al-Rasā'il* 9–13, 16–25. The unstinting praise of Maimonides' *Mishneh Torah* put forward by Aaron ben Meshullam of Lunel—above p. 265—was a reply to the letter that Abulafia addressed to R. Jonathan of Lunel. The occasion of Sheshet ben Isaac's praise of the *Mishneh Torah*—above p. 264—was also Meir Abulafia's attack on Maimonides. Like Abraham ben David, Abulafia was not at all a fundamentalist in respect to the rabbinic aggada; see B. Septimus, *Hispano-Jewish Culture in Transition* (Cambridge, Mass. 1982) 78–81.

[86]Letter of D. Qimḥi in A. Lichtenberg, *Qobeṣ Teshubot ha-Rambam* (Leipzig 1859) 3.4b. Statements in the same vein are reported by the scholars of Lunel in J. Shatzmiller, "*Li-Temunat ha-Maḥloqet ha-Rishona ᶜal Kitebe ha-Rambam*," *Zion* 34 (1969) 141–42, and by the scholars of Zaragosa in *Qobeṣ Teshubot ha-Rambam* 3.5b, column 1.

[87]J. Alfakar's letter in Lichtenberg, *Qobeṣ Teshubot ha-Rambam* 3.2b, column 1.

[88]M. Abulafia's letter in Lichtenberg, *Qobeṣ Teshubot ha-Rambam* 3.6b, column 1.

[89]Letter of Solomon ben Abraham in *Qebuṣat Miktabim*, ed. S. Halberstam (Bamberg 1875) 52–53, and letters of Qimḥi, Alfakar, and the scholars of Zaragosa in Lichtenberg, *Qobeṣ Teshubot ha-Rambam* 3.2b, column 1; 4b; 5b, column 1.

[90]Letter of Solomon ben Abraham in *Qebuṣat Miktabim* 52–53

[91]Letters of Naḥmanides and Baḥya ben Moses (quoting the scholars of Provence) in Lichtenberg, *Qobeṣ Teshubot ha-Rambam* 3.8b, column 1; 3.6a; Shatzmiller, "*Li-Temunat ha-Maḥloqet*" 128, 139, 140, 142, 144.

The ban promulgated by the rabbis of central France was soon rescinded,[92] but someone, whom a member of the rationalist camp names as Solomon ben Abraham himself, turned to Christian clerical authorities with the charge that Maimonides' works were an affront to religion. The upshot was that Christian clerics publicly burned both the Book of Knowledge and Maimonides' *Guide for the Perplexed*.[93]

To retaliate against Solomon ben Abraham, a ban was now pronounced against him by communities in southern France,[94] and those communities appealed to counterparts in Aragon and Castile for support in their action.[95] They met with little success, but some of the accounts—although not the version of events reported by the man who seems best informed—relate that a gruesome punishment was meted out from another quarter on persons who slandered Maimonides' works to the clerics. According to these accounts, the secular gentile powers put the slanderers to public shame[96] and cut off part of their tongues,[97] although there is nothing to suggest that Solomon ben Abraham himself was among those who suffered such punishment. With time, things quieted down.

Whatever exactly happened, a case could never be won in the forum of Jewish public opinion by bringing Church authorities into the fray and inducing them to

[92]Letter from the community of Lunel in Shatzmiller, "*Li-Temunat ha-Maḥloqet*" 142. The letter credits Moses Naḥmanides with helping convince the French scholars to rescind their ban; see Naḥmanides' letter in Lichtenberg, *Qobeṣ Teshubot ha-Rambam* 3.8a–10b. Naḥmanides, who had his own objections to Maimonides' rationalism, did his best to moderate the stands of both sides and comes out as the most attractive figure in the conflict.

[93]Letter of Qimḥi in Lichtenberg, *Qobeṣ Teshubot ha-Rambam* 3.4b (blaming Solomon ben Abraham); letters of the Ḥasdai brothers in *Qebuṣat Miktabim* 33–34; Y. Baer, *History of the Jews in Christian Spain* (Philadelphia 1971) 1.109, and note 60, where the sources are translated.

[94]Letter of Maimonides' supporters in *Qobeṣ Teshubot ha-Rambam* 3.1a, column 1; Shatzmiller, "*Le-Temunat ha-Maḥloqet*" 142.

[95]Letters of Solomon ben Abraham and the Ḥasdai brothers in *Qebuṣat Miktabim* 32–40, 50–53; Qimḥi letters in *Qobeṣ Teshubot ha-Rambam*; Shatzmiller, "*Li-Temunat ha-Maḥloqet*" 131–32, 140–44.

[96]Letter of the Ḥasdai brothers in *Qebuṣat Miktabim* 34–35.

[97]Shatzmiller, "*Li-Temunat ha-Maḥloqet*" 135, 141. Abraham Maimonides, *Milḥamot ha-Shem* (n. 6 above) 55, writes that in 1235, he received a written account of the events; included was the information about the cutting out of the tongues of the malefactors who slandered the Book of Knowledge and *Guide for the Perplexed* to the Church authorities and brought about the burning of the two books. David Qimḥi, who seems well informed concerning the events, names Solomon ben Abraham as the person responsible for bringing the Church into the dispute, but he says nothing about punishment at the hands of the secular authorities. A different account, which was written more than a half-century after the events and contains a number of false-sounding notes, relates that during the struggle between the two parties in the city of Montpellier, the antirationalists hired false witnesses to testify before the secular authorities against the Maimonidean camp, the plot was uncovered, and more than ten leaders of the antirationalist camp were punished by having their tongues cut out. See Lichtenberg, *Qobeṣ Teshubot ha-Rambam* 3.14a, column 1.

burn the works of an overtowering rabbinic scholar, no matter how objectionable his theological views might appear to conservatives. Criticism of the philosophic views put forward in the *Mishneh Torah* did not disappear in the centuries that followed, but the low point had been passed.[98] Significantly, when antirationalist sentiment erupted again in southern France at the turn of the fourteenth century and bans were pronounced against philosophic allegorizations of Scripture and the study of physics or metaphysics by anyone below the age of twenty-five,[99] Maimonides' works were not included in the prohibitions. Members of the antirationalist party were scrupulous in declaring their respect for the man whom a key figure among them extols as "the holy man, the lamp of Israel, the right-hand pillar, the comprehensive wise man, the great rabbi, the venerable, our master and teacher, Maimonides."[100] And one of the documents in which the bans were published makes a point of citing as support a passage from Maimonides' *Guide for the Perplexed*, a work in which he gave his rationalism even fuller rein than in the *Mishneh Torah*.[101]

c. The foregoing have been instances of the uncritical embracing of the *Mishneh Torah* and of critiques of it. The number of scholars involved in the two activities was not large.

From the fourteenth century onward, a trickle and then a veritable flood of rabbinic compositions started arranging themselves around the *Mishneh Torah* which undertook not to laud or criticize, but rather to understand and elucidate. Maimonides could scarcely have foreseen the need for such commentaries when he ventured in his introduction to the *Mishneh Torah* that henceforth "no one will ever require a further composition for any Jewish law,"[102] or when he predicted to Joseph ben Judah that "in the time to come . . . all Israel will use only my composition, and every other will undoubtedly be disregarded."[103] He was confident that the *Mishneh Torah* would be able to stand on its own two feet. Eventually, we saw, he did admit to Pinḥas of Alexandria that a supplement of some sort was needed, that he should have furnished the *Mishneh Torah* with a handbook listing his sources when they are not obvious; and he expressed the hope that he might still supply the lack. He moreover found that he had to justify three Sabbath rulings in

[98] See, for example, R. Elijah of Vilna, glosses on *Shulḥan ᶜAruk*, *Yoreh Deᶜa* 179:6, 246:4; S. Luzzatto, *Meḥqare ha-Yahadut* (Warsaw 1913) 1. 165–69.

[99] See above p. 245, where Maimonides himself writes that philosophy should wait until a person has advanced in his rabbinic education.

[100] Abba Mari ben Moses, *Minḥat Qena'ot*, in Solomon Adret, *Responsa*, 2 volumes, ed. Z. Dimitrovsky (Jerusalem 1990) 238, 250, 252, 711 (from which the quotation is taken), 783.

[101] Solomon Adret, *Responsa*, standard edition, §417, quoting *Guide for the Perplexed* 3.41, p. 92b.

[102] Above, p. 208.

[103] Moses ben Maimon, *Epistulae* (n. 7 above) 52.

the *Mishneh Torah* to Joseph ben Judah,[104] twenty-four rulings to the scholars of Lunel,[105] and additional rulings to other questioners.[106] In effect, he was thereby providing a commentary on a small segment of his code. But no one could have envisioned the literary effort that would, over the years, be lavished on the *Mishneh Torah.*

As the years passed, one well-disposed commentator after another set his hand to clarifying Maimonides' intent, identifying his sources, providing rationales for his opinions, resolving apparent discrepancies between Maimonides' rulings and what is indicated by the classic rabbinic texts, removing apparent inconsistencies between rulings within the *Mishneh Torah* itself, and defending Maimonides against the critics, particularly against Abraham ben David. Maimonides hoped that the *Mishneh Torah* would free readers from the trouble of working through the talmudic dialectic in order to determine what the halakic norm is in any given instance. History, in one more expression of its blithe unconcern for human expectations, decided on a different outcome. Rather than burying rabbinic dialectic, the *Mishneh Torah* became a catalyst for a new efflorescence of it, as commentators generated ever fresh layers of dialectical reasoning in the course of elucidating and defending the work. If Maimonides could have seen the future, he would have been gratified by the attention the *Mishneh Torah* elicited yet disconcerted by the code's failure to stand on its own, as he hoped it would.

The three best known of the hundreds of commentaries on the *Mishneh Torah* were done by two fourteenth-century writers and a writer in the sixteenth century: Shem Ṭob Ibn Gaon, the author of *Migdal ᶜOz*; Vidal of Tolosa, the—presumed—author of *Maggid Mishneh*;[107] and Joseph Caro, the author of *Kesef Mishneh*. Each of the three commentaries occupies itself with Maimonides' sources, his rationales for ruling as he did, and the critics' strictures, with Joseph Caro offering his commentary as a supplement to the *Maggid Mishneh.*[108] The three began to be printed together with the *Mishneh Torah* in the sixteenth century and have since then accompanied Maimonides' text in almost all printed editions.

Shem Ṭob Ibn Gaon and Vidal of Tolosa present a convenient contrast. The former was a highly partisan defender who refused to countenance criticism of the *Mishneh Torah* and could perform small contortions in defending it. Vidal of Tolosa—assuming that he is the genuine author of *Maggid Mishneh*—was the most judicious and most highly respected of Maimonides' commentators. He too admired the *Mishneh Torah*. But he eschews strained reasoning when defending it and concedes, where need be, that medieval rabbinists who differed from

[104]Above, p. 268.

[105]Above, pp. 269–70.

[106]*Responsa* §§251, 252, 423.

[107]It is not certain that Vidal of Tortosa is the author of *Maggid Mishneh*; see J. Spiegel, "*Sefer Maggid Mishneh*," *Kiryat Sefer* 46 (1970–1971) 556. The commentary was not widely known before it appeared in print in 1509; see Spiegel 554–55.

[108]*Kesef Mishneh*, introduction.

Maimonides had plausible grounds for their positions and occasionally even that rulings made by Maimonides may be indefensible.[109]

What Vidal of Tolosa thought of Maimonides' rationalism cannot be known, since, to judge from what has been preserved, he focused on Books of the *Mishneh Torah* which had legal relevance in his and Maimonides' day and passed over the first Book of the *Mishneh Torah*, where the theological matters are taken up. Shem Ṭob Ibn Gaon and Joseph Caro, despite their unbounded admiration for Maimonides, had, like most commentators on the *Mishneh Torah*, strong reservations about his rationalist and philosophic views. It may be instructive to look at the way in which they handle a few of the paragraphs in the *Mishneh Torah* where those views are expressed.

Maimonides maintained that in the world to come the souls of the righteous exist without a body like the ministering angels, and Abraham ben David objected: "This man's words are, in my view, close to [those of] a person who denies the resurrection of bodies."[110] Shem Ṭob Ibn Gaon and, later, Joseph Caro defuse the criticism by pointing out that the ancient rabbinic conception of the hereafter includes a phase of nonphysical immortality between the death of the human body and its future resurrection. The passage in the *Mishneh Torah* that Abraham ben David found upsetting is not, the two commentators contend, a rejection of the dogma of resurrection; Maimonides was just referring to a different phase of the afterlife.[111] The solution is simple, it brings Maimonides into line with what the two commentators and others deemed to be orthodox belief, and it became a topos among writers defending Maimonides' orthodoxy on the issue of resurrection and immortality.[112] Unfortunately, it obscures Maimonides' clearly stated position that nonphysical immortality and not resurrection is the ultimate end of human existence.

Again, as we saw, Maimonides asserted that the philosophic science of metaphysics was known to the rabbis and was identical with what they called the *account of the chariot*. He further quoted a passage from the Babylonian Talmud which ranks the account of the chariot as superior to talmudic dialectical argumentation,[113] and the implication was that the ancient rabbis ranked study of philosophic metaphysics higher than immersing oneself in the dialectic reasoning of the Babylonian and Palestinian Talmuds. Joseph Caro was plainly disturbed by Maimonides' statements and what they imply, but he preferred not to criticize the

[109]Tchernowitz, *Toledoth ha-Poskim* 1 (n. 52 above) 299–301, which is a warm appreciation of the *Maggid Mishneh*.

[110]Above, p. 274.

[111]Sh. Ibn Gaon, *Migdal ᶜOz*, and J. Caro, *Kesef Mishneh* on *Mishneh Torah*: *H. Teshuba* 8.2.

[112]The tactic already is used by Aaron ben Meshullam, *K. al-Rasā'il* (n. 5 above) 36–38. See also *Haggahot Maimoniyyot* on *Mishneh Torah*: *H. Teshuba* 8.1; *Leḥem Mishneh* on *Mishneh Torah*: *H. Teshuba* 8.1–2.

[113]Above, p. 245.

master directly. He makes his unhappiness known by quoting two medieval rabbinic authors, one of whom remarked ruefully that it would have been much better if what Maimonides wrote had not been written, while the other prayed that "God extend atonement" to persons—in other words, to persons like Maimonides—who represent the rabbis as having ranked the study of philosophy above traditional rabbinic study.[114]

One more example: The *Mishneh Torah* offers a rationalist interpretation of verses in the book of Exodus which relate that God did not grant Moses' request to see His "face" but did allow Moses to see His "back." In Maimonides' exegesis, seeing God's face signifies possessing fully adequate knowledge of "the true nature of God's existence" and seeing God's back signifies the possession of a lesser level of knowledge of God. Moses, as Maimonides read Scripture, was informed by God that the level of knowledge which he sought lies beyond the reach of mankind but he was nonetheless vouchsafed a degree of knowledge of God superior to anything ever attained by anyone preceding or following him.[115] Abraham ben David criticized the interpretation and concluded his criticism by writing: "*Face* and *back* are a great mystery, which is not to be disclosed to everyone, and the person who wrote these words [that is, Maimonides] probably did not know it." Shem Ṭob Ibn Gaon was a student of the cabala and he assumed that the great mystery alluded to by R. Abraham was cabalistic.

He comments on Maimonides' interpretation of seeing God's face and seeing God's back that "there are different aspects to Scripture, some hidden and some open. The method that Maimonides pursued in the present passage resembles his method in the *Guide for the Perplexed.* His aim was to put to rest the minds of [Jewish] philosophizers who were troubled by the literal meaning of [anthropomorphic] scriptural verses. . . . Maimonides himself realized that the true way is hidden and may be transmitted only orally, on an individual basis, and under conditions of the highest secrecy." That is to say, Maimonides was not at heart a philosopher, and his rationalist exegesis of Scripture was merely a tactic for rescuing Jews of a philosophic bent from loss of faith. In the present instance his allegorization of the scriptural anthropomorphisms "face" and "back" was intended solely for such Jews. The fantastic notion that Maimonides did not himself believe his rationalist exegesis of Scripture and other philosophic pronouncements and published them only to rescue persons who had been seduced by philosophy was picked up by other Jewish writers.[116]

Ibn Gaon goes on: "In my opinion, he came to know the mystery in later life. For I bear witness that I saw in Spain . . . the following written on a very old,

[114]Caro, *Kesef Mishneh* on *Mishneh Torah*: *H. Yesode ha-Torah* 4.13.

[115]*Mishneh Torah*: *H. Yesode ha-Torah* 1.10, with reference to Exodus 33:20-23. A similar interpretation is given in *Guide for the Perplexed* 1.21, where Maimonides notes that he had already "called attention to" the meaning of the scriptural passage in the *Mishneh Torah.*

[116]See I. Twersky, "*Li-Demuto shel ha-Rambam,*" *Asuppot* 10 (1995) 28.

soiled parchment scroll: 'When I Moses ben Maimon descended to the chambers of the chariot I understood . . . etc.'; and what he writes there is close to the views of the true cabalists [or: to the views of the true carriers of tradition]."[117] Ibn Gaon is telling us that Maimonides became a full-fledged cabalist at the end of his life.[118] The myth of Maimonides' conversion to the cabala raises its head elsewhere.[119] It commands as much credibility as would a report that at the end of their lives, Robespierre was converted to the royalist cause or Abraham Lincoln, to the cause of the secessionists.

As already said, commentaries on the *Mishneh Torah* eventually turned into a flood. In 1947, a researcher undertook a bibliographical study of printed commentaries of one sort or another on the *Mishneh Torah*, and he was able to identify a total of 341.[120] Additional commentaries on the *Mishneh Torah* remained in manuscript, of course, and during the past half century, rabbinic writers have expanded the genre still further. A few years ago a separate list was made of works that, without necessarily having the *Mishneh Torah* as their primary subject, discuss rulings made by Maimonides in it, and this time the figure came to 1,600.[121] Although Maimonides would have been disappointed that some of his expectations regarding the future recognition of the *Mishneh Torah* were not realized, it did become the most commented-on medieval Jewish literary work.

When Maimonides wrote that the *Mishneh Torah* would push all other rabbinic works off the stage, part of his expectation was that it would one day become the sole code of Jewish law, all others being relegated to oblivion. At certain periods, the *Mishneh Torah* was indeed recognized as the authoritative legal code in large sectors of the Jewish world, but it never became the universally accepted code that Maimonides foresaw.

At one point, he himself mentions having heard that the *Mishneh Torah* was accepted as authoritative in Baghdadi rabbinic courts.[122] In the early thirteenth century, Aaron ben Meshullam reported that the *Mishneh Torah* served as a code for deciding legal and ritual questions in Lunel.[123] In the fourteenth century, a number of Spanish Jewish communities formally recognized it as the code by

[117] *Migdal ᶜOz* on *Mishneh Torah*: *H. Yesode ha-Torah* 1.10.

[118] In *Migdal ᶜOz* on *Mishneh Torah*: *H. Yesode ha-Torah* 2.7, Ibn Gaon supposes that a statement of Maimonides' regarding the ten incorporeal intelligences associated with the celestial spheres and sublunar region reflects knowledge of the ten sefirot of the Cabalists.

[119] Examples in M. Shmidman, *On Maimonides' "Conversion" to Kabbalah*, in *Studies in Medieval Jewish History and Literature* 2, ed. I. Twersky (Cambridge, Mass. 1984) 383–85.

[120] Y. Rubenstein, last item of appendix, volume 5 of the *Mishneh Torah* published by Shulsinger (New York 1947).

[121] Frankel edition of the *Mishneh Torah*: *H. Shofeṭim*, appendix, *Sefer ha-Mafteaḥ*.

[122] *Responsa* §310, p. 573; 4.22. Maimonides heard that his "compositions," in the plural, were followed in deciding legal issues there.

[123] Above, p. 270.

which they would adjudicate all legal and ritual questions.[124] Writers describing circumstances at various times in the succeeding centuries relate that the *Mishneh Torah* served as the standard law code for Jewish communities in North Africa and Egypt in the fifteenth and sixteenth centuries,[125] that it was the standard code for Palestine in the sixteenth through the eighteenth centuries,[126] for Syria in the sixteenth century,[127] and—according to Joseph Caro, who was writing in the sixteenth century—for Jewish communities in all the Arab lands.[128] Yet just as Maimonides' *Book of Commandments* encouraged, rather than foreclosed, the production of additional works on the subject of the 613 commandments given to Moses, so too his *Mishneh Torah* had the effect of encouraging, rather than foreclosing, activity in the area of codification. A number of codes appeared after the *Mishneh Torah*, and one of them ultimately won the day.

The code of rabbinic law that established itself as authoritative throughout the Jewish world, with the notable exception of the land of Yemen, was a sixteenth-century work, R. Joseph Caro's *Shulḥan ᶜAruk*. Curiously, Caro intended it merely as a convenient halakic handbook and not as a full-fledged code; it nevertheless became the blueprint by which traditional Jews have for centuries conducted their lives and by which they still do today. For Jewish communities in Middle and Eastern Europe and their offshoots—the so-called Ashkenazic communities—it was Caro's *Shulḥan ᶜAruk* as supplemented by the glosses of a Polish rabbinist, R. Moses Isserles, that achieved supreme authority. In most of the Yemeni Jewish communities, the *Mishneh Torah* remained authoritative until organized Jewish life ceased in that country in the middle of the twentieth century, and even today there are Jews of Yemeni origin who follow it faithfully in religious matters. [129]

Joseph Caro was an admirer of the *Mishneh Torah*—or to be more precise, of the halakic side of the *Mishneh Torah*—and he went so far as to praise Maimonides' accomplishment in language that the Psalmist had applied to "the words of the Lord": Maimonides' words, like those of the Lord, are "pure and refined sevenfold."[130] Caro's commentary on the *Mishneh Torah* is one of the most useful and widely used, and he was among the witnesses for the acceptance of

[124] I. Kahana, "*Meḥqarim be-Sifrut ha-Teshubot*" (Jerusalem 1973) 8, 18–19 (the Jewish community of Toledo accepts Maimonides' code regarding all issues except two of a commercial nature, in which Maimonides' rulings were stricter than longstanding local custom); 21–24. With the passage of time, the code of Asher ben Jehiel attained higher authority than the *Mishneh Torah* in the Spanish communities; see Kahana 26–27.

[125] Kahana, "*Meḥqarim be-Sifrut ha-Teshubot*" 29, 31–33, 39–46, 52, 54.

[126] Kahana, "*Meḥqarim be-Sifrut ha-Teshubot*" 47–62, 65.

[127] Kahana, "*Meḥqarim be-Sifrut ha-Teshubot*" 54, 72, 74.

[128] Kahana, "*Meḥqarim be-Sifrut ha-Teshubot*" 51, 72.

[129] J. Kafah, "*Ha-Rambam we-Golat Teman*," *Sinai* 43 (1958) 257–58. R. Arussi, "*Ha-Gorem ha-ᶜAdati bi-Pesiqat ha-Halaka*," *Diné Israel* 10–11 (1981–1983) 131–48. A. Gaimani, " *Ḥadirat ha- Shulḥan ᶜAruk li-Teman*," *Peᶜamim* 49 (1991) 126–27, 131–33.

[130] Caro, *Kesef Mishneh*, introduction, adapting the language of Psalms 12:7.

Maimonides' code by various Jewish communities in the sixteenth century. His *Shulḥan ᶜAruk*, like all posttalmudic codes except for Maimonides', is of narrower scope than the *Mishneh Torah*, limiting itself to areas of law and ritual which were practiced in his day. It imitates Maimonides in omitting the sources for its rulings, although it occasionally makes an exception and does note its source; where it does not, the source can usually be ascertained by consulting another of Caro's works.[131] It keeps explanatory remarks to a minimum and in most instances simply lays down instructions, without ado and without adornment.

When the *Shulḥan ᶜAruk* addresses a legal or ritual issue that had previously been treated in the *Mishneh Torah*, it almost always follows Maimonides' opinion,[132] and by one estimate, almost a third of its wording is copied directly from Maimonides' code.[133] Joseph Caro's outlook on the world was, nonetheless, quite different from Maimonides'. In a very few instances, a rationalist thread from the *Mishneh Torah* has been carried over into the *Shulḥan ᶜAruk*, as when Caro writes, with Maimonides: It is "permitted to recite incantations over a [scorpion or snake] bite, even on the Sabbath and despite the incantation's having no effect at all, . . . in order that the victim does not become frantic."[134] The intent of the passage in the Babylonian Talmud on which the ruling is based was that incantations work. Maimonides introduced the qualification that the incantation has no effect at all, and Caro has repeated the qualification.[135] More frequently—and all in all we are speaking about a very small segment of the thousands of rulings in the *Shulḥan ᶜAruk*—Caro eliminates the rationalist touches with which Maimonides adorned the *Mishneh Torah*. I offer a few illustrations.

In the *Mishneh Torah*, Maimonides disregarded statements from the Babylonian Talmud to the effect that the parchment scrolls containing the "Hear O Israel" verses and mounted on the doorposts of Jewish houses protect the domicile and he branded as fools those who treat the scroll as an amulet designed for that purpose.[136] Instead, he explained that the affixing of the scroll to the doorpost was ordained by Scripture in order to teach a lesson in rationalistic faith: Whenever someone passes by the scroll and "encounters God's unity" inscribed therein, the

[131] J. Caro, *Bet Yosef.*

[132] Malachi ha-Kohen, *Yad Malachi, kelale ha-Shulḥan ᶜAruk*, §§2, 7. Ḥ. Madini, *Sede Ḥemed, kelale ha-poseqim* §13.3–4; Kahana, "*Meḥqarim be-Sifrut ha-Teshubot*" 69–71, 93; B. Benedikt, *Ha-Rambam le-lo Seṭiyya min ha-Talmud"* (Jerusalem 1985) 17–18.

[133] Ch. Tchernowitz, *Toledoth ha-Poskim* 3 (New York 1947) 7.

[134] J. Caro, *Shulḥan ᶜAruk, Yoreh Deᶜa* §179.6. See above, p. 225.

[135] Another instance of Caro's incorporating Maimonides' rationalism is *Shulḥan ᶜAruk, Ḥoshen Mishpaṭ* 425:2. It copies *Mishneh Torah*: *H. Roṣe'aḥ* 1.9, where a rationalistic explanation of a certain law is substituted for the talmudic explanation.

[136] BT *Shabbat* 32b; *ᶜAboda Zara* 11a; *Menaḥot* 33b; *Mishneh Torah*: *H. Mezuza* 5.4; 6.13. Maimonides could very well have regarded the view that the parchment scroll protects one's house as the opinion of an individual rabbi who was overruled by the majority. His language in fact contains an echo of the wording of what is represented in *Menaḥot* 33b as the opinion of the "rabbis," that is to say, as a majority opinion.

person will recall his love of God, shake off his concerns for the vanities of this world, and realize that nothing but knowledge of God is permanent—that the immortal part of man is human intellect at the stage where it possesses knowledge of God.[137] The *Shulḥan ᶜAruk*, for its part, disregards the spiritual and rationalist virtues that Maimonides ascribed to the parchment scroll and gingerly reaffirms the scrolls' protective powers. It states: When a person is scrupulous about affixing scrolls with the Hear O Israel verses to his doorposts, "his days will be multiplied and the days of his children"; when, by contrast, someone is careless about the commandment, his days and the days of his offspring will "be shortened."[138] It is worth noting that prominent law codes both prior and subsequent to the *Shulḥan ᶜAruk* combine the two stances. They yoke the rationalistic construction placed by Maimonides on the Hear O Israel scroll with the talmudic assurance of the scroll's apotropaic powers and explain: The scroll mounted on the doorpost inculcates consciousness of the unity of God in those who pass by, while also protecting the owner's house and multiplying his days and the days of his children.[139]

There are instances where the Babylonian Talmud prescribes actions to help guard against the dangers posed by demons or an evil spirit, where Maimonides' *Mishneh Torah* records the talmudic instructions but reinterprets them on rational instead of preternatural grounds, and where Caro's *Shulḥan ᶜAruk* goes back and again cites dangers posed by demons and evil spirits as the reason why the instructions must be obeyed.[140] Then, there are instances where the *Shulḥan*

[137]See above, p. 242.

[138]Caro, *Shulḥan ᶜAruk, Yoreh Deᶜa* §285. I write that Caro expresses himself gingerly, because he has restricted himself to what he could support from Deuteronomy 11:21, and has omitted the talmudic notion that the *mezuza* scroll guards one's house. His commentary on *Mishneh Torah*: *H. Mezuza* 5.4, does assert, on the basis of statements found in the Babylonian Talmud, that the *mezuza* scroll protects a person's house.

[139]R. Jacob ben Asher, *Ṭur, Yoreh Deᶜa* § 285, followed by M. Jaffe, *Lebush, ᶜAṭeret Zahab* (=*Yoreh Deᶜa*) §285, and R. Y. Epstein, *ᶜAruk ha-Shulḥan, Yoreh Deᶜa* §285. It is hardly surprising that none of the three alludes in any way to the doctrine of human intellectual immortality. Amazingly, however, a staunchly conservative nineteenth-century Hungarian rabbi, S. Ganzfried, *Qiṣṣur Shulḥan ᶜAruk* 11.23, copies Maimonides' words verbatim, writing: Whenever a person passes by a *mezuza* scroll affixed to a doorpost, he "encounters God's unity," which is inscribed therein, recalls his love of God, awakens from his spiritual slumber, shakes off his concerns about the vanities of this world, realizes that *nothing but knowledge of God is permanent*; to which Ganzfried adds: Affixing a *mezuza* scroll to the doorpost also multiplies one's days and the days of one's children. It is hard to imagine that Ganzfried grasped the import of the clause I have italicized. The notion that the *mezuza* scroll emblemizes God's unity found its way into the world of cabala. *Zohar* 3.263b (*Raᶜaya Mehemna*) states that the *mezuza* embodies "the secret of faith," that is to say, the proposition that the different aspects of God recognized by the cabalists coalesce in a single unity.

[140](1) BT *Shebuᶜot* 15b: Although one must not use biblical verses to heal diseases, one of the leading rabbis of the Amoraic period would recite verses from Scripture to protect himself when he went to sleep; Rashi explains: he was protecting himself against the demons (*mazziqin*) who attack men. *Mishneh Torah*: *H. Aboda Zara* 11.12: A healthy person is permitted to

ᶜAruk reinstates from the classic rabbinic corpus material with which Maimonides had not felt comfortable, which he had apparently taken to be nonbinding advice proffered by the rabbis, and which he had omitted entirely from the *Mishneh Torah*. The *Shulḥan ᶜAruk* thus includes such items passed over by Maimonides as the injunction to pour water three times on each hand in the morning in order to remove the evil spirit that settles on hands during the night;[141] the prohibition against eating meat and fish together because the combination can cause leprosy;[142] instructions regarding materials to be avoided when cleansing oneself after a bowel movement because they may cause hemorrhoids or render one susceptible to magical spells;[143] the injunction to consume salt when eating food and to drink water when drinking other beverages, because failing to do so may lead to halitosis and croup.[144] As an appendix to this last, Caro records a warning from a medieval source: Taking salt after meals with one's small finger, index finger, or thumb may lead to poverty, to having one's reputation besmirched, or to nothing less than the death of one's children; only the third and fourth fingers should be used.[145] Traditional Jews today still pour water on their hands three times each morning and avoid eating fish and meat together; the motivation is not so much actual fear of

---

recite scriptural verses in order that the *merit* of reciting them will protect him from trouble and harm (*neẓaqim*). *Shulḥan ᶜAruk, Yoreh Deᶜa* §179.10: A healthy man is permitted to recite scriptural verses to protect himself from demons (*mazziqim*). (2) BT *Berakot* 3a: One should not enter decrepit abandoned buildings because—*inter alia*—demons haunt such buildings. *Mishneh Torah*: *H. Roṣe'aḥ* 12.6 (cf. *H. Tefilla* 5.6): One should avoid such buildings because they are dangerous. *Shulḥan ᶜAruk, Oraḥ Ḥayyim* §90.6: One should avoid such buildings because—*inter alia*—demons haunt them. (3) BT *Pesaḥim* 112a: Food should not be left under the bed even in a closed container because an evil spirit settles on such food. *Mishneh Torah*: *H. Roṣe'aḥ* 12.5: One should not leave food under the bed because something harmful might fall in when no one is watching (see above, p. 225). *Shulḥan ᶜAruk, Yoreh Deᶜa* §116.5: One should not leave food under the bed because an evil spirit settles on such food. (4) BT *Ḥullin* 105b: Certain precautions have to be taken when disposing of water with which one washes one's hands after a meal because an evil spirit settles on the water. *Mishneh Torah*: *H. Berakot* 6.16: Certain precautions have to be taken when disposing of such water. *Shulḥan ᶜAruk, Oraḥ Ḥayyim* §181.2: Certain precautions have to be taken when disposing of such water because an evil spirit settles on it. Caro, in his commentary on *Mishneh Torah*: *H. Berakot* 6.16, points out a small difficulty in Maimonides' formulation of the rule about disposing of the water in instance (4) and then solves the difficulty by means of the astonishing conjecture that Maimonides was being ultracautious in matters involving evil spirits. M. Shapiro, "Maimonidean Halakah and Superstition," *Maimonidean Studies* 4 (2000) 71–72, lists traditional rabbinic scholars from the Middle Ages into modern times who refused to recognize that Maimonides rejected the existence of evil spirits and demons.

[141] J. Caro, *Shulḥan ᶜAruk, Oraḥ Ḥayyim* §4:2–3.

[142] Caro, *Shulḥan ᶜAruk, Yoreh Deᶜa* §116:2.

[143] Caro, *Shulḥan ᶜAruk, Oraḥ Ḥayyim* §3:11.

[144] Caro, *Shulḥan ᶜAruk, Oraḥ Ḥayyim* §179:6.

[145] Caro, *Shulḥan ᶜAruk, Oraḥ Ḥayyim* §179:6. There are alternate readings for the words "having one's reputation besmirched." The *Shulḥan ᶜAruk* contains a few additional items of a similar character.

being injured by an evil spirit or of contracting leprosy as respect for the ancient rabbis who promulgated the regulations. The other instructions just referred to are not observed in the most traditional of Jewish circles today and apparently were not regarded as binding even at the time when the *Shulḥan ᶜAruk* was published.[146]

To summarize: In the long run, the *Mishneh Torah* became authoritative after a fashion—through the medium of the *Shulḥan ᶜAruk* and not in itself. In Jewish communities of Middle and Eastern Europe and their offshoots, Maimonides' authority was, moreover, blunted by R. Moses Isserles' glosses, for these were designed specifically to balance Caro's rulings with the rulings and customs of the French and German rabbinic tradition. The rationalist threads that Maimonides wove into the *Mishneh Torah* are almost entirely ignored in the *Shulḥan ᶜAruk* and the other post-Maimonidean codes.

After the appearance of the *Shulḥan ᶜAruk* as supplemented by Isserles' glosses, codification activity by no means came to a halt, and in the traditional Jewish world it continues today. But almost all rabbinic codes that have appeared since the publication of the *Shulḥan ᶜAruk* are satellites revolving around it. They reword or reorganize some or all of the regulations recorded in the *Shulḥan ᶜAruk* in order to serve the needs of specific readerships; they fill in additional details; in rare instances they amend a decision made by the *Shulḥan ᶜAruk*; and they apply the *Shulḥan ᶜAruk*'s regulations to the exigencies of life and technology in each succeeding generation. For areas of law and ritual which are wholly theoretical and in particular for areas that fell into desuetude with the destruction of the Holy Temple in Jerusalem, Maimonides' code stands virtually alone.[147]

The *Mishneh Torah* made its mark in one more venue. From the beginning of the sixteenth century and extending into the eighteenth, some three dozen Christian Hebraists translated sections of Halakot into Latin,[148] and in the seventeenth century the available translations became a resource for Protestant theological speculation. The best-known personage who indulged in such speculation was none other than Isaac Newton. Not only was Newton familiar with sections of the code in Latin translation, but it has been shown that he drew from Maimonides in crystallizing his thoughts on the history of religion and perhaps in developing his own nontrinitarian theology.[149]

[146]See M. Isserles, glosses to *Shulḥan ᶜAruk*, *Oraḥ Ḥayyim* §§3:11; 179:6; M. Jaffe, *Lebush*, *Lebush ha-Tekelet* (=*Oraḥ Ḥayyim*) §§3:11; 179:6. A. Gombiner, *Magen Abraham*, gloss on *Shulḥan ᶜAruk*, *Oraḥ Ḥayyim* §§3:11; 179:6, explains: The nature of men today is different from what it was in earlier days, and the regulations therefore no longer apply.

[147]An exception: J. Epstein, *ᶜAruk ha-Shulḥan he-ᶜAtid*.

[148]J. Dienstag, "Christian Translators of Maimonides' *Mishneh Torah* into Latin," *Salo Wittmayer Baron Jubilee Volume*, English Section (New York 1974) 289–308.

[149]R. Popkin, "Newton and Maimonides," *A Straight Path*, ed. R. Link-Salinger (Hyman volume) (Washington 1988) 219–29. M. Goldish, *Judaism in the Theology of Sir Isaac Newton* (Dordrecht 1998) 30–31.

Legal Responsa. When rabbinic figures in talmudic times had difficulty in deciding a legal matter, they sometimes solicited the opinion of men who either had higher official status than they or were reputed to possess particular expertise in the subject.[150] The inquiry and response would be carried back and forth by messengers. Communication was generally done orally, in a reflection of the mandate to keep the Oral Law oral, although there is a bit of evidence in the Babylonian Talmud of written correspondence between Palestine and Iraq regarding legal issues.[151] After the redaction of the Babylonian Talmud, the asking and answering of questions of rabbinic law became an established literary genre, and questions and answers, often abbreviated, began to be gathered into collections of *responsa.*

During the heyday of the Iraqi rabbinic academies, the principals of the academies conducted a far-flung written correspondence on law and ritual. They invited inquiries from rabbinic judges and communal leaders in all corners of the Jewish world and were conscientious in answering, their motive being to put their knowledge at the disposal of others, to affirm and confirm their own institutional predominance over Jewish communities throughout the world, and at the same time to encourage financial support for their academies. With the waning of the Iraqi schools, legal questions were directed elsewhere. Questions were now sent to rabbinic authorities not because of any institutional status that they enjoyed, but simply because consensus recognized them as experts in rabbinic law. The greater the reputation of the man whose opinion was solicited, the wider, naturally, was the geographical circle of the persons who turned to him. As Maimonides' standing grew, he too received inquiries from a widening circle—from the cities and towns of Egypt, notably Alexandria, and also from Tyre, Aleppo, Damascus, Baghdad, Palestine, the "West," and southern France. His *responsa* were gradually gathered into partial, and then comprehensive, collections, the most recent and best of which comprises 480 items.[152] Some of his responsa have undoubtedly been lost and there is the possibility that responsa carrying his name have been attributed to him in error.

Those that have been preserved and published show Maimonides being asked, and making decisions, about a gamut of rabbinic topics. With the proviso that some of the inquiries addressed to him contain more than one question, and some cut across lines and hence resist hard and fast classification, I calculated that over two hundred of the questions concern litigation growing out of joint business

[150]Examples: BT *Giṭṭin* 59a; *Qiddushin* 44b; *Baba Qamma* 59b; *Baba Meṣiᶜa* 51a; *Baba Batra* 90b; *Ḥullin* 99b. PT *Berakot* 4:3, 8a; 6:1, 10b; 6:4, 10c; *Demai* 2:1, 22c.

[151]BT *Ḥullin* 95b.

[152]*Responsa* (n. 15 above) 4 vols. In most instances both the question and answer have been preserved, but occasionally only the one or the other have been. Most questions and responses were composed in Judeo-Arabic, some were composed in Hebrew, and sometimes what is preserved is a Hebrew translation from the original Judeo-Arabic. There are a small number of duplicates. A few of the responsa may be attributed to Maimonides erroneously, but the great majority contain an unmistakable reference to Maimonides either in the question or answer.

ventures, real estate partnerships, divorces, and inheritances; some twenty-five treat disputed family status, as, for example, the eligibility of women in a variety of predicaments to marry or remarry; another twenty-five relate to communal disputes; over a hundred and twenty-five are of a ritual character, most of these raised by questioners solely for their own edification, without there being any issue under adjudication; and some sixty-five are purely theoretical questions, sent to Maimonides by both scholars and novices who sought elucidation of niceties of Jewish law.

If we could have looked over Maimonides' shoulder as he sat and wrestled with the legal problems for which his counsel had been sought, we would have observed him carefully unraveling the conflicting claims of the litigants in dozens of financial disputes,[153] determining which portion of her marriage settlement a "cursed" wife must forfeit because she had failed to immerse herself in the ritual bath after her menstrual periods,[154] confirming the right of a husband to forbid his wife from working as a teacher of boys, because the husband regarded the unavoidable contact with the boys' fathers to be immodest,[155] explaining how a twice-widowed woman can maneuver around the rabbinic prohibition against such a woman's marrying a third time,[156] informing judges in Alexandria that he had followed their example and excommunicated a member of the priestly class and the divorcee whom the man had wed in violation of scriptural law,[157] advising a rabbinic court on the best way to handle a litigant who had behaved uncivilly to the judges,[158] determining the status of Muslims and Christians in Jewish law, listing the reasons why it is absolutely forbidden to weave verses from the Pentateuch into a prayer shawl,[159] explaining why one of the formulas by which God is blessed should be: Blessed art Thou O Lord, King of the universe "who giveth the Torah" rather than

[153]Examples: *Responsa* §§24–27; 29.

[154]*Responsa* §§321; 368–71.

[155]*Responsa* §45. In §34, after he received a different account of the circumstances, Maimonides suggested that the wife might announce that she was unwilling to live with her husband, whereupon he would be forced to divorce her—albeit with a loss of her marriage settlement—and she could then continue to support herself and her sons by teaching.

[156]*Responsa* §§15, 218.

[157]*Responsa* §349. See Leviticus 21:7. Maimonides had the excommunication announced in Fustat and Cairo and included in it everyone who would have business or social dealings with the priest and his "harlot."

[158]*Responsa* §450.

[159]*Responsa* §268. Maimonides gives two main reasons: (1) The Babylonian Talmud prohibits writing verses from Scripture in any other context than in a full Torah scroll. (2) The prayer shawl possesses only a minor level of sanctity and may be worn when entering a privy or utilized for nonsacred purposes; someone wearing a prayer shawl into which verses are woven might therefore enter a privy or use the shawl with the verses for an unclean purpose. He adds secondary considerations: Weaving verses into a prayer shawl is an innovation (*bid^ca*) with no precedent. Using the square script, which is intended for Torah scrolls, for any purpose other than writing a Torah scroll is "ugly."

"who teacheth the Torah,"[160] spelling out in detail how—this in a little treatise running seven pages—to make ritual ink,[161] instructing his correspondents how to prepare parchment for the small scroll attached to the doorpost (*mezuza*),[162] how best to knot the fringes that male Jews are instructed to tie to the corners of their garments (*ṣiṣit*),[163] when to stand during public prayers,[164] and what constitutes a rabbinically sanctioned haircut.[165]

As a rule, in monetary disputes, Maimonides' responsa follow the letter of rabbinic law—that is, talmudic prescriptions, with some allowance for posttalmudic usage[166]—even where equity might suggest that an exception should be made.[167] In the area of ritual, he tended to be punctilious about talmudic prescriptions[168] but dismissive of posttalmudic custom.[169] When dealing with communal disputes he

[160]*Responsa* §182. In some editions of *Mishneh Torah*: *H. Tefilla* 7.10, the formula is nevertheless: He "who teaches the Torah."

[161]*Responsa* §136.

[162]*Responsa* §137.

[163]*Responsa* §138. See Numbers 15:38.

[164]*Responsa* §263.

[165]*Responsa* §244.

[166]*Responsa* §§200, 363, 372, 381 (for the *geonic* sources, see the editor's notes. *Responsa* §§200 and 381 should be contrasted with *Mishneh Torah*: *H. Ishut* 14:14 and 16:8–9. Examples of posttalmudic prescriptions accepted by Maimonides' *Mishneh Torah* in the area of civil law are given by M. Havazelet, *Maimonides and the Geonites* (Hebrew) (Jerusalem 1967) 125–28, 132–34, 138–43.

[167]For example, *Responsa* §§23, 385. §23 cites the rabbinic maxim (Mishna, *Ketubbot* 9:2–3): "One does not practice mercy in matters of law." Maimonides was adamant about the cancellation of loans on the seventh, or sabbatical, year (see Deuteronomy 15:2) unless the old rabbinic stratagem for protecting them—the "prosbol"—had been followed, and he appears to have taken the lead in requiring that Egyptian judges enforce the cancellation. The questioner in *Responsa* §198 did not know whether the cancellation of loans was still to be observed in his day, for, he writes, some judges maintain that it is, others that it is not. *Responsa* §481, which includes the question of cancellation of debts in the seventh year, was addressed to Maimonides by one of his highly respected judicial colleagues. In his response, Maimonides rules that when a debtor is sued by another Jew in a gentile court for payment of a loan after the seventh year has passed, he may rely on the cancellation effected by the seventh year and take a solemn oath stating that he owes nothing. For additional questions addressed to Maimonides about the seventh-year cancellation, see Blau (n. 15 above) vol. 3, index, s. v. *shemiṭa*.

[168]For example, *Responsa* §§136–43. In §311, Maimonides wholeheartedly supports a Palestinian correspondent who excommunicated persons performing labor or conducting business on the intermediary days of the Jewish festivals.

[169]*Responsa* §114 rejects posttalmudic restrictions that segments of Jewish society placed on menstruating women. §138 rejects the manner in which certain posttalmudic scholars knotted the fringes on the corners of their garments. §§207, 208, and 254 reject various accretions that had infiltrated the rabbinically prescribed liturgy, notably, the recherché poetic pieces known as *piyyuṭ*. §244 dismisses male side curls (that is, *pe*ᶜ*ot*). §263 advises against standing when the Ten Commandments are read from the Torah in the synagogue. §267 advises against the entire congregation's reading certain verses aloud during the Torah readings. §313 and *Responsa* 4.23 advise against tying more than two willow branches to the palm branch carried by male Jews on

would counsel forbearance toward litigants who had shown contempt of religious officials[170] or toward officials who had behaved indiscreetly.[171] In questions of personal status, where the welfare of society or of an individual woman might be in jeopardy, he appears to have been as lenient as he thought that talmudic law might allow.[172]

Religious tolerance and ecumenism were not in fashion in Maimonides' day, and he was not favorably disposed toward either Christianity or Islam. Jesus is characterized by him as a renegade who tried to annul the Jewish religion, and he rules in his rabbinic works that there is a religious commandment to kill "Jesus of Nazareth and his students." He classifies the Christian religion, which he takes to be a later invention that attached itself to the name of Jesus, as a form of idolatry and he accordingly rules that Christians are subject to all the disabilities placed on idolaters by rabbinic law.[173] As for Muhammad, the founding prophet of the Islamic religion, Maimonides intimates—to speak more explicitly would be to risk life and limb—that he was much too given to the pleasures of the flesh, especially those involving members of the opposite sex, and that he deluded himself into imagining having been sent by God to establish a new religion.[174] The founders of non-Mosaic religions, in Maimonides' view, appropriated their ideas from the religion of Israel, adding here and subtracting there, and what they produced bears no more resemblance to the true religion than an inanimate statue does to a living human being.[175] In one context, he describes Christianity and Islam as propagated by their founders out of jealousy toward God's chosen people and for the purpose of eradicating the Jewish religion, although in another context, he writes that within

---

the Tabernacles holiday. In some of these instances, Maimonides counsels that those who insist upon observing erroneous customs should be left to act as they wish, and in *Responsa* §§152 and 181, he states the rule of thumb that when customs do no damage to religion, they may remain in place. Because of the lack of decorum he encountered in the Egyptian synagogues, Maimonides did make one conscious and substantial departure from the form of the talmudic liturgy; see above, p. 54, n. 214. For opposition to posttalmudic ritual innovations in Maimonides' Commentary on the Mishna, see the commentary on *Giṭṭin* 5:8. In the introduction to the *Mishneh Torah*, Maimonides states the rule that talmudic law is universally binding on all Jewish communities, whereas posttalmudic interpretations and innovations are not. The code itself takes a more complex stance vis-à-vis posttalmudic ritual customs than the responsa do, but it too criticizes posttalmudic innovations. See *Mishneh Torah*: *H. Ḥanukka* 3.14; Havazelet, *Maimonides and the Geonites* (n. 166 above), chapter 7; Twersky, *Introduction to the Code of Maimonides* (n. 23 above) 124–34.

[170] *Responsa* §§268 (end), 450.

[171] *Responsa* §§110, 111.

[172] Examples: *Responsa* §§3 (see editor's note 3); 15; 350.

[173] Moses Maimonides, *Epistle to Yemen*, ed. A. Halkin with English trans. B. Cohen (New York 1952) 12–15; English translation iii–iv. Commentary on the Mishna, *ᶜAboda Zara* 1:3; *Ḥullin* 1:2; *Mishneh Torah*: *H. ᶜAbodat Kokabim* (Frankel edition) 9.4; 10.1.

[174] *Guide for the Perplexed* 2.40.

[175] *Responsa* §448. *Guide for the Perplexed* 2.40. *Epistle to Yemen* 14–15; English translation iv.

the grand divine design, the two false religions serve a function: They prepare the ground for the ultimate triumph of the true religion.[176] Islam, in his opinion, is the cruelest and most implacable enemy that the Jewish people has faced in its entire history.[177]

Yet, notwithstanding his feelings, when he was asked for his legal opinion regarding Christianity and Islam, he judged matters on their merits. Someone once wrote to ask whether a talmudic statement to the effect that gentiles may not study the Torah is to be taken as a formal halaka and if so, whether the prohibition extends to teaching the commandments (*miṣwot*). He responds that the statement is indeed binding, and "when Jews have gentiles under their control, they must prevent them from studying the Torah until they convert to the Jewish religion." As for teaching the commandments to members of the two religions, Maimonides reasons as follows: Muslims do not recognize the divine origin of the Torah and if confronted with a text of the Torah which stands in opposition to their beliefs, they reject the text. They may moreover incorporate the discrepancy between Scripture and their beliefs into the battery of arguments that they employ in their polemics against Jews. Christians, by contrast, accept the divine origin of the text of the Torah, and although they willfully misinterpret it, there is always the possibility that they may see the light when given the correct interpretation. Even if they fail to see the light, no foreseeable harm can result from teaching them. Maimonides therefore answers the questioner that the commandments may be taught to Christians but not to Muslims.[178]

On a different occasion, Obadia, a recent convert to the Jewish faith, asked Maimonides to adjudicate a dispute that had arisen between him and his teacher regarding Islam. Obadia had asserted that Muslims are not idolaters, while the teacher had insisted that they are and, in exasperation, had called Obadia a fool. Maimonides responds that Obadia was right: Muslims are unquestionably monotheists and when they bow down to the stone in the Mosque of Mecca "their hearts are directed to heaven" and they do not worship the stone. "Just because they lie about us," Maimonides writes, "we shall not lie about them and assert that they are idolaters" if they are not. Obadia's teacher therefore owed him a full and heartfelt apology.[179]

Maimonides relied, in his repsonsa, on respectable precedents and, occasionally, on the broad discretion that talmudic law gives to properly constituted law courts.[180] He never would have perceived himself as deciding arbitrarily, as

[176]*Mishneh Torah*: *H. Melakim* (Frankel edition) 11:4. *Epistle to Yemen* 8–15; English translation iii–iv.

[177]*Epistle to Yemen* 94–97; English translation xviii.

[178]*Responsa* §149, where the editor gives references to sources in the Babylonian Talmud and to the pertinent ruling in the *Mishneh Torah*.

[179]*Responsa* §448. See below, p. 487.

[180]*Responsa* §§3; 211; 218; 350; 375 (to be compared to §470). It should go without saying that Maimonides allows himself discretion only toward regulations that, in the common talmudic

tailoring his reasoning to support predetermined results, or, to use a modern expression, as legislating from the bench, and he plainly took what he was doing seriously. To suppose that his rationalist cast of mind led him to treat rabbinic regulations, including minor regulations, cavalierly would be to harbor a wholly false image of the man.

Projected Works. Isaac Alfasi, as will be recalled, was the eleventh-century author of a highly regarded rabbinic code, known as his *Halakot*, which took the form of a digest of the Babylonian Talmud. After the *Mishneh Torah* had been published, a rabbinic judge wrote to Maimonides inquiring politely about a ruling there that did not agree with Alfasi's position on the same issue.[181] In response, Maimonides explains why his own opinion was "without doubt correct." He speculates that the erroneous ruling in Alfasi's *Halakot* was not a genuine part of the *Halakot* but a gloss written by someone in the margin which a scribe then mistakenly incorporated into the text. And in any event, even Alfasi was not immune from error; for Maimonides "disagreed with him at some thirty places or more,[182] [and those points of disagreement comprise] criticisms drawn up by Alfasi's own student, R. Joseph Ibn Migas, of blessed memory[183] . . . together with some to which I have called attention myself. . . . I have written fascicles on the items in question, but the project is not yet complete." Whereupon Maimonides goes on: "Time has also not allowed me to provide explanations for my commentary on difficult halakot throughout the [Babylonian] Talmud nor to explain the Halakot of the Palestinian Talmud which I have prepared [*ᶜasinu*], in the manner in which the master [Alfasi] did his *Halakot* of the Babylonian Talmud; I have not found the leisure to explain them."[184] Maimonides' reply to the questioner has been preserved only in an ungainly Hebrew translation from the Arabic original,[185] and I have intentionally translated the awkward last sentence in a manner that retains its ambiguities.

---

dichotomy, are classified as ordained "by the rabbis," and not toward any classified as "from the Torah."

[181]The question with which we are concerned here is the third of three unrelated questions that, according to the manuscript, Nahorai ben Hillel, a rabbinic judge, sent to Maimonides. The second of the three is dated 1196 and revolves around events that occurred in Damascus. Neither that question nor the present one contains the judge's name, and the present question mentions neither date nor place.

[182]In his Commentary on the Mishna, Maimonides wrote that he disagreed with Alfasi's opinion on fewer than ten issues. See above, p. 195.

[183]I. Ta-Shma, "*Yeṣirato ha-Sifrutit shel R. Yosef ha-Levi Ibn Migas*," *Kiryat Sefer* 46 (1970–1971) 144–45, quotes instances where Ibn Migas differed from Alfasi.

[184]*Responsa* §251.

[185]At a later point in Maimonides' reply, the Hebrew translation represents him as stating that the alternate and preferable reading in Alfasi's *Halakot* agrees with "what he wrote in the composition [or: compilation]." The composition, or compilation, is Maimonides' designation for his own *Mishneh Torah*, and he could hardly have referred to what *he*, that is, Alfasi, wrote

Three compositions are mentioned here: a critique of thirty or more rulings in Alfasi's *Halakot*, a commentary on difficult passages throughout the Babylonian Talmud, and a work on the Palestinian Talmud which was to parallel Alfasi's Halakot of the Babylonian Talmud. At the time of writing, Maimonides had not managed to complete any of the three.

Nothing further is known about the first, the critique of Alfasi's rulings. There is no way of knowing what its format was and how far it ever progressed.

As for the second, the commentary on difficult halakot in the Babylonian Talmud, Maimonides says that he had not yet furnished the requisite explanations. That might mean that the project had not gone beyond its preliminary stages or, possibly, that he had not completed it. In an earlier chapter, we saw that he reports having written commentaries on three orders of the Babylonian Talmud before he began his Commentary on the Mishna at the age of twenty-three.[186] Fragments of commentaries on the Babylonian Talmud have been preserved which have a fair probability of being his and, apart from one doubtful item, they all deal with the three orders of the Talmud that, Maimonides has told us, were the subject of the early commentaries. They, moreover, do not limit themselves to especially difficult passages.[187] Assuming them all to be authentic, they would appear to belong to the first cycle of Maimonides' talmudic commentaries, those completed before he began work on his Commentary on the Mishna, and they accordingly shed no light on the commentaries that concern us here. On a different occasion, Maimonides refers to "interpretative comments" (*perushim*) on talmudic topics which were to be found among his "compositions." There he could conceivably be referring to the projected commentary on difficult halakot in the Babylonian Talmud, but we shall never know, since he reveals nothing about the comments except for the single minor detail that one of the subjects discussed had to do with the Sabbatical and Jubilee years.[188] In the end it remains an open question whether he designed his comments on the difficult halakot as a refinement, completion, or expansion of the earlier cycle of talmudic commentaries or as something new, and we again have no way of determining how much of the plan ever come to fruition.

The third composition referred to in Maimonides' letter to the rabbinic judge is described by him as Halakot of the Palestinian Talmud. The same phrase also occurs at a certain point in his Commentary on the Mishna, where the context leads him to quote a statement from the Palestinian Talmud; he remarks that he had "recorded the statement in the Halakot of the Palestinian Talmud that" he had

---

there. Either the words "he said" are a scribal error or the Hebrew translator, who does not scintillate, took a passive verb in the Arabic text of Maimonides' responsum as active, and therefore where Maimonides in fact spoke about: "what *is written* [or: *said*] in the composition," the translator understood him as speaking about what *he*, that is, Alfasi, wrote there.

[186] Above, p. 141.

[187] Above, pp. 143–44.

[188] *Responsa* §389.

"collected."[189] From the language it would appear that he had not, at the time, gone beyond the stage of collecting material.

The trove of Cairo Geniza texts has produced two tantalizing manuscripts, both written in the same hand, which are pertinent. Each of the manuscripts contains a substantial part of an epitome of a tractate of the Palestinian Talmud.[190] Neither carries a title or gives the author's name, but a pair of experts on Maimonides' handwriting concluded that the writing is his.[191] By a happy chance, the statement from the Palestinian Talmud which, according to Maimonides' Commentary on the Mishna, was recorded in the Halakot of the Palestinian Talmud that he had collected, appears in one of the two preserved epitomes;[192] a further modicum of support is thereby lent to the identification of Maimonides as the author. The case has consequently been made that the two Geniza manuscripts are sections of two tractates of the promised Halakot of the Palestinian Talmud.[193]

In the letter where Maimonides refers to his Halakot of the Palestinian Talmud, making clear that he had not yet found the leisure to furnish the requisite explanations, he compares it to Alfasi's *Halakot* on the Babylonian Talmud. The two partial epitomes of tractates of the Palestinian Talmud rescued from the Cairo Geniza do not measure up to Alfasi's work.[194] Alfasi's *Halakot* copies out passages from each tractate of the Babylonian Talmud which it takes up, while omitting almost all the dialectical and nonhalakic elements, but it does more. It brings pertinent material from other tractates to bear on whatever topic it treats, it supplies brief explanations of the passages cited, and, with few exceptions, it states or indicates the halakic norm for each topic it deals with; marking or indicating the

[189]Commentary on the Mishna, *Tamid* 5.1. Kafah judges from the texts from which he worked that Maimonides' remark belongs to the original version of the Commentary on the Mishna.

[190]S. Lieberman, *Hilkhoth ha-Yerushalmi of Rabbi Moses ben Maimon* (New York 1947); supplemented by S. Hopkins, "A New Autograph Fragment of Maimonides' *Hilkhot ha-Yerushalmi*," *Journal of Semitic Studies* 28 (1983) 283–96.

[191]M. Lutzki in Lieberman, *Hilkhoth ha-Yerushalmi* 69. S. Sassoon, *A Comprehensive Study of the Autograph Manuscript of Maimonides' Commentary to the Mishnah* (Jerusalem 1990) 27.

[192]Lieberman, *Hilkhoth ha-Yerushalmi* 22.

[193]Lieberman, *Hilkhoth ha-Yerushalmi* 5.

[194]Maimonides writes that time constraints had not allowed him "to explain the Halakot of the Palestinian Talmud which I have prepared, in the manner in which the master [Alfasi] did his *Halakot* of the Babylonian Talmud; I have not found the leisure to explain them." The more obvious way of taking the sentence is that the *Halakot* written by Maimonides in the style of Alfasi's work on the Babylonian Talmud had not yet been supplied with the necessary explanations. The sentence might, however, equally mean that the raw material Maimonides had gathered was not even at the stage where it might be considered a counterpart of Alfasi's Halakot. The second reading of the sentence removes one of the objections to attributing the work to Maimonides which was raised by B. Benedikt, "*Moshe ben Maimon, Hilkot ha-Yerushalmi*," *Kiryat Sefer* 27 (1950–1951) 332.

norm was, after all, Alfasi's primary purpose. Everything is, moreover, sewn together expertly into a smooth, flowing fabric.

By contrast, the epitomes of the two tractates of the Palestinian Talmud which came to light in the Cairo Geniza do little beyond extracting passages from the halakic as well as the aggadic sides of the two tractates. The principle of selection governing the copying out of material is obscure, for the epitomes copy more nonhalakic material than would be appropriate if they were designed as works on halaka;[195] and although they usually avoid repeating statements that are likewise to be found in the Babylonian Talmud, they at times include such statements.[196] They disclose only minimal editing and supply only minimal explanations, and whatever editing and explanations they do contain seem to have been done at random.[197] At one revealing point, the author—or, to be more accurate, the compiler—has inserted the word "interpretation" into his catena of excerpts, but no interpretation is given;[198] he apparently was making a notation to remind him to add the needed interpretation at some time in the future. The epitomes from the Geniza twice quote opinions from the Palestinian Talmud that the latter itself labels as the normative.[199] They do not, however, mark any opinion as normative on their own, although the author could of course have thought that his choice of excerpts would suffice to indicate what the halaka is.

In short, the preserved epitomes from the Cairo Geniza look less like remnants of a literary composition than like preliminary note-taking. If the author was Maimonides, as is highly probable although not entirely certain,[200] he still had not gone beyond collecting material. He may have prepared these and other extracts as resources to be used in the writing of his Commentary on the Mishna and other rabbinic works, having in mind that they might eventually serve as raw material for

[195] L. Ginzberg, *Yerushalmi Fragments* (New York 1909) (in Hebrew) v. Benedikt, "*Moshe ben Maimon, Hilkot ha-Yerushalmi*" 346.

[196] Lieberman, *Hilkhoth ha-Yerushalmi* 5.

[197] To take one example: Lieberman, *Hilkhoth ha-Yerushalmi* 61–62 (=Hopkins, "A New Autograph Fragment" 288–89) explains a term in the text of the Palestinian Talmud (*peran/purna*) that is less difficult than other terms that come up in the text and are left unexplained.

[198] Lieberman, *Hilkhoth ha-Yerushalmi* 36.

[199] Lieberman, *Hilkhoth ha-Yerushalmi* 21, 40.

[200] Benedikt, "*Moses ben Maimon, Hilkot ha-Yerushalmi*" 329–49, although carping at times in his critique, succeeds in showing that Lieberman's arguments for Maimonides' authorship carry little conviction. The identification of the handwriting as Maimonides' by Lutzki and Sassoon nevertheless stands. I compared the facsimiles of the epitomes of the Palestinian Talmud with what have been identified as two autographs of Maimonides', namely, fragments from the *Mishneh Torah*, published by Lutzki in volume 5 of the Shulsinger *Mishneh Torah* (New York 1947), and a fragment of the Commentary on the Mishna published by J. Blau and A. Scheiber, *An Autograph of Maimonides, Publications of the Israel Academy of Sciences and Humanities* (Jerusalem 1981). To my untrained eye, the handwriting in the epitomes of the Palestinian Talmud is indeed the same as that of the two recognized Maimonides autographs.

a full-fledged work of Halakot of the Palestinian Talmud. However that may be, since Maimonides' letter to the rabbinic judge describes his Halakot of the Palestinian Talmud as unfinished, and since the partial epitomes of the two tractates of the Palestinian Talmud which have been preserved plainly do not come from a finished literary work, we are left one more time without evidence that any segment of the project was ever completed.

Maimonides speaks of additional literary plans in the rabbinic sphere: He acknowledges to Pinḥas of Alexandria that the *Mishneh Torah* should be accompanied with a list of sources and expresses the desire to furnish one; [201] and he writes that he wanted to translate his Commentary on the Mishna and *Book of Commandments* from Arabic into Hebrew.[202] Whereas in the previous instances, we cannot determine what progress he made, in these we cannot tell whether he ever took pen to paper.

The death of his brother in 1178 prevented Maimonides from devoting himself to his writing with the single-mindedness that had characterized his efforts until then, but his literary activity was far from over. Despite the worries pressing in upon him, he found time to compose his main philosophic work, the *Guide for the Perplexed*, as well as a series of medical texts. About the year 1199, he remarked plaintively that his first and true love had been God's Law, yet "many foreign women," who he had hoped would serve only as "ointment makers, cooks, and bakers," had forced their attentions on him and established themselves as "rival-wives." His "heart had become divided into many parts by all kinds of science," and his first love, the Law, had been neglected.[203]

As far as we can tell, the neglect persisted. After 1199 and until his death Maimonides continued to write on medical subjects but he is not known to have brought a single one of the rabbinic projects to completion.

Treatise on the Calendar (*Misattributed*). As was noted in the previous chapter, the classic rabbinic sources envisage a calendar in which the first day of each lunar month is fixed on the basis of eyewitness testimony, and a thirteenth month is added to lunar years ad hoc, when needed, so that they keep pace with the longer solar years. Well before Maimonides' day, a fixed calendar had been instituted, which operates with cycles of nineteen lunar years so designed that in each cycle, the same seven predesignated years are assigned a thirteenth month. Otherwise, the nineteen-year cycles are not identical with one another but they are easily generated through a set of rules that determine the day of the week on which each year starts as well as the months receiving twenty-nine days and those receiving thirty. Calendars based on rules and arithmetic calculations, rather than on eyewitness testimony, began to take hold around the time of the redaction of the

[201] See above, p. 267.
[202] *Responsa* §447; above, pp. 166, 185.
[203] *Responsa* 3.57.

Babylonian Talmud, although the procedure may not have fully established itself until centuries later. In the tenth century, the head of a Palestinian rabbinic academy was able to promulgate rules that differed slightly from those employed by rabbinic authorities in Iraq and elsewhere. His system produced a calendar that occasionally diverged from the one followed by the majority of the Jewish world, and for the period of a few years communities using his alternate calendar celebrated the festivals on different days from the mainstream.[204] After a fierce quarrel between the Palestinian scholar and the Iraqi authorities, the latter were victorious, and the calendarial rules that they insisted upon have ever since been universally recognized as the foundation for the Jewish calendar.

There exists a treatise on the subject of the fixed calendar which in the two primary manuscripts carries the heading: "A Composition of R. M. b. M on the Science of *ᶜIbbur*."[205] The term *ᶜibbur* strictly means the determination of the lunar months that should receive a thirtieth day and the lunar years that should receive a thirteenth month. But here as elsewhere it has the broader meaning of generating a calendar. The method of generating a calendar which it spells out is the one that had gained universal acceptance by Maimonides' time.

The "R. M. b. M." given as the treatise's author could be any rabbinic figure whose name and father's name both began with the letter M. Nevertheless, since only well-known and highly regarded scholars merited having their names reduced to acronyms, the manuscripts very likely wish to identify the author of the treatise as none other than R. Moses ben Maimon. In one of the two manuscripts, a different hand has in fact glossed the initials "R. M. b. M." with the words "R. Moshe ben Maimun."[206] An additional, fragmentary manuscript of the work also exists; I have not seen it, but according to the description in the manuscript catalogue, it too identifies the author as "R. M. b. M."[207] Editions of the treatise on the calendar routinely print it under Maimonides' name, and he is generally accepted as the author.

The treatise repeatedly illustrates the points it makes through what it calls "our year" and it adds that the year was 1158.[208] Maimonides began his Commentary on the Mishna in the Hebrew year corresponding to the end of 1160 and first two-thirds of 1161;[209] the treatise thus precedes the Commentary on the Mishna by two or three years. At one point in his Commentary on the Mishna, Maimonides is led to explain a few details of the Jewish calendar. After furnishing the explanations, he remarks: "My intent here is not to discuss all the factors or how they are

[204] See *Encyclopaedia Judaica*, art. *Ben Meir, Aaron.*

[205] Bibliothèque nationale, Paris, MSS #1058 and #1061.

[206] Paris MS #1061.

[207] E. Roth and H. Striedl, *Hebräische Handschriften* 3 (Wiesbaden 1984) 75. The manuscript is in the Levy collection, Hamburg.

[208] *Lettre de Maïmonide sur le calendrier hébraïque*, ed. and trans. R. Weil and S. Gerstenkorn (n.p. 1988) 43, 63, 67, 71.

[209] Above, p. 147.

calculated, for that could require an entire separate composition. Someone in Spain, other than I, did compose . . . a very fine composition" on the subject of the fixed calendar.[210] Maimonides does not state that he did not have to write a composition on the calendar because he had already done so. Rather, he says that to enter into the subject would require an entire treatise and, he implies unmistakably, he was not at the moment ready to undertake the task. He moreover tells his readers that there was no need for such a treatise because someone else had already done the job well. At two additional junctures in the Commentary on the Mishna, Maimonides refers to plans for treatises on subjects related to the calendar, and one of the passages can be read as referring to a plan for a treatise specifically on the method by which a calendar is generated.[211] In neither of the two passages does he betray the slightest indication of having written a treatise on the subject. Only by turning his words completely inside out might one accommodate them to the supposition that he had previously composed a treatise on the fixed calendar. He therefore cannot be the author of the treatise under consideration. The presence of his initials at the head of the treatise—assuming that he is the person intended—carries no weight, since dozens of works are known which bear not merely his initials, but his full name and yet are not accepted by the scholarly world as his.[212]

After completing his Commentary on the Mishna, Maimonides did devote half a dozen chapters of his *Mishneh Torah* to the subject of the fixed calendar,[213] plainly in order to render the *Mishneh Torah* complete.

Index of Midrashic Interpretations of Scripture (Probably Misattributed). This work, which according to the scribe was prepared by Maimonides for his own use, is an alphabetical index of thousands of biblical verses, accompanied by references to places in classic and medieval rabbinic literature where the verses are explained midrashically.[214] Lieberman rejected its authenticity, first, because

[210]Commentary on the Mishna, *ᶜArakin* 2:2. Maimonides could be referring to Bar Ḥiyya's treatise on the calendar.

[211]In Commentary on the Mishna, *Rosh ha-Shana* 2.7, the context leads Maimonides to refer to a projected composition dealing with the astronomical calculations for determining whether or not the new moon is visible on a given day. The subject of the calendar comes up again in the Commentary on the Mishna, *Sukka* 4.2, and there Maimonides remarks that "someday I may compose a separate composition" on the "subject of sighting [the new moon] and generating a calendar [*ᶜibbur*]." He appears to be looking forward there again to the projected composition on the astronomical calculations for determining whether or not the new moon is visible on a given day. But he could be referring to a general treatise on the fixed calendar.

[212]Below, pp. 312–13.

[213]*Mishneh Torah, Hilkot Qiddush ha-Ḥodesh* 5–10. See above, pp. 247–52.

[214]J. Fishman (Maimon), *Ḥayye ha-Rambam* (Jerusalem 1935), Part 2, iii–viii. I estimated that the index for the first ten letters of the Hebrew alphabet, which is as much as Fishman publishes, contains over 3,500 scriptural verses. He writes that he counted more than 20,000 references to rabbinic works.

Maimonides does not refer to it in any of his writings and no other writer mentions it as one of Maimonides' works, and secondly, because it cites books belonging to the Ashkenazic, and not the Sephardic, cultural orbit.[215]

Summary. Maimonides' major rabbinic works were a commentary on two-thirds of the tractates of the Babylonian Talmud, which he finished before the age of twenty-three; his Commentary on the Mishna, written in Arabic and completed when he was thirty years old; the *Book of Commandments*, an Arabic work that identifies what he believed were the 248 positive and 365 negative commandments given by God to Moses; and the *Mishneh Torah*, his code of Jewish law, which he wrote in Hebrew and completed at the age of forty. During the remaining twenty-six years of his life he continued to serve as a rabbinic judge and to answer halakic questions that were sent to him. But as far as is known, none of the additional rabbinic works that he planned saw the light of day.

The commentaries on the Babylonian Talmud did not circulate widely and, at most, fragments survive; Maimonides may not have been sufficiently satisfied with them to allow them to be disseminated. Each of the other major works left an indelible imprint on subsequent rabbinic thought and literature. Maimonides, despite having a clear understanding of their worth, failed to foresee the manner in which they would leave their mark.

Communal consensus chose not to enthrone Maimonides' Commentary as the standard commentary on the Mishna; it has nonetheless been consulted, usually in Hebrew translation, by every serious interpreter of the Mishna to whom it was known and accessible. Maimonides expected that the *Book of Commandments* would settle the issue of the 613 Mosaic commandments once and for all. Instead of foreclosing further speculation, it inspired, in its Hebrew translation, a new genre of rabbinic speculation as writers commented on Maimonides' enumeration of the commandments or tried their own hands at identifying them. Still, it is his rules for determining how a commandment qualifies as one of the 613 given to Moses and his actual enumeration of the commandments that stand at the center of all subsequent rabbinic thinking on the subject, even among writers who disagreed with him.

The *Mishneh Torah* is the preeminent literary achievement of the Jewish Middle Ages—the only competing claimant to the distinction being Rashi's commentary on the Babylonian Talmud—and admiration for it was soon compressed into the oft-repeated aphorism: "From Moses to Moses there arose none like Moses";[216] from the biblical Moses to Moses Maimonides, Jewish history has produced no equal. Maimonides, for his part, looked forward to a time when the *Mishneh Torah*

[215] *Midrash Debarim Rabbah*, ed. S. Liebermann (Lieberman), 2nd ed. (Jerusalem 1964) xiii–xiv.

[216] See Twersky, "*Li-Demuto shel ha-Rambam*" (n. 116 above) 17–19. Twersky records a wealth of other expressions of admiration for Maimonides.

would be recognized as a final summary of Jewish law and enthroned throughout the Jewish world as the single authoritative code for adjudicating legal issues. Events chose their own course. Rather than foreclosing further speculation, the *Mishneh Torah* helped engender an efflorescence of rabbinic literary activity and turned into the most commented-on Jewish work since the talmudic period. Rather than foreclosing further efforts at codification, it inspired a series of such efforts, which continues to our own day. Its authority as a legal code was in the end indirect, through the incorporation of many of its rulings in the *Shulḥan ᶜAruk*, the code that did become authoritative.

Integral to Maimonides' understanding of Jewish law was the belief that a tradition communicated by God to Moses had been handed down from generation to generation, received by the rabbis of the classic period, and preserved in Judah the Prince's Mishna and the Babylonian and Palestinian Talmuds; hand in hand with that proposition went a deemphasizing of the role of rabbinic dialectical reasoning. The transmission of the Oral Torah from Moses to subsequent generations was, Maimonides avers, unerring to the point that no dispute regarding its contents ever occurred among the ancient rabbis. To suppose such a thing would be "shameful and reprehensible, . . . incorrect, in conflict with [rabbinic] principles, and disparaging of the men through whom the Law has been transmitted. It is baseless." There have been readers in recent years who suppose that Maimonides was disingenuous when insisting on the unerring character of Mosaic tradition and the origin of that tradition in a communication directly from the deity to Moses. They should pay heed to the vehemence of the words just quoted, the indignation that Maimonides vents toward men who bungled the enumeration of the 613 commandments given to Moses by God, and the satisfaction he evinces in his own identification of the God-given commandments.

Maimonides was convinced, although the modern reader may think it preposterous, that the ancient rabbis were students of philosophy and science, and he envisaged a single cooperative enterprise in which philosophy, science, and Jewish law join forces. In his Commentary on the Mishna, he takes equal satisfaction in his comprehensive classification of the varieties of ritual impurity and in teaching that the object of human life and the road to human immortality consist in developing one's intellect. In the *Mishneh Torah*, he goes as far as to declare that study of science and philosophy constitutes study of the Law at the highest level. Mainstream rabbinic Judaism rejected his vision, not so much because of its historical inaccuracy as on ideological grounds, and in the half century after Maimonides' death, his welcoming of science and philosophy into the rabbinic universe evoked harsh opposition. As the standing of the *Mishneh Torah* grew and overt attacks on it became progressively less acceptable, the halakic portion established itself within the rabbinic canon, while Maimonides' vision of the union of Jewish law with science and philosophy was, more and more, treated like a family embarrassment, something that it is best simply to ignore. One element in the intellectualization of rabbinic religion insisted upon by the *Mishneh Torah* was, however, a signal success. Maimonides was not the first medieval Jewish author to teach the incorporeality of God, but it was his *Mishneh Torah* together with his list of thirteen principles of faith which persuaded scholars and laymen alike that the incorporeality of God is rooted in Scripture and forms a cardinal component of Jewish faith.

Although Maimonides is not known to have produced any major rabbinic work after the *Mishneh Torah*, the nonhalakic themes broached there and in the Commentary on the Mishna are taken up and further developed in his *Guide for the Perplexed*.

6

PHILOSOPHIC WORKS I

> The *Guide for the Perplexed* . . . a pearl that has no price. (Maimonides, describing his book in a letter to Joseph ben Judah)

> I am a man, who when . . . he finds no stratagem for teaching a demonstrated truth except by putting it in a manner appropriate for a single superior person but not for 10,000 ignoramuses, chooses to address the individual and disregard the outcry of the masses. (Maimonides, *Guide for the Perplexed*, introduction)

Maimonides' Philosophical Writings. There is a popular usage in which an outlook on life, on the world, or on a segment of either, whether sober or frivolous and whether espoused by a person or an institution, is dubbed his or its philosophy. We are treated to television interviews in which popular entertainers discuss their philosophy of life, and magazine advertisements in which distilleries and other commercial enterprises favor us with their business philosophies. That usage is not the one that interests us here. Scholars who concern themselves with Maimonides' philosophy have something more technical and academic in view, namely, the discipline in which men generally recognized through the ages as philosophers have made their mark and in which professors of philosophy ply their trade in the universities today. Since it is devilishly hard, however, to explain precisely what the technical and academic discipline is and how it differs from other disciplines, students of Maimonides' philosophy tend to choose the better part of valor. They simply take for granted that readers will understand what they are talking about and plunge *in medias res.*

To help fill the lacuna, I begin by quoting a definition from a well-regarded introductory textbook to the subject of philosophy. The book's authors acknowledge that "'philosophy' is a highly ambiguous and vague word [and] any definition of it

. . . will be arbitrary" and after conceding as much, they offer their definition. Philosophy, they venture, is "critical reflection on the justification of basic human beliefs and analysis of basic concepts in terms of which such beliefs are expressed."[1] The reason for the definition's clumsiness is that the authors were looking for a formula broad enough to cover the professional activity of Western philosophers of different periods and different orientations—Plato, Aristotle, Descartes, Kant, Wittgenstein, and others. It is far from certain that everyone for whom the coat was tailored would be willing to wear it, but the definition works nicely for Maimonides; it captures what he does when he sees himself as doing philosophy. As will appear, he invested a good deal of effort in critical reflection on ways in which the belief in the existence of God, the belief in the creation of the universe, and other basic human beliefs can be justified. And he invested no less effort in analyzing terms that people use when talking about basic beliefs.

Maimonides' philosophic writings will accordingly be those in which he himself engages in critical reflection and analysis of the sort described. They should also include writings in which he does not himself do the reflection and analysis but relies upon other thinkers who did. The thinkers from whom he almost invariably draws where philosophy is concerned are Aristotle and men who are known today as medieval Arabic Aristotelians. When he speaks of "the philosopher" without qualification, he means Aristotle; when he speaks of "philosophers" without qualification, he usually means the Arabic Aristotelians; and when he speaks of "philosophy" without further qualification—a term for which he never provides even an informal definition—he can mean both the process of critical reflection, analysis, and the rest, and also the body of doctrines that members of the Arabic Aristotelian school arrived at through critical reflection and analysis.[2]

Given what has been said, the following present themselves as candidates for recognition as Maimonides' philosophic writings: sections in his nonphilosophic works which turn from the primary subject of those works to propositions developed by either Maimonides or others through the discipline of philosophy; minor works of a philosophic character which are attributed to Maimonides; and most important, his *Guide for the Perplexed.* We shall find that not a single one of the minor works of a philosophic character which either represent themselves or are represented by the scribes as having been written by Maimonides is authentic.

[1] P. Edwards and A. Pap, *A Modern Introduction to Philosophy* (New York 1973) xiii–xiv.

[2] In medieval Arabic circles, the thinkers who are today known as the Arabic Aristotelians were simply called the *philosophers*, and their system of thought was called *philosophy* without further qualification. For an instance where Maimonides speaks of "philosophy" and means the system of the Arabic-Aristotelian school, see his *Treatise on Resurrection*, Arabic text and Hebrew translation, ed. J. Finkel, *Proceedings of the American Academy for Jewish Research* 9 (1939) 13. English translation: A. Halkin and D. Hartman, *Crisis and Leadership* (Philadelphia 1985) 211–33. Some of the places where Maimonides uses the term philosophy in his introduction to the *Guide for the Perplexed* can likewise be read as referring to the system of the Arabic-Aristotelian school.

The category of minor philosophic works is an empty box. His philosophic writings will therefore reduce themselves to the philosophic material found in his nonphilosophic works and the *Guide for the Perplexed.*

The philosophic material in Maimonides' nonphilosophic works consists of threads woven by Maimonides into his Commentary on the Mishna and, in particular, his introduction, known as the *Eight Chapters*, to the mishnaic tractate *Abot*, the tractate commonly called the *Ethics of the Fathers*; sections of a philosophical character in his *Mishneh Torah*; philosophic material found in a letter to Samuel Ibn Tibbon; and a section at the end of his *Medical Aphorisms.*

The pertinent elements in the Commentary on the Mishna and in the *Mishneh Torah* were touched on in earlier chapters. They reflect the thinking of the Arabic Aristotelian school of philosophy, and Maimonides could have learned virtually everything of a philosophic character appearing in the two rabbinic works from handbooks of philosophy written by men associated with that school. When the rabbinic works take up philosophic matters they avoid technicalities. The obvious reason is that the rabbinic works are designed for readers untrained in philosophy, but an additional reason could conceivably be that at the time of writing Maimonides had studied little philosophy apart from the handbooks and had not yet thought issues through to the extent he would in his *Guide for the Perplexed.*

The Commentary on the Mishna and the *Mishneh Torah* are nonetheless revealing. They establish that by the age of thirty, he had assimilated: the structure of the universe as pictured by the Arabic Aristotelian school; a conception of God and the angels as incorporeal beings consisting in pure intellect and existing outside of space and time; the Aristotelian theory of human ethics; the enshrinement of intellectual perfection as the goal of human life; the attendant subordination of other human activity, including religious and ethical behavior, to the service of the intellect. The philosophic elements in the Commentary on the Mishna and *Mishneh Torah* are particularly valuable for the light they cast on Maimonides' views concerning human free will and human immortality, subjects that make an appearance in the *Guide for the Perplexed* but are not fully developed there. The two rabbinic works unqualifiedly maintain the freedom of the human free, and as was seen in earlier chapters, each of them teaches that human immortality is a benison enjoyed solely by perfected human intellects.

Maimonides' letter to Ibn Tibbon offers an evaluation of a number of ancient and medieval philosophers and also clarifies philosophic details in the *Guide.* In the pertinent section at the end of his *Medical Aphorisms*, a work based primarily on Galen's medical writings, Maimonides puts aside his unbounded admiration for Galen the physician and endeavors to deflate the man's pretensions as a philosopher. He expresses particular annoyance at what he saw as Galen's confused criticism of the Mosaic—that is to say, the Jewish—position on miracles. In the course of exposing what he regards as Galen's errors, he spells out his own belief, according to which genuine miracles, such as the creation of "a horse or a bull instantaneously out of ashes," are not merely possible, but are compatible with a scientific conception of God and the universe. The subject of miracles leads Maimonides to Galen's statements on the paradigmatic miracle, the bringing into existence of the entire universe outside of God, and he excoriates Galen for inconsistency and incoherence on that issue as well.[3] The critique of Galen the philosopher constitutes a voice deserving to be heard, though rarely heeded, regarding a question that has especially exercised students of Maimonides' philosophy in recent years, the question whether he truly believed in the creation of the world or was disingenuous when repeatedly proclaiming his belief in creation.

There are five minor compositions of a philosophic character attributed to Maimonides, and the consensus of scholars today rejects Maimonides' authorship of all but one of them. The five are:

(1) A Hebrew work entitled *Nine Chapters on [Divine] Unity* (*Tish^c a Peraqim mi-Yiḥud*). Its initial chapters echo genuine rationalist pronouncements of Maimonides'. As the book proceeds, however, it betrays its non-Maimonidean provenance by unearthing profound secrets in such matters as the spelling of the sacred names of God, the biblical contexts in which the different divine names appear, the numerical value of the letters of the names, and anagrams that pop up when the letters of God's names are shuffled.[4] To take an example: The standard spelling of the divine name *elohim* is *alef, lamed, he, yod, mem*. Two of the five letters, *yod* and *he*, form a different name of God, a name that the *Nine Chapters on Unity* ranks above *elohim* in the hierarchy of divine names. And when the letters *yod* and *he* are removed from the lesser name, *elohim*, the three remaining consonants—*alef, lamed, mem*—spell out the Hebrew word for "mute"! Therein, the *Nine Chapters* teaches, lies a momentous cosmic truth: The higher name of God formed by the letters *yod* and *he* is the active speaking voice within the lesser name *elohim*, and when the voice of *yod he* is withdrawn from *elohim*, the latter is left mute.[5] Speculations of that sort on the letters of the divine names—which Maimonides would have dismissed as daft—as well as other material in the *Nine Chapters* have been shown to have been borrowed from a late thirteenth-century cabalist.[6]

[3] Maimonides, *Medical Aphorisms* (=*Pirqe Moshe*) ed. S. Muntner (Jerusalem 1959) (medieval Hebrew translation of *Fuṣūl Mūsā*) §§62–68. Arabic original and English translation of the sections from which I quote: J. Schacht and M. Meyerhof, "Maimonides against Galen on Philosophy and Cosmogony," *Bulletin of the Faculty of Arts of the University of Egypt* 5.1 (1937) 69–76, 82–88.

[4] *Tish^c a Peraqim mi-Yiḥud*, ed. G. Vajda, *Qobeṣ ^c al Yad* 15 (5) (1950) 128–37. English translation of the *Tish^c a Peraqim*: F. Rosner, *The Existence and Unity of God* (Northvale, N. J. 1990) 183–233.

[5] *Tish^c a Peraqim mi-Yiḥud* 133.

[6] *Tish^c a Peraqim mi-Yiḥud* 106. Vajda finds that these sections are copied from Joseph Gikatilla, *Sefer Ginnat ha-Egoz*.

(2) An Arabic work entitled *Chapters Regarding Eudaemonia* (*Peraqim ba-Haṣlaḥa*).[7] It consists of homiletic reflections on miscellaneous scriptural verses and incorporates passages copied verbatim from Maimonides. But it is flaccid; it deviates from Maimonides' position on prophecy,[8] the nature of the human soul,[9] and human immortality;[10] and it evinces other tell-tale signs of having someone of lesser stature than Maimonides as its author.[11]

(3) Another minor work containing philosophic material, known only through a European Jewish writer, Moses Taqu, who wrote in Hebrew. Taqu quotes from what he supposes to be a Commentary on the Book of Job composed by Maimonides. Maimonides is represented as having pictured existence as a descending chain wherein the highest level of being outside of God is the "Throne of Glory," which is followed by "the sphere of intellect," and then by the "sphere of angels." From the sphere of angels, the "rational soul" (*nefesh ha-ḥakama*) emanates, and when the rational soul "leaves the body," in other words, when an individual man dies, it returns to the sphere of angels, which is its source.[12] Such notions, with their distinctive neoplatonic coloring, are not merely foreign to Maimonides. When Samuel Ibn Tibbon solicited Maimonides' opinion concerning an earlier Jewish philosopher who had harbored notions of a similar sort, Maimonides informed Ibn Tibbon that the man's supposedly philosophic utterances were not worth wasting one's breath on.[13] Moses Taqu was active in the generation after Maimonides, and his testimony reveals that spurious compositions were already circulating in Europe under Maimonides' name only a few years after his death.

[7] *Peraqim ba-Haṣlaḥa*, ed. H. Davidowitz and D. Baneth (Jerusalem 1939).

[8] *Peraqim ba-Haṣlaḥa* 7-8, 13: The gift of prophecy is attained through fear of God, devoutness in prayer, and observance of the commandments. By contrast, Maimonides, *Guide for the Perplexed* 2.36, lays down three qualifications for prophecy: intellectual perfection, ethical perfection, and a healthy imaginative faculty.

[9] *Peraqim ba-Haṣlaḥa* 17: The rational soul is "hewn from the First Principle and Cause."

[10] *Peraqim ba-Haṣlaḥa* 25, 28, 30, 34: Human perfection consists in observing the "Torah of Moses," eudaemonia results from observing the Law, God releases the souls of the righteous from this "turbid world of misery" and transports them to the "world of spiritual beings," that is, the "world of intellects and of the spirits of the righteous," and each human soul has its own "compartment" there, which is commensurate with the perfection it attained in this world. Maimonides construes human immortality as a function of intellectual development; see above, pp. 164, 242.

[11] *Peraqim ba-Haṣlaḥa*, Baneth's introduction, viii, xvi–xxii. Despite the obvious signs, Steinschneider defended the composition's authenticity in *Die arabische Literatur der Juden* (Frankfurt 1902) and elsewhere. The possibility of its authenticity was defended by W. Bacher, "Treatise on Eternal Bliss Attributed to Moses Maimūni," *Jewish Quarterly Review* 9 (1897) 270–89. But after Baneth made the case for its inauthenticity, no informed scholar today would defend Maimonides' authorship.

[12] Moshe Taku (Taqu), *Ketav Tamim*, facsimile of Paris, Bibliothèque Nationale Heb. MS 711, published by J. Dan (Jerusalem 1984) 22a.

[13] Above, p. 116.

Not a single informed scholar today accepts Maimonides' authorship of the three foregoing works.

(4) An Arabic work entitled *The Treatise on Unity* (*Maqāla al-Tawḥīd*; *Ma*ᶜ*amar ha-Yiḥud*). The current scholarly consensus rejects its attribution to Maimonides as well,[14] but a recent study has argued that the issue of his authorship should not be considered closed.[15]

A small portion of the composition is known to have survived in the original Arabic, and the whole is available in an inept medieval Hebrew translation.[16] The *Treatise* opens with a short introduction turning on the notion—fully in the spirit of Maimonides—that God has no distinguishable qualities, and anthropomorphic descriptions of God must not be taken literally. The remainder is fashioned, with no mention of its source, out of selected chapters from Book One of Maimonides' *Mishneh Torah*, a work that, as will be recalled, was written in Hebrew. The author of the *Treatise on Unity* chose seven chapters, as well as bits of other chapters, from Book One,[17] translated and paraphrased into Arabic the parts he wished to use while omitting what did not suit his purpose, here and there supplemented what he borrowed, and provided transitions in order to mold the parts into a unity. When he had occasion to quote Scripture, he translated it too into Arabic. That feature of the *Treatise* is revealed indirectly by the Hebrew translation; for the translator—intent, it would seem, on probing the outermost limits of poor judgment—retranslated many of the scriptural verses back from Arabic into his own Hebrew instead of quoting the verses directly from the Hebrew Bible.[18] His retranslation of Scripture from Arabic into Hebrew does not improve on the biblical original.

[14]G. Vajda, *L'Amour de Dieu dans la théologie juive* (Paris 1957) 126, note; G. Scholem, *Ursprung und Anfänge der Kabbala* (Berlin 1962) 287, note 235; A. Altmann, "The Ladder of Ascension," reprinted in his *Studies in Religious Philosophy and Mysticism* (Ithaca 1969) 51, note; M. Kellner, Review of Rosner, *The Existence and Unity of God*, *Religious Studies Review* 18 (1992) 345.

[15]Tz. Langermann, "ᶜ*Iyyun me-Ḥadash be-Ma'amar ha-Yiḥud*," *Tarbiz* 65 (1995–1996) 109–28, whose position is not that Maimonides is the author but that the question should be left open.

[16]The Hebrew translation: Maimonides (?), *Ma'amar ha-Yiḥud*, ed. M. Steinschneider (Berlin 1846; reprinted in 1847). I used Munich, Hebrew MS 150, and Moscow, Hebrew MS 209, to correct the printed text. The preserved fragment of the Arabic text is published by Langermann, "ᶜ*Iyyun me-Ḥadash bi-Ma'amar ha-Yiḥud*" 125–26. English translation of *Ma'amar ha-Yiḥud*: Rosner, *The Existence and Unity of God* (n. 4 above) 37–87.

[17]*Mishneh Torah*: *H. Yesode ha-Torah* 2 (world of incorporeal beings); 3 (celestial region); 4 (sublunar world); 7; 8:3; 9:1 (prophecy). *H. De*ᶜ*ot* 1; 2:1 (ethical virtue). *H. Teshuba* 8 (immortality). *H. De*ᶜ*ot* 4 (healthy dietary regime).

[18]On pp. 9, 11, 18, 20, 21, 31, the medieval translator gives his own translation. On pp. 2, 3 (three verses), 15 (two verses), 16, 35, 38, he goes back and quotes from the Hebrew Bible. A colophon to one of the manuscripts states that in rendering biblical verses in his own words, the Hebrew translator followed the example of "the Master," presumably Maimonides, who translated Scripture into his own words in Arabic; see *Ma'amar ha-Yiḥud* 40.

If Maimonides were the author one would have to suppose that he for some reason selected sections from his own *Mishneh Torah* and recycled them into a small new work in Arabic. The scenario is scarcely convincing, but we do not have to resort to mere impressions. The *Treatise* bares its inauthenticity through statements it makes regarding the nature of the human soul, prophecy, and the afterlife. In each instance, the author thoughtfully slants positions taken in the *Mishneh Torah* in a direction alien to the genuine Maimonides, his object being to bring them, and hence Maimonides, into harmony with what he took to be orthodox Jewish theology.[19] To clinch matters, the Arabic author demonstrates that he is someone other than Maimonides by blundering when rendering a key Hebrew term in the *Mishneh Torah* into Arabic.[20] Maimonides, we may presume, would have understood what he had himself written and not misconstrued and mistranslated his own terminology. In fine, the *Treatise on Unity* is plainly the handiwork of an epigone, and the scholars who refuse to accept it as an authentic work of Maimonides' are correct.

None of the minor works considered so far therefore tells us anything about Maimonides himself. Yet, the spectacle of unknown writers' intertwining their

[19]*Ma'amar ha-Yiḥud* 15: The human soul is not a body, it does not stand in need of a body, and after it separates from the human body it returns to its supernal source, from which it is generated. P. 16: Wicked souls perish in hell while the good souls watch, as related in the books of Isaiah and Daniel. *Mishneh Torah, H. Yesode ha-Torah* 7.1, and 6, states: "It is a principle of the religion to know that God renders men prophets," and all prophets except for Moses receive their prophecy "through an angel," that is, through the supernal being known as the active intellect. *Ma'amar ha-Yiḥud* 18–19 corrects the statement as follows: "It is a principle of the Torah that God renders *whomever He wishes* a prophet *and speaks to whatever man He chooses* . . ."; a man who is fully qualified for prophecy rises to the level of the highest of the "angels," the level that the philosophers call "the active intellect."

[20]In the *Mishneh Torah*, Maimonides uses the term *de*^{c}*a* in the senses of intellect (*H. Yesode ha-Torah* 2.7, where the parallel passage in *Ma'amar ha-Yiḥud* 6 correctly has *sekel*; *H. Yesode ha-Torah* 4.8–9), intellectual knowledge (*H. Yesode ha-Torah* 2.8), and psychological characteristic. In *H. De*^{c}*ot* (*Halakot of Psychological Characteristics*) 1:1, Maimonides writes: "Every man has numerous psychological characteristics [*de*^{c}*ot*], and one psychological characteristic [that is to say, the psychological characteristic of one man] is different from another [that is to say, from that of another man]. . . . There are irascible men who are always angry, and men who . . . never get angry; and if they should be angry, they are only slightly so, once every few years." The Hebrew translation of the Arabic text of *Ma'amar ha-Yiḥud* paraphrases Maimonides as follows: "Men's *intellects* vary . . . and you find men who are irascible, difficult to placate . . . and others who are mild, easily placated, and hardly ever angry"; see *Ma'amar ha-Yiḥud* 29–30. The Hebrew translator, and hence the Arabic text from which he translated, misunderstood Maimonides and took *de*^{c}*ot*, which in this instance means psychological characteristics, in the sense of intellects. The Arabic term used elsewhere by Maimonides himself for psychological characteristic was *hay'a*, a term that could not be confused with intellect; see *Shemona Peraqim* (=Commentary on the Mishna [*Mishna* ^{c}*im Perush R. Moshe ben Maimon*] Arabic original and Hebrew trans. J. Kafah [Jerusalem 1963–1968]) 4, p. 379.

ruminations with the great man's ideas and sometimes with his very words is instructive. It testifies to Maimonides' impact on medieval Jewish thought and illustrates the power of his name. His stature was such that a magnetic field formed around him, and written material was drawn to him like metal filings to a magnet. The true, mediocre authors were forgotten, and the compositions attracted to the name "Maimonides" acquired a distinguished, spurious authorship.

Maimonides was not the sole medieval thinker to have his bibliography enhanced with unwanted titles. Other prominent medieval figures in both the Muslim and Jewish worlds were victims of misattributions; examples are Alfarabi, Avicenna,[21] and Ghazali[22] in the Islamic world, and Saadia[23] and Naḥmanides[24] in the Jewish world. Among medieval Jewish writers, Maimonides was, however, the most frequent victim. Here we have seen four minor philosophic works attributed to him in error. In earlier chapters, we found that a commentary on the tractate *Rosh ha-Shana* of the Babylonian Talmud and a composition on the Jewish calendar[25] are ascribed to him, although he could not possibly have written them. In the coming chapters, we shall encounter additional works carrying his name which contain statements that he could not have made; the works in question either are inauthentic or, at best, have been doctored after leaving Maimonides' hands.[26] And there are many more instances. The great Hebrew and Arabic bibliographer Steinschneider, who was by no means overly suspicious about compositions claiming Maimonides as their author, enumerated some thirty misattributions over and above those referred to here.[27] No scholar would step forward to defend Maimonides' authorship of a single one of them. And there are a few more items that Steinschneider, despite his encyclopedic knowledge of Jewish literature, overlooked,[28] giving us in all some forty works attributed to Maimonides which he

[21]The earliest list of Avicenna's writings, drawn up by a student, has forty-six items. A few centuries later, the number had doubled, and twentieth-century scholars are able to enumerate over two hundred titles attributed to Avicenna. See W. Gohlman, *The Life of Ibn Sina* (Albany 1974) 13–14, 46–49, 90–111.

[22]See M. Watt, "The Authenticity of the Works Attributed to al-Ghazālī," *Royal Asiatic Society* (1952) 24–43. One of Watt's assumptions in judging the authenticity of works attributed to Ghazali, namely, that his positions remained consistent throughout his various works, happens to be highly questionable.

[23]H. Malter, *Saadia Gaon* (Philadelphia 1942) 403–5.

[24]G. Scholem, "*Ha-im Ḥibber ha-Ramban et Iggeret ha-Qodesh?*" *Kiryat Sefer* 21 (1944–1945) 179–84.

[25]Above, pp. 144–46, 299–301.

[26]Below, pp. 470-75, 494–97, 501–9: *Epistle on the Length of Life*, *Epistle in Opposition to Astrology*, and *Epistle on Religious Persecution*.

[27]M. Steinschneider, *Catalogus librorum hebraeorum in Bibliotheca Bodleiana* (Berlin 1852-1860), columns 1932–37; *Die arabische Literatur der Juden* (Frankfurt 1902) 217–18. Steinschneider accepted the *Treatise on Unity* and *Chapters Regarding Eudaemonia* as authentic.

[28](1) A biological work attributed to Maimonides; see *Maqāla Tashtamil ᶜalā Fuṣūl min Kitāb al-Ḥayawān li-Arisṭū*, ed. J. Mattock (Cambridge 1966) x–xii. (2) A letter in which

could not have written. In addition, there are isolated pronouncements of one sort or another that medieval writers quote in Maimonides' name but that could not possibly have come from his pen or mouth.[29]

The misattributions occur in the areas of medicine, science, cabala, astrology, and alchemy, and they include a report of the appearance of a Messiah in the land of Persia. Some of the spurious pieces try to convince the reader that they come from Maimonides' hand. An author may, for example, remark that he had said such and such in the *Mishneh Torah* or *Guide for the Perplexed*, attempting to hoodwink the reader into believing that Maimonides was speaking. In instances of the sort, writers are palming off compositions and opinions as Maimonidean which would have enjoyed considerably less acceptance had they, the writers, spoken in their own voices. In other instances, works that do not themselves pretend to have come from Maimonides were labeled as such by scribes or readers who incorrectly guessed that he was the author.

Inasmuch as the compositions erroneously ascribed to Maimonides greatly outnumber his authentic works, a rule of thumb suggests itself: The circumstance that Maimonides' name is affixed to a composition creates no presumption of authorship, and compositions carrying his name must not be accepted as genuine until they prove themselves. Proof might take the form of a reference to his authorship of the doubtful composition in a work of his known to be genuine or testimony to the effect that he was the author by someone who was in close contact with him and familiar with his oeuvre.

The rule should be kept in mind when we consider one final minor philosophic composition that most of the manuscripts represent as having been written by Maimonides, namely:

(5) The *Treatise on Logic*. In contrast to the four compositions examined in the preceding paragraphs, the *Treatise on Logic* is today universally regarded as a genuine work of Maimonides'. The conclusion that I shall reach in regard to it, though inescapable, will therefore meet resistance.

The Treatise on Logic (Misattributed), Known in Hebrew as Millot ha-Higgayon. As just said, its authenticity is universally accepted today. Students of

---

Maimonides supposedly confirms the authenticity of a messiah who appeared in Isfahan; see Maimonides, *Epistle to Yemen*, ed. S. Halkin and trans. B. Cohen (New York 1952), appendix, 108–9. (3) A physician's prayer attributed to Maimonides but written in the eighteenth century; see F. Rosner, *The Medical Legacy of Moses Maimonides* (Hoboken 1998) 273–90.

[29] Shem Ṭob Ibn Gaon, *Migdal ᶜOz* on *Mishneh Torah*: *H. Yesode ha-Torah* 1.10, who quotes from a document where Maimonides supposedly states that he accepted the cabala in his old age. Meir Aldabi, *Shebile Emunah* (Warsaw 1887), 70b, column 1, who reports that Maimonides wrote: Every Israelite soul to be born in the future was present when the Torah was given at Sinai; pointed out by D. Schwartz, *Ben Shamranut le-Sikletanut*," *Daat* 32–33 (1994) 166, note 90. Tz. Langermann, "*Imrot u-Perushim mi-Yesodo shel ha-Rambam o ha-Meyuḥasim lo*," in *Me'ah Sheᶜarim* (Twersky memorial volume) (Jerusalem 2001) items 1, 2, 4, 5.

Maimonides, moreover, employ it regularly in their re-creation of his logical and philosophic views.[30]

Yet Maimonides himself never mentions it, even in contexts where he discusses issues of a logical nature and where a reference would be appropriate if he were the author.[31] Samuel Ibn Tibbon, the first translator of Maimonides' *Guide for the Perplexed* into Hebrew, drew up a glossary of philosophic terms that he used in his translation, and among them are terms defined in the *Treatise.* He too does not mention or allude to it. The *Treatise* contains nothing of a Jewish character and nothing indicating the slightest link to Maimonides. The sole evidence of his authorship is the presence of his name in most of the manuscripts. In the world of fine art, the appearance of a hitherto unknown painting claiming to come from the brush of one of the marketable old masters—Titian, Caravaggio, Rubens, Rembrandt, and their peers—immediately raises eyebrows among sober-minded cognoscenti. By the same token, critical scholars should have been wary from the moment that the *Treatise on Logic* attributed to Maimonides came to their attention. A nineteenth-century scholar did question the attribution to Maimonides[32] but he remained a lone voice.

The *Treatise on Logic* was written in Arabic and was translated into Hebrew three times in the Middle Ages. It circulated and was studied primarily in the latter language: Many more manuscript copies of the Hebrew translations have been preserved than of the original Arabic; one of the three translations was already in print in 1527, less than a century after the invention of movable type; and two dozen printed editions of one or another of the Hebrew translations followed before the Arabic original was finally published in its entirety in 1960.

[30]A few of many examples: A. Altmann, "Essence and Existence in Maimonides," reprinted in his *Studies in Religious Philosophy and Mysticism* (Ithaca 1969) 126–27; H. Wolfson, "The Classification of Sciences in Medieval Jewish Philosophy" and "Notes on Maimonides' Classification of Sciences," reprinted in his *Studies in the History of Philosophy and Religion* 1 (Cambridge, Mass. 1973) 510–43, 551–60; Wolfson, "The Amphibolous Terms in Aristotle, Arabic Philosophy and Maimonides," reprinted in *Studies in the History of Philosophy and Religion* 1.467–68; L. Strauss, "Maimonides' Statement on Political Science," *Proceedings of the American Academy for Jewish Research* 22 (1953) 115–30; L. Berman, "A Reexamination of Maimonides' Statement on Political Science," *Journal of the American Oriental Society*" 89 (1969) 106–11; J. Kraemer, "Maimonides on the Philosophic Sciences in His Treatise on the Art of Logic," *Perspectives on Maimonides* (Oxford 1991) 77–104. Strauss even suggests that when Maimonides—as we shall see, it was not actually Maimonides—mentioned eight items in a passage in chapter 14 and then only referred to seven of the eight when later summarizing the chapter, he was hinting at some deep, dark secret. In his inimitable fashion, Strauss does not deign to tell us what the secret might be.

[31]E.g., Maimonides, *Book of Commandments*, rule 8; *Guide for the Perplexed*, introduction; 1.52; 56; 58, p. 71b; 71, p. 96a; 2.33; and *Medical Aphorisms*, chapter 25. Maimonides did not complete chapter 25 of the *Medical Aphorisms* until shortly before his death. Consequently, his reason for failing to mention the *Treatise on Logic* there could not be that the *Treatise* had not yet been written.

[32]J. Reifmann, " *Prozdor*," *Ozar Tob* (1884) 18–21.

The Arabic original exists in two forms. The entire text has been preserved in Arabic characters, and a little more than half is preserved in Arabic written in Hebrew characters. Only a single manuscript of the Arabic in Hebrew characters contains the beginning of the *Treatise*, and there a title placed at the head of the work names Maimonides as the author.[33] The first translation into Hebrew was made about fifty years after Maimonides' death by Moses Ibn Tibbon, the son of the Hebrew translator of Maimonides' *Guide for the Perplexed*, and his translation is the one found in almost all the manuscripts and printed editions. In the majority of the Ibn Tibbon manuscripts, Maimonides is named as the author either as part of the title placed at the top or in the opening words of the first sentence. In some manuscripts, a colophon at the end likewise names him as the author. There nonetheless are at least two manuscripts that do not have Maimonides' name at the beginning,[34] a larger number do not name him in a colophon, and those that do not name him at the beginning do not do so in a colophon. In a word, at least two preserved manuscripts of Ibn Tibbon's translation do not attribute the *Treatise* to Maimonides.

The second translation into Hebrew, by a certain Aḥiṭub, includes Maimonides' name as part of the title at the head of the work, but the heading can hardly have come from the hand of the translator himself. It lauds the translator as "the sage, the man of intellect, his honor, our teacher, and our master," and even the most conceited writer knows enough not to describe himself in such a fashion.[35] The third translation, that of Joseph Ibn Vives, once again carries Maimonides' name in the title, and here the heading most likely was supplied by the translator. It relates that Vives did the translation for a friend, who is named, and it sounds as if the translator himself is speaking.[36] But with Vives we are well into the fourteenth century. Aḥiṭub's version has no colophon, and the Vives version has a brief colophon in which Maimonides' name does not appear.[37]

Vives, then, most probably took the *Treatise* to be a work of Maimonides'. It is not certain that the two earlier translators did.

Until the middle of the past century, the Arabic original of the *Treatise on Logic* was known solely from the partial text in Hebrew characters. Two complete copies of the treatise written in Arabic letters were then discovered in manuscripts owned

[33] I. Efros, *Maimonides' Treatise on Logic* (the Arabic text as preserved in Hebrew characters, the three medieval Hebrew translations, and Efros' English translation), in *Proceedings of the American Academy for Jewish Research* (New York 1938), Hebrew section 5. There are only two partial manuscripts of the Arabic text in Hebrew characters. Maïmonide, *Traité de logique*, trans. R. Brague (Paris 1996) is a French translation done from the Arabic original.

[34] Parma MS #402 and Sasson MS #1221.

[35] *Maimonides' Treatise on Logic*, Hebrew section 67. The introductory paragraph of Aḥiṭub's version in Vatican MS. Heb 349, which is recorded in the textual apparatus, was, as noted in Efros' introduction, p. 9, apparently copied from Ibn Tibbon's version.

[36] *Maimonides' Treatise on Logic*, Hebrew section 103.

[37] *Maimonides' Treatise on Logic*, Hebrew section 100, 129.

by libraries in Istanbul and Ankara, and an edition based on them was published in Turkey in 1960 and reissued the following year.[38] At the head of the printed edition stands the title: "Treatise on the Art of Logic by Moses the son of Maimon, the son of ᶜUbaydallāh, the Israelite, of Cordoba."[39] That would seem to be unambiguous enough.

A footnote in the editor's introduction to her edition discloses, however, that the first page of the Istanbul manuscript containing the *Treatise* provides a table of contents listing the items in the volume, and the table of contents describes the *Treatise* not as a composition of Maimonides' at all but instead as the "Book of the Terminology of Logic [*nuṭq*] by the Israelite Yaᶜqūb Abū Isḥāq ibn Yūsuf." The Turkish editor dismisses the attribution to Yaᶜqūb Abū Isḥāq out of hand as an "error," undoubtedly because she took for granted that the author was Maimonides.[40] I was able to acquire a photographic reproduction of the text of the *Treatise* as it appears in the Istanbul manuscript and a transcription of the opening lines of the text in the Ankara manuscript.[41] Neither of them names an author. (The apparatus of variant readings furnished by the editor in the Turkish printed edition indicates that the Istanbul text begins with the words "Book of the Terminology of Logic [*nuṭq*] by the Israelite Yaᶜqūb Abū Isḥāq ibn Yūsuf"; but the editor was apparently recording what she found in the manuscript's table of contents and not what she found at the head of the text itself.)

In short, the available evidence makes clear that the Istanbul manuscript attributes the work not to Maimonides but to a certain Yaᶜqūb Abū Isḥāq. It appears that the Ankara manuscript gives no author. And as far as one can tell, the ascription of the work to Maimonides in the printed Arabic edition is entirely the contribution of an editor who thought that she was being helpful. The editor, incidentally, was convinced by her examination of the two manuscripts that the text in the Ankara manuscript had served as the "model" for that in the Istanbul manuscript.[42] Yaᶜqūb Abū Isḥāq ibn Yūsuf is not otherwise known.

Attribution of the *Treatise* to Maimonides rests, then, on the appearance of his name in most of the manuscripts in Hebrew characters, whereas one of the

[38]M. Türker, "*Al-Maḳāla fī Ṣināʿat al-Manṭiḳ de Mūsā Ibn Maymūn*," *Review of the Institute of Islamic Studies* 3 (1959–1960) 55–60, 87–110; "*Mūsā Ibn-i Meymūn'un al-Maḳāla fī Ṣināʿat al-Manṭiḳ*," *Ankara Üniversitesi, Dil ve Tarih-Coğrafya Fakültesi Dergisi* 18 (1960) 14–18, 40–64. Efros printed an edition of the entire *Treatise* based both on the manuscripts of the parts of the Arabic original preserved in Hebrew characters, which he had published earlier, and on the edition of the text in Arabic characters that was published by Türker. See I. Efros, *Maimonides' Arabic Treatise on Logic*, *Proceedings of the American Academy for Jewish Research* 34 (1966), Hebrew section 9–42.

[39]Türker, "*Mūsā Ibn-i Meymūn'un al-Maḳāla fī Ṣināʿat al-Manṭiḳ*" 40.

[40]Türker, "*Mūsā Ibn-i Meymūn'un al-Maḳāla fī Ṣināʿat al-Manṭiḳ*" 16.

[41]The reproduction of the Istanbul text was obtained for me by Avner Ben-Zaken, and the transcription of the Ankara text was made thanks to the good offices of David Hirsch of Los Angeles and Phyllis Erdogan of Ankara.

[42]Türker, "*Mūsā Ibn-i Meymūn'un al-Maḳāla fī Ṣināʿat al-Manṭiḳ*" 16.

manuscripts in Arabic letters credits someone else, and the other, as far as I could ascertain, has no attribution.

The Arabic text of the *Treatise* which is written in Hebrew characters opens with a phrase from the Quran commonly used as an Islamic invocation: "In the name of Allah, the merciful and compassionate."[43] The text in Arabic characters from the library in Istanbul has the same invocation, and the Ankara text opens with an alternative invocation drawn from the Quran: "In the name of Allah, Lord of the worlds."[44] The three medieval Hebrew translations of the treatise naturally employ neither formula.[45] In all the versions, the *Treatise* proceeds to relate that a "leading figure [*sayyid*] from among the men of religious law and the masters of purity and elegance in the Arabic language asked a man" conversant with the art of logic—in other words, the author of the *Treatise*—to explain for him the different terms used in logic. The figure commissioning the *Treatise* requested that the explanations be "as concise as possible" and that the author should not "enter deeply into a clarification of the subject matter." He merely wanted to know what the terms meant. Since the author of the treatise is careful to bless the personage who commissioned the work, praying that his "strength be made permanent,"[46] it is reasonable to assume that he was someone actual and not a literary fiction of the sort occasionally invented by writers as an excuse for publishing their thoughts on one topic or another.

The author does what was required of him. He gives a brief explanation of the terms used in philosophic logic—the components out of which propositions are framed, the types of proposition, the types of syllogism, and so on. In a few places he ventures beyond logic and explains basic terms from other branches of philosophy.[47] As soon as the discussion verges on the overly technical, he heeds the instructions that he had received and stops short. In all, the author tells us, his small *Treatise* expounds no less than 175 terms, and they "include most of the terms occurring in the art of logic, as well as some employed in physical, metaphysical, and political science."[48] Recent scholars who have searched for the sources of the *Treatise on Logic* have discovered that much seems to be drawn from Alfarabi.[49] The finished product, though hardly scintillating, is a useful introduction to medieval Arabic logical and philosophical terminology, and neither Maimonides nor any other medieval philosopher would have reason to be em-

[43] *Maimonides' Treatise on Logic*, Hebrew section 5.

[44] Türker, "*Mūsā Ibn-i Meymūn'un al-Maḳāla fī Ṣināʿat al-Manṭiḳ*" 40, prints only the invocation found in the Ankara text and does not rccord the other reading. She was not the most meticulous of editors.

[45] *Maimonides' Treatise on Logic*, Hebrew section 23, 67, 103.

[46] *Maimonides' Treatise on Logic*, Hebrew section 5; English section 34. Türker 40.

[47] For example, chapter nine defines the different senses of cause; chapter fourteen distinguishes the branches of philosophy and delineates the subject matter of the several sciences.

[48] Türker 64. *Maimonides' Treatise on Logic*, English section 65.

[49] Kraemer, "Maimonides on the Philosophic Sciences" (n. 30 above) 81, and note 12.

barrassed at having written it. It should be observed that the author, whoever he was, had to accommodate a patron from a particular background who had set down strict guidelines and restrictions; the author's task was to explain the meanings of terms and not what he himself believed. The attempts that have frequently been made to recreate from the *Treatise* what the author himself—supposedly Maimonides—thought about the topics treated therefore skate on the very thinnest of ice.

Expertise in religious law was far more likely to be go hand in hand with purity and elegance in the writing of Arabic within medieval Islamic, than within medieval Jewish, society. Whether the person who commissioned the *Treatise on Logic* fully possessed the qualities or was being flattered is irrelevant; in either event, he sounds much more like a Muslim than a Jew.[50] If we could be assured that the Islamic invocation at the beginning came from the author, the surmise that the treatise was intended for a Muslim would become a certainty. The invocation, varying as it does in the versions of the Arabic original, seems however to be a scribal or editorial addition.

The information available prior to the publication of the full Arabic version in 1960 was thus insufficient to clinch the conclusion that the man commissioning the *Treatise* was a Muslim but certainly pointed in that direction. It is therefore astonishing that not only has the *Treatise on Logic* been accepted as a work of Maimonides'; the period in his life when he supposedly wrote it has been pinpointed as well. In 1835, a scholar ventured tentatively that the *Treatise* "appears to be a youthful work" of Maimonides.[51] Steinschneider subsequently threw caution to the winds and without a shred of evidence asserted that Maimonides "without doubt" wrote it "in his youth, perhaps in Spain . . . when still not fifteen years old."[52] The fancy that Maimonides wrote the *Treatise* when still in his teen years reechoes into our day.[53] Yet only a singularly unfettered imagination will be able to visualize a Muslim of rank selecting a teenage Jewish

[50] A similar observation is made by Kraemer, "Maimonides on the Philosophic Sciences" 77, although Kraemer hesitates to draw a firm conclusion. He further notes that manuscripts of genuine works of Maimonides' that circulated in Arabic sometimes open with an Islamic invocation.

[51] J. Derenburg, review of Beer, *Leben und Wirken des Rabbi Moses ben Maimon*, *Wissenschaftliche Zeitschrift für jüdische Theologie* 1 (1835) 424.

[52] M. Steinschneider, *Die hebräischen Übersetzungen des Mittlealters* (Berlin 1893) 434. Steinschneider expresses himself more cautiously in *Die arabische Literatur der Juden* 208.

[53] Examples: S. Zeitlin, *Maimonides, a Biography* (New York 1955) 216, note 9 ("before . . . his twentieth birthday"); Efros, *Maimonides' Treatise on Logic* 3 ("a young lad"); Türker, "*Mūsā Ibn-i Meymūn'un al-Maḳāla fī Ṣinā'at al-Manṭiḳ*" 14 ("seventeen years old"); J. Dienstag, "*Be'ur Millot Ha-Higgayon le-ha-Rambam*," *Areshet* 2 (1960) 7 ("when sixteen"); A. Heschel, *Maimonides* (New York 1982) 22 ("at sixteen"). Other writers, sensing that something was wrong, assign the *Treatise* to Maimonides' early twenties. While that dating is not quite so implausible as the supposition that Maimonides wrote the work when fifteen, sixteen, or seventeen years old, not a shred of evidence is, or can be, provided to support it either.

talmudic student as the "man," conversant with the art of philosophic logic, whom he would commission to prepare an introduction to the subject for him.[54] If Maimonides were actually the author, a less implausible guess would have been that he wrote it in the 1180s and 1190s, when he enjoyed the patronage of al-Qāḍī al-Fāḍil, Saladin's secretary and vizier. Al-Fāḍil had been trained in the religious law, he was renowned for his elegant Arabic literary style, and he commissioned one of Maimonides' medical works. In his later life, Maimonides wrote medical works for other prominent Muslims as well.

The copies of the Arabic version in Hebrew letters do not extend to chapter twelve, and the original text of that chapter therefore did not become known until the publication of the edition based on the manuscripts discovered in the two Turkish libraries. Chapter twelve treats the concepts of *priority* and *posteriority*. It explains that the two concepts are employed in five different senses, among which are priority and posteriority in time and priority and posteriority in nobility (*sharaf*). Something can be said to be prior to something else, the chapter teaches, inasmuch as it precedes the other in time; it can be said to be prior inasmuch as it precedes the other thing in nobility, that is, inasmuch as it is "more perfect" and "more excellent" than the other; and it can be said to be prior in three additional senses that do not concern us. The Arabic text illustrates temporal priority through the persons of Moses and Jesus, Moses having been prior to Jesus in time. Since the example is chosen to illustrate priority in time and the author contrasts priority in time with other senses of priority, the intimation is unmistakable: Moses was prior to Jesus solely in time and not in any of the other senses. Specifically, he was not prior to Jesus in the sense of nobility, perfection, and excellence. The name "Jesus" is given here as *ᶜĪsā*, which is a form employed by Muslims. When Jewish writers wrote for other Jews, whether in Hebrew or Arabic, they used the forms *Yeshu* or *Yashuᶜa*.

The illustration of temporal priority through Moses and Jesus must also have been in the Arabic text used by the three Hebrew translators. That is established by the circumstance that each of the translations illustrates temporal priority and posteriority in its own fashion; one translation employs Noah and Abraham as its example, the second, Reuben and Simon, and the third, Moses and Ezra. The translators plainly had before them a text with an illustration that could not be presented to a Jewish readership, and each chose a different pair of biblical figures as a substitute for the example in the original.[55] The cleverest of the substitutions is the third. The Babylonian and Palestinian Talmuds observe that if Moses had not already brought the Torah to the Israelites, Ezra the scribe was worthy of doing

[54]By the age of twenty-three and before leaving western North Africa, Maimonides completed commentaries on two-thirds of the Babylonian Talmud. He also found time to study medicine and astronomy during the same period.

[55]*Maimonides Treatise on Logic* 53, 91, 122. M. Ibn Tibbon, the earliest translator had the Arabic text in Hebrew characters; see Efros, *Maimonides' Arabic Treatise on Logic* (n. 38 above) 159, item 15.

so.[56] Ezra therefore fit perfectly, a man who was posterior to Moses in time, while comparable to him in perfection and excellence.

By itself, the example chosen by the author of the *Treatise* to illustrate temporal priority and posteriority suffices to show that he was writing for a Muslim. In Islamic doctrine, Moses and Jesus are two great prophets, of more or less equal rank, who served as links in the prophetic chain culminating in Muhammad; Muhammad is known in Islam as "the seal of the prophets." The notion of Moses and Jesus as men, one of whom preceded the other in time, but neither of whom is prior or posterior to the other in perfection and excellence, is therefore wholly apt in an Islamic context.[57] The illustration would have been problematic if the *Treatise* were written for a Christian. In Christian theology, Jesus is in one respect posterior to Moses in time, but in another may be viewed as preceding him, and the two men are by no means equal in perfection and excellence. In the medieval Jewish world, the bracketing of Moses and Jesus as men who differ in time, with the intimation that they are equal in respect to perfection, would verge on sacrilege. If the leading figure from among students of religious law who commissioned the treatise had been Jewish, the author could have looked forward to a most frigid reception when he delivered his handiwork, with its placing of Moses and Jesus on the same level. Anyone today who so wishes can make the simple experiment of reading the passage to a rabbinic scholar of the old school.

Although the personage for whom the *Treatise on Logic* was written was a Muslim, the *Treatise*'s author could conceivably have been Jewish. Someone lacking religious sensibilities and inhibitions could have borrowed the example of Moses and Jesus from the Muslim sources out of which he fashioned the *Treatise*, knowing that the illustration would suit the taste of his Muslim patron. The only evidence that the author was indeed Jewish is the name of the otherwise unknown "Israelite Ya^cqūb Abū Isḥāq ibn Yūsuf," which is attached to the version preserved in Arabic characters. The name, whose equivalent in English is "Jacob, the father of Isaac, the son of Joseph," an inversion of the genealogy of the biblical Jacob, sounds suspicious and could be a pseudonym. If there was such a man, he could conceivably have been a Jewish convert to Islam.[58]

[56]BT *Sanhedrin* 21b, and parallels.

[57]The point is made by L. Berman, "Some Remarks on the Arabic Text of Maimonides' 'Treatise on the Art of Logic,'" *Journal of the American Oriental Society* 88 (1968) 341. Berman stops short, however, of drawing the obvious conclusion that the treatise was written for a Muslim.

[58]Efros, *Maimonides' Arabic Treatise on Logic* 157–60, calls attention to five places where, he thinks, the reading in the text preserved in Arabic characters might suggest that the text was copied from an Arabic version written in Hebrew characters. If the *Treatise* was, perchance, originally composed in Hebrew characters, the author would obviously have to be Jewish. In three of the five items that Efros cites, namely, items 2, 6, and 15, in his complete list, the readings of the text in Arabic characters, far from reflecting a misreading of the text written in Hebrew characters, are superior to the latter. If anything, these items would suggest that the text in

What is out of the question is that the author was Maimonides. Maimonides believed that Moses was "the choicest of the human species,"[59] the greatest person ever to have lived,[60] and the greatest of the prophets.[61] When he had occasion to refer to Jesus, he appends a tag reserved for the archenemies of Israel and the wicked of mankind; he calls him: "Jesus [*Yashu*ᶜ*a*] of Nazareth, may his bones be crushed."[62] He places Jesus (*Yashu*ᶜ*a*) in the category of the "heretics" and "disbelievers, . . . whose minds have been extinguished by ignorance, and souls darkened by desire, so that they calumniate the Law and prophets . . . and scornfully neglect the commandments. 'May the name of the wicked rot.'"[63] It is scarcely imaginable that, merely for the purpose of illustrating a logical concept, Maimonides would have mentioned the greatest of the biblical prophets in the same breath with a heretic who calumniated the Law and prophets, a man whose bones should be crushed and whose name should rot. For him to have suggested that they were equal in perfection is inconceivable. Even if he should have encountered the illustration in a source from which he copied, he could easily have made a palatable substitution, as all three of the Hebrew translators from the Arabic did. The circumstance that a prominent Muslim commissioned the treatise would have been an added incentive for someone of Maimonides' stature to alter, rather than to retain, the illustration. Throughout the Middle Ages and into modern times, pressure was put on Jews in Muslim countries, especially men of prominence, to convert to Islam. Maimonides would hardly have placed ammunition in a Muslim patron's hands, hardly have put the chilling words in his patron's mouth: Ah, Mūsā, you recognize then that your biblical namesake was not the single greatest prophet, that he and ᶜ*Īsā* were links of equal standing in the chain of prophecy. I assume that you also recognize where the chain of prophecy ultimately led. May we not now expect you to draw the logical conclusion and join the true faith?

The *Treatise on Logic* has long been accepted as a work of Maimonides' and repeatedly been used in recreations of his thought—although, as already noted, doing so would be methodologically unsound even if he were the author. Rethinking its authenticity will therefore go against the grain, entrenched habits being hard to correct. But we have seen that the appearance of Maimonides' name in manuscripts of a given work creates no presumption of his having written it; there was consequently never a legitimate reason to suppose that he was the author of the *Treatise*. And the manuscript evidence is in any event contradictory.

Hebrew characters was copied from the one in Arabic characters. The remaining two of the five items do not support either alternative.

[59]Maimonides, *Epistle to Yemen* (n. 28 above) 66; English translation xiii.

[60]Maimonides, *Guide for the Perplexed* 2,33, 75b.

[61]Maimonides, *Guide for the Perplexed* 2.35; 3:51.

[62]Maimonides, *Epistle to Yemen* 12, 92.

[63]Maimonides, Commentary on the Mishna, *Ḥullin* 1:2; the verse is Proverbs 10:7. Maimonides expresses similar sentiments in *Mishneh Torah*: *H. Melakim* 11.4 (uncensored text).

Perhaps the *Treatise on Logic* was written by the Ya^c^qūb who is identified as the author in one of the Arabic manuscripts. If Ya^c^qūb Abū Isḥāq ibn Yūsuf happens to be a pseudonym, the author could have been the person hiding behind the pen name.

Maimonides' philosophic writings reduce themselves to the philosophic threads woven into his nonphilosophic writings and to his *Guide for the Perplexed*—or, to speak more precisely, to the philosophic sections of the *Guide for the Perplexed.*

The Guide for the Perplexed. In his *Treatise on Resurrection*, which he wrote in 1191, Maimonides repeatedly calls readers' attention to what he had "made clear" in his *Guide for the Perplexed* and in doing so, he refers to all three of the *Guide*'s parts.[64] The entire *Guide* must therefore have been in circulation at the time. In the introduction to the book itself he discloses that his plans for it had not yet taken definitive shape during the period when he was working on his Commentary on the Mishna. Immediately after completing the Commentary on the Mishna, he turned to his *Book of Commandments* and then, at once, to the *Mishneh Torah*, on which, he relates, he worked day and night for ten years. The finishing touches were put on the *Mishneh Torah* in 1178. He further recalls that after his brother died, in approximately 1177, he was bedridden and in a deep depression for a year. It follows that 1178 is the earliest possible starting date for the writing of the *Guide.*

A slightly later initial date is suggested by Maimonides' dedicatory preface to the *Guide* itself. He dedicates the *Guide* to his favorite student, Joseph ben Judah, and states that he decided to write it after Joseph left Egypt for Syria.[65] The scholarly supposition is that Joseph left Egypt in the mid-1180s,[66] and a letter Maimonides sent to him around 1191 lends a modicum of corroboration: He remarks that Joseph would remember Maimonides' situation in Fustat from the time when they were together, and the tone suggests that not too many years had passed. In short, Maimonides began the *Guide* no earlier than 1178, when he was forty years old, and probably in the 1180s. He completed it by 1191, when he was fifty-three or fifty-four. It was a period in which responsibility for his livelihood rested entirely on his own shoulders and during part or all of which he was supporting himself and his family through the practice of medicine. He consequently could not have worked on the *Guide* with the same concentration and single-mindedness that he devoted to his *Mishneh Torah*, a point not always appreciated.

[64] Maimonides, *Treatise on Resurrection* (n. 2 above) 8, 10, 22, 23, 30 (twice), 31, 32; Z. Diesendruck, "On the Date of the Completion of the Moreh Nebukin," *Hebrew Union College Annual* 12–13 (1937–1938) 468–70.

[65] Maimonides, *Guide for the Perplexed*, Dedicatory Preface.

[66] Moses ben Maimon, *Epistulae*, ed. D. Baneth (Jerusalem 1946), editor's introduction, 2.

After composing the *Mishneh Torah* in Hebrew, Maimonides expressed regret for not having written his Commentary on the Mishna and *Book of Commandments* in that language as well. He nonetheless returns to the Arabic language in the *Guide for the Perplexed.* One reason probably was that he foresaw different readers from those for whom his rabbinic works were intended, and a second may have been that he found Arabic an easier medium for articulating what he wished to convey.

The *Guide* is divided into three parts, and they are subdivided into some 175 chapters, which Maimonides left unnumbered;[67] the chapter numbers that we have today were furnished by the first Hebrew translator. The resulting volume is of considerable heft, extending 470 pages in a standard printed format. After Maimonides completed it, his literary achievements dropped to a lower plateau. He continued writing, and the last thirteen or more years of his life find him publishing a number of medical works and a pair of occasional pieces. None of them, however, compares in caliber with his rabbinic works or the *Guide for the Perplexed.*

As we saw, Maimonides' early literary activity was centered on Jewish legal texts, and the first work that he allowed to circulate was a Commentary on the Mishna corpus. At one point in the Commentary, he remarked that "the exposition of a principle [of belief] is preferable to anything else that I might expound";[68] and in both the Commentary and the subsequent *Mishneh Torah* he found opportunities to impart some of his thoughts on the nonlegal side of the Jewish religion.[69] But he envisaged something on a larger and more comprehensive scale. When still engaged in the Commentary on the Mishna, and hence more than a decade before he set to work on the *Guide for the Perplexed*, he reveals plans for complementing his treatment of the legal side of the Jewish religion with a full-fledged exposition of the nonlegal side. He was considering as many as three books.

He writes in the Commentary on the Mishna that he had "begun" a "Book of Prophecy," which would have among its topics: the unique character of Moses' prophecy, the extraordinary level of intellectual knowledge of God attained by Moses, and the reason why Moses' knowledge of God went no further than it did; inasmuch as Moses was "an intellect present in matter" and not an incorporeal being, it lay beyond his power, as it lies beyond the power of all humans, to know God in accordance with the "true nature of His being [*wujūd*]."[70] The *Book of*

[67] See Maimonides, *Dalāla al-Ḥā'irīn*, ed. I. Joel (Jerusalem 1931) 493–501.

[68] Above, p. 160.

[69] Above, pp. 155–57, 160–65, 231–62.

[70] Commentary on the Mishna (n. 20 above), *Sanhedrin*, 10:1 (the seventh of the thirteen principles of faith), p. 213; *Shemona Peraqim*, chapter 7, p. 395; English translation of *Shemona Peraqim*: Moses Maimonides, *Eight Chapters*, trans. J. Gorfinkle (New York 1912). In *Mishneh Torah*: *H. Yesode ha-Torah* 2.8, Maimonides stresses that even the incorporeal intelligences cannot attain a complete understanding of God's essence.

Prophecy would, moreover, be an "appropriate" place to examine the concepts *matter* and *form*, the sense in which the human intellect stands to the human soul as form to matter, the different stages of human intellect, and the process whereby man progresses from one of those stages to the next.[71] To judge from the description, the book would have situated the phenomenon of prophecy, and particularly the prophecy of the biblical Moses, within the larger context of human intellectual thought and would have explored the latter from the ground up.

Years later, Maimonides gave a different account. On that occasion he recalls that the *Book of Prophecy* was to have as its object the interpretation of "abstruse" (*gharīb*) points in the scriptural prophecies, and the context shows that he is talking about an allegorical reading of prophetic texts which would lay bare their scientific and philosophic core. The two accounts need not, of course, conflict. Maimonides could have planned to do both things, to situate the prophetic phenomenon within the framework of a philosophic theory of human intellect, while also offering an allegorical interpretation of individual prophetic texts. When he reminisces about the *Book of Prophecy* on the later occasion, he makes clear that the book had been intended for a broad readership.[72]

Secondly, he writes in the Commentary on the Mishna, he was "going to compose" a book of "interpretation of the *derashot*." By *derashot* he undoubtedly means the aggada of the ancient rabbis in general and not merely aggada that the rabbis were able to extract from Scripture by use of their midrashic tools.[73] We earlier found him—there too in his Commentary on the Mishna—making the far-reaching assertion: Rabbinic *derashot* contain all the "divine [or: metaphysical] matters and [all] the truths [*ḥaqā'iq*] . . . that men of science have opined and on which the philosophers have spent ages."[74] When he now describes the book he envisioned, he writes in a similar spirit that it would "assemble all the *derashot* found in the [Babylonian] Talmud and elsewhere . . . and interpret them in harmony with the truth [literally: the truths; *al-ḥaqā'iq*]"; he would show how rabbinic aggada reflects the truths on which men of science and philosophy have expended endless time and energy. In doing so, he would identify which pieces of aggada should be accepted at face value, which should be taken figuratively (*mathal*), and which, although apparently represented in the classic texts as events that actually occurred, in fact only portray things that had been dreamt.[75] The interpretations that Maimonides intended to offer would not be arbitrary, for he would support them from the "words" of the rabbis themselves. And all in all, his

[71] *Shemona Peraqim*, chapter 1, p. 376.

[72] *Guide for the Perplexed*, Introduction, p. 5b.

[73] For the term *derashot*, see above, pp. 126, 132–33.

[74] Commentary on Mishna, introduction 1.35; above p. 126.

[75] North African rabbinic scholars preceding Maimonides had read bizarre pieces of aggada as reflecting things that had been dreamt and had not actually occurred. See I. Ta-Shma, *Ha-Sifrut ha-Parshanit la-Talmud* (Jerusalem 1999) 1.135; 141.

book would "explain many beliefs."[76] Since his aim had been to disclose how rabbinic aggada embodies, and never contradicts, philosophic truth, Maimonides would later recall having decided on the title: "Book of Harmonization." On the later occasion he makes clear that the book on *derashot*, like his *Book of Prophecy*, had been intended for a broad readership.[77]

We get a glimmering of the kind of aggadic material that he planned to interpret when he singles out "the *derashot* of [the tractate of the Babylonian Talmud entitled] *Berakot* and the *derashot* of the chapter [of tractate *Sanhedrin* which is entitled] *Ḥeleq* " as prime instances of rabbinic aggada not to be taken literally.[78] Some of the aggadic passages in the two tractates which he would have had in mind are easy to spot.

In the tractate *Berakot*, for example, God is depicted as praying, as wearing phylacteries, as bemoaning the destruction of the Holy Temple and the exile of His people, as asking the high priest to bless Him, as roaring like a lion, and as causing earthquakes by letting enormous tears fall into the sea, by clapping his hands, by groaning, or by kicking the firmament.[79] Chapter *Ḥeleq* in the tractate *Sanhedrin* consists largely of miscellaneous midrashic and nonmidrashic aggada, some forty pages in all. We there encounter a debate that the "earth" and the "prince of the world" conducted in the presence of God with the object of persuading Him to undertake one action or another; a scene in which God took hold of Jeroboam ben Nebat's coat and invited him to join King David and Himself in a stroll through Paradise, whereupon Jeroboam declined because he learned that David would walk ahead of him; the experience of a seafarer who observed the "ministering angels" sawing slabs of jewels and pearls for the construction of the future Jerusalem; and the information that Northern Israel suffered its catastrophic drought because the prophet Elijah had been handed the "key to rain" and used it to punish King Ahab and his realm.[80] Maimonides could very well have read God's bemoaning the destruction of the Temple, the debate between the earth and the prince of the world, the "key to rain," and the story about Jeroboam ben Nebat—with its obvious ethical lesson—figuratively. He could have taken the story of the ministering angels' sawing slabs of jewels and pearls for the future Jerusalem as a dream. How he would have handled God's causing earthquakes by groaning, kicking the

[76]Commentary on the Mishna (n. 20 above), *Sanhedrin*, chapter 10, introduction, 4.209; 10:1 (seventh principle), 4.213.

[77]*Guide for the Perplexed*, Introduction, p. 5b.

[78]Commentary on the Mishna, *Sanhedrin*, chapter 10, introduction, p. 201. In the *Treatise on Resurrection* (n. 2 above) 3, Maimonides likewise calls attention to the errors into which one falls by taking the anthropomorphisms in tractate *Berakot* literally.

[79]BT *Berakot* 3a (taking Jeremiah 25:30 literally), 6a, 7a, 59a

[80]BT *Sanhedrin* 94a, 100a, 102a, 113a. Other passages in BT *Sanhedrin* that Maimonides undoubtedly thought needed to be interpreted are 103b, the abominations committed by King Jehoiakim, and 105a, the method whereby Balaam, the Midianite prophet, performed his soothsaying.

firmament, or performing the other actions that one would scarcely expect from an incorporeal deity is hard to guess.[81]

Besides the topics noted so far which—according to the Commentary on the Mishna—were earmarked for the *Book of Prophecy* and the book on the interpretation of *derashot*, there were still other subjects that Maimonides wanted to expound for readers. The ones he mentions are general philosophic propositions needed for understanding the phenomenon of prophecy and the difference between Moses' prophecy and the prophecy of the other biblical prophets. To cover them even concisely would, he avers, require more than "a hundred leaves," that is, two hundred pages. Since these other subjects revolved around the phenomenon of prophecy, we might suppose that he would have wanted to treat them in his *Book of Prophecy*. He nevertheless writes that he had not yet decided whether to take them up "in the book of the interpretation of *derashot* . . . , in the *Book of Prophecy*," or perhaps in still a third book devoted specifically to the "foundations" in question.[82]

His original plans for expounding the nonlegal side of the Jewish religion thus centered on sacred texts—prophecies recorded in Scripture and rabbinic aggada—and he planned to explore those texts within the framework of the Arabic Aristotelian philosophy that was regnant in his day.

Well over a decade passed before he brought his early plans to fruition, and by then he viewed things in a somewhat different light. In the Commentary on the Mishna, he states that he had already "begun" his *Book of Prophecy*. At a later date, in the introduction to the *Guide for the Perplexed*, he mentions that years earlier he had started work on two of the projects, the *Book of Prophecy* and the *Book of Harmonization*, and he had "written a little." It is here that he describes the *Book of Prophecy* as having had for its purpose the exegesis of abstruse parts of the prophecies recorded in Scripture. The *Book of Harmonization*, he writes here, was to have been an explication of rabbinic *derashot* "whose outer garb stands in contradiction with the truth and in opposition to reason."

Soon after starting on the two books, he continues in the introduction to the *Guide*, he found that he had placed himself in an impossible predicament. Their purpose was to set forth, for all to see, the inner meaning of prophetic texts and the inner meaning of aggadic statements that seem to contradict the truth. Yet the inner meaning is in both instances too sensitive to be disclosed to the unenlightened. The books would have had the function of revealing what may not be revealed, and Maimonides therefore decided to abandon them.

[81] R. Hai Gaon (tenth and eleventh centuries) and R. Hananeel (eleventh century) interpret the descriptions of the etiology of earthquakes as metaphorical expressions of God's concern for the fate of the Israelite nation. See *Oṣar ha-Geonim*, ed. B. Lewin (Haifa 1928), part 1 (*Responsa*) 131, and part 3 (*Appendix*) 63. In *Guide for the Perplexed* 1.29, p. 60a, Maimonides writes that the prophets' description of God as roaring is a metaphor for the downfall of some individual or group.

[82] Commentary on the Mishna, *Sanhedrin* 10:1 (seventh principle of faith) p. 213.

He nevertheless assures readers that he would, in the course of the *Guide*, clarify the nature of the prophetic phenomenon, the "degrees" of prophecy, and the figurative language employed by the scriptural prophets, albeit in a different fashion from what he originally planned. Although he makes no mention of salvaging anything from the project of explicating rabbinic aggada, he does, as occasions arise throughout the book, offer allegorical interpretations of a number of aggadic passages; a few will come up as we proceed. Finally, in what could be a reference to the additional topics requiring more than two hundred pages if they are to be covered properly, he writes that he would "restrict" himself to "stating the foundations of faith and [other] truths concisely and with an allusiveness bordering on explicitness, as I stated them . . . in the *Mishneh Torah*."[83]

Authors often write the introductions to their books after having completed the books themselves. Maimonides almost surely wrote the introduction to the *Mishneh Torah* after finishing the book and very possibly followed the same procedure in other works. He, however, composed the introduction to the *Guide for the Perplexed* in a form ready for circulation before writing the book.[84] When he spells out in the introduction precisely what he wanted to accomplish in the *Guide*, he is therefore telling us what his plans and motives were as he began to put pen to paper. He is not looking back after completing the book and recalling what he had done.

He states that he had two objects in view and that both of them concerned the prophecies recorded in Scripture. In pursuing the two objects, he would provide "the key to understanding everything that the prophets have said" and resolve "most of the difficulties" that a "man of intelligence" encounters in Scripture (*sharīᶜa*).[85]

The first object was to explain words in the prophetic books which are often understood wrongly, with the result that confusion sets in.[86] What he particularly has in mind is anthropomorphic descriptions of God. As he explains later in the book, Scripture describes God anthropomorphically because it addresses everyone, including the majority of mankind who cannot "at first thought" grasp the existence of anything apart from physical objects; in order to convince everyone of the existence of God, Scripture "speaks in conformity with the language of men" and describes God in physical terms.[87] It should be sressed that Maimonides refuses to allow even the uneducated and unenlightened to wallow in error. As soon as they learn to recognize the existence of God, they are to be weaned away from their false conceptions as far as possible and taught at the very least that God is not a physical being.[88]

[83] *Guide for the Perplexed*, Introduction, pp. 5b–6a.
[84] N. 93 below.
[85] *Guide for the Perplexed*, Introduction, pp. 6a, 9a.
[86] *Guide for the Perplexed* 2b–3a.
[87] *Guide for the Perplexed* 1.26.
[88] *Guide for the Perplexed* 1.35.

As examples of problematic words that are explained by Maimonides, we may take the terms *image* (*ṣelem*) and *likeness* (*demut*) in the verse where God announces: "Let us make man in Our image, after Our likeness." "People," Maimonides writes, "suppose that the term *image* in Hebrew denotes a thing's shape and outline" and they conclude that since God made man in His image, God has the shape and outline of a man, with a face, hands, and the like. God, in their benighted thinking, is merely larger and more luminous than man and composed not of flesh and blood but of a superior material. Those committing the error even suppose that to believe anything else would be to ignore an express pronouncement of Scripture and tantamount to denying the existence of God. In order to remove doubts arising out of the application of the terms *image* and *likeness* to God, Maimonides shows from Scripture itself that the primary sense of the Hebrew word *image* is not the external shape of a thing but its inner essence, and that the Hebrew word *likeness* denotes an inner, not an external, resemblance. When Scripture relates that God made man in His image and likeness, it therefore teaches not that God has a physical shape like man's but that, to a certain extent, man's essence resembles God's. The resemblance, in Maimonides' view, lies in man's having been created with the power to think intellectual thoughts, much as God consists in pure thought.[89]

Maimonides' second object in composing the *Guide for the Perplexed* builds on the first. Besides interpreting individual words in Scripture, he planned to clarify scriptural passages that were designed to be read figuratively but which again are often read wrongly. Scripture relates, for instance, that the patriarch Jacob dreamt of a ladder reaching to heaven, on which angels ascended and descended, and at the top of which God stood. The ignorant may regard the picturesque, Chagall-like tableau as an exact representation of the world above ours. In reality, God and the angels do not exist within physical space, angels do not climb, and God does not stand anywhere, certainly not on top of ladders. Jacob's ladder is a profound allegory, which Maimonides interprets in two ways. It epitomizes the structure of existence while also alluding to the process whereby prophets receive an inspiration from above and then "descend" to earth in order to instruct their less enlightened brethren.[90]

In connection with the second of his objects, Maimonides gives particular attention to two sections of Scripture which we have encountered before, the sections known as the *account of creation* and the *account of the chariot*, that is to say, the creation story at the beginning of the Book of Genesis and the vision of a divine chariot in the Book of Ezekiel. As the *Guide* progresses, he refers several times to his objects in writing the book and places more and more weight on his

[89] *Guide for the Perplexed* 1.1. Maimonides adds the qualification that "in truth" there is no resemblance between man and God.

[90] *Guide for the Perplexed*, Introduction, pp. 3a and 7b, taken together with *Guide* 1.15 and 2.10.

desire to explain "what can be explained regarding the account of creation and account of the chariot."[91]

The *Guide for the Perplexed* sets itself apart from Maimonides' original plan for a *Book of Prophecy*—where, he also said, he wanted to expound abstruse passages in the scriptural prophecies—by the readership he envisaged. He had foreseen a broad readership for the *Book of Prophecy*. By contrast, he stresses in the introduction to the *Guide* that his exegesis of Scripture is now not intended for the ordinary run of mankind, although it is possible even for them to benefit from it. Nor is his exegesis intended for complete beginners in philosophy or for students of rabbinic law who do not look beyond their legal studies.

The *Guide* is written instead for a "religious man" who believes in the truth of the Torah and is of good moral character, who has studied philosophy and assimilated the philosophic ideal, and who is torn in opposite directions. The man cannot decide whether to follow his intellect and reject the apparent meaning of words and problematic passages in Scripture when they conflict with what his intellect affirms, thereby—so he imagines—betraying the "foundations" of the Torah; or whether to accept the apparent meaning of the words and problematic passages and turn his back on his intellect. Maimonides will lead such a man out of his "bewilderment," his "heartache," and his "enormous perplexity," by showing that the problematic words have multiple meanings and when they are understood correctly, the conflict between them and the determinations of intellect vanishes; and, again, by deciphering passages in the prophetic books which are to be taken figuratively, not at face value, and often merely by pointing out that a given passage is to be read figuratively and letting the reader work things out for himself. Since Maimonides was not concerned with the general run of mankind who "go about in darkness" and cannot see the truth despite the brightness with which it shines, the

[91] In *Guide for the Perplexed* 2:2, Maimonides remarks: "The intent of the present work . . . [as] I made clear to you . . . in the introduction, . . . is to explain doubtful matters in Scripture [*sharī*ᶜ*a*] and to bring out the truth latent in Scripture's underlying core." He could have expressed himself more clearly; still, by "doubtful matters" he apparently is referring to words in Scripture with multiple meanings, while the "truths latent in Scripture's underlying core" are apparently philosophic and scientific propositions uncovered through allegorical interpretation. A few lines later in the same chapter, he writes: "You know from the introduction to the present work that its axis turns upon explaining what can be explained regarding the account of creation and the account of the chariot and in explaining doubtful matters related to prophecy and knowledge of God." The end of the sentence again leaves something to be desired. But the "doubtful matters related to prophecy" could, as before, be words in Scripture with multiple meanings, and "knowledge of God" could be the philosophic propositions regarding God which lead persons committed to the surface meaning of Scripture into perplexity. In *Guide* 2.29, Maimonides writes: "The first [that is to say, the primary] object of the present book is to explain what can be explained regarding the account of creation and the account of the chariot." The opening sentence of *Guide* 3, reads: "I have made clear more than once that the main object in the present work is to explain what can be explained regarding the account of creation and the account of the chariot, while taking into consideration the reader for whom the book is written."

number of those whom he expected to rescue from perplexity was tiny, as few as one in 10,000. He gives his book the title "Guide for the Perplexed" because it is written for persons beset with the perplexities described.[92]

Additional light on the kind of reader that Maimonides had in view is provided in the dedicatory preface preceding the introduction from which I have been quoting. He dedicates the *Guide* to Joseph ben Judah and promises to send portions to Joseph in Syria as they are completed. Evidence that he kept the promise comes in a subsequent letter in which he informs Joseph that he was now sending him six fascicles, comprising all of Part One.[93]

The dedication relates that Maimonides had for some time considered a composition along the lines of the *Guide for the Perplexed* but had left it in abeyance; whether he is thinking back to his original plans for two or three books on the nonlegal side of the Jewish religion or is referring to a subsequent conception closer to the *Guide* in its present form is unsaid. The immediate catalyst for his finally putting pen to paper was Joseph's departure from Egypt. Maimonides explains: When Joseph arrived in Fustat, he showed himself to be eager and deserving, worthy of being trained in science and philosophy and initiated into the "secrets of the prophetic books." Maimonides—perhaps utilizing the opportunity in order to test his ideas on pedagogy—devised a step-by-step curriculum for the newcomer. He had Joseph start with the study of mathematics and logic and looked forward to the day when his pupil would arrive at the culmination of the curriculum and enter upon the study of metaphysics. But Joseph never reached the final stage during his stay in Fustat. Maimonides recalls that Joseph pressed to be instructed in "metaphysical matters" and wanted in particular to learn whether the metaphysical arguments of the Kalam school are genuine "demonstrations" or possess lesser probative force. The young man was "perplexed" and in a state of "bewilderment," and Maimonides admired his "noble soul." Maimonides nevertheless remained firm and continued to insist on his pupil's plodding systematically through the curriculum designed for him.[94] Anyone who detects a patronizing tone in Maimonides' words has not misread.

Whenever a suitable occasion arose during the period that the two were together, he did allow Joseph glimpses into the meaning of abstruse scriptural and aggadic texts. But he never went beyond hint and allusion and he resisted Joseph's desire

[92]*Guide for the Perplexed*, Introduction, pp. 3a–b, 4b, 6a, 8b, 9b.

[93]Moses ben Maimon, *Epistulae* (n. 66 above) 67. Maimonides remarks that he was sending Joseph six fascicles making up the "whole" (*tamām*) of Part One of the *Guide*, as well as a copy of the introduction, since he could not recall whether he had already sent the introduction; that is to say, he could not recall whether he sent Joseph the introduction immediately after writing it. He thus composed the introduction in a form ready to be circulated before starting to write the book. Joshua Blau has informed me that at the time in Egypt a fascicle (*kurrāsa*) would contain twenty pages. Six fascicles would contain 120 pages, which could be enough for Part One in its entirety.

[94]*Guide for the Perplexed*, Dedicatory Preface; see, further, below, p. 522. Maimonides insists on the same step-by-step curriculum in his Commentary on the Mishna, *Ḥagiga* 2:1.

for a fuller exegesis of Scripture and aggada, just as he resisted the latter's desire to jump ahead in his scientific and philosophic studies. When Joseph left Egypt before completing the curriculum designed for him—there is no way of knowing how old he was at the time and how many years he had spent with Maimonides—Maimonides decided to communicate in written form what he had never reached the point of divulging face-to-face. The *Guide for the Perplexed* is the outgrowth of that decision.

The dedication of the *Guide* to Joseph ben Judah is more than a mere courtesy. Maimonides accompanied the *Guide* with a three-page letter in flowery rhymed Hebrew prose in which he expresses his affection for Joseph, extols his qualities, and states again that the book was written for him.[95] At frequent junctures in the body of the *Guide* he addresses the reader directly,[96] in a number of the instances Joseph is clearly the person being addressed, and Joseph could very well be the person addressed in all of them. One passage nicely brings out the attitude of master toward disciple. Maimonides reminds his reader, plainly Joseph, of a time when they studied astronomy together; he recalls that he explained certain technical features of celestial motion while withholding other features in order not to complicate what he wanted the student to take away from the lesson.[97] In a chapter where the context leads Maimonides to the physiology of the brain and the implications it has for medicine, he makes a few observations and remarks: "But you know all this, and nothing will be gained by explaining it at greater length";[98] Joseph had studied medicine. At another point, he warns his reader against being seduced by the doctrines of the Sabians, Chasdeans, and Chaldeans, and then appends the qualification that the warning was not in fact "necessary for someone of your caliber, . . . since you have sufficient knowledge of the sciences to protect your mind" against their inanity and myths.[99] The warning was only needed for persons lacking a scientific background into whose hands the *Guide* might fall. In a context where arguments from Aristotle's physics are at issue, Maimonides tells his reader: "I have composed the *Guide* based on what I know your attainments are" in the study of philosophy.[100] In still one more passage, he remarks: "I do not expect that you" will have any difficulty with statements that he had just made regarding the imaginative faculty of the human soul; for those statements presuppose "someone who has philosophized and understands . . . the [human] soul and its faculties."[101] The study of the human soul is a branch of physical science, and the last two quotations, assuming them to be intended for

[95]Moses ben Maimon, *Epistulae* 12–16.

[96]In addition to the passages that follow, see *Guide for the Perplexed* 1.65; 2.25; 3, introduction; 29, p. 64b; 41, p. 88b.

[97]*Guide for the Perplexed* 2.24, pp. 51b, 53a.

[98]*Guide for the Perplexed* 2.36, 78a.

[99]*Guide for the Perplexed* 3.29, p. 66a.

[100]*Guide for the Perplexed* 2.14 (beginning).

[101]*Guide for the Perplexed* 1.68 (end).

Joseph, therefore indicate that he had made progress in the physical sciences. The final lines of the last chapter of the *Guide* sound as if they too are intended for a specific person, who could only be Joseph ben Judah. Maimonides writes there that he had tried to convey what would be "particularly beneficial for persons who are of your type" and he expresses the hope that "through careful study, you grasp everything I have incorporated into the book."[102]

Very few books are composed solely for a single individual, and the *Guide for the Perplexed* was written with more than one reader in view. The dedication of the book to Joseph, the final lines of the book which were just quoted, and the accompanying letter in rhymed prose all include the information that Maimonides was writing as well for the "small number" of persons who resemble Joseph in background and education.[103] Furthermore, Joseph could not possibly have been in Maimonides' company for any period of time, or for that matter have read the first chapter of the *Mishneh Torah*, without learning that words in Scripture implying physical qualities are applied to God in an alternative, nonphysical sense. Thus even if Joseph was still disturbed by anthropomorphisms, he did not fully meet the description of the perplexed for whom Maimonides says that he produced the *Guide*. Maimonides' dedication of the book to his student should nonetheless not be ignored. It limns the physiognomy of an actual reader whom he had before his eyes as he wrote.

He has stated unequivocally that his two objects in the *Guide for the Perplexed* were exegetical. The book, he notes, will contain chapters that do not immediately and openly touch on the twin objects; he stresses at once, however, that those chapters are included solely because they prepare the ground for grasping a term in Scripture or for appreciating how a section of Scripture must be construed.[104] When "the foundations of faith and [other] truths" come up he planned to discuss them not in depth but "concisely and with an allusiveness bordering on explicitness," as he did in the *Mishneh Torah*.[105] If he is to be believed, the most influential work in the history of Jewish philosophy was conceived as an exercise in scriptural exegesis, not as a philosophic treatise, and philosophic issues were to be taken up in only a cursory and allusive manner. The "perplexed" in the book's title were not highly sophisticated intellectuals grappling with large questions such as the cataclysmic clash of reason and faith. They were men caught in a quandary of lesser dimensions—the skirmish between a naiveté that led them to read Scripture too literally and the demands of their intellect, which persuaded them, for instance, that God is incorporeal. The one reader whom the author identifies was a man who had made progress in philosophy and science yet had not, during the time

[102] *Guide for the Perplexed* 3.54 (end).

[103] *Guide for the Perplexed*, Dedicatory Preface. Similarly in a letter to Joseph, in Moses ben Maimon, *Epistulae* 16.

[104] *Guide for the Perplexed*, Introduction, p. 6a.

[105] Above, p. 327.

he and Maimonides were together, demonstrated that he was quite ready to enter the inner sanctum of metaphysics or to be exposed to a full-blown philosophic exegesis of Scripture.

Few students of the *Guide for the Perplexed* are willing to take Maimonides at his word. The great majority find it hard to accept that the book was designed as an essay in scriptural exegesis,[106] to recognize that the perplexity alluded to in the title is the consequence of nothing more momentous than an overly literal reading of Scripture, to acknowledge that the single identifiable reader for whom the book was geared was a man who had not completed the curriculum laid out for him, who had not, so to speak, graduated from college. Maimonides could, of course, have been dissembling in his introduction and misrepresenting his motives for writing the book; on occasion, authors behave in that perverse fashion. He could have himself been blind to his motives. Or, after starting to write with a certain aim, he could have turned aside and pursued other objects in addition or instead. Granted that any of those alternatives is conceivable—especially the last, since the finished product contains much more philosophy than Maimonides promised in the introduction—something is surely to be said for giving weight to what a highly intelligent author states were the reasons for which, and the readers for whom, he composed his book.

The following pages will treat the *Guide for the Perplexed* as a fabric woven in the main from three strands: the scriptural exegesis that Maimonides identified as his twofold object in writing the *Guide*; the strictly philosophic discussions, which are scattered through the book and turn out to be substantial; and sections that are more properly ideological than philosophical and carry forward Maimonides' efforts, met in his rabbinic works, to place a spiritualized and rationalist construction on the Jewish religion. Multiple themes in a literary work do not ordinarily wrap themselves in tightly sealed and isolated cocoons, and nothing of the sort happens in the *Guide for the Perplexed*. The exegesis of scriptural texts presupposes conclusions that will be reached in the strictly philosophic parts. The scriptural exegesis and the philosophical discussions contribute to the third strand, the spiritualizing and rationalizing of the Jewish religion. There are passages that can as plausibly be assigned to one of the strands as to another. The lines are blurred.

Moreover, while Maimonides was unusually successful at dissecting specific issues, breaking them down into their components, and bringing out their presuppositions, he could also lose focus and digress wantonly. Both his analytic skills and his penchant for digression were in evidence in his Commentary on the

[106]An exception is S. Klein-Braslavy, who has written two books on Maimonides' interpretation of the creation story—the account of creation—in the Book of Genesis. A. Ravitzky, "The Secrets of Maimonides," reprinted in his *History and Faith* (Amsterdam 1996) 284–85, detects a recent growth of interest in Maimonides' biblical exegesis. That, however, is by no means the same as the recognition that Maimonides' object in writing the *Guide for the Perplexed* was biblical exegesis.

Mishna[107] and they are openly in evidence in the *Guide for the Perplexed*, a work that he composed during a period when he was constantly distracted by day-to-day practical obligations. Where the *Guide* takes up neatly circumscribed philosophic or religious issues, the analytic and expository gifts shine forth. But as the book advances from chapter to chapter, it is poorly organized, and Maimonides' train of thought repeatedly meanders into byways. As a consequence, the three strands bob in and out and have to be extricated from one another. For a proper appreciation of the *Guide for the Perplexed*, they nonetheless must be given their due.

I shall assume that Maimonides understood what he was about in writing the *Guide for the Perplexed*, although his plans appear to have broadened considerably as the book developed. It follows that while the scriptural exegesis may strike the modern reader as the least interesting and least significant of the strands, that exegesis was the author's primary concern as he envisaged his book; and as the book turned out, it remains the warp into which the other strands are woven. I shall further assume that here as elsewhere Maimonides saw himself foremost as an educator and did his best to enlighten readers of the specific type he had in view, not to mystify or mislead them. He was in the first instance addressing persons who had studied philosophy but had not finished the course and was accordingly writing a book from which he expected that someone with such a background would benefit.

The Exegetical Strand in the Guide for the Perplexed. Maimonides has told us that his objects in composing the *Guide* were exegetical. There is scarcely a page on which he does not quote one or more scriptural verses, the total number of verses quoted exceeds 1,500, and whether expressly or implicitly, he interprets almost all of them. The interpretations start in the first line of the first chapter, where he immediately takes up the verse "Let us make man in Our image, after Our likeness," which had led some to suppose that God is a body. They continue to the closing lines of the final chapter. When problematic or thought-provoking biblical passages come up, he glides into extended exegesis.

Although Maimonides never formally spells out his method in interpreting Scripture, he insists that Scripture be read not with "the imagination," as is the habit of "homilists [*darshanin*] and the sorry commentators" who pride themselves on "wordiness and long-windedness." It must be read "with the true nature of the intellect, and after [one has attained] perfection in the demonstrative sciences and knowledge of the secrets of prophecy."[108] At the level of individual verses, he allows a degree of leeway, conceding that interpretations other than his which are in harmony with correct principles may also hit the mark.[109] And he himself interpreted verses differently on different occasions. He is adamant, however, that

[107] Above, pp. 152–55.
[108] *Guide for the Perplexed* 2.29, p. 65b.
[109] *Guide for the Perplexed* 1.21, 28.

only his approach to Scripture qualifies as the "science of the Law in the true sense."[110]

He is taking the position that Scripture must be read through the prism of what the philosophic sciences teach regarding the phenomenon of prophecy and what they demonstrate about other matters—the incorporeality of God, His being free of all qualities, and the like. Readers today will see Maimonides as forcing Scripture into alien molds, but that was not his perception, and he even warns against the "inanity" of reading things into Scripture.[111] He was sure that prophets prepare themselves for their calling by mastering the philosophical sciences and although he grants that the rabbis of the classic period sometimes erred in questions of natural science, he never betrays the slightest suggestion that prophets do. He accordingly views the philosophic sciences as indispensable exegetic tools for bringing the inner intent of Scripture to light.

The first of his two objects in writing the *Guide* is concentrated in the first forty-five chapters. These form a glossary, peppered with digressions, of more than forty words in Scripture which Maimonides fears might engender perplexity in a reader who fails to realize that they have multiple meanings.[112] Later chapters in the book add a few more entries to the glossary.[113]

Almost all are terms appearing in scriptural descriptions of God. Scripture calls God a "rock." It speaks of God's face, back, foot, eye, heart, and wing, each of which, in the more common usage of the word, is something possessed by corporeal beings. It employs a number of verbs of motion and rest in describing God—to come, go up, go down, go out, return, approach, pass, stand, sit, dwell. When taken in their ordinary sense, such verbs are applicable solely to beings that exist in three-dimensional space and hence have bodies. Then, there are sundry terms that Scripture uses in connection with God which imply physicality in one way or other, such as: speaking; grieving; seeing; giving birth; and being near, on high, in place, or in possession of a throne. On the opposite side of the ledger stands the conviction of Maimonides' and those for whom he was writing—a conviction confirmed by reason and scientific demonstration—that God is an incorporeal being.

[110]*Guide for the Perplexed*, Introduction, p. 3a, where Maimonides contrasts "the science of the Law in the true sense" with the "science of the Law" in the purely legal sense.

[111]*Guide for the Perplexed*, Introduction, p. 8b.

[112]The most recurrent theme in the digressions is the need to prepare oneself properly before entering upon the study of metaphysics and even physics and then to proceed step by step. See *Guide* 1.5; 17; 21; 32-35. If the digressions are intended for Joseph ben Judah, Maimonides could be encouraging him to complete the educational curriculum that had been devised for him or else he could be explaining why Joseph had not been allowed to go on to metaphysics when the two men were together in Fustat.

[113]*Guide* 1.65: *speech*; 1.70: *riding* (Deuteronomy 33:26 and Psalms 68:5, describe God as the one "Who rideth upon the heavens"); 3.54: *wisdom*.

His set procedure is to draw upon Scripture itself to prove that the problematic word has one or more nonphysical senses in addition to the common physical acceptation. Having established that, he submits that whenever Scripture uses the word in a description of God, one of the nonphysical senses is intended.

To take an example, he devotes a chapter in the *Guide* to the term *rock.* Scripture calls God "the Rock whose work is perfect," "an everlasting Rock," and "the Rock that begot thee." Maimonides cites a passage in the Book of Isaiah where the prophet characterized the patriarch Abraham as "the rock whence ye were hewn" and he infers from there that in an extended sense, *rock* means *source*. He concludes: When Scripture calls God a rock, it uses the word in the extended, not the physical sense and teaches that God is the source of all existence outside Himself.[114] No one, not even the most literalist reader in Maimonides' day, would doubt that Scripture speaks metaphorically when calling God a rock. How many would accept Maimonides' explication of the metaphor is less certain.

While almost all the entries in Maimonides' glossary are terms used by Scripture in connection with God, there are a few exceptions. An especially enigmatic chapter is devoted to the term *adam.* Everyone familiar with the Hebrew Bible knows that *adam* is both the personal name of the first man and one of the Bible's ways of saying *human being*. In a chapter conspicuous for its brevity, Maimonides makes the obvious observation that Adam was the name of the first human. He cites scriptural verses to establish that the term *adam* can, secondly, designate the "species" man and, thirdly, a specific segment of mankind, the lower class.[115] But he does not explain why he took the trouble to comment on the word or what problem his seemingly innocuous observations are designed to resolve. Since Scripture never employs the term in descriptions of God, he cannot, in the present instance, be worried about a mistaken supposition that God is a body.

The most plausible way of understanding what he wants to say turns on the observation that *adam* sometimes designates the entire human species. The creation story contains verses such as: "Let us make *adam* [man]"; "God created the *adam* [man]"; and "the Lord God formed the *adam* [man] of the dust of the earth." If what Maimonides says elsewhere in the *Guide* is accepted at face value, he recognized the existence of an actual man named Adam at the time of creation.[116] But in the present context he appears to be intimating that verses speaking about the making, creation, and formation of *adam* have in view not the individual man of that name but mankind in general.[117] God, in other words, immediately populated the world with the human species. Such indeed is the plain meaning of chapter one

[114]*Guide for the Perplexed* 1.16. The pertinent verses in order are Deuteronomy 32:4, Isaiah 26:4, Deuteronomy 32:18, and Isaiah 51:1.

[115]*Guide for the Perplexed* 1.14, which is adapted from Ibn Janaḥ, *Sefer ha-Shorashim*, art. *a-d-m*.

[116]*Guide for the Perplexed* 1.2; 7; 3.50.

[117]See S. Klein-Braslavy, *Perush ha-Rambam le-Sippur Beriat ha-ᶜOlam* (Jerusalem 1987) 201-2, who finds a similar interpretation of the term *adam* in Abraham Ibn Ezra.

of Genesis when read in isolation from chapter two; it is not until chapter two that Scripture describes the making of the first man and woman.

Later Maimonides would state openly and without hesitation that the biblical story of the creation of the world over a period of six days is not intended literally. He could speak openly there since he was able to point to opinions along the same lines recorded in the classical rabbinic sources.[118] But because he feared that his reading of the making of *adam* might raise hackles among literalists, he expresses himself obliquely here, just as he merely hinted at the true meaning of abstruse matters in Scripture during his discussions with Joseph ben Judah when the two were together in Fustat.

Maimonides' second object in the *Guide* builds on the first and consists in elucidating biblical passages that must be understood figuratively and, in some instances, merely identifying them and leaving the reader to work out the deeper meaning by himself. A scriptural passage that we found Maimonides taking figuratively was the description of the ladder extending up to heaven in Jacob's dream.[119] It may be worthwhile to consider a few additional examples.

To return once again to the verse in Genesis where God says: "Let us make *adam* in Our image and after Our likeness," Maimonides has determined that one sense of the term *adam*—and the sense apparently intended in the verse—is the "species" man. He moreover placed a philosophic construction on man's having been made in God's *image* and *likeness*; on his reading, those terms signify that man, the human species, was fashioned with an essence consisting in the ability to think intellectual thoughts much as God consists in pure thought. The scriptural verse poses still another problem that demands to be addressed: To whom could God have been speaking when He said "let *us* make *adam*"?

It is axiomatic for Maimonides that the deity does not literally talk to, or consult with anyone or anything.[120] The words "let *us* make," like so much else in Scripture, must therefore be taken figuratively. Maimonides interprets them as an allusion to the means whereby man was made. He explains that God acted through the mediacy of natural forces in the universe and particularly through the hierarchy of supernal incorporeal beings that bridge the gap between Him and the physical universe; those incorporeal beings are called *intelligences* in the language of the philosophers and *angels* in religious parlance.[121] If I have read Maimonides correctly, the sentence "Let us make *adam* in Our image and after Our likeness" says the following when fully understood: In the course of creation God brought forth the human species, a species whose essence embodies the ability to think

[118] *Guide for the Perplexed* 2.17, 36b; 2.30; 3.29, 66a; *Genesis Rabba* 1.14–15, and parallels.

[119] Above, p. 328.

[120] *Guide for the Perplexed* 1.65.

[121] See p. 241 above.

intellectual thoughts in a manner somewhat similar to the manner in which God consists in pure intellectual thought; and God carried out his plan through the intermediacy of the supernal incorporeal beings and other natural forces in the universe.[122] The scriptural verse has been freed of its problematic features and reemerges in precise rationalist garb. Some poetry may have been lost in the process.

When Scripture relates that Moses went up to Mount Sinai, he made certain requests and God responded to them. One was: "Show me now Thy ways that I may know Thee, to the end that I may find grace in Thy sight," and God presently replied: "I will make all My goodness pass before thee . . . and I will be gracious to whom I will be gracious and will show mercy on whom I will show mercy." In Maimonides' interpretation, Moses' request presupposes two truths, first that to find grace in God's sight, a person must not "merely fast and pray" but must acquire knowledge of God, and second that man can know God through His ways. Persons who, by contrast, are ignorant of God become the object of His anger—figuratively, of course, since the deity is not subject to emotions—and are rejected by Him. God's reply that He is gracious and shows mercy reflects the further proposition that God's gracious and merciful actions are instances of His ways: The actions through which God manifests Himself in the universe are His ways, and it is through them that He is known.[123]

Moses made a second request, with the words: "Show me, I pray Thee, Thy glory." God's reply is found in the sentences: "Thou canst not see My face. . . . Behold . . . thou shalt stand upon the rock. And . . . while My glory passeth by, . . . I will cover thee with My hand. . . . And I will take away My hand and thou shalt see My back, but My face shall not be seen." On Maimonides' reading, Moses was now requesting knowledge going beyond God's ways; he was appealing for knowledge of God's glory and face, His very essence. The reply he received was that not even he was capable of comprehending God's essence, for the divine essence is intrinsically unknowable to man.[124] Moses was nonetheless afforded a view of God's "back," and God's back symbolizes the things that He has created; the figurative language embodies the proposition that what God has created constitutes the data from which man can infer everything humanly possible to know about God. Moses' cryptic requests at Sinai and the cryptic replies he received hence teach that the aim of human life is knowledge of God, that man cannot attain knowledge of the divine essence, yet that man can know God indirectly, through His ways and through what He has created.

The scriptural passage says something further. It recounts that Moses stood "upon the rock," and that detail in Maimonides' hands is more than a colorful

[122] *Guide for the Perplexed* 2.6.

[123] *Guide for the Perplexed* 1.54. The scriptural passages are from Exodus 33, and I have matched God's replies to Moses' two requests as Maimonides does.

[124] In other words, the pure thought that God consists in is unknowable.

flourish. He has told us that when the term *rock* is applied to God, it means *source*. The instruction to Moses to "stand upon the rock" signifies that he would be able to grasp the manner in which God is a rock, the source of all existence outside of Himself.[125]

The *Guide for the Perplexed* interprets dozens of verses in a similar vein. In the divine names that God revealed to Moses at the burning bush, Maimonides finds an allusion to a technical philosophic proof for the existence of God; God taught the proof to Moses, and Moses would subsequently teach it to the elders of Israel as a step in establishing his credentials as God's chosen representative.[126] The adulterous wife in the Book of Proverbs is an allegory for the material substratum of the physical world. Like a promiscuous woman, matter in the physical world cannot exist without form—the male principle!—but it is unfaithful to any single form, for it constantly sheds one form and embraces another.[127] The biblical Book of Job becomes, in Maimonides' hands, a discourse on the different positions that can be taken concerning divine providence: Job himself takes the Aristotelian position, one of his so-called friends represents the position of the Mutazilite branch of Kalam, a second friend represents the position of the Asharite branch of Kalam, and the third friend, an unsophisticated version of the position of the Torah.[128] Various verses of Scripture speak of God's "good treasure house" and of the "books" in which God inscribes the names of those who find favor with Him and from which He blots out the names of those who sin against Him. "All that is metaphorical."[129] And so on.

Scripture sometimes labels what one or another prophet saw as a vision. Maimonides' understanding of the nature of prophecy and his conception of angels as incorporeal beings who exist outside of time and space entail that certain incidents ostensibly depicted by Scripture as taking place in the external world were also visions present solely to the consciousness of those who experienced them. Thus the three figures who appeared at the entrance to Abraham's tent and foretold the future birth of a son were not beings that occupied three-dimensional space, opened their mouths, and emitted sound waves. They were a vision experienced by Abraham. The angels who spoke to Sarah's maidservant Hagar in the desert, Jacob's wrestling with a numinous figure on his return from his father-in-law's house to the land of Canaan, the mysterious figure who directed Joseph to the location where his brothers were camping, Balaam's confrontation with his she-ass and the words they spoke to one another, the angel of the Lord who informed

[125] *Guide for the Perplexed* 1.16 (end); 21; 38; 54. Cf. *Mishneh Torah*: *H. Yesode ha-Torah* 1.10. I have assumed that Maimonides had the second half of Exodus 33:19 in mind even though he does not quote it.

[126] *Guide for the Perplexed* 1.63.

[127] *Guide for the Perplexed* 3.8. See Proverbs 7.

[128] *Guide for the Perplexed* 3.23.

[129] *Guide for the Perplexed* 2.47. The verses are Deuteronomy 28:12; Exodus 33:32–33; Psalms 69:29.

Samson's mother that she would bear a son, the appearance of the angel Gabriel to Daniel—these and other incidents recorded in Scripture were visions and not events that actually occurred in the external world.[130]

The exegetic strand in the *Guide for the Perplexed* reaches its climax for Maimonides when he takes up the *account of creation*, that is to say, the creation story in the Book of Genesis, and a number of chapters later in the *Guide*, the *account of the chariot*, that is, the vision of the prophet Ezekiel. The Mishna corpus and the two Talmuds know of an esoteric midrashic exposition of each of the scriptural sections, and writers have sometimes transferred the names of the two scriptural sections to the expositions of them: *Account of creation* sometimes becomes the name of the rabbinic exposition of the scriptural creation story rather than of the scriptural story itself, and *account of the chariot* becomes the name of the rabbinic exposition of Ezekiel's chariot vision rather than of the vision as Scripture depicts it. I did not detect that usage in the *Guide for the Perplexed*.

The Mishna discloses nothing, and the Talmuds little, about the rabbis' interpretation of the two scriptural sections. The classic rabbinic sources were intent on concealing, not disseminating the mysteries. They moreover insist on an even thicker veil of secrecy for exegesis of the account of the chariot than for exegesis of the account of creation. They prohibit expounding either of the two accounts to more than a single person at a time, but in the case of the former they add the further provisos that the student with whom secrets are shared must be "wise and capable of understanding things by himself" and that he is to be given only "subject headings" and left to work out the rest on his own.[131]

Maimonides assumes that the rabbis' arcane interpretation of the scriptural account of the chariot was never recorded in a book and the oral tradition through which it was once handed down from generation to generation had been lost with the passage of time; he makes a similar assumption about the rabbis' interpretation of the account of creation. He acknowledges that he had not had the benefit of "divine inspiration." Yet he was confident that his study of the prophets and rabbis together with his knowledge of philosophy and natural science had enabled him to lift the veil, penetrate the secret of the two scriptural sections, and reconstitute the rabbinic expositions of them from fragments preserved in the classic rabbinic texts.[132]

In his Commentary on the Mishna, Maimonides stated flatly that the "account of creation" is nothing other than the "science of physics," and the "account of the

[130]*Guide for the Perplexed* 2.42. A similar notion was expressed by Abraham Ibn Ezra, Commentary on Hosea 1:2.

[131]Mishna, *Ḥagiga* 2:1; BT *Ḥagiga* 13a. I am following Maimonides' understanding of BT *Ḥagiga* 13a, which suggests a different text from the one in the standard editions. R. Ḥananeel's commentary also seems to imply a different version of the talmudic text from the one that is preserved, and Maimonides may have had the same version.

[132]*Guide for the Perplexed* 3, introduction.

chariot" is the "science of metaphysics."[133] He expressed himself in like fashion in the *Mishneh Torah.*[134] In the *Guide for the Perplexed*, he puts the thought as follows: The scriptural account of creation recasts the "science of physics" in "metaphors, riddles, and dark language," and the rabbis likewise treated the subject in "riddles and metaphors." The scriptural account of Ezekiel's chariot and the rabbinic treatment of the scriptural account are a figurative version of the science of metaphysics. Maimonides does concede that he may be mistaken here and there in his reading of the scriptural accounts and in reconstituting the rabbinic interpretation[135] but he limits the concession to details at the most. He does not budge on his overall insight.[136]

Access, in his view, must be restricted not only to physics and metaphysics in their scriptural and rabbinic versions; it must be restricted to the versions taught by philosophers as well, the reason in the case of physics—the account of creation—being that it is the gate through which metaphysics is approached. He goes as far as to suggest that the very nature of physics and metaphysics conspires to conceal them: They are "great secrets," which no human mind can fathom fully. Authors of formal philosophic treatises cannot help but write so obscurely that it is hard to make out what they are saying. And philosophers who choose to set forth their thoughts in metaphorical language—Maimonides is thinking of works such as Plato's *Timaeus*, which we can safely assume he knew not directly but only through references to it in Aristotle or Alfarabi[137]—use that device to veil their meaning from the uninitiated.[138]

The rationale for keeping the two accounts secret is given by Maimonides in a variety of ways on different occasions. He writes that persons who lack the requisite intellectual gifts or have not prepared themselves through the requisite preliminary studies will be unable "fully to understand" what is placed before them;[139] they will fall into "idiocy and dementia";[140] they will lose respect for the rabbis who expounded the accounts of creation and the chariot;[141] they will "turn their backs" on the truth;[142] their "beliefs will become confused."[143] At one point, he resorts to an analogy between the human mind and the sense of sight. When

[133]Above, p. 161.

[134]Above, p. 244. Maimonides did not specify in either work whether he was talking about the scriptural texts or the lost rabbinic exposition of them.

[135]*Guide for the Perplexed* 1.28; 3, introduction; 4 (end).

[136]In *Guide for the Perplexed*, Introduction, 9b, Maimonides speaks of teaching "demonstrated truth" in the *Guide*.

[137]See above, p. 111.

[138]*Guide for the Perplexed*, Introduction, pp. 3b–5a; 1.17; 3, introduction, 7.

[139]*Mishneh Torah*: *H. Yesode ha-Torah* 2.12; 4.11.

[140]Commentary on the Mishna, *Ḥagiga* 2:1.

[141]Commentary on the Mishna (n. 20 above), introduction, p. 36.

[142]Commentary on the Mishna, introduction, p. 35.

[143]Commentary on the Mishna, *Ḥagiga* 2:1.

someone strains his sight by attempting to view objects beyond his power, the person loses the ability to see objects that previously caused him no difficulty; fantastic images (*khayālāt*) may, moreover, take shape in his field of vision. By the same token, a person who strains his mind trying to comprehend theoretical subjects that are beyond his power loses the ability to grasp what previously occasioned him no difficulty. The light of his intellect will be extinguished, and without the guidance of a healthy intellect, he will be overcome by irrational imaginings (*khayālāt*) and may even descend into immoral behavior.[144]

Circumstances joined forces to place Maimonides in a stark dilemma. God, he believed, has constructed the universe in such a fashion that "everyone who attains to a perfection" is "necessarily led to emanate it on others"; hence any human being who is able to unravel "a portion of these secrets" is driven to communicate "some" of what he discovers.[145] No less weighty was Maimonides' image of himself as the sole member of his generation to have discovered the key to the pertinent passages in the Books of Genesis and Ezekiel. If he selfishly withheld his discoveries from the "perplexed" and those discoveries went with him to the grave, he would despoil worthy coreligionists of what is rightfully theirs and begrudge the legitimate heirs their inheritance.[146] He was therefore inexorably drawn to do something that he asserts had never been done before, to become the first person to lay bare the scriptural and rabbinic secrets in written form and for posterity.[147] Yet he stood face to face with the various rationales for concealing the sciences of physics and metaphysics and, more important, with the rabbis' express prohibition against expounding the two scriptural accounts to more than a single qualified student at a time. How could he publish his discoveries in a book that might come into the hands of thousands, the vast majority of whom were unqualified for them?[148]

As a rule, commentators try to explicate the texts they study as transparently as possible. That was Maimonides' policy in his Commentary on the Mishna, and it has generally been his aim in the *Guide for the Perplexed*. He openly interpreted the dialogues between God and Moses as philosophic discussions although he realized that the unsophisticated might well be scandalized. He explicitly construed as internal visions incidents in Scripture which readers from time immemorial had been certain were events that occurred in the external world. An exception was his gingerly handling of the term *adam*, but *adam*, significantly, is a part of the scriptural account of creation.

To maneuver his way out of his dilemma, Maimonides developed a paradoxical commentatorial tactic. He would divulge what he had discovered regarding the

[144] *Guide for the Perplexed* 1.32.

[145] *Guide for the Perplexed* 2.29, in connection with the account of creation.

[146] *Guide for the Perplexed* 3, Introduction, in connection with the account of the chariot.

[147] *Guide for the Perplexed*, Introduction, p. 9b.

[148] *Guide for the Perplexed*, Introduction, p. 4a.

accounts of creation and the chariot in a book, while at the same time honoring the rabbis' directives by not speaking straightforwardly and fully. He would play hide-and-seek, as it were, convey his discoveries through subject headings, scatter even them through the *Guide for the Perplexed*, and unobtrusively call attention to scriptural phraseology that holds the key to underlying secrets, without spelling out what the phraseology signifies. Nonperceptive readers would miss the significance of the subject headings and overlook the hints. The perceptive would seize upon the headings, pick up the hints, and work things out by themselves.[149] Maimonides has not abandoned his role of educator and he remains intent on providing guidance to the perplexed. He settles, however, on a method for fulfilling that role without transgressing the rabbis' directives about limiting access to the two sensitive scriptural accounts. He will communicate his discoveries to those to whom he is giving guidance but will do so discreetly.

A few illustrations should again be helpful. I begin with the lesser mystery, the account of creation.

The Book of Genesis opens simply and elegantly: "In the beginning God created the heaven and the earth." It proceeds to describe the events of the first day of creation and in doing so refers to "darkness" and to the "spirit of God" that hovered over "the face of the waters." A few verses later, it recounts that on the third day, "God called the dry land 'earth.'" Maimonides makes clear that the sequence of days in the creation story is figurative and that creation in fact took place all at once.

He, like other medieval intellectuals, pictured the visible universe as geocentric and spherical, and he reads the opening verse of Genesis as a summary statement of the creation of the visible universe's two parts. "Heaven" is Scripture's designation for the immense outer region, consisting of the rotating celestial spheres and the stars and planets embedded in them; "earth" is the smaller, inner region, which comprises everything extending from the center of the world to the lower surface of the innermost celestial sphere, the sphere of the moon. The first verse of Genesis announces that God created both.

"Darkness" is Scripture's term for the physical element fire, pure elemental fire being colorless and hence dark. The "spirit of God" hovering over the waters stands for the element air, and the "waters" are obviously the element water. In subsequently declaring that God called the dry land "earth," Scripture imparts "one of the great secrets"—a secret that Maimonides shows no hesitation in disclosing. He explains that the locution "God *called* something such and such" is a scriptural device for differentiating between two things having the same name. The great secret in God's calling the dry land "earth" is that *earth* here means something different from what it did in the opening verse. In the opening verse, *earth* denoted the entire sublunar region, whereas now it denotes the fourth of the physical elements.

[149] *Guide for the Perplexed*, Introduction, p. 3b; 2.29 (end); 3, introduction.

The first few verses of Genesis teach, then, that in the act of creation, God created the two segments of the corporeal universe. Within the inner or lower segment, He created the four elements—fire, air, water, and earth—out of which all sublunar physical objects are composed.

Scripture further relates that on the second day God made a "firmament in the midst of the waters." Here again, Maimonides detects "extraordinary secrets," secrets that "must be hidden" from the "ordinary run of mankind" (*jumhūr*) yet that he again shows no qualms about disclosing: Since the four physical elements exist within the sublunar region, and since the firmament is situated in the midst of the waters, it too must be part of the sublunar region. Firmament in our verse is consequently something different from the heaven, which is Scripture's designation for the celestial region.[150] With the guidance of a couple of pieces of rabbinic aggada and what he learned from a scientific work on meteorology, Maimonides determines that the biblical firmament is a stratum of water vapor extending through the sublunar atmosphere. By locating it in the "midst of the waters," Scripture reveals that it is distinct in form both from the liquid water of oceans, rivers, and lakes, as well as from an additional stratum of water vapor situated at a higher altitude within the atmosphere.[151]

It is hard to avoid a sense of bafflement. Maimonides agonized over the propriety of making public what should be concealed. After beginning work on his *Book of Prophecy* and book on rabbinic aggada, he abandoned both because he found himself making public the inner meaning of scriptural prophecies and rabbinic aggada which are too sensitive to be disclosed to the unenlightened. He was torn between teaching what he had discovered regarding the scriptural account of creation and the rabbis' restrictions on such teaching, and his dilemma led him to design a tactic for communicating his discoveries without having the man in the street grasp the import of what he was saying. Yet he now openly discloses what he uncovered at the beginning of Genesis, repeating all the while that great secrets are at issue. And the content of his discoveries, as far as one can see, is banal and anticlimactic. One profound secret turns out to be the commonplace division of the visible universe into two parts, and a second set of secrets is the familiar Aristotelian physical theory of four sublunar elements. Maimonides discusses both straightforwardly and without obfuscation in his rabbinic writings and in the *Guide for the Perplexed* itself. A third set of secrets is the notion of two layers of water vapor in the atmosphere, which, if not exactly common knowledge, will slake the thirst of few souls craving for enlightenment in the mysteries of the universe.

As he goes on, Maimonides moves from the scriptural account of creation to pieces of rabbinic aggada which he apparently regarded as surviving fragments of

[150]Hence when Genesis 1:8 says that "God *called* the firmament heaven," it also differentiates between what *heaven* denotes here and what it usually denotes.

[151]*Guide for the Perplexed* 2.30. In *Mishneh Torah*: *H. Yesode ha-Torah* 3.10, and 4.1, Maimonides interprets the term *firmament* differently.

the ancient midrashic exposition of the scriptural account. These are aggadic items that may look bizarre but that, he assures us, are "absolutely perfect" and were "fully comprehensible" to the persons for whom they were originally intended. Because he has now turned to the rabbinic exposition and the rabbis insisted on restricting access particularly to it, and because he does not want to place himself in the category of a "revealer of a secret," he finally becomes circumspect. He nevertheless assures his reader that by presenting the aggadic items "in a certain order" and by dropping a few clues, he would render everything clear for a person "such as you."[152]

Three of the pieces of aggada should suffice for our purpose. All three revolve around the making of the first woman and the serpent's success in leading her into sin; Maimonides understood that the story of the tempting of Eve by the serpent is still part of the account of creation.[153] The scriptural narrative itself cannot help disquieting a reader of rationalist bent who is at the same time committed to the truth of Scripture, and the aggada quoted by Maimonides does not, at first appearance, improve matters.

The standard translations of the Bible recount that "God . . . took one of his [Adam's] ribs" and formed the woman, Eve, from it. The first piece of rabbinic aggada which concerns us reads Scripture differently and has it say instead that God took one of Adam's "sides." According to the rabbinic passage—which echoes a droll scene in Plato's *Symposium*—man was initially created with fully formed male and female sides that were "united back to back," like Siamese twins, the male side facing in one direction, and the female in the other. God cut the double-faced, four-legged Siamese creature down the middle, "took" the female half, and it became Eve. Maimonides quotes the rabbinic passage without interpreting it; he merely calls attention to certain features that he suggests are pregnant with significance, such as the aggadic stress on the two sides' being united with one another and yet distinct, and on Scripture's attaching the name "man" to both. Whereupon he exclaims: "How great is the ignorance of him who does not realize" that the notion of an originally androgynous human being is not frivolous but establishes a "necessary point." "The matter has now been rendered clear."[154] And he goes on to the next piece of aggada.

Whereas he was unexpectedly open in his interpretation of the initial verses of Genesis, he now has gone to the opposite extreme and expressed himself so obscurely that one cannot be entirely sure what he wants to say. At the very least, there can be no doubt that he is construing the piece of aggada figuratively. If evidence were needed, we have his citation, in the present connection, of a "great

[152] *Guide for the Perplexed* 2.30, p. 70a.

[153] *Guide for the Perplexed* 2:30, p. 70a.

[154] *Guide for the Perplexed* 2.30, pp. 70a–b. Maimonides' midrashic source is *Genesis Rabba* 8:1, and parallels. The notion of a race of originally double-faced humans who were subsequently cut in two by the deity is playfully put in the mouth of the comic poet Aristophanes by Plato, *Symposium* 189–90.

principle" laid down by the rabbis to the effect that everything at creation was made in "perfect size" and "perfect form."[155] It follows that God did not have to go back and correct his handiwork by slicing any of his creatures down the middle. We also have his earlier intimation that the creation of *adam* spoken of in Genesis is the bringing forth of the human species. The best that can be done with his hermetic remarks is to interpret them as medieval commentators on the *Guide for the Perplexed* did. He probably is hinting that the androgynous, double-faced creature from which the female segment was separated off is an allegory for the nature of the human soul. The male part of the double-faced creature represents man's intellect, and the female part, the soul's entire nonintellectual side, which faces in the opposite direction. The two aspects are united in each human being, yet they are distinct and separable.

Scripture recounts that after Eve was fashioned and the two first humans began their life together in the Garden of Eden, the wily serpent persuaded Eve to sin by eating of the tree of knowledge, whereupon she persuaded Adam to do the same. The next piece of rabbinic aggada taken up by Maimonides relates that Eve was led into sin not by the serpent itself, but by Satan, who sits astride the serpent. Maimonides quotes the aggadic statement, again does not interpret, and limits himself to a few more dark clues. The most plausible interpretation of what he is suggesting is that Satan sitting astride the serpent represents the human imaginative faculty, which sits astride the soul's faculties of sense perception,[156] and the temptation of Eve, in its aggadic version, is an allegorical depiction of man's psychological and moral condition: The imaginative faculty of the soul tempts the soul's entire nonintellectual side, and if it succeeds in its blandishments, the nonintellectual side can seduce the intellect and deflect it from pursuing its natural goal.

A few lines later Maimonides calls attention to a further piece of aggada whose surface meaning is "repulsive" but which is in truth "extraordinary." The item in question relates that "when the serpent had congress with Eve, he instilled pollution in her." Israel, which experienced the theophany at Mount Sinai, cleansed itself of the pollution, whereas the gentiles, who did not, remain polluted.[157] This time Maimonides quotes the aggadic passage without a single comment, but if we have read him correctly so far, his intent may be surmised: When the people of Israel received God's Torah at Sinai, they were furnished the means for controlling the nonintellectual part of their souls and protecting their intellectual faculty against

[155] *Guide for the Perplexed* 2.30, p. 69b, immediately before Maimonides takes up the aggadic passage concerning the creation of the double-faced man. The notion that everything was created in perfect size and with perfect form is his interpretation of another piece of aggada, found in BT *Rosh ha-Shana* 11a.

[156] See S. Klein-Braslavy, *Perush ha-Rambam la-Sippurim* ᶜ*al Adam* (Jerusalem 1986) 212–13.

[157] BT *Shabbat* 146a, and parallels. What Maimonides would well have found repulsive was the suggestion that the serpent had sexual intercourse with Eve.

distraction. Their intellectual faculty was thereby given free rein to develop. The gentiles, who did not receive the Torah, remain enslaved to their lower instincts and their intellectual faculty is hobbled.[158]

In fine, after Maimonides equated the scriptural account of creation with the philosophic science of physics and insisted on restricting access to them, he openly discloses what he himself discovered in Scripture, and his discoveries are anticlimactic. When he turns from the scriptural account of the creation of the world to the preserved remnants of the rabbis' exposition of the story of Adam, Eve, and the serpent, he is scrupulous in heeding the rabbis' instructions to restrict access. He presumably is so not only because of the rabbis' admonition; his allegorical reading of the making and temptation of Eve, as far as it can be deciphered, was bound to scandalize persons of a traditional bent. Nevertheless, the content of his allegorical reading—the propositions that man has an intellectual and nonintellectual side, that perfecting one's intellect is the goal of human life, that the human imaginative faculty may deflect man from his true goal, that the Torah gives man the means for controlling the nonintellectual side of his soul—includes nothing that Maimonides makes the slightest effort to hide either in his rabbinic works or elsewhere in the *Guide for the Perplexed.* While he may have had good reason to conceal the allegorization of the story of Adam and Eve, he had no discernible reason for hiding what, he hints, is conveyed by the allegory.[159]

The scriptural account of the chariot is the vision in which the prophet Ezekiel saw the heavens open and the "likeness of four living creatures" emerge from their midst. "Hard by the living creatures," the prophet saw four wheels. "Over the heads of the living creatures," he beheld the "likeness of a firmament"; above the firmament, the "likeness of a throne"; and above or on the throne, "a likeness as the appearance of a man."[160] The vision is known as the "chariot" because a firmament placed above four wheels suggests a vehicle.

Since the chariot is the more sensitive of the two accounts, Maimonides treats it more discreetly than he did the scriptural account of creation—as distinct from rabbinic aggada relating to the latter, which we just observed him handling with utmost discretion. He proposes merely to repeat what Scripture says, draw attention to certain significant features as he proceeds, and make unobtrusive but pregnant comments. Such, he expects, will hand perceptive readers the key for opening the door, while others will be left in the dark. In some of the particulars his language is so opaque that it is virtually impossible to determine what he is driving at, but the basic scheme is unmistakable.

[158] In Commentary on the Mishna, *Baba Qamma* 4:3, Maimonides intimates that gentiles are an inferior breed.

[159] The eleventh-century Spanish Jewish poet and philosopher Ibn Gabirol gave an allegorical interpretation to the Adam and Eve story which is similar in spirit to Maimonides' interpretation although it differs in detail. See Abraham Ibn Ezra, alternative commentary on Genesis 3:21.

[160] Ezekiel 1.

He calls attention to such details in the scriptural description as those to the effect that the four living creatures went "forward," "turned not when they went," yet "ran and returned," which when taken together, so Maimonides lets us understand, signify that they perform unvarying circular motion wherein each part repeatedly returns to the spot it previously occupied. The living creatures "sparkled," which, he intimates, means that they are transparent. "Their appearance was like coals of fire," which he construes as meaning that they give off light. He plainly takes the living creatures to represent transparent celestial spheres and specifically the eight spheres that contain stars and planets: The celestial spheres are living beings, they rotate continually, and the stars and planets, which give off light, are embedded in their surface. In an earlier chapter Maimonides had prepared the rationale for the prophet's portraying the eight spheres containing stars and planets as *four* angelic figures by showing how, from a purely scientific standpoint, the eight fall into four distinct categories.[161]

He further calls attention to Scripture's description of the wheels as "on the ground," as both one and four, as moving in tandem with the living creatures, and

[161]*Guide for the Perplexed* 3.2. In *Guide* 2.9–10, where Maimonides was concerned with astronomical matters, he observed that certain astronomers located the spheres of the planets Mercury and Venus between the sphere of the moon and the sphere of the sun, whereas the earlier astronomers located those two spheres, together with the spheres of Mars, Jupiter, and Saturn, beyond the sun. He opts for the second position, thereby arriving at the following order: the sphere of the moon, that of the sun, those of the five planets, that of the fixed stars, and a final, outermost sphere, which contains no stars and which pulls the other spheres around the earth once every twenty-four hours; the outermost sphere was known as the diurnal sphere. The scheme allows him to arrange the spheres containing stars and planets in four groups; and he speculates that from each of the four a power emanates into the sublunar region which, besides exercising an effect on the sublunar region as a whole, acts on one of the four physical elements in particular. Thus, from the sphere of the moon there emanates a power that acts on the element water in particular; from the sphere of the sun, a power that acts on the element fire; from the spheres of the five planets, a power that acts on the element air; and from the sphere of the fixed stars, a power that acts on the element earth. The scheme explains why Ezekiel's vision represents the spheres with stars and planets by four, rather than eight, living creatures and also why, in the vision, each of the four wheels, which stand for the four elements, is linked to one of the four living creatures. The living creatures are moreover described in the vision as each having four faces, and in *Guide* 2.9–10, Maimonides provides an explanation for that feature as well. In the same chapters, he further quotes passages from Scripture and rabbinic aggada, apart from Ezekiel's vision, which mesh with the astronomical scheme that he constructs. It is striking that he not only allows science to guide him in interpreting Scripture and rabbinic aggada, but in the present instance lets Scripture as well as rabbinic aggada guide him in deciding astronomical questions.

In *Guide* 2.8, Maimonides notes two astronomical issues in which the ancient rabbis erred, and in connection with one of them, he quotes a passage from the Babylonian Talmud which acknowledges that the gentile astronomers had been right and the rabbis wrong. (The passage does not appear in standard editions of the Babylonian Talmud.)

In *Mishneh Torah*: *H. Yesode ha-Torah* 2.7, Maimonides uses the term *living creatures* in a different sense. There *living creatures* is not a general term for celestial spheres, but a name for the highest of the ten incorporeal intelligences.

as going forward without turning as they go. He plainly takes them to represent the four physical elements of the sublunar world inhabited by man: The elements occupy the lowest region of the universe and accordingly are, as it were, on the ground. They arrange themselves naturally in four spherical layers around the center of the world—the element earth being surrounded by the layer of water, water by the layer of air, and air by fire—and hence can be pictured as four round wheels. They are one inasmuch as they share the same underlying matter, but four inasmuch as each has its distinctive form. Particles of each element are forced out of the element's natural place by the revolutions of the celestial spheres. And after the elements are set in motion by the spheres, they return in a straight line—without turning as they go—either upward or downward, toward their natural resting place.[162]

In the prophet's vision, the likeness of the firmament, the likeness of the throne, and the likeness as of the appearance of a man are situated one above the other. Maimonides points out that the appearance of the man is divided into two parts[163] and from that he infers that it does not represent God, for God does not have parts. The firmament, the throne, and the man must, as he reads the vision, represent rungs in the hierarchy of existence lying between the spheres containing stars, which are symbolized by the living creatures, and God, who does not enter the picture at all. The three likenesses somehow stand for the outermost celestial sphere, which has no stars, and the nine incorporeal intelligences, which are subordinate to God in the hierarchy of existence. Maimonides does not say enough to indicate which of the three stands for what.[164]

In short, he read Ezekiel's vision as a figurative depiction of the universe outside of God: the four elements, from which every physical object in the sublunar region is formed; the celestial spheres, which govern the four elements; and the incorporeal intelligences subordinate to God, which govern the spheres. While he may have had reason to conceal his reading of the prophet's vision as an allegorical representation of common scientific and philosophic notions, the tripartite scheme of the universe was common coin in his day and comes up without disguise more than once in his rabbinic works and the *Guide for the Perplexed*. He therefore had no detectable reason to conceal the content of the allegory. It moreover happens that despite his talk of being the first to rediscover the long lost secret of

[162]*Guide for the Perplexed* 3.2

[163]The prophet envisaged the likeness of a man as partly of "the appearance of electrum" and partly of "the appearance of fire." With the aid of a remark in the Babylonian Talmud, Maimonides finds in that description an echo of the Arabic Aristotelian notion that the incorporeal intelligences—or the first of the intelligences, if that is what the likeness of man is supposed to represent—contain two aspects, existence by reason of itself and existence by reason of its cause.

[164]*Guide for the Perplexed* 3.2 (end); 7. Perhaps the firmament stands for the outermost sphere, the throne stands for the rational souls of the spheres, and the man stands for the intelligences. Alternatively, the firmament might stand for the outermost sphere, the man might stand for the highest intelligence, and the throne for the other intelligences.

the account of the chariot, another Spanish Jewish philosopher had sketched an interpretation of Ezekiel's vision along similar, although not identical, lines, just a few years earlier.[165]

Resumé. If we respect what Maimonides himself tells us, he wrote the *Guide for the Perplexed* as an essay in scriptural exegesis. His plan for the *Guide* had its roots in an earlier plan for a Book of Prophecy, but he had become convinced that he should address a more select circle of readers than he originally had in mind, albeit persons who had not completed the full course of philosophic studies and were not overly sophisticated. He envisaged readers who possessed a certain amount of philosophic knowledge, had not yet been initiated into the science of metaphysics, and had been thrown into perplexity by words or passages in Scripture. His intent was to rescue them from their perplexity not by completing their philosophic education—although to a considerable degree he does that too—but by teaching them how to read Scripture.

The first of his two objects was defensive. He was concerned here with words in scriptural descriptions of God which when taken in their ordinary sense carry an implication of corporeality and he undertook to show from Scripture itself that such words have additional, nonphysical meanings. When the words are read correctly, the untoward implications disappear. His second object goes beyond individual words to problematic passages in Scripture, and now his stance is as much constructive as defensive: He undertakes to read problematic scriptural passages figuratively not merely in order to remove unacceptable implications, but to show as well that Scripture is replete with philosophic truths. God's statement "Let us make man in Our image" becomes a lesson in man's rational nature. Jacob's dream of a ladder extending to heaven on which the angels ascended and descended and on top of which God stood is a figurative representation of the structure of existence. When Moses encountered God at the burning bush, the divine names he was taught embody a philosophic proof of the existence of God. The dialogue between Moses and God at Sinai teaches that man's natural goal in life is to know God, with the proviso that God's essence is unknowable and He has to be known through His "ways," that is to say, through what He does in the universe. The creation story imparts basic principles of Aristotelian physics as well as propositions, which Maimonides for some reason regarded as highly significant, concerning layers of water vapor in the atmosphere. Rabbinic aggadic comments concerning the formation of Eve out of Adam's body and the serpent's temptation of Eve are allegories that allude to the nature of man and the relation of man's nonintellectual, to his intellectual side. Ezekiel's vision is a figurative representation of the tripartite universe outside of God.

[165]Abraham Ibn Daud, *Emuna Rama* 1.8. Ibn Daud treats Ezekiel's prophecy even more allusively than Maimonides does out of respect for the rabbis' directives to conceal the interpretation of the account of the chariot.

Maimonides tells us that the scriptural accounts of creation and the chariot are equivalent to the sciences of physics and metaphysics, and for that reason the rabbis restricted access to them. What he discovers in the accounts of creation and the chariot is nonetheless a series of commonplace notions that he treats without compunction in other contexts, and it is hard to see just where he thought the sensitivity in the account of creation and the account of the chariot lay.[166]

[166]In *Guide for the Perplexed* 1.35, Maimonides lists a number of "secret" matters that should be withheld from the uneducated because of their difficulty, yet they are all subjects that he discusses openly in one section or another of the *Guide*.

7

Philosophic Works II

> [Avoid] the great inanity . . . animating the writings of most schools of thought in the world today. For every one of them tries to discover in an author's statements meanings that the author had not the slightest intent to convey. (Maimonides, *Guide for the Perplexed*, introduction)

The Philosophic Strand in the Guide for the Perplexed. Maimonides did not expect his mode of scriptural exegesis to appeal to large numbers of readers, but he was confident that there would be some, and there were. As the years passed, a time however came when his rationalistic exegesis, especially where it moves beyond problematic words in Scripture to the allegorization of whole passages in the spirit of medieval Arabic Aristotelianism, was seen by all to be wrongheaded. Today, the exegesis in which Maimonides took such pride fails to speak to a single reader and is something of an embarrassment to Maimonides' admirers.[1] The genuinely philosophic side of the book has worn better. Although Maimonides' scientific conceptions are outdated and his philosophic attitude is out of fashion, the philosophic strand still continues to engage the interest of readers of various stripes.

The philosophic sections start making their appearance midway through Part One of the book and continue, intermixed with a variety of other matters and extending like islands in an archipelago, to midway through Part Three. In them, Maimonides

[1] See Maimonides, *Moreh Nebukim*, ed. and trans. J. Kafah (Jerusalem 1972) 2.378, note 23, and 3.454, note 22. In the latter passage, Kafah insists on translating in a way that precludes what is obviously the correct interpretation of Maimonides' understanding of the "living creatures." J. Faur, *Homo Mysticus* (Syracuse 1999) 18, refuses to accept what he calls the "standard interpretations" of Maimonides' exegesis of the account of the chariot "offered by the commentators of the *Guide*," giving as his reason: Maimonides' exegesis, as interpreted by the commentators, stands "in such flagrant contradiction with the biblical text that to accept" those interpretations "the reader must presume that Maimonides was scripturally illiterate." What Faur calls the commentators' interpretations is simply what Maimonides himself obviously meant. Faur offers no alternative interpretation of Maimonides' exegesis of the account of the chariot.

does not, as he promised in the introduction to the *Guide*, discuss the foundations of faith and the truths of philosophy with "an allusiveness bordering on explicitness" as he did in the *Mishneh Torah.* On the contrary, he enters into those subjects far more fully and explicitly, and in far more technical detail, than he did in the *Mishneh Torah* or anywhere else. Still, when he was well along in the *Guide* and had explored a couple of key philosophic issues much more thoroughly than on any previous occasion, he continued to insist that his object was not to compose a work on physics, not to outline a system of metaphysics, and not to demonstrate propositions belonging to those two philosophic disciplines. He deems books already written on such matters to have done a "sufficient" job and—he adds with comely modesty—if there should happen to be a topic that had not been dealt with adequately by others, "what I would say . . . would not be superior to what has already been said." Philosophic issues come up in the *Guide for the Perplexed* only insofar as they are a "key" for understanding "figurative" passages and "secrets" in the books of the prophets and, again, insofar as they contribute to an understanding of the account of creation, the account of the chariot, fundamental aspects of prophecy, and beliefs of the Torah (*al-sharᶜiyya*).[2] The genuinely philosophic chapters in the *Guide for the Perplexed*, which are found by readers to be the most intriguing and stimulating, are thus included in the book not for their own sake. They are there because they aid Maimonides in his scriptural exegesis, which he saw as his great contribution to Jewish thought yet which appeals to today's readers least.

Centuries after Maimonides, Western philosophers, usually in the guise of devil's advocate, would propose odd scenarios regarding the relationship of the human consciousness to what lies around us. Such scenarios are not to be looked for in the philosophic chapters of the *Guide*. It never crossed the mind of the Arabic Aristotelians from whom Maimonides drew or of Maimonides himself that the existence of a world independent of the human consciousness might be a mirage. He never doubted that the human sense organs are translucent windows through which reliable data concerning the external world enter the human soul,[3] that the perceptive apparatus of one human being is the same as that of another, and that the world therefore presents itself to one member of the human species in the same way as it does to another. He knew of Kalam thinkers who maintained that when—to supply an illustration—a moving physical object is perceived to strike a stationary object and the latter is immediately perceived to move, the first object is not the *cause* of the second object's motion; in Kalam doctrine, God invariably intervenes and sets the second object in motion. But Maimonides was confident that everyone with a modicum of good sense grasps instinctively that when an object begins moving after being struck by something else, the latter is the *cause* of

[2] *Guide for the Perplexed* 2.2.
[3] See *Guide for the Perplexed* 1.71, pp. 97a–b; 73 (12).

the motion of the first. He upbraids proponents of the Kalam position in the words of Scripture: "'As one mocketh a man, will ye mock Him?' For what they say is, truly, sheer mockery."[4]

A substantial set of philosophic topics is explored in the *Guide for the Perplexed.* They are, in the order in which Maimonides takes them up: the problem of divine attributes, that is to say, the question of the extent to which human language is capable of describing God; the structure of the corporeal universe; the demonstration of the existence, unity, and incorporeality of a first cause of the universe, or God; reasons for concluding that the translucent celestial spheres, which are nested one within the other like the layers of an onion, which have the stars and planets embedded in their surface, and which rotate around the earth, are living beings endowed with intellect; reasons for recognizing that a hierarchy of wholly incorporeal beings subordinate to God and commonly known as *intelligences* parallels the celestial spheres and maintains them in motion; the mechanism whereby the incorporeal God and incorporeal intelligences can act on the corporeal universe; the question whether, and how, it can be proved that the corporeal universe was brought into existence after not having existed, that is to say, was created; the nature of prophecy; the purpose, if any, for which a universe outside of God exists; the manner in which God has knowledge of beings outside Himself; the manner in which God exercises providence over His creatures. The issues are characteristically medieval, and Maimonides, not surprisingly, handles them with an array of tools borrowed from the medieval Arabic Aristotelian school of philosophy. Taken together, they cover a broad terrain. And the positions at which Maimonides arrives fit together into a well-knit and comprehensive conception of God, the universe, and man. He could, nevertheless, have justified the inclusion of each of the topics on the grounds that it relates to the twin objects—the exegesis of terms and of figurative passages in Scripture—that he said he had in view when writing the *Guide for the Perplexed.*

Considered logically, the first philosophic issue that Maimonides treats, the problem of divine attributes, is out of place. The possibility and propriety of describing God cannot be determined before God is known to exist and certain propositions about Him are known, and those subjects are not taken up until a later stage of the *Guide*. If Maimonides had proceeded in a systematic and logical fashion, he would have first established the existence and nature of God and only then gone on to the subject of divine attributes. Such is the order that he in fact followed in his law code, the *Mishneh Torah*: The opening paragraphs of that work briefly sketch a demonstration of the existence of God and then proceed to an equally brief discussion of divine attributes. It is likewise the order that Thomas Aquinas, the preeminent medieval Christian philosopher, followed in his monumental and carefully constructed *Summa Theologiae.*

[4]*Guide for the Perplexed* 73 (6); the verse is Job 13:9. Maimonides gives different examples to illustrate the Kalam position.

Maimonides was by no means insensitive to the necessity of tackling subjects in their proper sequence. In the *Mishneh Torah*, he gives considerable attention to the order in which he treats halakic matters. In the *Guide for the Perplexed*, he dwells on the necessity of having the demonstration of the existence of God precede arguments for the creation of the world. He explains: The existence of God can be established with a higher degree of certainty than the creation of the world; and the thesis that God exists is more fundamental for philosophy and religion than the thesis that the world was created. Kalam thinkers, in topsy-turvy fashion, inverted the order. They started with arguments for creation and then inferred from the world's having come into existence after not existing that there is a creator who brought it into existence.[5] It should be obvious, however, that what has a higher degree of certainty and is more fundamental—the existence of God—must come first and not be made to depend on what is less certain and less fundamental—the creation of the world.

Although the subject of divine attributes is out of its logical place within the sequence of philosophic issues discussed in the *Guide*, Maimonides did have a rationale for putting it where he does. In the first half of Part One of the book, he focuses on words used by Scripture when describing God. It made sense to cap a discussion of terms actually used to describe God with a theoretical examination of the way in which God can, in principle, be described. The possibility nonetheless remains that as Maimonides found himself drawn into the theoretical implications of the issue of attributes more deeply than he originally foresaw, he rethought his plan for the book and undertook to demonstrate the existence of God, as well as to explore other philosophic subjects, with comparable thoroughness and in comparable depth. In other words, the awkward placing of the subject of divine attributes may furnish a modicum of support for the hypothesis that Maimonides' plan for the *Guide* expanded as he proceeded.

In what follows, I offer a few examples of Maimonides' treatment of philosophic issues in the *Guide for the Perplexed*. My aim will be to illustrate his style of handling philosophic issues, the sorts of positions he takes, and the way in which those positions add up to a distinctive conception of God and the nature of man.

As was seen in an earlier chapter, the opening paragraphs of Maimonides' *Mishneh Torah* offer a demonstration of the existence of God. It is a version of Aristotle's proof from the motion of the celestial spheres to a cause of their motion, and because of the readership that Maimonides envisaged for the *Mishneh Torah*, he reduced the argument to a barest minimum. He reasoned simply that "the celestial sphere rotates continually, and it is impossible for it to move without a mover"; hence a first being, or "God," must "move the sphere with an infinite power." An accompanying argument, similarly condensed to a minimum, deduced from the infinite power of the mover of the spheres that the mover, or God, is not a

[5] *Guide for the Perplexed* 1.71.

body, that He is incorporeal. In one further step, Maimonides deduced from the incorporeality of the mover of the sphere that only one such being, only one God, exists.[6]

In the *Guide for the Perplexed*, Maimonides goes beyond the single bare-bones proof of the existence of God from the motion of the celestial spheres. He now offers four proofs of the existence, unity, and incorporeality of God—as well as additional, auxiliary proofs of God's unity and incorporeality—and one of the four is a much more fully articulated version of the proof from celestial motion. Maimonides never tires of repeating that all four proofs are "demonstrations" (*burhān*).[7] That is to say, they establish the existence of God with the same degree of certainty possessed, for example, by geometrical demonstrations; the existence and unity of God can be known with the same certainty that the angles of a triangle are known to add up to 180º. Of one of the four proofs, Maimonides writes: It "is a demonstration and free of doubt, and only someone who is ignorant of the demonstrative mode could reject or dispute it."[8]

Before getting to the proofs, Maimonides clarifies a few methodological matters.

First, as already noted, he stresses that the question of the existence of God should be settled before the question of the creation or eternity of the world is broached. Secondly, he posits that what can exist is divisible into two classes, the corporeal and the incorporeal, and the corporeal is accessible to sense perception, whereas the incorporeal obviously is not. The corporeal must therefore be the starting point for all human science, and a philosopher seeking to prove the existence of an incorporeal being must begin with what the human senses report regarding corporeal being and proceed from there. A demonstration of the existence of God must rest on an empirical foundation.[9]

[6] Above, pp. 235–36.

[7] *Guide for the Perplexed* 1.58 (not of all four); 71; 2.1; 2; 3.45, p. 99a. Ghazali, *Maqāṣid al-Falāsifa* (Cairo, n.d.) 46, distinguishes two kinds of "demonstrative syllogism," namely a "why-demonstration," which reasons from the cause to the effect and explains not only that the conclusion is so but also why it is so, and a "that-demonstration," which reasons from the effect to the cause and establishes only that the conclusion is so. He gives as an example of the former: Where there is a fire, there is smoke; there is a fire; therefore there is smoke; and as an example of the latter: Where there is smoke, there is a fire; there is smoke; therefore there is a fire. Aquinas, *Summa Theologica* 1.2.2, draws a similar distinction in preparation for his demonstrations of the existence of God. In *Maqāṣid* 147, Ghazali offers a proof of the existence of God which, like Maimonides' proofs, reasons from the world to God, and which he expressly calls a "demonstration." It is plainly a demonstration of the second type, a "that-demonstration," and Maimonides' demonstrations of the existence of God are also plainly of the same type.

[8] *Guide for the Perplexed* 2.1 (3).

[9] *Guide for the Perplexed* 1.71. Maimonides is excluding what are known as ontological or a priori proofs for the existence of God, that is to say, arguments which, on purely logical grounds and without evidence drawn from the external world, conclude that a deity must exist. The philosophic tradition in which he stood had no notion of such proofs, and one may surmise that he would have dismissed them as preposterous.

Thirdly, he adds a qualification to what he said about leaving the issue of the creation or eternity of the universe in abeyance until the existence of God is demonstrated. The "correct method," he now writes, is to demonstrate the existence of God on parallel tracks, employing the eternity of the world as a premise on one track and the creation of the world on the other, while not yet committing oneself to either premise. The thinking should be that if the world was created, it plainly stood in need of a creator who brought it into existence, and the creator is God; if, by contrast, the world has existed forever, a demonstration employing the eternity of the world as a premise likewise leads to God's existence. The existence of God will accordingly be arrived at on each alternative—by immediate inference, on the assumption that the world was created, and through a chain of philosophic reasoning, on the assumption that it is eternal. Since proving the existence of God on the second track, on the premise of eternity, is more challenging, Maimonides directs his efforts there, even though he insists that he believes the world was created.[10]

He regarded the proof that reasons from the motion of the celestial spheres to the existence of an incorporeal mover of the spheres as the primary proof of the existence of God. It was Aristotle's proof. Anachronistically, he credited the biblical Abraham with having formulated it over a thousand years before Aristotle.[11] He deployed it himself in the *Mishneh Torah*. Before getting to it in the *Guide for the Perplexed*, he comments that the "rotation of the sphere" is the "strongest sign [*dalīl*] whereby the existence of God can be known . . . as I shall demonstrate."[12] And his remarks about assuming the eternity of motion for the sake of argument when proving the existence of God have the proof from motion especially in view. It is the only one of the four proofs that truly requires the premise of eternity, whereas the other three can easily make do without the premise.[13]

Despite his characterization of all four of his proofs for the existence of God as demonstrations, they are hardly of uniform quality. One of the four is so feeble that the reader will be hard put to see how Maimonides could have supposed it to be a demonstration.[14] His primary proof, the proof from the motion of the celestial spheres, carries the baggage of what would be jettisoned a few centuries later as wholly discredited natural science. Maimonides, like his Greek and Arabic predecessors, could envision the revolutions—today we would say the apparent revolutions—of the stars and planets around the earth only by locating them in transparent rotating spheres, and the proof from the motion of the spheres hinges on the question of what causes the spheres to rotate. Since Maimonides' day, the

[10]*Guide for the Perplexed* 1.71.

[11]Above, p. 238.

[12]*Guide for the Perplexed* 1.70 (end).

[13]Maimonides employs the premise of eternity in the third of his four proofs, but that proof could easily be formulated without the premise.

[14]*Guide for the Perplexed* 2.1 (b).

science of astronomy has of course done away with celestial spheres. Further, the proof needs more than the common-sense proposition that objects begin to move only if something sets them in motion. It requires the less obvious premise that objects *continue* to move only as long as something maintains them in motion. The thinking here was that the longer an object moves, the more power—the more fuel, as it were—is needed in order to keep it in motion, and when something such as a celestial sphere moves over infinite time, the cause maintaining it in motion must be of infinite power. The science of physics eventually learned how to account for the continued motion of objects without positing that any *thing* constantly keeps them in motion.

If we put the weakest of Maimonides' four proofs aside and abstract from the particularities of the remaining proofs, the three—including the proof from the motion of the spheres—can be reduced to a common skeleton. Each focuses on something, be it a process, an event, or an aspect of the world, which is dependent on a cause. Each then discovers that the cause is dependent on a further cause, which activates it. And each proof reasons that the series of causes behind the phenomenon with which we started cannot extend back indefinitely, that a first cause of all the links in the chain must be reached. Expressed more technically, each rests on the principle that an *infinite regress of causes* is impossible.[15]

Philosophers since David Hume have dismissed the principle that an infinite regress of causes is impossible as a fantasy plucked out of thin air by muddled heads.[16] The principle does have a rationale, however. It at least deserves to be met on its own terms and only then, if one finds the reasoning specious, to be rejected. Maimonides explains the rationale in the following manner; I expand a little on what he says:

Take a chain of causes and effects in which B causes A, C causes B to cause A, and so on. Inasmuch as each link in the chain performs its function because the link behind it induces it to do so, the earlier, and not the later link in the chain is the true cause of the outcome: Since it is only by virtue of C that B acts, C and not B is the true cause of A; the man who lights a match and applies it to a log, and not the match, is the true cause of the log's catching fire. But if a D—let us say, the cold weather that motivated the man to set the log on fire—induces C to act, it and not C is the true cause of A. Should there also be an E—perhaps the atmospheric conditions producing the cold weather—then E will be the true cause. And so forth. The first link in the chain is always the true and ultimately responsible cause of all the links that follow. Consequently—and here is the core of the matter, or the legerdemain, if one does not like the principle—should there be no first cause, the supposed series of causes and effects would have *no* true cause. And without a true cause, which is responsible for all the intermediate links and for the ultimate

[15] H. Wolfson, "Notes on Proofs of the Existence of God in Jewish Philosophy," reprinted in his *Studies in the History of Philosophy and Religion* 1 (Cambridge, Mass. 1973) 572–73.

[16] D. Hume, *Dialogues Concerning Natural Religion*, Part 9.

effect, the effects in the chain would be causeless and hence would not exist.[17] Every chain of causes must therefore be traceable back to its first and true cause.

To repeat, the three more serious of Maimonides' proofs of the existence of God deploy the principle that an infinite regress of causes is impossible and thereby establish a first cause in whatever variety of causation they focus on. Each proof then reasons in its own way that a first cause, which is nowise dependent on any other cause, must be incorporeal. And from there, each proof goes on to show that only a single absolutely first cause can exist.[18] The single incorporeal first cause of the universe is what is known as God.[19] Maimonides, it cannot be said too many times, insists that his proofs are watertight demonstrations.

By Maimonides' prescription, a complete proof of the existence of God must establish that there exists a first cause of the corporeal universe, that the first cause is incorporeal, and that the incorporeal first cause is one.[20] Those propositions by themselves do not support the uncompromising stance to which he was drawn on the next topic, a topic that modern readers may find hopelessly arid but that was of the utmost concern for him—the possibility of man's framing descriptions of God. He had already adumbrated his position in the *Mishneh Torah*, where he stated that no being apart from God Himself can know God's "true nature"; that God does not possess *life* or *wisdom* in the sense in which man possesses such qualities; that God exists outside of time and space and hence cannot properly be described through use of temporal or spatial language; that God never changes, neither speaks nor is silent, is never either angry or pleased.[21]

In the course of proving the existence, unity, and incorporeality of the first cause, in the *Guide*, Maimonides deduces a critical corollary, namely, that the first cause "exists by reason of itself."[22] The notion of *existing by reason of itself* joins forces with a tactic that he learned from his Arabic Aristotelian predecessors to give him the tool he wanted for analyzing descriptions of God.[23]

His thinking goes: To say that something exists wholly by reason of itself is to say that it exists by virtue of nothing else whatsoever. But if something exists by

[17] *Guide for the Perplexed* 1.69, pp. 89a–b; 2, introduction, proposition 3.

[18] For the incorporeality and unity of God in the proof from the motion of the celestial spheres, see above, p. 236. In the simplest of the four proofs, *Guide for the Perplexed* 2.1 (d), the reasoning goes: If the first cause contained potentiality, something would have to cause it to pass from potentiality to actuality and it would not in fact be the first cause. Potentiality and matter go hand in hand, and therefore the first cause, which is free of potentiality, contains no matter; it is incorporeal. Since there would be nothing to distinguish two incorporeal first causes from one another, it follows that only one first cause exists.

[19] *Guide for the Perplexed* 2.1 (d).

[20] *Guide for the Perplexed* 1.71.

[21] *Mishneh Torah*: *H. Yesode ha-Torah* 1.11; 2.8.

[22] *Guide for the Perplexed* 2.1 (c), (d).

[23] The tactic goes back to Greek neoplatonism. See H. Davidson, *Proofs for Eternity, Creation, and the Existence of God* (New York 1987) 294–96.

virtue of nothing else whatsoever, not only does it not exist by virtue of factors outside it. It also does not exist by virtue of factors internal to it; in other words, it is entirely free of components that combine to make it what it is. And since God is such a being, a being existing by reason of itself, He contains no components.[24] God is not merely one in the sense that no more than a single deity exists. To do full justice to divine unity, we have to embrace the "belief in a single, simple essence, containing no composition or multiplicity of factors." "No matter how you consider God's being, you find it to be one, not divisible into two in any respect whatsoever. . . . It has no multiplicity, either in actuality or in[asmuch as] the mind [is able to discern distinctions in it]."[25]

We have been led, almost unawares, from the tautology that a first cause does not have an external cause, to the much stronger proposition that the first cause, or God, does not even have internal causes, and thence to the still stronger proposition that the first cause, or God, contains no internal composition or multiplicity whatsoever. The ground is now prepared for the further conclusion that while man can know the existence of God with certainty, man cannot comprehend or enunciate what God is.[26]

In the first place, Maimonides reasons that man cannot comprehend or express God's very essence. Human minds know the essence of a thing through logical definition; and a logical definition is framed by starting with the larger class to which the thing to be defined belongs and adding the distinguishing characteristic that sets it apart from everything else in the class. To define *man*, we take *animal*, which is the larger class to which man belongs, add the characteristic that sets him apart from other animals, namely, *rationality*, and arrive at the definition of man as *rational animal.* Since God does not belong to any larger class, He cannot be defined. In the second place, God cannot be known or described through a part of His essence, for, as just seen, He contains no components or parts. In the third place, since God is wholly unitary, He does not have nonessential qualities—*accidents* in the technical language of philosophy—added to His essence and making Him what He is.[27]

Yet, as everyone knows, Scripture is replete with descriptions of God. As Maimonides reads Scripture, those descriptions cannot have the intent of disclosing what God is, for that is impossible. Scriptural descriptions of God must be construed in one of two ways, either as attributes of action, that is, as reports of

[24]*Guide for the Perplexed* 2.1 (c) and the appendix to 2.1 (d).

[25]*Guide for the Perplexed* 1.51, p. 58a.

[26]The unknowability of God's essence was a commonplace in pre-Christian Greek, and in medieval Christian, Islamic, and Jewish thought. See, for example, D. Kaufmann, *Geschichte der Attributenlehre* (Gotha 1877) 277–78, 444-45; H. Wolfson, *Philo* (Cambridge, Mass. 1948) 2.153–60; B. Abrahamov, "Faḫr al-Dīn al-Rāzī on the Knowability of God's Essence and Attributes," *Arabica* 49 (2002) 204-30.

[27]*Guide for the Perplexed* 1.52.

what God *does*; or as expressions of God's general "perfection, in accordance with what man regards as a perfection."[28]

Take the verse in which God represented Himself to Moses as "merciful and gracious, long-suffering, and abundant in goodness and truth, keeping mercy unto the thousandth generation, forgiving iniquity," and so forth.[29] Scripture, on Maimonides' reading, is there describing God's actions and not God Himself; and it does so by applying to God terms that are commonly used to describe human beings who perform actions with a surface resemblance to the actions performed by God. God exercises "tender care," as it were, in bringing a fetus into existence and furnishing the fetus with the limbs and organs that it needs in order to survive and function. When parents supply the needs of a newborn infant, they act from the psychological characteristic and emotion of *mercy*. Hence Scripture applies the adjective *merciful* to God as well. Its intent is that God performs actions resembling actions flowing from human mercy, although with the critical reservation that in the case of God, the actions do not flow from a characteristic or emotion of the soul. God does not possess a soul in any proper sense and is not subject to emotions.

God brings creatures into existence and provides for them without the obligation to do so. When a human agent lavishes gifts on another without obligation, he acts from the psychological characteristic of graciousness. Scripture accordingly applies the adjective *gracious* to God, its intent being not that God acts through a characteristic or emotion but rather that He performs actions similar to those flowing from human graciousness. Not everything that occurs in the world will strike the human observer as benign. Plagues, natural disasters, and wars sometimes lay large regions waste and destroy entire populations, and God, as the first cause of the universe, is ultimately responsible for such phenomena too. A man who does things of the sort acts out of jealousy, anger, or revenge. Scripture accordingly calls God *jealous*, *angry*, and *vengeful*, its intent again being that God's actions resemble the human actions in question, not that He has a soul subject to emotions.[30] Other descriptions of God in Scripture are to be construed along the same lines.

Maimonides says less about scriptural descriptions of God of the other type, those designed merely to express His perfection in accordance with what man considers to be a perfection. But he does offer a few examples. At one juncture in the *Guide*, he remarks that when Scripture describes God as undergoing movement of various kinds—going up, going down, standing, seating Himself, and the like—it is speaking in accordance with the popular supposition that the ability to

[28]*Guide for the Perplexed* 1.52; 60 (end). Maimonides also goes to some length in ruling out descriptions of God which are construed not as saying anything about God Himself but as referring to His relationship to other beings.

[29]Exodus 34:6–7.

[30]*Guide for the Perplexed* 1.54.

move is a perfection.[31] In another place, he writes that when Scripture and Jewish liturgy call God a "great God," "mighty," and "awe-inspiring," they again apply to God the language of human perfection. Scripture and the liturgy employ terms of the sort because the unsophisticated must be given some notion of the deity to hold on to, although it of course would have been better if they had no such need. The danger in the descriptions is that if understood wrongly, they will imply the presence of qualities in God.[32]

Scriptural descriptions of God should be taken, then, either as conveying what God does, rather than what He is, or as teaching the unsophisticated that He is perfect.[33]

Maimonides does not stop here. He goes "deeper," as he puts it, and calls attention to a subtle procedure for saying something obliquely about God Himself: The correct mode of describing God, a mode that is free of "looseness" and "contains no defect whatsoever vis-à-vis God," is through negative statements. Negative statements are those reporting what the thing described is not, rather than what it is, and Maimonides submits that they can impart almost as much information as incomplete positive descriptions. There is, he maintains, somewhat dubiously, little difference between saying that an object is neither mineral nor vegetable and saying that it is animal, apart from the critical detail that the positive attribute *animal* denotes something in the object described, whereas the negative attributes are free of the implication.[34]

The more negations one is able to assemble about a thing, the more indirect knowledge one has of it. Consider, Maimonides writes, a series of men who have heard the word "ship" but do not know what the word means. The first of the men ascertains that a ship is not an accidental quality. The second goes on to ascertain that it is not an animal, a third that it is not mineral, a fourth that it is not a plant still growing out of the ground, a fifth that it is not a body in a natural state. A sixth, seventh, eighth, ninth, and tenth successively determine that the shape of a ship is not flat, spherical, conical, circular, or equilateral, and an eleventh man discovers as well that a ship is not solid. Each succeeding man has attained to a further approximation of what a ship is, and the last man is not far behind someone who has the positive conception of a hollow elongated body, fitted together from a number of pieces of hewn wood. By the same token, the more negations one learns about God—the more negations known in the form of demonstrated propositions, not the more words that are merely mouthed—the closer one approximates a conception of what God is.[35] Increasing one's indirect knowledge of God is of such value that a person may spend years mastering a science solely in

[31] *Guide for the Perplexed* 1.26.
[32] *Guide for the Perplexed* 1.59.
[33] *Guide for the Perplexed* 1.60 (end).
[34] *Guide for the Perplexed* 1.58.
[35] *Guide for the Perplexed* 1.60.

order to demonstrate for himself how an additional characteristic is to be negated of God.[36]

How do negative attributes work in practice?

With a single exception, the illustrations that Maimonides offers are not negative terms at all but positive terms construed negatively. He explains: When we demonstrate the existence of a first cause who is radically different from everything else, we state that "He is existent." What we should be thinking when uttering those words is that "His failure-to-exist is impossible" (literally: "His *absence* is impossible"): In predicating the positive term *existent* of God, we should have in mind the negative phrase *not such-as-fails-to-exist.* Similarly, when we ascertain that God's existence is different from the existence of inanimate being, we state that "He is alive"; our intent should be that "He is not dead." When we go on to realize that God's manner of existence is different from the manner of existence of the celestial spheres, which are living beings but corporeal, we state: He is "not corporeal." When we further discover that God's existence is also different from that of the supernal incorporeal intelligences, inasmuch as they are caused whereas He is not, we state: He is "from eternity," by which we should understand "not caused." When we discover that beings emanate from God in a well-ordered manner, we state that He is "powerful, knowing, and possessed of will." In saying that God is "powerful," we should think: He is "not impotent," which in turn means that His existence suffices to bring other things into existence. In saying that God is "knowing," we should think "not ignorant," which in turn means "comprehending, that is, alive." In saying "possessed of will" our intent should be "not inattentive and heedless," which in turn means that the beings He produces do not exist in a haphazard and random fashion but are well ordered. When we establish that God is unique and nothing else is like Him, we state that He is "one," by which we mean, or should mean, the "negation of plurality."[37]

In two of these instances, the negative constructions placed on descriptions of God are just way stations leading to what Maimonides earlier identified as attributes of action: Stating that God is "powerful" and "possessed of will" is taken as equivalent, in the end, to saying that His existence is sufficient to bring other things into existence in a well-ordered fashion. In a third instance, Maimonides starts with the positive term "knowing," construes it negatively, and goes on to interpret his negative construction in such a fashion that he arrives back at a new positive attribute—"comprehending, that is, alive." It sounds very much as if he is juggling with words.

For his part, Maimonides was confident that he was favoring us with an invaluable philosophic and religious insight. To describe an object as alive, powerful, knowing, and so on would ordinarily imply that the qualities, or *accidents*, of life, power, or knowledge, are attached to the object's essence.

[36]*Guide for the Perplexed* 1.59.
[37]*Guide for the Perplexed* 1.58.

Maimonides moreover accepted the view of Avicenna, which he mistakenly took to be the view of Aristotle, that in the case of everything except the first cause, existence and unity are likewise accidental qualities attached to an object's essence: When the accidental quality of existence becomes attached to the essence of man, a human being enters the realm of actual existence, and when the accidental quality of unity is attached to a created essence—a notion that, Maimonides acknowledges, is almost impossible for the human mind to fathom[38]—a single exemplar of the essence is present in the realm of actual existence. By contrast, God's essence, unlike the essences of other beings, is free of qualities, including the accidents of existence and unity. To imagine anything else would be to harbor a wholly mistaken concept of what God is.

Life, knowledge, power, existence, unity, and the like are therefore radically different in the case of God from the accidental qualities, denoted by the same words, which attach themselves to the essences of beings other than God. They are identical with God's essence. Describing God negatively and construing affirmative statements about Him negatively, even if the negative statement turns into something else in the end, accommodates that fundamental truth. By teaching the profound and difficult proposition to his readers, Maimonides believed that he was equipping them to talk about God while avoiding the pernicious implication of God's being subject to accidental qualities.

He makes yet one more point. When attributes are negated of God, they must be negated as "we say of a wall [that it is] 'not seeing.'" In uttering those words, we do not mean that the wall happens not to see as an unconscious or blind person, who by his nature should be able to see, happens not to. We mean that the wall belongs to the class of entities which by their nature could not possibly see. By the same token, when we say "failure-to-exist is impossible" for God, God is "not dead," God is "uncaused," and so on, we should have in mind that God is not merely free of the qualities being negated. His nature is such that the qualities negated could not conceivably be present in Him.[39]

Maimonides was convinced that the existence, unity, and incorporeality of God can be known with the same demonstrative certainty as the theorems of geometry. He tells us that what God is, as distinct from whether He exists, is beyond the grasp of human knowledge and beyond the reach of human speech.[40] Where Scripture ostensibly describes God, the descriptions should be construed either as attributes of actions, that is, as descriptions of what God does, or as general expressions of God's perfection. The most correct mode of describing God is

[38]*Guide for the Perplexed* 1.57.

[39]*Guide for the Perplexed* 1.58, p. 71b.

[40]In *Guide for the Perplexed* 1.68. Maimonides—following, as he so often does, the Arabic Aristotelian school of philosophy—describes God, without reservation, as pure intellect, and he never explains how the attribute of intellect should be construed negatively. It apparently went without saying for him that incorporeal beings consist in pure intellect, and he had no qualms in applying that positive term to God.

through negations, through negating characteristics of God which He could not conceivably have. Maimonides remarks in passing that scriptural descriptions of God are likewise amenable to the negative mode of interpretation.[41]

The deity, as Maimonides conceives of Him, is plainly very different from the paternal, merciful, loving, sometimes angry, sometimes hating, yet always approachable and always concerned God whom most readers encounter in Scripture and rabbinic literature, and to whom those who pray, pray. A measure of personality is salvaged for God when Maimonides explores the issue of the creation or eternity of the universe.

In setting forth the range of positions that merit being taken into account regarding the origin of the universe, Maimonides makes clear that the one carrying the greatest philosophic prestige in his day was Aristotle's: "Aristotle, his followers, and commentators on his books"—it would have been more accurate to have said: Aristotle as read through the medium of his medieval Arabic followers—held that the universe has a cause of its existence, and the cause, God, acts in a necessary and unvarying manner through all eternity. "Even though Aristotle did not put it in so many words," God never wills anything that He did not will before. Because God is eternal and immutable and therefore always acts in an identical way, what He produces, the universe, is equally eternal and immutable. The same celestial spheres have always performed, and in the future will always perform, the same revolutions around the earth. Although changes obviously take place on earth, the earth as a whole and the natural laws governing events on it are eternal and immutable as well.

A second view, espoused by Plato and other philosophers of lesser rank than Aristotle, held that the universe was created, but since "it is impossible for something to come out of nothing," the matter from which the universe is made must have already existed. Matter exists side by side with God from all eternity, although at a subordinate level inasmuch as God is the eternal "cause of its existence."[42] Then God created—that is to say, fashioned—the universe out of the preexistent matter.

The third view, which Maimonides writes is held by "everyone who believes in the Law of Moses" and which he undertakes to defend, is that God created both the universe and the matter out of which He made it. "God brought everything existing outside of Himself into existence after complete and absolute nonexistence." Creation after absolute nonexistence is "unquestionably a fundamental principle [*qāᶜida*] of the Law of Moses, our teacher, coming immediately after the unity [of

[41] *Guide for the Perplexed* 1.59, p. 74b.

[42] I find it hard to understand how God's bringing matter into existence from eternity would not be tantamount to something's coming from nothing. Since Maimonides understands that for Aristotle, God is the eternal cause of the existence of the universe, the question comes up there too: How would God's bringing the entire universe into existence from eternity not constitute something's coming from nothing?

God]. You must not imagine anything else. Our father Abraham was the first to proclaim the doctrine, to which he had been led by [philosophic] deliberation."[43]

Maimonides speaks here of creation *after* nonexistence, but a more common name for the position he defends is creation *out of* nothing, or *ex nihilo*, that is to say, creation not from anything already existent.[44] Still another label appears in a disconcerting number of recent authors who have written about Maimonides. They term the position he defends as "creation in time," and that phrase has even found its way into the widely used English translation of the *Guide for the Perplexed.*[45] The scholars in question have made an unfortunate choice of words, and one can only hope that it does not reflect a failure to grasp the thought behind the words. From Maimonides' standpoint, creation of the physical universe could not conceivably have taken place *in* time, and nothing in the Arabic text of the *Guide for the Perplexed* ever justifies the translation "creation in time."

Time, as understood by Aristotle and the medieval Arabic Aristotelians, is possible only in a corporeal universe and hence is not present unless a corporeal

[43]*Guide for the Perplexed* 2.13, supplemented by 2.19, pp. 39b–40a. I have changed the order in which Maimonides presents the three positions. Maimonides' grounds for stating that Abraham was led to the doctrine of creation by philosophical investigation are aggadot according to which Abraham discovered God through observing the heavens; see *Guide for the Perplexed* 2.19, pp. 44a–b; and above p. 238, n. 205. Maimonides understands that Abraham was a prophet but that he prophesied only for himself. Thus when Abraham taught mankind the existence of God and the creation of the world, he did so through the medium of philosophic proofs and not in the role of prophet; see *Guide for the Perplexed* 2.39.

In the list of thirteen principles of faith which Maimonides incorporated into his Commentary on the Mishna, the proposition that God alone is "from eternity" is placed fourth, directly after the principles of the existence, unity, and incorporeality of God. Later, after he finished the *Guide*, he went back and added to that fourth principle the statement: "Know that the great fundamental principle of the Law of Moses is the universe's having been created . . . after absolute nonexistence." See Commentary on the Mishna, Arabic original and Hebrew translation, ed. and trans. J. Kafah (Jerusalem 1963–1968) *Sanhedrin* 10.1, p. 212. In the *Mishneh Torah*: *H. ᶜAbodat Kokabim* 1:3, where Maimonides advances the notion that the patriarch Abraham discovered the existence of God through the proof from the motion of the spheres, he mentions creation only in passing. It is possible that he did not fully appreciate the importance of the doctrine of creation for the nature of God until he came to write the *Guide for the Perplexed.*

[44]The formula *creation after nonexistence* had an advantage over *creation ex nihilo* for Maimonides, since the latter formula might be construed as *eternal creation ex nihilo*, that is, the continual and eternal bringing forth of the universe from nothing. Such, in effect, was the position of Alfarabi, of Avicenna, and of Averroes in an early stage of his thought. It is what Maimonides understood to be Aristotle's position. Maimonides' formula nevertheless has not withstood the irresistible need of commentators to have him say something different from what he actually said, and he has been interpreted as maintaining that creation took place after nonexistence only in a "causal" sense. He was, in other words, understood to have adopted the awkward position that creation took place eternally but also *after nonexistence* inasmuch as the first cause is causally prior to the world. See Joseph Kaspi, Commentary on *Guide for the Perplexed* 2.13.

[45]See Pines' translation, pp. 179, 281, 329, et passim. As far as I could see, Munk's French translation and Friedländer's earlier, generally inferior English translation avoid the error.

universe exists.[46] Maimonides accordingly stresses that since no corporeal universe existed before creation, there was no time before creation and creation did not take place, and could not have taken place, "in a temporal beginning"; on the contrary, "time is one of the things created" as part of the created universe. Maimonides turns to his reader, very possibly Joseph ben Judah, the man to whom he dedicated the *Guide*, and warns against language implying the existence of time prior to creation. Use of such language, he cautions, leaves "you" open to "refutations from which there is no escape." Your opponent will drive you into a corner by pointing out that when you admit the prior existence of time, you in effect concede the existence of a physical universe before the universe was supposedly created. You thereby refute your own belief in creation.[47]

Maimonides' stated position, then, is that God brought the universe outside Himself into existence after nonexistence; and *after* has to be construed in such a manner that it carries no implication of prior time. His position is not that God created the world *in* time.

The confrontation between the opposing positions on the origin of the world is pivotal for Maimonides, and the reason, he tells us, is not the handful of biblical verses in the Book of Genesis and elsewhere declaring that God created the heavens and the earth. Those verses do carry weight for him. But he had no difficulty in interpreting the myriad anthropomorphic descriptions of God in Scripture metaphorically. Had it been necessary—had the eternity of the world been demonstrated as the incorporeality of God had been—the handful of scriptural references to creation could likewise be allegorized away. What is truly at stake and what makes creation a fundamental principle of the Mosaic Law, coming right after the existence, unity, and incorporeality of God, is the implications that the thesis of creation, on the one hand, and eternity, on the other, have for God's nature.

He explains: If the universe was created, if God exercised His will and performed the paradigmatic miracle of bringing a universe into existence after it did not exist, God is capable of exercising His will again and intervening in the universe at any time. "All the miracles [recorded in Scripture] become possible, and the Law [*sharīᶜa*] becomes possible." Questions that might be raised about God's giving the Law to Israel—why He chose a certain man as His primary prophet, why He had His prophet perform certain miracles rather than others, why He gave His Law to a particular nation and at a particular time rather than to another nation or at another time, why He included certain commands and prohibitions in the Law rather than other commands and prohibitions, what His overall aim was in giving the Law—are disposed of at one fell swoop. The solution in every instance

[46]According to Aristotle's definition, *Physics* 4.11, 219b 2–3, time is the "number of motion in respect to before and after," which he explained as meaning that it is neither movement itself nor number itself but "movement insofar as it admits of enumeration." Hence, unless there exists a corporeal being that moves—and specifically the celestial region, which undergoes continual and unvarying circular motion—there can be no time.

[47]*Guide for the Perplexed* 2.13.

is: "thus did God will" or, what comes to the same since God's unfathomable will and unfathomable wisdom are identical with His essence and hence with one another: "Thus did His wisdom determine."

By contrast, the thesis that the world is eternal and events never deviate from their necessary course "undercuts the Law at its root." God could not have intervened in the course of history and communicated the Torah to Moses, every miracle recorded in Scripture will be "false," and Scripture's promises of reward and threats of punishment will be "idle."[48] Maimonides did not believe that miracles are frequent, and in reading Scripture, he systematically minimized them. He nevertheless insists that miracles are possible and that the authenticity of Scripture depends on the possibility of God's intervening in the universe.[49] Whereas the handful of scriptural verses speaking of creation could have been allegorized away with little difficulty, to allegorize away all the miracles in Scripture and especially God's choosing Moses to lead the Israelites out of Egypt and to Mount Sinai, where He gave them the Torah through Moses, would be nothing less than "inanity."[50] In a bit of corroborating rhetoric, Maimonides remarks that if the causal relationship between God and the universe is eternal and immutable, then God, whom every intelligent person considers to be absolute perfection, would be unable to alter the length of the wing of a fly or the leg of a worm.[51]

At stake, then, is the conception of a deity who can intervene in nature and interrupt the natural course of events. The thesis of creation entails, and the eternity of the world excludes, such a deity.

How does the foregoing bear on Plato's intermediate view?

In the intermediate view, God performed the paradigmatic miracle of bringing the world into existence after it did not exist, yet He did so from a preexistent matter. In one of the contexts from which I have quoted, Maimonides acknowledges that since the intermediate position recognizes an act of creation on the part of God, it is compatible with the possibility of further interventions by God and does not contradict the miracles recorded in Scripture. Maimonides merely adds there that as long as creation from a preexistent matter is not demonstrated, "we shall not incline toward it or give it any heed"; we "shall take the scriptural texts at face value" and affirm creation *ex nihilo*. In another context, he by contrast writes: "There is no difference for us between those [like Plato] who believe that the heavens can only come into existence from something else . . . and Aristotle, who believes that they do not come into existence at all. . . . For everyone who follows the Law of Abraham and Moses . . . believes that nothing whatsoever is co-eternal with God and it is not impossible for Him to bring what exists into existence out of

[48]*Guide for the Perplexed* 2.25. As we shall see, Maimonides did not in fact believe that God ordinarily plays an active role in the rewarding and punishing of human beings.

[49]*Guide for the Perplexed* 2.29, pp. 64b–65a.

[50]*Guide for the Perplexed* 2.25.

[51]*Guide for the Perplexed* 2.22, p. 49b.

nonexistence."[52] In one context, Maimonides acknowledges that creation from a preexistent matter is compatible with the scriptural conception of God; in another, he asserts that from the Jewish viewpoint, creation of the universe from an eternal matter is no more acceptable than the eternity of the universe as a whole. The two statements would appear to be irreconcilable and they pose a problem for interpreters of the *Guide for the Perplexed.* Perhaps Maimonides simply expressed himself carelessly.

Notwithstanding the bearing that the issue has for Scripture and religion, he treats it as a philosophic problem, and the chapters of the *Guide* which adjudicate between creation and eternity make up—in my judgment, at least—the most carefully reasoned philosophic sequence in the book. Maimonides, as just seen, explains why the issue is crucial: The nature of God is at stake. He notes that the authority of Aristotle had become dominant in intellectual circles and many of his contemporaries blindly embraced everything the Greek master was thought to have held. To reduce Aristotle to size, he therefore cites evidence showing that while what that greatest of philosophers wrote about things in the lower, sublunar region is well argued and correct, his understanding of the celestial region is riddled with holes.[53]

Maimonides further searches out passages in Aristotle's philosophic works where he found Aristotle himself recognizing that the arguments in favor of the thesis of eternity fall short of full-fledged demonstrations. Although Maimonides—whose knowledge of Aristotle was seen in an earlier chapter to have been surprisingly incomplete—refers to Aristotle dozens of times in the *Guide for the Perplexed*, he quotes a sentence or more from one of his works on only seven occasions. Five of the seven quotations serve the present purpose; they are designed to show that Aristotle realized he was offering only plausible arguments, and not true demonstrations, for the thesis of eternity. To drive the point home, Maimonides graces one of the passages he quotes from Aristotle with an interpretation that he had "not seen in any commentator." His failure to have discovered the interpretation in a Greek or Arabic commentator is hardly astonishing, seeing that it consists in teasing out the sense of superfluous wording in the pertinent Aristotelian text exactly as a midrashist would tease out the sense of superfluous words in a text of Scripture.[54]

[52]*Guide for the Perplexed* 2.13 (end); 25.

[53]*Guide for the Perplexed* 2.22, pp. 49b–50a; 24, p. 54a.

[54]The five quotations from Aristotle designed to show that he realized he had not demonstrated eternity are (a) what is more properly a paraphrase than a quotation of *On the Heavens* (*De cealo*) 2.12 in *Guide for the Perplexed* 1.5; (b) *Physics* 8.1, (c) *On the Heavens* 1.10, and (d) *Topics* 1.11, all quoted in *Guide* 2.15; and (e) *On the Heavens* 2.12, quoted in *Guide* 2.19. This last is the place where Maimonides puts his quasi-midrashic interpretation on the words "in accordance with our *intelligence*, our *understanding*, and our *opinion*." He found those words in his text of Aristotle's *On the Heavens*; the preserved Greek text does not have them, and the printed Arabic text has "in accordance with our understanding and our opinion" but not "our intelligence." The

Before proceeding to his own arguments, Maimonides examines those of his opponents. He records, analyzes, and rebuts two sets of arguments for eternity, one set that he identifies as genuinely Aristotelian and another that, he correctly observes, was formulated not by Aristotle but by post-Aristotelian philosophers. As for what he calls his own "proofs" (*dalā'il*) for creation after nonexistence, he concedes that they, like Aristotle's arguments for eternity, fall short of being full-fledged demonstrations, but he believes that they "approach" the level of demonstration.[55]

His proofs conform to a single mold, each calling attention to an aspect of the universe which would be inexplicable if the relationship between God and the universe outside of God were necessary and immutable. To take just one example: The distribution of the stars across the heavens discloses no plan or order and appears to be entirely random. If the universe had no cause, the locations of the stars in the heavens—that is to say, in the celestial sphere in which they are embedded—could be a matter of pure chance; but Maimonides' demonstrations of the existence of God established that the visible universe does have a cause and does not exist by chance. Now, if the cause of the universe acted immutably and through necessity, the stars should be arranged in accordance with some necessary law and reveal a uniform pattern. The fact that they do not and are instead scattered randomly across the heavens indicates that God, for reasons known to Himself, exercised His will and deliberately chose a patternless arrangement.

But acting through will and choice goes hand in hand with acting after not having acted. Maimonides' conclusion is therefore that the world was brought into existence after not having existed; as will be noted, the argument says nothing about creation's having occurred *ex nihilo*.[56] More important than the conclusion that the world was created is what the argument reveals about the nature of God. If God possesses will and performed the miracle of creation, He can intervene in the universe and perform the lesser miracles recorded in Scripture.

The incorporeal, unknowable, indescribable deity resulting from Maimonides' demonstrations of the existence of God and his theory of divine attributes has now been shown, through the arguments for creation, to be possessed of will and hence to be a deity capable of intervening in the universe and steering events in new directions should His wisdom decide on such a course.

---

remaining two quotations of a sentence or more from Aristotle are *Guide* 2.20, quoting *Physics* 2.4; and *Guide* 3.43, quoting *Nicomachean Ethics* 8.9.

[55] *Guide for the Perplexed* 2.19, p. 40a.

[56] *Guide for the Perplexed* 2.19, pp. 43b–44a. For Maimonides' other arguments, including one that does conclude with creation *ex nihilo*, see. H. Davidson, "Maimonides' Secret Position on Creation," *Studies in Medieval Jewish History and Literature*, ed. I. Twersky (Cambridge, Mass. 1979) 27–35. Students of philosophy will note that Maimonides has inverted the procedure of arguments from design. Arguments from design look for order in the universe and draw inferences from that. Maimonides' arguments for creation reason from an absence of order in the celestial region.

When Maimonides, in the Commentary on the Mishna, originally outlined plans for two or three works on the nonlegal side of the Jewish religion, one of the topics that he said he wanted to expound was the general philosophic propositions needed for understanding the phenomenon of prophecy. Even after rethinking his plans, he writes again in the introduction to the *Guide for the Perplexed* that the "nature" of prophecy would be one of the topics he would take up in the book.[57]

In the chapters of the *Guide* that fulfill the promise, Maimonides starts, as the basis of discussion, with what he calls the "view of the philosophers" regarding the nature of prophecy; he does so without citing or even alluding to the reasoning underlying that view. He makes a couple of critical adjustments, which rest on scriptural and theological, not philosophic considerations. And he asserts that "the view of our Law and the fundamental principle of our religion" is identical with the view of the philosophers once the adjustments are made. His treatment of the subject may be categorized as philosophical—first, because it builds on theories evolved by the Arabic Aristotelian school of philosophy, and, secondly, because what he defines as the "view of our Law" regarding prophecy is an extension and application of the concept of God that he arrived at on philosophic grounds.

The last rung in the hierarchy of transcendent incorporeal beings consisting in pure thought and subordinate to God in Maimonides' picture of the universe is an incorporeal being known as the *active intellect*. Maimonides further understood—and here he was following the Arabic philosopher Avicenna in particular—that the active intellect continually and invariably emanates the entire range of abstract human thoughts. Human beings tap into the transmission of the active intellect to the extent that their intellects are attuned for doing so. Although the active intellect is the immediate source, the emanation may be said to come from God. Since God is the ultimate, and hence the true cause of everything in the universe, He is the ultimate and true cause of the existence of the active intellect and of the emanation that it emits.

The conception cannot help striking today's reader as bizarre. Maimonides is saying that when a human being thinks an abstract thought, the thought is not formed by the person himself but comes to him, fully fashioned, from outside. The human being's role consists in preparing his intellect for thinking the abstract thought and thereby attuning himself for receiving the emanation, or transmission, or broadcast, of the active intellect. When a human intellect is properly prepared, it automatically taps into that emanation and thinks the thought—just as in the modern world, a properly attuned radio or television receiver immediately receives whatever signal it is attuned for.[58] Prophecy occurs when a human soul receives the emanation of the active intellect in a certain manner.

[57] See above, pp. 323–24, 327.

[58] *Guide for the Perplexed* 2.4, p. 14a; 3.8, p. 12a. For Avicenna's position, see H. Davidson, *Alfarabi, Avicenna, and Averroes, on Intellect* (New York 1992) 86–89.

The candidate for prophecy has to possess an intellect that is capable of comprehending abstract thoughts at the highest level, in other words, an intellect that has mastered philosophy and science. Consummate knowledge of philosophy and science is therefore a precondition. The person must further possess an especially strong and healthy imaginative faculty; the imaginative faculty is one of several faculties of the soul having a physical seat in the brain, and among its functions is the ability to fashion images. Thirdly, he must have attained a level of morality that secures him against the distractions of sensual desires and allows him to focus his attention on the supernal realms. The highly developed intellect of such a soul is attuned for receiving a full measure of the ever-present emanation of the active intellect, and when it does, the emanation filters through the soul's intellectual faculty into its healthy and powerful imaginative faculty. The human subject will then "conceive nothing other than highly abstruse divine matters and will see nothing other than God and His angels"; his imaginative faculty will convert abstract truths about God and the lesser supernal incorporeal beings into visual as well as audible images. The prophet will also be able to formulate rules whereby society can be governed for the benefit of its members. And he will have the gift of grasping the laws of nature governing human affairs, of applying those laws instantaneously to facts at hand, and of thereby foreseeing the direction that events are going to take. He will thus be able to predict the future. "This," Maimonides tells us, "is the highest degree attainable by man, the culminating perfection of the human species."[59]

Thus far, he has sketched for us the philosophic view of prophecy. He finds the view of the Mosaic Law and Jewish religion to be identical with the philosophic view "in all but one respect." If nature (*al-amr al-ṭabīᶜī*) were left to its own devices, everyone who satisfies the conditions would prophesy. "We," however, believe that God can, by an exercise of will, miraculously block the course of nature. God can intercede, halt the process, and prevent someone who is attuned for receiving the emanation of the active intellect in a prophetic mode from prophesying.[60] Since that is the only role played by God in the prophetic process, it remains unclear how Maimonides would explain—and for that matter whether he believed in—the ability of prophets apart from Moses to perform and foresee genuine miracles.

The view of the Mosaic Law adds a further reservation to the philosophic theory of prophecy: A single man in the history of mankind, the biblical Moses, prophesied without the aid of his imaginative faculty and without attuning himself to the ever-present emanation of the active intellect. God Himself communicated directly with Moses' intellect.[61]

[59] *Guide for the Perplexed* 2.32; 36; 38.

[60] *Guide for the Perplexed* 2.32 (3).

[61] *Guide for the Perplexed* 2.35, which refers back to Commentary on the Mishna, *Sanhedrin* 10:1, seventh principle, and *Mishneh Torah*: *H. Yesode ha-Torah* 7.6.

In the introduction to the *Guide for the Perplexed*, Maimonides informed us that he had decided not to discuss certain aspects of prophecy openly because they were inappropriate for unsophisticated readers. In one of the early chapters of the *Guide* he lists "the essence [*ma^c^nā*] of prophecy" among topics that are "secrets of the Torah" and not to be fully revealed to the ordinary run of mankind.[62] Yet he apparently sees no impropriety in allowing the unsophisticated who happen upon the *Guide* to read there that a prerequisite of prophecy is developing one's intellect through the study of philosophy and science; that prophecy comes about through a natural process and automatically; that, with the sole exception of Moses, prophets receive their inspiration not directly from God but from the ever-present emanation of the active intellect; that God plays a direct role only when he stays the natural process; and hence that when Scripture depicts God as speaking to a prophet, such speech occurred solely in a vision or dream evoked by the emanation of the active intellect.[63] Maimonides had in fact already exposed readers to an unambiguous, albeit less detailed, version of the theory both in the list of thirteen principles of faith that he incorporated into his Commentary on the Mishna and in his *Mishneh Torah*.[64]

The concept of God that Maimonides was seen to develop earlier has here been carried over to the phenomenon of prophecy. In treating the earlier issues, he taught that God usually allows nature to follow its course, yet the possibility always remains that He might exercise His will and intervene miraculously, as He once did in the miracle of bringing a universe into existence. Maimonides now tells us that as long as events are allowed to run their course, every soul attuned for prophecy will receive the inspiration from the ever-present emanation of the active intellect which renders it a prophet. But God can exercise his will and intervene miraculously, and when He does, His action consists in preventing events from proceeding naturally. During one period of human history, God intervened positively and more dramatically by communicating directly with the intellect of the greatest man ever to have lived.

What Maimonides has told us about prophecy forms the background for a final philosophic topic that we ought to consider: the manner whereby God exercises providence over the universe and particularly over man. As in his treatment of creation and prophecy, Maimonides begins by setting forth positions that had been adopted on the issue. He dismisses all but one, which he characterizes variously as "our view," the view of "our Law," and the view of the "Law of Moses." We may leave aside the alternative positions and consider only that.

It is, he writes, "one of the foundations of the Law of Moses that God cannot possibly be unjust and that every ill or good fortune affecting mankind individually

[62] *Guide for the Perplexed* 1.35, p. 42a.

[63] For the last point, see *Guide for the Perplexed* 2.41.

[64] Above, p. 156.

or communally is in accordance with the deserts of the persons concerned, through a just judgment." "If a thorn pricks someone's hand,[65] . . . that is a punishment, if someone has the slightest pleasure, that is a reward, and everything is in accordance with a person's deserts. As Scripture says: 'All His ways are justice.'" The manner whereby a man's deserts lead to the result is, however, "beyond our comprehension."[66]

Whereupon Maimonides takes the uncommon step of placing his personal "belief" and "opinion" alongside the view of the Law of Moses. He rejects nothing said so far—he is after all adding his twist to nothing less than a doctrine of the divine Law. When speaking in his own name, he too affirms that everything occurring to members of the human species, whether pleasant or painful, is "in accordance with what the person deserves; as Scripture says: 'All His ways are justice.'" But he adds a critical nuance that transforms divine providence into something very different from what the vast majority of his coreligionists understood it to be. While he has no "demonstration" for the nuance, he cites a passage in the Arabic philosopher Alfarabi which, he thinks, lends it support and he ventures that it both meets the demands of reason and harmonizes with statements found in Scripture.[67]

Providence, in Maimonides' version, "follows upon the divine emanation," that is, the emanation coming from the "most perfect intellect," or God. And the instrument by which one taps into the divine emanation and partakes of providence is the human intellect. To the extent that a human being perfects his intellect, the divine emanation makes contact with him and he gains the protection of divine providence. At the apex, when "everything revealed to a man of intellect" is revealed to a person, the divine emanation "associates itself with him and directs all his actions by way of reward and punishment."[68]

The sinking of a ship with its passengers and the collapse of the roof of a house on those inside serve as illustrations. Events of the sort, Maimonides writes, occur by pure chance, yet the decision to enter or avoid the ship or the house is "not . . . in our view accidental." A person makes that decision "through divine will, in accordance with his deserts, by way of God's judgments, which operate through laws beyond our understanding."[69] Maimonides is saying once again that the workings of providence are beyond human comprehension, but theories found in other medieval Jewish writers suggest the type of notion that he likely had in mind. The writers in question explain that when someone perfects his intellect to the level where it is attuned to the forces in the universe affecting his life, he receives intimations of what is in his interest, and the intimations direct him away from

[65]Cf. BT *Ḥullin* 7b: "No one injures his finger here below unless it is so decreed from above."

[66]*Guide for the Perplexed* 3.17, pp. 34b–35a. The verse is Deuteronomy 32:4.

[67]*Guide for the Perplexed* 3.17, pp. 35b–36a; 18, pp. 38b–39a.

[68]*Guide for the Perplexed* 3.17, pp. 36a, 37b.

[69]*Guide for the Perplexed* 3.17, p. 36a.

dangerous situations and toward actions that benefit him.[70] Maimonides, for his part, seems to be suggesting that when someone perfects his intellect and comes into contact with the divine emanation, he receives intimations directing him away from ill-fated ships, unstable roofs, and similar dangers.

In the list of "secrets of the Torah" which should not be divulged to the unsophisticated, Maimonides includes the secret of "how God's providence" operates.[71] We have nonetheless seen more than once that he can in one breath insist on something's being hidden and in the next breath be surprisingly open regarding it. From the standpoint of conventional religion, the implications of the nuance that he has added to the view of the Mosaic Law on divine providence are more radical than anything else we have encountered in the *Guide*, yet he makes no great effort at concealment. He states openly that since "providence follows intellect," it is proportional to a human being's intellectual attainments and consequently "not . . . equal in all men." Providence is very strong in the case of the prophets, although even there variations occur, inasmuch as different prophets reach different levels of perfection. Providence over "the virtuous and righteous" is proportional to their attainments. "As for the sinful ignorant, insofar as they lack" contact with the divine emanation, they are exposed to happenstance and left unprotected, "like him who walks in total darkness and whose ruination is guaranteed" or, in the language of Scripture, "like the beasts that perish."[72] The punishment of such persons is not something that God or any other higher being decides upon and executes; it is simply their being exposed to the vagaries of everyday life as a consequence of having only negligible contact with the emanation from above. The thesis that the degree of providence one enjoys depends on one's degree of intellectual perfection and that the sinful ignorant enjoy no providence at all belongs, in Maimonides' opinion, to the "fundamental principles of the Law," and he cites passages of Scripture to support his contention.[73]

Not merely does someone of superior intellectual accomplishments enjoy a larger measure of divine providence than someone of lesser accomplishments. The same person may partake of different degrees of providence at different times. As long as an individual worthy of providence keeps his mind and attention focused on intellectual matters, the divine emanation is in firm contact with him and his degree of providence is high. Should he, however, let his mind and attention stray to

[70] Abraham Ibn Ezra, Commentary on Exodus 33:21; Levi Gersonides, *Milḥamot ha-Shem* 4.5. Moses Ibn Tibbon proposes a similar explanation of Maimonides' conception of divine providence; see Z. Diesendruck, "Samuel and Moses Ibn Tibbon on Maimonides' Theory of Providence," *Hebrew Union College Annual* 11 (1936) 363–64.

[71] *Guide for the Perplexed* 1.35, p. 42a.

[72] *Guide for the Perplexed* 3.18, quoting Psalms 49:13. Maimonides adds that in principle there is little reason not to destroy "the sinful ignorant" and when circumstances require—as when men and women professing idolatrous beliefs threaten the true faith—Scripture indeed commands that they be put to death.

[73] *Guide for the Perplexed* 3.18

mundane matters, the degree of providence he enjoys is diminished—although without disappearing completely. Therein lies the key to the misfortunes that befall the prophet, the wise man, and the righteous. When their minds turn away from intellectual matters and lose contact with the emanation from God which exercises providence over mankind, they too fall prey to the random slings and arrows of everyday life.[74] One can scarcely help wondering whether events that Maimonides observed in his own lifetime—the suffering of the Jewish communities in the West at the hands of the Almohads, the death of his brother at sea—may not have had a part in his thinking.

Some of the words that I have quoted have to be decoded in order to complete the picture, but the decoding is not difficult. In the first place, the "virtuous and righteous" who partake of divine providence are plainly not so in a merely ethical sense. They are persons who have perfected their intellects. Secondly, when Maimonides writes that an emanation from the most perfect intellect in existence, or God, exercises providence over man, his meaning must be only that God is the ultimate source. We saw earlier that all abstract human thought comes to man from the active intellect and its emanation, that the emanation from the active intellect inspires the prophet, and that the ultimate source of the emanation is God. Maimonides now writes in connection with providence that the emanation protecting the virtuous man is identical with the emanation providing him with scientific knowledge (*ᶜulūm*) and that the emanation protecting the prophet is identical with the emanation inspiring the prophet "to speak."[75] A single emanation coming from the active intellect is the source of human abstract thought, prophecy, and divine providence; they are related phenomena. God is responsible in the sense that He is the ultimate cause of the existence of the active intellect and hence the true cause of the emanation emitted by it.

Thirdly when Maimonides says that in the view of the Law of Moses, everything pleasant or unpleasant, even being pricked by a thorn, is a reward or punishment imposed by God's judgment and the divine will, he does not mean that God holds daily court and decides who is to be pricked by a thorn or vouchsafed pleasure on a given day and who is not to be. When he wrote in his *Mishneh Torah* that God judges the wicked and condemns the worst of them to death on the spot or again that God decides during the New Year season who is to be inscribed for life and who is to be inscribed for death, he cannot have meant those words literally.[76] In his scheme, being pricked by a thorn and other mishaps are punishments in the sense that they result from being out of contact with the emanation of the active intellect. As for the assertion that every pleasure a human being enjoys is a reward, that can hold water only for the enlightened few as long as they are in contact with

[74] *Guide for the Perplexed* 3.51, p. 127b.

[75] *Guide for the Perplexed* 3.18, p. 38a. Maimonides further writes, perhaps disingenuously, that the emanation "directs the actions of the righteous."

[76] *Mishneh Torah*: *H. Teshuba* 3:2–3.

the emanation of the active intellect, not for the unenlightened many whose contact with the emanation is negligible.

The centrality of intellect for Maimonides and the attendant minimizing of a direct role of God in human affairs cannot be stressed too often or too strongly: Before a human being may hope for the gift of prophecy, he must perfect his intellect, for only then will he receive the emanation of the active intellect in the desired fashion; God limits His direct role in the process to denying prophecy to some who would otherwise prophesy. Divine providence is contingent on a person's perfecting his intellect and establishing contact with the same emanation from the active intellect; in explaining how providence works, Maimonides makes no mention of a direct intervention by God in the lives of ordinary human beings, although we did see that he recognizes divine miracles during the period of the exodus of the Israelites from Egypt. His rabbinic works made clear that the only part of man to survive the death of the body and gain immortality is a developed human intellect and they gave an inkling of the procedure whereby intellectual immortality is achieved. While the subject of human immortality does not come up formally in the *Guide for the Perplexed*, when Maimonides touches on it in passing, he takes the predictable stance: The "sole . . . cause" of human immortality is perfecting one's intellect through acquisition of all knowledge that a human being is capable of.[77] We hear nothing in any of Maimonides' works of a great assize in which God judges each individual human being and decides who will and who will not be allowed to pass through the gates of paradise.

The Rationalizing and Spiritualizing Strand in the Guide for the Perplexed. The *Guide for the Perplexed* is Maimonides' most comprehensive exposition of the nonlegal side of the Jewish religion. Since that meant for him the rationalized and spiritual side, a plausible case could be made for taking the rationalizing and spiritualizing of religion not as one of several strands in the *Guide for the Perplexed* but as its entire warp and woof. I have ventured that a more illuminating picture emerges when three main strands are distinguished.

[77] *Guide for the Perplexed* 3.27, p. 60a; similarly 1.70, p. 92b.

In *Guide for the Perplexed* 3.51, p. 129b, when speaking of the postmortal human intellect, Maimonides can write that after a perfected intellect separates from the body and enters the immortal state, it experiences "enormous pleasure." In *Guide for the Perplexed* 1.74 (7) (to be taken together with *Guide* 2, introduction, proposition 16), he refers to the opinion of the Islamic philosopher Ibn Bājja according to which human intellects entering the immortal state coalesce into a single collective intellect in which all individuality is lost and he appears to endorse that position; if all individuality is lost, it would be senseless to speak of the pleasure of an individual intellect. The dissonance between the two statements is discussed by A. Altmann, "Maimonides on the Intellect and the Scope of Metaphysics," in his *Von der mittelalterlichen zur modernen Aufklärung* (Tübingen1987) 87–90, and Altmann contends that Maimonides did recognize a degree of individuality in the immortal state.

Continuing on the premise, the present section offers a few illustrations of Maimonides' rationalizing and spiritualizing of the Jewish religion where he goes beyond the exegesis of problematic terms and figurative passages in Scripture and beyond philosophy in the strict sense.

His thoughts on the Torah, which he shares with the reader from the beginning of the *Guide for the Perplexed* to the end, make a good place to start. Maimonides characterizes the Torah as a unique and perfect fount of wisdom for the Jewish people and for everyone else who has the good sense to turn to it.[78] It is the "book that guides everyone who seeks guidance, toward the truth."[79] And since what is perfect cannot be improved upon, there has never been a divine Law like it and it will never be replaced by another.[80] Although a legion of Jewish thinkers before and after Maimonides would heartily endorse those sentiments, considerably fewer would agree with his understanding of the guidance that the Torah provides.

He posits, with recourse to Aristotelian terminology, that man has two perfections (ἐντελέχεια), one of the human body and the other of the human soul. As could easily have been predicted, he ranks the latter above the former. Perfection of the body consists in physical health, and that of the soul, in man's becoming an "actual intellect" through knowledge of "everything a man can possibly know about all things that exist"; "it clearly contains neither deeds nor qualities [of the soul] [*akhlāq*]." Perfection of the soul is, in a word, perfection of the human intellect.

The Torah comes to man's aid at both levels: It has "two things as its aim, namely, the welfare of the [human] soul and the welfare of the [human] body." It brings about the former by providing "mankind [*al-jumhūr*] with correct views [*ārā*ᶜ], in accordance with their capabilities," examples being the affirmation of the existence and unity of God, of God's knowledge, power and will, of His having existed from all eternity, and of His not being a body. Because the Torah addresses persons whose capacities vary, it leaves certain things unsaid; it teaches, for example, that God exists and is one without entering into all the premises whereby those propositions can be demonstrated. And because it ministers in particular to "ordinary mankind," who cannot always fully comprehend the truths that they must accept, it conveys "some [propositions] explicitly and some, metaphorically." Maimonides at one juncture adduces the scriptural representations of God in anthropomorphic language as an instance of a metaphorical conveying of an essential truth—the truth that God exists: Novices find it hard to conceive of incorporeal being, and by using anthropomorphic language, Scripture can more easily convince them of the existence of God;[81] and this is so even though everyone must be disabused of the notion that God is a body as soon as possible,

[78]*Guide for the Perplexed* 2.39; 3.27, p. 60a.
[79]*Guide for the Perplexed* 3.13, p. 25a.
[80]*Guide for the Perplexed* 2.39.
[81]*Guide for the Perplexed* 1.26.

since to hold that erroneous belief is sheer heresy.[82] A set of truths that is conveyed metaphorically in a later book of the Bible would be the account of the chariot in the book of Ezekiel, where the science of metaphysics is cast in figurative language.

It will be no surprise that the welfare of the human body, the other part of the Torah's aim, is a precondition of the welfare of the soul. Man, being a compound creature, cannot devote himself to intellectual pursuits "as long as he is in physical pain, unduly hungry or thirsty, or suffering from severe hot or cold." And since no single individual is able to provide for all his physical needs—food, clothing, shelter, and the like—men cannot be islands unto themselves; they must live in societies. Maimonides, with his predilection for dividing and subdividing, distinguishes two ways in which the Torah ministers to the human body: First, it promulgates laws that check violence among the members of society, and, secondly, it inculcates qualities of the soul (*akhlāq*) that members of society must possess if peace and cooperation are to reign.[83]

Human legal codes also, of course, endeavor to create a nonviolent, well-ordered society. The critical difference for Maimonides is that the human codes go no further and are unconcerned with the soul. Counterfeit religious codes—he is thinking particularly of Islamic religious law, which discretion prevented him from naming—pretend to be divinely given. They copy from the Torah, adding here and subtracting there, with the object of creating a verisimilitude of originality, and they, like the authentic revealed law, address both man's physical and his spiritual needs. But the alterations mar the product, and false prophets reveal themselves to be such through their sullied personal lives and especially their inability to rein in their sexual drives. Maimonides calls attention to a couple of obscure false prophets in Scripture who took an unhealthy interest in their neighbors' wives[84] but he was undoubtedly thinking not so much of them as of the Muslim prophet Muhammad; the Islamic sources themselves relate that Muhammad had a weakness for attractive women.[85]

The Torah concerns itself, then, with the welfare of the human body and human soul, or intellect, and it has the goal of bringing about the perfection of both body and soul, particularly the latter. If Maimonides had been asked whether he was not reducing the Torah to a propaedeutic for the study of philosophy, he would have

[82] *Guide for the Perplexed* 1.35; 36, p. 44a; see above, p. 289.

[83] *Guide for the Perplexed* 3.27–28. *Guide* 3.39, p. 85a, shows that *akhlāq* are not necessarily *moral* qualities.

[84] *Guide for the Perplexed* 2.39–40, referring to Zedekiah the son of Maaseiah and Ahab the son of Kolaiah, who appear in Jeremiah 29:21–23.

[85] The Islamic sources describe repeated instances where Muhammad caught sight of an attractive woman and quickly added her to his considerable harem of wives and concubines. In one notorious instance, the woman was already married and her husband divorced her so that Muhammad could take her. See W. Muir, *The Life of Moḥammad* (Edinburgh 1923) 290–92, 298, 319, 377–78, 383, 427–28, 515.

replied that on the contrary he was showing it to be a unique, divinely designed system for educating all levels of mankind.

To bring out in detail how the Torah does its work, he devotes a series of chapters—one-seventh of the entire book—to the Torah's commandments. Readers of the *Book of Commandments* and *Mishneh Torah* had already been told that divine commandments are not arbitrary, that their rationale is not simply to drill men and women in blind obedience to God, and that each has its specific purpose. In the *Mishneh Torah*, Maimonides explicated what he took to be the purposes served by a handful of commandments. The *Guide for the Perplexed* goes into the subject systematically.[86]

It posits that "every one of the 613 commandments" received by Moses has its reason and purpose, and to suppose otherwise would be demeaning to God, the author of the Torah; such a supposition would imply that God behaves without purpose and hence irrationally.[87] Maimonides proceeds to consider, one by one, about a quarter of the 613 commandments and to bring out the reason for which he thinks they were instituted. In his interpretation, they all contribute in some way to the welfare of either the human body or human soul by, either directly or indirectly, teaching essential truths, checking violence, or inculcating human qualities necessary for a smoothly working society.

For example, the first of the Ten Commandments, "I am the Lord your God," is, in Maimonides' account, the obligation to *know* the existence of God, and the commandment to recite[88] the Hear O Israel passage is the injunction to *know* God's unity. Both commandments guide the human intellect to its perfection and promote the welfare of the human soul.[89] The prohibitions against swearing in the name of any but the true God, against breaking a divine oath, and against swearing in vain train man in honoring and exalting God and thereby promote the belief in a perfect deity.[90] Observance of the Sabbath day teaches—as Scripture itself states—that God created the world, and the Sabbath also provides the body with a needed period of rest after the labors of the week.[91]

Commandments of the Torah that prescribe punishments for murder, robbery, and other crimes plainly check violence and contribute to a stable society. The commandments to love one's neighbor and refrain from bearing grudges inculcate socially desirable character traits. Regulations for slaughtering animals in the least painful manner, for chasing away the mother bird before removing its young or its eggs from the nest, for refraining from cutting off a segment of a live animal as food, and for refraining from slaughtering a cow or ewe and its young both on one

[86]He divides the commandments into fourteen classes which only in part match the fourteen Books of his *Mishneh Torah*.

[87]*Guide for the Perplexed* 3.31.

[88]As the Oral Torah understands Scripture.

[89]*Guide for the Perplexed* 3.27, and 3.52 (end). See above, p. 234.

[90]*Guide for the Perplexed* 3.36.

[91]*Guide for the Perplexed* 2.31; 3.28; 36; 41, p. 90b; 43, p. 95a.

day all instill a desirable character trait, the quality of compassion.[92] They thereby contribute to the welfare of the human body.

Then there are the seemingly unfathomable commandments such as the prohibitions against wearing garments in which wool and linen have been spun or woven together, the wearing of women's clothes by men and of men's clothes by women, grafting a branch from one species of tree on a tree of another species, sowing two species of seed together, and the like. Maimonides interprets commandments of the sort as stratagems in the Torah's campaign to "separate [the Israelite nation] from idolatry."[93] Arabic books circulated in his day which described actual or imagined ancient pagan beliefs and practices,[94] and those descriptions present an array of rituals. Pagan priests shaved their beards and wore garments of mixed materials, and that, Maimonides explains, is reason why the Torah forbids the practices. Since the pagans had rituals in which men and women wore one another's garments, the Torah forbids such practices too; at the same time it undoubtedly also wants to discourage the licentiousness accompanying cross-dressing. Pagans, Maimonides found in the books he examined, performed a ceremony in which a beautiful girl grafted a branch from one species of tree on a tree of a different species at the very moment when a man was performing an unspeakable sexual act with her. To extirpate the practice completely, the Torah, on Maimonides' interpretation, forbids not only grafting a branch from one species on a tree of another species but forbids even sowing seeds belonging to multiple species together.[95] By rooting out idolatrous practices and false beliefs regarding the divine, these commandments and others of a similar character further the welfare of the human intellect.

A good number of the Torah's commandments deal with the construction of a divine sanctuary, the erection of an altar on the sanctuary grounds, the offering of divers communal and private sacrifices to God, and the establishing of a priestly class with responsibility for the Temple, the altar, and the sacrificial service. Maimonides makes no effort to hide his opinion that offering animal sacrifices, bringing meal offerings, and pouring out wine libations are not the most refined mode of divine worship. He quotes such scriptural verses as the one in which God, speaking through the mouth of the prophet, asks rhetorically: "To what purpose is the multitude of your sacrifices unto Me?" And he cites as further evidence the limitations Scripture places on the venues where sacrifices may be offered—only in the holy sanctuary—and the narrow class of men it allows to serve as priests—only descendants of Aaron, the brother of Moses. By limiting the

[92] *Guide for the Perplexed* 3.28; 48. In *Mishneh Torah*: *H. Tefilla* 9.7, following BT *Berakot* 33b and parallels, and Maimonides' own Commentary on Mishna on the relevant passages, he states that sending away the mother bird is a divine decree and leaves it at that.

[93] *Guide for the Perplexed* 3.49, p. 119a. He deploys the same sort of explanation in *Mishneh Torah*: *H. ᶜAbodat Kokabim* 12:7, 11, 13.

[94] *Guide for the Perplexed* 3.29, pp. 64b–66b.

[95] *Guide for the Perplexed* 3.37.

bringing of sacrifices to a single holy sanctuary, and persons who officiate to a single family, God obviously wanted to "restrict this type of worship" to what His "wisdom determined should not be completely abandoned."

On Maimonides' reading, the dozens of commandments concerned with sacrifices have an educational function: When the ancient Israelites received the Torah, the nations around them worshiped images, or, at the very best, worshiped the stars, through sacrifices and the burning of incense in temples, and those were the religious rites with which the Israelites were familiar. It is a law of human nature that men resist being violently wrenched away from the forms in which they have been brought up; prohibiting sacrifice outright and immediately instituting a more intellectual mode of worship would therefore have been too great a shock. To wean the Children of Israel away from the worship of images and stars and to turn their hearts toward the true God, the Torah accordingly instructs them to build a sanctuary and an altar, to establish an elaborate system of sacrifices, and to install a priestly class, with the critical proviso that everything be done solely for the sake of God. The Torah's sacrificial system thereby ingrains the belief in the existence and unity of the true God, who transcends the stars.[96] It too contributes to the welfare of the human intellect.

Maimonides, it should be noted, nowhere draws the inference that inasmuch as sacrifices have done their job, they will be dispensed with in the future. When he describes the messianic age in the concluding chapter of the *Mishneh Torah*, he repeats, with no apparent qualms, the talmudic belief that the Messiah will rebuild the Holy Temple and reinstitute the sacrificial service.[97] He incorporates in his code of Jewish law a sketch of the daily liturgy and liturgies for the Sabbath, New Moon, and Festivals, and he includes there the traditional prayers for the restoration of animal sacrifices;[98] he undoubtedly recited those prayers himself. Neither in the *Mishneh Torah*, the *Guide for the Perplexed*, nor anywhere else does he in any way hint that since Temple sacrifice is an inferior form of worship and has fulfilled its original purpose, it will never be reinstated. What his full thinking on the subject may have been can only be conjectured. Perhaps, like other Jews of a rational bent who, until the present day, recite the prayers for the rapid rebuilding of the Holy Temple and restoration of the sacrificial service, he was not sure what to think.

The reasons uncovered by Maimonides for other commandments run along similar lines. Those commandments in some manner promote the welfare of the human body or human intellect.

[96]*Guide for the Perplexed* 3.32; the scriptural verse quoted by Maimonides is Isaiah 1:11. The function of sacrifices in weaning Israel away from idolatry is expressed, in homey language, by *Leviticus Rabba* 22:8, as pointed out by M. Margulies in the notes to his critical edition of *Leviticus Rabba*.

[97]*Mishneh Torah*: *H. Melakim* 11.1.

[98]*Yedi^cot ha-Makon le-Ḥeqer ha-Shira ha-^cIbrit* 7 (1958) 196, 202–5.

It is not just worshiping God through sacrifices that Maimonides deems less than ideal. "Crying out to God [in personal supplication], reciting the [formal, fixed] liturgy, performing other practices that are part of divine worship"—wearing "fringes [on one's garments, affixing] parchment scrolls to the doorpost, [wearing] phylacteries, and the like"—are "closer" to the ideal than sacrifice is. That can be seen in the Torah's ordaining that not merely a single clan but all members of the nation, or in some cases all males, pray, affix parchment scrolls containing the appropriate biblical verses to their doorposts, wear phylacteries, and the like; and from its prescribing that prayer and the ritual practices be observed everywhere and not merely in a single sanctuary. Nevertheless, even worshiping God through the fixed liturgy and ritual acts that Jews are instructed to recite and perform daily—prayers and rituals that Maimonides himself observed punctiliously—falls short of the highest form of worship. The highest form is "thought [*fikra*] unaccompanied by any act whatsoever,"[99] and "the more one increases thought of God, . . . the more worship [of God] increases."[100] The adulatory descriptions of God permeating the liturgy become in Maimonides' hands a grudging concession to human frailty, an artifice for giving man at least a partial notion of the deity to whom he prays, and they should be kept to a minimum. Where God is concerned, "to keep silent is to praise."[101]

There is no suggestion anywhere in Maimonides' writings that the Jewish liturgy, replete as it is with praises of God and the marking of sections to be recited aloud, would ever be abolished. Instead he appeals to readers not to run through the fixed liturgy or act out the obligatory rituals (*miṣwot*) as matters of rote without paying attention to what their tongues are saying and their hands are doing, "like someone digging a hole in the ground or gathering firewood in the forest." Prayers and rituals should be a vehicle for ascent to what lies behind them. When a person recites the daily prayers, performs the obligatory ritual acts, and reads Scripture, his object should be to train himself in turning away from the world and focusing his attention exclusively on God.[102]

The exhortation to focus attention exclusively on God is scarcely a new theme in devotional literature.[103] What sets Maimonides' version of the exhortation apart is his stress on science and intellect. Worship at its highest, he tells us, consists in "applying one's thought to God alone after having attained scientific knowledge of Him," that is, after mastering the demonstrations of God's existence, unity, incorporeality, and freedom from attributes. As for persons who "think about God and talk about Him at length without scientific knowledge, following nothing but an imaginative concept of God or a belief received on the authority of somebody else,

[99]*Guide for the Perplexed* 3.32, pp. 70a, 71b–72a.
[100]*Guide for the Perplexed* 3.51, p. 124b.
[101]*Guide for the Perplexed* 1.59, pp. 73a–74b.
[102]*Guide for the Perplexed* 3.51, p. 125b.
[103]See, for example, G. Vajda, *La Théologie ascétique de Baḥya* (Paris 1947) 86–87.

such persons in my view are . . . not only distant [from God]; they are not truly talking about God and thinking about Him at all. For what they have in their imagination and talk about corresponds to nothing whatsoever that exists and is merely a figment of their imagination." The words could not be more biting: Persons who worship without knowledge of basic demonstrated propositions about God—a category that would include over 99 percent of senior rabbinic scholars through Jewish history, and a larger percentage of nonscholars—worship a figment of their imagination. Since the human faculty by which God is truly worshiped is a perfected intellect, Maimonides calls the form of worship that he recommends "intellectual worship" of God.[104]

Intellectual worship converges with what he views as human life at its acme. In his rabbinic works, he presented as the ideal, a life in which all human activities are directed toward a single goal: knowledge of God. If a person eats, drinks, and even goes to sleep, with the sole intent of maintaining a healthy and strong body that will enable him to devote his intellect to knowing God, then, Maimonides wrote, the person serves God through eating, drinking, and sleeping.[105] In the *Guide for the Perplexed*, he carries the notion further.

He exhorts his readers to mobilize not only all their activities, but every moment of their time, toward the true goal of life. A person should allow his thoughts to turn to the "needs and amenities of life," such as planning his business, running a household, and caring for his body, only during periods when he is in any event distracted, as when he is at meals, in the bathhouse, or conversing with his "wife, his small children, or . . . common people [*jumhūr al-nās*]." He should be forewarned, however, that as long as he turns his attention to everyday needs and desires, his link with the divine emanation is interrupted and he loses the protection of divine providence. When a person discharges his fixed religious obligations—praying, performing the religious actions ordained by the Torah, reading Scripture—he should set everything extraneous aside and focus his thought exclusively on them and their deeper purpose. The most precious moments are those in which a person is by himself during the day or lies awake in bed at night.[106] At those times his thought should be on God alone, he should approach God, and he should present himself before Him. Maimonides believes that the style of life outlined thus far lies within the power of men of science who train themselves systematically.

A still higher rung remains, one attained by Moses and the three patriarchs, Abraham, Isaac, and Jacob, and one that Maimonides confesses was beyond his

[104]*Guide for the Perplexed* 3.51, pp. 124b, 126a.

[105]*Shemona Peraqim* (=Commentary on the Mishna, introduction to *Abot*) 5. English translation: Moses Maimonides, *Eight Chapters*, ed. and trans. J. Gorfinkle (New York 1912). *Mishneh Torah*: *H. De*ᶜ*ot* 3.2–3.

[106]Maimonides is undoubtedly thinking of Psalms 4:5: "Commune with your heart upon your bed." He had already quoted the verse as a prescript for ideal worship in *Guide for the Perplexed* 1.59, 73b.

own powers. Moses and the patriarchs raised "true knowledge and joy in what they knew" to a level where they were able to "converse with people, take care of their physical needs," and conduct their daily affairs, while "their intellect remained all the time with God." No matter what they may have been doing, even when their bodies and tongues were in the company of men, they were with God in their hearts and minds. Theirs is the very highest form of worship and the perfect life.[107]

In one of the closing chapters of the *Guide for the Perplexed*, Maimonides asks us to picture a ruler's palace located in the center of a city. Outside the city, people live who are so benighted that they have no notion of the existence of the ruler. They represent the primitive segments of mankind, such as the Turks of the North and the Negroes of the South, who neither through beliefs conveyed to them by others nor through the conclusions of their own reasoning have any inkling of the existence of God. Within the city there are some who turn their backs to the ruler's residence.[108] These represent persons who do have a notion of the existence of higher beings, but whose beliefs are false. They have been misled either by "an enormous error" in their own reasoning or through having received their beliefs from others who were themselves misled; as a consequence they worship the stars or, even worse, graven images. They are much more pernicious than the previous class because they can infect additional men and women with their error, and to prevent the disease from spreading, it is sometimes necessary to destroy them.

People are also to be found in the city who would like to go to the palace and join the ruler there yet have never even seen the palace's outer wall. They are the multitude of followers of the Law (*sharīᶜa*), the "unlettered who observe the commandments [*miṣwot*]." The term that Maimonides uses here for Law can denote Muslim religious law as well as the Jewish Law. But since he puts the words "unlettered who observe the commandments" in Hebrew rather than Arabic, he must be speaking specifically of uneducated pious Jews. At the next level are men who have reached the ruler's residence yet keep going around it in search of the entrance. They are the experts in law (*fuqahā*; Ibn Tibbon translates: *talmudiyyim*, "talmudists") who have received correct beliefs from others but do not themselves ever investigate those beliefs and the principles of religion. They do nothing but study legal texts in order to determine the precise legal and ritual obligations of every member of the community; they concern themselves exclusively with subjects that occupied Maimonides in the larger part of his *Mishneh Torah*.

Some inhabitants of the city do succeed in entering the ruler's residence; these are people who use their intellect to study the principles of religion, and the greater

[107] *Guide for the Perplexed* 3.51, pp. 126a–27a.

[108] Very likely a conscious echo of Ezekiel 8:16, where the prophet sees in a vision some twenty-five men "with their backs toward the Temple of the Lord, and their faces toward the East; and they worshiped the sun toward the East."

their mastery of science, the closer they come to the throne room. Persons who know "the demonstration of everything that can be demonstrated," who have "reached certainty about every metaphysical matter for which certainty is possible," and who have "approached certainty in matters for which it can only be approached," have found their way to the central area of the palace, where the ruler sits. A still smaller and more select number proceed to "turn away from everything except God, and place all their intellectual efforts on examining what exists in order to draw up proofs of [the existence and nature of] God and to understand how God governs what exists. . . . It is they who enter the chamber where the ruler holds court" and, as it were, see the ruler. They are the genuine prophets. The member of the human species who attained the greatest possible knowledge of God, who turned away most steadfastly from everything else and kept his thoughts most single-mindedly on God, was the greatest of the prophets, Moses.[109]

In his *Mishneh Torah*, Maimonides stated unambiguously, albeit obliquely, that the ancient rabbis themselves accorded philosophy a place in their own rabbinic curriculum and indeed regarded philosophic metaphysics as talmudic study at its highest level. What he has said now in the *Guide for the Perplexed* is similar in spirit but is put much more provocatively: Simple Jews who worship God merely by observing the divine commandments have never seen the outer wall of the palace in which God, metaphorically, resides. More shocking, experts in religious law who accept correct beliefs on the authority of others and never investigate those beliefs themselves cannot find the entrance to the palace. The vast majority of posttalmudic[110] rabbinic scholars are thereby relegated to a rank inferior to that of philosophers—and there are no grounds for supposing that Maimonides is referring only to Jewish and not to gentile philosophers—who have "reached certainty about every metaphysical matter for which certainty is possible and . . . approached certainty in matters for which it can only be approached."

Resumé. If medieval writers gave their books subtitles, Maimonides might have given his the subtitle: *In Praise of Intellect.* Scripture, he insists, must be read with "the true nature of the intellect, and after [one has attained] perfection in the demonstrative sciences and knowledge of the secrets of prophecy." Scriptural exegesis must, in other words, rest on a scientific picture of the universe and on propositions demonstrated by the intellect such as the propositions that God is an incorporeal and wholly unitary being; that God can be properly described only in negative terms; that the prophet prophesies by tapping into an emanation emitted by the active intellect; that prophetic experiences are visions and not perceptions of anything outside the prophet's soul.

[109] *Guide for the Perplexed* 3.51, pp. 123a–24a. Close readers of the *Guide* should note that the "ruler" of 3.51 is not identical with the "king" of 3.52.

[110] Maimonides, it will be remembered, believed that the rabbis of the talmudic period knew the sciences of physics and metaphysics.

Maimonides takes God's words "Let us make man in Our image, after Our likeness" to mean that man's essence resembles God's inasmuch as man is created with the power to think intellectual thoughts, much as God consists in pure thought. When Moses encountered the deity at the burning bush, he was taught a demonstration for the existence of God. Moses' dialogue with God at Sinai concerned the extent to which the human intellect can attain knowledge of the essence of God.

The first prerequisite for tapping into the emanation of the active intellect and acquiring the gift of prophecy—according to the properly philosophic sections of the *Guide*—is possession of an intellect that comprehends abstract thoughts at the highest level, that has, in other words, mastered philosophy and science. When explaining how divine providence operates in the universe, Maimonides identifies the instrument by which a person partakes of it as, once again, the human intellect: By perfecting his intellect and to the degree that he does so, a human being comes into contact with the emanation emitted by the active intellect and ultimately deriving from God, the most perfect intellect; he thereby automatically receives his share of providential protection. As for human immortality, it is gained exclusively through perfecting one's intellect.

In what I have called the rationalizing and spiritualizing strand of the *Guide for the Perplexed*, Maimonides teaches that worship at its highest consists in applying one's intellect and thought to God. The more a person perfects his intellect, the closer to God he comes. Those who, by contrast, think and talk about God without having scientific knowledge of Him—and they include the vast majority of post-talmudic authorities on Jewish law—talk about a figment of their imagination and not about anything that exists. Prophets have reached "perfection in metaphysical [or: divine] matters" and "place all their intellectual efforts on examining what exists in order to draw up proofs of [the existence and nature of] God and understand how God governs what exists." The acme of the human species is the man who at all times, single-mindedly and without interruption, sets his thought on God, that is to say, who focuses his thought on what his intellect has demonstrated about God.

The Esoteric Issue. The rabbis of the mishnaic and talmudic periods had restricted access to their exposition of the *account of creation* and the *account of the chariot*, and Maimonides, to an extent that readers today may find hard to appreciate, regarded every rule promulgated by the ancient rabbis with utmost seriousness. He was incapable of shrugging the restrictions off. Yet he also could not bring himself to deprive the nation of its rightful inheritance. His solution, he has said, would be to convey his discoveries through intimations that nonworthy readers would miss but that the perplexed for whom he wrote would pick up. It is to be noted that Maimonides speaks of veiling what he had discovered, not of misrepresenting it. We further saw that he was in actuality much more open about his discoveries than he led us to expect he would be.

The most frequently cited sentence in the *Guide for the Perplexed* is commonly read as saying something a good deal stronger. The sentence comes in a section at the end of the introduction, where Maimonides lists reasons why contradictions and contrary statements occur in compositions of various types. "The stove is hot" and "the stove is not hot"[111] would be contradictory statements. "The stove is hot" and "the stove is cold" would be contrary statements.

Maimonides enumerates seven reasons in all. The first four cover contradictions and contrary statements that "are found" (*mawjūd*) in the halakic side of rabbinic literature or "appear" in Scripture. It is not they, but the fifth, sixth, and seventh reasons for such statements that have engrossed students of the *Guide for the Perplexed*, especially in recent years.

The fifth reason is pedagogical and expository: An author may, in an early stage of what he is writing, address an issue that rests on a highly difficult proposition. In order to avoid confusing readers, the author formulates the proposition in a simplified, imprecise fashion, having in mind that he will articulate it more precisely at a later stage. And the early, imprecise formulation may be in conflict with the later, more precise formulation. The sixth reason for problematic statements in written works is error on the part of the author. Authors who blatantly contradict themselves are dismissed by Maimonides as not worth wasting breath on, but he explains that the following can happen even among better authors. Someone may, in the course of what he is writing, make two statements, A and Z. Statement A is such that if combined in a syllogism with another proposition known to be correct, it leads to the conclusion B; if B, in turn, should be combined in a syllogism with a further proposition known to be correct, it would lead to C; and should the same be done with C, the conclusion would be D. Then should the same be done with statement Z, it would lead to Y, which would lead to X, which would finally lead to W. And D may contradict or be the contrary of W. By failing to work out all the syllogisms, the author does not see that D and W are implied by A and Z, that they conflict with one another, and that A is therefore not consistent with Z.

The seventh situation is that in which an author deals with "very recondite matters," parts of which have to be hidden while other parts have to be revealed. The author finds it necessary in one context to conduct his discussion in accordance with a given proposition and in another context to do so in accordance with a different proposition, which contradicts the first one. It is then essential "that the multitude [*jumhūr*] in no way sense the contradiction [between the two propositions], and the author will accordingly deploy tactics to hide it from them at all costs." Maimonides does not explain how a reader will be able to determine which of the propositions better reflects the author's intent.

He goes on: "Inconsistency" in the writings of genuine philosophers is due to the fifth reason, that is, the need to formulate statements imprecisely for the sake of exposition and pedagogy. True philosophers, he is indicating, do not commit

[111] Or, to speak more technically: "It is not the case that the stove is hot."

errors in reasoning and do not deliberately make contradictory statements in order to hide recondite matters. "Contradiction" that "may be found" (*yūjad*) in most other writers, in commentators on Scripture, and in the aggadic side of rabbinic literature is due to the sixth reason, mistakes in reasoning. The aggadic side of rabbinic literature contains contradictions due to the seventh reason as well, that is, contradictions dictated by the necessity of veiling recondite matters from the multitude. Maimonides raises, and leaves open, the possibility that the words of the prophets may also contain contradictions of this last sort.

Whereupon, he makes the remark upon which all the ink has been expended: Any "inconsistency"—Maimonides does not use the more precise terms *contradiction* and *contrary statements*—that "may be found" (*yūjad*) in the *Guide for the Perplexed* is due to either the fifth or the seventh reason, that is, to the requirements of exposition or to the necessity of hiding things from the multitude. Maimonides advises readers to keep the warning in mind as they read the book in order to avoid becoming confused.

Manuscripts of the *Guide for the Perplexed* preserved by the Jewish communities of Yemen have the remark in a different version. They have Maimonides attribute any inconsistency in the *Guide* to either the fifth, the *sixth*, or the seventh reason[112]—to pedagogical requirements, mistakes, or the need to conceal sensitive matters. Somebody in Yemen must have been annoyed by opinions Maimonides advanced which the unknown person deemed unacceptable as well as by Maimonides' self-assurance in implying that the *Guide* contains no errors of reasoning. He annotated his copy of the book to read that, despite what Maimonides thought, the book may indeed contain inconsistencies of the sixth sort. A scribe incorporated the caustic annotation into the text, and it was then copied by other scribes. Thanks to the annotator and the Yemeni scribes, users of the Yemeni manuscripts find Maimonides incongruously advising readers of the *Guide* to be on their guard for mistakes in his reasoning.

The truth is that Maimonides conformed in practice, if not consciously, to Emerson's *bon mot*: "With consistency a great soul has simply nothing to do"; and he left anomalies in his wake in everything he wrote. Even his *Mishneh Torah*, on which he worked intensely and without distraction, slips and falls into inadvertent inconsistencies. It should scarcely be surprising that the *Guide for the Perplexed*, which he wrote when he was for the first time constantly distracted by the demands of earning a living, does so as well.[113]

[112]Maimonides, *Moreh Nebukim*, ed. and trans. J. Kafah (n. 1 above) 1.21, textual note.

[113]A couple of examples: (1) As a result of confusing Aristotle and Avicenna, Maimonides is led to state both that the first cause is the mover of the celestial spheres and that the first cause exists beyond the mover of the celestial spheres; see *Guide for the Perplexed* 2.1 (1); 2.4, pp. 13a, 14a-b. (2) At the beginning of the introduction to the *Guide*, Maimonides treats equivocal terms (an example in English would be the noun *sage* as a designation for a wise person and a particular herb) and derived terms (an example would be the term *eye* as a designation for the organ of sight and the center of a storm) as two parallel linguistic categories. Later, however, in *Guide*

If the *Guide* also contains intentional inconsistencies, the place to begin looking for them should be obvious. Maimonides said clearly in the introduction that his object in writing the book was to interpret perplexing terms and figurative passages in Scripture, while he would touch on theological and philosophical topics in only a cursory fashion. The exegetic sections, which he regarded as the heart and marrow of the book when he wrote the introduction, should accordingly be the place to start in the search for intentional inconsistencies. A learned medieval commentator assumed as much insofar as the fifth category, the exigencies of exposition and pedagogy, is concerned. He speculated that Maimonides' reference to inconsistencies belonging to that category had in view the "explanation of terms that he undertook at the beginning [of the *Guide*], the treatment of those terms being imprecise in comparison to what Maimonides explained later."[114] The commentator offers no examples, but possible instances are not hard to find.

When Maimonides interprets a scriptural verse in which Moses is said to "behold . . . the similitude of the Lord," he explains it as meaning that Moses had knowledge of "the true nature of God"; later chapters state that the true nature of God lay beyond the comprehension even of Moses.[115] Again, the term *face* in verses such as the "The face of the Lord is against them that do evil" is interpreted by Maimonides as a metaphor for "God's anger and wrath"; later he would assert that God is not subject to anger or other emotions.[116] Scriptural verses in which God is described as "hearing" are interpreted by Maimonides as meaning that God answers human supplications. But the theory of divine providence which he presents later excludes the possibility of God's answering ordinary human supplications in any literal sense.[117] In each case, he can be viewed as expressing himself imprecisely at an early stage of the book, because the pertinent proposition was a difficult one, and as formulating the proposition more precisely at a subsequent stage. In the last instance, we might be tempted to view him as making inconsistent statements belonging to the seventh category, that is, as at first concealing the proposition that God does not literally answer ordinary human supplications, in order to avoid scandalizing the unsophisticated.[118] That reading

---

1.37; 43, he describes certain biblical terms as *equivocal* by virtue of being used in a *derived* manner. Derived terms would accordingly be a subclass of equivocal terms.

[114]Shem Ṭob Falaquera, *Moreh ha-Moreh* (Pressburg 1837) 10.

[115]*Guide for the Perplexed* 1.3, with reference to Numbers 12:8. See above, p. 338. The commentaries of Ibn Kaspi, Efodi, and Shem Ṭob also take the statement in *Guide* 1.3 to be an instance of the fifth category of contradiction.

[116]See *Guide for the Perplexed* 1.37 (and in the same vein, 1.24), and above, p. 361.

[117]See *Guide for the Perplexed* 1.45, and above pp. 374-76. In *Guide* 3.28, Maimonides distinguishes beliefs taught by the Torah which are true from those that are not literally true but are "necessary"; and he classifies the beliefs that God becomes angry and that He answers supplications of the oppressed among the latter.

[118]The last instance might also be read as a case of an inconsistency in the words of the prophets themselves due to the seventh reason for contradictions.

is not satisfactory, however, since Maimonides does nothing to hide the inconsistency. He is entirely open in his opinion that God does not, in the ordinary sense of the word, respond to prayer.

In any event, there are instances where pedagogical requirements may have led him to make statements in the early chapters on scriptural terms which he had in mind to correct in later chapters. As for contradictions due to the necessity of hiding very recondite matters from the multitude, I have not met a single instance in either the exegetic or philosophic sections of the *Guide for the Perplexed* which meets Maimonides' specifications—an instance where he might be seen to deploy tactics in order to conceal an intentional contradiction from the multitude at all costs.

A further consideration, thus far ignored by students of the *Guide*, should be taken into account: The search for intentional inconsistencies that has occupied so many could be a wild goose chase. Since Maimonides composed and published the introduction before writing the body of the book,[119] the inconsistencies that he warned "*may* be found" may never actually have materialized. In the course of writing the book, he may never have become conscious of the need to introduce intentional inconsistencies of either of the two sorts that he warned readers to be on their guard for.

Be that as it may, a small brigade of scholars whose interest has been piqued by Maimonides' remarks have taken up the challenge. The search, especially in recent decades, has focused almost exclusively on the philosophic, as distinct from the exegetic, sections. And although Maimonides stated that inconsistencies occurring in the writings of serious philosophers belong to the fifth category and are due to pedagogical factors, scholars generally look for inconsistencies that might fall under the seventh category and be attributable to a desire to hide his innermost beliefs.

Soon after Maimonides' death, his contemporary Averroes was hailed in Jewish philosophic circles as the authoritative interpreter of Aristotle, and a small number of commentators on the *Guide* undertook to bring Maimonides into as close a harmony as possible with Averroes and his version of Aristotelian philosophy. A rationale is articulated by Moses Narboni, who read Aristotle through the filter of Averroes' commentaries and was the most accomplished Jewish philosopher of the Averroist school. Narboni determined that Maimonides had represented Aristotle's position incorrectly on a matter bearing on the crucial question of the creation or eternity of the world. After giving "close consideration to what Maimonides wrote," Narboni decided that Maimonides "did not fail to understand Aristotle's position as thoroughly as might appear, his efforts at hiding secrets led him to express himself in this problematic manner, and his words are amenable to an interpretation bringing them into harmony with the [philosophic] truth. Commentators have the obligation to interpret Maimonides in a fashion that harmonizes with the truth, as long as Maimonides' words permit. Particularly in instances where something he wrote does contain statements in harmony with the truth, the

[119] Above, p. 330, n. 93.

commentator must construe, combine, and integrate the words until they are . . . completely in harmony with the truth, which is reflected in the [occasional] statements."[120] In short, it is a pious duty to mold Maimonides' words so that they agree with Averroes' version of Aristotle's philosophy, especially when something Maimonides wrote lends itself to such an interpretation.

Since Aristotle and Averroes affirmed the eternity of the world, commentators of an Aristotelian and Averroistic persuasion ascribed the belief in eternity to Maimonides. They supported their exegesis through real or imagined signposts in the *Guide* and through what they saw as inconsistencies in the book due to the "seventh reason."[121] Maimonides was thereby given a radically new face. He had made clear that the significance of the creation of the world lay not so much in the historical fact of the world's having come into existence after not existing as in the implications: If God created the world, He is capable of intervening in the world at any time—although he rarely does—and the "Law becomes possible." God could have chosen Moses and communicated the Torah to him. If, by contrast, the world is eternal, God is bound by necessity, His relationship to the world is unalterable, and the Law is undercut "at its root." God could not conceivably have communicated directly with Moses. Maimonides' conception of God stood at no small remove from the popular conception, but his defense of the creation of the world retained volition and a critical measure of personality in the deity. The medieval commentators who taught that Maimonides was dissimulating and in actuality believed in the eternity of the world attributed to him a belief in a God who is bound by necessity and is wholly impersonal.

As the Middle Ages drew to a close and Averroes' reputation relaxed its hold, the Averroist exegesis of the *Guide for the Perplexed* receded into the mists of the past. Scholars within the academic community who took a renewed interest in Maimonides' *Guide* during the nineteenth century did not all view the book in the same way. But no one any longer considered it a pious duty to twist Maimonides' words so that they agree with what Averroes and Aristotle held. And the search for

[120] Moses Narboni, Commentary on *Guide for the Perplexed* (Vienna 1853) 3.13, p. 52a.

[121] See A. Ravitzky, "The Secrets of Maimonides," reprinted in his "*History and Faith* (Amsterdam 1996) 254.

To consider one of the most cogent points made by a medieval commentator who read Maimonides as accepting the eternity of the world: Narboni, Commentary on *Guide for the Perplexed* 2, introduction, proposition 18, puts forth an argument that amounts, in effect, to the following: Maimonides held that the first incorporeal cause of the world never changes. But if God created the world after not having done so, He would have undergone change. Maimonides therefore contradicted himself in ostensibly maintaining that God created the world; he presumably did so intentionally, and must have believed in eternity. It happens that Thomas Aquinas, whom nobody has—yet—suspected of contradicting himself intentionally, argues both for God's never changing and for God's having created the world after not doing so; see Aquinas, *Summa Theologica* 1.9.1; 1.46.1, ad 5 and 6. A medieval philosopher of Maimonides' rank thus could consider creation to be compatible with the unchanging nature of God. Other points made by the Averroist commentators on the *Guide for the Perplexed* are, in my judgment, weaker.

signs and inconsistencies in the text of the *Guide* which lead to a web of secrets buried deep below the surface of the book became a historical curiosity.[122]

The search returned with a vengeance in the mid-twentieth century, and the standard bearer was now Leo Strauss. Strauss is so central to discourse about the *Guide for the Perplexed* and has brought about so great a sea change in the study of the book that no one can hope to appreciate the way in which the *Guide* is read today without taking account of him, his method, and his watchword. The watchword is esotericism.

Strauss was born and educated in Germany and spent the second half of his life teaching in American universities until his death in 1973. He had a number of faces—to mention just two, he conducted an unremitting campaign against modern social science and, whether through design or not, helped inspire the American political movement known as neo-conservatism, for which he remains a venerated icon—and his methodological stance evolved over the years. Of interest to us is not what one of his devoted former students dubbed the "pre-Straussean Strauss"[123] but the mature Strauss who made the discovery for which he is best known. He arrived at the conviction that a long line of eminent thinkers through the centuries wrote their books with exoteric façades, beneath which they concealed their socially unacceptable, esoteric teachings; one of Strauss's works is pointedly entitled *Persecution and the Art of Writing*. Strauss and his disciples were further convinced that he alone had refined the art of reading written materials to a precision never reached before in the history of human literacy and hence he was uniquely qualified for deciphering texts and bringing their underlying esoteric messages to light. Esoteric teachings popped up in Socrates, Plato, Xenophon, Alfarabi, the fictional spokesman for philosophy in Judah Hallevi's *Kuzari*, Machiavelli, Spinoza, Locke, Leibniz, Montesquieu, Rousseau, and undoubtedly others whom I have missed. The capstone of the tradition of esoteric writing was Strauss himself. Although he would hardly have risked life and limb had he expounded his thoughts candidly in twentieth-century America, it was one of his principles that the intellectual elite—the "philosophers," as he called them—must always be circumspect toward the "vulgar" in order to avoid damaging the fabric of society.[124] Therefore he too concealed his personal opinions and beliefs under an opaque façade. What interests us is that a key link in Strauss's chain of esoteric

[122]S. Luzzatto did complain that Maimonides had not been wholly forthright and he cited medieval commentators who understood Maimonides to have hidden certain of his beliefs. See A. Motzkin, "On the Interpretation of Maimonides," *Independent Journal of Philosophy* 2 (1978) 42–44. A Hebrew version of Motzkin's article appeared in *ᶜIyyun* 28 (1978).

[123]A. Bloom, *Giants and Dwarfs* (New York 1990) 246. Even the pre-Struassian Strauss showed interest in the esoteric character of philosophy for Maimonides. See L. Strauss, *Philosophie und Gesetz* (Berlin 1935) 88–89; English translation: *Philosophy and Law*, trans. F. Baumann (Philadelphia 1987) 82.

[124]See S. Drury, *The Political Ideas of Leo Strauss* (London 1988) 33–34.

writers was, much as the medieval Averroist commentators on the *Guide for the Perplexed* had earlier assumed, Maimonides.[125]

Strauss must have had charisma in the classroom. A former student writes: "Those of us who knew him saw in him such a power of mind, . . . such a rare mixture of the human elements resulting in a harmonious expression of the virtues, moral and intellectual, that our account of him is likely to evoke disbelief or ridicule from those who have never experienced a man of this quality."[126] Another rhapsodizes: "Today I know that books and Leo Strauss, who turned books into a cosmos for us, are responsible for much of the happiness in my life. . . . What I, and others, owe to Leo Strauss is beyond repayment. . . . Years . . . after I had stopped attending classes, someone . . . said: 'You ought to thank God for having had a teacher like that.'"[127] A third speaks in a similar vein, while in the same breath letting out that Strauss could also be perceived in a different light: "He was the greatest of teachers." Sadly, his views on philosophy and political science and his method of reading classic texts caused him to be "despised, ridiculed, misrepresented, envied, and"—apparently the ultimate indignity—"sometimes even ignored. But not for long, and not forever, and never by those who studied under him."[128]

Not every reader fell under the spell. An expert on Plato found that Strauss "turns upside down the meaning of . . . [Plato's] *Republic*."[129] Another classical scholar judged Strauss's posthumously published study of Plato's *Laws* to be "an utter disaster"; Strauss had a "misguided obsession with perfectly natural and unimportant silences on Plato's part" and his "overinterpretation of nonsignificant detail in defiance of simple common sense vitiates the entire book."[130] A third wrote of a book of his on Xenophon: "Strauss's 'interpretation' consists of a tedious paraphrase. . . . No coherent line of interpretation emerges from his enigmatic asides."[131] Even scholars who were less negative—or who addressed books of Strauss's which allowed them to be so—expressed grave reservations. A reviewer of his *Thoughts on Machiavelli* was of the opinion that "the splendid line of reasoning which Strauss develops is at times weakened by his penchant for . . . a species of learned gobbledegook . . . such as speculations based on the numbers of chapters or their titles and the like."[132] A specialist in

[125]For explicit statements of the exoteric/esoteric dichotomy by medieval commentators on the *Guide for the Perplexed*, see Ravitzsky, "The Secrets of Maimonides," reprinted in his "*History and Faith*, 251–52.

[126]Bloom, *Giants and Dwarfs*, 235.

[127]W. Dannhauser, "Becoming Naïve Again," *The American Scholar* 44 (1975) 640.

[128]W. Berns, in the *National Review*, December 7, 1973, 1347.

[129]M. Burnyeat in the *New York Review*, May 30, 1985, 36. Burnyeat's critical review, which is invaluable, guided me to the some of the references in the following notes.

[130]T. Saunders, in *Political Theory* 4 (1976) 239, 241.

[131]T. Irwin, in *The Philosophical Review* 83 (1974) 409.

[132]C. Friedrich, in *The New Leader*, October 12, 1959, 27.

John Locke acknowledges, in an effort to be fair, that Strauss's "kind of intellectual cryptography . . . can sometimes yield—and undoubtedly has yielded in the case of his studies of Locke—historical insights of remarkable power." Strauss's cryptography is, however, "necessarily capricious," and Locke's "private papers . . . impugn the reality not just of individual elements of the [esoteric] interpretation but of the entire construction."[133]

Strauss made much of a passage in the introduction to the *Guide for the Perplexed* for which he offered the following translation: "Connect its [the book's] chapters one with another; and when reading a given chapter, your intention must be not only to understand the totality of the subject of that chapter but also to grasp each word [*lafẓa*] which occurs in it in the course of the speech, even if that word does not belong to the intention of the chapter. For the diction of this treatise has . . . been chosen . . . with great exactness and exceeding precision."[134] The translation serves as a *raison d'être* for Strauss's approach to Maimonides but it is tendentious, and a much more plausible rendering of what Maimonides says is given in an admirable new Hebrew translation of the *Guide.* Maimonides, in the new translation, charges readers "not only to understand each chapter in a general way, but also to grasp every *expression* appearing within the chapter in the course of the discussion, even when the expression does not bear directly on the chapter's subject. . . ."[135] He is, in other words, not announcing that the *Guide for the Perplexed* is a cryptogram, every word of which has to be deciphered. He is making the more mundane, though scarcely inconsequential, statement that what he writes about a term taken up incidentally in one chapter may illuminate what he says in another chapter. When the passage is read in that way, it dovetails nicely with Maimonides' plan to scatter subject headings and hints throughout the book.

Instances can indeed be found where a remark made in an early chapter of the *Guide* regarding a term can illuminate what Maimonides says in a later chapter. Here is an example.

In one of the chapters dealing with scriptural terms that might engender perplexity, Maimonides digresses and mentions a biblical verse reporting a vision experienced by the nobles of Israel at Mount Sinai. The nobles beheld the divine throne and under the throne they saw "a work of the whiteness of sapphire stone."

[133]J. Dunn, "Justice and the Interpretation of Locke's Political Theory," *Political Studies* 16 (1968) 69–70.

[134]L. Strauss, *Persecution and the Art of Writing* (Glencoe 1952) 65; preface to Pines' translation of *Guide of the Perplexed*, p. xv.

[135]Maimonides, *Moreh Nebukim*, trans. M. Schwarz, 1 (Tel Aviv 2002) 13. In Maimonides' Commentary on the Mishna, *Nega^{c}im* 7:2, *lafẓ* has the meaning of *terminology* or *sense*. Munk translated *lafẓa* into French as *parole*, very likely with the conscious intent of avoiding the more neutral and all-inclusive *mot*, which would be the exact French equivalent of *word*. Friedländer translates: "term." Pines incorporates Strauss's translation of the passage into his own translation of the *Guide*.

Maimonides explains that the sapphire stone stands for the underlying matter of the physical world.[136] Later, in his exegesis of the scriptural account of the chariot, he equates the expression "beryl stone" in the vision of Ezekiel with the sapphire stone in the earlier vision. He presumably expected careful readers to remember that the sapphire stone symbolizes the material substratum of the world, to apply that knowledge when reading the account of the chariot, and to realize that the beryl stone in the vision of Ezekiel is also a symbol of the underlying matter of the physical world.[137] The information is, perhaps, conveyed obliquely out of respect for the ancient rabbis, who insisted on covering the account of the chariot with a heavy veil of secrecy.

We previously saw how statements made at a later stage of the *Guide* can be read as corrections of less precise statements made at an earlier stage. Here we have seen how a digression made in an earlier chapter can cast light on a later chapter. What is involved in each instance is Maimonides' rationalistic exegesis of Scripture. Nothing we have encountered is likely to cause a modern reader's heart to pound and adrenalin to run.

At all events, when Strauss gives his instructions for deciphering the *Guide for the Perplexed*, he mandates that attention be paid not merely to every word in the book—even though Maimonides allowed himself rhetorical flourishes and, like most authors, varied language and style in order to avoid ennui.[138] Strauss mandates that attention also be given to parts of words, the position of words, the structure of sentences, the absence of words that Maimonides might have used, chapter numbers, and similar features.

He insists that there is significance in instances where Maimonides prefixes the Arabic article *al-* to Hebrew nouns, in Maimonides' devoting the very first chapter of the book to the term *image*, and in his opening the last chapter with the phrase "the word *wisdom*"; Maimonides' choice of the phraseology "the word wisdom" instead of simply "wisdom" makes all the difference. Some of the chapters where Maimonides interprets scriptural terms start by putting the term to be discussed in the form of a noun while other chapters put the term in the form of a verb. Sometimes Maimonides quotes a scriptural verse in full but elsewhere he abbreviates a verse and instead of completing it writes "etc." When he refers to a person from the past, he sometimes adds the tag "may he rest in peace" to the

[136] *Guide for the Perplexed* 1.28, referring to Exodus 24:10. I have translated the biblical phrase as Maimonides understood it.

[137] *Guide for the Perplexed* 3.4. Additional examples: (1) *Guide* 1.43, which explains the term *kanaf* (wing) when applied to angels and throws light on *Guide* 3.2, 4a, which discusses the vision of the prophet Ezekiel in Ezekiel 1.11. (2) What Maimonides writes about Adam's son Seth in *Guide* 1.7, which throws light on *Guide* 2.30, 71b.

[138] To take one example, in chapters where Maimonides expounds biblical terms that might occasion perplexity, he usually calls the item to be expounded—face, rock, back, foot, to sit, to stand, to go out, and the like—a "term" *(ism)*. But for the sake of variety, he sometimes calls the item to be expounded a "word" (*kalima*) or an "expression" (*lafẓ*). See *Guide* 1: 4; 7; 30; 45; 70.

person's name and sometimes does not. Each of these peculiarities is, for Strauss, fraught with significance.

Notice, in his view, must be taken of Maimonides' discussing natural science precisely in the seventeenth chapter of Part One and thereby linking the numeral seventeen to natural science. In fact, Maimonides did not assign numbers to chapters of the *Guide* and undoubtedly gave not the slightest thought to whether he was engaged in writing the fifteenth, seventeenth, or nineteenth chapter. Strauss wants readers of the *Guide* to ask themselves why Maimonides discusses the scriptural term *foot* but fails to discuss the scriptural term *hand*; why the book has "a chapter devoted to [Scripture's use of the term] 'grief' but none to 'laughter'"; why Maimonides quotes the verse "[Hear O Israel,] the Lord is our God, the Lord is one" only once in the *Guide* and moreover does not do so in sections where he discusses divine unity; why Maimonides fails to mention the immortality of the soul in the section dealing with divine providence.[139]

Strauss's own esoteric and enigmatic pose prevented him from stating outright what any of these clues is supposed to signify. His insinuation regarding Maimonides' failure to mention immortality where he thought it should be mentioned is fairly obvious: He is hinting, that Maimonides was hinting, that no part of man, including the human intellect, can gain immortality.[140] What he is insinuating regarding Maimonides' failure to quote the "Hear O Israel" verse where he thought it should be quoted can, as we shall see, also be guessed.[141] In the other cases we are left in the dark. What, for instance, is momentous about the numeral seventeen, about *foot*, and about *grief*?

At the very minimum, Strauss suggests that Maimonides did not in his heart of hearts believe in the creation of the world after its nonexistence, in the possibility of God's intervening miraculously in the universe, and in God's having once done so by choosing Moses as His prophet; that is to say, Maimonides did not believe in the Mosaic revelation.[142] Although Strauss's reading of Maimonides is inextricably tied to his peculiar notions about the history of Western thought and the place of the intellectual elite—the "philosophers"—in human society, those wider theories have been almost entirely ignored by students of medieval Jewish philosophy. But his suggestions regarding Maimonides' position on the creation of the world have brought about a revolution. From the beginning of the nineteenth century, when Maimonides began to be studied in academic settings, until the middle of the

139 Strauss, *Persecution and the Art of Writing* 74–78, 89; preface to Pines' translation of the *Guide* xxiv–xxvi, xxx, xlvii–xlviii.

140 Strauss, *Persecution and the Art of Writing* 15 similarly points out Alfarabi's failure to mention immortality where, in Strauss's view, he might be expected to. The omission, Strauss concludes, "places beyond any reasonable doubt" Alfarabi's own rejection of the belief.

141 Below, p. 401.

142 Strauss, *Persecution and the Art of Writing* 40–41, which has to be read with the realization that it is laced with Straussian irony; preface to Pines' translation of the *Guide* xxxvi–xxxvii, xxxix.

twentieth century, scholars[143] assumed that when he argued for the creation of the world after its not having existed, he was advocating creation after nonexistence. Then, largely thanks to Strauss, the tide turned. The majority of those studying Maimonides in academic settings today are convinced that when he argued for creation, he meant that the world was *not* created after not existing—or, in some nuanced versions, he was surreptitiously expressing doubts as to whether or not the world was created. More than twenty books and articles written during the past half century can be named which are designed to prove one or the other proposition or which simply take one or the other for granted. A few years ago, a respected scholar could assert flatly: "It is not one of the deeper secrets of the *Guide* that Maimonides really prefers the Aristotelian notion of eternity *a parte ante*, . . ." that is, of the past eternity of the world.[144] Members of the academic community who cannot shake off the eerie notion that Maimonides may actually have meant what he said hesitate to "come out" lest they be viewed as gullible and naive.

A variety of features in the *Guide for the Perplexed* have been brought forward to show that the creation of the world was not Maimonides' true position.[145] As I

[143] With the possible exception of S. Luzzatto and Aḥad ha-ᶜAm.

[144] W. Harvey, "Why Maimonides Was Not a Mutakallim," *Perspectives on Maimonides*, ed. J. Kraemer (Oxford 1991) 113.

[145] Examples: (1) J. Bekker, *Sodo shel Moreh Nebukim* (Tel Aviv 1955): Maimonides distinguishes between "true beliefs" and a few "necessary beliefs," which are not literally true; whereupon Bekker extrapolates and posits a full complement of necessary beliefs in the *Guide* and classifies the belief in creation among them. J. Levinger's devastating review in *Beḥinot* 11 (1957) shows that Bekker repeatedly misrepresents what Maimonides actually wrote. (2) J. Glicker, "*Ha-Beᶜaya ha-Modalit ba-Pilosofia shel ha-Rambam*," *ᶜIyyun* 10 (1959) 188–91: Maimonides criticizes thinkers of the Kalam school for selecting whatever theories from ancient philosophy would serve their purpose—he was thinking of atomist theories—instead of taking their departure from the way things are in the external world and building on that; yet, Glicker contends, Maimonides himself lets external, religious considerations give direction to his arguments for creation instead of taking his departure from the way things are in the external world; whereupon Glicker concludes not that Maimonides saw the mote in the other fellow's eye and failed to see the beam in his own, but that he was creating a smoke screen and in actuality accepted the Aristotelian position on eternity. (Maimonides would have pointed out the difference between what he criticizes in the Kalam and what he does himself.) (3) A. Nuriel, *Ḥiddush ha-ᶜOlam o Qadmuto ᶜal pi ha-Rambam*, reprinted in his *Galuy we-Samuy* (Jerusalem 2000) 30–40: Maimonides uses the term *creator* as a synonym for God in contexts where he restates the position of believers in the eternity of the world and where, Nuriel thinks, he hints that he himself believed in eternity; Nuriel concludes therefrom that Maimonides used the term *creator* as a signpost to awaken the attention of the perspicacious and as a smoke screen for concealing his true views from the multitude. Answered by I. Ravitsky, *Tarbiz* 35 (1966) 341–47. (4) W. Harvey, "A Third Approach to Maimonides' Cosmogony-Prophetology Puzzle," *Harvard Theological Review* 74 (1981) 295: Maimonides proves the existence of God on the basis of the premise that the world is eternal; Harvey dismisses Maimonides' explanation that he was demonstrating the existence of God on the parallel tracks of creation and eternity. (5) H. Kreisel, in *History of Jewish Philosophy*, ed. O. Leaman and D. Frank (London 1997) 260–61: To will the creation of the world after not having done so would involve a change in God's essence, and Maimonides rules

already noted, I have not been able to identify a single contradiction in the *Guide* which fits the specifications for deliberate contradictions of the seventh type laid out by Maimonides in his introduction to the book.

And something can be said on the other side. In Maimonides' conception of human history, mankind originally recognized a single incorporeal deity; it soon stumbled into the erroneous belief that the physical heavens are the first cause of the universe; the patriarch Abraham helped a segment of mankind to emerge from the error; and the biblical Moses completed the task as far as the Israelite nation was concerned.[146] That scheme makes sense only in a framework in which the world and human history had a beginning. As seen in an earlier chapter, Maimonides is indignant at posttalmudic rabbinists who blundered when enumerating the 613 *sui generis* commandments given to Moses by God and he evinces palpable satisfaction in his rules for identifying the privileged commandments and enumerating them. If he did not believe that God intervened in human history, favored Moses with a unique revelation, and communicated the 613 commandments directly to Moses—that Moses' prophecy differed essentially from the prophecy of prophets who depend on the active intellect for inspiration—then the heated rhetoric, the efforts to identify the commandments possessing privileged status, and the satisfaction in the result, are hollow and meaningless; and, Maimonides has told us, divine intervention in the world is possible only on the assumption of creation. In the present chapter, we saw him taking pains to immunize his position against refutation by avoiding language implying that creation took place "in time"; and he warned his readers to avoid such language. Why would he have warned those whom he undertook to enlighten against language that might open their belief to refutation, if he was simultaneously intimating to them that the belief was false? Since he knew of persons who would be unreceptive to the thesis of creation after nonexistence if they thought Aristotle had proved the contrary, he searched out passages where Aristotle himself acknowledged that the eternity of the world cannot be demonstrated. Most of the substantive quotations from Aristotle in the *Guide for the Perplexed* serve that purpose.

The threads out of which Maimonides wove his arguments for creation derive from the Islamic thinker Ghazali, and he conceded that the arguments fall short of being apodictic demonstrations. They nevertheless constitute the most original set of proofs for creation in medieval Jewish philosophy. What odd cast of mind would lead someone to design a new set of arguments and present it to those whom he was trying to enlighten if by doing so he was inducing them to embrace a position opposed to the one he himself held?[147] Within the *Guide*, Maimonides

---

out the possibility of such change. See n. 121 above, where I point out that Aquinas too combined an insistence on God's unchangeability with a belief in creation.

[146]Maimonides, *Mishneh Torah*: *H. ᶜAbodat Kokabim*, chapter 1.

[147]Drury, *The Political Ideas of Leo Strauss* (n. 124 above) 188, understands that Strauss divided his own disciples into two classes, deliberately hid his inner beliefs from the inferior class, and allowed only the elite class to glimpse them. Perhaps Strauss thought that Maimonides did

repeatedly and in a variety of contexts finds opportunities to stress his belief in creation.[148] In the last section of his main medical work he turns aside from the subject of medicine and goes out of his way to castigate Galen for his skepticism regarding the prophecy of Moses and the possibility of miracles.

Could we be in the presence of one of those vertiginous intrigues in which the countervailing evidence suggesting that there was no intrigue merely demonstrates how deep the plot ran?

The esoteric engine is driven by an inner momentum. If one can accept that Maimonides devoted a tenth of the *Guide for the Perplexed* to a meticulous and original defense of the creation of the world while secretly believing that the world is eternal, why not go the whole hog and conclude that he believed nothing he wrote in the *Guide for the Perplexed*? When the mature Strauss is read with the care that he demanded of readers of serious writing, he points precisely in that direction. Maimonides, he remarks nonchalantly, "took . . . for granted that being a Jew and being a philosopher are mutually exclusive,"[149] and he goes further. He repeatedly hints, that the *Guide for the Perplexed* hints, that besides not believing in a deity capable of intervening in the world and affecting the course of human affairs, Maimonides did not believe in the existence of God at all.[150] The esoteric message that Strauss uncovered in Alfarabi, Machiavelli, and Spinoza[151] revolved around atheism, and he found varieties of atheism in such diverse

---

something similar and placed Joseph ben Judah and everyone else for whom he was ostensibly writing in the inferior class.

[148]Examples: (1) *Guide for the Perplexed* 1:28: Scripture singles out the underlying matter of the world as God's handiwork, because that matter was the first thing He brought into existence. (2) *Guide* 2.19, pp. 44a–b: The prophets made a point of adducing the heavens when proving the existence of God because the heavens also provide proof of the creation of the world. (3) *Guide* 3.43, p. 95a: One purpose of the commandment to observe the Sabbath is to ingrain the belief in creation. (4) *Guide* 3.50, p. 120a: The book of Genesis incorporates the genealogies of the first humans in order to show that mankind can be traced back to a beginning; support is thereby given to the proposition that the world was created, which is a "foundation of the Law."

[149]Strauss, *Persecution and the Art of Writing* 19, and, in different words, 43. By contrast, the pre-Straussian Strauss recognized that for Maimonides "the aim of the Law is identical with the aim of philosophy" and "the Law commands philosophizing"; see Strauss, *Philosophie und Gesetz* (n. 123 above) 76–77; English translation 69.

[150]Strauss, *Persecution and the Art of Writing* 83, 124–26 (which echoes what Strauss writes about Machiavelli; see his *Thoughts on Machiavelli* [Chicago 1958] 217). Preface to Pines' translation of the *Guide* xxi–xxii, xli, xlviii, li–lii.

[151](1) L. Strauss, "How Farabi Read Plato's *Laws*," reprinted in Strauss, *What Is Political Philosophy*? (Glencoe 1959) 147–50. (The statement, p. 148, that "Farabi drops Plato's repeated reference to the gods" in "literally the central chapter" of his summary of Plato's *Laws* is pregnant with meaning; one of Strauss's rules was that esoteric writers bury their true beliefs in the center of their works in order to make them less conspicuous. When Strauss writes on p. 150: "We would be foolish to claim that we are in a position to explain these difficulties" he is being ironic.) (2) *Thoughts on Machiavelli* (Chicago 1958) 209, 216–17. (3) "How to Study Spinoza's *Theologico-Political Treatise*," reprinted in *Persecution and the Art of Writing* 189.

personages as Socrates[152] and Locke.[153] Atheism moreover seems—one always has to say "seems" when talking about Strauss because of his idiosyncratic manner of expressing himself—to have lain at the core of his own esoteric thinking.[154] Maimonides was joining good company.

Strauss would have us understand, then, that the author of the preeminent medieval Jewish philosophic work regarded the concept of *Jewish philosopher* as a contradiction in terms. Not only would Maimonides' system of Jewish philosophy be a sham, but since Maimonides considered himself to be a philosopher, and Strauss certainly considered him to be one, the inescapable implication would be that Maimonides did not see himself as Jewish. Strauss further gives us to understand that the author of the preeminent work on the commandments given by God directly to Moses and the author of the preeminent medieval code of Jewish religious law not only saw himself as non-Jewish. He did not believe that God exists.

Because the ultimate esoteric interpretation of the *Guide for the Perplexed*, which makes Maimonides a covert atheist, is so outlandish and since Strauss conveyed it in his habitually enigmatic and opaque fashion, it has failed to register in academic circles. It has survived, however, in a more straightforward and somewhat less radical version. Here Maimonides is represented as having concluded that not only is knowledge of God's essence impossible but all knowledge of God, including knowledge of His existence, is impossible. No longer a full-fledged atheist in the mold of Friedrich Nietzsche, he now becomes an agnostic in the mold of Immanuel Kant.[155]

Both theses—that Maimonides was an atheist and that he was an agnostic—transform the *Guide for the Perplexed* into one of the most grotesque books ever

[152] H. Neumann, "Civic Piety and Socratic Atheism," *Independent Journal of Philosophy* 2 (1978) 33–37; Drury, *The Political Ideas of Leo Strauss* 83, 88–89.

[153] Strauss, *What Is Political Philosophy*? 205–10.

[154] Drury, *The Political Ideas of Leo Strauss* 52–56, 60, 170–74, 195; R. Brague, "Leo Strauss and Maimonides," in *Leo Strauss's Thought*, ed. A. Udoff (Boulder 1991) 103–5; intimated by S. Pines, "*ᶜAl Leo Strauss*," *Molad* 247–48 (1976) 455–56. There is a reading of Strauss which ascribes to him a more benevolent and sympathetic attitude toward religious faith. See W. Harvey, "The Return of Maimonideanism," *Jewish Social Studies* 42 (1980) 254–55, and note 35; Drury 186–92; A. Ivry and K. Green, in *Leo Strauss's Thought* (Boulder 1991) 86–89, 55–58, and note 121. Drury, I believe correctly, reads statements of Strauss's in that vein as intended for the nonphilosophers in the Straussian scheme, that is, for the nonelite.

[155] S. Pines, "The Limitations of Human Knowledge According to Al-Farabi, ibn Bajja, and Maimonides," *Studies in Medieval Jewish History and Literature*, ed. I. Twersky (Cambridge, Mass. 1979); "Les limites de la métaphysique selon al-Farabi, Ibn Bājja, et Maïmonide." Summarized in Pines, "The Philosophical Purport of Maimonides' Halachic Works and the Purport of the *Guide of the Perplexed*," in *Maimonides and Philosophy*, ed. Pines and Yovel. The connection with Kant is made in "Limitations of Human Knowledge" 94 and 100. Pines' interpretation is analyzed in H. Davidson, "Maimonides on Metaphysical Knowledge," *Maimonidean Studies* 3 (1992–1993) 49–99.

written. Maimonides states that one of his two objects in the *Guide* was to show how scriptural anthropomorphisms may be squared with the philosophically demonstrated proposition that the first cause is incorporeal, the "perplexed" in the book's title being persons who cannot work out the harmonization by themselves and need guidance. He puts forward what he calls four "demonstrative methods" for establishing the existence of a single incorporeal cause of the universe, in other words, four incontrovertible demonstrations of the existence of God. A series of chapters in the *Guide* is devoted to explaining how, seeing that God's existence is knowable while His essence is not, God may be described; another series to the phenomenon of prophecy, which Maimonides characterizes as an effect of the emanation originating in God and mediated through the incorporeal active intellect; a third series to God's knowledge of the universe; and a fourth to divine providence, which he again makes dependent on the emanation ultimately traceable to God. Over and over again, Maimonides defines the goal of human life as mastering "divine science," that is, the science of metaphysics, and learning as much as humanly possible about God, notwithstanding the unknowability of God's essence. He maintains that man approaches God by acquiring as much knowledge about Him as possible, that the highest form of worship consists in acquiring such knowledge and keeping it before one's eyes at all times. Yet we are to suppose in one version that Maimonides rejected the existence of a single incorporeal God altogether and in the other that he placed the possibility of knowing whether God exists beyond human competence. The 470-page volume was written in order to conceal a few ethereal clues which overturn virtually every word in the book and which would have to wait more than seven and a half centuries before anyone noticed them.

At one spot, when talking about exegesis of Scripture, Maimonides warns against "interpreting things that have no interpretation and were not meant to be interpreted." Overinterpretation of Scripture parallels "the great inanity . . . animating the writings of most schools of thought in the world today. For every one of them tries to discover in an author's statements meanings that the author had not the slightest intent to convey."[156]

The Reception of the Guide for the Perplexed. Although the numbers of those who read and studied rabbinic texts in the Middle Ages and afterwards is hundreds of times greater than the number of those who read and studied philosophy, the mark that the *Guide for the Perplexed* made on the latter was proportionately as strong as the mark made by Maimonides' *Mishneh Torah* on the former. The *Guide* generated most interest in Jewish communities in Spain, southern France, and areas allied with them culturally. But it was also welcomed, studied, and taught, and commentaries on it were written, elsewhere—including such out of the

[156]*Guide for the Perplexed*, Introduction, p. 8b.

way locales as Prague in the fourteenth and fifteenth centuries[157] and Poland in the sixteenth.[158]

If we set aside writers who limited their activity to commenting on Greek and Arabic philosophic works, it is hard to find a single medieval Jew writing in the area of philosophy after Maimonides upon whom the *Guide for the Perplexed* did not leave its imprint. Some eighty commentaries on all or part of the book are known.[159] Moses Narboni, Levi Gersonides, and Ḥasdai Crescas, the sole medieval Jewish thinkers apart from Maimonides who can lay claim to being philosophers of rank, not only read and borrowed from the *Guide*; each worked out his own system of thought through his encounter with it and its author. Narboni wrote a dense commentary on the book. Gersonides can regularly be seen to have Maimonides and the *Guide* at the back of his mind, and Maimonides' importance for him comes out indirectly as well, in the catalogue he left of his personal library: The first items listed by Gersonides in the scientific and philosophic section of the catalogue of books he owned are two complete and two partial manuscripts of the *Guide for the Perplexed*, and Gersonides notes that he had done one of the complete copies of the *Guide*, a manuscript on vellum, in his own hand.[160] Crescas' claim to philosophic standing rests on an analysis and critique of the twenty-five physical and metaphysical propositions that Maimonides' laid down as a prolegomenon to his demonstrations of the existence of God.

It was by no means the case that all who studied and used the *Guide* understood it fully or were faithful to Maimonides' spirit. The most egregious were writers who forced Maimonides into unnatural marriages with modes of thought that would have made him wince: We find hotchpotches in which themes from the *Guide* are

[157] E. Kupfer, "*Li-Demutah ha-Tarbutit shel Yahadut Ashkenaz*," *Tarbiz* 42 (1972–1973) 117–21, and note 14a.

[158] Especially notable is R. Moses Isserles of Krakow, whose glosses on the *Shulḥan ᶜAruk* enabled it to become the authoritative code for Ashkenazic Jews. Isserles incorporated the picture of the universe found in the *Guide for the Perplexed* into his homiletic writings and he initiated his student, R. Mordecai Jaffe, a halakist of equal stature, into study of the *Guide*; Jaffe wrote a commentary on the book. Isserles' commitment to philosophy was not unqualified. In defending himself to another eminent rabbinic scholar, who had berated him for the "sin" of citing the "impure" Aristotle in deciding a halakic issue, Isserles replies that he had never studied "the books of the cursed Greeks, such as the *Physics* and *Metaphysics*," that his knowledge of philosophy came solely through the medium of the *Guide for the Perplexed* and other respected Jewish works, that he studied such works on the Sabbath and festivals, when ordinary folk "go out for a stroll," and that he paid attention only to conclusions and did not go into the demonstrations whereby Maimonides and others arrived at their conclusions. See M. Isserrles, *Responsa*, ed. A. Ziv (Jerusalem 1970) §§6–7, pp. 25, 31–32. Isserles' ambivalent attitude toward philosophy comes out in the awkward opinion he attaches to *Shulḥan ᶜAruk*: *Yoreh Deᶜa* §246.4.

[159] M. Steinschneider, "Die hebräischen Commentare zum Führer des Maimonides," *Festschrift zum siebzigsten Geburtstage A. Berliner's*, ed. A Freimann (Frankfurt 1903) 345–63; a few additional items are listed by J. Dienstag, "*Moreh Nebukim le-ha-Rambam*," *Gevuroth Haromaḥ* (Weiler Festschrift) (Jerusalem 1987) 207–37.

[160] G. Weil, *La bibliothèque de Gersonide* (Louvain 1991) 46, 87.

yoked to Abraham Ibn Ezra, astral magic, and astrology,[161] to a simplistic neoplatonism,[162] to Karaite theology,[163] or to cabalistic doctrines.[164] But, quite apart from the out-and-out eclectics, a long line of authors managed to construe the *Guide* as saying something different from what, at least on the surface, the words do say.

In classifying the ways in which medieval Jews who made an effort to come to grips with the *Guide for the Perplexed* reacted to it, the first line to draw is between adherents and opponents. It was adherents in particular who failed to give unqualified credence to Maimonides' express words regarding God, the world, and man.

Some admirers—notably, Samuel Ibn Tibbon, the Hebrew translator of the *Guide*—did try to ascertain, as best they possibly could, the meaning of every statement in the book and to tread in Maimonides' footsteps.[165] There were the commentators of the Averroist school who placed a more radical construction on the

[161]The fourteenth-century Spanish Jewish thinkers studied by D. Schwartz, *Yashan be-Qanqan Ḥadash* (Jerusalem 1996), especially 28–34.

[162]D. Blumenthal, *The Commentary of R. Ḥoṭer ben Shelomo to the Thirteen Principles of Maimonides* (Leiden 1974) 17–41. Ḥoṭer, a fifteenth-century Yemeni Jew, combines Maimonides' picture of incorporeal intelligences, the first of which emanates from God and the others from one another, with a system in which the divine One emanates a cosmic Intellect, which in turn emanates a Cosmic Soul. Blumenthal, "Was There an Eastern Tradition of Maimonidean Scholarship," *Revue des études juives* 138 (1979) 65–66, gives a couple of additional examples of Yemeni writers who created eclectic miscegenations.

[163]Aaron ben Elijah, *Eṣ Ḥayyim*; see Davidson, *Proofs for Eternity, Creation, and the Existence of God* (n. 23 above), index, s. v. Aaron ben Elijah. D. Lasker, "Maimonides' Influence on the Philosophy of Elijah Bashyazi the Karaite" (in Hebrew), *Jerusalem Studies in Jewish Thought* 3 (1983–1984) 406–22.

[164]Examples: A. Altmann, "Maimonides' Attitude toward Jewish Mysticism" (translated from the German), in *Studies in Jewish Thought*, ed. A. Jospe (Detroit 1981) 207–9 (Abraham Abulafia). M. Idel, "Maimonides and Kabbalah," *Studies in Maimonides*, ed. I. Twersky (Cambridge, Mass. 1990) 56–78 (Abulafia and cabalists associated with him). S. Heller Wilensky, "Isaac Ibn Laṭif—Philosopher or Kabbalist?" in *Jewish Medieval and Renaissance Studies*, ed. A. Altmann (Cambridge, Mass. 1967) 200–201. I. Tishby, *Mishnat ha-Zohar* (Jerusalem 1949) 1.97 (knowledge of God as the goal of human life); 102 (unknowability of the infinite God); 113 (God's freedom from attributes); 220 (functions of Maimonides' active intellect ascribed to the tenth aspect of God; R. Jacob Emden, *Mitpaḥat Sefarim* [Lvov 1871] 67, recognizes a parallel between the philosophic active intellect and the cabalistic tenth aspect of God but supposes that the philosophers borrowed the concept from Jewish sources). G. Scholem, *Major Trends in Jewish Mysticism* (New York 1954) 184, 194, 203, 240 (the *Zohar*). J. Ben-Shlomo, *Torat ha-Elohut shel R. M. Cordovero* (Jerusalem 1965) 23–25, 44–46.

[165]Maimonides acknowledged that interpretations of Scripture other than his can be acceptable as long as they are in accord with correct principles, and Ibn Tibbon sometimes allows himself to disagree with Maimonides on the interpretation of individual verses; a list is drawn up by Ravitzky, *History and Faith* (n. 121 above) 242. Ibn Tibbon does not, however, differ on any matter of substance. He states his attitude to Maimonides in *Ma'amar Yiqqawu ha-Mayim* (Pressburg 1837) 114.

Guide than Maimonides' explicit language warranted. They, as we saw, read it as surreptitiously espousing an eternal, necessary, and unchanging nexus between God and the world, hence a wholly impersonal deity who could be concerned with nothing whatsoever outside of Himself. And at the opposite end of the spectrum of adherents stood others—generally men of lesser philosophic prowess than the Averroists—who also viewed themselves as devoted followers of Maimonides while considering it their pious duty to place a more traditional construction on the *Guide* than warranted by the words. They were exercised by Maimonides' statements on such subjects as human perfection, providence, the afterlife, and the purpose of the religious commandments. A few examples from writers belonging to this group:

Abraham Shalom, a fifteenth-century Spanish Jew, was a self-styled devotee of Maimonides. At one juncture, Shalom takes up the question of the nature of the human soul and its bearing on basic Jewish beliefs. He determines that orthodox doctrine mandates construing the human soul as a substance capable of existing independently of the body; for observance of the religious commandments will have intrinsic value only if it enables the soul to survive the body's demise.[166] Yet Maimonides stated that the human soul perishes together with the body and nothing apart from an intellect in possession of thought of God and other supernal incorporeal beings survives.[167] Shalom therefore "girds up the loins of reasoning and analysis" and "with strength of hand"—he perhaps should have said: sleight of hand—interprets Maimonides' language as affirming something different from what it says. Notwithstanding Maimonides' statements to the effect that the human soul perishes and the human intellect alone survives, Shalom tells us that Maimonides in fact viewed the human soul as a "divine spiritual substance" capable of existing independently of the body.[168]

Joseph ben Shem Ṭob Ibn Shem Ṭob, a Spanish Jewish contemporary of Shalom's, was certain that the scriptural commandments have a "peculiar property [*segula*]," which is able to elevate persons who study and observe them to a higher level of perfection than study of philosophy can. Yet the *Guide for the Perplexed* ascribes to the commandments only purposes of a pragmatic, rationalistic character. Joseph gives Maimonides the "benefit of the doubt [*le-kaf ẓekut*]." He explains that the rationalizing of the commandments in the *Guide* has in view just one of two functions served by the commandments, and the lesser function at that: In addition to their practical function, Maimonides, despite his failure to put it in so many

[166]Abraham Shalom, *Neweh Shalom* (Venice 1575) 8:2, 123a; H. Davidson, *The Philosophy of Abraham Shalom* (Berkeley 1964) 81–84. Shalom does not argue, as someone might today, that only if the entire human soul survives will the human personality survive.

[167]Maimonides, *Guide for the Perplexed* 1.70, p. 92b; above, p. 242.

[168]Shalom, *Neweh Shalom* 8:3, pp. 123b–24a; 8:9, p. 144a. In *Neweh Shalom* 8:5, p. 130b, he glosses over Maimonides' implacable opposition to astrology in any and all forms and attributes to him the belief that astrological forces do control human life, with the proviso that Jews who observe God's commandments escape those forces.

words, also recognized that the commandments serve a higher function thanks to a peculiar property they possess.[169]

Maimonides had explained that divine providence operates through the human intellect's coming into contact with the emanation radiating from the active intellect, that providence is therefore contingent on intellectual perfection, and that the degree of providence enjoyed by each human being is proportional to his intellectual attainments. Several writers—Moses Ibn Tibbon, Shem Ṭob Falaquera, Abraham Shalom, Joseph ben Shem Ṭob—nonetheless uncover an additional and complementary form of divine providence in Maimonides' language, a providence that comes to the aid of those who love God, have faith in Him, and perform the divine commandments, quite apart from intellectual development.[170]

To take one more example: Moses Almosnino, a sixteenth-century follower of Maimonides who lived in Turkey but whose origins went back to Spain, construes Maimonides' insistence on the primacy of human intellectual perfection as affirming that such perfection is not desirable in itself but only as a means to something else. On Almosnino's reading of Maimonides, intellectual perfection is of value insofar as it prepares man for the separate and higher goal of loving God.[171]

We can hardly help wondering how far these apologists deluded themselves into imagining that they were bringing Maimonides' true intent to light and how far they were conscious of twisting the master's words into an uncomfortable harmony with their own notions of Jewish orthodoxy. The question cannot be answered.

The exegetic strand in the *Guide for the Perplexed* likewise had its impact, inspiring allegorical interpretations of Scripture which may or may not have gone further than Maimonides would have been willing to go. I offer a couple of illustrations.

[169]Joseph ben Shem Ṭob, *Kebod Elohim* (Ferrara 1556) 21b–22a (the pagination appears to have been added in the recent photographic reprint). In a similar vein, R. Yom Ṭob ben Abraham Ishbili, *Sefer ha-Zikkaron* in *Kitebe ha-Riṭba*, ed. M. Blau (New York 1963) 37, writes that in stating the purposes of various commandments, Maimonides "did not believe it was the true reason for the commandment in question." He was merely supplying the multitude with "somewhat rational considerations" that could be used when "answering skeptics." Abi^cad Sar Shalom Basilea, an Italian cabalist active at the turn of the eighteenth century, considers Maimonides to be a "wise and very pious man" and gives him "the benefit of the doubt" on the issue of the reasons for the commandments in much the same way that Joseph ben Shem Ṭob does; see Basilea, *Emunat Ḥakamim* (Warsaw 1888) chapter 11, p. 24a.

[170]Moses Ibn Tibbon, in Diesendruck, "Samuel and Moses Ibn Tibbon on Maimonides' Theory of Providence" (n. 70 above) 364; Shem Ṭob Falaquera, *Moreh ha-Moreh* (n. 114 above) 146–48; Abraham Shalom, as quoted in Davidson, *The Philosophy of Abraham Shalom* 74–76; Joseph ben Shem Ṭob, *Kebod Elohim* 21a. A variation in Kalonymous, *Mesharet Moshe*, is quoted by D. Schwartz, "The Debate over the Maimonidean Theory of Providence," *Jewish Studies Quarterly* 2 (1995) 193–94.

[171]Moses Almosnino, *Pirqe Moshe* (Salonika 1563) 26a. Similarly in Kalonymous, *Mesharet Moshe*, as quoted by D. Schwartz, 194–95.

Maimonides had hinted that the scriptural story of the creation of *adam* has in view the bringing forth of the entire human species, in other words, mankind in general; that in the rabbinic account of the formation of Eve out of Adam's side, the male aspect of the original Adam symbolizes the human intellect, and the female aspect, man's nonintellectual nature; that the serpent's temptation of Eve and Eve's temptation of Adam are an allegory for the deflection of the human intellect by the lower faculties of the human soul; that the names of Adam's first sons, Cain and Abel, have allegorical significance; and that there is significance in Seth's being the son of Adam from whom the entire human species is descended.[172] David Qimḥi, one of the most accomplished medieval Bible commentators, was also one of Maimonides' staunchest defenders in the early dispute concerning the *Mishneh Torah* and *Guide for the Perplexed.* Qimḥi accompanied his sober, philological commentary on the Book of Genesis with an exegesis of the "hidden" sense of the narrative that opens with the words "And the Lord God formed man [*adam*]" in Genesis 2:7 and that extends to the end of Genesis 4.

Qimḥi begins by stating that the term *adam* in the pertinent chapters of Genesis is, in its surface sense, the name of the first man created by God, while in its deeper sense, *adam* stands for the entire human species. The narrative thus speaks on two levels, addressing the multitude and telling the story of Adam, the first man, and at the same time addressing the elite and adumbrating the condition of mankind in general. Both levels, Qimḥi stresses, "are true."

He goes on: When Scripture relates that "the Lord God planted a garden in Eden," Eden, on the hidden level, symbolizes the supernal active intellect; the active intellect "is the true, spiritual Eden." The garden located *in* Eden is a symbol for the power the active intellect possesses for emanating forms. And the tree of life, which the Lord made grow "in the midst of the garden," symbolizes the active intellect's emanation specifically of human intellect. Eden, the garden, and the tree are thus allegories for the part of the supernal world which most directly affects man, namely, the active intellect's power of emanating forms and, most important, its power of emanating the human intellect and human intellectual thoughts. When man eats of the tree of life, that is, when he masters metaphysical science, perfects his intellect, and thereby conjoins with the active intellect, he lives forever.

The woman, who was formed out of Adam's side, represents, in Qimḥi's allegorical interpretation, the portion of the man which is not intellect, including, in particular, the faculty of desire.[173] Scripture relates that man cleaves to woman so that they are "one flesh"; at a deeper level, Scripture is saying that men typically allow their intellects to succumb to physical desire. Further, "they were both naked, the man [*adam*] and his woman, and were not ashamed." That is, when the human intellect cleaves to the lower side of human nature, it denudes itself of

[172]*Guide for the Perplexed* 2.30.

[173]Qimhi, in a strange choice of terminology, sometimes calls these parts of the human soul "material intellect."

intellectual thought, reduces itself to the level of the beasts, and loses its sense of shame. Although Qimḥi had written that the woman represents the part of the man which is not intellect, he is not deterred from stating much the same of the serpent. It represents the nonintellectual part of the human soul and the faculty of desire in particular. The serpent tempts the woman; she tempts the male, or purely intellectual, aspect of man; the intellectual aspect of man is deflected from pursuing intellectual perfection and fails to attain immortality.

Adam's son Cain (in Hebrew: *Qayin*) symbolizes the segment of mankind that busies itself only with acquiring (*qinyan*) land. Abel (in Hebrew: *Hebel*) symbolizes the segment that expends time and energy on the vanities (*hebel*) of business and politics. Qimḥi says nothing about the symbolism of the name of Adam's third son, Seth, but—following Maimonides—does note that Seth was, in the words of Scripture, begotten in man's (*adam*'s) "own likeness, after his image." That is a figurative way of saying that Seth and his offspring partake of man's authentic essence, which is intellect, and they alone eat of the tree of life. There is fortunately a consolation for the Cains and Abels of the world. Qimḥi assures us that Cain, Abel, and Seth, stand not only for different kinds of men, but also for different stages in individual lives—Cain, for youth, Abel, for adulthood, and Seth, for mature old age. When a human being entering his later years turns over a new leaf, frees himself from earlier errors and passions, and focuses his energies on intellectual matters, he is able to redirect his life and perfect his intellect in anticipation of its approaching release from the confines of the body.[174]

Maimonides had remarked that *woman* can be a metaphor for physical matter. In a notorious incident that occurred in southern France around the turn of the fourteenth century, someone characterized as a member of the Jewish aristocracy and as the "offspring of holy men" but never named—it probably was Levi ben Abraham, who is known as the author of several books of a rationalist and allegorizing character—was given the podium at a wedding. He took the opportunity to set forth his interpretation of the biblical story of Abraham and Sarah and of a strange piece of rabbinic aggada: The aggada relates that one of the ancient rabbis once came upon the cave where Abraham and Sarah are interred and there he beheld Abraham lying with his head in Sarah's arms while she lavished her full attention on her beloved.[175] Sarah, Abraham, and their embrace, the speaker explained to the wedding guests, are allegories for matter, form, and the coalescing of the two which gives rise to physical objects.[176] The public allegorization of the

[174]L. Finkelstein, *The Commentary of David Kimhi on Isaiah* (New York 1926) liv–lxxiv, on Genesis 2:7–4.26. See Maimonides, *Guide for the Perplexed* 1.7.

[175]BT *Baba Batra* 58a.

[176]Abba Mari ben Moses, *Minḥat Qena'ot* in Solomon Adret, *Responsa*, 2 volumes, ed. Z. H. Dimitrovsky (Jerusalem 1990) 226, 443. Letter of Simeon ben Joseph, published by D. Kaufmann in *Jubelschrift zum neunzigsten Geburtstag des L. Zunz* (Berlin 1884), Hebrew section 147. Y. Bedersi in Solomon Adret, *Responsa* §418. For the identification of the allegorist as Levi ben Abraham, see *Minḥat Qena'ot* 380–81, 390–91.

patriarch and matriarch of the Israelite nation as two abstract philosophic concepts occasioned an uproar, and a member of the community, Abba Mari, sent an indignant account of the incident to R. Solomon Adret, a rabbinic authority of unchallenged standing, in Barcelona.

R. Solomon was duly scandalized. After letters went back and forth for a time, he assembled a number of rabbinic figures and together they pronounced a ban, first, on any member of their own community who studied Greek philosophy before the age of twenty-five,[177] and secondly, on anyone, anywhere, "who asserts that Abraham and Sarah are form and matter," who asserts "that Jacob's twelve sons are the twelve signs of the zodiac or that Moses established legislation [and did not act as God's spokesman]," or who interprets the scriptural prohibition against eating the flesh of the pig through health considerations. Persons making those assertions were declared to be excommunicated until they repent, the authors of books advancing the proscribed opinions were branded as heretics, and such authors as well as persons in possession of their books were declared to be excommunicated until the books were "committed to flame, never again to be mentioned by name."[178] The Abba Mari and Adret camps were careful to avoid criticizing the man whom Abba Mari calls "our master and teacher, Maimonides," and the document promulgating the ban against the allegorists goes out of its way to quote for support a passage from the *Guide for the Perplexed*[179]—even though Maimonides was undoubtedly the inspiration for the allegorical interpretation at the eye of the storm.

A resolution was found, and no bonfires are known to have been lit. Relatives of the allegorist interceded with Abba Mari and assured him that the man had not intended to deny the literal truth of the scriptural story of Abraham and Sarah; he was only trying to make sense of the strange piece of aggada.[180] The allegorist himself confessed deep regret for what had occurred. R. Solomon thereupon withdrew his curse and in its stead bestowed a blessing on the penitent together with the hope that "Abraham and Sarah will place their hands on the man's head and bless him. It is, after all, from their loins that he has come."[181]

[177] Solomon Adret, *Responsa*, standard edition §415; *Minḥat Qena'ot* 721.

[178] Abba Mari ben Moses, *Minḥat Qena'ot* 721, and the slightly different versions in *Minḥat Qena'ot* 734–35; Solomon Adret, *Responsa* §417. Yedaiah Bedersi wrote to Adret that he had never heard of the allegorization of the twelve sons of Jacob as the signs of the zodiac; see A. Halkin, "Yedaiah Bedershi's Apology," in *Jewish Medieval and Renaissance Studies*, ed. A. Altmann (Cambridge 1967) 167. That allegorical interpretation as well as the taking of Abraham and Sarah as symbols for form and matter have, however, been found in a work of Levi ben Abraham; see C. Touati, "La controverse de 1303–1306," *Revue des études juives* 127 (1968) 30–31.

[179] Solomon Adret, *Responsa* §417, quoting *Guide for the Perplexed* 3.41.

[180] Abba Mari ben Moses, *Minḥat Qena'ot* 443.

[181] Abba Mari ben Moses, *Minḥat Qena'ot* 468–69. Others who took their cue from Maimonides and interpreted Scripture in a similar allegorical spirit included Samuel Ibn Tibbon, Jacob Anatolio, Joseph Ibn Kaspi, and Levi Gersonides.

The story has a curious coda. A commentary on talmudic aggada has been preserved which is attributed to R. Solomon Adret and is generally recognized as his; and the commentary has no qualms about deploying concepts borrowed from the Arabic Aristotelian school of philosophy to allegorize away awkward elements in the material with which it deals. At one juncture, it takes up a problematic piece of aggada concerning the male Leviathan and his female consort. The male and female Leviathans were, according to the aggada, among God's first creations, and after creating them, God killed the female, salted her body, and stored it to be served to the righteous at their banquet in the world to come. The Adret commentary offers the following interpretation: The female Leviathan represents the human soul, and the male Leviathan, the human intellect. "The soul is like matter, and the intellect is its form; hence intellect is masculine and soul is feminine," perhaps an allusion to the circumstance that the Hebrew word for intellect is masculine in gender, and the Hebrew word for soul is feminine. The lesson taught by the aggada is that the human soul, represented by the female Leviathan, has a potentiality for receiving actual intellectual thought thanks to its intellect, which is represented by the male Leviathan. As for the salting away of the flesh of the female Leviathan to be eaten at the future banquet of the righteous, it signifies that "the soul of the righteous is immortal and will survive into the time of the resurrection and the world to come."[182] Notwithstanding Adret's denunciation of the allegorizing of the matriarch Sarah as the material principle in the physical world and the patriarch Abraham as form, he—or, to speak more precisely, the commentary attributed to him—did not hesitate to use the same conceptual tools to allegorize away a puzzling piece of rabbinic aggada.

Self-styled orthodoxy, like radicalism, sometimes has difficulty calling a halt. In the sixteenth century, an ultrafundamentalist berated Adret, the man who had been at the forefront of orthodoxy's opposition to the allegorization of Scripture, for his own allegorization of rabbinic aggada. The critic insisted on taking the most bizarre sounding rabbinic aggada at face value.[183]

We have been looking at the reception of the philosophic and exegetic sides of the *Guide for the Perplexed* among adherents. The *Guide* also stirred up opposition; approbation and opposition travel down through the centuries, intertwined, as it were, in a double helix. On several occasions, a dialectic can be observed, as a heated attack on Maimonides elicited an equally heated response.

The most virulent attacks occurred in the early thirteenth century, soon after Maimonides' death, when rabbis in central France placed "everyone who reads the *Guide for the Perplexed* and the Book of Knowledge [of the *Mishneh Torah*]

[182]Solomon Adret, *Ḥiddushe ha-Rashba ᶜal Aggadot ha-Shas*, ed. Sh. Weinberger (Jerusalem 1966) 87, 91, 93.

[183]See G. Scholem, "*Yediᶜot Ḥadashot ᶜal R. Yosef Ashkenazi*," *Tarbiz* 28 (1958–1959) 233, with reference to Adret, *Ḥiddushe ha-Rashba ᶜal Aggadot ha-Shas* 61.

under the ban," and then a few years later when Jewish opponents of Maimonides complained to church authorities about the *Guide* and the Book of Knowledge, and the authorities accommodated by burning both.[184] The burning of Jewish books by Christians was sobering. More than once in the years that followed, opponents of the *Guide* would lob intemperate language at it, and Maimonides' defenders would reply in kind. The excommunication threat was brandished a couple of times. But disagreements never again descended to the same depths of incivility.

The *Guide* was nevertheless criticized for specific perceived errors: for identifying intellectual perfection as the aim of human life;[185] for interpreting the *account of creation* and *account of the chariot* as a condensation of the philosophic sciences of physics and metaphysics rather than as a repository of ancient theosophic lore;[186] for construing prophetic experiences solely as visions and not as events that occurred in the real world and outside the mind of the prophet;[187] for maintaining that Moses was the only prophet with whom God communicated and the remaining prophets received their prophecy from the active intellect;[188] for ascribing rationalistic, pragmatic purposes to the commandments[189] and in particular for viewing the sacrificial rites as merely a stratagem to wean the Israelites away from idolatry and not as something of value in its own right.[190] The common denominator was unhappiness with Maimonides' rationalizing of the Jewish religion, and the criticisms were largely an inverted image of the efforts of adherents of Maimonides to bring his words into line with what both they and the

[184] Above, p. 279.

[185] The "rabbinic scholars" referred to by Shem Ṭob, Commentary on *Guide for the Perplexed* 3.51; Isaac Arama, *ᶜAqedat Yiṣḥaq* (Pressburg 1849) 1.261b–62b.

[186] Daniel Ibn al-Māshiṭa, writing in Judeo-Arabic in 1223, cited by P. Fenton, "Le *Taqwīm al-Adyān* de Daniel Ibn al-Māshiṭa," *Revue des études juives* 145 (1986) 282. The cabalists cited by Idel, "Maimonides and Kabbalah" (n. 164 above) 35–41, 47. Basilea, *Emunat Ḥakamim* (n. 169 above), chapters 13–15, gives Maimonides the "benefit of the doubt" (*le-kaf zekut*), "forces" (*doḥeq*) his words, and interprets him as recognizing two levels of inquiry into the universe. In identifying the account of creation with philosophical physics, and the account of the chariot with metaphysics, Maimonides, according to Basilea, was talking only about the lesser of the two levels.

[187] Naḥmanides, Commentary on Genesis 18:1; a poem published by H. Brody, "*Shire Meshullam ben Shelomo*," *Yediᶜot ha-Makon le-Ḥeqer ha-Shira ha-ᶜIbrit* 4 (Berlin 1938) 100, lines 16–18; the German Jewish rabbinic figures from the fifteenth and sixteenth centuries quoted by E. Kupfer, "*Hassagot min Ḥakam Eḥad*," *Kobez al Yad* 21 (1985) 222.

[188] Naḥmanides, Commentary on Genesis 18:1.

[189] The writers cited by Idel, "Maimonides and Kabbalah" notes 44, 45, 46, 51, 54; Brody, "*Shire Meshullam ben Shelomo*" 102, lines 49–53; the German Jewish rabbinic figures from the fifteenth and sixteenth centuries quoted by Kupfer, "*Hassagot min Ḥakam Eḥad*" 222; S. R. Hirsch, *The Nineteen Letters of Ben Uziel* (New York 1942) 183–84.

[190] Naḥmanides, Commentary on Leviticus 1:9; the cabalists quoted by Idel, "Maimonides and Kabbalah" note 51, and p. 49; Arama, *ᶜAqedat Yiṣḥaq* 3.3b–4a; the German Jewish rabbinic figures from the fifteenth and sixteenth centuries quoted by Kupfer, "*Hassagot min Ḥakam Eḥad*" 222.

critics agreed was orthodox doctrine. A substantial number of the critics were cabalists or had cabalistic leanings.

Not every opponent was satisfied with calling attention to specific errors in the *Guide for the Perplexed*. Some leveled their guns at Maimonides himself and at the book as a whole, and on two occasions, matters threatened to get out of hand again.

In the last quarter of the thirteenth century, the "prince and exilarch of all Israel" residing in Damascus was informed that a European Jew—a man named Solomon ben Samuel, who was also known as Solomon Petit—was agitating in Acre, Palestine, against "the great gaon, our teacher Moses ben Maimon." He was "imputing things that were incorrect unto" the *Guide for the Perplexed*, a book in which Maimonides "battled to refute the heretic [*apikoros*] and every denier of our true Torah." The complaint against Solomon had very likely been sent to Damascus by Maimonides' grandson David, who lived in Acre during a good part of the period and took upon himself to defend his grandfather's honor.

The Damascus exilarch and his law court issued a warning in which they advised Solomon that he would be excommunicated if he did not desist. Solomon was not deterred. He traveled to Europe to muster support for his position and was there able to collect statements from European rabbinic scholars which, he made known, prohibited the study of the *Guide for the Perplexed* and instructed that it be "sealed away forever." On his return to Acre, he resumed his campaign, now wielding the written statements that he had brought back as weapons.

In 1286 if the date is correct—scholars have pointed out problems in it—the exilarch and his rabbinic judges proclaimed that their patience was exhausted. They solemnly excommunicated anyone who "utters wickedness against the gaon, our teacher Moses, or his book, the *Guide for the Perplexed*, . . . who asserts that it contains heresy [*minut*], who asserts that those who read it have walked the path of heresy, . . . who prevents the reading of the book, or who commands that it be sealed away," as well as anyone who keeps in his possession a letter or document enunciating the aforementioned sentiments or attempting to accomplish the aforementioned goals. The declaration of excommunication concludes with the extreme step of permitting recourse to gentile authorities should that be necessary in order to enforce the decree. Rabbinic figures from Safed and Acre followed the example of Damascus, albeit, according to the preserved reports, in less detail. They are simply reported to have excommunicated anybody who kept the forbidden documents in his possession.[191]

[191] A. Lichtenberg, *Qobeṣ Teshubot ha-Rambam* (Leipzig 1859) 3.21b–22b. The declaration of the rabbis of Safed is problematic. It reports that the signatories stood at Maimonides' grave when making their declaration, yet the first signatory is named Moses ha-Cohen (the priest), and Jewish law does not allow members of the priestly class to enter cemeteries; see Leviticus 21:1, BT *Nazir* 53b–54a, Tosefta, *Makkot* 4 (3):17, and Maimonides, *Mishneh Torah*: *H. Abel* 2:15. Other documents reporting aspects of the incident also raise questions. Nevertheless, there is so much interlocking evidence that the essential outline may be accepted as accurate.

Damascus was not the only city that boasted an exilarch of *all* Israel. Mosul, 400 miles to the northeast, also had one, and in 1288, the "exilarch of all Israel" who resided in Mosul entered the picture.

He and his retinue had heard that Solomon ben Samuel was trying to "seal away" the *Guide for the Perplexed* on the grounds that it "inclines toward heretical books." The Mosul group issued an excommunication of Solomon and anyone else of a similar mind should they in the future "utter wickedness" against Maimonides, direct that the *Guide for the Perplexed* or other books of Maimonides' be sealed away, try to prevent the reading of Maimonides' books, keep in their possession documents encouraging any of those actions, and so on.[192] Five months later, the principal of the rabbinic academy in Baghdad informed Maimonides' grandson that he had received the latter's complaint against Solomon ben Samuel. The Baghdadi principal and his colleagues contributed their own excommunication of Solomon and Solomon's allies, making it contingent on the miscreants' failing to repent forthwith.[193] Whether Solomon was silenced by the phalanx facing him is unknown. No reports have been preserved of an open clash between the Near Eastern authorities who came to the defense of Maimonides and the *Guide* and the European rabbinic figures who supplied Solomon Petit with the written statements prohibiting study of the book.[194]

Around the middle of the sixteenth century, communal peace was threatened in a different part of the Jewish world. A young rabbinic scholar named Joseph ben Joseph[195] tried to foment opposition to the *Guide for the Perplexed* in the city of Prague. According to the report, he was called before the "membership of the yeshiva"—the precise meaning of the phrase is unclear—and instructed to desist, which he did.[196] When his father-in-law, who had held a rabbinic position in Prague, was subsequently appointed rabbi of the Poznan district in Poland, Joseph joined him there and renewed his attacks on Maimonides, informing those willing to listen that Maimonides was a "total heretic" and that not a single chapter of the *Guide for the Perplexed* was free of heresy.[197] The father-in-law was drawn into the fray: In 1559, he took advantage of his annual pre-Passover sermon to advise his flock that the *Guide* was a forbidden book, that the burning of the Talmud in Italy in 1553 had been divine punishment for the printing of the *Guide* in Venice

[192]Document published in *Jeschurun* (Bamberg) 7 (1871) 73–74.

[193]Document published in *Jeschurun* 7.76, 78–79.

[194]Jewish life in Acre came to an end a short time afterwards when the Muslims retook the city from the Christians, who had been in control.

[195]Later in life he was known as Joseph Ashkenazi.

[196]Ph. Bloch, "Der Streit um den Moreh des Maimonides in der Gemeinde Posen," *Monatsschrift für Geschichte und Wissenschaft des Judenthums*" 47 (1903) 264. Since Eastern European Jews did not name children after living persons, Joseph's father must have died before Joseph was born; the point is made by Kupfer, "*Hassagot min Ḥakam Eḥad*" (n. 187 above) 220.

[197]Bloch, "Der Streit um den Moreh" 264, 268.

two years earlier, and that in the olden days, the pious of Austria used nonrabbinic works such as the *Guide* as floor mats or stools or simply burned them.[198]

A pamphlet was thereupon circulated in the Jewish community spelling out the imbecilities of the rabbi and his son-in-law. The pamphlet states that Joseph was a fool and an ox, that his mouth was impure and his brain defiled, that he spoke foolishness and idiocy; and it makes the scurrilous insinuation, if I understood correctly, that he had been born out of wedlock. The rabbi was a "great jackass," a fool, and vile, he had obtained his appointment to the rabbinate of Poznan through "slyness," and—to cap matters—had "through slyness" induced a wealthy widow to marry him after his wife died.[199]

The author of the pamphlet discloses that both opponents and followers of Maimonides had their supporters in Poznan and he appeals to the communal authorities in that city to call the rabbi to account.[200] How things turned out is again unknown.

Maimonides and the *Guide* were not only blamed for the public burning of the Talmud in Italy. They were held responsible for the disasters that befell the Jewish community in Spain prior to, and culminating in the trauma of 1492.

An early fifteenth-century Spanish cabalist, Shem Ṭob Ibn Shem Ṭob—whose son Joseph ben Shem Ṭob Ibn Shem Ṭob was earlier seen to have given Maimonides the "benefit of the doubt" concerning the special "property" of the religious commandments—recognized the excellence of the codifying side of Maimonides' *Mishneh Torah.* He moreover acknowledged that Maimonides was not the most extreme of the Jewish philosophers.[201] He nonetheless condemns Maimonides for doctrines advanced in the *Guide for the Perplexed* and elsewhere.

Worst of all in Shem Ṭob's judgment was Maimonides' thesis that the soul with which man is born perishes upon the death of the human body, only intellectual thought acquired from the emanation of the active intellect survives, and the surviving intellectual thought of all men who perfect their intellect coalesces into a single incorporeal whole. The implication for Shem Ṭob is that a future

[198]Bloch, "Der Streit um den Moreh" 167, 273, 275, 346. The rabbi did not identify the *Guide for the Perplexed* by name, but as the author of the pamphlet attacking him insists, his intent was clear.

[199]Bloch, "Der Streit um den Moreh" 164 (where there seems to be an insinuation that Joseph's name—Joseph *ben Joseph*—shows him to have been a *shetuqi*, a child with no known father), 166, 273, 275, 346, et passim. The author of the pamphlet was apparently Abraham Horowitz, the author of a commentary on Maimonides' *Eight Chapters*; see Bloch 263. He probably was not a resident of Poznan; see pp. 273, 275. It is hard to imagine that anyone in sixteenth-century Eastern Europe could revile the rabbi of his own community in the way the pamphlet does and escape scot-free.

[200]Bloch, "Der Streit um den Moreh" 267, 270, 271, 273, 275, 276.

[201]Shem Ṭob Ibn Shem Ṭob, *Sefer ha-Emunot* (Ferrara 1556) 1.1, p. 5a. In Shem Ṭob's judgment, Isaac Albalag was the worst of the Jewish philosophers.

resurrection of the dead, a day of divine judgment, and the punishment of the wicked in Hell would all be impossible. "The rabbis of France, . . . R. Abraham ben David, R. Meir [Abulafia], . . . and R. Samuel [ben Eli], the head of the yeshiva in Iraq," were all therefore correct in denouncing Maimonides for denying essential Jewish doctrine.[202] Other errors of Maimonides' to which Shem Ṭob calls attention are the proposition that ritual commandments such as the dietary laws and prohibitions of certain sexual relations serve only to ingrain desirable beliefs and qualities and remove undesirable ones, thereby preparing man for the intellectual life;[203] that the Temple, its implements, and the sacrificial service, are nothing more than artifices for uprooting false beliefs;[204] that providence follows solely from intellectual perfection;[205] and that most of the miracles recorded in the Bible were not actual events.[206]

It was not, however, merely errors here and there that aroused Shem Ṭob's ire. He berates Maimonides for contradicting the "entire Torah," the Oral as well as the Written, and for having "walked in the paths of those who reject the Torah of Moses," in other words, Aristotle and the Aristotelian school.[207] Maimonides was even more blameworthy than Aristotle. Aristotle excluded the possibility of God's knowing what occurs in the world and he therefore at least freed God of responsibility. Maimonides, by contrast, maintained that God created the world and knows everything taking place within it, that the prophets exhort mankind to obey God's commandments, and yet that God remains blithely unconcerned whether people do or do not observe them. God, in Maimonides' view, never rewards those who obey or punishes those who do not, and such a "belief is without doubt thousands of times" worse than Aristotle's. Nor is that all. Maimonides' views led the "majority of Jews" astray, and thereby became the cause of "Israel's denying the Lord God of their fathers." The allusion is reasonably clear. Shem Ṭob is saying that the rationalism of the *Guide for the Perplexed* discouraged Jews from martyring themselves for their faith and hence contributed to the mass conversions to Christianity in Spain during and after the anti-Jewish riots of 1391.[208]

[202]Shem Ṭob, *Sefer ha-Emunot*, introduction, pp. 2b–3a; 1:1, pp. 5b–6b; 1:4, pp. 10b–11a. Maimonides' position on human immortality is unacceptable for Shem Ṭob for an additional reason—because it is incompatible with the cabalistic doctrine of the transmigration and rebirth of souls. Shem Ṭob had convinced himself that divine justice can be harmonized with the suffering of the innocent only on the assumption that souls atone for sins they commit in one life by returning again to earth in a subsequent life. The suffering of the innocent is accordingly a punishment and atonement for misdeeds that their souls committed in a previous life. See *Sefer ha-Emunot* 7:4.

[203]Shem Ṭob, *Sefer ha-Emunot* 1:1, 7a; 1:4, 11a; 2: 3, 15a (erroneously numbered as 13a).

[204]Shem Ṭob, *Sefer ha-Emunot* 2: 3, 15a.

[205]Shem Ṭob, *Sefer ha-Emunot* 1:3, 9a; 1:4, 11a.

[206]Shem Ṭob, *Sefer ha-Emunot* 1:2, 8a; 1:4, 11a.

[207]Shem Ṭob, *Sefer ha-Emunot* 2:1, 12b; 2:3, 15a.

[208]Shem Ṭob, *Sefer ha-Emunot* 2:4, 15b.

Shem Ṭob did not go unanswered. When his book was printed posthumously in Ferrara in 1556, one of the town's rabbis arranged for it to be followed almost at once by the publication of a refutation that had been written some time earlier by Moses al-Ashkar, an Egyptian rabbinic judge.[209] The tone is shrill. Shem Ṭob's critique of Maimonides consists, in al-Ashkar's words, of "imaginations," "false inferences," "lies," "inanities," "idiocies," and "falsifications." Shem Ṭob "perverts the truth and invents things." The placenta should have folded back over his face and suffocated him when he was in the womb, and he should have been stillborn. How, al-Ashkar wonders, could previous authorities have neglected to decree that his book be burnt even "on a Day of Atonement that coincided with the Sabbath"?[210] As for Shem Ṭob's specific arguments, al-Ashkar refutes them one by one, largely in the style of the defenders of Maimonides who showed him to have held precisely the beliefs that they understood orthodox Jewish doctrine demands. Al-Ashkar thus cites statements in Maimonides' genuine works as well as in some falsely attributed compositions which, as he reads them, affirm that men enjoy divine providence in accordance with their behavior and not just their intellectual attainments, that the religious commandments and animal sacrifices serve purposes of a higher character than those assigned them in the *Guide*, and so forth.[211]

In 1492, two or three generations after Shem Ṭob wrote his attack on Maimonides, Jews and Muslims who refused to convert to Christianity were expelled from Spain, and the Spanish Jewish community met its end. Joseph Jabez was one of those who submitted to the tribulations of exile.

Jabez took a jaundiced view of the human intellect and denigrates it as one of the elements in man's makeup that lead him astray and must be resisted. In Jabez's words: The "evil inclination . . . loves the commission of sins and despises the negative commandments," and in the same way, "the human intellect . . . loves intellectual thoughts, . . . and despises the true opinions of the Torah," such as the belief "in [divine] retribution, the revelation of the Torah, resurrection, and the Great Judgment Day, all of which stand in opposition to intellectual syllogism." Jews are therefore "commanded" by religious law to resist the allurements of syllogistic reasoning.[212] That being the case, Jabez asks himself how Maimonides, of whom it is commonly said that "from [the biblical] Moses to Moses [Maimonides] no one like Moses arose," could have promoted the philosophic ideal in the *Mishneh Torah* and composed the *Guide for the Perplexed.*

His answer is that Maimonides was a unique exception and not to be imitated. Maimonides was "holy and pious from the womb, . . . going back several gen-

[209]Moses al-Ashkar, *Hassagot she-Hissig . . . ᶜal Ma she-Katab R. Shem Ṭob be-Sefer ha-Emunot* (Ferrara 1556), unpaginated, identical with al-Ashkar, *Responsa* §117.

[210]Moses al-Ashkar, *Responsa* (Jerusalem 1959) §117, pp. 303, 305, 311, 314–16.

[211]Moses al-Ashkar, *Responsa* §117, pp. 303, 307.

[212]J. Jabez, *Or ha-Ḥayyyim* (Lemberg 1850), chapter 8, p. 22b.

erations," "a righteous man the son of a righteous man, a pious man the son of a pious man." He alone was able to travel terrain frequented by "troops of beasts and highway robbers, that is to say, the philosophers, who declare that the Lord hath forsaken the land, who deny the creation of the world and bring a [supposedly] apodictic demonstration for its eternity. . . . The wild beasts did not devour or harm him, nor did the highway robbers despoil him. He extracted onyx stones from the poisons [or: heads] of asps in the vipers' den of the chief of the philosophers. He put out his hand, and he [the viper-philosopher] harmed him not." A little more patience with the florid metaphors and biblical rhetoric, and we get to learn what the onyx stones extracted from asps in the vipers' den are: Maimonides "girded on his sword, . . . delved into their books, and did battle with those gentiles. The spirit of the Lord came mightily upon him, . . . he tore the arm, yea the crown of the head, and he saw from the words of the viper himself [that is, from Aristotle] that he had not produced a demonstration of eternity." Maimonides accordingly "held fast to his tradition and produced proofs for the belief in creation, albeit not an apodictic demonstration, for such does not exist." Providence did its part too by preventing Maimonides from ever seeing Averroes' demonstrations for the eternity of the world. Had he been exposed to Averroes' demonstrations, who knows? He might have succumbed.[213]

Although Maimonides had sufficient reason for studying philosophy and composing the *Guide for the Perplexed*, although his own merit and the merit of his ancestors protected him from the mortal dangers of philosophy, and although he was able to extend that protection to his immediate students, damage began to set in, Jabez writes, when the *Guide* passed from Maimonides' immediate students to the students of the latter.[214] In the closing years of Spanish Jewish life, conditions reached a pass where pupils would sharpen their intellects through six, seven, or eight years of studying the Torah in rabbinic academies and then employ the "holy tool" perfected through rabbinic studies for the purpose of "donning filthy garments," that is, "cleaving to the science of philosophy." The sin of rabbinic students who left their studies for philosophy was a primary reason for God's visiting the disasters of 1492 on Spanish Jewry.[215] When the bitter day came, the corrosive forces that Maimonides inadvertently put in motion continued their mischief. Among those who were unable to escape from the Iberian peninsula, simple, uneducated Jewish women persuaded their husbands to chose martyrdom. By contrast, Jews infected by the "great leprosy" of philosophy deserted their ancestral faith in order to save their skins.[216] Historians have followed Jabez in

[213]Jabez, *Or ha-Ḥayyyim*, chapter 9, pp. 24a; 26a–b. The image of extracting onyx stones from the poisons, or heads, of asps appears in Abba Mari, *Minḥat Qena'ot* (n. 176 above) 653, as pointed out by G. Freudenthal, "Holiness and Defilement," *Micrologus* 9 (2001) 175. Freudenthal also calls attention to a different version of the image in *Minḥat Qena'ot* 510.

[214]Jabez, *Or ha-Ḥayyyim*, chapter 9, p. 26a

[215]Jabez, *Or ha-Ḥayyyim*, introduction, pp. 2b–3a; chapter 9, p. 23b.

[216]Jabez, *Or ha-Ḥayyyim*, chapter 5, p. 19b; chapter 12, p. 28b.

crediting a prevailing philosophic ethos for the choice of apostasy over martyrdom or exile by masses of Spanish Jews in 1391 and 1492—in contrast to the greater willingness of German Jews to accept martyrdom during the crusades. There is no way of determining whether the diagnosis is correct.

That the author of the magnificent *Mishneh Torah* also wrote the *Guide for the Perplexed* was a hard nut to crack for those who saw it as a book overflowing with heresy. Two implacable opponents of philosophy—both of whom, as it happens, were excellent talmudists and demonstrated keen textual skills when treating rabbinic works—believed that they discovered the solution to the puzzle.[217]

Joseph ben Joseph, the man who in the sixteenth century tried to persuade the community of Poznan that Maimonides was a heretic and every chapter of the *Guide* is imbued with heresy—he was also the man who rebuked R. Solomon Adret for allegorizing rabbinic aggada[218]—eventually set his views down in a small volume.[219] There he evinces a fundamentalism of a pitch that we have not encountered yet. He rejects Maimonides' position that the human soul and the angels are "intellect," since he finds Scripture and the rabbis describing both in physical terms.[220] He rejects the astronomers' and philosophers' conceit that the world is round, since a well-known rabbinic passage assumes it to be flat.[221] And he traces "the denial of *all* the principles of faith" to the newfangled notion that God is pure intellect and unchangeable. His contention is that if God were intellect and unchangeable, He could not do the things that Scripture and the ancient rabbis describe Him as doing: God could not see what happens in the world, hear sounds, speak, forgive, reward and punish, write in a book, feel pity, love those who serve Him, hate the sinner, take vengeance, rest on the Sabbath, pass through

[217]Shem Ṭob ben Joseph—the grandson of the Shem Ṭob who stated that Maimonides contradicted the "entire Torah"—remarks in his Commentary on *Guide* 3.51: "Many rabbinic scholars say" that Maimonides did not write the lines comparing experts in rabbinic studies who fail to investigate religious principles philosophically to persons who go around the ruler's palace without ever finding the entrance. And, they further say that if he did write the chapter, "it should be sealed away or, better, burned."

[218]Above, p. 410.

[219]Sections were published by Scholem, "*Yediᶜot Ḥadashot ᶜal R. Yosef Ashkenazi*" (n. 183 above) 59–89, 201–35. The composition does not carry the name of the author, but Scholem, 69–74, shows convincingly that it was written by Joseph, the son-in-law of Aaron, the rabbi of Poznan. Kupfer, "*Hassagot min Ḥakam Eḥad*" (n. 187 above), published a sixteenth-century refutation of the composition, and the refutation, p. 127, confirms that the author was indeed named "Joseph ben Joseph." Joseph seems to have composed his critique of Maimonides over a period of years: He writes several times that he was still young and immature, which would suggest that he had not yet left Europe. But he also makes a number of observations concerning a Bible manuscript that was kept at the time in Damascus and that he presumably saw after leaving Europe and moving to Palestine when already in his thirties or forties.

[220]Scholem, "*Yediᶜot Ḥadashot ᶜal R. Yosef Ashkenazi*" 216–17.

[221]Scholem, "*Yediᶜot Ḥadashot ᶜal R. Yosef Ashkenazi*" 220.

Egypt, descend to Sinai, reascend to heaven, or sit "upon a throne high and lifted up"; those are actions performed by "corporeal bodies." In opposition to Maimonides and his followers, who allegorized away scriptural and rabbinic descriptions that are incompatible with a philosophic conception of God, Joseph opts for a God who is corporeal and subject to change.[222]

The *Mishneh Torah*, in Joseph's judgment, is "careful" throughout and "takes the strict," which for him is the exemplary, view in questions of religious law. That it could have been written by someone who subscribed to a gamut of heretical beliefs was therefore mind-boggling. Joseph had once "heard" that the solution lay in the code's being commonly called—as, we may add, it is in some contexts still called today—"Maimuni"[223] rather than either "the code of Moses ben Maimon" or the *Mishneh Torah*, the name Maimonides chose. He notes something even more telling: Maimonides wrote his Commentary on the Mishna and the *Guide for the Perplexed* in Arabic, from which Hebrew translations had to be made, whereas the code of law was written in Hebrew. And there is something else: When Maimonides did write Hebrew, he mixed in incomprehensible neologisms derived from the Arabic, whereas the Hebrew of the body of the code is clear and pure. Joseph concludes: "Therefore, let him who understands, understand."[224] He is plainly intimating that the Arabic Commentary on the Mishna, the Arabic *Guide for the Perplexed*, and the opening Book of the *Mishneh Torah*, which is in Hebrew but contains outlandish terminology and philosophic theories, were written by Maimonides. The body of the *Mishneh Torah* is the work of a different person, Maimonides' father, Maimon. Although Maimonides arrogated the *Mishneh Torah* to himself, the name *Maimuni* has stubbornly and providentially attached itself to it in order to keep the truth alive.

The dialectic of response to critique operated again here. A few years later, an unknown author of cabalistic sympathies wrote a "small composition" of some seventy pages, about half the length of Joseph's work, to refute the charge that Maimonides rejected every iota of "our holy Torah and the tradition of the rabbis." The refutation is not as feverish as the pamphlet excoriating Joseph which circulated in Poznan; it does not brand him a foolish ox with an impure mouth and defiled brain but, on the contrary, grants that, though misguided, he acted out of pious motives and "for the sake of heaven."[225] As the refutation goes through Joseph's criticisms one by one, it defends Maimonides on the grounds that his positions were no less legitimate than the positions of others, and the Torah, after all, has "seventy faces."[226] It observes that Maimonides cannot be blamed for not having had access to cabalistic knowledge and, for good measure, it gives credence to the

[222]Scholem, "*Yedi^c ot Ḥadashot ^c al R. Yosef Ashkenazi*" 227–29.

[223]For instances, see Avida, *Sefer Mishneh Torah le-ha-Rambam ke-Sefer Limmud*, *Aresheth* 3 (1961) 34, note 13.

[224]Scholem, "*Yedi^c ot Ḥadashot ^c al R. Yosef Ashkenazi*" 83.

[225]Kupfer, "*Hassagot min Ḥakam Eḥad*" 226.

[226]Kupfer, "*Hassagot min Ḥakam Eḥad*" 226–27, 272.

fable that Maimonides learned about the cabala in his old age and was won over.[227] And it has recourse to the familiar tactic of interpreting Maimonides in a manner that, willy-nilly, brings him into line with what the author considers to be orthodox Jewish doctrine. The Maimonides coming out of the anonymous defense had no thought of combining the Torah and philosophy; the calumny that he intended to do so is an invention of commentators on the *Guide*.[228] The genuine Maimonides, we are informed, believed that the religious commandments possess intrinsic value beyond the pragmatic functions assigned to them in the *Guide*; that man enjoys providence thanks to both his intellectual attainments and his observance of the commandments and not, God forbid, solely through the former; that myriad angels exist apart from the intelligences which move the celestial spheres; that the miracles recorded in the Bible all took place in the real world as described.[229] As for the supposition that Maimonides "stole" his father's work and turned it into the body of the *Mishneh Torah*, yet the theft went unnoticed for centuries until detected by Joseph ben Joseph, the anonymous refutation brushes that aside as preposterous.[230]

The puzzle—how both the superb *Mishneh Torah* and the disastrous *Guide for the Perplexed* could have been written by the same person—was solved in the opposite way by R. Jacob Emden, an erudite rabbinic author of the eighteenth century. In his version, it is the *Guide* that Maimonides could not conceivably have written.

Jacob Emden had wider interests, and was more broad-minded, than Joseph ben Joseph. He does not, for instance, hesitate to use the philosophic term "necessarily existent" as a cognomen for God, he takes for granted that God is a nonphysical being, and he explains away the attribution to God of human emotions with the favorite stratagem of the rationalists: "Scripture speaks in conformity with the language of men." He realized that the earth is round, although, two centuries after Copernicus, he still visualized a universe in which celestial spheres carrying the sun, moon, and planets rotate around the earth.[231] When corresponding with a Jewish medical student, he asks the man to provide him with definitive works on alchemy, whether written by Jews or non-Jews.[232] In a quarrel with a former friend who had begun learning French, he concedes that Jewish law does not prohibit study of the language, with the proviso, however, that French erotic novels be excluded. He himself read non-Jewish works, usually, of course, in the privy,

[227] Kupfer, "*Hassagot min Ḥakam Eḥad*" 242–43.

[228] Kupfer, "*Hassagot min Ḥakam Eḥad*" 226, 245.

[229] Kupfer, "*Hassagot min Ḥakam Eḥad*" 241, 248, 249, 254–55, 268.

[230] Kupfer, "*Hassagot min Ḥakam Eḥad*" 259.

[231] Jacob Emden, glosses on the Babylonian Talmud, *Sukka* 52b; *Migdal ᶜOz: Oṣar ha-Ṭob* (Zhitomir 1874) 22a, column 2. Emden calls the belief in the corporeality of God a "disease" in *Iggeret Purim*, quoted by J. Schacter, "Rabbi Jacob Emden's *'Iggeret Purim*," *Studies in Medieval Jewish History and Literature* 2, ed. I. Twersky (Cambridge, Mass. 1984) 445.

[232] Jacob Emden, *She'ilat Yabeṣ* 1, §41 (end).

where the Written and Oral Laws may not be studied and recourse must be had to books of a secular character.[233]

Emden was a contentious figure with a string of quarrels to his name, and when the Muse of Vituperation inspired him, speaking, as a rule, in an opulent biblical or rabbinic idiom, he could be carried away. Consider, for instance, the title page of a book in which his principal object was to mark interpolations that had infiltrated the canonic text of the cabala, the *Zohar*. He begins by venting his spleen through imagery used by Scripture to castigate persons who go a whoring after false gods and from there he soars: A scribe who allows interpolations to enter a book under his care opens his "legs wide [like a strumpet] to every passerby, consents to every adulterer, lies with every animal and has it lie with" him. The irresponsible scribe "swallows all [kinds of] refuse and dirt, draws in all filth, and is never satiated." "Like a hog rooting in garbage, getting fat on the dung," such a scribe "enjoys, and delights in the excrement of men." There is more, all put prominently on the title page of what is ostensibly a scholarly work.[234]

In his earlier writings, R. Jacob Emden took for granted that the Maimonides of the *Mishneh Torah* was also the author of the *Guide for the Perplexed*. He was not happy with elements in both works, especially with Maimonides' use of the premise of eternal celestial motion in proving the existence of God. But he repeated a time-honored exculpation: Maimonides wrote during a period when "heresy was in the ascendant," and his "intent was for the sake of heaven, considering the times."[235] People were studying philosophy, and Maimonides defended religion in a form they could comprehend.

At a later stage, Emden came to see things in a different, more lurid light. In Part Two of the book in which he exposes what he judges to be interpolations in the *Zohar*, he has occasion to refer to the *Guide for the Perplexed* and when he does, "a fire is closed up" in his "bones with crushing pain. . . . Why is my pain perpetual?"[236] He finds the *Guide*'s treatment of scriptural miracles to be "strange and perverse."[237] When he reflects upon the purposes assigned to the religious commandments in the *Guide*, his "soul fainteth within" him and collapses; for what the book says on the subject is "a mocking, a joke, ridiculous. Can there be any taste in drivel?"[238] The rationale given in the *Guide* for the Temple sacrifices "in particular" has the "taste of drivel." It is like the "vexing dripping of rain on a raw

[233]Emden, *Mitpaḥat Sefarim* [n. 164 above) 74, column 2—75, column 2. *She'ilat Yabeṣ* 1, §10, treats the question of what may and what may not be studied in the privy.

[234]Emden, *Mitpaḥat Sefarim*, title page. Y. Rafael, "*Kitebe R. Ya*ᶜ*akob Emden*," *Aresheth* 3 (1961) 259, quotes a slightly superior text from the first edition, Altona, 1768.

[235]Emden, *She'ilat Yabeṣ* 1, §41 (end); Commentary on Mishna *Abot* 2:14; 5:22 (end); *Migdal* ᶜ*Oz*: *Oṣar ha-Ṭob* 22a, column 1; 22b, column 1; *Migdal* ᶜ*Oz*: *Bet Middot* 119b. Additional references in Schacter, "Rabbi Jacob Emden's *'Iggeret Purim*" 442, note 12.

[236]Emden, *Mitpaḥat Sefarim* 62.

[237]Emden, *Mitpaḥat Sefarim* 64.

[238]Emden, *Mitpaḥat Sefarim* 56, 61.

rainy day." Only someone who "has gone mad" and has no "cure for his malady" could be seduced by it. "This by itself . . . justifies decreeing that the book be burnt."[239] Nothing, however, raises R. Jacob Emden's hackles as much as the notion that the ancient *account of creation* and *account of the chariot* are identical with the philosophic sciences of physics and metaphysics.

The *Guide for the Perplexed* replaces the "divine wisdom [and] hidden delight" of the genuine account of the chariot—which for Emden is nothing other than the secret doctrine of the cabala—with "inanities, empty words, striving after wind, and vanities . . . drawn from treasure houses of falsehood and lies of . . . philosophy." In place of true wisdom, the *Guide* palms off a "fabricated divine science, invented by ne'er-do-wells who put one patch on another and plastered one muddle on another." Only a totally blind man could compare that "trivial counterfeit science, full of fetid stupidities, raising a stench like ordure," with "true wisdom, . . . abundant in grace and beauty. With it are enduring riches and its wealth has no end, no pleasantness is stronger than it and no delight more mighty; it is sweeter than honey and the juice of the honeycomb." Anyone "who supposes that the vanities of the philosophers are identical with the *account of creation* and *the account of the chariot* is without doubt a heretic and unbeliever."[240]

The list of crimes of the *Guide for the Perplexed* goes on: "Who knows how many hundreds and thousands left the faith" because of the book? "It was the proximate cause for the destruction of many large and mighty Jewish communities," particularly in Spain and France.[241] "This ruin," this field "all grown over with strange thistles," cannot possibly be harmonized with Maimonides' "holy" *Mishneh Torah*, a work whose "mouth is most sweet and which is altogether lovely"—although R. Jacob adds that the *Mishneh Torah* too is open "to objection" on the issue of the eternity of the world, "may the Lord forgive" Maimonides.[242]

His solution is that whereas the *Mishneh Torah* is an authentic work of Maimonides', there is "undoubtedly a duty" to protect Maimonides' reputation and not hold him responsible for "the empty earthenware jars of the *Guide for the Perplexed*." The *Guide* must be the "handiwork of another philosopher," who attached Maimonides' name to it out of a desire "to hang himself on a great tree" and thereby "strangle himself."[243]

[239]Emden, *Mitpaḥat Sefarim* 61–62.

[240]Emden, *Mitpaḥat Sefarim* 56.

[241]Emden, *Mitpaḥat Sefarim* 62. Emden also blames the destruction of the Spanish Jewish community on the *Guide* in his *Iggeret Purim* and there quotes Joseph Jabez as a source. Quoted by Schacter, "Rabbi Jacob Emden's *'Iggeret Purim*" 445.

[242]Emden, *Mitpaḥat Sefarim* 64–65.

[243]Emden, *Mitpaḥat Sefarim* 64, 70. Emden comes to the same conclusion in: (1) *Migdal ᶜOz: Bet Middot* 121b, column 1, just a few pages after he recognized that Maimonides was indeed the author of the *Guide*; the subsection denying that Maimonides was the author must accordingly have been added to the book after Emden wrote the earlier passage. (2) A gloss to his Commentary on Mishna *Abot* 3:15, which refers to *Migdal ᶜOz: Bet Middot* 121b, column 1

The twentieth century offers yet one more exchange between a critic and a defender of the *Guide*. The slant is somewhat different from what we have seen thus far, and neither party engages in verbal pyrotechnics; but the improvement in tone is not paralleled by an improvement in intellectual level. The protagonists barely go beyond hazy generalities.

Wolf Jawitz was the author of a comprehensive, multivolume history of the Jewish people from ancient times to the nineteenth century, his object being to counterbalance and correct Heinrich Graetz's earlier, path-breaking history by presenting men and events in a more traditional light. Like Graetz, he had no inhibitions about historians' making value judgments. Graetz had lionized the rationalist and enlightened Maimonides, whom he called the "Jewish Aristotle."[244] Jawitz's admiration for Maimonides knows no bounds as far as the rabbinic works are concerned, but he cannot contain his astonishment that a man of Maimonides' stature could have written a book as un-Jewish in character as the *Guide for the Perplexed*.

Jawitz descries a yawning gulf between "Greek philosophy" and the "Torah of Israel." Greek philosophy, as he understands it, is concerned only with knowledge and regards "the virtues, whose choicest fruit is obligation, commandment, behavior, and service, . . . as practically nothing, with the exception of the small amount necessary" for preparing oneself to acquire knowledge. The "perfect Torah of the Lord," as expounded at all times by "our prophets and rabbis through their holy spirit . . . is the complete opposite," for the Torah and its expounders teach that virtue and behavior are primary, and knowledge, secondary. Jawitz acknowledges that Maimonides' aim in the *Guide for the Perplexed* was "pure"; he wanted "to prove to his contemporaries, many of whom were beginning to have doubts about the Torah and religious commandments, that God's Torah is true and eternal." It is nonetheless incredible that Maimonides' "sharp pure eye" should have failed to recognize the chasm between the two worldviews and that he represented the "philosophizer" as pious and pure, the one whom God desires, while dismissing the perfect, innocent man who fails to philosophize as "wicked" and "impure," abandoned by God, banished from His presence, and an object of divine anger.[245]

When the volume of Jawitz's *History of Israel* expressing these sentiments was published posthumously in 1935, it contained a rebuttal by R. Abraham Isaac Kook, the Ashkenazi Chief Rabbi of Palestine.

(the Commentary itself was written before *Migdal ᶜOz* and in the original version recognizes Maimonides as the author; see n. 235 above). (3) *Iggeret Purim*, quoted by Schacter, "Rabbi Jacob Emden's *'Iggeret Purim*" 445.

[244]H. Graetz, *Geschichte der Juden*, 3rd ed., 6 (Leipzig 1894) 263–65. English version: H. Graetz, *History of the Jews* 3 (Philadelphia 1894) 448–49.

[245]W. Jawitz, *Toledot Yisrael* 12 (Tel Aviv 1935) 32–34.

Rabbi Kook submits that the storm swirling around the *Guide for the Perplexed* for centuries after it was published had abated in recent generations. He envisages a corpus of "sacred books" which accompanies the Torah and, he writes, now that the controversy over the *Guide* was resolved, the *Guide* had been welcomed into the sacred canon. "Our duty today is therefore not merely to give Maimonides' words the benefit of the doubt but also to plumb their profundity and examine [all of] Maimonides' qualities [*middot*] exhaustively, [treating them] as qualities of the Torah" itself.[246]

That is not to say that everyone must accept Maimonides' opinions. The Jewish religion, as conceived by Rabbi Kook, has a wide embrace and recognizes alternative paths through which Jews can "attach their hearts to holiness, purity, faith, [divine] service, the Torah, and the commandments." Maimonides' approach suited "the spirit of his holiness, the power of his faith, and the intensity of his holy, true service" and it met the needs of persons of a similar temperament. Alternative approaches of additional "great men of Israel"—among whom Kook undoubtedly included the cabalists[247]—serve the needs of other temperaments. All approaches are legitimate as long as they are guaranteed by authoritative personages; whether or not they are compatible with one another is presumably immaterial. God forbid, then, that the labels "Grecism and foreignness" should be affixed to Maimonides' views![248]

Jawitz, the Chief Rabbi goes on, was misinformed when he asserted that Greek philosophy as a whole regards human virtue and behavior as worthless: It is false that "all of Greek philosophy belittles the content of behavior." And while "we may find among the philosophers" some who took such a position, the "great" Maimonides did not follow the philosophers blindly. He "put their words to the test, purified them," and accepted "the good content," that is to say, what "agrees with the Torah, with righteousness, and with justice."[249] He winnowed out the philosophic wheat, the portion in agreement with the Torah, and discarded the philosophic chaff.

The *Guide for the Perplexed*, we further read, has the enormous merit of "raising up the foundation of the holiness of faith in all its purity" by driving "the dreadful idiocy of divine corporeality out of the territory of Israel." If Maimonides had not performed the "holy service" of "rescuing the soul of the [Jewish] faith from the depths of that error," from divine corporeality, God alone knows "how far unbelief and negativity would have consumed us." Maimonides, "in his wisdom and great holiness," has another merit: He laid down three principles that separate the Torah "absolutely" from Greek wisdom and erect "an eternal wall between the holy and the profane." The three principles are: "individual providence over the

[246]Jawitz, *Toledot Yisrael* 12.211.

[247]See Jawitz, *Toledot Yisrael* 12.218.

[248]Jawitz, *Toledot Yisrael* 12.211–12.

[249]Jawitz, *Toledot Yisrael* 12.216.

human species, extending to all individuals and their actions"; the creation of the world, which uproots "the idolatrous Greek *Anschauung* concerning existence" and "restores to us the holy ways of the Torah," that is, "the original Judaic *Anschauung* concerning all existence"; and the recognition that prophetic knowledge comes from "God's word through the holy spirit" and has a "source more exalted than anything man's spirit can grasp through his human intellect."[250]

Maimonides would have been neither surprised nor annoyed at the *Guide*'s being treated as a constituent of a Jewish sacred canon; he regarded the book as no less essential for an enlightened Jewish religion than his code of Jewish law. Whether he would have read the misguided defenses of the *Guide* drawn up by Chief Rabbi Kook and earlier authors with amusement, resignation, or horror can only be guessed.

Describing the language of the *Guide for the Perplexed* as Judeo-Arabic means that it is basically Arabic, that it is shot through with Hebrew terms and Hebrew and Aramaic quotations from Scripture and rabbinic literature, and that the Arabic is written in Hebrew, not Arabic characters. A reader of Arabic unfamiliar with Hebrew writing who wished to gain access to the *Guide* could learn the letters with a little effort and once he did, would feel at home in the Arabic substratum; Maimonides wrote a good quality medieval Arabic.[251] But the hundreds of terms and quotations in Hebrew and Aramaic would remain a formidable obstacle. An analogy would be a book composed in English but written in Cyrillic script. The script could be mastered without too much time and effort, although the English words would look strange in Slavic dress. If, however, the author peppered his book with Russian terms and quotations from the Russian classics in the original language, an English reader would be hard put to follow what was set before him.

When Maimonides sent a segment of the *Guide* to Joseph ben Judah, he made a point of asking him not to lose it and to be chary about letting others see it; for there are many "wicked Jews" and he did not wish to come to "harm at the hands of the gentiles."[252] He says nothing about a transcription into Arabic characters. But if he was concerned about having the version in Hebrew characters fall into the possession of unfriendly Jews who might inform on him to Muslims, he would hardly have wanted such a transcription to be made.

Transcriptions were made nevertheless, and two manuscripts of the *Guide* in Arabic characters have been identified. The first, which has been tentatively dated to the thirteenth century and exists only in fragmentary form, has the Hebrew citations from the Bible in Arabic translation and hence was probably done, or goes

[250]Jawitz, *Toledot Yisrael* 12.212–15. Kook himself rejected Maimonides' manner of explaining the reasons for the divine commandments. See Y. Cherlow, "Maimonides' View on the Reasons for the Sacrifices as Reflected in the Teaching of Rav Kook," *Daat* 39 (1997) 130–31.

[251]I. Friedlaender, "Die arabische Sprache des Maimonides," *Moses ben Maimon*, ed. W. Bacher et al., 1 (Leipzig 1908) 427–28.

[252]Moses ben Maimon, *Epistulae*, ed. D. Baneth (Jerusalem 1946) 68.

back to a text that was done, by a Jewish scribe.[253] The second was copied in the fifteenth century by a Yemeni Muslim who was engaged in the book trade, and in it the Hebrew citations and words are transliterated into Arabic characters and not translated.[254] Transliterating Hebrew into Arabic characters requires a knowledge of the Hebrew language and cannot be done mechanically.[255] The Yemeni Muslim writer therefore also probably copied from a text that goes back to a Jewish scribe.

A few non-Jewish Arabic readers of the *Guide* are known. The first was ᶜAbd al-Laṭīf, a Muslim visitor to Egypt who met Maimonides there and took a dislike to him. ᶜAbd al-Laṭīf remarks sourly that Maimonides "produced a book for the Jews which he called *The Book of the Guide* and he pronounced a curse on anyone who would write it in non-Hebrew characters. I, however, examined it [*waqaftu ᶜalayhi*] and found it to be an evil book, destructive of the principles of religious laws and beliefs, which the author thought he was enhancing."[256] A second Muslim who read at least a small part was Muḥammad al-Tabrizi, a thirteenth-century Persian writer. Tabrizi composed an Arabic commentary on the twenty-five philosophic propositions used by Maimonides to prove the existence of God; he knows that the exact title of the book from which the propositions come is *The Guide for the Perplexed*, but what he says about the *Guide* suggests that he had not seen it in its entirety.[257] There is a report concerning a third Muslim, an eccentric Sufi who lived in the thirteenth century, stating that "Jews studied" the *Guide* "with him" (*yashtaghil ᶜalayhi*);[258] the report seems to say that the Muslim Sufi in fact taught the book to Jewish students, but that is hard to imagine. Finally a Coptic priest who wrote in Arabic quotes passages from Part Three.[259] The information taken together falls well short of a picture of Muslim thinkers' coming to grips with the issues at the heart of the *Guide*.

[253] S. Munk, "Notice sur Joseph ben-Iehouda," *Journal asiatique* (1842) 27.

[254] F. Rosenthal, "From Arabic Books and Manuscripts V," *Journal of the American Oriental Society* 75 (1955) 14–15, 20. Tzvi Langermann was kind enough to provide me with a copy of the first couple of pages and he informed me that Hebrew words and quotations are transliterated, and not translated, throughout the manuscript.

[255] Hebrew words in a Judeo-Arabic text written in Hebrew characters use the same sign for the consonants *shin* and *sin*. In transliterating, only someone with a knowledge of Hebrew will know where to use an Arabic *shin*, and where an Arabic *sin*.

[256] ᶜAbd al-Laṭīf, quoted by Ibn Abī Uṣaibiᶜa, *ᶜUyūn al-Anbā* (Beirut 1965) 687.

[257] A. M. Tabrīzī, *Commentary on the Twenty Five Premises from the Guide of the Perplexed* (Arabic and Persian), ed. M. Mohaghegh (Tehran 1981) 3. Tabrīzī's account of Maimonides' position on the human soul is badly flawed.

[258] I. Goldziher, "Ibn Hūd, the Mohammedan Mystic, and the Jews of Damascus," *Jewish Quarterly Review* 6 (1894) 220. Goldziher translates the pertinent sentence from a medieval Muslim source as follows: "Under his [Ibn Hūd's] guidance the Jews were wont to occupy themselves with the study of the *Kitāb al-dalālat*." Ibn Hūd was an unconventional Muslim—see J. Kraemer, "The Andalusian Mystic Ibn Hūd," *Israel Oriental Studies* 12 (1992) 69–73—but it is hard to imagine that he taught the *Guide* to a circle of Jews.

[259] Munk, "Notice sur Joseph ben-Iehouda," 27.

The most influential translations of the *Guide* were those into Hebrew, for they made it accessible to Jews who did not read Arabic and permitted its dissemination throughout the Jewish world. The early thirteenth century saw two Hebrew translations, the first being that of Samuel Ibn Tibbon, a man whose name has already come up a number of times. Ibn Tibbon went to lengths to guarantee the correctness of his translation: He corresponded with Maimonides about errors that copyists may have introduced into the Arabic text of the *Guide* which reached him in southern France; he asked Maimonides for direction in interpreting passages with which he had difficulty; in doing his translation, he kept as close as he could to the word order of the original Arabic in order to convey exactly what Maimonides had said; and after completing the translation, he went back and made improvements. The final product is a faithful reflection of the original, although it has the drawback of doing violence to Hebrew syntax. A few years after Ibn Tibbon, Judah al-Ḥarizi, a Spanish Jew who was both a poet and a translator, produced a stylistically more congenial, but less precise and sometimes simply incorrect Hebrew translation. Ibn Tibbon's translation overshadowed Ḥarizi's version as well as the original Arabic and became for centuries the primary medium in which the *Guide* was known. Although Ibn Tibbon was not himself a thinker of any depth, his translation of the *Guide* became the most widely read medieval Jewish philosophic text in the Middle Ages, and the choices he made in translating Arabic philosophic terms played the pivotal role in standardizing Hebrew philosophic terminology.

The *Guide for the Perplexed* entered the world of medieval Christian thought in several guises. The Latin version in most common use in the Middle Ages was made around 1240 from al-Ḥarizi's Hebrew translation. Not only is it a translation of a translation, and not only does it derive from the less reliable of the two medieval Hebrew translations; it is incomplete. The translator merely summarizes chapters that are devoted to the Hebrew language and biblical exegesis and that he thought would not interest, or be understood by, the readership he envisaged; he may not have fully understood them himself.[260] There exists a separate Latin translation of the twenty-five philosophic propositions used by Maimonides to demonstrate the existence of God together with the first chapter of Part Two of the *Guide*, which contains Maimonides' four demonstrations. The preserved manuscripts name "Rabbi Moses the Hebrew philosopher" as the author but do not identify the *Guide for the Perplexed* as their source.[261] Then there exists a translation and reworking of about twenty chapters of Part Three of the *Guide* which can be dated to 1223–1224 and hence more than a decade before the fuller

[260]W. Kluxen, "Literargeschichtliches zum lateinischen Moses Maimonides," *Recherches de Théologie ancienne et médiévale* 21 (1954) 34–35.

[261]Kluxen, "Literargeschichtliches zum lateinischen Moses Maimonides" 36–38. The reasons Kluxen gives for supposing that the translation was made from Ibn Tibbon's Hebrew version do not hold water, and the translation may well have been made from the original Arabic. It is accordingly tempting to speculate about a possible connection with the text of the twenty-five propositions which Tabrizi used.

translation done from al-Ḥarizi's Hebrew.[262] Finally, evidence from an author who lived in the last third of the thirteenth century suggests that yet another translation of the *Guide* into Latin circulated in Christian circles.[263]

Scholars have identified a dozen medieval Christian philosophers and theologians who cite, or borrow from, the *Guide for the Perplexed*,[264] and of these, Thomas Aquinas, the central figure in medieval Christian philosophy and theology, has attracted the most attention. Aquinas, who read both the Islamic and Jewish philosophers with interest—naturally, in Latin translation—borrows substantially from the *Guide* in his demonstrations of the existence of God and his analysis of the issue of the creation of the world; and in working out his positions on such issues as divine attributes, prophecy, and providence, he constantly wrestles with what the Latin translations told him regarding Maimonides' treatment of those subjects. The notion of a confrontation across the decades between the leading medieval Jewish, and leading medieval Christian philosopher has intrigued scholars, and a small library of articles and books has sprouted up which set the positions taken by the two on a range of issues side by side.

The *Guide* was retranslated into Latin in the seventeenth century and has been translated, in most instances more than once, into Spanish, Italian, French, German, Hungarian, English, Yiddish, and modern Hebrew. Besides the other feathers in its cap, it is the medieval Jewish work with the largest number of translations to its name.[265]

[262]Kluxen, "Literargeschichtliches zum lateinischen Moses Maimonides" 41.

[263]Giles of Rome, *Errores philosophorum*, ed. and trans. J. Koch and J. Riedl (Milwaukee 1944) xlvii–xlviii.

[264]J. Riedl, "Maimonides and Scholasticism," *The New Scholasticism*" 10 (1936) 22–23; W. Kluxen, "Die Geschichte des Maimonides im lateinischen Abendland," *Miscellanea Mediaevalia* 4 (1966) 161–62. There were scholastics who did not have a clear picture of what Maimonides actually wrote in the *Guide*; see S. Feldman, "Did the Scholastics Have an Accurate Knowledge of Maimonides?" *Studies in Medieval Culture* 3 (1971) 145–50.

[265]J. Dienstag, "Maimonides' *Guide for the Perplexed*: A Bibliography of Editions and Translations," *Orient and Occident* (Scheiber memorial volume) (Budapest 1988) 95–128, lists translations that have appeared in print. Regarding a fifteenth-century Spanish translation, see Maimonides, *Guide for the Perplexed: A 15th Century Spanish Translation*, ed. M. Lazar (Culver City, Cal. 1989). Regarding a sixteenth-century Italian translation, see D. Kaufmann, "Maimonides's *Guide* in World Literature" (translated from the German), *Studies in Jewish Thought*, ed. A. Jospe (Detroit 1981) 240–41.

8

MEDICAL WORKS

> The art of medicine [although it treats only the body] plays a very large role in [acquiring] both the [ethical] virtues and knowledge of God, and hence in attaining true eudaemonia. Learning and studying medicine is an important form of divine worship. . . . For through medicine we calibrate our bodily actions so that they become genuinely human actions, actions [that render the body a tool] for [the acquisition of] the virtues and scientific truths. (Maimonides, *Shemona Peraqim*, Chapter 5)

> I guarantee that all who obey the rules [of diet and hygiene] which I have laid down will stay free of disease . . . until they die at an advanced age without ever needing a physician, while their bodies will be healthy and remain so throughout their lives. (Maimonides, *Mishneh Torah*: *H. De*^{c}*ot* 4.20)

Maimonides' Medical Writings. Maimonides knew of persons who deprecated reliance on the medical art for the reason that it implies lack of trust in God. The subject comes up in connection with a paragraph that appears in some but not all versions of the Mishna Corpus and that Maimonides did not judge to be a genuine part of the Mishna.[1] He nevertheless discusses it in his Commentary on the Mishna because of the "benefits" it contains.

[1] It appears today in all the standard printed texts of the Mishna.

The part of the paragraph which is of primary interest to Maimonides and hence to us relates that the biblical King Hezekiah removed a work entitled *The Book of Medicines* from circulation, and the religious authorities of the time gave their approval. The mishnaic or pseudo-mishnaic paragraph fails to reveal either what *The Book of Medicines* was or the objections raised against it. Maimonides, in his Commentary, takes note of an interpretation that he had encountered, according to which the book was a collection of medical advice and was removed from circulation by Hezekiah because he found people relying on it to cure disease rather than trusting in God. That interpretation, Maimonides writes, is both ridiculous on its face and reprehensible inasmuch as it ascribes extreme ignorance to the king and to the authorities around him who approved of the king's action. If the "nonsensical and foolish reasoning" of the unnamed interpreters were carried to its logical conclusion, anyone who is hungry and eats is equally blameworthy for failing to trust God to assuage his hunger without food. The truth, of course, is that we eat when we are hungry and thank God for providing us with what we eat. By the same token we should cure disease and thank God for providing us with the means to do so.[2]

In Maimonides' highly intellectualized picture of human nature, the health of the body is nonetheless not a goal. The ideal human life took the shape of a pyramid for him, with human intellectual perfection constituting the apex, perfection of the soul standing at a second level, and a healthy body forming the base. A healthy body is accordingly desirable not for itself but only as the platform upon which the soul can strive toward its proper perfection. Nor is a human soul possessed of ethical virtue an end in itself; such a soul is desirable because it will serve, and not distract, its highest faculty, the intellect. Perfection of the intellect is what God and nature intend as the goal of human life. "Man must direct his heart and every one of his actions *solely* toward knowing God."[3]

Maimonides makes the same point specifically in connection with the practice of medicine. He lauds medicine inasmuch as through it "we calibrate our bodily actions" so that they mold the body into a tool for the acquisition of "the virtues and scientific truths." It accordingly "plays a very large role in [acquiring] both the [ethical] virtues and knowledge of God, and hence in attaining true eudaemonia,"[4]

[2]Maimonides, Commentary on Mishna, *Pesaḥim* 4:10. Maimonides' explanation of King Hezekiah's action is that the *Book of Medicines* was either a theoretical study of forbidden magical charms and was withdrawn from circulation because people attempted actually to use the charms in order to cure disease; or that the book dealt with noxious potions and their antidotes and was withdrawn from circulation because some were using it to poison their enemies rather than to cure those who had been poisoned.

[3]Maimonides, *Mishneh Torah*: *H. De ᶜot* 3. 2–3; 4.1.

[4]Maimonides, *Shemona Peraqim* (=*Mishna ᶜim Perush R. Moshe ben Maimon*, Arabic original and Hebrew translation, ed. and trans. J. Kafah [Jerusalem 1963–1968], introduction to *Abot*), chapter 5. English translation: Moses Maimonides, *Eight Chapters*, ed. and trans. J. Gorfinkle (New York 1912).

genuine human well-being. Medicine creates a strong and healthy body and thereby provides man with an indispensable tool for the acquisition of ethical virtue and scientific knowledge; the culmination is knowledge of God and the other supernal beings, and with it a person attains eudaemonia.[5]

The statements just quoted come from Maimonides' Commentary on the Mishna and *Mishneh Torah.* His primary philosophic work, the *Guide for the Perplexed*, evidences an unmistakable drift in the direction of asceticism over against the rabbinic works, and at one spot in the *Guide* he asserts, perhaps with conscious hyperbole, that no "benefit" accrues to the human soul from a well-constituted and constructed body.[6] Yet he could scarcely ignore the intractable circumstance that nobody devotes himself to intellectual pursuits "as long as he is in physical pain, unduly hungry or thirsty, or suffering from severe hot or cold." Even in the *Guide* Maimonides therefore continues to regard a minimum level of physical well-being as a precondition for intellectual perfection.[7] Intellectual perfection, he never tires of exhorting readers of the *Guide*, is the goal toward which they must strive.

The ideal presented in all these contexts is not a sound mind in a sound body but rather a sound mind, preceded by whatever soundness of body may be necessary for achieving soundness of mind. Medicine's value lies in helping to create the tool for pursuing the higher end.

There is still another way in which Maimonides expresses the notion that the human body and material goods in general have a subordinate function within the ideal life. He prescribes, once again in a rabbinic context, the manner in which men should divide their time and he takes an artisan as his example. He envisages the artisan's working at his craft three hours a day in order to support himself and then spending nine hours, the lion's share, in the study of the Law and philosophy.[8]

If the human body is only a means to a higher end, and if Maimonides contemplated such an allocation of time from an ordinary artisan, we might expect that he conformed to no less a standard himself. We might expect that he spent no more time than was necessary in earning enough to satisfy his minimal bodily needs and the needs of his family and that he set aside the remaining hours for the care of his intellect, for the study of the Law and philosophy. Up until a certain age he did essentially that. Then he discovered that ideals are one thing and the pressures of life, another.

When writing to his student Joseph ben Judah around 1190, he describes the routine into which his life had fallen. He was practicing medicine and spent a good part of each day with his aristocratic patients in Cairo. Upon returning home to Fustat, he would devote his remaining daytime hours as well as the evening to

[5]See above, pp. 164, 233.

[6]*Guide for the Perplexed* 3.54 (second kind of perfection). In the *Guide,* the ethical virtues of *Mishneh Torah*: *H. De^cot* serve only other persons and not him who possesses them.

[7]*Guide for the Perplexed* 3.27.

[8]*Mishneh Torah*: *H. Talmud Torah* 1.12.

studying "what was pertinent [to his cases] in the medical literature. For you know how long and difficult the medical art is for one who is faithful and precise and wishes to say nothing without knowing a proof of what he says and without knowing where the proof is stated." Medical matters were so demanding that from the beginning to the end of the week he could not find an hour for "the Law" apart from what he read on the Sabbath. "As for the other sciences," he did not have time to give them a thought.[9] In a different, often quoted passage, which was written later in the 1190s, Maimonides relates that his medical obligations in Cairo occupied him until the afternoon. "When I arrive [home], overcome by hunger, I find my courtyard full of Jews and non-Jews of every class." I ask them to "wait until I eat a light meal, [my sole meal] for the entire day.[10] . . . They are not gone before nightfall and sometimes, I swear, until two or more hours after dark. I give them instructions lying prostrate from fatigue and when night falls, I am so weak that I can no longer talk."[11] He was allotting not three, but many more exhausting hours of the day to his professional activities. Those activities were focused on the welfare of human bodies, which he had insisted play only an instrumental role in the good life.

The event that impelled Maimonides into the full-time practice of medicine was undoubtedly the death by drowning of his younger brother in approximately 1177. The tragedy left Maimonides with debts and the responsibility for the family's livelihood, and that, as he wrote to an old acquaintance, included the burden of the widow and her young daughter. We saw in an earlier chapter that rabbinic law, in his reading, unambiguously prohibits receiving payment in exchange for one's rabbinic knowledge and he fulminates against those who ignore the prohibition. Accepting a regular salary for the performance of his rabbinic judicial duties was consequently out of the question. There was little market for his scientific and philosophic expertise. He may have invested money in commercial ventures conducted by others and may also have had an income from the teaching of medicine.[12] But the obvious way out of his financial straits was the practice of medicine, a subject that he had studied in his youth, before arriving in Egypt. The

[9]Moses ben Maimon, *Epistulae*, ed. D. Baneth (Jerusalem 1946) 69–70. English translation of the letter: R. Weiss and C. Butterworth, *Ethical Writings of Maimonides* (New York 1975) 115–23.

[10]In his treatise *On Asthma*, Maimonides states that persons of strong constitution, but not the elderly and those recovering from an illness, may restrict themselves to a single full meal a day without damaging their health, although he advises them to eat something in addition before going to sleep and indicates that such had been his own custom. See *On Asthma*, ed. and trans. G. Bos (Provo 2002), chapter 6, §§1, 4. Medieval Hebrew translation of the Arabic text: Moshe ben Maimon, *On Hemorrhoids*, *On the Increase of Physical Vigour*, *On Asthma* (in Hebrew), ed. S. Muntner (Jerusalem 1965).

[11]A. Marx, "Texts by and about Maimonides," *Jewish Quarterly Review* 25 (1935) 376–77. Translation in B. Lewis, *Islam* (New York 1974) 2.192.

[12]See above, pp. 34, 36.

beginnings of his professional career are hidden from view. Since he informs us, however, that he worked day and night on his *Mishneh Torah* during the decade leading up to 1177 or 1178, he could hardly have conducted a medical practice during those years; and by the early 1190s, he had become a well-known physician with a clientele in the highest echelons. He must have developed his practice between the two dates.

Not only did he now fail to allocate the hours of the day between his livelihood and his intellectual pursuits in the manner that he advocated, and not only had his attention been usurped by the treatment of human bodies, which are only a means to a much higher end; the sole substantial writings known to have come out of the years from 1191 to the end of his life are medical works. Preparing books on medicine for both laymen and physicians swallowed up whatever productive time remained after he had treated his patients and pored over the medical literature pertinent to their cases. His literary energy was henceforth directed toward instructing readers not in the care of their intellects, nor even in the care of their souls, but in the care of the instrument that soul and intellect must employ—the human body. The rabbinic books that he planned and, as far as is known, never wrote[13] were sacrificed in favor of his writings on the lesser subject.

There is good evidence that ten preserved medical texts carrying Maimonides' name in the manuscripts are authentic compositions of his. Two additional medical texts attributed to him in the manuscripts are usually recognized as genuine as well, but the authenticity of one of the two is uncertain and that of the other, highly doubtful.[14]

Six of the apparently genuine works link themselves together through cross-references to one another,[15] and one of the six is the *Medical Aphorisms*, an incontrovertibly authentic book of Maimonides'. There are instances where writers pretending to be Maimonides incorporated cross-references to authentic works of his into their forgeries for the purpose of adding verisimilitude. But those deliberate forgeries were ideological in character. The writers wrapped themselves

[13]See above, pp. 295–99.

[14]M. Steinschneider, *Die arabische Literatur der Juden* (Frankfurt 1902) 213–17, lists nine items, because he treats the two treatises on sexual matters under a single heading, did not know of the existence of the glossary of drug names, and did not include the *Epistle on the Length of Life* among the medical works; see also Steinschneider, *Die hebräischen Übersetzungen des Mittlealters* (Berlin 1893) 762–74. M. Meyerhof, "The Medical Work of Maimonides" in *Essays on Maimonides*, ed. S. Baron (New York 1941) 274–87, similarly combines the two pieces on sexual matters and does not take account of the *Epistle on the Length of Life*; he accordingly lists ten items. F. Rosner, *The Medical Legacy of Moses Maimonides* (Hoboken 1998), chapter 1, also lists the ten items but rejects the authenticity of the second piece on sexual matters. In chapters 2–4, he summarizes the contents of three of the ten.

[15]They are the *Compendia of Galen's Books*, Commentary on *The Aphorisms of Hippocrates*, *Medical Aphorisms*, *On Asthma*, *Regimen of Health*, and *On the Causes of Symptoms*.

in the cloak of the great man in order to further the acceptance of beliefs that they felt were sufficiently important to justify the dishonesty. It is harder to imagine writers on medical subjects inventing cross-references to Maimonides' medical works in order to attach his name falsely to their books and thereby lose the opportunity for developing their own professional credentials. Maimonides' authorship of the six items that link themselves together may therefore be accepted as more or less certain.

The authenticity of a seventh composition, a treatise on sexual performance which carries Maimonides' name, is likwise reasonably certain. Fragments of the original draft have been found which, in the judgment of a scholar familiar with Maimonides' handwriting, are in his hand,[16] and in two preserved manuscripts, the treatise appears in the company of other medical works of Maimonides.[17]

Additional information is supplied by Ibn Abī Uṣaybiᶜa, who came to Egypt after Maimonides' death, studied and worked there as a physician, and was acquainted with Maimonides' son. Ibn Abī Uṣaybiᶜa's biographical dictionary lists some of Maimonides' medical writings and in doing so vouches for three more of the works carrying his name in the manuscripts.[18] There is thus very strong evidence for the authenticity of seven medical works attributed to Maimonides and reasonable evidence for the authenticity of three more.

An eleventh item, a second composition on sexual matters, carries Maimonides' name in the preserved Arabic manuscript, and most, although not all, recent scholars have accepted the attribution. It is dedicated to a personage who belonged to the house of Saladin and who lived at the time when Maimonides was acquiring his reputation at court as a physician.[19] But it neither cites anything written by Maimonides nor is mentioned in anything that he wrote. Since copyists had a penchant for attaching Maimonides' name to books that are not genuinely his, we must allow the possibility that here his name was affixed erroneously.[20] The twelfth item attributed to Maimonides is known as the *Epistle on the Length of*

[16] S. Stern, in *Maimonidis commentarius in Mischnam* (Copenhagen 1956–1966) 3.18. The draft is in Arabic written in Hebrew characters. Stern draws the plausible inference that Maimonides wrote in Hebrew characters and then had a scribe transcribe the text into Arabic characters for the Moslem personage who commissioned it.

[17] Stern, *Maimonidis commentarius in Mischnam* 3.17.

[18] Ibn Abī Uṣaibiᶜa, *ᶜUyūn al-Anbā'* (Beirut 1965) 583, attributes five medical works to Maimonides: the *Compendia of Galen's Books* and *Regimen of Health*, both of which are authenticated on other grounds, to which he adds: the *Explanation of the Names of Drugs*, the treatise *On Hemorrhoids*, and *Poisons and Their Antidotes.*

[19] H. Kroner, *Ein Beitrag zur Geschichte der Medizin* (Oberdorf 1906) 8, 73, reports that Tifashī, a Muslim writer on sexual matters—whose work is not available to me—both cites Maimonides as one of his sources and draws material from the present treatise.

[20] S. Muntner, *Sexual Life* (*ᶜAl ha-Ḥayyim ha-Miniyyim*) (Jerusalem 1965) 19–20, summarized in Maimonides, *Treatises on Poisons, Hemorrhoids, Cohabitation*, trans. F. Rosner (Haifa 1984) 158, submits arguments, which are not wholly convincing, against the treatise's authenticity.

Life. As will appear, it contains features rendering the attribution extremely doubtful.

Besides the foregoing, Maimonides devotes a chapter of his code of rabbinic law, the *Mishneh Torah*, to diet and hygiene. There he offers advice in the spirit of Galenic medicine which is similar to the advice he gives in his formal medical works.[21]

All ten of the well-attested medical works, as well as the two questionable ones, were originally written in Arabic, and most are still preserved in that language. Those that can be dated belong to the later years of Maimonides' life, and death intervened before he could put the finishing touches to the most comprehensive, the *Medical Aphorisms*. Five of the compositions were written in response to requests by men of standing in the Muslim community for help with their personal medical problems, a sixth describes Maimonides' treatment of another prominent Muslim, and a seventh was commissioned by a Muslim patron for the public welfare. The remaining compositions, with the exception of the questionable *Epistle on the Length of Life*, were designed as textbooks and reference works for the use of students of medicine and also, Maimonides says, for his own use. Most were translated into Hebrew one or more times in the Middle Ages,[22] and at least half were translated into Latin, either from the original Arabic or from the Hebrew.[23] Over the last few decades, all of them have been translated into English, at least in part,[24] but the translations are not always satisfactory.[25]

[21] *Mishneh Torah*: *H. De*^{c}*ot* 4.

[22] All except the *Compendia of Galen's Books*, the *Explanation of the Names of Drugs*, the second treatise on sexual matters, and the *Epistle on the Length of Life*. See M. Beit Arié, "*Targumim bilti Yedu*^{c}*im*," *Kiryat Sefer* 38 (1962–1963) 567–74, for newly discovered Hebrew translations of four of the works.

[23] See Steinschneider, *Die arabische Literatur der Juden* (n. 14 above) 213–17.

[24] Information on medieval and modern translations of the medical works is given by J. Dienstag, "Translators and Editors of Maimonides' Medical Works," *Memorial Volume in Honor of Prof. S. Muntner*, ed. J. Leibowitz (Jerusalem 1983) 95–135.

[25] Examples: (1) The first sentence of chapter 1, §72, of Maimonides' *Medical Aphorisms* was translated into English (see reference in the next note) as follows: "The force in semen which can be found in material within blood is capable of making bones. It is material capable of making nerves and similar to other materials which make flat appearing organs. This is called the *procreating force*." The correct translation is: The power in semen whereby there come into existence from the blood [of the female] a matter that is suitable for the generation of bone, a matter suitable for the generation of nerves, and similarly a matter for each of the other homeomerous parts of the body [literally: the remaining matters of the homeomerous organs], is called the generative power. *Homeomerous* is a Greek philosophic and scientific term meaning: having, or consisting of, similar parts. (2) The beginning of chapter 3 of the second treatise on sexual matters reads in the translation of M. Gorlin, *Maimonides "On Sexual Intercourse"* (Brooklyn 1961): "It is known that this act is not only instinctive, meaning that erection would be according to the nature of activity represented by nutrition or growth, so that the processes of the Soul would have to be discounted. Rather it helps greatly in this respect. . . ." The correct translation is: It is known that this function is not solely a natural function [in other words, a

The entire body of Maimonides' medical books contains just a single passage—found in a section where he ventures beyond medicine into the realm of theology—in which he alludes to one of his nonmedical writings.[26] His nonmedical works, by contrast, commonly refer to one another but never to the medical works. The reason for the wall separating the two corpuses is undoubtedly the circumstance that one corpus was intended largely for a Muslim readership, and the other, exclusively for Jewish readers.

In composing his medical works, Maimonides drew extensively from his predecessors and makes no claim of originality. The second-century physician Galen was his primary source. He deemed Galen to be the greatest medical scientist ever to have lived[27] and he saw the human body, its health, and its maladies, as Galen did. The first three items in the list that follows are textbooks or reference works, which could easily have grown out of Maimonides' efforts to search the medical literature for what was pertinent to his clinical practice. They consist mainly of citations from, or paraphrases of Galen.

I turn to the ten apparently authentic medical compositions and then to the two whose authorship is uncertain.

1. *Compendia of Galen's Books* (described by Maimonides as a collection of passages that he copied verbatim from Galen).[28] Ibn Abī Uṣaybiᶜa calls it "a

---

function of the natural soul, or the natural power of the soul; see Maimonides, *Shemona Peraqim*, chapter 1]; that is to say, erection is not like the functions of nutrition or growth, in which the animal soul has no part. Rather, it [erection] is also an animal function and indeed peculiar to the animal soul. (3) Maimonides' diagnosis of the condition that forms the subject of the treatise *On Asthma* is purged of its Galenic elements by S. Muntner, whose translation reads [*On Asthma*, introduction]: "This disorder starts with a common cold, especially in the rainy season, and the patient is forced to gasp for breath day and night, depending on the duration of the onset, until the phlegm is expelled, the flow completed, and the lung well cleared." The translation should read: The cause of this respiratory disorder [*rabw*] is catarrh descending from the brain, usually in the winter [or: rainy season]. The orthopnea and pain do not cease day and night as long as the attack continues—until the catarrh decreases, what has reached the lungs is matured, and the lungs are cleansed.

[26]Maimonides, *Medical Aphorisms* (*Pirqe Moshe*) ed. S. Muntner (Jerusalem 1959) (medieval Hebrew translation of *Fuṣūl Mūsā*) 25, §64; English translation, with same chapter divisions: *The Medical Aphorisms of Moses Maimonides*, trans. F. Rosner and S. Muntner, 2 volumes (New York 1970-1971). Except for the introduction and the end of chapter 25, which are not divided into paragraphs, I cite the *Medical Aphorisms* by chapter and paragraph. G. Bos was kind enough to let me consult a prepublication version of his edition of chapters 1–5 of the Arabic text together with his English translation of those chapters. For the remaining chapters, I have corrected the Hebrew with the aid of the Arabic original in Leiden MS Or. 128 (#844 in the Jong-de Goeje catalogue).

[27]*Medical Aphorisms* 25, §59.

[28]*Medical Aphorisms*, introduction, Hebrew text 12; English translation of the passage, based on the manuscripts: Y. Tz. Langermann, "Maimonides on the Synochous Fever," *Israel Oriental Studies* 13 (1993) 177. M. Steinschneider, "Die Vorrede des Maimonides zu seinem Commentar

compendium of Galen's sixteen books,"[29] with the unmistakable expectation that readers would understand which books were meant. Galen's body of writings was enormous, and medieval Arabic writers on medicine relate that in the sixth or seventh century, the medical schools of Alexandria had selected sixteen of Galen's works to serve as a curriculum embodying the nucleus of the entire system.[30] Those undoubtedly are the sixteen from which, Ibn Abī Uṣaybiᶜa tells us, Maimonides decided to make his excerpts.

A second Muslim physician, ᶜAbd al-Laṭīf, who was a contemporary of Maimonides' and once met him, is reported—by the same Ibn Abī Uṣaybiᶜa—to have characterized Maimonides' *Compendia* somewhat differently, namely, as "a book on medicine which he culled from Galen's sixteen and from five other books."[31] A third Muslim, al-Qifṭī, writes that Maimonides "composed a compendium of twenty-one of Galen's books," the twenty-one books in question consisting of "sixteen" with "the addition of five."[32] Taken together, the three accounts indicate that Maimonides' excerpts were drawn from the sixteen works of Galen forming a curriculum for the study of medicine as well as from five of Galen's other compositions.

No complete manuscript of Maimonides' *Compendia of Galen's Books* is known to have survived and only small segments of the still extant parts have been published.[33] Scholars who examined the surviving manuscripts have found that they contain compendia of three works of Galen from among the sixteen constituting the Alexandrian canon; fragments in Maimonides' own hand of compendia of two more items from the list of sixteen; compendia of four additional compositions of Galen; and a fragment of a compendium of a fifth additional composition.[34]

über die Aphorismen des Hippocrates," *Zeitschrift der Deutschen Morgenländischen Gesellschaft* 48 (1894) 222, 234.

[29]Ibn Abī Uṣaibiᶜa, *ᶜUyūn al-Anbā'* (n. 18 above) 583.

[30]Steinschneider, *Die hebraeischen Übersetzungen des Mittlealters* (Berlin 1893) 654–55; F. Sezgin, *Geschichte des arabischen Schrifttums* 3 (Leiden 1970) 142, 144–45. O. Temkin, "Geschichte des Hippokratismus im ausgehenden Altertum," *Kyklos* 4 (1932) 76–79, shows that the existence of a list of precisely sixteen Galenic works in sixth-century Alexandria is uncertain and that the medieval Arabic writers were not unanimous about the works of Galen which belonged in the list. M. Ullmann, *Die Medizin im Islam* (Leiden 1970) 65–67, 343.

[31]ᶜAbd al-Laṭīf, quoted by Ibn Abī Uṣaybiᶜa, *ᶜUyūn al-Anbā* 687.

[32]Qifṭī, *Ta'rīkh al-Ḥukamā'*, ed. J. Lippert (Leipzig 1903) 319. I have followed the emendation of the text suggested by Stern, *Maimonidis commentarius in Mischnam* (n. 16 above) 3.12.

[33]Stern, *Maimonidis commentarius in Mischnam* 3.13–17, supplemented by S. Hopkins, "A New Autograph Fragment of Maimonides's Epitomes of Galen," *Bulletin of the School of Oriental and African Studies* 57 (1994) 126–32. U. Barzel, *Moses Maimonides' The Art of Cure* (Haifa 1992) gives an English translation of one of the twenty-one sections.

[34]Stern, *Maimonidis commentarius in Mischnam* 3.12–13. Information on some of the pertinent works of Galen is found in Sezgin, *Geschichte des arabischen Schrifttums* 3.96–98,

Galen was notoriously prolix, and Maimonides undertook to compress the original texts, plainly in order to make them more usable. His *Compendia*, notwithstanding the title, were nevertheless far from compendious. Of the preserved parts that are complete or more or less so, the three drawn from the collection of sixteen Galenic works fill 284 pages in manuscript,[35] and three of those drawn from the additional five run 552 pages.[36] Six of the twenty-one parts thus extend to more than 800 pages. Qifṭī belittles the *Compendia* on the grounds that Maimonides carried "excerpting to the extreme," made only minute changes, and produced nothing of value.[37] The sentiment may have been shared, since as far as is known no one took the trouble to translate Maimonides' effort into either Hebrew or Latin.

A note consisting of a few pages has recently been identified wherein Maimonides offers his own solution to a pair of problems arising in connection with one of the Galenic books of which he made a compendium, this on the subject of "continuous"—that is, nonintermittent—fevers.[38]

2. Commentary on *The Aphorisms of Hippocrates*.[39] The *Aphorisms* itself is a poorly organized collection of more than 400 terse, miscellaneous statements on physiology, health, and medicine, attributed to the ancient Greek physician Hippocrates. A range of topics is covered: diagnosis through examination of urine, stools, vomitus, and perspiration; pain; prognosis through those and other physical signs; the significance of weather and the seasons of the year for diagnosis and prognosis; the role of age and sex in susceptibility to various diseases; fevers; the four humors; menstruation and pregnancy; growths and inflammations; indications for bloodletting through venesection; indications for administering purgatives and emetics; and more.

The quality of the statements is uneven. Some of them would have been illuminating in their day, although today they naturally are no longer so, some are platitudes, others are enigmatic, and some are grotesque. It should, for instance, have been instructive for the ancient reader to be told that blood or pus in the urine

---

119–21.

[35]Langermann, "Maimonides on the Synochous Fever" (n. 28 above) 176.

[36]See W. Ahlwardt, *Verzeichniss der arabischen Handschriften (zu Berlin)* 5 (Berlin 1893) MS 6231.

[37]Qifṭī, *Ta'rīkh al-Ḥukamā* 319.

[38]Langermann, "Maimonides on the Synochous Fever" 181–84, 192–98.

[39]Edition of the preface in Arabic, Hebrew, and German translation: Steinschneider, "Die Vorrede des Maimonides" (n. 28 above) 218–34. Medieval Hebrew translation of the whole: *Commentary on the Aphorisms of Hippocrates* (*Perush le-Firqe Abuqraṭ*), ed. S. Muntner (Jerusalem 1961), which is to be read in conjunction with M. Plessner's penetrating—and devastating—review in *Kiryat Sefer* 38 (1963) 302–10. English translation, with the same chapter and section divisions as the Hebrew: Maimonides, *Commentary on the Aphorisms of Hippocrates*, trans. F. Rosner (Haifa 1987).

is a symptom of damage to the kidneys or bladder,[40] that when foamy blood is spit up, it comes from the lungs,[41] and that convulsion following a wound is a fatal symptom (because it is a probable sign of tetanus).[42] But few readers, even in ancient times, should have needed the great Hippocrates—or whoever the author of the *Aphorisms* was—to inform them that in the case of severe diseases, predictions of death and recovery are uncertain.[43] The modern reader, for his part, will not know whether to be more puzzled or amused upon hearing the following: Bald people do not contract large varicose veins and if by chance they do, their hair grows back.[44] Women do not become ambidextrous.[45] It is a favorable sign when persons suffering from melancholy or kidney disorders contract hemorrhoids.[46] When chronic hemorrhoids are cured and not a single one is allowed to remain in place, the patient is at risk of becoming ill with dropsy or consumption.[47] Persons with jaundice will probably not suffer from flatulence.[48] If someone has a speech defect he is likely to suffer from serious diarrhea.[49] And diarrhea helps to cure eye disorders.[50]

Notwithstanding its uneven character, the *Aphorisms of Hippocrates* was enormously popular in ancient and medieval medical circles, and a number of Arabic medical writers composed commentaries on it.[51] Maimonides, although expressing reservations here and there, shares the ancient and medieval assessment. He states in an introduction that he was motivated to compose a commentary on the *Aphorisms* because he found it to be "the most useful of Hippocrates' books," a book the contents of which every physician should know by heart, one that he had seen studied by nonphysicians and even taught to schoolboys.[52] As for the procedure he would observe, he states that he would speak in his own voice in just a small number of instances. Galen had already written a commentary on the *Aphorisms*, and most of Maimonides' comments, including all that are not

[40]*Aphorisms of Hippocrates* 4:75; cf. 4:81.

[41]*Aphorisms of Hippocrates* 5:13.

[42]*Aphorisms of Hippocrates* 5:2.

[43]*Aphorisms of Hippocrates* 2:19.

[44]*Aphorisms of Hippocrates* 6:34.

[45]*Aphorisms of Hippocrates* 7:43.

[46]*Aphorisms of Hippocrates* 6:11.

[47]*Aphorisms of Hippocrates* 6:12.

[48]*Aphorisms of Hippocrates* 5:72.

[49]*Aphorisms of Hippocrates* 6:32.

[50]*Aphorisms of Hippocrates* 6:17.

[51]A list of other Arabic writers who composed commentaries on the *Aphorisms of Hippocrates* is given by M. Steinschneider, *Die arabischen Übersetzungen aus dem Griechischen* (Graz 1960) p. (305). Quotations from some of the Arabic commentaries are given by F. Rosenthal, "Life Is Short, the Art Is Long," *Bulletin of the History of Medicine* 40 (1966) 226–45.

[52]Maimonides, Commentary on *The Aphorisms of Hippocrates*, introduction, Hebrew text 5; English translation 12.

otherwise marked, would convey the kernel of Galen's more wordy interpretations.[53]

Only the very first aphorism in the book leads Maimonides to provide more than a brief paragraph. The first aphorism, which is by far the best known, reads according to the translation used by Maimonides: "Life is short, the art is long, time is limited, experience is dangerous, and judgment is difficult."[54] He approaches the two opening clauses as he might a passage in the Mishna or the Babylonian Talmud.

His analysis, which apparently is to a large degree original,[55] goes as follows: If Hippocrates' meaning were that human life is short considering the demands of the medical art, and mastery of the medical art is long considering the extent of human life, then the second clause repeats what the first clause said and is redundant. The redundancy vanishes, however, when the two clauses are construed as affirming different things, namely, that human life is short considering what *any* art requires, whereas medicine is not merely long, but longer than all other arts. The intent will then be that human life is *a fortiori* short when measured against the demands of medicine. To further make the point, Maimonides lists the subjects that a physician must master. They include the physiology, nature, health, and disease of the human organism and each of its parts; the methodology of medical diagnosis; preventative medicine; treatment of disease; nutrition; the impact of climate on health; the utilization of medical implements; what physicians through the centuries have discovered experimentally about the qualities of various medicaments; and other matters. Nor is it enough merely to know those subjects from books. Once a student of medicine has assimilated what the books teach, he should learn how to apply his knowledge in practice. No wonder that medicine is deemed to be longer than any other art![56] Maimonides goes on to explicate the aphorism's remaining clauses in the same spirit.[57]

He speaks in his own voice in comments on about twenty of the 400 aphorisms. When he does, it is usually to reject an aphorism, to reject Galen's interpretation of an aphorism, or to do both, that is, to complain that Galen had performed acrobatics to save Hippocrates' honor instead of simply conceding that the latter had

[53]Commentary on *The Aphorisms of Hippocrates*, introduction, Hebrew text 5; English translation 12.

[54]*Aphorisms of Hippocrates* 1.1. The aphorism has an echo in Mishna, *Abot* 2.16: "The day is short, the work is great, the workers are lazy, the reward is large, and the employer is impatient"; but Maimonides does not take notice of the similarity.

[55]Rosenthal, "Life Is Short, the Art Is Long," 236–37. Maimonides' interpretation is not completely original, for part of it had been suggested by an earlier Muslim commentary on Hippocrates; see Rosenthal 232–33.

[56]Commentary on *The Aphorisms of Hippocrates* 1, §1, Hebrew text 7–10, on the authority of Alfarabi; 12–13, on the authority of Galen. English translation 15–20.

[57]For example, he explains the words "time is limited" as meaning that when a physician is faced with an actual sick patient, he has no time to experiment and must be ready to act.

slipped.[58] Maimonides nevertheless does not even hint at a reservation concerning the curious aphorisms that I listed a few paragraphs earlier except for recording a qualification placed by Galen on the one regarding baldness and varicose veins. That aphorism, Maimonides reports, was restricted by Galen to loss of hair resulting specifically from scabies. On Galen's reading, which Maimonides tacitly accepts, Hippocrates recognized that the noxious humors concentrated in the head and causing scabies on the skull are drawn away from the legs, and the person affected is left free of varicose veins. The converse is equally true: Should someone suffering from scabies on the skull develop varicose veins, the noxious humors will be drawn in the opposite direction and the scabies will disappear. When Maimonides explains the failure of women to become ambidextrous, he expressly and without reservation cites Galen: The reason, according to Galen, is the physical weakness of the female sex. Without mentioning Galen, he ascribes the beneficial effect of hemorrhoids—in melancholy, dropsy, and consumption[59]—to their ability to attract noxious black bile and unhealthy blood away from other parts of the body. A person with jaundice is unlikely to suffer from flatulence because an excess of yellow bile is the cause of the former, the humor phlegm is the cause of the latter, and an excess of yellow bile in the system suppresses phlegm. Speech defects are accompanied by diarrhea because both are manifestations of overly soft humors. As for the therapeutic benefit of diarrhea for eye disorders, Maimonides merely remarks that the link is "clear."[60] Diarrhea presumably helps by draining harmful humors from the system.

In some of his critical comments, Maimonides surmises that Hippocrates had noticed a chance coincidence and wrongly generalized from it. Thus one aphorism states that it is a sign of mental disease when a woman's breasts become engorged with blood. Maimonides dismisses the connection, writing: "It seems likely to me that Hippocrates saw such a situation once or twice and drew the unqualified inference";[61] Hippocrates must have seen one or two women with engorged breasts who were mentally disturbed and he jumped to the conclusion that all such women suffer from a mental disorder. When calling attention to another unjustified generalization by Hippocrates, Maimonides concludes, with discernible sarcasm: "If you want to place a patina of verisimilitude on this false statement by adding

[58]Alfarabi had also complained that Galen went to extremes in interpreting the text of Hippocrates in order to twist it into accordance with scientific truth. See J. Bürgel, *Averroes "contra Galenum," Nachrichten der Akademie der Wissenschaften in Göttingen, Philologisch-historische Klasse* (1967) 287. In fact, Galen could be mildly critical of Hippocrates. See *Galen's Hygiene* (*De sanitate tuenda*), trans. R. Green (Springfield, Ill. 1951) xxiii.

[59]Maimonides' text of *Aphorisms* 6:11–12 did not have "kidney disorders" as one of the conditions benefited by hemorrhoids.

[60]Commentary on *The Aphorisms of Hippocrates* 6, §17. In the introduction, p. 5, Maimonides writes that a number of the aphorisms are "self-explanatory'"

[61]Commentary on *The Aphorisms of Hippocrates* 5, §40.

conditions and assumptions [that will be able to salvage it], go and take what Galen said about it."[62]

Besides the small number of comments articulating Maimonides' personal opinion and the small number in which he quotes Galen by name, there are some in which—although Galen may have written a page or more—he merely observes that a given Hippocratic aphorism "is clear." In his introduction, he stated that the remainder of his comments, and they make up by far the greater number, would convey the nub of Galen's explanations. I chose a small sample[63]—instances where Maimonides does not speak in his own name, mention Galen, or remark that an aphorism is self-explanatory—restricting myself to comments that say something distinctive, and I compared them with interpretations of the same aphorisms in Galen's commentary.[64] Included were the aphorisms on the importance of retaining at least one hemorrhoid, the inverse relationship between jaundice and flatulence, and the link between speech defects and diarrhea. In each instance, Maimonides does what he promised to do. He gives the gist of Galen's interpretation, invariably in briefer form. Where the prolix Galen had needed a paragraph, Maimonides may make do with a line or two, and where Galen wrote a page or more, a short paragraph suffices for Maimonides.

His interpretation of one further aphorism merits attention because of the window it opens on his understanding of the human organism and his style of reasoning in medical matters. The Hippocratic aphorism at issue here states that when someone suffers from a continuous—that is to say, nonintermittent—fever, if the surface of the patient's body should be cold and the body's interior burning hot, and if the patient is moreover thirsty, it is a fatal sign. Galen, as Maimonides reports, explained that the cause of the phenomenon, when it occurs, is the formation of a hot swelling—or: inflammation—in one of the internal organs: The hot swelling [or inflammation] draws blood and pneuma, the airlike substance that circulates through the body and animates it, to the diseased internal organ and away from the body's surface, leaving the surface cold. Maimonides finds no fault with the aphorism, but he rejects Galen's interpretation as demonstrably "not true." For, he submits, hot internal swellings [or inflammations] are often found to be accompanied by a hot, rather than a cold, bodily surface.

"In my opinion," he writes, the explanation of the aphorism is as follows: The materials making up the surface of the human body are thick and by nature cold. In the present instance, the heat of the corrupt humor that is responsible for the fever cannot overcome those materials. When the heat of the humor travels to the surface of the body and seeks pores to cool itself, the cold surface blocks its efforts and the heat is reflected back into the interior of the body. The heat is thereby rendered

[62]Commentary on *The Aphorisms of Hippocrates* 2, §20.

[63]Maimonides' comments on eighteen of the aphorisms.

[64]Galen, Commentary on *The Aphorisms of Hippocrates*, in *Opera Omnia*, ed. C. Kühn, 2nd ed. (Hildesheim 1964–1965), volumes 17.2 and 18.1.

more intense, the fever is stoked, and the patient's thirst increases. "This," Maimonides assures us, "is a true, natural cause," in other words, an explanation of the phenomenon wholly in accordance with the nature of the human organism. "There can be no doubt concerning it."[65]

In the course of his Commentary, Maimonides cites an additional book of Hippocrates' by name,[66] Galen's Commentary on the *Aphorisms of Hippocrates*, seven further books of Galen's,[67] and the Muslim writer Alfarabi.[68] He refers to his own *Compendia of Galen's Books*[69] and to his *Medical Aphorisms*,[70] the next item in the present list. These last two references do not necessarily establish that Maimonides wrote the present work after the other two.[71] He is known to have gone back and corrected certain of his writings after completing them and he could have inserted the references to the two compositions some time after the Commentary on Hippocrates had been finished.

3. *Medical Aphorisms* (*Fuṣūl Mūsā*)[72] (a large and comprehensive medical text—not, however, approaching the dimensions of Maimonides' *Compendia of Galen's Books*—written to serve him and others as a reference work).[73] It comprises twenty-five chapters, each consisting not so much of aphorisms, as of brief paragraphs. The number of paragraphs in a given chapter varies, and the book contains some 1,500 in all. Each chapter except for the last is devoted to a specific medical topic. Chapter one, for example, is concerned with physiology,[74] chapter

[65]Maimonides, Commentary on *The Aphorisms of Hippocrates* 4, §48.

[66]Commentary on *The Aphorisms of Hippocrates* 5, §40 (the *Epidemiae*).

[67]Steinschneider, "Die Vorrede des Maimonides" (n. 28 above) 220–21, 232–33; *Commentary on the Aphorisms of Hippocrates*, introduction, pp. 3–5; 1, §1, pp. 10, 13; 1, §14; English translation 9–12, 18, 21, 31.

[68]*Commentary on the Aphorisms of Hippocrates* 1, §1, p. 8; English translation 15.

[69]Steinschneider, "Die Vorrede des Maimonides" 222, 234.

[70]Commentary on *The Aphorisms of Hippocrates* 2, §33.

[71]Below, p. 458. it will appear that Maimonides refers to the Commentary on the *Aphorisms of Hippocrates* in the treatise *On Asthma*, which shows signs of being an early medical work.

[72]Arabic original of introduction and colophon, edited with German translation by P. Kahle, in H. Schröder, *Galeni in Platonis Timaeum commentarii fragmenta* (Leipzig 1934) 89–96. Arabic original of the final section with English translation: J. Schacht and M. Meyerhof, "Maimonides against Galen on Philosophy and Cosmogony," *Bulletin of the Faculty of Arts of the University of Egypt* 5.1 (1937). An edition of the entire Arabic text with English translation is being prepared by G. Bos. Medieval Hebrew translation: *Pirqe Moshe*, ed. S. Muntner (n. 26 above). A Latin translation was published in 1489 under the title of *Aphorismi*, and other Latin editions followed. For a list of Arabic writers of works similar in nature to Maimonides' *Aphorisms*, see Steinschneider, *Die arabischen Übersetzungen aus dem Griechischen* (n. 54 above) (360)–(362).

[73]*Medical Aphorisms*, introduction, Hebrew text 13; English translation 1.25.

[74]Maimonides is following precedent in beginning with physiology. See Sezgin, *Geschichte des arabischen Schrifttums* 3.145; N. Siraisi, *Medieval and Renaissance Medicine* (Chicago 1990) 85.

two with the four humors, and other chapters with inspection of urine, diagnosis by means of the pulse, sundry diseases, fevers, conditions affecting women, medications, laxatives, emetics, bloodletting through venesection, surgery, exercise, diet, going to the bath, and so on.

In the introduction Maimonides notes that he did not, in the strict sense, "compose" the present work but instead "chose" and "culled" it "from Galen's words" in "all of his books."[75] That is to say, he extracted short excerpts from whichever texts of Galen's happened to have said something pertinent to the subjects that he wished to cover. He then rearranged the excerpts under his own chapter headings. The paragraphs in chapter one, on physiology, thus come from a dozen different works of Galen's, and those in chapter two, on the humors, come from fifteen.

He further explains somewhat pedantically how the procedure he observed here differs from his procedure in the "*Compendia [of Galen's Books]*." There, everything was copied word for word from Galen. Here, "most [of the paragraphs] are in Galen's words" or in cases where Galen was commenting on a Hippocratic text, in the words of both; some of the paragraphs are a mixture of verbatim quotation and paraphrase; some are pure paraphrase; a few are taken from "later" physicians; and a few are Maimonides' own comments.[76] Notes appended by Maimonides to each of the paragraphs identify his sources. They reveal that nine-tenths of the book comes, indeed, from writings by, or attributed to, Galen, that Maimonides drew from no less than ninety such works, that he included material from a half dozen Muslim medical authors, and that he interjects occasional comments of his own.

In short, he draws not from a limited number of Galen's works, as he did in his *Compendia of Galen's Books*, but from ninety, which may have been all that were available to him. He sometimes paraphrases Galen, he includes information from other medical authors, and he rearranges the excerpts under subject headings of his own making.

Since the introduction to the *Medical Aphorisms* carefully compares the procedure to be pursued in it with Maimonides' procedure in his *Compendia of Galen's Books*, all or a good portion of the latter must have been complete before he wrote the introduction to the *Aphorisms*. By itself, that does not necessarily establish relative dates for the two compositions, since introductions are as often

[75] *Medical Aphorisms*, introduction, Hebrew text 12; English translation 24.

[76] *Medical Aphorisms*, introduction, Hebrew text 12, 14; English translation 1.24, 26. Extended sections drawn from medical writers other than Galen are: (1) 20, §§67–81 (properties of various foods) and 22, §§35–56 (properties of various foods and drugs), which are cited in the name of Abū Marwān Ibn Zuhr; (2) 20, §§82–89 (properties of certain foods) and 22, §§57–70 (properties of various foods and medicaments), which are cited in the name of al-Tamīmī; and (3) 21, §§67–89 (effects of various drugs), which are cited in the name of Ibn Wafīd—who was also one of the sources for Maimonides' work on the *Explanation of the Names of Drugs*—and Avicenna.

done after, as before, the books they introduce, and we do not know when the introduction to the *Medical Aphorisms* was written. It can safely be assumed that the *Compendia* is not later than the *Aphorisms*, since it furnished raw material for that work, and Maimonides was still engaged with the *Aphorisms* at the time of his death. He could, however, have worked on the two simultaneously.

The date when Maimonides started writing the *Medical Aphorisms* cannot be determined, but a pair of parallel passages makes clear that he spent years on it. In chapter eight, he comments on the disease that he calls "diabetes," using the Greek term; the condition, he reports elsewhere in the name of Galen, expresses itself through a fierce thirst and heavy urination.[77] Here he quotes Galen to the effect that diabetes is extremely rare and, speaking for himself, he remarks that he had neither encountered it in the "West" nor heard of instances from his teachers. Yet during "about ten years" in Egypt he had seen more than twenty cases. He conjectures that the higher incidence in Egypt was related to the hot climate and perhaps also to the population's drinking the sweet water of the Nile.[78] A parallel passage in the twenty-fourth chapter of the book makes no reference to the earlier statement. It again quotes Galen on the rareness of diabetes, no longer mentions the West, states that during a period of twenty—and not ten—years in Egypt Maimonides had seen three women and almost twenty men suffering from the disease, and conjectures, with no mention of the sweetness of Nile water, that the condition was caused by the hot Egyptian climate.[79] The readings "ten years" and "twenty years" are confirmed by the Arabic manuscripts.[80]

The first of the two passages does not prove that Maimonides was already working on the *Medical Aphorisms* ten years after coming to Egypt, in other words, by 1178 at the latest. Such a hypothesis is not, in fact, likely, considering his words about toiling day and night on the *Mishneh Torah* during the decade leading up to 1177 or 1178. Nor need we assume that he wrote the second passage ten years after the first. The ten years in the first passage could conceivably be the time that had elapsed after Maimonides began practicing medicine in Egypt, while the twenty years in the second could be the time elapsed since his arrival in the country. Yet no matter how the passages are taken, we get a considerable span. If the ten years in the first passage and the twenty years in the second measure from the same point, he spent at least ten years on the book. Even if the ten years refer to his service as a physician and the twenty to his residence in Egypt, he was working

[77]These two symptoms are given in the second of the passages, *Medical Aphorisms* 24, §39. The Greek term *diabetes* means a siphon, and the disease got that name because persons suffering from it incessantly siphon out urine.

[78]*Medical Aphorisms* 8, §§68–69.

[79]*Medical Aphorisms* 24, §§39–40.

[80]Namely, the version written in Hebrew characters found in Bodleian, MS Pococke 319 (=Neubauer 2113), the version in Arabic characters in Gotha, MS 1937 (both checked for me by Y. T. Langermann), the version in Arabic characters in Leiden, MS Or. 128, and the version in Hebrew characters in Paris Hebrew MS 1210.

on it by 1188. Maimonides' nephew informs us that as Maimonides finished each chapter, he would polish it for him and put it into a final form, and that his uncle died before revising the twenty-fifth chapter. Only after Maimonides' death did he, the nephew, incorporate that chapter into the book;[81] the *Medical Aphorisms* therefore had not been completed by 1204. The book could, of course, have been finished in large part before then, and Maimonides could have returned and written the final chapter, which is different in character from the rest, at the end of his life. When he refers to the *Medical Aphorisms* in his Commentary on the *Aphorisms of Hippocrates*, he obviously could not have had in view a version that contained the final, semi-posthumous chapter.

The *Medical Aphorisms* is Maimonides' most ambitious medical composition, and it has been characterized as a medical equivalent of the *Mishneh Torah*, his most ambitious rabbinic work.[82] The two works do have a superficial resemblance. Both wrestle with a vast number of particulars belonging to a self-enclosed system of thought, Galenic medicine in the one instance, Jewish law in the other; and for each, Maimonides created a new arrangement that, he was confident, persons interested in the subject would find more useful than the original. Although he worked less intensely on the *Medical Aphorisms* than on the *Mishneh Torah*, it occupied him over an even longer period. He plainly invested a good deal of labor in combing thousands of pages of Galen's oeuvre and the works of others for the excerpts he wanted and in rearranging the excerpts under rubrics of his own design.

In conception and execution, the *Medical Aphorisms* nevertheless falls miles short of the rabbinic work. Maimonides decided on the normative status of every legal item that went into the *Mishneh Torah*. He devised a comprehensive logical scheme for presenting the items there. At appropriate junctures he furnished—as he did in all his preserved rabbinic compositions—introductions and general rules to illuminate the minutiae. And he constructed a theological, ethical, and spiritual accompaniment to the code's legal side. Apart from the final chapter of the *Medical Aphorisms*, Maimonides virtually never judges the correctness of the excerpts he records, and sometimes he includes excerpts within a single chapter which do not sit well with one another. While each chapter is devoted to a specific topic, the order of the paragraphs within the chapters is largely haphazard. We await in vain introductory remarks and general rules that might help readers assimilate what is set before them.

In a few of the chapters, Maimonides was able to find an excerpt from Galen that could serve as an appropriate opening statement. The chapter on pulse, for example, begins by identifying the pulse's two functions: First and more importantly, the pulse regulates the body's innate heat and, secondly, it is

[81] *Medical Aphorisms*, end of introduction.

[82] *Medical Aphorisms*, the editor's Hebrew introduction to the medieval Hebrew translation, xi; English introduction xii.

responsible for respiration.[83] The chapter on bloodletting begins by calling attention to three factors that a physician should take into account before undertaking the procedure: He should ascertain that the patient's medical condition truly calls for bloodletting, that the patient is neither too old nor too young for the procedure, and that he is sufficiently strong.[84] There are a few more such instances.[85] Most of the chapters, however, begin with statements chosen at random, and even when Maimonides does find a pertinent opening statement, the remaining excerpts inevitably follow one another haphazardly and without any discernible plan.

A look at a few of the paragraphs dealing with the four humors may convey something of the flavor of the work while expanding our picture of Maimonides' understanding of the human organism and its health. We have already encountered the humors' significance for human health in his Commentary on the *Aphorisms of Hippocrates.*

Chapter two of the *Medical Aphorisms*, which is devoted specifically to the subject of humors, opens with a passage where Galen distinguished between blood in the ordinary sense of the term and the blood that constitutes one of the four humors: The red liquid that drips out of a vein when it is cut is composed of all the humors, that is, the humor blood, black bile, yellow bile, and phlegm. The compound is called *blood* because the humor blood is the predominant component.[86] An excerpt later in the chapter explains that each humor is characterized by a pair of qualities: Yellow bile has a hot and dry power; black bile, a cold and dry power; phlegm, a power that is cold and moist; and blood, one that is hot and moist.[87]

Other excerpts, appearing in no particular order, teach that food undergoes its first stage of digestion in the stomach and a second stage in the liver.[88] A third stage of digestion, we learn elsewhere, occurs after the product of the first two stages is distributed by the veins[89] to the various organs of the body.[90] On the completion of the stage of digestion effected by the liver, there precipitate out material resembling the foam that floats on the surface of fresh wine and other material resembling the lees that fall to the bottom of the wine. The former is yellow bile and the latter, black bile; and, Maimonides tells us, phlegm and blood

[83] *Medical Aphorisms* 4, §1.

[84] *Medical Aphorisms* 12, §1. For the source in Galen, see P. Brain, *Galen on Bloodletting* (Cambridge 1986) 87.

[85] *Medical Aphorisms* 10, §1; 18, §1; 20, §1; 22, §1.

[86] *Medical Aphorisms* 2, §1.

[87] *Medical Aphorisms* 2, §12.

[88] *Medical Aphorisms* 2, §10.

[89] Regarding the veins, see R. Siegel, *Galen's System of Physiology and Medicine* (Basel 1968) 29.

[90] *Medical Aphorisms* 1, §§58, 59; see *On Asthma* (n. 10 above), chapter 2; *Regimen of Health*, chapter 1.

are additional products of the digestive process occurring in the liver.[91] Besides natural yellow bile, which performs a necessary function in the living organism, the body can contain four or five varieties of unnatural yellow bile.[92] Besides natural black bile, which also serves a function, the body can contain an unnatural, noxious black bile as well as certain secondary black "chymes";[93] chymes, in Maimonides' reading of Galen's physiology, are the juices produced by the digestive process and are distinct from humors.[94] Phlegm too makes its appearance in "many varieties," healthy and unhealthy.[95] Galen does not seem to have recognized an unhealthy form of the final humor, blood.[96]

Maimonides further quotes Galen to the effect that an excess of a natural, healthy humor in the organism or the presence of an unnatural, unhealthy humor causes disease.[97] Black bile—Galen, as Maimonides quotes him, does not make clear whether he means the unnatural variety or an excess of the natural variety—is most virulent of all. It is responsible for cancer, leprosy, quartan fever (probably the disease known today as malaria), peeling of the skin, dementia, thickening of the spleen, and hemorrhoids.[98]

The supposition that irregularities in the humors, and particularly in black bile, cause disease underlies a number of Galen's therapies. Maimonides records the following from his source: Leprosy and cancerous growths in their initial stages can be cured by repeatedly emptying the body of its black humor by bleeding and at

[91]*Medical Aphorisms* 2, §§7, 10; 3, §34 (blood).

[92]*Medical Aphorisms* 2, §§3, 5, 10. Siegel, *Galen's System of Physiology and Medicine* 220, finds a total of seven kinds of yellow bile in Galen.

[93]*Medical Aphorisms* 2, §§10, 14.

[94]The Greek term for *humor* is χυμός (English *chyme*), and the Arabic equivalent is *khilṭ*. The Arabic translations of Galen used by Maimonides did not handle the Greek term χυμός consistently. Usually they translate it as *khilṭ*, the Arabic equivalent. Sometimes, however, rather than translating the term, they transliterate and write *kaymūs*; see *Medical Aphorisms* 2, §§11, 17, 25, and the sources in Galen noted in Bos's translation. As a consequence, Maimonides appears not to have realized that *kaymūs* and *khilṭ* are synonyms and supposed instead that they have different denotations. He thus understands Galen to have recognized five primary chymes, in other words, five primary fluids produced by the digestive process, namely: "phlegm, yellow bile, black bile, [the humor] blood, and the watery part of blood [in the ordinary sense of the term *blood*]" (*Medical Aphorisms* 2, §27). Maimonides also adduces an excerpt from Galen to the effect that a "thin watery moistness" is present in each of the humors (*Medical Aphorisms* 2, §2). He simply sets these statements down, without any apparent effort to integrate them into a consistent scheme. But since he brings them together in the same chapter, he may—and I am speculating—have been intimating that each of the four humors is a chyme, a postdigestive fluid, composed of a watery substratum and a substance dissolved within it. The substantive side of the humor, which exists in solution, is what possesses the hot-dry, cold-dry, cold-moist, or hot-moist power.

[95]*Medical Aphorisms* 2, §§6, 13a.

[96]Brain, *Galen on Bloodletting* (n. 84 above) 7–8.

[97]*Medical Aphorisms* 2, §§6, 10, 22.

[98]*Medical Aphorisms* 2, §§16, 25.

the same time having the patient observe a healthy regimen.[99] Melancholic dementia is a consequence of the presence of blackish blood—apparently, blood containing an excess of black chymes—in the veins. When the condition pervades the body, blood should be drawn from "the vein," and when the blackish blood causing dementia is limited to the brain, efforts should be focused on the troublesome blood in that region.[100] Maimonides, as he cites Galen, does not specify which vein should be opened in the former instance and how the blackish blood is to be removed from the area of the head in the latter instance. The first step in treating both "the cold growth on the brain known as lethargy and the warm growth on the brain known as phrenitis" is to remove from the head whatever humors may be causing the problem; that can be accomplished by drawing blood and applying rose oil and vinegar.[101] In cases where fainting results from yellow bile's spilling into the "orifice of the stomach"—the aperture at the juncture of the stomach with the esophagus—the patient should drink thin, cold, aromatic wine; where the cause of the fainting is an excess of insufficiently digested humor, he should be given strong, light colored or yellow wine.[102] Plucking body hair draws humors from the body's interior to the surface and thereby helps cure forgetfulness and narcolepsy.[103]

The theory of humors is ignored in the most bizarre paragraphs of the *Medical Aphorisms*; these are devoted to materials that act on the body not in accordance with the laws of medical science but through extraordinary properties.[104] Maimonides lists over seventy materials of the sort, and among those that he copies from Galen are compounds to be ingested and embrocations to be applied to the body which are made of roasted mouse heads kneaded in honey, bat brains, camel or lamb brains, fox lung, the spleen of the wild ass, crabs, worms, or the dried excrement of dogs, wolves, cattle, sheep, goats, pigeons, or chickens.[105] Among the items that he cites from the Muslim physician al-Tamīmī are such oddities as an eye ointment made with roasted bladder stones and kidney stones, a potion of burnt crystal mixed with ass's milk for curing tremors and tuberculosis, and a mouthwash for halitosis consisting of vinegar in which gold has been repeatedly dipped.[106] Maimonides had been in contact with the son of the renowned

[99]*Medical Aphorisms* 9, §107.

[100]*Medical Aphorisms* 9, §16.

[101]*Medical Aphorisms* 9, §17.

[102]*Medical Aphorisms* 9, §49.

[103]*Medical Aphorisms* 9, §35.

[104]In the Commentary on the *Aphorisms of Hippocrates* (n. 39 above) 1, §1, pp. 12–13, English translation 20, Maimonides quotes Galen as stating that medicaments in general act on the human body through what in medical terminology is called their "properties." He does not draw a distinction between the properties of the present items and those of standard medicaments, but the present items are certainly bizarre.

[105]*Medical Aphorisms* 22, §§2, 3, 6, 10, 15, 20, 22–26, 28–30, 32.

[106]*Medical Aphorisms* 22, §§ 68, 69, 70.

physician Abū Marwān Ibn Zuhr, and the son revealed to him some of the "wonders" that Ibn Zuhr had discovered by observation. Vision, he had found, can be strengthened by looking into the eyes of the wild ass or by applying an ointment made of rose water and sugar. Wearing rabbit fur strengthens the bodies of elderly people and children, wearing the fur of sheep strengthens the bodies of youths, while just being in the vicinity of cats causes consumption. Dripping mustard oil into the ear heals deafness. Sexual performance can be improved by eating birds' heads, especially if they are male birds, turnips cooked with meat, or the testicles of animals of the sort whose flesh is naturally warm and moist. Hedgehog fat when applied topically produces a "strong . . . male erection" and enhances sexual pleasure; and the penis of the hedgehog or ram, when dried, ground, made into a potion, and drunk, likewise has the property of producing a strong erection. The inner membrane of a bustard's gizzard, when dried and mixed with kohl, has the property of healing watery eyes. When an emerald is worn as a pendant, it alleviates epilepsy and cures diarrhea and dysentery, when worn in a finger-ring, it strengthens the orifice of the stomach and stops vomiting, and when ground and drunk in a mouthful of water, it acts as an antidote to poison.[107]

Although Maimonides does not expressly endorse each of the above, he says nothing to cast the slightest doubt on their efficacy, and we shall see that in another of his works he explicitly recommends substances that act through the same and similar properties. His gullibility is perhaps extenuated by the great Galen's having been equally guilty.[108] It is striking, however, that he had been more levelheaded in a purely rabbinic context. When commenting on a mishnaic passage dealing with medical procedures, he had stressed that rabbinic law recognizes only "what is true" and is grounded in "logical reasoning and accessible experience." Since the efficacy of materials that act through extraordinary properties cannot be "comprehended by logical reasoning" and the sole evidence for their efficacy is "far-fetched experience," rabbinic law does not recognize them as genuine medicaments.[109]

Perhaps the best piece of advice in the book is a further excerpt from Galen. Galen stated that when the Greeks did not know how to treat a disease, they left the patient in the hands of nature and did nothing.[110]

[107]*Medical Aphorisms* 20, §71; 22, §§36, 38, 40, 42, 44, 47, 48, 50.

[108]I made no attempt to determine whether all the works of Galen's from which Maimonides quotes are authentic.

[109]Commentary on the Mishna, *Yoma* 8:4. At issue is a medicament made of a substance the ingestion of which is prohibited by Jewish dietary laws, yet which was thought by one of the ancient rabbis to have a property that could save the lives of persons bitten by a rabid dog. The rabbinic rule is that ritual prohibitions are waived where human life is endangered. Nevertheless, Maimonides explains, the prevailing rabbinic view did not allow a waiver in the present instance because the supposed medicinal properties of the prohibited substance lie beyond the ken of science.

[110]*Medical Aphorisms* 8, §75.

Most of the twenty-fifth and final chapter of the *Medical Aphorisms* is devoted to contradictions and inconsistencies in Galen's medical works. There was nothing original in criticizing Galen,[111] and Maimonides observes that the medieval Arabic physician Ibn Zakariyyā Rāzī (Rhazes) had also drawn up a critique. But Rāzī, he writes, introduced extraneous, nonmedical considerations, while Maimonides assures readers that he would restrict himself exclusively to considerations of a medical nature. Before entering upon an examination of the contradictions and inconsistencies, he suggests three possible reasons for their occurrence: slips on Galen's part, for "only prophets" are exempt from error; bad translations from the Greek original into Arabic; or his own failure to understand Galen's words. Where he is not sure of the reason for a discrepancy, he writes that he will simply call attention to the problematic passages and leave things at that.[112]

The chapter sets forth about fifty instances where statements in Galen's medical works openly contradict, or are inconsistent with, one another. In regard to some, Maimonides adjudicates between the incompatible statements, explaining why he considers one of the statements to be more correct. In a few instances, he writes that the discrepancy is most likely due to the translators. In the remaining, and they are the majority, he simply notes the discrepancy.

To take a few examples: He finds that in one of Galen's works, a putrefied humor giving rise to fever is said to circulate throughout the body, while in the same work as well as in another, such humors are said to be restricted to a specific spot. Maimonides reasons that the second opinion must be correct. Inasmuch as persons are sometimes found who suffer simultaneously from several distinct fevers, the humors responsible for them must be circumscribed in separate, clearly defined locations within the body.[113] Again, Galen once states that a physical constitution inclining from the mean toward immoderate warmth or immoderate cold is easier to cure than a constitution inclining toward immoderate moistness or dryness; but a different passage in the same work asserts that in the case of the stomach, the easiest imbalance to correct is an imbalance in the direction of immoderate moistness. Maimonides concedes that the first statement was probably intended in a general sense, while the second applies only to the stomach. Galen was nonetheless remiss, for if the stomach is indeed an exception to the rule, he should not have formulated the first statement in a blanket fashion and without qualification.[114] A third example: Galen writes in one place that the four humors do not exist in a pure form within the body but are virtually always mixed with each other, while elsewhere in the same work he maintains that the humors usually do exist in pure form in the bodily organs and are only occasionally mixed. In

[111]See O. Temkin, *Galenism* (Ithaca 1973) 118–22; Bürgel, *Averroes "contra Galenum"* (n. 58 above) 279–97.

[112]*Medical Aphorisms* 25, §1.

[113]*Medical Aphorisms* 25, §5.

[114]*Medical Aphorisms* 25, §7.

Maimonides' opinion, observation lends support to the former alternative.[115] Throughout the chapter, as in these examples, his critique of Galen is conceived and conducted wholly within the framework of Galenic medicine.

The conclusion of chapter twenty-five of the *Medical Aphorisms* turns away from medicine to castigate Galen for cavalier remarks that he made about the Mosaic belief in miracles and for incoherent statements on the issue of the creation of the world. Maimonides supposes that Galen's unquestionable preeminence in medicine led him to arrogate authority to himself in areas where he had no expertise; the opinions he expressed where he had no right to speak show him to have been "ignorant" and "wrongheaded."[116]

Despite its limitations, the *Medical Aphorisms* is a convenient distillation of Galen's self-indulgently verbose writings on medicine—albeit a version in which the original Greek texts have been filtered through Arabic translations, the translations have been refiltered through Maimonides' understanding of them, and the upshot may sometimes diverge from the way in which modern scholars read Galen.[117] It became a popular medical text. The Arabic original has been preserved in a half dozen manuscripts, it was translated into Hebrew twice in the thirteenth century, and a good number of manuscripts of each of the translations have been preserved. Curiously, no Hebrew version was printed until the nineteenth century, by which time the book held interest only for historians and not for practicing physicians; while neither of the two Hebrew translations would win a prize for accuracy and clarity, the poorer of the two was unfortunately the one chosen for publication.[118] The book was also translated into Latin twice in the Middle Ages and was published in Latin for the use of physicians no less than four times in the fifteenth and sixteenth centuries.[119]

4. *On Hemorrhoids*[120] (a composition written for a young man of a noble family who suffered periodically from severe hemorrhoids and whom Maimonides

[115] *Medical Aphorisms* 25, §38. Cf. 2, §§12, 13.

[116] *Medical Aphorisms* 25, §§59–68, which addresses Galen, *De usu partium* 11.14, in particular. The distinction between Galen the superlative physician and Galen the unreliable philosopher had become something of a topos in Maimonides' time; see Temkin, *Galenism* 74–80.

[117] See, for example, n. 94 above.

[118] B. Richler, "Manuscripts of Moses ben Maimon's Pirke Moshe in Hebrew Translation" *Korot* 9 (1986) 345*–56*. G. Bos, "Maimonides' Medical Aphorisms," *Korot* 12 (1996–1997) 35–79.

[119] J. Leibowitz, "*Targumim le-Latinit shel Pirqe Moshe*," *Korot* 6 (1973) 275–81.

[120] Arabic original, medieval Hebrew translation, and German translation: H. Kroner, "Die Haemorrhoiden in der Medicin des XII und XIII Jahrhunderts," *Janus* 16 (1911). Reedition of the medieval Hebrew translation: Moshe ben Maimon, *On Hemorrhoids, On the Increase of Physical Vigour, On Asthma* (n. 10 above) (pp. 6–7, give some information about other medieval works on the same subject). English translation from the Hebrew: Maimonides, *Treatises on Poisons, Hemorrhoids, Cohabitation*, trans. F. Rosner (Haifa 1984). The references that follow

had treated). After each occurrence, the patient's swelling would recede, but the condition would flare up again later. The patient therefore inquired about effecting a permanent cure by removing the protruding hemorrhoids surgically. Maimonides, wisely without doubt, advised against surgery; for "danger" would be involved inasmuch as it was "unclear whether or not the protruding tissues were of the sort that should be excised." If they were not, and if the underlying cause persisted, new tissues would simply replace those that had been cut away. The solution, Maimonides informed the young man, was to address the underlying cause, and to that end he prescribed a dietary regimen. The man asked Maimonides to give him the regimen in written form, and Maimonides complied with the present twenty-page composition.[121]

He begins by explaining that "most diseases, and especially the more serious" result from poor digestion. When food is not properly digested in the stomach, then the second stage of digestion, which takes place in the liver, and the third stage, which takes place in the other parts of the body, will also be defective. To avoid disease one must consume food correctly: One must be careful to eat food of good quality, refrain from overeating, and observe the correct order, taking, for example, light food before heavy food. Meals must be eaten at the correct time. That is to say, a person should eat only when genuinely hungry and after exercise, so that the body's inner heat is aroused and facilitates the digestive process, and never immediately before exercise and other vigorous movement, since physical activity interferes with digestion.[122]

As for hemorrhoids, Maimonides writes, "it is known" that they usually result from an excess of black bile in the body, and such is invariably the situation when hemorrhoids protrude beyond the rectum. Only in a small number of instances are they the result of an excess of the humor blood, and in even a smaller number, of the humor phlegm. Black bile causes the problem by thickening the blood—not the humor blood, but blood in the ordinary sense. The limbs and organs reject such blood, and, being weighed down by black bile, it gravitates to veins in the vicinity of the rectum and distends them, the result being hemorrhoids. To prevent the condition, a person should avoid foods that produce black bile and thicken the blood, including beans, lentils, dates, aged cheese, goat meat, beef—especially the head—salted meat, aquatic fowl, unleavened bread, pastas, and others.[123] Maimonides goes on to list the foods that may be eaten safely, herbal medications to be ingested, ointments to be applied to the sensitive area or inserted as suppositories, and herbs that can be placed on hot coals to create a fumigant over which the patient sits.[124] He recommends warm baths, warns against allowing anything cold

---

refer to the chapter and section divisions of the Muntner edition.

[121] Maimonides, *On Hemorrhoids*, introduction.

[122] *On Hemorrhoids* 1.5.

[123] *On Hemorrhoids* 2.

[124] *On Hemorrhoids* 3; 4; 5; 7.

to touch the area, and adamantly opposes using harsh laxatives without the advice of an expert physician.[125] Chronic diseases are, he states, especially dangerous, and when they recur, action must be taken. When hemorrhoids recur, the indicated treatment is to bleed the patient immediately from the basilic vein in the arm or the vein at the back of the knee, and if bloodletting is not possible because of the patient's age or the season of the year, to treat him by cupping on the lower back.[126] It will be observed that Maimonides has combined a complete misunderstanding of the cause of the malady with a mixture of common sense, harmless advice, and some very bad advice, for treating it.

5. *On Asthma* (*Fī al-Rabw*). Maimonides is writing for another unidentified Muslim of high standing—he calls him a nobleman and addresses him as "your honor" [*ḥaḍra*]—who lived most of the time in Alexandria, was about forty years old, and suffered from a condition called *rabw* in Arabic. The patient's symptoms were recurrent attacks of catarrh, orthopnea, and pain, usually in the winter, and he found relief if he moved to a drier part of the country when he felt that an attack was coming on;[127] orthopnea is extreme difficulty in breathing in any but an upright position. In the *Medical Aphorisms*, Maimonides quotes Galen as having defined *rabw* as a situation involving breathing difficulties[128] and he notes in the present treatise that certain medicaments he was prescribing would alleviate breathing problems and coughing.[129] He does not, however, mention wheezing in either context, and wheezing is the distinctive symptom of asthma as the term is used today. Consequently, while the illness that he was being asked to treat may have been the bronchial condition known in modern medicine as asthma—which is the word I shall use for the sake of convenience—it could also have been some other respiratory disorder.

A number of physicians had prescribed regimens for the man to follow, all without success, and he was now turning to Maimonides for advice. Maimonides writes that he would not enter into a full account of the disease, since doing so would require too lengthy a tome, and the etiology of asthma as well as the circumstances under which attacks occur were already covered in the medical literature. He would limit himself to what he had been asked to do and prescribe a better regimen for his patient.[130]

From examining the patient and from what the man had told him, Maimonides had established that the immediate cause of the attacks was the flowing out of catarrh from the brain;[131] in Galenic physiology, the brain communicates with the

[125] *On Hemorrhoids* 5; Postscript.

[126] *On Hemorrhoids* 6.

[127] Maimonides, *On Asthma* (n. 10 above), introduction.

[128] See *Medical Aphorisms* (n. 26 above) 23, §79.

[129] E.g., *On Asthma*, chapter 11, §5, chapter 12, §2.

[130] *On Asthma*, introduction, §1.

[131] *On Asthma*, introduction, §2.

respiratory tract.[132] Fumes rising from the stomach and filling the brain were also somehow implicated.[133] Maimonides does not explain here how the fluid triggering the symptoms forms in the brain, but another of his medical works traces the source of such fluid once again to humors: Catarrh results when humors accumulated in the brain are dissolved by inordinate heat or cold and drip into the nose, throat, lungs, stomach, and other internal organs.[134]

The attacks, Maimonides goes on, were on each occasion resolved when the flow of fluid from the brain stopped, what drained into the lungs was "matured," and the lungs were cleansed.[135] He further quotes Galen's observation that weak bodily organs become ill either through an excess of healthy humors in the body or through the presence of unhealthy humors.[136] It follows that the best way to manage periodically recurring maladies, such as gout, pain in the joints, migraine, and asthma is to forestall them by controlling the body's humors through good hygiene.[137] In the instance at hand, efforts have to be taken to cleanse the entire body, and the brain and lungs in particular, of excess and thick humors and then to ensure that the brain no longer accepts or produces such humors.[138]

The importance of a correct, comprehensive regimen for health had been an established motif in the medical literature from the time that the Hippocratic corpus was put together,[139] and the treatise *On Asthma* places itself within that tradition. It consists largely in instruction for controlling humors, with annotations to the effect that this or that measure will be especially beneficial for persons suffering from asthma or persons with the patient's constitution. The patient, it seems, would become indisposed by hot breezes, could not bear to let his hair grow long, and found it difficult to wear head coverings, whence Maimonides had inferred that his bodily constitution inclined toward heat and the constitution of his brain was overly hot.[140] Only toward the end of the treatise does Maimonides finally devote a few pages to his patient's specific medical problem.[141] Some of the general advice is similar to what Maimonides offers in the composition on *Hemorrhoids*,

[132]Galen, *De usu partium* 8.6; Maimonides, *Medical Aphorisms* 1, §§41–42; Siegel, *Galen's System of Physiology and Medicine* (n. 89 above) 105–6; G. Bos, "Maimonides on the Preservation of Health," *Journal of the Royal Asiatic Society*, 3rd series, 4 (1994) 233.

[133]*On Asthma*, chapter 2, §3.

[134]Maimonides, *Regimen of Health*, Arabic text, ed. H. Kroner, *Janus* 28 (1924) 148–49. English translation: *The Regimen of Health*, trans. A. Bar Sela, et al., *Transactions of the American Philosophical Society*, n.s. 54.4 (1964) 30b.

[135]*On Asthma*, introduction, §2.

[136] See above, p. 448.

[137]*On Asthma*, chapter 1, §§1, 2.

[138]*On Asthma*, chapter 11, §§1, 5.

[139]Bos, "Maimonides on the Preservation of Health," 216–18.

[140]*On Asthma*, introduction, §2.

[141]*On Asthma*, chapters 11 and 12. Maimonides instructs his patient to begin with herbal potions, starting with the least potent and progressing to the more potent as necessary. If those steps are insufficient he should go on to enemas, and if even they do not suffice, to laxatives.

and much is similar to what we shall meet in his *Regimen of Health*, the next item to be considered; the treatise *On Asthma* and the *Regimen of Health* even share a section of around four pages. Maimonides is candid about relying largely on his predecessors and especially Galen; he cites Galen repeatedly and also cites Hippocrates, Rāzī, Alfarabi, and Ibn Zuhr.[142] Much, although not all, of what he says can be matched with excerpts from Galen that are recorded in his *Medical Aphorisms*.[143]

The regimen that he outlines covers a range of rubrics—food, drink, exercise, quality of air, mental hygiene, sleep, the elimination of superfluities from the body, bathing, massage, and sexual intercourse—and just pointing out the relevance of those categories for health goes back to Galen.[144] Nourishment, Maimonides stresses, must be taken in moderation, and satiety avoided, inasmuch as it distends the stomach and overburdens the digestive system. Food that generates thick or viscous humors should be avoided entirely, for humors of the sort—and even an excess of good humors—are excreted from the body only with difficulty and hence clog the body's organs and passageways. Because of his patient's problem, Maimonides also rules out nourishment generating fumes that might rise and fill the brain.[145] Among the excluded foods are bread made of refined wheaten flour; wheaten pastas; unleavened bread, which, Galen declared, "does no one any good"; legumes; beef; mutton, because "Galen said that it is worse than beef"; milk since it "fills the head"; aged cheese; and aquatic fowl. Healthy foods include bread made of unrefined wheat, which is well leavened, well kneaded, salted, and oven-baked; young barnyard fowl; lean ocean and river fish; and the forequarter of year-old male lamb. The fat around the stomach should be avoided as should the flesh of the female lamb, since it is viscous and deposits superfluities in the body. Maimonides goes on to list fruits, vegetables, and condiments that are healthy or unhealthy in general and those that are healthy or unhealthy for persons who are affected by the present malady or have a hot constitution. Most fresh fruit is relegated to the unhealthy category, because Galen had become convinced that the fevers from which he himself once suffered were caused by eating fresh fruit.[146]

Maimonides warns the man for whom he was writing that overindulging in wine is harmful, because it heats the brain. "A small amount" taken while food is being digested nonetheless improves the digestive process, feeds the body's innate heat, and helps rid the body of superfluities through perspiration and urine. By a small amount Maimonides means "about three or four cups" per meal—presumably

[142]See *On Asthma*, introduction, §4, and Bos's index to his edition.

[143]See Maimonides, *Medical Aphorisms*, chapters 17 and 20.

[144]For the Galenic source, see *Companion Encyclopedia of the History of Medicine* 288–89; Bos's note to his English translation of *On Asthma*.

[145]*On Asthma*, chapter 2, §§1, 3.

[146]*On Asthma*, chapters 3 and 4. Regarding unleavened bread, see *Medical Aphorisms* 20, §16, and regarding fruit, *Medical Aphorisms* 20, §51. Regarding the best way of baking bread, see Galen, *Hygiene* (n. 58 above) 209.

envisaging something more modest than eight-ounce tumblers. Since Islamic law prohibits the drinking of wine, he also supplies a recipe for a seasoned drink of honey and crushed chickpeas, preferably black ones, which has virtues similar to those of wine and which he had observed senior physicians prepare. "As many know," water drunk during the meal or directly afterward interposes itself between the stomach and the food that the stomach is trying to digest and thereby interferes with the digestive process. Maimonides therefore prescribes that water not be drunk during meals and for about two hours afterward, until digestion is complete. Otherwise, he approves of fresh clean water that has been boiled and cooled. But lukewarm water is ruinous. It reduces appetite, interferes with digestion, weakens the stomach and the rest of the body, destroys the body's constitution, and leads to damage of blood, liver, and spleen.[147]

He strongly discourages sleeping after meals, because sleep at that time fills the brain with fumes. Persons affected by the present disorder in particular are advised to limit their sleep as much as possible, all the more when they are suffering an attack, and always to wait three or four hours after eating before going to sleep.[148] Frequenting the bathhouse is also to be avoided, inasmuch as it "corrupts the humors"; Maimonides informs his patient that the "later" physicians recommended going to the bath no more than once every ten days, to which he adds that bathing is especially damaging for asthmatics. Anyone who does bathe should use the hottest water that he can bear and allow only hot water to touch his head, for hot water "sustains the brain's functions and eliminates its superfluities," whereas lukewarm or cold water weakens the brain and increases humors in it.[149] After bathing, a person should immediately sleep for an hour, because sleep "matures what can be matured" in the digestive system and otherwise dissolves noxious humors in the body.[150] Going considerably beyond Galen, Maimonides warns in dire tones about the danger of sexual intercourse for the great majority of men, his explanation being that ejaculated semen carries healthy, natural humors along with it and hence dries out and cools the body's organs.[151] He recommends exercise before meals on the authority of Hippocrates and Galen, while labeling physical activity after eating as yet one more thing to be avoided: It causes the nutrients in the stomach to

[147]*On Asthma*, chapter 7. Regarding wine, see Galen, *Hygiene* 34.

[148]*On Asthma*, chapter 10, §1. In chapter 6, §4, Maimonides warns against sleeping on an empty stomach and writes that he would himself take light food before going to bed. (By coincidence, accepted medical opinion today recommends that persons suffering from laryngopharyngeal reflux do not eat for several hours before going to sleep.)

[149]Maimonides does not seem to take into account that the patient for whom he was writing suffered from an overly hot brain.

[150]*On Asthma*, chapter 10, §§2–4.

[151]*On Asthma*, chapter 10, §8. Galen had warned that the ejaculation of semen has a drying effect on the body and can harm men of dry constitution but, as the excerpts from Galen in Maimonides' *Medical Aphorisms* 17, §§8–9, 12–13, show, he had no thought of discouraging sexual intercourse in a wholesale fashion.

be released to the rest of the body before being fully digested, thereby clogging passageways with chymes.[152]

Galenic medicine was fixated on superfluous materials in the human body, and Maimonides, quoting Galen, recommends not only looseness of the bowels, but periodic enemas and self-induced vomiting as well. Keeping the bowels loose, for which Maimonides furnishes a variety of recipes, helps to eliminate superfluities and prevents the development of thick, viscous humors. Prophylactic enemas serve to cleanse the brain, purge the intestines, improve digestion, delay old age, and forestall "many diseases." And self-induced vomiting performed regularly—at monthly or more frequent intervals—cleanses the stomach of the humor phlegm. For those who find vomiting difficult, Maimonides prescribes medicaments to be ingested which accomplish the same purpose; one, which he himself used,[153] consists simply of sugar mixed with anise or swallowed with lemon juice, and he found that it was wonderfully effective in keeping his own stomach phlegm-free. In the view of the best medical opinion, he writes, bloodletting should not be part of routine hygiene. It should be performed only when needed to treat disease and it should be done, and harsh laxatives taken, only if prescribed by an expert physician.[154] He does encourage his patient to use one of the milder laxatives prophylactically once or twice a year—something that the man was already doing—in order to evacuate unwanted humors and keep his brain and lungs clear.[155]

He refers by name to his Commentary on *The Aphorisms of Hippocrates*.[156] As already pointed out, cross-references of the sort do not establish relative dates for the works involved, since he could have gone back and added a reference after a given work was completed.

Some of what he says in the treatise *On Asthma* suggests, indeed, an early date within his medical career. He describes how a condiment with medicinal value is, or was, prepared "among us in Spain"[157] and speaks of things "known among us in the West"[158] as well as of medical recipes that he had "received from masters [of the art of medicine] in the West."[159] At a certain point, he comments on the unusual relationship between patients and physicians which he had "seen . . . in

[152] *On Asthma*, chapter 5, §5.

[153] BT *Shabbat* 147b, prohibits self-induced vomiting. Alfasi, *Shabbat*, chapter 22 (end), qualifies the prohibition. In *Mishneh Torah*: *H. Shabbat* 21.31, Maimonides records a prohibition against ingesting emetics on the Sabbath as part of the wider prohibition against ingesting medicaments on the Sabbath day but he does not state a general prohibition against emetics. *Mishneh Torah*: *H. De*^{c}*ot* 4, the chapter dedicated to hygiene, which unlike the treatise *On Asthma* is directed to a Jewish readership, makes no mention of self-induced vomiting.

[154] *On Asthma*, chapter 9.

[155] *On Asthma*, introduction; chapter 11, §4; chapter 12, §8.

[156] *On Asthma*, chapter 13, §19. The reference to the *Regimen of Health* in chapter 10, §5, has in view not Maimonides' *Regimen*, but rather a work of Galen's. See Bos's translation.

[157] *On Asthma*, chapter 4, §6.

[158] *On Asthma*, chapter 4, §4; chapter 12, §2.

[159] *On Asthma*, chapter 12, §§9, 10.

the land of Egypt,"[160] sounding much like a newcomer, although he must have been in the country for a period of years. His other works on medicine also mention how things were in the lands of his youth, but—with the exception of the *Explanation of the Names of Drugs*, to be discussed below—none of them has an array of statements that identify him to such an extent with Spain and the lands of the West over against Egypt.

He recalls two actual cases, one of which he had himself seen when he was a student of medicine in the West, while the other was a notorious incident that he heard about during the same period. The first patient died a few hours after being bled, and the second, a few hours after the medicament theriac was administered. Maimonides asked an experienced physician with whom he was studying about the error in the former case, and his teacher told him that the bloodletting had been performed before the patient was ready for it. As for the latter case, the sons of a Jewish and a Muslim physician informed Maimonides what their fathers thought.[161] One son stated in the name of his father, who had been among the attending physicians, that the dose of theriac administered to the patient had been too large. The other son reported that his father, the distinguished Abū Marwān Ibn Zuhr—whose own father had been another of the attending physicians—was of the opposite opinion: The dose had been too small. Maimonides naturally was not satisfied with the answers. In order, as he writes, to advance his medical understanding, he pressed the sons of the two physicians to explain why the dosage was too large or too small, but they either could not or would not reveal anything more. It is rare for Maimonides to reminisce about his student days in any written context.

He further relates that he had once cared for an unnamed young woman who suffered from a respiratory problem similar to his present patient's condition. He prescribed a medication for cleansing the woman's lungs and brain and for stopping the catarrh and he kept track of her progress for at least three years.[162] Plainly, he had practiced medicine—where and when is unclear—for a period of time before he sat down to write the composition that we are concerned with.

One passage nevertheless sounds like an attempt to establish his medical credentials and certainly not like the words of a physician with a solid practice who enjoyed renown in the very highest circles. After citing Hippocrates and Galen at length on the danger of engaging physicians who are not fully competent, Maimonides warns the man for whom he was writing: "I call God as my witness that I know myself well and realize that I am one of those who are not perfect in the art of medicine and are terrified by it. . . . I, nonetheless, know myself better than others [know themselves] and can evaluate my knowledge and the knowledge

[160] *On Asthma*, chapter 13, §47. §§41–46, offer further comments on the style of medical practice in Egypt.

[161] *On Asthma*, chapter 13, §§33, 38.

[162] *On Asthma*, chapter 12, §5.

of others better than someone can who is inferior to me in medical theory. . . . I have made these comments lest you . . . fail to appreciate my counsel or suppose that it involves personal interest. I do not want you to take what I have said lightly and dismiss it."[163] It is hard to visualize Maimonides writing those lines, with their uncomfortable mixture of self-deprecation and self-promotion, after he had become important enough to have his medical advice solicited by royalty. He never felt the need to recommend his rabbinic qualifications to Jewish readers in anything resembling the same tone.

6. The *Regimen of Health* (*Fī Tadbīr al-Ṣiḥḥa*).[164] It was prepared for Saladin's eldest son al-Afḍal, who had sent a messenger to Maimonides asking for advice regarding his constipation, poor digestion, and depression.

Al-Afḍal was born in 1170, spent most of his adult life in Syria and Palestine, but in 1199 lived for a time in Egypt, where he served as regent for his brother's small son; he was soon deposed and banished from the country. Ibn Abī Uṣaybiᶜa, writing several decades after Maimonides' death, describes "King [or: Prince] al-Afḍal" as one of Maimonides' patients, without, however, making clear whether Maimonides treated him in person or, perhaps, only advised him on medical matters in writing.[165] The *Regimen of Health* must have been commissioned at a time when al-Afḍal was away from the country, for if he were in Egypt, he could simply have summoned Maimonides from Fustat to Cairo rather than sending his request by messenger. Maimonides includes advice on appropriate times for sexual intercourse, and that would indicate that al-Afḍal was no longer a child. Apart from those considerations, there is no way of dating the composition.

His reply to al-Afḍal opens with the words: "The command of the royal, most excellent [*afḍalī*, a flattering play on al-Afḍal's name] master [*mawlā*], may God exalt him and keep him strong, has reached the most humble slave [*mamlūk*], Moses ibn Ubaydallah the Israelite. . . ."[166] As was just seen, Maimonides' treatise *On Asthma* was written for a man who requested help for a specific malady, yet it consists largely of general advice on hygiene and health, with only digressions and a final few pages devoted to the patient's condition. The present work is, in the main, another regimen for healthy living as well as an overall guide for the treatment of disease, and only one of its four chapters focuses on al-Afḍal's

[163] *On Asthma*, chapter 13, §27. The passage is quoted at greater length above, p. 36.

[164] Arabic original and German translation: Maimonides, *Fī Tadbīr aṣ-Ṣiḥḥat*, ed and trans. H. Kroner, *Janus* 27-29 (1923–1925). Medieval Hebrew translation: *Regimen sanitatis* (*Hanhagat ha-Beriut*), ed. S. Muntner (Jerusalem 1957). English translation: *The Regimen of Health*, trans. A. Bar Sela et al. (n. 134 above). A Latin translation was published in Florence, 1476, and in Venice, 1514.

[165] Above, p. 68.

[166] As Maimonides penned the mandatory courtesies, one can visualize him recalling the courtesies that Judah the Prince employed when writing to the Roman official Antoninus. See *Genesis Rabba* 75:5.

specific problems. Here, however, since the prince's physical complaints were poor digestion and constipation, and since the core of hygiene for Maimonides was good digestion and the avoidance of excess materials in the body, almost all of the *Regimen* would have had immediate pertinence for the patient.

Maimonides cites the expected authors—Hippocrates, Rāzī, Ibn Zuhr, Alfarabi, and especially Galen—and he acknowledges that many of the things he says in the *Regimen* had been said in previous "compositions" of his.[167] One of them may very well have been the treatise *On Asthma*. The two works evidence a similar cast of mind, and most of the advice offered in the present work matches what Maimonides said in *On Asthma*, although there are a few divergences. The connection is especially striking in a section of about four pages which forms half of the last chapter of the *Regimen of Health* and appears word for word toward the end of the other book.[168] In the *Regimen*, the section moreover betrays signs of having been copied mechanically.[169]

As he did in the treatise *On Asthma*, Maimonides quotes Galen's remark about the Greeks' leaving matters in the hands of nature when they were not sure how to treat a disease.[170] He warns, as he did there, against the prescribing of even a mild medicament or procedure unless the physician is certain that it is the appropriate treatment and also that it is needed, in other words, that nature, left to itself, will not correct the problem;[171] for Galen pointed out that making a mistake in even such minor matters as drink and bathing can have disastrous consequences.[172] He insists that bloodletting should be performed, and harsh laxatives, harsh emetics, harsh enemas, and other strong measures taken, only on the advice of expert physicians.[173] And he stresses that digestion is the key to health. If, as Galen warned, the first stage of digestion in the stomach is not completed properly, then

[167]*Regimen of Health*, Arabic text, *Janus* 27.287; English translation 16b.

[168]*Regimen of Health*, Arabic text, *Janus* 28.70–74, 143–45; English translation 27a–29b. *On Asthma*, chapter 13, §§1–16. In both works, the common section concludes with the words: "Ibn Zuhr stated in a well-known, available book of his: I never administered a laxative without thinking about it for days before and afterwards." The *Regimen of Health* also shares material with Maimonides' *Medical Aphorisms* and echoes some of the medical advice given earlier in his law code, *Mishneh Torah*: *H. De*^{c}*ot*, chapter 4.

[169]The first half of *Regimen of Health*, chapter 4, the section that is identical with part of the treatise *On Asthma*, contains a paragraph repeating almost word for word something already cited from Rāzī in *Regimen*, chapter 1. See *Regimen of Health*, Arabic text, *Janus* 27.295, 28.74; English translation 20b–21a, 28a–b.

[170]*Regimen of Health*, Arabic text: *Janus* 27.295; English translation 20b. Cf. *On Asthma*, chapter 13, §25.

[171]*Regimen of Health*, Arabic text, *Janus* 28.72–73; English translation 27b–28a Cf. *On Asthma*, chapter 13, §5 (part of the section where the two works are identical); chapter 13, §22.

[172]*Regimen of Health*, Arabic text, *Janus* 28.144; English translation 28b–29a. Cf. *On Asthma*, chapter 13, §18.

[173]*Regimen of Health*, Arabic text, *Janus* 27.296–97; English translation 21a–b. Cf. *On Asthma*, chapters 12, §8; 13, §§32, 38.

the second stage in the liver will likewise fall short, and the third stage, which takes place throughout the body, will be even more faulty. In order to digest food properly, one should exercise regularly, stop eating before reaching satiety lest the stomach become extended, and avoid physical activity, sexual intercourse, and bathing, after meals. Sleeping after meals is now, however, accepted as an aid for digestion.[174]

Foods that produce superfluities should, we have heard more than once, be avoided. Hence wheat should be eaten only in the form of bread made of unrefined flour that has been well leavened, well kneaded, salted, and oven-baked. Unleavened bread and pastas are excluded. Fresh, not overly fat milk is here considered good, as is lean white cheese, while aged cheese is extremely unhealthy because it is a "thick" food; butter is acceptable. Fat from all kinds of meat is unhealthy, as is fresh fruit. And so forth. Drinking water during or immediately after eating is harmful, with the exception—in contrast to what Maimonides wrote in the treatise *On Asthma*—of pure cold water during the meal. Wine is again highly praised when taken in moderation: It facilitates the digestion of other foods, is itself easily digested, expels superfluities through the pores, and makes urine and perspiration flow. It has still other virtues that Maimonides forbears from mentioning because Muslims are prohibited from drinking it. From what is known regarding al-Afḍal, no one would need to have had qualms about recommending wine to him, and Maimonides may have been more concerned about the sensibilities of Muslim clerics into whose hands the *Regimen* might fall.[175]

He qualifies the opinion of "the physicians"—which he accepted in his treatise *On Asthma*—that bathing daily corrupts the body's humors and that one should go to the bathhouse no more than once every ten days. In the present work he permits a brief daily bath, on the condition that the bather's stomach is empty yet hunger pangs have not set in.[176] We again hear the warning against washing one's head with cold or even lukewarm water—because residues will be retained and because the nerves originating in the brain will turn sluggish. Hot water, by contrast, helps release residues and improves the composition of the brain, "with the result that [the organism's] movements and sense faculties are strengthened."[177] Water applied to

[174]*Regimen of Health*, Arabic text, *Janus* 27.288–90, English translation 17a–18a.

[175]On food: *Regimen of Health*, chapter 1. On wine: *Regimen*, Arabic text, *Janus* 28.146; English translation 29. Maimonides, *On the Causes of Symptoms*, Arabic original, facsimile of the medieval Hebrew translation, English translation, and partial medieval Latin translation, ed. J. Leibowitz and S. Marcus (Berkeley 1974) 133r (references in this form apply equally to the Hebrew, English and Arabic texts), reveals that al-Afḍāl later asked Maimonides to instruct him on the advisability of heeding physicians who recommended taking wine for therapeutic purposes.

[176]*Regimen of Health*, Arabic text, *Janus* 28.147; English translation 30a. Cf. *On Asthma*, chapter 10, § 4, which also recommends bathing once every ten days, and *Mishneh Torah*: *H. De*ᶜ*ot* 4.16, which recommends bathing once a week. Maimonides has in mind sessions in a bathhouse where perspiring was an integral part of the procedure.

[177]*Regimen of Health*, Arabic text, *Janus* 28.147–48; English translation 30a.

the head should therefore almost burn the skin. Maimonides notes with regret that men engage in sexual intercourse for no other purpose than physical pleasure and he emphasizes that the discharge of semen is unhealthy for all except young men who have a moist constitution. It is particularly harmful for the elderly, the sick, those recovering from illness, and other men of dry constitution; for men who are hungry, thirsty, or intoxicated; when food is being digested; after the bath, before and after exercise, and on the day before and after bloodletting.[178]

Since removing superfluous materials from the body is essential, he lists a number of compounds that keep the stools soft; these were especially appropriate, since constipation was one of the problems for which al-Afḍal solicited Maimonides' advice. At the same time he repeats the warning about the use of cathartic laxatives unless absolutely needed.[179] When he mentions the physicians' "proposition that vomiting once or twice a month is very good" for maintaining health, he expresses neither approval nor disapproval, but only appends the qualification that self-induced vomiting must be restricted to patients who are strong enough to perform it and to times when the weather is not overly cold.[180] He lists materials that can be used for mild enemas, warns against enemas that are administered with harsh materials, but does not prescribe regular prophylactic use of the procedure, as he did in the treatise *On Asthma*.[181] It is tempting to speculate that he had become a little more skeptical and cautious about the medical measures at his disposal than he was in the treatise *On Asthma*. The evidence is too thin, however, to permit such a conclusion with any confidence.

Maimonides' tactic for drawing al-Afḍal out of his depression takes the form of a brief sermon on fortitude and the insignificance of the imagined goods and evils of this world.[182] In the closing paragraphs of the treatise, he turns in a different

[178]*Regimen of Health*, Arabic text, *Janus* 28.145-46; English translation 29b. Commentary on the *Aphorisms of Hippocrates* (n. 39 above) 6, §30, quotes Galen to the effect that sexual intercourse contributes to podagra. *Medical Aphorisms* (n. 26 above) 17, §9, quotes him to the effect that intercourse dries the body, and therefore benefits those whose bodies contain a surplus of vapors. *On Asthma*, chapter 10, §8, states that intercourse is very harmful for most men, that it is especially damaging to the elderly, and that overindulgence is harmful for all men. Maimonides' rabbinic and philosophical works also recommend limiting sexual activity, although there the stress is on moral and religious considerations; see *Mishneh Torah*: *H. De*ᶜ*ot* 4.19; *Guide for the Perplexed* 3.35, 49. *The Inner Secret* on sexual matters written for a member of Saladin's circle and attributed to Maimonides concedes that one select class of human males benefits from sexual intercourse, namely, men who have a hot, moist, irascible disposition, have hairy bodies, eat and drink heartily, live idle lives, and lack intellectual interests; see Arabic text and German translation in H. Kroner, *Ein Beitrag zur Geschichte der Medizin* (n. 19 above), Arabic text 7–8; German translation 32–34. Modern Hebrew translation: *Sexual Life* (n. 20 above) 27–28.

[179]*Regimen of Health*, chapter 3.

[180]*Regimen of Health*, Arabic text, *Janus* 27.299; English translation 22a. Arabic text *Janus* 27.297; English translation 21a, gives a recipe for a mild emetic.

[181]*Regimen of Health*, Arabic text, *Janus* 27.296–97; 28.145; English translation 21a, 29a.

[182]*Regimen of Health*, Arabic text, *Janus* 28.66–70; English translation 25a–27a.

direction. He recommends various substances that act through unusual properties, some of them resembling items that he cited from Ibn Zuhr in the *Medical Aphorisms*, and none so unappealing as the more distasteful concoctions that he reported there in the name of Galen.[183] Thus on the authority of skilled physicians, he informs al-Afḍal and other readers that eating rabbit flesh is shown by experience to be beneficial in cases of palsy and nerve disease, eating the brains of rabbits is helpful in cases of palsy, wearing rabbit fur is "beneficial in diseases of the nerves, especially for the elderly," and wearing sheep fur or squirrel pelts contributes generally to human health. Wearing fox fur or cat fur is, on the contrary, harmful. Just to smell the breath of cats is unhealthy, while smelling that of pigeons protects one against a variety of nervous conditions. Experience has moreover established that the wild ass has an "extraordinary property in strengthening vision." Eating its flesh and exposing one's eyes to vapors rising from cooked ass meat strengthens vision and opens blocked nerves, and human vision benefits merely from looking constantly into the eyes of the wild ass.[184]

The *Regimen of Health* enjoyed considerable popularity. It circulated in Arabic, Hebrew, and Latin, and the Latin translation was printed a number of times in the fifteenth and sixteenth centuries.[185]

7. *A Treatise Setting Forth Certain Symptoms and Answering Them* (known in English under the title: *On the Causes of Symptoms*).[186] It was intended for the same person, Saladin's son al-Afḍal, for whom the *Regimen of Health* was written and in half a dozen places it asks the addressee to refer back to the *Regimen*.[187] Al-Afḍal had on this occasion sent Maimonides a very detailed account of his current symptoms. Maimonides, who continues to observe the etiquette of speaking as a "most humble slave" to his "master," flatters al-Afḍal with the assurance that highly proficient physicians of the day could not have described symptoms so comprehensively and meticulously as the prince had done.[188] Since al-Afḍal's message to Maimonides has not been preserved and Maimonides does not mention what the patient's symptoms now were, we cannot tell how far the medical problems forming the subject of the *Regimen of Health* had been resolved. It is nonetheless evident from Maimonides' advice that al-Afḍal still suffered from depression and that hemorrhoids together with a real or imagined heart condition had added themselves to his woes. Whatever the prince's medical problems, they

[183]Above, p. 449.

[184]*Regimen of Health*, Arabic text, *Janus* 28.151–52; English translation 31b. For the medicaments with unusual properties in the *Medical Aphorisms*, see above, p. 450.

[185]Steinschneider, *Die hebraeischen Übersetzungen des Mittlealters* (n. 30 above) 771, lists one incunabulum of the *Regimen* and four sixteenth-century imprints of the Latin translation.

[186]Maimonides, *On the Causes of Symptoms* (n. 175 above).

[187]*On the Causes of Symptoms* 136v, 142v, 144v, 156r, 141, 150, 184, 186. Al-Afḍāl's name is alluded to at the end of the Arabic text.

[188]*On the Causes of Symptoms* 131r.

scarcely seem to have been life-threatening. He had a good three decades of life before him.

Al-Afḍal asked Maimonides to review measures that had been recommended to him by other physicians, and much of Maimonides' treatise consists in comments on the recommendations; he accepts some but rejects or corrects more than half. The prince apparently requested or intimated that he would like Maimonides to come to see him. Maimonides declares that nothing could have afforded him more delight, nor could any experience have been more sublime, than presenting himself before al-Afḍal and treating the prince in person.[189] Nothing, in other words, could be more delightful and sublime than leaving the comfort and safety of home, submitting to the arduous and dangerous journey to Syria or Palestine, and joining the circle of physicians in attendance on the young, idle hypochondriac. Unfortunately, Maimonides informs the prince, old age and weakness prevented him from making the trip.[190]

A look at Maimonides' opinion regarding a couple of the measures proposed by the other physicians may be illuminating. One physician had advised al-Afḍal to employ hot sitz baths and poultices in order to open veins—plainly hemorrhoids—that were causing him trouble and thereby release the blood they contained, while another physician wanted to let nature take its course without human intervention. Maimonides replies that the former opinion was in error and the latter, correct; first, hot baths and poultices could heat the body's constitution and "scorch the humors," and secondly, nature knows best what, and how much, to expel from the body. There is a possible advance here over the treatise *On Hemorrhoids*, where Maimonides not only prescribed hot baths for hemorrhoids but also stressed the need to bleed persons suffering from the condition in order to remove excess black bile from their systems. He has not, however, become as enlightened as might be hoped, since he does not completely rule out treatment by bleeding: He concedes that he himself had encountered situations like the present one in which the affected parts were so swollen and painful that he had to employ medications to open the veins and extract blood.[191] At a later point in the treatise, he remarks that certain medical conditions "unquestionably" require bloodletting through venesection.[192]

A second example: One of al-Afḍal's physicians had recommended that he take a potion made from chicory, sandalwood, tamarind, plums [or: pears], and jujube. That, Maimonides writes, was a terrible mistake. The combination, and especially the inclusion of plums—or: pears—and jujube, is appropriate only for persons in whom yellow bile is predominant. From al-Afḍal's letter, Maimonides had determined that the prince suffered from the presence of black fumes in his system, which would ascend to his heart and brain. Such fumes must have been generated

[189] *On the Causes of Symptoms* 151, 187.
[190] *On the Causes of Symptoms* 151, 187.
[191] *On the Causes of Symptoms* 131v–33r.
[192] *On the Causes of Symptoms* 142r–v.

from black bile, which in turn must have been generated from the periodic "burning" of phlegm;[193] whence Maimonides inferred that phlegm, not yellow bile, was the predominant humor in al-Afḍal's constitution. Administering the potion described to someone in whom phlegm is predominant idles and moistens the person's stomach, cuts short the digestive process that takes place in the stomach, and results in the corruption of all three stages of digestion.[194]

The cynosure of the treatise is a recipe for a cardiac medicine copied from Avicenna. The recipe requires more than thirty ingredients, namely: pearls, amber, coral, gold filings, "Armenian rock," lapis lazuli, shredded silk, roasted river crab, the herb oxtongue, saffron, cardamom, cubeb, chicory seed, cucumber seed, nard, red rose, musk, camphor, two kinds of cinnamon, and a dozen other materials. The compound can be formed into lozenges or mixed with honey to make a paste. Besides the basic formulation, which is the one that Maimonides prescribes for al-Afḍal, he also describes variant versions drawn up by Avicenna for persons whose constitution is hotter or colder than average.[195]

He concludes by providing al-Afḍal with two daily schedules, one to be followed in the summer and the other in the winter. Al-Afḍal is to arise by sunup in the winter and an hour after sunup in the summer. Maimonides prescribes tonics that he should drink during the day, medicaments, including Avicenna's heart remedy, that he should take during the week, and what he should eat both on the assumption that he was used to having one full meal a day and on the assumption that he was used to having two. He should go riding each morning, rest until his breathing returns to normal, eat his main meal, then lie down and have a musician sing and play for an hour, whereupon he should fall into a deep sleep. In the afternoon he should either read or converse with congenial friends, with the object of "expanding" his spirit and creating pleasant thoughts. In the evening he should sip wine buffered with rose water and oxtongue. After a second full meal or a snack, depending on what he was accustomed to, he should summon the musician to play for two more hours and fall into another deep sleep for the night.[196] Music and pleasant conversation were generally recognized therapies for depression.[197]

Al-Afḍal had informed Maimonides that he had reduced his sexual activity, and Maimonides congratulates him on the wise step.[198] The prince was not yet ready for complete celibacy, however, and Maimonides therefore sets times for him to engage in sexual intercourse: either in the early evening before supper, or at night

[193]*Medical Aphorisms* 2, §28, by contrast, quotes Galen as saying that phlegm is the only humor from which black bile cannot be generated. Avicenna held that black bile could result from phlegm's being burnt; see R. Klibansky, E. Panofsky, F. Saxl, *Saturn* and *Melancholy* (London 1964) 88.

[194]*On the Causes of Symptoms* 135v–36r, taken together with 156v.

[195]*On the Causes of Symptoms* 145r–46v.

[196]*On the Causes of Symptoms* 152v–56v.

[197]Klibansky, *Saturn and Melancholy* 85, 267.

[198]*On the Causes of Symptoms* 143v.

after he had digested his evening meal, but in both instances when his stomach was not entirely empty. Maimonides also instructs him how to adjust his exercise, nap, and tonic on days on which he goes to the bath.[199]

It will be remembered that al-Afḍal was in his twenties or early thirties at the time. Maimonides undoubtedly had reason to assume that the prince's official duties were not overly taxing.

The present *Treatise*, like the *Regimen of Health*, was translated into Hebrew and Latin, and an incomplete version of the Latin was published together with the *Regimen of Health* a half dozen times in the fifteenth and early sixteenth centuries.

8. A short, untitled treatise on improving sexual performance[200] written for an unnamed Muslim who must have been a figure of standing. Maimonides addresses him as his "exalted master" (*mawlā*), calls himself the man's "servant" (*khādim*), and writes that the man "commanded" him to solve the problem.[201]

The unnamed Muslim personage asked Maimonides to recommend measures for increasing his sexual potency. His ability to have sexual intercourse had flagged, he had become extremely thin, and he was concerned about the condition of his body. Nevertheless there were a number of young ladies to whom he had responsibilities, and he made clear to Maimonides that he did not want to hear a word about reducing his sexual activity. He also did not want a difficult regimen.[202] Maimonides recommends mental attitudes to cultivate, the types of partners to choose and avoid, foods that increase blood volume and thereby increase the supply of semen, foods to be avoided, compounds to be ingested for their aphrodisiac virtues, bathing schedules, massage of the lower extremities designed to keep them warm, and ointments that, when applied regularly, make it possible for an erection to be sustained after ejaculation. A few of the recipes are cited in the names of Avicenna and Ibn Zuhr. The former, for example, prescribed a patty made of the brains of fifty small birds, thirty egg yolks, fifty dirham weights of butter, small amounts of onion juice and carrot juice, juice from a piece of chopped lamb, salt, and spices;[203] cholesterol was not a concern in those days. The latter prescribed a "medication . . . beneficial for deficient erections, semen,

[199] *On the Causes of Symptoms* 139–43, 184.

[200] Arabic original and German translation: H. Kroner, "Eine medicinische Maimonides-Handschrift aus Granada," *Janus* 21 (1916) 203–47. Medieval Hebrew translations: Kroner, *Ein Beitrag zur Geschichte der Medizin* (n. 19 above), and Moshe ben Maimon, *On Hemorrhoids, On the Increase of Physical Vigour, On Asthma* (n. 10 above). English translation from the Hebrew: Maimonides, *Treatises on Poisons, Hemorrhoids, Cohabitation* (n. 20 above). Fragments of a draft in Maimonides' own hand are edited by Stern, *Maimonidis commentarius in Mischnam* (n. 16 above) 3.18–21. Manuscripts of a Latin translation have also been preserved.

[201] Kroner, "Eine Medicinische Maimonides-Handschrift aus Granada," chapters 1, 10.

[202] Kroner, "Eine Medicinische Maimonides-Handschrift aus Granada," chapter 1.

[203] Kroner, "Eine Medicinische Maimonides-Handschrift aus Granada," 225, 235; English translation 172.

and desire," the most distinctive ingredient of which is fox testicle (perhaps a plant).[204] Maimonides endorses both recipes, and several of the dozen and a half additional compounds that he recommends for ingestion contain ingredients of a similar character.[205]

Compositions on enhancing sexual potency had a considerable history in Arabic medical literature.[206] Maimonides repeatedly advises his readers to limit sexual intercourse for both medical and ethical reasons, and just how comfortable he felt about contributing to the potency genre can only be guessed. However that may be, medieval Hebrew readers must have found the subject to have a certain interest. The present composition was translated from Arabic into Hebrew three or four times in the Middle Ages.[207]

9. *Explanation of the Names of Drugs* (*Sharḥ Asmā' al-ᶜUqqār*),[208] which is not so much a medical text as a pharmaceutical glossary. Lists of pharmaceutical materials for the use of practicing physicians are as old as Greek medicine, and Arabic writers prior to Maimonides produced a number of them.[209] Maimonides' glossary is concerned not with the medical use to which the various materials can be put but only with what the terms denote. Drawing upon five Arabic authors, whom he names, he lists 405 pharmaceutical terms, mostly for materials derived from plants, but some for materials of mineral and animal origin. He gives equivalents in Arabic, Greek, Syriac, Persian, Spanish, and Berber, yet never in Hebrew. In a number of places, he notes what a given term meant "among us in the West" and in some instances, furnishes the equivalent in the Egyptian Arabic dialect.

10. *On Poisons and Their Antidotes* (commissioned by al-Qāḍī al-Fāḍil, Saladin's vizier and Maimonides' patron).[210] Maimonides writes that in Ramadan,

[204]Kroner, "Eine Medicinische Maimonides-Handschrift aus Granada," 228, 238; English translation 177–78.

[205]Similarly, Maimonides, *Medical Aphorisms* 22, §§42, 50.

[206]See Ullmann, *Medizin im Islam* (n. 30 above) 193–98; G. Bos, "Ibn al-Jazzār on Sexuality and Sexual Dysfunction," *Jerusalem Studies in Arabic and Islam* 19 (1995) 250–51.

[207]Beit Arie, "*Targumim bilti Yeduᶜim*" (n. 22 above) 567–68; Tz. Langermann, "Some New Medical Manuscripts from Moscow," *Korot* 10 (1993–1994) 55.

[208]Arabic original and French translation: Maimonides, *Un glossaire de matière médicale*, ed. and trans. M. Meyerhof (Cairo 1940); Meyerhof's introduction traces a series of works on the same subject. Modern Hebrew translation: Maimonides, *Lexicography of Drugs*; *Medical Responses*, trans. S. Muntner (Jerusalem 1969). English translation from the French: Moses Maimonides, *Glossary of Drug Names*, trans. F. Rosner (Philadelphia 1979).

[209]See M. Levey, *Early Arabic Pharmacology* (Leiden 1973), chapters 6 and 9.

[210]A facsimile of the composition from an Arabic manuscript written in Hebrew characters is reproduced in Moses Maimonides, *Treatise on Poisons and Their Antidotes*, trans. S. Muntner (Philadelphia 1966). Medieval Hebrew translation: Moses ben Maimon, *Same ha-Mawet*, ed. S. Muntner (Jerusalem 1942). German translation: M. Steinschneider, "Gifte und ihre Heilung," *Archiv für pathologische Anatomie und Physiologie* 57 (1873) 62–120. English translation:

1199, six years after Saladin's death and some time after al-Fāḍil had retired from public office, he instructed Maimonides, "the least of his slaves," to compose a manual for the population on the treatment of poisonous bites. Since Maimonides makes a point of noting that the work was commissioned in Ramadan, he plainly understood that al-Fāḍil's intent was to perform a charitable act on the occasion of the sacred Muslim month. Maimonides' introduction opens with fulsome flattery of his patron. He recalls that on a previous occasion al-Fāḍil had, at considerable expense to himself, arranged to have two antidotes, "the great theriac and the electuary of Mithridates," prepared for victims of poisonous bites in Egypt. Theriacs and mithridate are strange concoctions of miscellaneous materials which entered the history of medicine prior to Galen and maintained an astonishing popularity into eighteenth-century Europe; they were originally intended as antidotes for poisons but they also came to be used prophylactically and therapeutically for other purposes.[211]

Maimonides stresses that he was making no pretense of originality.[212] The most acceptable pieces of advice that he gives had, like the dubious theriac and mithridate, a millennium long history: In the case of poisonous bites, he counsels that a tourniquet be applied above the wound, incisions made, and the poison sucked out; and for ingested poisons, he counsels that vomiting be induced.[213] The remainder of the work is devoted primarily to compounds that may be taken as antidotes against different poisons.

11. *The Inner Secret*: *A Memorandum for Noblemen, and Tried and True Devices for the Highborn*[214] (of uncertain authenticity). It is a comprehensive treatise on sexual matters, dedicated to "al-Muẓaffar b. Ayyūb, king of Ḥamāt [in Syria]," who in turn may be identical with a nephew of Saladin's better known as Taqī al-Dīn ᶜUmar b. Nūr al-Dawla Shāhanshāh b. Ayyūb.[215] Taqī al-Dīn was born in 1139, died in 1191, and spent time in Egypt. The author begins by discussing the benefits and damage that come from sexual intercourse and then

---

Maimonides, *Treatises on Poisons, Hemorrhoids, Cohabitation* (n. 20 above). Bibliographical information on the genre is given by M. Steinschneider, "Die toxicologischen Schriften der Araber bis Ende XII. Jahrhunderts," *Archiv für pathologische Anatomie und Physiologie* 52 (1871) 340–75, 467–503; Ullmann, *Medizin im Islam* 321–42.

[211]On the history of theriacs and mithridate from ancient to early modern times, see G. Watson, *Theriac and Mithridatium* (London 1966) 10–44, 106–8, 140–48, 150.

[212]Maimonides, *Same ha-Mawet* 93–94; English translation 33–36.

[213]*Same ha-Mawet* 97, 140; English translation 39, 82. These practical measures, which continue to be employed in our day, go back to ancient medicine; see Watson, *Theriac and Mithridatium* 1, 17.

[214]For the Arabic text, German translation, and modern Hebrew translation, see above, n. 178. English translation: Maimonides "*On Sexual Intercourse*" (n. 25 above) 61–82. The English translator, like Muntner (n. 20 above), rejects the attribution to Maimonides.

[215]The identification of al-Muẓaffar with Saladin's nephew was made by M. Steinschneider in *Jeschurun* 5 (1865) 185.

prescribes multiple concoctions and ointments for a variety of purposes—for either increasing the sexual drive or suppressing it, for creating good mouth odor in order to attract sexual partners or bad odor in order to repel them, for strengthening penile erections and sustaining them, for preserving youthful feminine breast shape, encouraging or discouraging sexual desire in one's partner, restoring the hymen of a nonvirgin, promoting hair growth in armpits and the genital area, removing hair, and treating insomnia. This is the composition whose attribution to Maimonides depends solely on the heading in the manuscripts and the authenticity of which has been questioned.

12. *Epistle on the Length of Life* (probably misattributed). An anonymous Arabic commentary on Maimonides' *Mishneh Torah*, preserved in a manuscript of Yemenite provenance,[216] digresses at one point and records a question that, it relates, "the Moses of the age" was asked by "his student Joseph ben Judah." The answer to the question, which then follows, was given the title "On the Length of Life" by its first modern editor. The answer is substantial, extending 115 lines in the printed edition, and a little more than half is medical in character. Neither the question nor the answer is known from any other source.

Although the commentator on the *Mishneh Torah* who has preserved the question and answer attributes the former to Joseph ben Judah and the latter to "the Moses of the age," by which he plainly means Maimonides,[217] the question and answer themselves do not mention either name. Nor does the answer refer to any of Maimonides' works, despite Maimonides' having dealt with the core of the issue elsewhere, and despite his habit, when writing one work, of referring to others in which he dealt with the same topics. As far as I know, doubts have never been expressed regarding his authorship of the *Epistle*.

The anonymous commentator on the *Mishneh Torah* writes: "I thought it appropriate to record for you a matter about which the Moses of the age was asked. His student Joseph ben Judah asked him: 'Is the life of a man in the present world set at a fixed span [*ajal*], which the man must reach, and are deleterious factors unable to destroy the man [before he reaches it]? Or are such factors able to destroy the man [before his time] . . . should he fail to protect himself against them."[218] The notion of a predetermined life span that cannot be diminished or exceeded is common in Islam, where it ordinarily is God who is understood to ordain the length of life.[219] The notion can fit as comfortably into an astrological framework, where

[216]Oxford, Bodleian Library, Hebrew MS Opp. Add 8vo 46 (=Neubauer 2497b).

[217]See above, p. 62, n. 258.

[218]Maimonides, *Über die Lebensdauer*, ed. and German trans. G. Weil (Basel 1953) 12, 16. It was reedited as: *Teshubat ha-Rambam Bi-she'elat ha-Qeṣ ha-Qaṣub*, ed. and Hebrew trans. G. Weil and M. Schwarz (Tel Aviv 1979) 18, 27 (henceforth cited as: *Lebensdauer*, Hebrew edition). English translation: Rosner, *Medical Legacy of Moses Maimonides* (n. 14 above) 249–58.

[219]See *Encyclopedia of Islam*, 2nd ed., s.v. *adjal*.

the agents determining the length of a person's life would be the stars.[220] And rabbinic midrashic literature also knows of the opinion that "from the moment a person is born, it is decreed how many years he will live; if he merits, he completes his years, and if not, they are reduced." The reason given there is not theological or astrological but simply a pair of biblical verses.[221]

After reporting the question, the commentator quotes the answer that constitutes the *Epistle on the Length of Life*. The answer begins with an unambiguous declaration: "Our position is that there is *no* fixed life span" (*ajal*). "A living being continues to live as long as whatever diminution occurs in his essential moisture is resupplied, . . . in accordance with Galen's statement that the cause of death is a loss of equilibrium in the innate heat."[222] The *Epistle*, as we have it, proceeds to list a number of physical conditions that can upset a person's innate heat and thereby bring about his demise. If, for example, the body becomes inordinately hot, the innate heat may be "dissolved." An inordinate cooling of the body can "freeze" the innate heat.[223] The shock of sudden pleasure may dissipate the innate heat and thereby extinguish it, in the way that a strong draft extinguishes a candle.[224] The breathing in of noxious fumes may smother it, as a candle's flame is extinguished by smoke.[225] And so on. As a final consideration, the *Epistle* observes that severe physical trauma can also cause death by sundering the organism's unity.[226]

The first part of the *Epistle* arrives at the conclusion that if someone protects himself against the conditions listed, factors tending to shorten human life will not "destroy him" and he will reach his maximum "natural life."[227] In order to make

[220]For a suggestion of that usage, see A. Ibn Ezra, alternate Commentary on Genesis 6:3. The term *ajal* had a natural sense as well, namely, the maximum life span that a particular person's physiology permits; see the passage from Avicenna's *Qānūn* quoted in *Über die Lebensdauer*, Hebrew edition 60. In that sense of the term, the actual length of the person's life is not unalterable; that therefore cannot be the sense in which the term is used in the question addressed to the author of the present *Epistle*. *Über die Lebensdauer* at one point contrasts the term *ajal* in the sense of "length of life" with *ajal maḥtūm*, "fixed length of life"; see Hebrew edition 25.

[221]*Ecclesiastes Rabba* 3.3, citing Ecclesiastes 3:2, and Proverbs 10:27. The opposing opinion cited there is that "if he merits, years are added, and if not his years are reduced." BT *Yebamot* 49b cites a different biblical verse showing that a person's life cannot exceed the number of years set for him at birth.

[222]*Über die Lebensdauer*12, 16; Hebrew edition 18, 27.

[223]*Über die Lebensdauer* 12, 17; Hebrew edition 19, 27–28.

[224]*Über die Lebensdauer* 13, 17–18; Hebrew edition 20, 28.

[225]*Über die Lebensdauer* 13–14, 18–19; Hebrew edition 21, 29. The role of the essential moisture of the body in longevity and the metaphor of the candle could have been learned by the author from a pseudo-Galenic work or from Avicenna. See *Über die Lebensdauer*, Hebrew edition 98–101; M. McVaugh, "The 'Humidum Radicale' in Thirteenth-Century Medicine," *Traditio* 30 (1974) 267–68.

[226]*Über die Lebensdauer* 14, 19; Hebrew edition 22, 30.

[227]*Über die Lebensdauer* 14, 19–20; Hebrew edition 22–23, 30.

sense of what has been said thus far, we must understand that every human being has a natural maximum length of life, although not a predetermined and unalterable life span.[228]

At this point, after having completed his medical arguments, the author of the *Epistle* is quoted as making the following statement, which sounds like the introduction to the entire treatise: "I shall adduce two kinds of proof to support my position—first, proofs from Scripture, and, second, proofs from nature." The *Epistle* goes on to cite a number of scriptural passages implying that actions taken by human beings can affect the length of life. Scripture, for instance, instructs the home owner: "Make a parapet for thy roof that thou bring not blood upon thy house should any man fall from thence"; if erecting parapets prevents premature accidental death and extends human life, while the failure to do so shortens life, the human life span is not fixed. The prophet Jeremiah warned in the name of the Lord: "He that abideth in this city shall die by the sword and by the famine and by the pestilence; but he that goeth out and falleth away to the Chaldeans . . . shall live."[229] If decisions by the city's inhabitants could shorten or extend their lives, the human life span is, again, not predetermined. After presenting all its arguments from Scripture, the *Epistle* ends. A problematic closing sentence from the hand of the commentator who preserved the *Epistle* seems to say that he had not copied the work in its entirety.[230]

As the modern editor of the text observed, the original order of the arguments is apparently reversed in the version that has reached us. Whereas the author of the *Epistle* is quoted as stating that he would present his arguments from Scripture first, they are the second of the two sets of arguments in the preserved version. The medical arguments, presumably identical with the proofs from nature which the author said would come second, have been moved to the first position. And the introductory statement in which the author lays out the procedure that he intended to pursue has been plumped down between the two sets of arguments and not left where it belongs, at the beginning. Why the anonymous commentator on the *Mishneh Torah* or the source from which he copied should have inverted the order is unclear.[231]

Joseph ben Judah was in correspondence with Maimonides during two periods. Maimonides first heard from him when Joseph arrived in Alexandria from his home

[228] A notion of the sort is found in: (1) Averroes, Middle Commentary on Aristotle's *De Generatione*, Hebrew text, ed. S. Kurland (Cambridge, Mass. 1958) 90; English translation: Averroes, Middle Commentary on Aristotle's *De Generatione*, trans S. Kurland (Cambridge, Mass. 1958) 102. (2) The commentary on the Book of Proverbs attributed to Ibn Ezra, 10:27; 11:4, 17.

[229] *Über die Lebensdauer* 14–15, 20, 22; Hebrew edition 23, 25, 30, 32; Deuteronomy 22:8; Jeremiah 21:9.

[230] *Über die Lebensdauer*, Hebrew edition 26, 32, and note 47.

[231] Weil, *Über die Lebensdauer* 26; Hebrew edition 36 offers a possible, although not overly convincing explanation.

in the West and sent "letters" and literary compositions to Maimonides in order to introduce himself. Nothing is known about those letters apart from a page of one which has been discovered and is replete with rhetoric but says nothing specific[232] and a remark of Maimonides' to the effect that before meeting Joseph, he had been impressed by the latter's eagerness to study science.[233] After Joseph left Egypt for Syria, probably in the mid-1180s, the two were in correspondence again. Several of Maimonides' letters to Joseph from the second period have been preserved and they are infused with particular warmth for his favorite student. By contrast, the *Epistle on the Length of Life*, as we have it, is completely impersonal and devoid of the slightest hint that the author knew the man to whom he was writing. We thus have one indication that the present exchange did not take place between the two after Joseph left Egypt.

Joseph became close to Maimonides when he lived in Egypt and during that time studied Maimonides' *Mishneh Torah*.[234] No one familiar with Maimonides and the *Mishneh Torah* would need to solicit his opinion on the question whether the human life span is fixed unalterably by God, the stars, or some other factor; anybody who had been privileged to associate with Maimonides would realize, without asking, that he would dismiss the proposition out of hand. Joseph was, moreover, trained in medical theory by the early 1190s, and a letter of Maimonides' written around then advises him to support himself by teaching medical texts.[235] Yet the medical information in the *Epistle* which is represented as having been sent by Maimonides to Joseph is elementary and hardly what one educated physician would need to expound in detail to another.

It can therefore be taken as more or less certain that the question about a fixed human life span was not addressed by Joseph to Maimonides, and the present *Epistle* not sent by Maimonides to Joseph, after they had parted and Joseph had moved to Syria. If the question was indeed sent by Joseph to Maimonides, it would have to have been included among the letters that he dispatched from Alexandria before the two met. Although Maimonides sometimes did not bother to answer questioners, he will have to be assumed on this occasion to have generously penned a substantial reply to a question from a complete stranger. When he reminisces about the letters sent to him by Joseph from Alexandria he mentions no such question nor any reply on his part.

Having come this far, we must ask whether the names of Joseph and Maimonides may not have been attached to the *Epistle* in error. The circumstance that the anonymous commentator on the *Mishneh Torah* who has preserved the question and answer attributes them to Maimonides and his student is hardly probative; we are already familiar with the penchant of scribes for attaching

[232]Moses ben Maimon, *Epistulae* (n. 9 above) 5–6.

[233]Maimonides, *Guide for the Perplexed*, Dedicatory Preface.

[234]Moses ben Maimon, *Epistulae* 68–69.

[235]Moses ben Maimon, *Epistulae* 68.

Maimonides' name to compositions that he did not write. After someone in the chain of transmission—whether the commentator himself or someone preceding him—guessed that Maimonides was the author of the *Epistle*, either he or another helpful party could have taken the further step of affixing Joseph's name to the question on the supposition that Joseph was a logical person to have addressed it to Maimonides.

The following should be taken into account. The *Epistle* opens by stating that human beings continue to live as long as their essential moisture is maintained but then it jumps, without transition, to the proposition that the cause of death is a disturbance in the equilibrium of the innate heat. No effort whatsoever is made to link the two factors—although it is known from Avicenna that a link could be made[236]—and, as the *Epistle* proceeds, the role of essential moisture is forgotten. Moreover, as we have seen, Maimonides' authentic medical works focus almost obsessively on the digestive process and the modulation of the four humors and consistently identify the humors as the critical factor in human health and illness. Maimonides barely mentions the role of innate heat and, as far as I could discover, never mentions the body's essential moisture as factors in human physiology.

Most telling, however, are the words with which the author of the *Epistle* introduces his arguments from Scripture. He writes that he will present those arguments before offering arguments from nature because Scripture "is the end to which we attain after the propaedeutic sciences [*ᶜulūm riyāḍiyya*], namely, [after] the mathematical, the natural [or: physical], and the metaphysical [sciences], . . . and it [that is, Scripture] leads man to his final eudaemonia."[237] The statement runs counter to Maimonides' outlook, for he never relegated the philosophic sciences to a subservient status vis-à-vis Scripture. He viewed the relationship as synergistic, with Scripture supplying knowledge of the universe not accessible to physical and metaphysical science, such as the creation of the world[238] and the uniqueness of the Mosaic prophecy; and with science leading man to a correct understanding of Scripture, by guiding him, for example, to the allegorization of anthropomorphic descriptions of God. When Maimonides outlined the process whereby man attains intellectual perfection and hence eudaemonia, he unambiguously represented

[236]Weil, *Über die Lebensdauer* 46; Hebrew edition 59, points out that for Avicenna, the inborn heat modulates the essential moisture of the body. Aristotle, *De Longitudine et Brevitate Vitae* 5, states that the "moist" and the "hot" are the factors in the body determining length of life.

[237]*Über die Lebensdauer* 14, 20; Hebrew edition 23, 30. An alternative translation: The scriptural arguments "are the end to which we attain . . . and they lead man. . . ." By—apparently—labeling the mathematical, physical, and metaphysical sciences all as propaedeutic, the *Epistle* commits an additional inaccuracy, for in medieval Aristotelian usage, the mathematical sciences alone are propaedeutic sciences. Maimonides, Commentary on the Mishna, *Rosh ha-Shana* 2:7 (end), thus uses the term "propaedeutic sciences" as a designation for mathematics and the mathematical side of astronomy.

[238]Maimonides' position is that the arguments in favor of creation are stronger than those against, but no strict demonstration is possible. See above, p. 370.

mathematics and physical science as a *preparative* (*tawṭi'a*) and metaphysics as the *end* (*ghāya*), with no hint that the study of Scripture forms a further, crowning stage.[239]

Someone, we have seen, apparently meddled with the order of the arguments in the *Epistle on the Length of Life*, and the commentator who preserved the *Epistle* seems to have abbreviated it. Features in the *Epistle* which can be squared only with difficulty or not at all with Maimonides' authorship could conceivably be additional mischief wrought by the commentator or another busybody, who preceded him. Behind our version there may conceivably have stood an authentic composition of Maimonides' which was better thought out and did not clash with Maimonides' genuine views. Whether or not that is the case, the version of the *Epistle* which has come down to us cannot be from his hand. If wholly inauthentic, as seems probable, the *Epistle* furnishes additional evidence of the powerful magnetic field that formed around Maimonides' name and attracted works to him which he did not write.

So much for the medical works written by or commonly attributed to Maimonides.

Maimonides' System of Medicine. Maimonides stresses to Joseph ben Judah that a physician should say "nothing [regarding his patients' conditions and treatments] without knowing a proof of what he says, without knowing where the proof is stated and what the reasoning underlying it is."[240] The implied premise that medical practice must be grounded in medical theory had been championed by Galen,[241] and Maimonides defends it anew in his treatise *On Asthma.*

Immediately after the sentences quoted earlier from the treatise *On Asthma* which sound like an application for employment,[242] he writes: The "art of medicine" rests on both "experience and reasoning, and the things known by experience are much more numerous than those known through reasoning." Because experience plays a quantitatively larger role, people tend to consider nothing else. They say: "Consult the experienced man, not the physician." Or: "So and so may not be a man of science but he has experience, training, and practical skill." Maimonides discerns a twofold error here. First, since any individual's experience is inevitably limited, the physician must go beyond his own experience and call upon that of the ages; consequently, study of the writings of prior physicians going back to Galen and Hippocrates is integral even to the experiential side of medicine. Secondly, although the empirical details in medicine are numerically greater than the theoretical principles, "science is the root, whereas the practical [part] is the branch; and there

[239]See *Guide for the Perplexed* 1:34; 3:51.

[240]Letter to Joseph ben Judah, quoted above, p. 68.

[241]For example, Galen, *On Examinations by Which the Best Physicians Are Recognized*, ed. and trans. A. Iskandar (Berlin 1988) 151–52.

[242]Above, pp. 459–60.

can be no branch without a root." Consequently, while it is possible for someone to "know the art of medicine and control its roots and branches" through studying books and without undergoing clinical training under "masters in the art," the converse, that a man might acquire expertise solely through having "seen and observed practice," is wholly "impossible." More rhetorically: The practitioner who is possessed of experience but does not know the logic of medical science is "blind," and a patient placing himself in the hands of such a practitioner is like the seafarer who surrenders himself to the "blowing of the winds, which do not follow a logical pattern." It will be a matter of pure chance whether the man survives or drowns. Maimonides, as is his wont in medical contexts, lays no claim to originality in what he has said. He makes clear that he is drawing on the authority of Hippocrates and Galen.[243]

Today, we have come to expect dramatic advances in medical science by the month, and medical textbooks are discarded as obsolete every few years; the theory that Maimonides is talking about is, by contrast, almost exclusively the thousand-year-old Galenic heirloom. When Galen is considered within the context of his own age, he can be seen to have taken admirable steps in the direction of a scientific account of the human organism. He could be a fine observer, he performed experiments on living beings in order to test hypotheses, and he was able to correct some misconceptions of his predecessors.[244] But when measured against what the science of medicine means today, his efforts are as the halting infantile steps of a future marathon runner. From Galen's time to Maimonides'—and for centuries thereafter—medical theory remained stalled at the point where Galen left it. Maimonides' mental makeup was such that it was congenial for him to look to the past for the acme of human achievement in a given area. Although he did not hesitate to attack Galen when he found him crossing the line from medicine into philosophy, he never dreamt of breaking out of the hoary Galenic framework in the area of medicine itself.[245]

He almost certainly never performed, or was present at, a human autopsy. His knowledge of physiology came from Galen's reports of dissections of apes and other animals,[246] supplemented by his own rabbinic studies and actual examination of slaughtered animals in order to determine whether they satisfied ritual standards. Although he thereby gained familiarity with the major internal organs, he, like Galen, badly misread the organs' functions. He had no understanding of the

[243]*On Asthma* (n. 10 above), chapter 11, §3; 13, §§28–31. The analogy between medicine and piloting a ship was old; see Galen, *On Examinations by Which the Best Physicians Are Recognized* 147.

[244]Siegel, *Galen's System of Physiology and Medicine* (n. 89 above) 160, 163. D. Furley and J. Wilkie, *Galen on Respiration and the Arteries* (Princeton 1984) 47–52; the authors point out that Galen was not the first to perform physiological experiments.

[245]*Medical Aphorisms*, 25, §59.

[246]See M. May's introduction to her edition of *Galen on the Usefulness of the Parts of the Body* (Ithaca 1968) 40–41.

purpose of respiration,[247] assigned the brain a direct role in the respiratory process,[248] had no inkling of the circulation of the blood,[249] believed that what is carried in the arteries, as distinct from the veins, is primarily pneuma and to only a smaller extent a rarefied form of blood.[250] He supposed that the liver receives juices produced by digestion in the stomach and transforms them into humors for the use of the rest of the body,[251] that the spleen and gall bladder have the function of cleansing blood of unhealthy yellow and black bile.[252] Blood corpuscles, female ova, bacteria, viruses, and all the other microscopic or barely visible components of the animal organism lay well beyond the horizon.

He had not the slightest reservation about the tradition, even older than Galen,[253] which reduced body chemistry to the four humors, which regarded maintenance of the humors in a proper state and correct proportions as the cardinal factor in health, and which attributed a long list of diseases to the presence of unhealthy humors in the body or an excess of healthy ones.[254] In his Commentary

[247]*Mishneh Torah*: *H. Roṣeaḥ* 3.9.

[248]*Medical Aphorisms* 1, §§41–42.

[249]See *Medical Aphorisms* 1, §§3–6, 19–20, 50, 53. No reputable historian of medicine imagines that Galen recognized the circulation of blood. He thought that all blood flows outward, from its source in the center of the body—through veins stemming from the liver and through arteries stemming from the heart—to the body's periphery. See Siegel, *Galen's System of Physiology and Medicine* 47–56, 83–87. It has been argued that Galen did have some understanding of the "minor circulation" of blood between heart and lungs, but the texts of Galen do not bear that supposition out either; see C. Harris, *The Heart and the Vascular System in Ancient Greek Medicine* (Oxford 1973) 314–22. Ibn al-Nafīs, a thirteenth-century Egyptian physician, has also been credited with recognition of the "minor circulation" between heart and lungs. See *Encyclopedia of Islam*, 2nd ed., s.v. Ibn al-Nafīs.

J. Leibowitz, "Harveian Items in Hebrew Language," *Harofé Haivri* (1957) 2.138, calls attention to Maimonides, *Medical Aphorisms* 4, §44, as having possible bearing on the movement of the blood, but he makes clear that Maimonides' statement is "far from being identical with Harvey's revolutionary concept of the circulation." Rosner, *Medical Legacy of Moses Maimonides* (n. 14 above) 51, cites the same passage in the *Medical Aphorisms* as evidence that Maimonides—Rosner should instead have written "Galen," whom Maimonides is quoting— did furnish an "unbelievable description of blood circulation." In fact, Maimonides is talking there about the "movement," perhaps the pulsation, of the arteries—Galen believed that the arteries are themselves responsible for their pulsation—and makes no mention of blood.

[250]*Medical Aphorisms* 1, §19. Maimonides appears to go beyond Galen; see Galen, *De usu partium* 6.16; *De facultatibus naturalibus* 3.14. One of Galen's significant discoveries was that the arteries carry blood, something not previously understood; see Siegel, *Galen's System of Physiology and Medicine* 93, 159.

[251]*Medical Aphorisms* 1, §§ 51, 58; 3, §§34, 88; 6; above, p. 447. See Siegel, *Galen's System of Physiology and Medicine* 243–46.

[252]*Medical Aphorisms* 1, §61; 2, §9; 3, §34. Siegel, *Galen's System of Physiology and Medicine* 258–61, points out Galen's misconceptions regarding the spleen's functions; on p. 270, he discovers what he does consider to be an intuition by Galen into one of its true functions.

[253]Klibansky, *Saturn and Melancholy* (n. 193 above) 8–10.

[254]*Medical Aphorisms* (quoting Galen) 2, §§20, 22–23, 30; 7, §§10, 13–14; 9, §15. *On*

on the Mishna, he goes as far as to explain certain animal conditions that, according to rabbinic law, do or do not render meat ritually unfit for consumption as the outcome of imbalances in the animals' humors.[255] Historians of medicine have noted that while the blood, yellow bile, and phlegm of Galen, his predecessors, and his followers can be related to actual entities in the human organism, black bile is a figment of the ancient imagination.[256] Yet it was precisely black bile that Galenic medicine fingered as the primary villain in human disease, as the cause, for example, of leprosy, quartan fever, podagra, peeling of the skin, dementia, thickening of the spleen, hemorrhoids, and cancer.

Maimonides can, it is true, demur from Galen on a trifle here and there, but his animadversions are not grounded in new knowledge and certainly not in new medical paradigms. Without questioning the presuppositions of Galenic medicine, he merely calls attention to a detail that Galen overlooked and then reasons from it to a different conclusion.[257] He thus rejects Galen's opinion that a putrefied humor giving rise to fever spreads throughout the body; for, as is commonly known, patients can exhibit several distinct fevers at the same time, and if the putrefied humor were spread through the entire body, discrete fevers could not be differentiated from one another.[258] He rejects the notion that internal inflammations cool down the body's surface by drawing blood and pneuma to the interior; for, as is likewise commonly known, internal inflammations are sometimes accompanied by a hot, and not a cold, bodily surface, and if inflammations drew blood and pneuma to the body's interior, they would always do so.[259]

Recent writers, qualified physicians among them, have lauded medical discoveries that they convinced themselves Maimonides made. One author ventured: "It would do well for contemporary Medicine if Maimonides' Medical Writings could be carefully scrutinized and his suggestions subjected to experiment." It would be no surprise "if some new approach to one of the . . . illnesses.which he discusses would result."[260] Writers expressing sentiments of the sort abandon critical judgment and enter hagiography. The sad fact is that Maimonides, like Galen and the better medieval physicians, did not have the data and conceptual tools that

---

Asthma. chapter 1, §2. See Brain, *Galen on Bloodletting* 7–8, 11–12.

[255]Commentary on the Mishna, *Ḥullin* 3:5.

[256]Siegel, *Galen's System of Physiology and Medicine* (n. 89 above) 220-21; Brain, *Galen on Bloodletting* 7.

[257]See *Medical Aphorisms*, 25, §69: Should someone, even a person whom you regard as consummately honest and impeccably moral, cite observations that he made and then use the observations to support a thesis, it is incumbent on you not to be swayed by the reported observations and to weigh the thesis on purely theoretical grounds.

[258]Above, p. 451.

[259]Above, p. 442.

[260]Maimonides, *Treatise on Poisons and Their Antidotes* (n. 210 above), translator's introduction xxvi–xxviii. Similar sentiments are expressed by H. Kook, *Peraṭim Urogeniṭaliyyim be-Mishnato shel ha-Rambam,*" *Korot* 6 (1973) 216, 220–21; Rosner, *The Medical Legacy of Moses Maimonides* (n. 14 above) 17, 40, 43, et passim.

would enable them to grasp the most basic workings of the human body and the etiology of a single human disease recognized by modern medicine. Maimonides' understanding of the human body, its health, and its diseases was incomparably inferior to what an average Western student entering high school knows today.[261]

On the authority of those whom he calls "men of theory," Maimonides distinguishes, within "the art of medicine," a "regimen for the healthy" as well as a "regimen for the sick," in other words, a preventative and a therapeutic side; and he judges the preventative side to be the more "noble."[262] Even compositions that he prepared for persons suffering from specific disorders, such as the treatise *On Asthma* and the *Regimen of Health*, pay more attention to general diet and hygiene than to the maladies constituting their ostensible subject matter. Maimonides' reason for placing so much weight on prevention was that "most diseases and the more serious ones result from poor digestion in the stomach," and poor digestion, in turn, is a consequence of eating the wrong foods or eating the right foods in the wrong manner.[263] He guarantees that all who observe his dietary and hygienic rules will "stay free of disease . . . until they die at an advanced age without ever needing a physician, while their bodies will be healthy and remain so throughout their lives." The only exceptions are unfortunates born with a bad constitution and victims of pestilence or drought.[264]

The broadest advice that he gives on the preventative side, put forward in several of his works and offered on the authority of Hippocrates and Galen, is to eat moderately and engage in regular exercise.[265] Although his justification will strike us as outlandish—overeating distends the stomach thereby impairing its ability to digest food; exercise fans the body's natural heat, which then expels superfluities from the body[266]—here, surely, few of his patients would regret having heeded his counsel.

Faithful to the Galenic tradition, he had an obsession with undesirable materials in the body. Physicians, he writes, know that constipation generates "extremely harmful fumes, which rise to the heart and brain, destroy the humors, and disturb the vital spirits, the outcome being melancholy, bad thoughts, apathy, lassitude,

[261] *Medical Aphorisms*, 25, §59.

[262] *Regimen of Health* (n. 164 above), Arabic text, *Janus* 27.295; English translation 20b. On Galen's authority, Maimonides distinguishes a third "regimen" as well, namely, the "restoration" of convalescents and the elderly to full health.

[263] Kroner, "Die Haemorrhoiden" (n. 120 above) 646, 658, 671; English translation 127.

[264] *Mishneh Torah*: *H. De^c ot* 4.20. Similarly *On Asthma*, chapter 5, §5; *Regimen of Health*, Arabic text, *Janus* 27.288; English translation 17a.

[265] *Medical Aphorisms* (n. 26 above) 17, §2. *Regimen of Health*, Arabic text, *Janus* 27.287; English translation 16b. *On Asthma*, chapter 5, §5. Maimonides, *Mishneh Torah*: *H. De^c ot* 4.15. For the stress on exercise in the Hippocratic Corpus, Galen, and Arabic medical literature, see Bos, "Maimonides on the Preservation of Health" (n. 132 above), 221–22.

[266] *Regimen of Health*, Arabic text, 27.289; English translation 17b.

and retention of the residues of digested food."[267] To avoid such untoward consequences, everyone should "examine himself" at frequent intervals to see whether his bowels need to be evacuated—namely, before and after meals, before and after the bath, before and after sexual intercourse, before and after sleeping, and before and after exercising, a total of ten junctures.[268] In one work after another, Maimonides prescribes potions for keeping stools soft, albeit with a caveat against the use of cathartic laxatives.[269] His concern with residues' clogging the body sometimes goes further, extending to regular self-induced vomiting and prophylactic enemas—although he may have become wary of those measures by the time he wrote the *Regimen of Health* for al-Afḍal. Merely repeating his instructions brings a snicker to one's lips.

He also offers numerous individual pieces of advice on diet and hygiene, almost all drawn again from his predecessors. Some items may happen to coincide with medical opinion today, such as his advice to breathe fresh, and not polluted, air,[270] to avoid spoiled food and meat that has been left out overnight,[271] to take wine in moderation, use unrefined flour, prefer chicken and related fowl over aquatic birds, such as duck and geese, and avoid animal fat. The other column in the ledger is, however, longer. We are told that very young lamb and female lamb damages the body, yet the yearling is healthy. White fat from properly raised chicken—in contrast to fat from four-legged animals—is highly nutritious.[272] Sugar and honey help to clear the body of unwanted residues. Smelling incense strengthens the brain.[273] Drinking lukewarm water destroys the digestive system. Fresh fruit, cabbage, peas, and beans are deleterious to the human constitution. Washing one's head with anything but very hot water, bathing except on the correct schedule—a schedule that varies from one of Maimonides' medical works to another—sleeping at the wrong times, and discharging semen are all harmful. Most of what Maimonides recommends is represented as beneficial because he imagines that it produces good humors or rids the body of undesirable ones, and most of what he rules out is harmful because he imagines that it does the opposite.

[267] *Regimen of Health*, Arabic text, *Janus* 28.61; English translation 23a. *On Asthma*, chapter 9, §9. Alluded to in *Mishneh Torah*: *H. De^c^ot* 4.13.

[268] *Regimen of Health*, Arabic text, *Janus* 27.290; English translation 18a; *Mishneh Torah*: *H. De^c^ot* 4.16.

[269] *Regimen of Health*, Arabic text, *Janus* 27.297–98; English translation 21b–22a. *On Asthma*, chapter 9, §§1-3. *Mishneh Torah*: *H. De^c^ot* 4.13-15.

[270] *On Asthma*, chapter 13, §§1, 4; *Regimen of Health*, Arabic text, *Janus* 28.70–71; English translation 27a–b (good air is essential because the bodily pneumas are formed from it); Hippocrates as cited by G. Bos, "Maimonides on the Preservation of Health," 225–26; *Galen's Hygiene* (n. 58 above) 35.

[271] *Regimen of Health*, Arabic text, *Janus* 28.149–50 ; English translation 31a. Spoiled food produces poisoned humors; see *Medical Aphorisms* 7, §15; 20, §10.

[272] *On the Causes of Symptoms* (n. 175 above) 149v.

[273] *On Asthma*, chapter 11, §5; *Regimen of Health*, Arabic text, *Janus* 28.149; English translation 31a.

When he turns from the preventative to the therapeutic side of medicine, his watchword is caution. The physician's mandate, as he quotes Hippocrates, is to help and not harm.[274] He counsels readers to consult only the truly expert. A physician "who is less than perfect in the medicinal art produces more harm than benefit. . . . It is better not to follow the advice of any physician at all than to follow the advice of a physician who leads one astray."[275] He quotes what he thought was an authentic text of Aristotle's to the effect that "the majority of persons who die do so as a consequence of medical treatment."[276] Where possible, weaker medications should be preferred to stronger ones because of the dangers inherent in the latter.[277] Ibn Zuhr, he relates, would agonize for days both before and after prescribing a laxative.[278]

He never tires of citing Galen's dictum: Whenever the Greeks were uncertain about treating a disease, they left the patient in the hands of nature; to which he adds in the name of Hippocrates and the early Arabic physician Rāzī: Nature is "clever, and does what is required, . . . the physician being needed only to buttress it." "When the disease is stronger than the patient's strength . . . no physician can help him"; when the patient's strength is greater, "nature heals him . . . and there is no need at all for a physician"; only "when the disease and the patient's strength are equal is a physician needed in order to buttress the patient's strength" and tip the scales.[279] Even where there is no danger of mistake, "the most accomplished physicians" would not hurry in administering medications for minor disorders, lest the workings of nature be interfered with.[280] The caution Maimonides counsels in administering medications was fortunate. Of the dozens of compounds designed for ingestion which he prescribed, the only ones that we can conceive of working consistently as intended are the laxatives, some of the emetics, and perhaps one or two analgesics. Consider the sugar water, the medicaments distinguished by extraordinary properties, the beneficial and harmful furs, the wondrous property of the wild ass in strengthening vision, and the compound of pearls, amber, coral, gold filings, shredded silk, roasted river crab, cucumber seed, and a score of other

[274]*On Asthma*, chapter 13, §17. Bos's translation gives the source in Hippocrates.

[275]Commentary on *The Aphorisms of Hippocrates* (n. 39 above) 1, §1, pp. 10–11; English translation 18. Similarly in the treatise *On Asthma*, chapter 13, §22.

[276]*Regimen of Health*, Arabic text, *Janus* 27.296; English translation 21a; *On Asthma*, chapter 13, §§20, 21.

[277]*Regimen of Health*, Arabic text, *Janus* 27.298–300; English translation 21b–23a.

[278]Above, n. 168.

[279]*Regimen of Health*, Arabic text, *Janus* 27.295–96; English translation 20b–21a. The Galen passage and quotations from Hippocrates on leaving matters to nature are also found in the treatise *On Asthma*, chapter 13, §§23, 25. The Galen passage appears in *Medical Aphorisms* 8, §75. The Rāzī passage reappears a second time in the *Regimen of Health*, Arabic text, *Janus* 28.74; English translation 28a–b. For Galen's appreciation of the power of nature, see Brain, *Galen on Bloodletting* (n. 84 above) 4.

[280]*On Asthma*, chapter 13, §5; *Regimen of Health*, Arabic text, *Janus* 28.72; English translation 27b.

ingredients, which he prescribed for Prince al-Afḍal's actual or imagined heart condition.[281]

Bloodletting was an essential element in Galenic therapy. It was the ultimate tactic for purging the body of undesirable and harmful humors as well as a plethora of blood, and Galen conducted an unrelenting polemic against physicians of his day who refrained from performing the procedure.[282] Maimonides quotes Galen as having prescribed bloodletting for curing and even preventing inflammation of the lungs, diaphragm, spleen, liver, stomach, bladder, womb, and kidneys; as well as for treating podagra, arthritis, hemoptysis, ophthalmia, hemorrhoids, headache, fever, dementia, insufficient menstruation, and nosebleed.[283] Only in very recent times did the procedure relax its uncanny grip on the Western medical mentality. Dostoyevsky, in a xenophobic caricature, could still have "a precise little old" German physician come to the bedside of a man who had lost large amounts of blood after being run over by a carriage and make the perceptive prognosis: "He's at his last gasp. His head's badly injured too. I could bleed him I suppose, but it won't be of any use."[284]

Although Maimonides by no means rules bloodletting out entirely, he surrounds it with a blessed rampart of caution. He quotes Galen regarding the safeguards to be observed before performing it[285] in addition to citing instances where patients were mistakenly bled and either died soon after or were left invalids for life.[286] He himself remembered an instance from his student days in which a strong young man suffering from a fever was bled and died a few hours later. He may also have heard the story that circulated regarding Saladin's last hours: As Saladin lay ill in Damascus in the year 1193, one of the court physicians insisted on bleeding him over the objections of the other attending physicians and thereby hastened the Sultan's demise. When the story came out, the dolt barely escaped the wrath of the mob.[287]

Bloodletting is placed by Maimonides at the head of the list of strong forms of therapy which should be avoided if possible because of their danger and which should only be performed under the direction of an expert physician.[288] If the

[281] Above, pp. 449–50, 464, 466.

[282] Brain, *Galen on Bloodletting* 13–15, 38–41, 100–103.

[283] *Medical Aphorisms* 12, §§22. For the source in Galen, see Brain, *Galen on Bloodletting* 25, 29, 32, 33, 37. Brain 158–72 cites some medical evidence indicating that certain infections may need iron in the body on which to feed and he suggests that bloodletting, with the resulting reduction of iron in the system, may in fact have a beneficial effect in inhibiting infection.

[284] F. Dostoevsky, *Crime and Punishment*, Magarshack translation, 201–2.

[285] *Medical Aphorisms* 12, §§1–11; *On Asthma*, chapter 13, §§32, 36. See Brain, *Galen on Bloodletting* 67, 102–3, 131–32.

[286] *On Asthma*, chapter 13, §36. See Brain, *Galen on Bloodletting* 86.

[287] A. Ehrenkreutz, *Saladin* (Albany 1972) 230.

[288] Maimonides ignores the talmudic descriptions of bloodletting by nonphysicians who were specialists in the procedure.

reservations he expresses dissuaded physicians who read his medical works in Arabic, Hebrew, or Latin from performing the procedure rashly, he may have saved more than one poor soul from being bled to death by the very person who was charged with bringing about a cure.

The insistence on caution in bloodletting and in prescribing the medications available at the time certainly reflects good sense. But caution in extending questionable treatment scarcely suffices to explain Maimonides' fame as a physician. We cannot help asking how, with the medical knowledge at his disposal, the treatment he administered could have brought him the renown that he enjoyed.

In the end, his success and the success of others of similar training in winning the confidence of their patients, even allowing for placebo effects, remains a mystery. Some light is perhaps cast on the mystery by Maimonides' explication of a passage at the beginning of the *Aphorisms of Hippocrates.* A physician, as Maimonides' expands on the Hippocratic passage, must not "just say what should be done and depart" but must supervise every detail of the patient's treatment. He must make sure that the patient and persons tending him follow instructions to the letter and commit no error when the physician is not present, that the patient be given support if he has to take a bitter medicament or undergo a painful treatment. Should the patient be too poor to provide for his needs, it is the physician's responsibility to furnish food and medication, and when the environment is not salubrious and the patient cannot afford to move to better quarters, the physician must arrange for the move.[289] The words may still be read with profit.

The healer, Maimonides is teaching in effect, must be as concerned with the person who is ill as with the illness. It is a reasonable guess that Maimonides and other successful physicians in the Middle Ages—and maybe also successful practitioners of homeopathy, osteopathy, chiropractic, herbalism, acupuncture, reflexology, aromatherapy, and the other forms of hopelessly unscientific medicine in our own day—comprehended the human side of medicine better than do many who are trained in modern medical science. While cells, tissues, and organs are undoubtedly the locus of disease, and medieval, as well as today's unconventional, medicine are immeasurably worse equipped than modern scientific medicine for treating them, it is, as has been noted more than once, human beings who become ill and need to be cared for.

[289]Commentary on *The Aphorisms of Hippocrates* (n. 39 above) 1, §1, pp. 14–15; English translation 22–23.

9

MISCELLANEOUS WRITINGS

> Disputation and refutation are permitted to him who wishes to travel those routes, but may God prevent me from doing so. (Maimonides, *Treatise on Resurrection*)

> Homiletic exegeses and far-fetched anecdotes [repeated] verbatim, in the way that women recite to one another in a house of mourning. (Maimonides' characterization of his opponent's book, in the *Treatise on Resurrection*)

> It can happen that a man intends to set forth a proposition in clear, plain language, wherein he makes every effort to remove doubts and any possibility of an interpretation's being placed on the proposition, yet persons of unhealthy soul read out of his language the opposite of the proposition that he intended to set forth. (Maimonides, Preface to *Treatise on Resurrection)*

Side by side with his other literary activities, Maimonides conducted an extensive correspondence with coreligionists in Egypt and abroad. First, there are his legal responsa, that is, his written answers to questions sent to him from locations throughout the Jewish world regarding practical or theoretical issues of Jewish law. As noted in an earlier chapter, the most complete collection comprises 480 items. Secondly, are his personal letters, a valuable source for re-creating his life and personality. The line between the two categories is not always clear-cut, and personal information can sometimes be mined from what are, in form, legal responsa.

Among the noteworthy personal letters is Maimonides' reply to a letter from a rabbinic judge in Palestine who had extended hospitality to the Maimon family when it visited the Holy Land years earlier. Maimonides alludes to the time that he, his father, his brother, and the Palestinian judge had spent together. He does not disguise his annoyance with the judge for not having sent condolences on the death of Maimonides' father, which occurred shortly after the Maimon family and their host went their several ways. And he recalls the devastating blow that his brother's death, which occurred years earlier, dealt him both emotionally and financially.[1]

Several letters from Maimonides to Pinḥas, a rabbinic judge in Alexandria, have been preserved. Each of them in some way concerns legal issues, but a few go into other matters as well, and one is of special interest. Here Maimonides explains and defends the method he followed in the *Mishneh Torah*, his code of Jewish law. He expresses displeasure at unflattering statements reportedly made about him by Pinḥas, while insisting that, despite what people said, he for his part had not spoken disparagingly of the Alexandrian.[2] This is the occasion on which he remarks that he had not answered a previous communication from Pinḥas because when people "cling to their stupidity and are unwilling to change their minds" his rule was to "keep silent and leave them to do as they please."[3] Letters from Maimonides to his favorite student, Joseph ben Judah, depict with palpable satisfaction his life as a successful physician in Egypt, discuss Joseph's ambitions, and furnish a glimpse of the tense relationship that had developed between them, on the one side, and Samuel ben Eli, the principal of the Baghdad rabbinic academy, on the other. Maimonides stresses to Joseph that he always tried to behave with humility, he encourages Joseph to do the same in his relationship with Samuel ben Eli, but he also recalls times in his younger years when he did not live up to that standard. Notwithstanding the humility on which he prides himself, he vents his bitterness toward the ignoramuses and blockheaded, dull-witted pietists who had criticized his *Mishneh Torah*. Maimonides' correspondence with Samuel Ibn Tibbon describes his medical practice and a typical week in his life a few years after the description in the letters to Joseph. And it provides Maimonides evaluation of Greek, Muslim, and Jewish philosophers and answers Samuel's philosophic inquiries.[4]

Letters to a rabbinic scholar in Lunel in southern France reveal Maimonides at his gentlemanly best; he congratulates the scholar and the scholar's circle on their rabbinic acumen and, in sharp contrast to the instances when he took umbrage at criticism, encourages those with whom he is corresponding to examine the

[1] I. Shailat, *Letters and Essays of Moses Maimonides* (in Hebrew) (Jerusalem 1987–1988) 228–30.

[2] Shailat, *Letters and Essays of Moses Maimonides* 436–54.

[3] Above, p. 44.

[4] A. Marx, "Texts by and about Maimonides," *Jewish Quarterly Review* 25 (1935), 374–81; Shailat, *Letters and Essays of Moses Maimonides* 525–54.

Mishneh Torah with as critical an eye as possible.[5] In the *Mishneh Torah* he instructs rabbinic judges and communal leaders to behave with "modesty and awe" toward their communities,[6] and his own sense of *noblesse oblige* comes to the fore in letters that he wrote in that spirit to nonscholars.[7] He radiates particular warmth toward Obadia, a convert to the Jewish faith, addressing him as "our master and teacher Obadia, the man of intelligence and understanding, the bona fide convert, may the Lord requite his deed and may his reward be complete from the Lord, the God of Israel, under whose wings he has come to take refuge."[8] Obadia once wrote to Maimonides about a dispute that took place between him and his Jewish teacher concerning the question whether Muslims are idolaters. When Obadia had ventured that Islam is not a form of idolatry, the teacher lost patience and blurted out in the language of Proverbs: "Answer a fool according to his folly." Maimonides assures the convert that he was correct but even if he had been wrong, it is incomprehensible that anyone would call him a fool—"a man who abandoned his father and the place of his birth, . . . perceived with his heart's eye, came and cleaved to this people, which today is abhorred of nations and a servant of rulers, realized that its religion is the true, righteous religion . . . while all other religions have been plagiarized from its religion, . . . who understood it all, followed after the Lord, . . . and entered under the wings of the divine presence, . . . whose heart stirred him up to come and be enlightened with the light of the living. Can someone at that level be called a fool?" Obadia's teacher had committed the "grave sin" of transgressing the scriptural command: "A convert shalt thou not wrong." Maimonides assumes that the transgression was inadvertent, but the teacher still had the obligation to go and beg Obadia for forgiveness, to fast, cry out to the Lord and pray, hoping that God will pardon him.[9]

In addition to his legal responsa and personal correspondence, Maimonides wrote a short treatise in response to questions that had been sent to him by a leader of the Jewish communities in Yemen. It takes the form of a letter to the Yemeni leader, and since Maimonides asks that it be read throughout Yemen, it may be characterized as a circular letter. He composed a second treatise, this time not in the

[5]Maimonides, *Responsa*, ed. J. Blau, 2nd ed. (Jerusalem 1986) 3.55–57; 4.32–34. J. Kafah, "*She'elot Ḥakme Lunel u-Teshubot 'ha-Rambam,' Kelum Meqoriyyot Hen*?" *Sefer Zikkaron le-ha-Rab Yiṣḥaq Nissim* 2 (Jerusalem 1985) 235–52, rejects the authenticity of the legal responsa ostensibly sent by Maimonides to Lunel.

[6]*Mishneh Torah*: *H. Sanhedrin* 25.1, quoting and expanding on BT *Rosh ha-Shana* 17a. Maimonides expresses a similar sentiment in his Commentary on the Mishna, *Abot* 4:12.

[7]*Responsa* §§66, 306; D. Baneth, "*Mi-Ḥalifat ha-Miktabim shel ha-Rambam*," *Sefer Zikkaron le-Asher Gulak uli-Shemuel Klein* (Gulak and Klein Memorial Volume) (Jerusalem 1942) 53, 55–56; Shailat, *Letters and Essays of Moses Maimonides* 404–18.

[8]*Responsa*, §§293, 436, 448.

[9]*Responsa*, §448. See above, p. 295. Exodus 22:20 reads: "A *ger* shalt thou not wrong." The standard English translation is: "A stranger shalt thou not wrong," but the Oral Torah understands the term *ger* in the verse as a convert to the Jewish religion.

form of a letter, in response to the criticisms of his position on resurrection which had been raised by Samuel ben Eli and forwarded to him by friends in Iraq. Two more small treatises are also attributed to Maimonides, both of which look again like circular letters. One of them expressly represents itself as a work of Maimonides', and the other is commonly credited to him. Although both are ordinarily included in lists of his works, close inspection shows them to be of doubtful authenticity. In the remainder of the present chapter, I examine the two authentic and two probably spurious treatises.

Epistle to Yemen. A certain Jacob ben Nathaniel, who like his father before him was a Jewish leader in Yemen, wrote to Maimonides bewailing the hard times that had befallen his community and appealing to Maimonides for guidance. Jacob turned to Maimonides because he had heard of his scholarly stature, particularly from an Egyptian Jew who had come to Yemen and whom Maimonides, in his reply, calls a "friend and student."

Maimonides informs the Yemeni leader that the reports of his attainments were exaggerations spread abroad by well-meaning acquaintances and he was in fact the very least of the scholars of Spain.[10] He then sheds the obligatory cloak of modesty and with total self-assurance spells out to Jacob and his community the way they should deal with the problems facing them. At one juncture, he introduces his advice by writing: "Know well" that just as the blind place themselves in the hands of a man of sight and follow him implicitly, and persons ignorant of medicine allow the physician to direct them, so the multitude must place itself in the hands of a prophet and accept implicitly what he declares to be true and false. Today, when prophecy is no longer available, the multitude are to follow the direction of scholars, men who have spent their days and nights investigating truth and falsehood.[11] Whereupon Maimonides spells out his instructions. He plainly expected Jacob ben Nathaniel and Jacob's associates to view him as a member of the class of scholars who are competent to direct the multitude and whom they have an obligation to heed.

The style of the introduction, the personal allusions found there, the self-confidence suffusing the *Epistle*, the patronizing, yet courteous, attitude to Jacob, the allusions to philosophic notions—watered down to suit the expected readership[12]—all fit Maimonides to a tee. His authorship is confirmed by an

[10]Moses Maimonides, *Epistle to Yemen*, Arabic and Hebrew versions, ed. A. Halkin with English trans. B. Cohen (New York 1952) (a singularly handsome edition, unfortunately marred by typographical and other errors) 1–3. English translation [i]–[ii].

[11]*Epistle to Yemen* 74; English translation [xiv].

[12]See *Epistle to Yemen* 16–18 (the Written Law inculcates ethical and intellectual virtue); 64 (there are scientific objections to astrology, but the present *Epistle* is not an appropriate occasion for exploring them); 70 (the biblical Abraham taught the existence and unity of a first cause); 88 (an allusion to the intellectual and ethical prerequisites for prophecy); English translation [iv], [xiii], [xvii].

express reference to it in a legal responsum of his own son.[13] Samuel Ibn Tibbon reports that a copy of Maimonides' *Epistle to Yemen* reached him about ten years after he translated Maimonides' *Guide for the Perplexed* into Hebrew, that is, in about 1214.[14] Ibn Tibbon was the first to translate the *Epistle* into Hebrew, and his translation shows that he had the composition in essentially the same form in which the Arabic original has reached us.

The *Epistle* jumps from one issue to another, and the editor of the most complete edition, published a half century ago, accordingly suggested that it may not have been written as a single whole but could be a mosaic pieced together from separate segments, each of which dealt with a discrete subject.[15] The suggestion has not been taken up by other scholars. If it happens to be correct, not all the components need be from Maimonides' hand; one or more sections written by someone else could conceivably have been combined with the authentic sections to form the treatise as we have it today. Should that be the case, when Maimonides' son refers to the *Epistle*, he could be referring to only part of what now forms a single whole.

To determine a date for the *Epistle*, a circular letter, or treatise, purportedly written by Maimonides in 1194 or 1195, has been cited.[16] There, Maimonides or someone pretending to be Maimonides refers to an incident that had occurred about twenty-two years earlier. The description of the incident resembles, although it does not entirely match, the description of one of the events that, according to the *Epistle to Yemen*, led Jacob ben Nathaniel to turn to Maimonides for advice.[17]

[13]Abraham Maimonides, *Responsa*, ed. A. Freimann and S. Goitein (Jerusalem 1937) §94. Abraham Maimonides calls it his father's *Book to Yemen*.

[14]Maimonides, *Moreh ha-Nebukim* (Ibn Tibbon's Hebrew translation of the *Guide*), ed. Y. Even Shmuel (Jerusalem 1946 or 1947), appendix 58.

[15] *Epistle to Yemen*, editor's introduction (in Hebrew) ix.

[16]A. Marx, "The Correspondence Between the Rabbis of Southern France and Maimonides About Astrology," *Hebrew Union College Annual* 3 (1926) 357. The manuscripts differ on the date; see Shailat, *Letters and Essays of Moses Maimonides* 490. English translation of the document, which I call the *Epistle in Opposition to Astrology*, with pagination of Marx's edition indicated: R. Lerner and M. Mahdi, *Medieval Political Philosophy* (New York 1963) 227–36.

[17]The 1194-1195 treatise narrates the following: About twenty-two years earlier, a man who "represented himself as a harbinger preparing the way for the king Messiah" had appeared in Yemen and announced that the Messiah was already present in the country. "Many Jews and Arabs had congregated" around the messianic harbinger, and he "wandered about in the mountains." The Yemeni Jewish community thereupon had—according to the treatise—sent Maimonides a long letter describing the prayers introduced by the man and the marvels he had performed. From what they reported, Maimonides, if he is accepted as the author, immediately realized that the man was a deluded ignoramus and everything he had done was "a falsehood." Maimonides thereupon replied to the Yemeni Jews in "three or four fascicles" in which he exhorted the Yemeni community to "warn" the man to cease his activities because of the damage he might cause. See Marx, "The Correspondence . . ." 356–57. The *Epistle to Yemen* in fact relates that Maimonides had been asked about the appearance of a self-styled Messiah—not a harbinger of the Messiah—in the towns of Yemen. Maimonides realized that the man was demented and recommended that he be

From Maimonides' apparent reference in the later treatise to the event occurring twenty-two years earlier which led up to the writing of the *Epistle*, it has been concluded that he wrote it in about 1172. We shall presently see that the circular letter or treatise carrying the 1194 or 1195 date and claiming Maimonides as its author is probably spurious. The 1172 date is therefore based on a dubious premise.

A date of roughly the same order can nevertheless be reached from a different direction. The *Epistle to Yemen* recommends that the recipients consult Maimonides' Commentary on the Mishna and hence—assuming the *Epistle* to be a single, unified composition—postdates that work.[18] Maimonides completed the Commentary on the Mishna in the Hebrew year corresponding to the last third of 1167 and first two-thirds of 1168; the end of 1167 would therefore be the earliest possible date for the *Epistle*. Jacob ben Nathaniel, the man whom Maimonides is addressing, wrote to him that the Yemeni Jewish community had suffered at the hands of one of the local Muslim princes who persecuted the Jewish population under his control and attempted to force it to accept the religion of Islam. In replying, Maimonides urges the Yemeni Jews to be strong in adversity, for God always eventually rescues His people from their troubles. Not long after 1173, Maimonides' words proved prophetic, for Saladin's brother conquered the land of Yemen, and the persecutor, whoever he was, could no longer have been a threat.[19] Since the *Epistle* does not yet know of the change for the better, it could not have been written much after 1173. It accordingly dates itself between 1167 and approximately 1173. Maimonides was at most thirty-five years old at the time, yet his reputation had already grown to the point where the Yemeni community considered him the most appropriate person to turn to for guidance, even though the community had strong links to the Iraqi rabbinic academy and no previous contact with Maimonides.

The *Epistle* opens with a flowery and effusive introduction in rhymed Hebrew prose in which Maimonides praises Jacob ben Nathaniel and the Jews of Yemen and disclaims the reports of his own scholarly attainments. Other writings of Maimonides show that he was skilled in the style of rhymed prose displayed here.

---

incarcerated—and not merely warned—until his defective mental condition could become public knowledge; at that point he could be released, since no one would pay further attention to him. See *Epistle to Yemen* 84, 92–94; English translation [xvi], [xviii]. To complicate matters further, the section on the Messiah in the *Epistle to Yemen* makes statements that conflict with what Maimonides writes about the Messiah in the *Mishneh Torah*, a work in which he was engaged during the time that he wrote the *Epistle*; see below.

[18] *Epistle to Yemen* 56; English translation [xi]. Maimonides calls the Commentary: "my large composition on the interpretation of the Mishna." After he issued the *Mishneh Torah*, he called that work his "large composition"; see above, p. 203.

[19] *Epistle to Yemen*, editor's introduction vi. Halkin identifies a certain ᶜAbd al-Nabīy as the Muslim persecutor. The invading army led by Saladin's brother is known to have put ᶜAbd al-Nabīy to death.

After the Hebrew introduction, the *Epistle* shifts to Arabic so that all members of the Yemeni community could understand.

Maimonides had been told that the hostile Muslim prince "decreed religious persecution for Israel and coerced [the inhabitants of] all the areas under his control to leave their religion"; while some members of the Jewish community remained firm, others lost faith.[20] How much territory the unnamed prince controlled and how harshly his decree was enforced cannot be ascertained from the *Epistle*, and no independent record of the events is known. The first third of the *Epistle* deals with the persecution.

"My brothers," Maimonides exhorts the Yemeni Jews, "you must all give ear, contemplate what I say, and teach it to the children and women." When God chose the Sons of Israel as His people, the jealousy of the gentiles was aroused. Kings attempted to destroy God's Law and religion with the sword. Thinkers—Syrian, Persian, and Greek—tried to undermine it with their writings. Then new enemies—the Christians and Muslims—appeared who combined both tactics, force together with persuasion. In order to entice Jews into apostasy, they cunningly promulgated their new religions, which they proclaimed as a divine revelation superseding the Mosaic Law.[21]

God has, however, promised never to forsake his people. Every persecution directed against the Jewish people and its religion has failed, and every persecutor has been destroyed by God.[22] In the current instance, one must not lose heart but instead accept the ordeal as a trial and purification, in which the faithful can demonstrate their mettle. To suffer and lose one's possessions for the sake of God is an honor, and therefore everyone should, if need be, forsake family and possessions and flee into the desert. Any who are delayed in doing so must be careful not to transgress a single divine commandment; for each transgression, whether large or small, will be punished even if committed under duress. As for those who submit to the enemy and forsake the Law, they declare for all to hear that they are not descendants of the men and women who were present at Sinai when the Law was given to the Israelites.[23]

Jacob ben Nathaniel had further informed Maimonides that a Jewish convert to Islam cited passages in Scripture which, the apostate contended, foretold the mission of the prophet Muhammad. The *Epistle* refutes the supposed scriptural proofs. Doing so leads it to lay down criteria for judging when a claimant to prophecy is a genuine prophet. A prerequisite is that the claimant does not dispute the immutability of the Law of Moses, whereas anybody—Maimonides is careful not to mention the name of Muhammad—diverging from the Law of Moses is a false prophet. The subject of the Law of Moses, in turn, leads the *Epistle* to warn

[20] *Epistle to Yemen* 4–6; English translation [ii].
[21] *Epistle to Yemen* 6–12; English translation [ii]–[iii].
[22] *Epistle to Yemen* 22; English translation [v].
[23] *Epistle to Yemen* 26, 34–36; English translation [vi]–[vii].

the Yemenite community about Karaite attacks on the Oral Law. Karaite propaganda, Maimonides stresses to the Yemeni Jews, constitutes an even greater threat to a small and weak Jewish community such as theirs than Muslim religious persecution.[24]

In regard to another matter of concern for Jacob, the *Epistle* asserts that the date of the coming of the Messiah cannot be ascertained, that Scripture warned against calculations of the date and the rabbis forbade them, and that when Saadia Gaon nonetheless did calculate the date, communal exigencies undoubtedly impelled him to act in opposition to the directives of Scripture and the rabbis.[25] Jacob ben Nathaniel had betrayed an inclination toward astrology in his letter to Maimonides, and Maimonides disabuses him of it.[26]

Then comes the strangest passage in the treatise and one of the strangest in Maimonides' entire oeuvre. The *Epistle* informs Jacob and other readers that an ancient family tradition, going back to the beginning of the exile of the Jews from Palestine to Spain, inferred from a certain scriptural phrase the year when prophecy would reappear in Israel; and the reappearance of prophecy, the *Epistle* makes clear, will be a precursor of the Messiah's coming. The date inferred from the scriptural phrase is 1210, and the author writes: My fathers "forbade us absolutely to publicize it." "I think it is true. . . . God, however, knows the truth."[27] The notion of Maimonides' recommending a calculation of the reemergence of prophecy, which will be the precursor of the Messiah, just a few pages after insisting categorically that the date of the messianic age cannot and must not be calculated, of his moreover divulging in a communication to be read by men, women, and children throughout Yemen a secret that his fathers absolutely forbade making public, verges on the incredible. That is not all. The ancient, highly secret family tradition regarding the reemergence of prophecy turns out to be a variation on a midrashic comment already recorded for everyone to see in the Palestinian Talmud.[28] On these grounds, a scholar in the nineteenth century concluded that

[24]*Epistle to Yemen* 36–48, 52–54, 58. English translation [viii]–[xii]; on p. [viii], where "apostle" is a typographical error for "apostate." The *Epistle* makes the harsh statement that "in my judgment," Jewish law permits killing Karaites, since they deny the part of the Mosaic prophecy which mandates observance of the Oral Law. In Commentary on the Mishna, *Ḥullin*: 1.2, Maimonides states that the founders of the Karaite movement deserved to be put to death for their heresy, but that contemporary Karaites, who follow the movement because of indoctrination, are exempt from such drastic punishment.

[25]*Epistle to Yemen* 60–64; English translation [xii]–[xiii].

[26]*Epistle to Yemen* 64–78; English translation [xiii]–[xv].

[27]*Epistle to Yemen* 82–84; English translation [xvi].

[28]In Numbers 23:23, the prophet Balaam declares: "As of this time it will be said in Jacob and in Israel: 'What hath God wrought!'" In PT *Shabbat* 6:9, 8d, a midrashist explains the verse as follows: When as many more years pass in the future as have passed from creation until *this time*, the course of human history will come to an end and people will marvel saying: See what God hath wrought. The tradition Maimonides received from his forefathers explains the verse as meaning that when as many more years pass in the future as have passed until this time, prophecy,

"the passage in question must absolutely be excised as an audacious falsification."[29]

Despite the cogency of the scholar's conclusion, it unfortunately has a vulnerable chink. Maimonides' son Abraham was later questioned by Yemenite Jews—perhaps after 1210 had come and gone and the momentous events failed to materialize—about his father's tradition regarding the date of the Messiah (*al-qeṣ*). The letter in which Abraham was asked about the calculation has not been preserved, and we have only his brief reply: He informs the questioners that his father's *Epistle to Yemen* had already disclosed everything Maimonides knew about the matter. Although the details of the calculation are not discussed, the reply confirms that Maimonides did indeed share an eschatological calculation with the Yemeni Jews. Abraham Maimonides betrays some discomfort with the subject, for he immediately adds: The tradition that I myself know is what is expressly stated in the Written Law, namely, that the coming of the Messiah will be contingent on repentance by God's people.[30]

The final section of the *Epistle to Yemen* deals with a self-styled Messiah who had recently appeared in Yemen. The *Epistle* explains to Jacob that the man in question was a demented soul and it outlines criteria for identifying a genuine Messiah. According to those criteria, the Messiah will be a prophet close to the level of the biblical Moses and hence someone who excels in intellectual and ethical virtue; he will be completely unknown until he is revealed; he will first appear in Palestine; and he will establish his credentials through "signs and marvels." God will bring about that all the nations of the world will stand in awe of him.[31] The description raises additional problems. At the time when he wrote the *Epistle to Yemen*, Maimonides was working on his *Mishneh Torah*, and the *Mishneh Torah* flatly rejects the notion "that the Messiah will have to perform signs and marvels" to establish his credentials: He will prove himself instead by enforcing observance of the Written and Oral Laws among Jews, conducting a successful war against the gentiles, rebuilding the Holy Temple, and gathering in the exiles. The section outlining criteria for identifying a genuine Messiah therefore looks suspicious.[32] If

---

which reveals what God has wrought and which will be a precursor of the messianic age, will be restored. As Maimonides calculates the number of years that had passed from creation to Balaam's prophecy, the addition of an equal number comes to the year 1210.

[29]D. Kaufmann, "Une falsification dans la lettre envoyée par Maïmonide aux juifs du Yemen," *Revue des études juives* 1892 (24) 114.

[30]Abraham Maimonides, *Responsa* §94. On the role of repentance for the coming of the Messiah, see BT *Sanhedrin* 97b.

[31]*Epistle to Yemen* 88–92; English translation [xvii]. For the Messiah's prophetic gifts, see *Mishneh Torah*: *H. Teshuba* 9.2.

[32]*Mishneh Torah*: *H. Melakim* 11:3–4. Shailat, *Letters and Essays of Moses Maimonides* (n. 1 above) 157–58, struggles to harmonize the description of the Messiah in the *Epistle* with the description in the *Mishneh Torah*.

It may also be noted that the section on the Messiah in the *Epistle* calls the Hebrew Bible "the twenty-four," that is, the twenty-four books, whereas that expression does not appear in any of

we reject it as spurious, we shall have to assume that an unknown person fabricated it and he or another party combined it with the authentic sections to piece together the *Epistle* as known today. The situation remains puzzling.

The *Epistle to Yemen* has been preserved in slightly different versions, and precisely in which form it circulated among those for whom it was originally intended is unknown. One of the versions was translated into Hebrew three separate times by European Jews in the Middle Ages.[33] As preserved, the *Epistle* is scarcely profound. Notwithstanding its modest intrinsic virtues, it is of interest

---

Maimonides' authenticated works; see W. Bacher, *Die Bibelexegese Moses Maimūni's* (Budapest 1896) 8.

[33]Two more or less complete manuscripts of the Arabic text have been preserved, both written in Hebrew characters; see *Epistle to Yemen*, editor's introduction xxxi. They differ from one another in several places, the most significant difference being *Epistle to Yemen* 98–102; see the textual apparatus. The section in question deals with false messiahs who had appeared and is the completion of the *Epistle's* discussion of the Messiah, which has already been seen to be problematic. One of the Arabic manuscripts, which I shall call the shorter, devotes a single sentence to each false messiah while the other describes them much more fully. A strong argument has been offered for viewing the fuller account as spurious; see Rabbenu Moshe ben Maimon, *Iggarot*, ed. J. Kafah (Jerusalem 1972) 57, note 91.

All three Hebrew translations give the account of the false messiahs in the briefer form and in general they show themselves to have been made from an Arabic text that was close to the shorter of the two Arabic versions. In one notable instance, a line omitted in the shorter Arabic version through homoeoteleuton is omitted in the three Hebrew translations as well; see *Epistle to Yemen* 56, lines 9–10, and the Arabic textual apparatus. There is nevertheless a significant difference between the shorter Arabic version and the translations. The *Epistle* mentions the founder of the Muslim religion ten times, and all the versions generally avoid using the name "Muhammad"; the exceptions that I noted are *Epistle* 44, where the letters of Muhammad's name are at issue and his name therefore had to be given, and *Epistle* 81, where one of the Hebrew translations does use the name Muhammad. The shorter Arabic version speaks of "the individual" (*al-shakhṣ*) or "so-and-so" (*peloni*) instead of Muhammad. The longer Arabic version usually speaks of "madman" (*meshugga*^{c}) when it means Muhammad (see Quran 52:28 and 81:21, where Muhammad is suspected of being mad [*majnūn*]). In several passages, the longer version speaks of "so-and-so." And in one passage, it speaks of "the unfit one" (*pasul*, a play on *rasūl*, God's "apostle"); see *Epistle* 38, line 17, and apparatus. The three Hebrew translations generally call Muhammad "madman," and in the passage where the longer Arabic version calls him "the unfit one," the Hebrew translations do so as well. The correlation of the Hebrew translations among themselves and with the longer Arabic version is not, however, perfect in this respect. There is, moreover, a single passage in which both Arabic versions speak of the Quran. All three Hebrew translations substitute the epithet "disgrace" (*qalon*, a pun); see *Epistle* 38, line 8. Virtually the only thing to be said with any confidence about the snarled situation is that the copy of the *Epistle* sent by Maimonides to the Yemenite Jewish community could not possibly have called Muhammad "madman," or called the Quran "disgrace." As it is, the *Epistle* is highly critical of the Muslims, and for that reason, the author requests that it be kept away from anyone who might deliver it into Muslim hands; see *Epistle to Yemen* 106; English translation [xx]. To imagine the consequences should a text containing the ugly epithets have fallen into twelfth-century Muslim hands, one may extrapolate from the predicament of Salman Rushdie in our own day.

because it testifies to the extent that Maimonides' reputation had spread when he was still in his thirties. It reveals the confidence, firmness, and tact that he could deploy when responding to what he viewed as an unsophisticated Jewish community in need of help. It also deposits in our laps an intractable building block—the messianic calculation—as we try to piece together a full picture of Maimonides.

Maimonides' solicitousness toward the Yemenite Jews endeared him to them, and the name of Moshe ben Maimon was soon incorporated into Yemeni public prayers.

Epistle in Opposition to Astrology or Letter to the Scholars of Montpellier (Probably Misattributed). This is the circular letter, dated 1194 or 1195, which I referred to when discussing the *Epistle to Yemen*. It exists only in Hebrew, and since those for whom it was intended did not know Arabic, Hebrew was presumably the language in which it was composed.

Two pieces of evidence would seem to support its authenticity. First, a letter from a group of men in southern France, which has been preserved independently, addresses Maimonides by name and pleads for answers to a number of questions regarding astrology. The *Epistle in Opposition to Astrology*, as we have it, is a response to the questions posed in the letter.[34] Secondly, Jonathan ha-Kohen of Lunel, who had a connection with the authors of the letter inquiring about astrology,[35] once extolled Maimonides in the following extravagant scriptural phraseology: "Thou hast rendered the wonders of the diviners foolish with thy demonstrations and dried up [or: put to shame] the astrologers with . . . the work of thy fingers. Thou hast shed thy dew upon us and sent thy offering to thy people

[34]The letter from southern France to Maimonides is published by Marx, "The Correspondence Between the Rabbis of Southern France and Maimonides About Astrology" (n. 16 above) 338, 343–49. (According to the single mediocre manuscript of the letter, the writers inquire in a postscript, 349, about a report that men had come from "a distant [*merḥaq*] land" and informed Maimonides of the appearance there of a messianic harbinger. The letter does not identify the distant land, but the *Epistle in Opposition to Astrology*, p. 356, which replies to the letter, assumes that the questioners were asking about a harbinger of the Messiah who appeared in "the East [*mizraḥ*], in Isfahan." The reading *merḥaq* in the preserved manuscript of the letter is presumably an error for *mizraḥ*.)

[35]The manuscript of the letter to Maimonides, Marx, "The Correspondence . . ." 348, §26, asks that he address his reply in care of R. Jonathan ha-Cohen in "Motl . . . which is near Dadbonne and Marseilles." The editor corrects this to read: "Montpellier, which is near Narbonne and Marseilles." When Jonathan later wrote to Maimonides, he made clear that he represented a circle of scholars in Lunel. Montpellier and Lunel both lie between Narbonne and Marseilles, and they are only about twenty miles apart. The authors of the letter to Maimonides may possibly have thought that it would be easier for the messenger carrying Maimonides' reply to deliver it to Montpellier than to Lunel; or perhaps Jonathan changed his place of residence from one town to the other in the interval; or, a third alternative, the place name that has been corrupted in the preserved manuscript may, in fact, be Lunel.

in the day of thy warfare."[36] Jonathan would appear to have known of a composition that he was certain came from Maimonides' hand and that offered Maimonides' "people" a demonstration of the groundlessness of astrology. We shall see that the *Epistle in Opposition to Astrology* in fact contains nothing that can be deemed a demonstration.

The author of the *Epistle* refers to what he calls his own *Mishneh Torah* as well as to his "large composition in Arabic" on theological topics; the statements regarding the latter make clear that he is talking about the *Guide for the Perplexed.*[37] There are, however, serious discrepancies between the *Epistle* and the *Guide*.

At a certain point, the *Epistle* is led to digress on the subject of the creation of the world and it asserts: Most "philosophers" held that the world is eternal, some that it was created from a preexistent matter, and still other "philosophers" agreed with the prophets of Israel that the world was created *ex nihilo*.[38] In the *Guide for the Perplexed*, Maimonides had written that "every philosopher of whom I have heard a report or whose words I have seen" ruled out the possibility of something's coming out of nothing. He thus knew of no philosopher who accepted the creation of the world *ex nihilo*.[39] The *Epistle* further states that philosophers taking the three positions—the eternity of the world, creation from a preexistent matter, and creation *ex nihilo*—viewed individual events in the sublunar world inhabited by man exclusively as matters of chance.[40] In the *Guide for the Perplexed*, Maimonides stated that construing individual human events as a matter solely of chance was a corollary of Aristotle's belief in the eternity of the world, with the intimation that thinkers accepting creation in any guise would not attribute human events entirely to pure chance.[41] The *Epistle* presents as additional propositions accepted by all philosophers that the "celestial spheres and stars possess souls and knowledge [*madda*^{c}]" and "God makes everything [in the sublunar world] through

[36]Maimonides, *Responsa* (n. 5 above) 3.53. The connection—or possible connection—between Jonathan's words and the *Epistle in Opposition to Astrology* was pointed out by I. Sonne, "*Iggeret ha-Rambam le-Shemuel Ibn Tibbon*," *Tarbiz* 10 (1938–1939) 140–41.

[37]Marx, "The Correspondence . . ." 349–51, 353.

[38]Marx, "The Correspondence . . ." 352–53, §§12–15. The *Epistle* cannot be extending the term *philosopher* to include the adherents of the Kalam, since in §§17, 19, it states that philosophers taking all three of the aforementioned positions on creation rejected individual divine providence, and no one could ascribe a rejection of individual providence to the Kalam.

[39]*Guide for the Perplexed* 2.13 (b).

[40]Marx, "The Correspondence . . ." 353–54, §§17, 19.

[41]*Guide for the Perplexed* 3.17 (b), and see above, p. 367. Maimonides states and then repeats that the chance nature of events is a corollary of a belief in eternity. One of Alfarabi's compositions on astrology argues that some, but not all, individual events in the world are "accidental"; and Alfarabi, as Maimonides knew, believed in the eternity of the world. His intent, however, was only to establish that human events are not predetermined. See F. Dieterici, *Alfarabi's philosophische Abhandlungen* (Leiden 1890) 106; German translation: F. Dieterici, *Alfarabi's philosophische Abhandlungen aus dem Arabischen übersetzt* (Leiden 1892) 174.

a power coming from the spheres and stars";[42] *stars* here means both stationary and wandering stars, that is to say, both what we would today call stars and what we would call planets. In the *Guide for the Perplexed*, Maimonides did write that philosophers and Jewish tradition alike understood the celestial spheres to possess rational souls and that both understood the celestial spheres and perhaps the stars as well to exercise an effect on the sublunar region.[43] But he followed the Arabic philosopher Avicenna in crediting a being of a different order, the incorporeal active intellect, with a more weighty role than the spheres or stars: The active intellect, for Maimonides, is the source of the forms of natural material objects in the sublunar world.[44] The omission of the role of the active intellect in the *Epistle* would have been gross carelessness on his part, for that omission, taken together with the magnifying of the role of the spheres and stars, undermines the *Epistle*'s rejection of astrological theory.

Other anomalies stand out. The *Epistle* speaks of "a thousand books" that had been written defending one or another position on the issue of eternity and creation,[45] yet no medieval Jewish thinker knew of anything remotely approaching that number of books on the subject. The author of the *Epistle* could have been expanding either on a statement of the genuine Maimonides to the effect that philosophers had been debating the issue of eternity and creation in their writings for 3,000 years or on another statement of his to the effect that believers in creation from a preexistent matter are subdivided into "subgroups, which it is useless to list."[46] But the hyperbole is ludicrous; it subverts the author's credibility, and Maimonides was too sober to have uttered it. The *Epistle* speaks of "compositions" written by the "scholars of Greece, Persia, and India" on astronomical science,[47] whereas the authentic works of Maimonides do not, as far as I know, disclose familiarity or interest in Indian astronomy. The *Epistle* informs the writers of the letter from southern France that astrology is shown in the *Mishneh Torah* to be the foundation of idolatrous belief. One of Maimonides' rabbinic works does call faith in astrological predictions and various sorts of magic the "root and branches of idolatry," but the work doing so is his Commentary on the Mishna and not the *Mishneh Torah*.[48]

[42]Marx, "The Correspondence . . ." 353, §17.

[43]*Guide for the Perplexed* 2.5; 10.

[44]*Guide for the Perplexed* 2.4.

[45]Marx, "The Correspondence . . ." 353, §15. The *Epistle* allows itself another gratuitous hyperbole, p. 350, §6, where it states that "fools have composed thousands of books full of vanity and emptiness."

[46]*Guide for the Perplexed* 1.71, p. 96a; 2.13 (b).

[47]Marx, "The Correspondence . . ." 352, §11.

[48]Maimonides, Commentary on the Mishna (=*Mishna* ^{c}*im Perush R. Moshe ben Maimon*, Arabic original and Hebrew trans. J. Kafah [Jerusalem 1963–1968]), ^{c}*Aboda Zara* 4:7, p. 357. *Mishneh Torah*: *H.* ^{c}*Abodat Kokabim* 11.8–9, 16, links astrology with idolaters, but does not characterize it as the foundation or root of idolatry.

There are thus strong, if not overwhelming, grounds for rejecting the *Epistle in Opposition to Astrology* as a forgery. Should it be rejected as inauthentic, however, we face less than appealing alternatives. We shall have to assume either that Maimonides failed to answer the letter from southern France soliciting his views on astrology, just as, we shall see, he failed to answer earlier letters from the same circle,[49] or that his reply was lost; and then that a person opposed to astrology supplied the lack by fabricating a reply. Or else we shall have to suppose that Maimonides' reply fell into the hands of someone who found it perfunctory and expanded and reworked it into its present shape. We shall further have to assume that Jonathan ha-Kohen knew of a reply from Maimonides which is no longer extant or accepted the spurious reply as genuine.[50] Wherever the truth lies, the *Epistle* seems already to have existed more or less in its current form by the fourteenth century. A Jewish writer active in southern France in the first half of the fourteenth century speaks of the "Epistle" that "Maimonides . . . sent to the scholars of Montpellier," and a paragraph that he quotes from it is found in the *Epistle in Opposition to Astrology* as preserved today.[51]

To return to the letter addressed to Maimonides: The writers evince distress at the thought that the position of the heavenly bodies at a person's birth should determine the course of his entire life, for such a notion throws the efficacy of prayer and religious observance into doubt.[52] The letter thereupon asks a series of questions about the determination of events by the heavens and about possible tactics for escaping from what the heavens ordain. The writers of the letter confess that they themselves did not understand astrological theory and were simply repeating what they had heard from others; but they ask Maimonides to reply in full all the same so that his answer might be shown to experts in the subject who lived nearby. It was not their first letter to Maimonides. They relate that they had written to him on previous occasions regarding the issue and were uncertain whether their letters never arrived or whether Maimonides had not considered their questions worthy of his attention. They express the very highest regard for Maimonides, plead for a response, and promise to accept whatever he says as if it came from the mouth of the biblical Moses.[53]

In the *Epistle*, the real or fictitious Maimonides confesses a reluctance to answer, the reason being that he was overburdened with other cares. In the end, he

[49] See immediately below.

[50] When Jonathan of Lunel wrote the complimentary letter to Maimonides in about 1190, the *Guide for the Perplexed* had not yet reached southern France; see Maimonides, *Responsa* (n. 5 above) 3.52. And it was not translated into Hebrew until 1204. Since the *Epistle in Opposition to Astrology* refers to the *Guide,* if it is spurious, its author either lived in an area where the *Guide* was accessible in Arabic and he was able to read it in the original language or else he acquired his knowledge of it through an intermediary.

[51] Moses Narboni, Commentary on the *Guide for the Perplexed* (Vienna 1853) 3.49.

[52] Marx, "The Correspondence . . ." 344, §§4, 6.

[53] Marx, "The Correspondence . . ." 345, §§7, 8, 9; 346, §§13, 18; 347, §§21, 24; 348, §28.

answered only because "R. Pinḥas"—the intent undoubtedly being Pinḥas of Alexandria, who had come to Egypt from France and appears here as an intermediary between the men of Southern France and Maimonides—had sent a messenger, and the messenger refused to leave until Maimonides yielded and quickly wrote out the *Epistle*.[54] If the *Epistle* is completely spurious, the person representing himself as Maimonides fabricated the story about Pinḥas and the messenger to add an air of verisimilitude.

The author of the *Epistle* touches on a number of matters that circle around the central issue. He distinguishes three sources of human knowledge,[55] outlines the three philosophic positions on the question of the creation or eternity of the world,[56] acknowledges that the celestial spheres and stars exercise an influence on the lower world,[57] contrasts the different ways in which philosophy, astrology, and Mosaic religion explain the success of some men and the failure of others,[58] and states that philosophy and Mosaic religion agree in affirming human free will.[59] He defines the subject matter of the true science of the heavens, that is, what we call astronomy, in order to distinguish it from astrology.[60] There was a precedent here: The Arabic philosopher Alfarabi had defined the subject matter of astronomy in order to differentiate between true astral science and astrological pseudo science.[61]

As for the questions regarding astrology which the letter from southern France posed, the *Epistle* responds that they are branches growing out of a single tree. The tree is the belief in the truth of astrology, and once that belief is uprooted, the questions branching out from it wither away. The *Epistle* does not separate the two basic senses of astrology, neither of which necessarily entails the other, namely: the doctrine that the positions of the stars determine human events, and the doctrine that man can predict the course of human events by observing the positions of the stars. It nonetheless plainly opposes both.[62] It characterizes astrology as a discipline embraced only by "Chasdeans, Chaldeans, Canaanites, and Egyptians," whereas the philosophers of Greece ridiculed those four ignorant nations, and the wise men of Persia likewise dismissed their pseudo sciences.[63] The *Epistle* fur-

[54]Marx, "The Correspondence . . ." 357, §30.

[55]Marx, "The Correspondence . . ." 350, §4.

[56]Marx, "The Correspondence . . ." 352–53, §§12–15.

[57]Marx, "The Correspondence . . ." 353, §§17–18.

[58]Marx, "The Correspondence . . ." 354–55, §§ 19–20, 22–25.

[59]Marx, "The Correspondence . . ." 354, §21.

[60]Marx, "The Correspondence . . ." 351–52, §11.

[61]Th. Druart, "Astronomie et astrologie selon Farābī," *Bulletin de philosophie médiévale* 1978 (20) 44.

[62]Marx, "The Correspondence . . ." 351, §9; 355, §23; 356, §26.

[63]Marx, "The Correspondence . . ." 351, §§9–10. In *Guide for the Perplexed* 3.37, the Chasdeans, Chaldeans, Egyptians, and Canaanites are named as nations that indulged in magical practices as part of their idolatrous religions.

ther informs the men of southern France that the opponents of astrology have clear and certain proofs refuting astrological belief, but gives no hint of what the proofs are.[64] Statements attributed to certain talmudic rabbis in the classic rabbinic texts do, the *Epistle* concedes, suggest that "at the moment of a man's birth, the stars determine" the course of his life. But what has been established by demonstration must not be discarded just because an individual ancient rabbi, who may have nodded momentarily, happens to have expressed a contrary opinion. Furthermore, the rabbinic statements are not necessarily meant to be taken at face value; they may have been designed for a purpose unknown to us today and not meant literally.[65] Such is the sum and substance of what the *Epistle* says about astrology. The subject obviously is not explored very deeply.

The failure to spell out the distinction between the two senses of astrology—the determination of events in this world by the stars and the foretelling of the future by looking at the stars—together with an uncompromising opposition to both harmonizes with the stance taken by Maimonides in his genuine writings. In his Commentary on the Mishna, Maimonides rejects the proposition that the stars determine human events and sketches a brief scientific argument refuting one of the two premises on which, he submits, the proposition rests.[66] In the *Mishneh Torah* he notes that Scripture prohibits "soothsaying" and he maintains that the Oral Torah understands the soothsaying prohibited by Scripture to be the predicting of events in this world from the positions of the stars. He rules there that Scripture prohibits both making astrological predictions and acting in accordance with the predictions made by others.[67] He further writes: "Men of science . . . know by clear proofs" that astrological predictions are "emptiness and vanity" but he does not disclose what the proofs are.[68] His *Epistle to Yemen* speaks out against what are apparently both senses of astrology, asserting that "accomplished wise men [or:

[64]Marx, "The Correspondence . . ." 351, §10.

[65]Marx, "The Correspondence . . ." 356, §26. Astrological influences on human life are recognized in BT *Shabbat* 156a, and *Mo^ced Qaṭan* 28a.

[66]Commentary on the Mishna, *^cAboda Zara* 4:7: Astrology has two premises, both of which are disproved by physical science. The first is that some stars are favorable and some unfavorable, and the second is that when stars are aligned with specific areas of the outermost sphere, those areas intensify or lessen the effect of the stars. Maimonides says nothing that might reveal what the scientific argument against the first of the premises might be. He does indicate what the argument against the second is: All areas of the undifferentiated outermost sphere are of the same nature, and therefore none could intensify or lessen the effect of a star more than another does. Similar reasoning is found in Alfarabi. See Dieterici, *Alfarabi's philosophische Abhandlungen* (n. 41 above) 112; German translation 183.

[67]*Mishneh Torah*: *H. ^cAbodat Kokabim* 11.8–9. The commentaries give Maimonides' rabbinic sources. Maimonides may have connected the prohibition against making astrological predictions to Deuteronomy 18:10: "There shall not be found among you . . . a soothsayer"; and the prohibition against acting in accordance with them to Leviticus 19:26: "Ye shall not. . . practice . . . soothsaying." See Book of Commandments, negative commandment #32.

[68]*Mishneh Torah*: *H. ^cAbodat Kokabim* 11.16.

scientists]," both Jewish and non-Jewish, reject the belief, and scientific proofs refute it. Here too, he does not reveal what the scientific proofs are, giving as his reason the inappropriateness of the forum, although he does cite Scripture to show that certain astrological predictions of events in biblical times failed miserably.[69] His opposition to astrology places him solidly in the tradition of the Arabic Aristotelians Alfarabi and Avicenna, both of whom drew up refutations of astrological theory, and when he speaks in his genuine works of refutations of the pseudo science[70] he could have those of Alfarabi and Avicenna in mind. Although the *Epistle in Opposition to Astrology* distorts Maimonides' views on ancillary issues, it thus represents his stance on astrology correctly.

His implacable opposition failed to bring the issue to a close within the Jewish world. Astrology had adherents[71] and opponents[72] among Jewish thinkers before he appeared on the scene, and it continued to do so afterwards. To judge from medieval works subsequent to Maimonides which touch on the subject and have been preserved, adherents of astrology easily outnumbered the opponents.[73] In

[69]*Epistle to Yemen* (n. 10 above) 64–68; English translation [xiii].

[70]Th. Druart, "Astronomie et astrologie selon Farābī," (n. 61 above) 43–47; "Le second traité de Farābī . . . ," *Bulletin de philosophie médiévale* 21 (1979) 47–51; M. Mehren, "Vues d'Avicenne sur l'astrologie," *Le Muséon* 3 (1884) 383–403. It is not absolutely certain that the attributions to Alfarabi and Avicenna are correct.

[71]Abraham bar Ḥiyya addressed an apologia for astrology to the rabbinic authority Judah b. Barzilai. Abraham Ibn Ezra wrote treatises on astrology, and his Bible commentaries are permeated with astrological assumptions; see for example his commentary on Exodus 3:15. Both men gave practical astrological advice. Horoscopes and astrological almanacs written in Hebrew letters have been found in the Cairo Geniza with dates from the tenth to the fourteenth centuries, but mostly from the eleventh and twelfth centuries. See B. Goldstein and D. Pingree, "Horoscopes from the Cairo Geniza," *Journal of Near Eastern Studies* 36 (1977) 113–14; "More Horoscopes from the Cairo Geniza," *Proceedings of the American Philosophical Society* 125 (1981) 155–56; "Astrological Almanacs from the Cairo Geniza," *Journal of Near Eastern Studies* 38 (1979) 153–54; "Additional Astrological Almanacs from the Cairo Geniza," *Journal of the American Oriental Society* 103 (1983) 673.

[72]Saadia expressed implicit opposition to the belief in astrology in *Sefer ha-Emunot we-ha-De^c^ot* 10.13, and explicitly opposes it in his Commentary on the Book of Job. Judah Hallevi rejects at least the predictive side of astrology in *Kuzari* 4.9.

[73]Among those who recognize astrological forces are: Naḥmanides, Commentary on Genesis 1:18; Leviticus 18:25. Ibn Malka; see G. Vajda, *Juda ben Nissim Ibn Malka* (Paris 1954) 34–37. R. Solomon Adret, *Responsa* §19. The writers described as belonging to the "circle" of R. Solomon Adret and quoted by D. Schwartz, "*Ben Shamranut le-Sikletanut*," *Daat* 32–33 (1994) 160–61. Judah ben Solomon ha-Cohen; see G. Freudenthal, "Providence, Astrology, and Celestial Influences," in *The Medieval Hebrew Encyclopedias of Science and Philosophy*, ed. S. Harvey (Dordrecht 2000) 357, and Tz. Langermann, "Some Remarks on Judah ben Solomon," in the same volume, 383. Levi ben Abraham; see W. Harvey, "Levi ben Abraham of Villefranche," in *The Medieval Hebrew Encyclopedias of Science and Philosophy* 187. M. Meiri, Commentary on BT *Shabbat* 156a (despite Meiri's tendency to follow Maimonides in ideological matters; see M. Halbertal, *Ben Torah le-Ḥokma* [Jerusalem 2000] chapter 1). Gersonides, *Milḥamot ha-Shem* 2.2, et passim (Gersonides gave practical astrological advice).

one respect, Maimonides did succeed. Although the authors of subsequent comprehensive codes of Jewish law do not all accept his rejection of the theory of astrology, they follow him in ruling that Jewish Law prohibits consultations with astrologers.[74]

Epistle on Religious Persecution (Iggeret ha-Shemad), also called the Treatise on Sanctifying God's Name (Ma'amar Qiddush ha-Shem) (Probably Misattributed). It was originally written in Arabic, but the original is no longer extant; and it was translated at least twice into Hebrew. The better known translation, which is found in all except one of the manuscripts and which has been published a number of times, has a heading that attributes the work to Maimonides, while the other translation, which is found in only a single manuscript and breaks off in the middle of a sentence about half-way through the text, does not name an author.[75] The *Epistle* deals with the same sort of issue that occupied Maimonides in the first third of his *Epistle to Yemen* and it makes a couple of distinctive

---

Moses Narboni, who took astrological factors into account in his medical practice; see G. Bos, "R. Moshe Narboni: Philosopher and Physician," *Medieval Encounters* 1 (1995) 240–43. The circle of fourteenth-century admirers of Abraham Ibn Ezra studied by D. Schwartz, *Yashan be-Qanqan Ḥadash* (Jerusalem 1996) 31–32, et passim. R. Judah ben Asher, quoted by D. Schwartz, *Astrologia u-Magia* (Ramat Gan 1999) 266–67. Ḥasdai Crescas, *Or ha-Shem* 4.4. Joseph Ḥabiba, *Nimmuqe Yosef*, BT *Sanhedrin* 7 (end), quoted in full, and with sympathy, by J. Caro, the author of the *Shulḥan ^{c}Aruk*, in his commentary on *Ṭur*: *Yoreh De^{c}a* §179. Zeraḥiah ha-Levi, quoted by Schwartz, *Astrologia u-Magia* 189. The Yemeni writers cited by Tz. Langermann, "Yemenite Philosophic Midrash," in *The Jews of Medieval Islam*, ed. D. Frank (Leiden 1995) 338. Moses Almosnino, *Tefilla le-Moshe* (Salonika 1563) 40a, 54b; *Pirqe Moshe* (Salonika 1563) 93a. See also next note.

The most outspoken opponent was I. Polgar, *Ezer ha-Dat*, ed. J. Levinger (Tel Aviv 1984), chapter 3. Another opponent was Jacob ben Asher (see next note), who quotes and apparently accepts Maimonides' statement that only "fools imagine" astrological predictions to be true. A third was Abraham Bibago; see A. Bivach (Bibago), *Derek Emuna*, ed. Ch. Fraenkel-Goldschmidt (Jerusalem 1978) 129–33. Abraham Shalom was able to echo Maimonides and speak of "the stupid astrologers," to praise the biblical Abraham and Moses for their battle against astrological beliefs, yet at the same time to recognize that astrology does have a stratum of truth. See Abraham Shalom, *Neweh Shalom* (Venice 1575) 2.9–10, 39b–40a; 5.6, 71b–72a; 8.5, 130b; H. Davidson, *The Philosophy of Abraham Shalom* (Berkeley 1964) 6–7, 94.

[74]Jacob ben Asher, *Ṭur*: *Yoreh De^{c}a* §179 (quoting from Maimonides the prohibition against both making astrological predictions and acting on them). J. Caro, *Shulḥan ^{c}Aruk*: *Yoreh De^{c}a* §179.1. M. Jaffe, *Lebush ^{c}Aṭeret Ṣebi* (=*Yoreh De^{c}ah*) §179, who states, borrowing language from Joseph Ḥabiba, *Nimmuqe Yosef*, BT *Sanhedrin* 7 (end): Although God governs the world through the medium of the stars and although astrology is a great science and the astrologers sometimes make accurate predictions, the ancient rabbis forbade consulting astrologers. Some of the rabbinic figures cited here adduce BT *Pesaḥim* 113b, as their grounds for prohibiting consultation with astrologers.

[75]*Iggeret ha-Shemad*, in Shailat, *Letters and Essays of Moses Maimonides* (n. 1 above) 30, apparatus. English translation: A. Halkin and D. Hartman, *Crisis and Leadership* (Philadelphia 1985) 15–34.

are virtually identical with statements appearing there.[76] In his writings, Maimonides often referred to places where he treated subjects similar to the one before him at the moment. Yet the *Epistle on Religious Persecution* does not refer or allude to the *Epistle to Yemen*, nor does the *Epistle to Yemen* or any of Maimonides' other works refer or allude to it. Over a century ago, a scholar adduced this together with additional considerations as grounds for rejecting the attribution to Maimonides[77] but he has been ignored.

Neither of the Hebrew translations has qualms about calling Muhammad "the madman" (*meshugga*^{c}).[78] If that term or an equivalent—such as the Arabic word *majnūn*—was used in the Arabic original, the author could hardly have been living under the oppressive conditions he describes or, indeed, have been an easily identifiable person dwelling in any Muslim land. Although Jews writing to one another in Arabic invariably wrote in Hebrew characters, the stratagem, as Maimonides himself observes,[79] was only partial protection against having the contents divulged to the Muslim populace and authorities. A person might have enemies within the Jewish community, and Jewish converts to Islam were always hovering nearby. There was consequently the danger that even something in Hebrew characters might become public knowledge, and ridiculing Muhammad in a Muslim country was not conducive to a long and trouble-free life in the Middle Ages. As we learn from recent news reports, it still is not.

R. Isaac ben Sheshet, a well-regarded rabbinic authority active in Spain and North Africa in the late fourteenth and early fifteenth centuries, furnishes the first known reference to our *Epistle*. He had received a question concerning the status in Jewish law of persons who had been forced to convert to Christianity during the Spanish persecutions. The questioner thought that what he calls Maimonides' *Epistle on Religious Persecution* (*Iggeret ha-Shemad*) would be relevant to the issue and he quotes from it. Both he and R. Isaac, who answers at some length, treat the *Epistle* as a piece of formal jurisprudence issued by Maimonides and cite it side by side with Maimonides' law code as they weigh the legal matter before them.[80] The exchange of letters occurred around the turn of the fifteenth century,

[76](1) *Iggeret ha-Shemad* 55, and *Epistle to Yemen* (n. 10 above) 36; English translation [viii]: If a man commits a serious sin he should not suppose that it no longer makes a difference if he proceeds to commit minor sins; King Jeroboam, for example, was punished both for setting up two golden calves and for lesser matters. The two works differ in their examples of Jeroboam's minor sin. (2) *Iggeret ha-Shemad* 55 and *Epistle to Yemen* 34; English translation [vii]: When someone is prevented from observing the Jewish religion, he must abandon family and possessions and flee the country.

[77]Maimonides, *Guide of the Perplexed*, trans. M. Friedländer (London 1881–1885) 1.xxxv–xxxvii.

[78]*Iggeret ha-Shemad* 42. See above, p. 493, n. 33.

[79]Above p. 425, and p. 493, n. 33.

[80]R. Isaac ben Sheshet, *Responsa* §11. A few years later, R. Simeon Duran, *Tashbeṣ* 1, §63, reports a statement that he had been told was made by Maimonides in the "Treatise on Sanctifying God's Name" and he is apparently referring to our *Epistle*.

in other words, 200 years after Maimonides' death. The *Epistle* itself contains no date.

It portrays a situation in which an unnamed Muslim ruler conducted a widespread "religious persecution" (*shemad*)[81] against his Jewish subjects and apparently against Karaites and Christians as well.[82] Non-Muslims were coerced by the governing authorities, under threat of death, to acknowledge the "apostlehood" of Muhammad and his rank as a "true prophet."[83] At one point, reference is made to a popular Jewish hope that the Messiah would appear in the West and lead the suffering Jews to Palestine.[84] That suggests that the West may have been the epicenter of the persecution. It is therefore quite possible, although by no means certain, that the *Epistle* has the twelfth-century Almohad persecutions in view.

The *Epistle* represents itself as a refutation of an earlier pamphlet written by someone, again unnamed, who did not live in the lands affected by the religious persecution. It relates that the pamphlet's author had been asked whether Jews are permitted to acknowledge Muhammad as God's apostle and prophet in order to save their lives or whether they must undergo martyrdom to avoid doing so. He had answered apoplectically, branding anyone who acknowledges Muhammad's apostlehood even under duress as wicked, a denier of the God of Israel, a denier of the entire Torah, and disqualified from serving as a witness in Jewish legal proceedings. Such a person, in the judgment of the unnamed author, is a non-Jew, any Jewish prayers that he might recite are sinful, and any Jewish religious acts he might perform in secret are worthless.[85] The intemperance of the pronouncements verges on caricature, and it is hard to imagine their being expressed orally or in writing by a rabbinic authority of any standing. Moreover, although the *Epistle* states here and there that it is quoting verbatim from the otherwise unknown pamphlet, the quotations are sparing and the rationale the *Epistle* gives for not reproducing more is lame.[86] There are therefore grounds for suspecting that the lost pamphlet and its author are a straw man, a fictional mouthpiece for attitudes the person who wrote the *Epistle* sensed around him. On the other side of the coin, the quotations, inadequate though they are, and the manner in which the *Epistle* speaks about the "man" who wrote the pamphlet are consistent with its being an actual document and not a literary fiction.

Whether the author of the pamphlet being attacked was real or fictitious, the *Epistle* does not mince words. It accuses him, among other things, of "blasphemy and sacrilege, . . . stupidity and foolishness." He had made empty statements

[81]On the term *shemad*, see above, p. 11, n. 24.

[82]*Iggeret ha-Shemad* 33.

[83]*Iggeret ha-Shemad* 30–33.

[84]*Iggeret ha-Shemad* 57.

[85]*Iggeret ha-Shemad* 30–32.

[86]*Iggeret ha-Shemad* 30–31: Human speech is a gift of God, and the author of the pamphlet has misused it. It is therefore inappropriate to publicize what he said.

that "even women lacking a brain" would not have uttered. Specifically, he had failed to see the difference between worshiping another deity voluntarily and acknowledging, out of fear of death, that God chose Muhammad as His apostle and prophet, between worshiping an image as a deliberate act of apostasy and entering, under duress, a mosque where the worshipers' intent is to venerate the one God. [87] If the *Epistle* is a genuine work of Maimonides', it would reveal him to be highly sensitive to the tribulations of his coreligionists—although a lesson or two in gender sensitivity would not have hurt. It would also buttress the case for his having himself acknowledged the apostleship of Muhammad when he dwelled in the lands of the West. At one juncture the *Epistle* repeats the words of the prophet Jeremiah: "Let us lie down in our shame and let our confusion cover us, for we have sinned against the Lord God, we and our fathers." At another juncture, some—but not all—manuscripts of the *Epistle* have the writer speak about the counsel he gives to "myself and to my friends" when caught up in conditions such as had been described.[88] It sounds as if he was one of those who had performed acts that, according to the pamphlet he castigates, would reduce a Jew into a non-Jew.

From an intellectual point of view, the *Epistle* is badly flawed. It is guilty of disingenuousness when reporting what the Muslim authorities demanded of their Jewish subjects and of inaccuracy when applying the pertinent rabbinic legal categories to the situation it discusses.

The writer relates that although Jews caught up in the religious persecution were offered the choice of acknowledging Muhammad as the apostle of God or being put to death, the situation was unlike earlier religious persecutions. To save oneself in the present instance, one merely had to utter a few words: "Nothing is required . . . except a statement to the effect that one believes in that man [Muhammad]. The person is not required to perform any action, and if he wishes to fulfill the 613 [Mosaic] commandments clandestinely [after saying the words] he can do so, and nobody will interfere." The Muslims "know full well that we do not believe the statement and that a person mouths it only to save himself from the king by appeasing him and exalting his religion."[89]

Now, the formula "there is no god but Allah, and Muhammad is his apostle" is nothing less than the Islamic declaration of faith, and recitation of the formula is the mechanism whereby one converts to Islam. Muslim legists in the West at Maimonides' time did require something more to complete the conversion process: They required assurance of the voluntary nature of the conversion, explicit acceptance of the Islamic ritual obligations, immediate performance of a few basic rituals, and, perhaps, formal registration of the conversion in the judicial

[87] *Iggeret ha-Shemad* 30–32.

[88] *Iggeret ha-Shemad* 43, quoting Jeremiah 3:25.

[89] *Iggeret ha-Shemad* 53.

archives.[90] But fanatics who would allow themselves to ignore the nicety that conversion must be voluntary could easily ignore the remaining elements in the process and regard everyone who uttered the formula as a full-fledged Muslim. Moreover, the *Epistle* itself calls persons who acknowledged Muhammad as God's apostle and prophet the "religiously coerced" (*anusim*). He lets slip that they henceforth had to attend services in the mosque.[91] It looks very much as if the Jews who acknowledged Muhammad's apostlehood were not just mouthing a few innocuous words to please the king; they were, at least in the eyes of their persecutors, converting to the religion of Islam.

A few lines after asserting that Jews were allowed to observe their 613 religious commandments in private without interference once they acknowledged Muhammad to be God's apostle, the *Epistle* exhorts its readers to "fulfill the commandments as far as possible. Should someone, perchance, transgress a number of commandments or desecrate the Sabbath," he should not conclude that having sinned in more serious ritual matters he no longer need trouble himself about the less serious. "He should rather be as scrupulous as he can" in observing whatever he can.[92] The writer further indicates that those who observed the Jewish religious commandments would "lose their life and all their possessions, should what they did become known."[93] It thus turns out that the Muslim authorities were not at all as indulgent as they had been represented. They did not smile benevolently on persons who continued to observe the 613 commandments of the Law clandestinely after reciting the requisite words about Muhammad. Rather than living their lives as before after mumbling a few words to appease the Muslim ruler, those who submitted would be able to observe their ancestral religion only if they were willing to live the dangerous life of crypto Jews. So much for the circumstances of the persecution.

The Babylonian Talmud prescribes that in times of religious persecution, if a Jew should be presented with the choice between committing the smallest infraction of Jewish law and custom—even something, in the words of the Talmud, as minute as changing the style of one's shoelace—or suffering death, he must remain steadfast and choose death.[94] The author of the *Epistle* is familiar with the rule. But he evades it by drawing a distinction between infractions involving actions—whether the performance of actions that the Written and Oral Torahs prohibit or the failure to perform actions that the twin Torahs mandate—and infractions solely involving speech. Martyrdom, he contends, is demanded by Jewish law only when someone is forced to commit a transgression involving action; when forced to commit a

[90]M. Abumalham, "La conversión segun formularios notariales andalusíes," *Miscelanea de estudios arabes y hebraicos* 34 (1985) 72, 76–80.

[91]*Iggeret ha-Shemad* 32.

[92]*Iggeret ha-Shemad* 54–55.

[93]*Iggeret ha-Shemad* 58.

[94]BT *Sanhedrin* 74a–b; Alfasi, *ad locum*; Maimonides, *Mishneh Torah*: *H. Yesode ha-Torah* 5.3.

transgression involving only speech, a person should submit and not suffer martyrdom. The *Epistle* therefore advises coreligionists to recite the requisite words and acknowledge Muhammad as God's apostle if necessary to save their lives.[95]

The *Epistle*'s author cites no legal source for his distinction between infractions that involve an action and for which one should martyr oneself during a period of persecution, and infractions involving speech and for which one should not martyr oneself. In actuality, the classic rabbinic sources—in contexts that do not involve religious persecution and martyrdom—expressly exclude a distinction between action and words where apostasy from the Jewish religion is concerned, and, what is relevant for us, Maimonides followed the rabbinic sources in his *Mishneh Torah*.[96] Maimonides morover ranked commandments involving mental processes and not actions as the foundations of the Jewish religion.[97] Most significantly of all, he created a category of persons who "deny the Law" and lose their portion in the world to come because of the enormity of their sins; and among them he included those who sin through speech, notably, the man who "*says* that God has exchanged one law for another and the Torah is no longer binding, . . . as the Christians and Muslims [maintain]."[98]

In short, when the *Epistle* applies the rabbinic regulations governing martyrdom, it distinguishes between infractions involving actions and those involving speech, whereas the classic rabbinic sources and Maimonides' code in particular exclude any distinction between recognizing another religion by actions or by speech. The *Epistle* specifically exempts the persecutors' demand that Jews mouth the words "Muhammad is the apostle and prophet" from the mandate of martyrdom and in fact encourages Jews to make the declaration in order to save their lives; reciting those words is part of the mechanism whereby one converts to Islam, and the ancient rabbis expected Jews to martyr themselves when compelled to convert to another religion. Apart from the conversion aspect, accepting Muhammad as a prophet would imply a denial of the eternally binding nature of the Law of Moses and, at least according to Maimonides' *Mishneh Torah*, would be an infraction of the most serious proportions. To cap it all, the *Epistle* has been seen to concede that Jews who submitted to Muslim demands did in fact commit infractions involving actions; for they had to refrain from performing certain religious commandments. Even granting the quibble about infractions involving speech, persons presented with the bitter choice should, by a rabbinic rule that the

[95] *Iggeret ha-Shemad* 53–54.

[96] Mishna, *Sanhedrin* 7:6; Maimonides, *Mishneh Torah*: *H. ᶜAboda Zara* 3.4: To *say* to any physical object "you are my god" is a form of idolatry. According to the accepted halakic rule, one must under all conditions martyr oneself rather than commit idolatry.

In the *Book of Commandments* (*Sefer ha-Miṣwot*), introduction, rule 9, Maimonides recognizes four areas with which the religious commandments are concerned: beliefs, actions, ethical qualities, and speech.

[97] *Mishneh Torah*: *H. Yesode ha-Torah*, chapter 1.

[98] Maimonides, *Mishneh Torah*: *H. Teshuba* 3.6, 8 (Frankel edition).

Epistle itself recognizes, have chosen death. Maimonides had stated in his *Epistle to Yemen* that anyone who submits to the enemy and forsakes the Law declares before the world that he is not a descendant of the men and women who were present at Sinai when the Law was given to the Israelites.[99]

We can easily sympathize with the unfortunates who found themselves in the frightening predicament and were too weak to resist. We can likewise sympathize with the author of the *Epistle* as he offered support and comfort to his coreligionists. It is nonetheless obvious that in doing so he circumvented the demands of rabbinic law.

In the course of its treatment of martyrdom, Maimonides' *Mishneh Torah* lays down the rule that in situations where rabbinic law prescribes that one should submit to an oppressor, commit the infraction demanded, and *not* suffer martyrdom, a person who nonetheless martyrs himself through a delusion of supererogatory heroism "is guilty of a capital sin."[100] No source for Maimonides' opinion has been discovered in the classic rabbinic texts. It would seem to be his own conclusion and it was one with which not all rabbinic authorities concurred.[101] The author of the *Epistle* for his part knows the rule and accepts it. He writes: Where the rabbis do not mandate martyrdom, "should someone see himself . . . as more scrupulous than the sages and allow himself to be killed, . . . thereby sanctifying God's name, as he supposes, such a man is a sinner, . . . his blood is on his own head, and he is guilty of a capital sin."[102] As already seen, the *Epistle* not only permits, but recommends acknowledging Muhammad's apostlehood when necessary in order to save one's life. Yet immediately after stating the rule about submitting and not martyring oneself when the Law does not require that to be done, the *Epistle*—undoubtedly because the writer realized that he had stretched matters in sanctioning the acknowledgment of Muhammad's apostlehood—states: A Jew who refuses to acknowledge Muhammad and martyrs himself "has done a religious good deed [*miṣwa*] and will receive a great reward from God, because he has surrendered his soul for the sanctification of God's name."[103] The *Epistle* tells us that it is a capital sin to martyr oneself when such is not required, that Jewish law does not require one to martyr himself in order to avoid acknowledging Muhammad as God's prophet, yet that those who do martyr themselves rather than acknowledge Muhammad's prophethood perform a religious good deed and will receive a great reward. The writer is not merely guilty of inaccuracy regarding the halakic rules covering the situation he describes; he maneuvers himself into a blatant self-contradiction.[104]

[99]Above, p. 490.

[100]Maimonides, *Mishneh Torah*: *H. Yesode ha-Torah* 5.4. These would be instances when there was no general religious persecution and certain additional conditions also obtained.

[101]See Caro, *Kesef Mishneh*, on *Mishneh Torah*: *H. Yesode ha-Torah* 5.4.

[102]*Iggeret ha-Shemad* 52.

[103]*Iggeret ha-Shemad* 53–54.

[104]The point is made by Friedländer, *Guide of the Perplexed* (n. 77 above) 1.xxxvi.

The writer either had a poor legal and logical mind or allowed extra-legal considerations to sway him. As we have seen on more than one occasion, Maimonides was capable of expressing himself rhetorically. But when deciding issues of rabbinic law, he put extra-legal considerations aside and was scrupulous about applying only legal criteria. If the *Epistle* is an authentic work of Maimonides', he was therefore acting out of character. A recent scholar dedicated a valuable study to the halakic side of the *Epistle* and called attention to shortcomings in its halakic reasoning including points that I have mentioned here. The scholar in question started, however, by taking Maimonides' authorship for granted. He consequently could find no way of making sense of the *Epistle* except as an instance where Maimonides consciously "distorted the facts to whose ascertainment he had dedicated his life, in the hope of saving a host of sinners from despair. . . ."[105]

In the final third of the *Epistle*, the author writes that he had "collect[ed] . . . chief spices from the books of the early [scholars]" (*sifre ha-qadmonim*) in order to clarify the subject at hand and he divides his clarification into five short sections.[106] Since the Arabic text is lost, we cannot know what Arabic term underlies the Hebrew word *qadmonim*, "early [scholars]." As it stands, the Hebrew word could mean *earlier*, in the sense of a just few years previously,[107] but also *ancient*; it might, in other words, designate either recent scholars or the rabbis of the classic period, the period up to the completion of the Babylonian Talmud.[108] Maimonides, as far as I could discover, does not use the term *qadmonim* as a designation for rabbinists of either the talmudic or the posttalmudic periods.[109] Nor was it his habit to preface a legal discussion by saying that he was now going to collect what posttalmudic works had said and rule on the basis of them.

Virtually all the halakic elements in the five sections with which the *Epistle* concludes have parallels in either Maimonides' *Book of Commandments* or his *Mishneh Torah*, and several of the pertinent statements cannot be traced to any source earlier than Maimonides.[110] At the same time, the *Epistle* subtly adapts

[105]H. Soloveitchik, "Maimonides' *Iggeret ha-Shemad*: Law and Rhetoric," in *Lookstein Memorial Volume*, ed. L. Landman (New York 1980) 281–319. I quote from p. 319.

[106]*Iggeret ha-Shemad* 46–59.

[107]Ibn Ezra, Commentary on Genesis 24:59.

[108]For example, Ibn Ezra, Commentary on Genesis 15:6 and 16:3. Other examples of both senses are given in Ben Yehuda's dictionary, sub voce *qadmoni*.

[109]In the *Mishneh Torah*, he typically calls the rabbis of the classic period *ḥakamim* but calls neither them nor posttalmudic rabbinic authorities *qadmonim*.

[110](1) *Iggeret ha-Shemad* 47–49 (and see p. 51) divides desecration of God's name into two general and two particular categories, thereby developing a distinction drawn by Maimonides, *Book of Commandments*, negative commandment #63, between two general categories and one particular category of desecration of God's name. The *Iggeret's* scheme is awkward, because one of its

legal opinions of Maimonides' in order to accommodate them to its own purpose.[111] If Maimonides was himself the author of the *Epistle*, it is unclear what the books of the early scholars on which he relied might have been. But if the author of the *Epistle* was someone who drew from Maimonides—and if the Arabic underlying the Hebrew phrase that I have translated as *early scholars* should permit such a reading—the books of which he speaks would most plausibly be Maimonides' *Book of Commandments* and *Mishneh Torah.* On that scenario, the unknown author fashioned the five sections with which he completed the *Epistle* mainly or wholly from Maimonides, while adjusting what he found there in order to serve his purpose.

Perhaps Maimonides was the author of the *Epistle* and allowed himself to obfuscate the anti-Jewish persecution that he was dealing with. Perhaps he was acting out of character, twisted the rabbinic rules that he was applying, and went as far as blatantly to contradict himself. Perhaps the Arabic words underlying the expression "books of early [scholars]" are a designation Maimonides would use for talmudic and midrashic literature, and he is saying that he fashioned the sections with which the *Epistle* concludes out of inferences somehow made by him from the classic rabbinic texts. Or perhaps the Arabic words are a designation that Maimonides would use for early posttalmudic writings and he was acting out of character again—or maybe he was still very young and unsure of his legal judgment—and he relied not on the classic texts themselves but on posttalmudic writers whose works have unfortunately evaporated into thin air without leaving a trace.

Perhaps. But the bottom line is that there are very strong, although maybe not conclusive, grounds for rejecting the authenticity of Maimonides' authorship of the *Epistle.* There are no grounds for affirming his authorship apart from his being named as the author in manuscripts of one of the two Hebrew translations and by persons writing two centuries after his death. We have seen more than once that the attribution of a work to Maimonides in a manuscript commands little credibility.

---

particular categories repeats one of the general categories. (2) *Iggeret ha-Shemad* 51–52: Somebody who commits an infraction where the rabbis said he should have chosen martyrdom has desecrated God's name under compulsion, which is different from desecrating God's name voluntarily; he is not subject to punishment and is not called a "sinner" or "wicked man"; supported by a passage from Sifra. Maimonides, *Mishneh Torah H. Yesode ha-Torah* 5.4, citing the same passage from Sifra: Someone in such a situation has desecrated God's name and transgressed but is exempt from punishment. There is a difference in emphasis between the *Iggeret* and *H. Yesode ha-Torah.* (3) *Iggeret ha-Shemad* 52: The sin of undergoing martyrdom when not required by the rabbis; discussed earlier in the text. (4) *Iggeret ha-Shemad* 54–55: Jews should mouth the statement about Muhammad and then leave the country at once in order to observe their religion freely. Maimonides, *Mishneh Torah H. Yesode ha-Torah* 5.4: A person who desecrates God's name by not choosing martyrdom in instances where the rabbis mandated martyrdom is not subject to punishment. But if he is able to leave the country and fails to do so, he is "as a dog that returneth to his vomit" and is classified as a willful sinner.

[111] Examples (3) and (4) in the previous note.

Treatise on Resurrection. The *Treatise on Resurrection* is the most personal of Maimonides' works and goes to the heart of his innermost beliefs. Unfortunately, as happens elsewhere in his writings, after it has been read and reread, divergent opinions about it remain.

The chain of events that induced Maimonides to compose it was set in motion by statements he had made in his Commentary on the Mishna and *Mishneh Torah.* Those statements refer back, in turn, to a few lines in the Mishna tractate *Sanhedrin* and to the segment of the Babylonian Talmud constructed around the Mishna passage.

The tractate *Sanhedrin* of the Mishna has as its primary topic the imposition of different types of death penalty by law courts. Toward the end of the tractate, an association of ideas leads away from death penalties imposed by human courts to the "world to come" and those who are excluded therefrom—those who, as it were, are subject to the ultimate death penalty imposed by God. The pertinent Mishna paragraph states the general rule: "All Israel have a portion in the world to come" and then lists certain exceptions. Among those losing their portion in the world to come is he "who says that there is no resurrection of the dead,"[112] that is, who denies a future restoration of the souls of the dead to resurrected bodies.

The Mishna corpus does not explain what the "world to come" is, but the Babylonian Talmud appears to equate it with a future state of existence that will begin with the resurrection of the dead and continue with a new, either lengthy or unending, life for the resurrected righteous. On the Talmud's reading, the Mishna accordingly asserts that as a form of poetic justice, anyone who denies resurrection of the dead forfeits the future resurrection of his own body and the state of existence which then ensues.[113]

The meaning of the term *world to come* became one of the bones of contention between Maimonides and his opponents. The opponents identify the world to come with the resurrection of the dead—as the Babylonian Talmud appears to do—and a subsequent unending life enjoyed by those who are resurrected. Maimonides, we shall see, unqualifiedly affirms his belief in a future resurrection of the dead but treats resurrection as only a passing, secondary episode within the scheme of human postmortal existence. The world to come, the ultimate goal of human existence, is, for him, something quite different, namely, the eternal, incorporeal state of existence enjoyed by perfected human intellects. He will moreover insist that the ancient rabbis intended by the "world to come" precisely what he understands by the term.

[112]Mishna, *Sanhedrin* 10:1. Maimonides did not have, or did not accept, the alternate reading in the Mishna according to which the person who loses his portion in the world to come is he "who says that resurrection is not *affirmed in the Torah.*"

[113]BT *Sanhedrin* 90a (he who denies resurrection will be punished measure for measure by being deprived of it); 92a (the resurrected bodies will live forever); 92b (perhaps they will not live forever). *Tanḥuma*, *Vayiqra* (standard version) §8, states that the world to come exists alongside this world, and righteous souls go there immediately upon the death of their bodies.

As was noted in an earlier chapter, Maimonides halts at a number of places in his Commentary on the Mishna and provides an introduction to the section of the Mishna that he is about to interpret before proceeding to an exegesis of the text itself. The chapter of the Mishna containing the declaration that all Israel have a portion in the world to come is one of the places where he considered such an introduction to be called for. He prepares the ground for the Mishna text by setting forth his understanding of the *world to come* and the *resurrection of the dead* together with several other terms, notably, the *Garden of Eden* and the *Age of the Messiah*. The latter two are drawn into the discussion because of their eschatological character and because they are mentioned in the section of the Babylonian Talmud that is constructed around the pertinent Mishna paragraph.

Different schools of posttalmudic thought, Maimonides writes, view the Garden of Eden, the Age of the Messiah, and the resurrection of the dead as one or another form of eternal physical existence in a future happy state—a state, for example, in which immortal physical human beings will drink from ever-flowing streams of wine and oil or in which they will pick already baked bread and fully tailored clothes from trees. Each school of thought regards one such physical state or a combination of them as God's final reward to persons who obey His Law. But few, he laments, ask precisely what the term *Garden of Eden* and the other terms, especially the *world to come*, mean. Few ask what the purpose of human existence is and which of the eschatological states are merely steps on the path to the ultimate aim of human life.[114]

Before entering on the subject of human immortality and explaining what he took the rabbis to have intended by the various eschatological terms they used, Maimonides—still in the introduction to the Mishna paragraph with which we are concerned—offers an analogy and makes a methodological statement regarding rabbinic aggada. Both the analogy and the methodological statement are relevant for us.

The analogy is that of a schoolboy. When a boy begins his study of the sacred Law, Maimonides writes, he cannot yet appreciate the true object of such study. The teacher therefore initially motivates him by giving him sweets as a reward for success in his studies. When the boy outgrows sweets, the teacher motivates him by promising attractive clothes, then money, and eventually the prospect of becoming a "rabbi and judge" and basking in the respect and honor attendant upon those titles. In truth, the goal to be pursued in studying the Law is neither material reward, professional titles, nor honor. The goal is the resulting knowledge of God's Law.[115]

Maimonides' methodological statement regarding the sayings (*aqwāl*, *kalām*) of the ancient rabbis, in other words, rabbinic aggada, stresses that none of those

[114]Maimonides, Commentary on the Mishna, *Sanhedrin* 10.1, introduction (n. 48 above) pp. 195–97.

[115]Maimonides, Commentary on the Mishna, *Sanhedrin* 10, introduction pp. 197–99.

sayings, no piece of aggada, may be dismissed; the ancient rabbis were great and wise men, and some of their dicta embody profound wisdom. Many of the rabbis' sayings are nonetheless impossible and indeed embarrassing when taken at face value, for the literal sense of the language sometimes depicts things that no intelligent person would desire even if they were possible.[116]

Although the analogy of the schoolboy by no means conflicts with the methodological statement on aggada, each suggests a different way of viewing what Maimonides is going to do in the present section. The analogy suggests that the Garden of Eden, the messianic age, and the resurrection of the dead are real places and events but they are means to a higher end, their function being to motivate mankind along the path toward the ultimate goal of human existence. The methodological statement suggests that at least some rabbinic remarks about the Garden of Eden, the Messiah, and the resurrection of the dead are impossible when taken literally and must be construed in a metaphorical sense. When illustrating aggada that has to be taken metaphorically, Maimonides remarks that what the ancient rabbis said about trees bearing already baked bread and tailored clothes symbolizes nothing more than the plenty with which the earth will be blessed at the time of the Messiah.[117] The rabbinic statement to the effect that in the world to come the righteous sit with crowns on their head and enjoy the splendor of the divine presence envisages not literal crowns, but "the immortality of the soul through the immortality of its object of thought . . . as maintained by expert philosophers."[118] The pivotal question is how far Maimonides went in reading rabbinic aggada in a nonliteral fashion. Was he perhaps hinting that it is not merely certain statements about the Garden of Eden and resurrection, but rather the entire notion of a Garden of Eden on earth and a future resurrection of the dead which must be read as metaphors?

Whatever the correct answer to the question, Maimonides asserts that the rabbinic expression "world to come" does not mean resurrection of the dead: When the rabbis spoke of the world to come, they had no thought of anything relating to man's physical side nor even of anything occurring at some future date. By the world to come, they meant the immortal state that human souls or, to be more precise, the intellectual faculty of human souls, can attain at any and all times. When a human intellect attached to a body is perfected and separates from the body at death, the intellect becomes immortal forthwith and—as Maimonides interprets the rabbis—immediately enters the world to come.

The mishnaic assurance that *all* Israel have a portion in the world to come would seem to be run counter to what Maimonides has been saying; all Israel surely do not

[116]Maimonides, Commentary on the Mishna, *Sanhedrin* 10, introduction pp. 201–3. See BT *Sanhedrin* 100a.

[117]Maimonides, Commentary on the Mishna, *Sanhedrin* 10, introduction p. 207. The description of bread and clothes growing on trees is found in BT *Shabbat* 30b.

[118]Maimonides, Commentary on the Mishna, *Sanhedrin* 10, introduction p. 205, discussed above, pp. 156, 164.

perfect their intellects to the required level. He explains the assurance as follows: When the people of Israel accept the words of the prophets as coming from God, they are moved to pursue virtue and to develop their intellects; they labor to acquire intelligible thought; their intellects are thereby rendered immortal and they gain their portion in the world to come.[119] The rabbis' promise of a portion in the world to come is thus an oblique way of saying that the Torah furnishes the needed tools for pursuing the intellectual life and, as a by-product, of achieving intellectual immortality.

As for the *Garden of Eden*, Maimonides submits that there is no reason why an idyllic location of such a sort cannot exist somewhere on earth. The *Age of the Messiah*, as he construes it, will be an era when the yoke of the gentiles will be thrown off and the people of Israel will live independently in their own land. It will be an age of material and intellectual prosperity, but the laws of nature now governing the world will remain in effect. As for a future resurrection of the dead, Maimonides stresses that it is one of the principles of the Law of Moses, and Jews who reject it cut themselves off from the Jewish nation. Resurrection will, however, be enjoyed only by the righteous, and since all bodies must eventually decompose, the bodies of the resurrected will inevitably die again.[120] Maimonides goes into no more detail. The introductory section in his Commentary on the Mishna which I have been citing is the one that concludes with his well-known list of thirteen principles of the Jewish faith.[121] The last item in the list is put most crisply: "The thirteenth principle is the resurrection of the dead, and I have already explained it."[122]

Maimonides' position in the Commentary on the Mishna is, then, that resurrection is a dogma of the Jewish faith. A resurrection of the bodies of the righteous will definitely occur at some future time, but the resurrected bodies will not live forever, and restoration of souls to bodies is not the goal of human existence. The ultimate goal is human intellectual perfection, and although no one should pursue intellectual perfection in order to obtain a reward, the reward will come in the form of the immortality of the human intellect. When the rabbis spoke of the world to come, they were talking about immortality of the intellect.

Maimonides' *Mishneh Torah* likewise affirms a future resurrection of the dead but it deals with the subject even more tersely than the Commentary on the Mishna did. "All Israel," Maimonides writes in the *Mishneh Torah*, "have a portion in the world to come." There are exceptions and one of them, he specifies—on the basis of the Mishna paragraph already referred to—is the person who denies the

[119]Maimonides, Commentary on the Mishna, *Sanhedrin* 10, introduction pp. 208–9.

[120]Maimonides, Commentary on the Mishna, *Sanhedrin* 10, introduction pp. 206–7; see above, n. 113.

[121]See above, p. 156.

[122]Maimonides, Commentary on the Mishna, *Sanhedrin* 10, introduction p. 216.

resurrection of the dead.[123] That is all the *Mishneh Torah* has to say about resurrection. By contrast, Maimonides gives considerable attention to the subject of the world to come.

"The goodness laid away for the righteous," he states, "is the life of the world to come." It is not a future era in human history, something not yet existent, but rather the state of immortality gained by every properly developed human intellect upon the death of its body. In the world to come, there "is no body or corporeality; only the souls [*nefesh*] of the righteous, [existing] without body, like the ministering angels." The "soul [*neshama*] that stands in need of a body," that is to say, the subrational segment of the human soul, does not participate. Since the human body and the subrational segment of the human soul play no part, the rabbinic portrayal of the world to come as a place where the righteous "sit with crowns on their heads" is perforce "allegorical." By the righteous' wearing crowns in the afterlife, the rabbis meant that the intellectual thought acquired by human souls during the life of the body and "thanks to which they gain the life of the world to come remains with them."[124]

In both his Commentary on the Mishna and the *Mishneh Torah*, Maimonides, in sum, recognizes a future resurrection of bodies but says virtually nothing about it beyond affirming that it will occur. He in no way explains what function it serves, apart from suggesting that it has been promised in order to motivate man to choose the correct path in life. And he focuses his interest not on resurrection but on the world to come, which he construes in harmony with philosophic theories of the immortality of the human intellect; the "righteous" who gain the world to come are persons who perfect their intellect. We are left with the question whether he genuinely believed, or did his best to believe, in a literal resurrection of the dead, despite any discomfort he may have felt with the notion; or whether he perhaps took rabbinic references to resurrection metaphorically and saw resurrection as a symbol for the immortality of the human intellect, in much the same way that he took the rabbis' notion of crowns on the heads of the righteous as an allegory.

It was Maimonides' account of human immortality in the *Mishneh Torah*, where his treatment of resurrection is even more meager than in the Commentary on the Mishna, that became the eye of a hurricane. Because he there conspicuously distinguishes the world to come and the goodness laid away for the righteous from the

[123] *Mishneh Torah*: *H. Teshuba* 3.5–6. Maimonides further states that "the pious from among the gentiles likewise have a portion in the world to come"; for his rabbinic sources, see above, p. 242, n. 219. In *Mishneh Torah*: *H. Melakim* 8.11, Maimonides distinguishes between the *pious* among the gentiles, who partly accept the direction of the Mosaic Law, and the *wise* among the gentiles who do not. If in the present passage, he still has in mind what he wrote in the Commentary of the Mishna about the sense in which all Israel have a portion in the world to come, his meaning could be that the pious among the gentiles have a portion there because they too follow the guidelines of the Mosaic Law and accordingly develop their intellects.

[124] *Mishneh Torah*: *H. Teshuba* 8.1–3, 8. Cf. H. Yesode ha-Torah 4.8–9.

resurrection of bodies, the suspicion arose that he did not in his heart of hearts believe in a future resurrection of human bodies.

His arch-critic, Abraham ben David, reacted to the account of the world to come in the *Mishneh Torah* with the comment: "This man's words are, in my view, close to [those of] him who denies the resurrection of bodies. . . . By the life of my head, that was not the rabbis' opinion."[125] Other critics in southern France and Spain joined the fray.[126] As far as is known, none of the criticisms from the western half of the Jewish world came to Maimonides' attention, but criticisms from the eastern half did. Samuel ben Eli, the principal of the Baghdadi rabbinic academy, stood at the forefront of the controversy in the East, and Maimonides' response to Samuel's critique was caustic.

Samuel wrote a twenty-page treatise in Arabic, which has been preserved only in a medieval Hebrew translation. In it, he recalls how he became involved in the resurrection issue and he lays out a veiled criticism of Maimonides. Courtesy and tact prevented him from mentioning Maimonides by name, but it is unmistakable whom he had in mind.

Some time earlier, Samuel relates in the opening paragraphs of his treatise, Jews in the land of Yemen wrote informing him that they had received "a composition by a certain scholar, . . . may God further his well-being," which rejected the resurrection of the dead in the traditional Jewish sense of the return of the souls of the dead to their bodies.[127] Maimonides, it will be recalled, commonly called the *Mishneh Torah* his "composition."[128] The letter from Yemen further reported that in the composition in question, the unnamed scholar interpreted ultimate human reward and retribution as something reserved for the soul alone; he took the resurrection of the body described in Scripture as a "metaphor" (*mashal*) for the survival of the human soul; and the appearance of his book brought about a deterioration of faith among the Jews of Yemen.[129] Maimonides does maintain in the *Mishneh Torah* that the ultimate human reward is enjoyed exclusively by the human soul or, to be precise, the human intellect. He takes the rabbinic portrayal of the righteous' sitting with crowns on their heads to be an allegory and some scriptural depictions of what will occur in the messianic age to be metaphors.[130] He never, however, writes in the *Mishneh Torah* or anywhere else that the resurrection of the body described in Scripture is a metaphor for the immortality of the soul.

Samuel had been perturbed by the letter he received, because lack of faith in the resurrection of the dead leads to "doubts about the truth and about the dogmas of

[125]Above, p. 274.

[126]Above, pp. 277–78.

[127]Samuel ben Eli, *Iggeret be-ᶜInyan Teḥiyyat ha-Metim* (*Ma'amar be-Teḥiyyat ha-Metim*), ed. Tz. Langermann, "*Qobeṣ ᶜal Yad*, n.s., 15 (2001) 66.

[128]Above, p. 203.

[129]Samuel ben Eli, *Ma'amar be-Teḥiyyat ha-Metim* 66.

[130]*Mishneh Torah*: *H. Melakim* 12.1.

religion." He apparently had not yet himself seen Maimonides' *Mishneh Torah*, but he answered the Yemeni Jews on the basis of what they quoted from it. He assured them that the doctrine of resurrection must be taken literally, that God will in the future restore human souls to their bodies. At the same time, he defended the unnamed author of the composition occasioning the doubts by showing how the quotations sent to him by the Yemeni Jews can be harmonized with orthodox belief. He also cited another work of the author of the composition in order to defend him against charges of heterodoxy. The other work, Samuel pointed out to the Yemeni Jews, expressly declared the belief in resurrection to be a principle of the Mosaic Law and denied all connection with the Jewish nation to anyone who fails to embrace the belief; at the same time it represented resurrection as a boon enjoyed by the righteous alone. The words cited by Samuel from the author whose name he avoids mentioning are a verbatim quotation from Maimonides' Commentary on the Mishna.[131] Samuel is reporting, in effect, that he had defended Maimonides' orthodoxy to the Yemeni Jews by quoting from Maimonides' Commentary on the Mishna.

At a later date, Samuel continues, the composition that occasioned the uproar in Yemen—in other words, Maimonides' *Mishneh Torah*—reached Iraq, and members of Samuel's circle informed him that local Jews who read it had begun to question the literalness of the doctrine of resurrection. At the request of the faithful, he thereupon composed the present treatise, in which he repeated some of the things that he had written earlier to the Yemeni Jews and in which he expanded on the subject.[132]

The bulk of Samuel's treatise undertakes to establish two propositions, first, that the human soul in its entirety survives the body's death and, second, that at some time in the future, souls of the dead will be restored to their bodies.[133] Unaided human speculation, he submits, is helpless when faced with issues of the sort, for philosophers are incapable of agreeing on the nature of the human soul or the soul's fate. To make the point, he quotes a half dozen divergent opinions of "men of reason [*sekel*]" regarding the nature of the human soul and contends that if human speculation were capable of discovering what kind of entity the soul is, philosophers would not have disagreed sharply on the issue.[134] Somewhat inconsistently, after having disqualified human speculation as an arbiter, Samuel adduces the support of philosophy for both propositions that he wishes to establish. "The wisest philosophers," he informs readers, showed "with rational [*sikliyyot*] proofs and true demonstrations that the [human] soul . . . is an incorporeal, self-subsistent substance,"[135] from which it follows that the death of the human body

[131] Samuel ben Eli, *Ma'amar be-Teḥiyyat ha-Metim* 67, quoting Maimonides' thirteenth principle of faith, Commentary on the Mishna, *Sanhedrin*, introduction, p. 206.

[132] Samuel ben Eli, *Ma'amar be-Teḥiyyat ha-Metim* 67.

[133] Samuel ben Eli, *Ma'amar be-Teḥiyyat ha-Metim* 70.

[134] Samuel ben Eli, *Ma'amar be-Teḥiyyat ha-Metim* 67-68.

[135] Samuel ben Eli, *Ma'amar be-Teḥiyyat ha-Metim* 68.

does not entail the death of the soul. Moreover, "the most precise of the philosophers" and, again, "one of the wise philosophers at the end of his book on the soul" maintained that human reason does not exclude the possibility of God's restoring human souls to bodies.[136]

The half dozen divergent opinions of men of reason on the nature of the human soul turn out to be verbatim quotations from a prolix and voluminous philosophic work entitled *K. al-Mu^c^tabar*, written by a Jewish physician named Abū al-Barakāt, who was active in Baghdad during the early twelfth century.[137] The pair of theses that Samuel cites from the wisest and most precise of the philosophers—namely, that the human soul is a self-subsistent substance, and that reason does not exclude the possibility of a future resurrection—are positions that Abū al-Barakāt advanced in his own name in the same work.[138] And the passage cited by Samuel from the end of the wise philosopher's book on the soul is a word-for-word quotation from the penultimate chapter in the section of *K. al-Mu^c^tabar* which deals with the human soul.[139] Samuel never mentions either Abū al-Barakāt's name or the name of his book.

Since the philosophers had not spoken with one voice, Samuel concludes that reliance must be placed on Jewish sources—on Scripture, on rabbinic tradition, and on the consensus of the Jewish nation, which is rooted in the other two.

To take a few samples of Samuel's reasoning from the Jewish sources: He argues for the immortality of the human soul from the fact that the biblical heroes Abraham, Moses, Elijah, Isaiah, and others all suffered for their callings despite having no expectation of being rewarded in this world. Since they could expect no reward in the present life, they must have looked forward to their reward in an existence beyond the grave.[140] Scripture, as rabbinic tradition and Samuel understand it, warns that God will demand the blood of a person who commits

[136]Samuel ben Eli, *Ma'amar be-Teḥiyyat ha-Metim* 82–83.

[137]Abū al-Barakāt, *K. al-Mu^c^tabar* (Hyderabad 1939) 2.355.

Qifṭī, *Ta'rīkh al-Ḥukamā'*, ed. J. Lippert (Leipzig 1903) 343, 346, reports that Abū al-Barakāt converted to Islam and repeats two different accounts of his motive for having done so. The passage is summarized by S. Poznanski, "Die jüdischen Artikel in Ibn al-Qifti's Gelehrtenlexikon," *Monatsschrift för Geschichte und Wissenschaft des Judentums* 49 (1905) 50–52. The fact that Samuel ben Eli calls Abū al-Barakāt a wise and precise philosopher and that Joseph ben Judah, who criticized Samuel for every minor slip, does not cry out against Samuel's relying on, and even praising, an apostate suggests that here too Qifṭī was mistaken. Regarding Qifṭī's unreliability, see above, pp. 17–18. In the early thirteenth century, a copy of Abū al-Barakāt's commentary on the Book of Ecclesiastes was made for a principal of the Baghdad rabbinic academy; see Langermann, *Iggeret R. Samuel ben Eli be-^c^Inyan Teḥiyyat ha-Metim* (n. 127 above) 57; that too strongly suggests that Abū al-Barakāt was not known as a convert to Islam. My colleague Hossein Ziai informs me that medieval Persian works refer to Abū al-Barakāt as a Jew, without further qualification.

[138]Abū al-Barakāt, *K. al-Mu^c^tabar* 2.364, 440, 449–50.

[139]Abū al-Barakāt, *K. al-Mu^c^tabar* 2. 443–44.

[140]Samuel ben Eli, *Ma'amar be-Teḥiyyat ha-Metim* 70–71.

suicide. Plainly someone who commits suicide can be punished only in a postmortal state, from which it again follows that the human soul survives the body.[141] The Babylonian Talmud records anecdotes in which living persons converse with the dead; they must have conversed with souls that survived the death of their respective bodies.[142] It is common knowledge that Jews pray for the welfare of their dead relatives; such everyday behavior proves that the consensus of the nation, which is rooted in Scripture and the rabbinic sources, takes the survival of the soul for granted.[143]

To demonstrate that bodies will be restored to life at some time in the future, Samuel quotes a number of scriptural verses, for example, the sentence in Deuteronomy wherein God announces: "I kill and I make alive; I have wounded and I heal." He further quotes the talmudic analysis of the Deuteronomy verse, where it is argued that just as God causes the very same person to be wounded and healed, so too, Scripture must be saying, God does not cause the death of one person and the birth of another, but makes the very same person die and live again.[144] As for the consensus of the Jewish nation, Samuel finds it in the liturgy. When a Jew awakens in the morning, he recites a prayer acknowledging that God will take his soul and expressing the expectation that God will "restore it to me in the future to come." The matinal formula concludes: "Blessed art thou O Lord, who restorest souls to dead corpses." The Babylonian Talmud instructs anyone finding himself in the vicinity of Jewish graves to bless God who created those now dead and who will "one day quicken and maintain" them. The formula concludes much as the previous formula did: "Blessed is He who quickeneth the dead."[145]

As Samuel pictures the end of days, the inaugural event will be the coming of the Messiah. God will at once resurrect the faithful and conduct them into a new Garden of Eden located near Jerusalem; Samuel was in good company here, since Jewish theologians commonly linked resurrection with the messianic age.[146] In the new Garden of Eden, the resurrected will lead a blissful life. A stream of water will spring forth from under the "threshold of the Holy Temple" and will swell as it

[141]Samuel ben Eli, *Ma'amar be-Teḥiyyat ha-Metim* 71, with reference to Genesis 9:5. Cf. BT *Baba Qamma* 91b, *Genesis Rabba* 34:5, and Rashi on Genesis 9:5. Ibn Ezra, Commentary on Deuteronomy 32:39, notes that Genesis 9:5 had been cited by some to prove that souls undergo postmortal punishment.

[142]Samuel ben Eli, *Ma'amar be-Teḥiyyat ha-Metim* 73, referring to anecdotes in BT *Berakot* 18b.

[143]Samuel ben Eli, *Ma'amar be-Teḥiyyat ha-Metim* 70.

[144]Samuel ben Eli, *Ma'amar be-Teḥiyyat ha-Metim* 76. The verse is Deuteronomy 32:39, and the rabbinic analysis is found in BT *Sanhedrin* 91b, and parallels. Saadia, *Sefer ha-Emunot we-ha-De^{c}ot* 7:3, whom Samuel here cites as further support, also quoted the verse together with the talmudic analysis, although without mentioning that his source was talmudic. Abraham Ibn Ezra, Commentary on Deuteronomy 32:39, notes that "many" had cited that verse as a proof-text for the "life of the world to come."

[145]Samuel ben Eli, *Ma'amar be-Teḥiyyat ha-Metim* 80, alluding to BT *Berakot* 58b.

[146]For example, Saadia, *Sefer ha-Emunot we-ha-De^{c}ot*, appendix, 7.8.

flows forth. Wondrous trees will grow on each side of the stream, including the trees of life and of knowledge, as well as other trees that had perhaps been present in the original Garden of Eden without being mentioned in the Book of Genesis; Samuel says nothing, however, of trees from which clothing can be picked. After about a thousand years, the resurrected bodies of the righteous will be translated into a new existence, the *world to come*, and there they will live forever, partaking of a form of bodily pleasure superior to the eating and drinking of our present world. The world to come is thus the climax of both the Age of the Messiah and the resurrection of the dead and it will be enjoyed by resurrected bodies.[147] Samuel deflects the objection that by the law of nature every composite body must decompose: Divine power can overcome any law of nature.[148]

The sitting of the righteous with crowns on their heads and their enjoying the splendor of the divine presence will occur, in Samuel's scheme, when resurrected bodies enter the world to come. "Anyone who maintains" that the description is a metaphor for the immortality of disembodied souls has not, he contends, read the sources carefully. For the talmudic passage containing the description draws a parallel between the righteous with crowns on their heads and the Israelite nobles who, after God gave Israel the Ten Commandments at Sinai, "beheld God and did eat and drink." The comparison of the righteous in the world to come to the Israelite nobles at Sinai makes clear that the former, like the latter, will be not disembodied souls but living bodies, which are able to partake of a form—albeit a higher form—of bodily pleasure.[149]

As already mentioned, Samuel's treatise never refers to Maimonides by name; his only obvious references are his initial remark regarding a composition by a certain author which arrived in Yemen and later in Iraq and his quotation from Maimonides' Commentary on the Mishna. Maimonides was nonetheless plainly his target. Samuel rejects the "position of him who says" that the world to come is not temporally later than the current world, but is rather the state of immortal souls at all times through human history;[150] the formulation he rejects was that of Maimonides'. He criticizes the position of "anyone who maintains" that the rabbinic description of the righteous' sitting with crowns on their heads is an allegorical depiction of the immortality of the soul;[151] it was Maimonides who construed the description as allegorical.[152] Samuel links resurrection to the Age of

[147]Samuel ben Eli, *Ma'amar be-Teḥiyyat ha-Metim* 81, citing Ezekiel 47:1–12. The prophet envisions a stream that will originate under the threshold of the Temple and flow eastward and trees that will grow on each side of the stream.

[148]Samuel ben Eli, *Ma'amar be-Teḥiyyat ha-Metim* 78.

[149]Samuel ben Eli, *Ma'amar be-Teḥiyyat ha-Metim* 78. The righteous who in the future will sit with crowns on their head are compared to the nobles of Israel described in Exodus 24:11, in BT *Berakot* 17a.

[150]Samuel ben Eli, *Ma'amar be-Teḥiyyat ha-Metim* 74–75.

[151]Samuel ben Eli, *Ma'amar be-Teḥiyyat ha-Metim* 78.

[152]Above, pp. 512, 514.

the Messiah; Maimonides avoided making such a link in both his Commentary on the Mishna and his *Mishneh Torah*.[153] In Samuel's eschatological scheme, the righteous whose souls are restored to their bodies will live in their resurrected condition forever,[154] and the possible objection that everything composed of the four physical elements must by the laws of nature eventually decompose is countered by the consideration that God can overcome the laws of nature. Maimonides asserted flatly that every physical body must at some time decompose.[155]

Samuel concludes by asserting that persons who reject resurrection do so because they do not believe in the divine origin of the Torah. Divine punishment will be visited upon them for their disbelief, they will be excluded from God's mercy, and they will lose their own portion in the world to come.[156] Nothing suggests that the harsh words are directed against those who believe in resurrection but fail to accept his specific account in all its details. Thus while he criticizes Maimonides' position on resurrection and the world to come, he nowhere places Maimonides among the unbelievers. Maimonides could easily have treated Samuel's treatise as a naive, alternative version of resurrection and the world to come and ignored the veiled criticisms of his own version.

Maimonides' student Joseph ben Judah also entered the controversy. Joseph lived on and off in Baghdad, and relations between him and Samuel ben Eli were not good. He clashed with Samuel on several occasions, and Maimonides had to restrain him, warning against insulting a man who, with all his limitations, was much older, held a dignified post, and was respected by society.[157]

Joseph recalls that during one of his stays in Baghdad, he and Samuel debated matters relating to the subject of resurrection. The debate, as he describes it, did not touch on resurrection itself, but rather on interpretations of biblical verses and rabbinic anecdotes that Samuel thought proved the immortality of the soul.[158] Joseph was sure that he had shown Samuel's interpretations to be worthless.

[153]See *Mishneh Torah*: *H. Melakim* 11.3: The Messiah will not have to resurrect the dead, as "fools" suppose.

[154]Samuel ben Eli, *Ma'amar be-Teḥiyyat ha-Metim* 78, 81. An explicit statement to the same effect is found in BT *Sanhedrin* 92a, but *Sanhedrin* 92b can be understood as indicating that such was not the majority rabbinic opinion.

[155]Above, p. 513. Samuel, *Ma'amar be-Teḥiyyat ha-Metim* 81, also objects strenuously to taking the creation story allegorically, for, he contends, such an approach completely undermines the Torah. In the *Guide for the Perplexed*, Maimonides did take a good portion of the creation story allegorically; see above, pp 343–47. If Samuel was familiar directly or through report with the *Guide*, Maimonides could be his target here too.

[156]Samuel ben Eli, *Ma'amar be-Teḥiyyat ha-Metim* 83.

[157]Moses ben Maimon, *Epistulae* (Jerusalem 1946) 61–62.

[158]S. Stroumsa, *The Beginnings of the Maimonidean Controversy in the East* (Jerusalem 1999) (the Arabic text of Joseph's refutation of Samuel, a medieval Hebrew translation of Joseph's refutation, and Stroumsa's modern Hebrew translation of the refutation) §§71–84.

Behold now, to his astonishment upon returning to Baghdad after an absence of several years, a small treatise in which Samuel stubbornly repeated the same foolishness! Joseph thereupon sat down and wrote a full refutation.[159] Although he is careful to avoid using Samuel's name, there can be no question about whom he has in view. The medieval translator of Joseph's refutation tells us that it was directed against Samuel's treatise,[160] and Joseph's quotations from the treatise he was refuting corroborate that he was arguing against the treatise of Samuel's which I just summarized. As will be recalled, Samuel copied several passages from a philosophic work that he did not name. Joseph correctly identifies the source of the passages as *K. al-Mu*ᶜ*tabar*, although he too does not name the book's author.[161]

By far the larger part of Joseph's refutation is concerned with the quality of Samuel's argumentation and with the aspersions that, he thought, had been cast on Maimonides. Maimonides, in Joseph's words, is "the enlightener of our eyes, . . . our teacher and master, . . . unique in his age, the central pillar, the light of the world, the sign and wonder of his generation from the rising of the sun in the east even until its going down in the west," and so on.[162] Joseph reminds readers that in the Commentary on the Mishna, Maimonides had affirmed the dogma of resurrection without reservation and he acknowledges that Samuel ben Eli did not deny that. Still, by repeating the gist of the letter he received from the Yemeni Jews, Samuel associated himself with those who falsely accused Maimonides of denying the dogma of resurrection in the *Mishneh Torah*.[163] Further, by arguing at length and repeatedly that resurrection is possible and will occur, Samuel planted the false suspicion that his adversary believed otherwise.[164] He was thereby guilty of harboring and disseminating groundless suspicions of a fellow Jew and deserved to be punished severely by God for his sin.[165]

As for Samuel's argumentation, Joseph objects, for example, to the arguments from anecdotes in which the dead speak: Seeing that the souls of the dead do not have the organs of speech, they cannot actually speak, and the anecdotes must be narrating things that occurred in dreams.[166] The willingness of Abraham, Moses, and other biblical figures to suffer in fulfilling God's commands does not prove that they expected a reward in the hereafter; those great men, as the rabbis teach us, worshiped God out of love and not through any hope for reward.[167] The biblical

159 Stroumsa, *Beginnings of the Maimonidean Controversy in the East* §§71, 85.

160 Stroumsa, *Beginnings of the Maimonidean Controversy in the East*, introduction, 12.

161 Stroumsa, *Beginnings of the Maimonidean Controversy in the East* §§54–57, 146. For the pertinent passages in Abū al-Barakāt, see above, nn. 137–39, and the notes in Stroumsa's edition of Joseph's refutation.

162 Stroumsa, *Beginnings of the Maimonidean Controversy in the East* §4.

163 Stroumsa, *Beginnings of the Maimonidean Controversy in the East* §31.

164 Stroumsa, *Beginnings of the Maimonidean Controversy in the East* §6.

165 Stroumsa, *Beginnings of the Maimonidean Controversy in the East* §147.

166 Stroumsa, *Beginnings of the Maimonidean Controversy in the East* §§75–76.

167 Stroumsa, *Beginnings of the Maimonidean Controversy in the East* §§62–66.

verses quoted by Samuel to prove the dogma of resurrection, such as "I kill and I make alive," are the wrong verses. They only establish that God has the power to bring people back to life, not that He will actually do so, whereas other biblical verses prove what is required, namely, that a general resurrection will occur.[168]

Joseph goes on at some length in the same fashion, and a good number of his criticisms do not rise above mere carping.[169] In matters of substance, he differs from Samuel on only one point: Samuel had maintained that the world to come spoken of by the ancient rabbis was the eternal state of existence of resurrected bodies. Joseph responds in the spirit of Maimonides that after resurrection, the bodies to which souls are restored will die again; and he construes the rabbinic world to come as immortality of the soul. Sometimes Joseph differs even from Maimonides.[170] He infers from Scripture, and states repeatedly, that the resurrection of the dead will occur in the time of the Messiah, whereas Maimonides avoided making such a link. More significantly and surprisingly, he embraces the position of *K. al-Mu^c^tabar* that the human soul is a self-subsistent substance and intrinsically immortal, whereas Maimonides held that human souls are not intrinsically immortal and only the intellectual faculty of the human soul, when developed, survives the death of the body.[171] Joseph, as will be recalled, never completed his course of philosophy with Maimonides, and it would seem that he had not yet received a a complete copy of the *Guide for the Perplexed.*

What can scarcely be doubted is that he genuinely believed, and understood Maimonides to have believed, in a future resurrection of human bodies which will take place in the age of the Messiah.[172]

A letter addressed by Maimonides to Joseph in about 1190 reveals that Joseph had recently sent him a copy of Samuel's treatise, but it makes no mention of Joseph's refutation.[173] Maimonides does not disguise his opinion of Samuel. He

[168]Stroumsa, *Beginnings of the Maimonidean Controversy in the East* §§13–14.

[169]See Stroumsa, *Beginnings of the Maimonidean Controversy in the East* §§26–28, 32, 42, 135.

[170]In §19, Joseph argues, precisely as we shall see Maimonides do, that since the rabbis insisted that there will be no eating and drinking in the world to come, the world to come is not a place where bodies exist. In §134, Joseph singles out BT *Berakot* and *Sanhedrin* 10 as sections of the Talmud that contain especially problematic aggada. Maimonides had done the same in the Commentary on the Mishna; see above, p. 325.

[171]Stroumsa, *Beginnings of the Maimonidean Controversy in the East* §§9, 24, 51–58, 127, 144, 147. The self-subsistent nature of the soul goes back to Avicenna; see H. Davidson, *Alfarabi, Avicenna, and Averroes, on Intellect* (New York 1992) 83, 106.

[172]Stroumsa, *Beginnings of the Maimonidean Controversy in the East* §§147–48.

[173]In the letter to Joseph, Maimonides writes that he had heard from Yemen about persons there who understood his *Mishneh Torah* as denying resurrection, and we learn from Maimonides, *Treatise on Resurrection*, Arabic text and medieval Hebrew translation, ed. J. Finkel, *Proceedings of the American Academy for Jewish Research* 9 (1939) 11, that he received the information from Yemen in 1189. The Arabic original, although not the medieval Hebrew

calls him a "poor soul" (*miskīn*). Samuel's status, he writes, was due not to his own worth but to his years, to genealogy, to the absence of men of discrimination in Baghdad, and to an ability to feed people a "noxious pottage," leading them to hang on every word coming out of the Baghdadi rabbinic academy and on the preposterous titles that it distributed.[174] Turning to Joseph, Maimonides writes in an intimate and informal tone: "I am amazed at you, my son; how could you have sent it [that is, the treatise] to me? In order to let me see how little the man knows? Did you suppose that I thought . . . he understands anything?" "In my opinion he is like any other purveyor of homiletic interpretation [*darshan*], and he thrashes around as the others do. God knows, I was genuinely amazed that he could speak such . . . ridiculous and disgraceful . . . nonsense. . . . If he had stuck to drawing proofs from the hundred blessings [recited by Jews every day] or from the blessing recited in the vicinity of Jewish graves, it would have been more in his line than talking about the soul and the views of the philosophers." In doing so, "he must be repeating somebody else's inanity."[175] Maimonides sensed that the list of philosophers' views on the soul in Samuel's treatise could not have been assembled by a man of his caliber and he assumes that Samuel was relying on someone else's work. He did not realize that the source was Abū al-Barakāt's *K. al-Muᶜtabar.*

Samuel's criticism of Maimonides' position on resurrection comes up another time in an exchange of letters between the two men. Maimonides once confided to Joseph that he hesitated to answer Samuel's letters, because he supposed that Samuel merely wanted to elicit a response. Since etiquette would require him to answer courteously, Samuel could thereupon display the written response and demonstrate to all and sundry that Maimonides belonged to the company of scholars who pay respect to the distinguished head of the Baghdadi rabbinic academy.[176]

Maimonides nevertheless did answer Samuel a couple of times. The exchange of interest to us involved a question of rabbinic law having nothing to do with resurrection. Maimonides had issued a legal opinion permitting travel by riverboat on the Sabbath, and Samuel had respectfully set forth his objections to that opinion. Before getting to his objections, Samuel opened with a polite and ingratiating preface. It was, he reminded Maimonides, public knowledge that when Jews in Yemen "were pained by something said in your composition," in other words, by

---

versions, of the letter to Joseph, which are shorter, further states that Maimonides had not yet composed his *Treatise on Resurrection*; and even when the statement in the Arabic version referring to the still unwritten *Treatise* is left out of account, the tenor of the part of the letter testified to by both the Hebrew and Arabic versions indicates that Maimonides had not yet composed it. See Moses ben Maimon, *Epistulae* (n. 157 above) 66–67, 75, 79. The *Treatise on Resurrection* itself gives the last third of 1190 and first two-thirds of 1191 as the Jewish year in which it was written; see immediately below. An English translation of the *Treatise on Resurrection* is found in Halkin and Hartman, *Crisis and Leadership* (n. 75 above) 211–33.

[174]Moses ben Maimon, *Epistulae* 54–55, 60.

[175]Moses ben Maimon, *Epistulae* 65–66.

[176]Moses ben Maimon, *Epistulae* 60.

Maimonides' statements about resurrection and the world to come in the *Mishneh Torah*, Samuel had poured oil on the troubled waters and defended Maimonides to the Yemeni Jews.[177]

In his reply to Samuel, Maimonides points out, with only slightly disguised satisfaction, an elementary blunder in his adversary's reasoning on the river travel issue; the letter was not one that Samuel would be eager to put on display as evidence of Maimonides' respect for him. Then, in a final paragraph, he sets the halakic question aside and informs Samuel that he indeed knew of the way in which Yemeni Jews and others "lacking in sense or desiring to belittle me . . . construed what I wrote. . . . And I explained to them how they misunderstood my words." He had, in other words, been apprised of the uproar regarding resurrection which the *Mishneh Torah* occasioned in Yemen and had written to the Yemeni Jews clarifying his position. He goes on: "I also have received your treatise, may God keep watch over you, which contains all the homiletic interpretations [*derashot*] recorded [in the Talmud] regarding resurrection. I have myself composed a treatise in which I clear myself of the evil name being circulated about me and there I explain what you will [presently] see." As may be inferred from Maimonides' remarks to Joseph, quoted a few paragraphs earlier, the reference here to *all* the homiletic interpretations recorded in the Talmud is an oblique way of dismissing Samuel's treatise as jejune scribbling. Maimonides concludes his letter to Samuel with irony neatly wrapped in the *pro forma* courtesy that, he told Joseph, he would have to deploy when addressing the head of the Baghdadi academy: "I pray that your well-being and the well-being of your sacred academy and entire pure retinue will increase and grow. Amen." He gives the summer of 1191 as the date.[178]

Maimonides' rejoinder to Samuel ben Eli's treatise on resurrection is known as his own *Treatise on Resurrection*. In it, he mentions that he was writing in the Jewish year corresponding to the last third of 1190 and first two-thirds of 1191;[179] we just saw that in the summer of 1191, he describes the *Treatise* as already written.

He was in his fifties, the preeminent Jewish judge in Egypt, and established as a physician in the Sultan's court. His major rabbinic works had long been in circulation, and his reputation extended to the ends of the Jewish world. References in the *Treatise on Resurrection* to the several parts of his *Guide for the Perplexed* disclose that that work had also been completed. On more than one occasion he had asserted that criticism had no effect on him. Even more to the point, he writes to Joseph ben Judah that it was not merely his nature to ignore "fools"; he did so out of a sense of self-dignity as well.[180] And he considered

[177] Maimonides, *Responsa* (n. 5 above) §309; supplemented by *Responsa* 4.16.

[178] *Responsa* §310.

[179] Maimonides, *Treatise on Resurrection* 12.

[180] Moses ben Maimon, *Epistulae* 56.

Samuel to be a nonentity. Yet the *Treatise* reveals that he had been stung to the quick by Samuel's criticism.

The *Treatise* falls into three distinct sections: a preamble, the body of the work, and a postscript.[181]

The preamble recalls Maimonides' constant efforts to make his coreligionists aware of the spiritual underpinning of the Jewish religion. He writes that when he designed his rabbinic works, he decided not to limit himself to the "branches of religion" and neglect religion's "roots." By the branches, he means the legal side of the Jewish religion, and by roots, its beliefs; he is saying that he determined not to neglect the doctrinal side of religion in favor of the legal side. The urgency of defining the basic beliefs of the Jewish religion had been borne in upon him when he once encountered an accomplished rabbinic scholar who was unsure whether God is a physical being with "eyes, hands, feet, and intestines." In his lifetime, he had even encountered Jews who were certain that God is a body and who branded persons thinking otherwise as nonbelievers and heretics.[182]

In both his Commentary on the Mishna and his *Mishneh Torah*, Maimonides accordingly undertook to delineate the roots of the religion. He was concerned for the edification of "those who are called scholars, or *geonim*, or whatever you want to call them." He wanted to encourage them to "build their branches," that is, their legal studies, on "roots of the law," on true beliefs; to dissuade them from "throwing knowledge of God behind their backs"; and to direct their efforts toward what "perfects them and brings them close to God, rather than to what the common people suppose [human] perfection to be."[183] In a word, Maimonides incorporated the doctrines of the Jewish religion into his rabbinic works in order to instruct everyone, especially rabbinic scholars, and especially the *geonim* "or whatever you

[181]The opening lines of the body of the *Treatise* form a logical starting point for the whole, and the body of the work (pp. 17–18) repeats a pair of considerations already put forward in the preamble (pp. 6–8). It is therefore possible that the preamble was written independently of the other two parts and attached to them when the *Treatise* was published.

The authenticity of the *Treatise on Resurrection* was rejected by J. Teicher, "*Ziyyuf Sifruti*," *Melilah* 1 (1944) 81–92, and, following in his tracks, L. Goldfeld, *Moses Maimonides' Treatise on Resurrection* (New York 1986). Teicher, 88, 91, and Goldfeld, 39, 45, had the bizarre notion that the inspiration for the *Treatise* was Christian. Teicher's specific arguments are refuted by I. Sonne, "A Scrutiny of the Charges of Forgery Against Maimonides' 'Letter on Resurrection,'" *Proceedings of the American Academy for Jewish Research* 21 (1952) 101–17. The web of interrelated writings—Samuel's treatise, Joseph ben Judah's refutation of it, Maimonides' letter to Joseph, the interchange between Samuel and Maimonides—are ample evidence of the authenticity of the *Treatise*. Teicher knew of Maimonides' letter to Joseph, and of Maimonides' reference to the *Treatise* at the end of his letter to Samuel regarding river travel. His tactic for accommodating those items with his rejection of the authenticity of Maimonides' *Treatise* was simple and straightforward. He wielded his razor and rejected their authenticity as well. See J. Teicher, "Maimonides' Letter to Joseph ben Jehudah," *Journal of Jewish Studies* 1 (1948) 41, 48.

[182]Maimonides, *Treatise on Resurrection* 3.

[183]Maimonides, *Treatise on Resurrection* 4.

want to call them," in the roots, the principles, on which the religion rests. The title of *gaon*, it will be remembered, was proudly borne by heads of the Iraqi academies such as Samuel ben Eli, and Maimonides himself sometimes uses the title when addressing Samuel.[184] One can easily picture the appreciation and gratitude with which Samuel and other rabbinic scholars of his standing welcomed the elementary instruction in the Jewish faith proffered by Maimonides.

As part of his educational project, Maimonides goes on, he expounded, in both of his main rabbinic works, the concept of the world to come, which, he was certain, is the immortality of the human intellect.[185] He felt that intellectual immortality demanded particular attention, because the general run of mankind has difficulty in grasping the nonphysical nature of the human hereafter, just as it has difficulty in grasping the nonphysical nature of God and the angels. Most people can imagine only the existence of physical bodies and the qualities inhering in bodies, whereas the existence of the incorporeal is foreign to them—this, although incorporeal beings in fact possess a higher degree of existence than the corporeal does.[186] These comments of Maimonides' are not wholly apt if aimed at Samuel ben Eli, since Samuel expressly recognized that the angels are "free of matter," that God is "exalted above the attributes of bodies,"[187] and that human souls survive the death of their bodies. Yet they are not inapt either. Samuel did not restrict human survival to the intellectual faculty of the soul, as Maimonides did, and he held fast to the belief that at the culmination of human existence souls will be restored to resurrected bodies and continue to exist in a physical condition forever.

Giving more attention to the immortality of human intellects in the world to come did not, Maimonides insists, have the object of casting doubt on resurrection. His recognition of the dogma of resurrection should be clear, first, from the passage in his Commentary on the Mishna where he stated that although resurrection is not the "final end," no one can deny it and still maintain a connection with the Mosaic Law; and secondly, from the passage in his *Mishneh Torah* where he listed failure to believe in the resurrection of bodies as one of twenty-four transgressions that cause a person to forfeit his portion in the world to come.[188] He is saying that he affirmed the truth of resurrection, although without elaboration, and then turned his attention to intellectual immortality as part of his plan to educate readers in the neglected, spiritual side of the Jewish religion.

When all has been said, Maimonides is willing to concede that should the masses foolishly persist in regarding angels as bodies, or the ultimate end of human existence as the immortality of human bodies and not human intellects, they do not compromise their faith.[189] "Would that the ignorant were ignorant of nothing

[184]Maimonides, *Responsa* §310; *Treatise on Resurrection* 12–14.
[185]Maimonides, *Treatise on Resurrection* 5.
[186]Maimonides, *Treatise on Resurrection* 7–8.
[187]Samuel ben Eli, *Ma'amar be-Teḥiyyat ha-Metim* (n. 127 above) 73.
[188]Maimonides, *Treatise on Resurrection* 6.
[189]Similarly in Shailat, *Letters and Essays of Moses Maimonides* (n. 1 above) 414.

more, . . . that their belief remained free of ascribing corporeality to the Creator."[190] For believing that God is a corporeal being is a mortal sin and not forgivable.

Such is the preamble to Maimonides' *Treatise on Resurrection.*

The body of the *Treatise* opens, much as Samuel's treatise did, with an account of the circumstances that led up to its composition. Maimonides writes that after his *Mishneh Torah* was disseminated throughout the Jewish world, he heard that the account he gave there of the world to come was construed by a "student" in Damascus as a rejection of the dogma of resurrection. He treated the incident as isolated and disregarded it. Then in the Jewish year corresponding to the last third of 1188 and first two-thirds of 1189, he received a letter from Jews in Yemen reporting that members of the Yemeni Jewish community had denied resurrection and supported their stand by adducing statements regarding the world to come in the *Mishneh Torah.* He wrote back that resurrection in the sense of a future return of souls to human bodies was a "principle of the Law" and cannot be allegorized away. Two years later, he received letters from "friends in Baghdad," and they informed him that a Yemeni Jew had sent an inquiry to "the head of the academy, R. Samuel [ben Eli] ha-Levi, may God watch over him." Samuel had replied in the form of a "treatise on the subject of resurrection" in which he informed the Yemeni Jewish community that some of Maimonides' statements were in error, but some were defensible; Maimonides acknowledges that Samuel had shown moderation in his reply. Subsequently Maimonides received the "treatise that this *gaon*, may God watch over him, composed" and there found "all the homiletic exegeses and haggadot" that Samuel had compiled.[191] There is a blurring here of the distinction drawn by Samuel between his reply to the inquiry sent from Yemen and the fuller treatise he later wrote when the issue erupted in Baghdad. The composition that Maimonides received must have been the latter. At one juncture he states that he is quoting from Samuel's treatise, and what he quotes is a sentence precisely as it appears in the treatise of Samuel's which has survived, in other words, the treatise that Samuel said he composed for the Jews of Baghdad.[192]

This time, Maimonides decided not to let matters rest, and before the year was out, he wrote his own *Treatise on Resurrection.* Although he makes clear that Samuel's "bizarre" essay was the catalyst, his direct refutation of Samuel occupies only a few pages. It boils down to two main objections: Samuel argued simplistically from undigested rabbinic aggada. And he confused philosophy with Kalam and showed no grasp of what philosophers actually hold. Maimonides is using the term *philosopher* not in the meaning of a practitioner of the philosophic

[190]Maimonides, *Treatise on Resurrection* 9.

[191]Maimonides, *Treatise on Resurrection* 11–12.

[192]Maimonides, *Treatise on Resurrection* 13, quoting Samuel ben Eli, *Ma'amar be-Teḥiyyat ha-Metim* 69. Pointed out by Tz. Langermann, "*Qobeṣ Ḥadash ba-Pilosophia ha-Yehudit,*" *Kiryat Sefer* 64 (1992) 1432.

method but in the specific sense of a member of the Arabic Aristotelian school of philosophy.

Maimonides liked to contrast the right and wrong approaches to rabbinic aggada: The latter consists in reading aggada literally, and the former, in realizing that it compresses into a nutshell truths that scientists and philosophers have reached only with great effort.[193] Samuel chose the wrong approach. "Everyone knows that men of science do not . . . repeat the homiletic exegeses and far-fetched anecdotes [of the ancient rabbis] verbatim in the manner in which women recite to one another in a house of mourning." The "aim" of men of science "is to interpret the [rabbinic] exegeses and explain their sense so that it agrees with, or approaches, what is known rationally [*ma*ᶜ*qūl*]."

When Samuel ventured to talk about philosophy, the outcome was still worse. The views on the nature of the soul which he attributed to philosophers are, in fact, theories of the Kalam school, and Kalam thinkers are not genuine philosophers. In particular, Samuel's statement that "wise" philosophers do not deny the possibility of the resurrection of the body betrays confusion regarding the two schools; in other words, gentile philosophers do deny the possibility of resurrection, and it is Kalam thinkers who do not. "If this *gaon*, may God protect him, had limited himself to collecting those aggadot [or: homiletic exegeses; *derashot*] and anecdotes, and to the interpretation of the scriptural verses by which he supposedly proved that resurrection is affirmed explicitly in the Torah, it would," in Maimonides' judgment, "have been something more seemly and appropriate for a person of his sort."[194] Notwithstanding Samuel's failure to appreciate the inner meaning of

[193]See above, pp. 126, 133, 324–25, 511–12.

[194]Maimonides, *Treatise on Resurrection* 12–14. The last sentence echoes a sentence in Maimonides' letter to Joseph ben Judah, above, p. 523.

Maimonides, p. 13, further mentions "things taken [by Samuel] from Avicenna's *The Hereafter* [*al-Ma*ᶜ*ād*] and from the *al-Mu*ᶜ*tabar*, which was written there in Baghdad," and he complains that Samuel regarded those things as "purely philosophic propositions." But he shows no realization that *K. al-Mu*ᶜ*tabar* was Samuel's source for the key statement about wise philosophers who recognize the resurrection of the body. He therefore probably had only indirect knowledge of the book.

Two books carrying Avicenna's name have been published which contain the words *The Hereafter* (*al-Ma*ᶜ*ād*) as part of their titles, namely: Avicenna, *al-Risāla.al-Aḍḥawiyya fī al-Ma*ᶜ*ād*, ed. and Italian trans. F. Lucchetta as *Epistola sulla vita futura* (Padua 1969); and *al-Mabda' wa-al-Ma*ᶜ*ād*, ed. A. Nurani (Teheran 1984). There may, moreover, have been yet a third treatise attributed to Avicenna and entitled precisely *The Hereafter* (*al-Ma*ᶜ*ād*). See the bibliographies of Avicenna in G. Anawati, *Essai de bibliographie avicennienne* (in Arabic) (Cairo 1950) 255, and W. Gohlman, *The Life of Ibn Sina* (Albany 1974) 94–95. It is impossible to tell whether Maimonides was referring to either of the two books that have been published. Both repeat Avicenna's well-known proposition that the human soul is a self-subsistent substance; Maimonides did not accept that thesis and while he would not be justified in asserting that it is not philosophic in the general sense of the term, he could have thought that it did not belong to mainstream Arabic Aristotelianism. The two published books attributed to Avicenna embrace the proposition—which Maimonides would accept as in every sense philosophic—that intellectual

rabbinic aggada, he would have embarrassed himself less if he limited himself to playing homiletic games with Scripture and aggada, kept quiet about philosophy, and avoided theological discourse with scholars of Maimonides' rank.

After the brief, acerbic critique of Samuel, Maimonides announces that his "intent in the present treatise is not to oppose anything" in Samuel's treatise nor even to make any further reference to it. He is above that: "Disputation and refutation are permitted to him who wishes to travel those routes, but may God prevent me from doing so." His object in the remainder of the *Treatise on Resurrection* will be merely to repeat what he had written about resurrection in his Commentary on the Mishna and *Mishneh Torah* without "anything whatsoever added." The *Treatise* will offer nothing new and is consequently—in undoubtedly the only instance of Maimonides' characterizing one of his works in such a fashion—"without value." It will merely provide "prolixity for the masses" and "added explanation capable of being understood by women and the ignorant, nothing else."[195] We have the anomaly of Maimonides' composing a fairly substantial *Treatise* in reaction to Samuel ben Eli's criticism of him, and yet of his addressing not Samuel, but the masses, women, and the ignorant. We surely may be excused if we sniff here a heavy measure of sarcasm—the implication that Samuel's proper place is among the masses, women, and ignorant.

Regarding resurrection, Maimonides is unequivocal: Resurrection, as "agreed on" by the Jewish nation, as repeatedly referred to "in prayer, sermons, and supplications," as recorded by "the prophets and leading ancient rabbis," as expressly defined in the "Talmud and midrashic compilations," means the "return of the human soul to the body after its having been separated" from the body at death. "Nothing different and no allegorical interpretation whatsoever [of the doctrine] have ever been heard within the nation." "It is forbidden to suppose that any member of the [Jewish] religion believes the contrary"—the reason undoubtedly being that one would thereby commit the sin of placing an innocent fellow Jew under suspicion.[196]

Although Maimonides thus bases his belief on roughly the same sources as Samuel, he considers his use of the sources to be more cautious. Scriptural verses speaking of a resurrection of the body which are amenable to metaphorical interpretation are not sufficient to settle the issue for him, and talmudic and midrashic inferences of a homiletic character also are not.[197] He is willing to credit

---

perfection is the goal of human existence and both reserve the highest level of pleasure in the afterlife to souls that develop their intellectual faculty. Both, however, also defend the possibility that the surviving souls of good persons who never develop their intellect may, after death, imagine that they are experiencing the physical delights—including the garden and the black-eyed maidens—promised by the Islamic prophet. See *al-Risāla al-Aḍḥawiyya* 225; *al-Mabda' wa-al-Ma^{c}ād* 114–15.

[195] Maimonides, *Treatise on Resurrection* 14–15, 26.

[196] Maimonides, *Treatise on Resurrection* 15.

[197] See below, p. 532.

only scriptural verses that are unambiguous. Nevertheless a single verse will do; once a single biblical verse affirms resurrection unambiguously, the doctrine is validated and the matter is settled.[198] And he finds two verses that pass muster, both of them at the end of the Book of Daniel—whom he classified as a prophet, albeit a prophet in one of the lower categories of prophecy.[199] First there is the verse stating: "Many of them that sleep in the dust of the earth shall awake, these to long-lasting life, and these to reproaches and everlasting abhorrence." Secondly is the instruction given by the angel to Daniel: "But go thou thy way till the end be, and thou shalt rest, and shalt stand up to thy lot at the end of days."[200] The first of the two verses would seem to suggest that both the righteous and wicked will be resurrected, but Maimonides relies instead on a rabbinic source to justify restricting resurrection to the righteous.[201]

As for himself, Maimonides proclaims with undisguised emotion: I "deny, and declare my innocence before God of the proposition that the soul will never be restored to the body and that for such to occur is impossible." "Whoever deliberately chooses to malign me and attribute to me an opinion that I do not believe, . . . whoever places a far-fetched interpretation on what I say in order to find me at fault, . . . falls into the class of those who harbor suspicions of the innocent . . . and will have to face the bar of [divine] justice."[202] The allegation that "I said that references to resurrection in Scripture are metaphorical is a blatant lie and unadulterated calumny on the part of whoever makes the statement. My books are available. . . . Let it be shown where I said such a thing."[203]

While the body of the *Treatise on Resurrection* does largely what Maimonides said it would do—repeating and expanding on what he had written regarding resurrection in earlier works—he makes a few small new points.

"It seems" to him from what the rabbis said "that those whose souls return to bodies will eat, drink, have sexual intercourse, bear children, and die after an extraordinarily long life." [204] He leaves undecided whether the miracle of resurrection will take place "during the days of the Messiah, before the Messiah, or after his death."[205] He explains why he had considered resurrection of the dead to be so

[198]Maimonides, *Treatise on Resurrection* 19–20.

[199]Maimonides, *Guide for the Perplexed* 2.45 (2).

[200]Maimonides, *Treatise on Resurrection* 15, 19, quoting Daniel 12:2, 13. Maimonides' justification for understanding the words *ḥayye ᶜolam* in the biblical verse as "long-lasting life" rather than "everlasting life"—and hence for his not reading the verse as an affirmation of the eternal life of resurrected bodies—would be verses such as Exodus 21:6.

[201]See Maimonides, Commentary on the Mishna (n. 48 above), *Sanhedrin* 10, introduction p. 207, and editor's note. Saadia, in his commentary on Daniel (see Ibn Ezra's commentary), similarly reads Daniel 12:2 in such a way that only the righteous are resurrected.

[202]Maimonides, *Treatise on Resurrection* 19.

[203]Maimonides, *Treatise on Resurrection* 16.

[204]Maimonides, *Treatise on Resurrection* 16.

[205]Maimonides, *Treatise on Resurrection* 21.

basic a dogma that it deserved being included in his list of thirteen principles of faith: A denial of the possibility that God can resurrect the dead leads to a denial of the possibility of all other scriptural miracles—such as Aaron's staff's turning into a serpent, the descent of the manna, the theophany at Sinai, and the pillars of fire and cloud that accompanied the Israelites in the desert—and a total denial of the possibility of miracles is tantamount to "a denial of the fundamental doctrine of religion [*kefira ba-ᶜiqqar*] and a rejection of the Law."[206] He speculates that his position had been misunderstood because he had felt the need to pay more attention to the unfamiliar doctrine of immortality of the human intellect in the world to come than to the familiar dogma of resurrection of the body.[207]

At one spot we find a veiled riposte to a veiled criticism that Samuel had directed against him. Samuel had insisted that the rabbinic description of the righteous' sitting in the world to come with crowns on their heads relates to the world of resurrected bodies and he had adduced a proof-text from the Babylonian Talmud to refute "anyone who holds" otherwise. The very same passage of the Babylonian Talmud now furnishes Maimonides with a proof-text for his own position that the world to come is a state in which bodies play no role. The talmudic passage includes the sentence: "In the world to come there will be no eating, drinking, or sexual intercourse." Maimonides reasons that without eating, drinking, or sexual intercourse, a human body would exist in vain; God, however, does nothing in vain; inasmuch as the rabbis stress that those activities will be absent, the world to come must be a nonphysical state of existence.[208]

He concludes the body of his *Treatise* by announcing that since he had thus far said nothing not already found in his earlier works, he would add a postscript, which solves two scriptural-theological problems. Readers will thereby be able to come away from the *Treatise* without feeling that they had completely wasted their time.

The first problem is why so many biblical verses deny the possibility that human souls might return to human bodies. Job, for example, declaimed: "If a man die, may he live again?" "As the cloud is consumed and vanisheth away, so he that goeth down to the grave shall come up no more." And additional verses express the same sentiment. Maimonides' solution is that scriptural verses denying resurrection look at things from the natural point of view, and plainly by the laws of nature, human souls do not return to bodies after having separated from them.

[206]Maimonides, *Treatise on Resurrection* 19. I have taken the examples of miracles from the postscript, p. 30, where Maimonides cites creation as the paradigmatic miracle; see Exodus 7:10; 16:14–15; Numbers 14:14. It is to be noted that the reason Maimonides gives for enumerating resurrection as a principle of faith is not the mishnaic statement to the effect that denying resurrection causes one to lose one's portion in the world to come.

[207]Maimonides, *Treatise on Resurrection* 24.

[208]Maimonides, *Treatise on Resurrection* 17–18. Maimonides' version of the talmudic passage BT *Berakot* 17a differed from the version in our editions.

What survives, from the natural viewpoint is only the human soul, or, more precisely, the human intellectual faculty when perfected.[209]

The second problem is why the Pentateuch never mentions the resurrection of the dead expressly and at the very most does so in obscure and oblique allusions.[210] Maimonides' solution here is that the Pentateuch addresses the Israelites who had just come out of Egypt. During their sojourn there, pagan religious attitudes had been so firmly ingrained in them that they were not temperamentally ready for miracles performed by a transcendent deity who is possessed of will.[211] They were at first unable to grasp anything beyond "natural" immortality, that is, "immortality of the soul." Only "with the passage of generations," after the Israelites had become fully convinced of the reality of prophecy and the possibility of miracles, could they accept prophetic predictions of a future resurrection of human bodies.[212] Educating the Israelite nation must have been singularly difficult. The earliest prophetic book in which Maimonides finds references to the resurrection of the dead is the Book of Isaiah, which he would have dated some seven centuries after the exodus from Egypt. The only book of Scripture that, in his opinion, affirms resurrection unambiguously is the Book of Daniel, which he would have dated two centuries still later.

The second of the two questions raised by Maimonides contains a subtext with one more barb for Samuel. As Maimonides summarized Samuel's treatise, Samuel contended that resurrection is affirmed "explicitly" in the Torah.[213] In just posing the second question, Maimonides takes for granted that, at the most, the Pentateuch alludes to resurrection of the dead obliquely and obscurely. Samuel's reading of the Pentateuch is ignored as not worthy of discussion.

Whereas Samuel treated Maimonides with scrupulous tact and courtesy, Maimonides, despite his words about being above disputation, has sniped at his opponent from the start. Early on, he dropped the remark about his efforts to instruct the "*geonim*, or whatever you want to call them." He criticized Samuel for compiling rabbinic homiletic exegeses verbatim and without expounding their inner sense, whereas "everyone knows that men of science" do not proceed in such a fashion. Samuel presented his homiletic materials in the way that "women recite to one another in a house of mourning." The *Treatise on Resurrection*, which was occasioned by Samuel's critique, would address the "masses," "women, and the

[209]Maimonides, *Treatise on Resurrection* 26–28. The verses quoted here are Job 7:9 and 14:14, and Maimonides quotes additional scriptural verses in the same vein. He writes that some authors offered far-fetched interpretations of the problematic verses in order to bring them into harmony with the dogma of resurrection; he could be thinking of Saadia, *Sefer ha-Emunot we-ha-De^{c}ot* 7:5.

[210]Maimonides' concession that the Torah may refer to resurrection in obscure allusions has BT *Sanhedrin* 90b in view.

[211]See above, p. 381.

[212]Maimonides, *Treatise on Resurrection* 27, 31–32.

[213]Above, pp. 517–18, 528.

ignorant"; Samuel, the only identifiable target of the *Treatise*, is allowed to decide in which group he would like to place himself.

Maimonides could simply have ignored Samuel's carefully modulated critique of his position on resurrection, just as he ignored the student in Damascus who read the *Mishneh Torah* as rejecting the dogma of resurrection. Alternatively, he could have answered Samuel in a few lines as he indicates he responded when he first heard that some Yemeni Jews had cited the *Mishneh Torah* for support in rejecting the belief in resurrection: He could have said that in his view, as stated in his Commentary on the Mishna and the *Mishneh Torah*, a resurrection of the dead will occur, but the culmination of human existence, what the rabbis called the world to come, is immortality of the human intellect. Or, again, he might have published the preamble to the *Treatise on Resurrection* and left things at that. The *Treatise on Resurrection*, which extends some thirty pages in the printed edition, in which Maimonides solemnly declares that everyone who maligns him will have to answer at the bar of divine justice, in which he repeatedly disparages the principal of the Baghdad academy, reveals a hypersensitivity to criticism which was scarcely to be foreseen. He had been stung too deeply to bring himself to shrug off the aspersions on his orthodoxy.

Maimonides has assured his readers that Scripture promises a future restoration of the souls of the righteous dead to reconstituted bodies. He has stressed that resurrection is a principle of the Jewish religion, that it must not be allegorized away, and that like every faithful Jew, he believes it will take place. The resurrected, in his account, will live for a long, but finite, period of time, they will most likely eat, drink and reproduce, and they will die again. Their perfected intellects will then revert to a condition of disembodied immortality. Resurrection is obviously not, for Maimonides, the climax of human history as it is for writers like Samuel ben Eli. The sole indication he gives of its possible role in the divine scheme of things is his remark in the Commentary on the Mishna that certain eschatological states are means to an end, and not the end itself; he thereby suggests that the promise of resurrection motivates unsophisticated persons to obey God's commands and eventually to move on to the true purpose of human existence, which is the development of the human intellect.

In the preamble to the *Treatise on Resurrection*, Maimonides writes ruefully: "It can happen that a man intends to set forth a proposition in clear, plain language, wherein he makes every effort to remove doubts and any possibility of an interpretation's being placed on the proposition, yet persons of unhealthy soul read out of his language the opposite of the proposition that he intended to set forth."[214] The very word of God suffered such a fate. Moses, speaking at God's behest, declared "Hear O Israel, the Lord God, the Lord is one" and thereby taught God's absolute unity; yet Christians perversely infer from Moses' words that the deity is

[214]Maimonides, *Treatise on Resurrection* 1–2.

triune, consisting of Lord, God, and Lord. Maimonides is ostensibly saying that in previous writings he had tried to put his espousal of the doctrine of resurrection in clear language, yet persons of unhealthy soul took him to have meant the opposite of what he intended.[215] The *Treatise on Resurrection*, for its part, states unequivocally that a miraculous future restoration of souls of the dead to physical bodies is integral to Jewish doctrine and that Maimonides believes it will occur. Even so, and despite his protests, there still remain those who "read out of his language" in the *Treatise* the opposite of the proposition that he sets forth, readers who remain unconvinced that he believed in a future resurrection of the dead.[216]

The truth is that he has not been completely forthcoming. There is the unanswered question: What benefit can accrue to human intellects through being recalled for a time from their ultimate immortal state to a second physical life, the pleasures of which are, in Maimonides' words, "foolishness," "vanity" and "of no value"?[217] Then consider the following: He has explained that the nonintellectual faculties of the soul do not survive the death of the body; only the intellect survives.[218] When he speaks of the restoration of "souls" (*nafs*) to bodies,[219] he must consequently be using the term *soul* in the specific sense of *intellect*. Yet we saw him writing: "It seems to me from what the rabbis said that those whose souls return to bodies will eat, drink, have sexual intercourse, bear children, and die after an extraordinarily long life." Eating, drinking, sexual intercourse, and bearing children are, in his conceptual framework, functions performed through the lower faculties of the soul. Resurrected human beings would therefore have to possess those faculties, faculties that, in Maimonides' view, did not survive the death of their original body. In his framework, resurrection would accordingly be more

[215] Maimonides applies the observation to himself, with curious imprecision. One would have expected him to write: In my rabbinic works, I affirmed the proposition that bodies will be resurrected, yet persons of unhealthy soul thought that I was denying resurrection. Instead, he writes: In my rabbinic works, I called attention to the neglected proposition that the ultimate human fate is immortality of the intellect, yet as a consequence, people began to doubt a *different* proposition, which is clear to all Jews, namely, that the dead will be resurrected.

[216] The school of interpretation that construes Maimonides as having denied creation, God's involvement in the world, and the possibility of miracles will perforce interpret him as denying the miracle of resurrection. See, for example, R. Lerner, "Maimonides' Treatise on Resurrection," *History of Religions* 23 (1983) 140–55. But doubts have often been expressed about Maimonides' belief in resurrection apart from the radical esoteric interpretation of his philosophy. See S. Luzzatto, *Meḥqare ha-Yahadut* (Warsaw 1913) 1.166; J. Finkel, "Maimonides' Treatise on Resurrection," *Essays on Maimonides*, ed. S. Baron (New York 1941) 114–16; Y. Leibowitz, *Emunato shel ha-Rambam* (Tel Aviv 1980) 44; O. Leaman, *Moses Maimonides* (London 1990) 117–18, who assumes that Maimonides could not have believed in resurrection "given what we know about the nature of corruptible matter and the individuality of the person"; L. Goodman, *Jewish and Islamic Philosophy* (New Brunswick 1999) 105.

[217] See below, p. 536.

[218] Above, pp. 242, 514.

[219] Maimonides, *Treatise on Resurrection* 15, 16, 29.

nuanced than has been disclosed thus far. God would not simply restore souls to reconstituted bodies. He would have to reconstitute a body together with the lower faculties of a human soul, retrieve an immortal human intellect from the happy disembodied state in which it had existed since its original body died, and attach the human intellect to the reconstituted complex of body and lower soul.

Does Maimonides' failure fully to spell out the implications of his position therefore bespeak disingenuousness, and did he, even when heatedly reaffirming his belief in resurrection, inwardly subscribe only to intellectual immortality?

Consider now the other side. As far as his rabbinic works are concerned, Maimonides could conceivably have used the term *resurrection* metaphorically and spoken of resurrection with the mental reservation that he meant immortality of the intellect. But the *Treatise on Resurrection* eschews every shred of ambiguity. Maimonides here categorically affirms his belief in resurrection in the sense of a restoration of souls—which, we have just seen, must mean *intellects*—of the dead to physical bodies and he evinces a good deal of emotion in making the declaration. If he did not believe in a genuine resurrection, he was not equivocating in the *Treatise*, not employing language designed to be taken literally by the unsophisticated and metaphorically by the cognoscenti. He was simply lying, and his indignant protestations of belief in a genuine resurrection of the body would be an out-and-out hoax. Maimonides saw himself as a consummate educator. To envisage him publishing a treatise with the sole object of lying brazenly about his beliefs and consciously misleading readers who looked to him for guidance does not create an appealing—nor, I would venture, a convincing—picture, especially when he could simply have avoided writing the *Treatise* altogether.

The case for taking him at his word is strengthened by a statement in the letter that he wrote to Joseph ben Judah regarding Samuel ben Eli's criticism of his position on resurrection. In the letter, Maimonides exclaims: "How could anyone of sound mind suppose that a person who adheres to the religion of Israel can fail to believe in the principle" of resurrection, seeing that it is "clear and universally known . . . Who could place a nonliteral interpretation" on the scriptural verses affirming resurrection? "Who has ever dared to lay hands" on the dogma?[220] Joseph was Maimonides' favorite student and had unmeasured respect for his master. Maimonides could be expected not to mislead him at least. Joseph's refutation of Samuel's treatise shows, moreover, that Joseph himself believed in the dogma and thought that Maimonides did so too.

If Maimonides believed, or did his best to believe, in the miracle of resurrection despite any discomfort that we may imagine him feeling about it, he accepted the possibility of God's intervening in the world through miracles and he accepted the paradigmatic miracle, creation. If he did not believe in the resurrection of the dead, he was capable of duping those who depended on him for guidance—his favorite student and his readers.

[220]Moses ben Maimon, *Epistulae* (n. 157 above) 66–67.

No matter how Maimonides' position on resurrection is read, an instructive contrast can be drawn between the treatment of the hereafter by him and by Avicenna, the Islamic philosopher who had the greatest impact on his conception of the universe. Avicenna ruled out the possibility of a resurrection of dead bodies while at the same time praising the prophet Muhammad for hiding "true eudaemonia" from the masses and preaching a fairy tale that they could grasp. Muhammad taught that the reward for socially desirable behavior in this world will be a future state in which the resurrected righteous dwell forever in luxurious pavilions, are served delicious cool drinks by immortal young boys, and take their pleasure with fetching black-eyed maidens.[221] Those were promises to which the man in the street could respond. By contrast, Christianity—in Avicenna's judgment—betrays a total ignorance of human psychology. Its doctrine that the resurrected bodies of the righteous will exist forever in a stark, joyless state or, no better, will live the life of angels, demonstrates a total failure to understand human nature. As the vast majority of mankind views things, though few are bold enough to make their feelings known, the angels lead a doleful existence. The poor creatures are miserable; they are never able to indulge in food, drink, and sexual intercourse; and they are subject to the unending drudgery of "praising and worshiping [God] day and night." Promises of a resurrected existence in the Christian mode will hardly motivate the masses to behave in a manner beneficial to society.[222]

Maimonides refuses to make the concessions that Avicenna sardonically believed human nature demands. Although he recognizes that looking forward to an idyllic resurrected existence may motivate people at a certain stage of their development, he is uncompromising in presenting the austere truth to his readers. He writes on one occasion: "These stupid and ignorant Arabs who are swept up in lust" may imagine that a person is rewarded for living a religious life only if he "eats and drinks well, has sexual relations with attractive beings, wears fine linen garments and embroidery, and dwells in ivory dwellings. . . ." Maimonides' Jewish readers, by contrast. are told bluntly that those physical pleasures are "foolishness," "vanity" and "of no value." The ultimate reward for mankind is the permanent existence of perfected human intellects.[223]

In our own day, the resurrection of the dead no longer stands at the center of the consciousness of even the most traditional of Jewish thinkers. In one of those curious games that history plays, it has been Maimonides' inclusion of resurrection in his list of thirteen principles of faith which, more than anything else, has prevented resurrection from being shunted still further to the outer periphery of Jewish religious consciousness.

[221] See Quran 56.

[222] Avicenna, *al-Risāla al-Aḍḥawiyya fī al-Maᶜād* (n. 194 above) 87–97.

[223] *Mishneh Torah*: *H. Teshuba* 8.6.

Summary. The *Epistle to Yemen* reveals how Maimonides on one occasion instructed an unsophisticated Jewish community on the proper way to conduct itself during a period of tribulation: He addressed the Yemeni Jews sympathetically, firmly, and a bit patronizingly. The *Treatise on Resurrection*, besides revealing that he could be unexpectedly sensitive regarding criticism of his religious correctness, holds a key for settling much that one would want to know about him. Depending on the direction in which the key is turned, whether as Maimonides tells us we must turn it or as many readers think it should be turned, it either opens a window on his unshakable attachment to rabbinic tradition or reveals something very unpleasant about his character. The other two minor treatises attributed to Maimonides are probably inauthentic and therefore cannot be used in accounts of Maimonides' activities, personality, or views. If they are indeed inauthentic, they provide further evidence of the magnetic field that formed around him and attracted the writings of others into his orbit.

10

CONCLUSION

> When the reason for something is set forth clearly and its truth is known through faultless proofs, we do not rely on the author, but on the proof that was clearly set forth and the reason that was made known. (*Mishneh Torah*: *H. Qiddush ha-Ḥodesh* 17.24)

> Those who think about God and talk about Him at length without scientific knowledge, following nothing but an imaginative concept of God or a belief received on the authority of someone else, such persons in my view are . . . not truly talking about God and thinking about Him at all. (*Guide for the Perplexed* 3.51)

Maimonides' Worldview. In Maimonides' picture of the universe, the region inhabited by man—what we would now call the earth and its atmosphere—lies at the center and is surrounded by nine transparent celestial spheres, nested one within another. The innermost celestial sphere has the moon embedded in its surface and it is followed by: the sphere of the sun; five spheres, each containing one of the planets that were known in the Middle Ages;[1] an eighth sphere, in which the fixed stars and constellations are embedded; and an all-encompassing ninth sphere, which contains no planets or stars. The spheres carrying the moon, sun, and planets rotate around the earth, each with its own velocity, and give rise to the movements

[1]There was a version in which the spheres of the planets Venus and Mercury are located below the sphere of the sun. The version placing them above the solar sphere appealed to Maimonides because he found that it harmonized with his interpretation of the vision of the prophet Ezekiel. See Maimonides, *Guide for the Perplexed* 2:9; 2:10 (end).

peculiar to the bodies that they contain—the monthly movement of the moon around the earth, the yearly apparent movement of the sun around the earth, and so on. An infinitesimal movement of the eighth sphere is responsible for the phenomenon of precession. The ninth sphere functions as a mirror image of what we today understand to be the daily rotation of the earth on its axis. It revolves around the stationary earth once every twenty-four hours and draws all the other spheres with it, thereby bringing about the daily rising and setting of the moon, sun, planets, and stars.

In fact, of course, the sun, moon, and planets, do not—considered from the vantage point of an earthbound observer—move around the earth in precise circles. To account for their full observed motion, secondary spheres had to be added to the basic scheme. The secondary spheres belonging to each primary sphere interact like cogs with one another and with their primary sphere, and the upshot is that the heavenly bodies describe not circles but either ellipses or convoluted curlicues around the earth. What I have outlined, if minor variations are ignored, was common coin among intellectuals in the medieval Arabic world. It was taken for granted in educated circles, just as the movement of the earth around the sun is taken for granted today.

Maimonides weighed different possible systems of secondary spheres and in the end found them all wanting. He never reached the point of questioning the existence of celestial spheres but came to the conclusion that attempts to determine how many there are and how they operate are problematic. His mature position was that the science of astronomy must to some extent make do with tentative working hypotheses and be satisfied as long as it finds a hypothesis enabling it to predict celestial phenomena accurately.[2]

The closed universe pictured by Maimonides lent itself to proofs for the existence of a first incorporeal cause, or God. He repeatedly and unambiguously affirms that the existence of an incorporeal first cause, who consists in sublime, undifferentiated thought and whose essence is unknowable and indescribable, can be demonstrated beyond all question. The possibility of such a demonstration lies at the heart of both his philosophic and his religious thinking.

God does not govern the universe by Himself. Maimonides followed the philosophers of the medieval Arabic Aristotelian school in positing a hierarchy of incorporeal beings known to the philosophers as *intelligences*, inasmuch as they consist in pure thought, and identified by Maimonides and others with the angels of religion.[3] In the *Mishneh Torah*, he set the number of incorporeal intelligences at ten, nine paralleling the nine main celestial spheres, and a tenth, called the *active intellect*, which parallels the inner, sublunar region inhabited by man. In the

[2]Maimonides, *Guide for the Perplexed* 2:24, 53b–54a.
[3]*Guide for the Perplexed* 2.4, p. 14a; 2.6, p. 16a.

Guide for the Perplexed, he hesitates to fix the number exactly. But he betrays not a shadow of a doubt about the existence of incorporeal intelligences, just as he did not doubt the existence of celestial spheres.[4] The existence of angel-intelligences and especially of the active intellect is, like the possibility of demonstrating the existence of God, integral to his philosophic and religious thinking.[5]

God brings the first incorporeal intelligence into existence through a process of emanation;[6] the intelligence springs fully formed, as it were, out of God's thought. The first intelligence is the cause, again through a process of emanation, of the existence of the second intelligence as well as of the existence of the outermost celestial sphere; the second intelligence emanates the third intelligence as well as the second of the celestial spheres; and so on, down until the active intellect which emanates the sublunar region inhabited by man. It is through the medium of the intelligences and active intellect that God is the cause of the existence of the celestial and sublunar regions and hence of everything taking place within them. In earlier chapters, we saw Maimonides tracing human intellectual thought, prophecy, and divine providence to the active intellect and only ultimately and indirectly to God.

If Maimonides is taken at his word, the universe outside of God has not existed from all eternity: God switched on the process of emanation and brought the incorporeal intelligences and, through them, the spheres and the lower world into existence after they did not exist. Since God performed the greatest of miracles by creating the universe, He can intervene miraculously in the created universe whenever His wisdom and will determine that such is called for. Miracles occur only rarely in Maimonides' universe, but by defending their possibility, he preserves a measure of personality in God. He thus recognizes that God communicated directly with Moses, redirected the course of history by having Moses lead the Israelites out of Egypt, brought the Israelites to Sinai, and there gave them the Written Torah and the interpretation of it known as the Oral Torah. A key area in which God intervenes to redirect the natural course of events is prophecy; God can, and sometimes does, prevent persons who are qualified for prophecy and are about to prophesy from doing so. Another area in which God will intervene, if Maimonides is taken at his word, is the resurrection of the dead, which will take place at some point in the indefinite future.

In both his rabbinic and philosophic works, Maimonides emphasizes that the goal of human life is intellectual perfection. The emotional and empathic side of human life receives short shrift throughout his writings and particularly in the

[4]*Guide for the Perplexed* 2:3–4, 6; H. Davidson, "Maimonides on Metaphysical Knowledge," *Maimonidean Studies* 3 (1992–93) 77.

[5]Calling the higher links in the hierarchy *intelligences* and the last link the active *intellect* is merely a convenient convention; Greek, Arabic, and Hebrew have a single word for both *intelligence* and *intellect*.

[6]*Guide for the Perplexed* 2:12.

Guide for the Perplexed, where some of his statements will make more than one reader uncomfortable. He writes, in the *Guide*, that the man of intellect suppresses desire for the "bestial" pleasures of food, drink, and sexual intercourse. Such a man focuses his attention on science and knowledge and gives thought to his livelihood, the running of his household, and the care of his body only when he is in any event distracted, as when at meals, in the bathhouse, or conversing with his "wife, his small children, or . . . common people." A person who, by contrast, neglects his or her intellect is not truly human, but rather "an animal in the shape and outline of a human being." The superior person therefore looks upon the general run of mankind as if they were either animals of prey, who are to be avoided, or cattle, who may be useful for supplying his inescapable physical needs.[7]

The theme of intellect extends its tentacles still further. Maimonides teaches that human beings approach God, who consists in pure intellectual thought, by expanding their own intellectual thought and specifically by acquiring as much knowledge about God and the other supernal incorporeal beings as is possible, that is, demonstrative knowledge of their existence and whatever other knowledge about them might lie within man's power. The highest form of divine worship is thought focused on God and unaccompanied by either ritual acts or speech; "where God is concerned, to keep silent is to praise."[8] Divine providence is enjoyed automatically by persons who perfect their intellect and to the extent that they do so. A highly developed intellect is a prerequisite for prophecy. Immortality is enjoyed by human intellects that reach the level at which they have a being belonging to the imperishable incorporeal realm—presumably the active intellect[9]—as the object of their thought, become identical with that imperishable object of their thought, and become equally imperishable and immortal.[10]

The Torah and its commandments are accordingly not ends in themselves. Their purpose is to provide man with the guidance he needs for perfecting his intellect and to create social conditions that promote the intellectual life. The unlettered who observe the ritual side of the Written and Oral Torahs while ignoring the intellectual side—who attend only to the means and ignore the end—resemble inhabitants of a city who wish to go to the ruler's palace and behold the ruler in his chambers yet do not even get to see the palace's outer wall. Men who devote their lives to the study of religious law while relying on others for the beliefs and principles of religion and never bothering to investigate those beliefs and principles are not much better. They—the vast majority of rabbinic scholars—are like inhabitants of the city who do succeed in reaching the palace yet keep walking around it and never find the entrance. Put still more strongly, persons who think and talk about God at length

[7]*Guide for the Perplexed* 1:7; 2:36, pp. 79a–b; above, p. 384.
[8]Above, pp. 383–84.
[9]*Guide for the Perplexed* 2.4, p. 14a.
[10]Above, pp. 156, 164, 242.

without having scientific knowledge of Him are not merely distant from God. They in fact talk and think not about God at all but about something nonexistent, a figment of their imagination.[11]

Thus far, we have Maimonides the scientist and philosopher.

During the time that he pursued his philosophic interests and preached the philosophic way of life, Maimonides studied rabbinic law, observed the commandments of the Written and Oral Torah, and conscientiously recited the prayers in the fixed liturgy. That he did so is scarcely surprising; his family background, the society in which he lived, and his position in it would lead one to expect little else. What is worthy of note is the implicit credence that he gave to God's having presented Moses with exactly 613 commandments at Sinai and to God's having communicated to Moses the interpretations of the commandments of the Written Torah which make up the Oral Torah. No less noteworthy is the manner in which he allocated his own time and energy: His study of rabbinic law, which he characterized as a means, was more thorough than his study of philosophy, which is the end; as a consequence, his mastery of rabbinic literature was much more solid than his mastery of the philosophic literature. He invested more time and energy in composing his rabbinic writings than his philosophic writings. He even studied medicine, which has the menial task of ministering to the human body, more intensively than philosophy, which ministers to the human intellect. And despite maintaining that the highest form of divine worship is thought unaccompanied by any ritual act, he was ultra-meticulous in observing the rituals. Here are a few illustrations.

When he discusses the commandment to wear phylacteries, Maimonides stresses the lesson that they convey: A man who wears phylacteries containing the four prescribed scriptural passages written on parchment—and who keeps the scriptural passages constantly before his mind's eye—becomes modest, God-fearing, and resistant to laughter and idle talk. He "does not contemplate evil thoughts, but rather turns his mind exclusively to truth and justice," that is, to the pursuit of knowledge and morality.[12] The order in which the parchments are positioned within the boxes would hardly seem to affect the lesson they teach. Nevertheless, after Maimonides' rabbinic studies led him to conclude that the parchments in his own personal pair had not been written and inserted in the correct order, he discarded his phylacteries, acquired a correctly fashioned pair, and advised others to follow his example.[13]

When enumerating the 613 commandments believed to have been communicated by God to Moses, Maimonides determined that every Jewish man has the obligation

[11] Above, pp. 384–85.

[12] Above, p. 258.

[13] Maimonides, *Responsa*, ed. J. Blau, 2nd ed. (Jerusalem 1986) §289.

to write a Torah scroll or at least to arrange for one to be written for him.[14] Jewish law codes coming after Maimonides continue to record the obligation, but the command is infrequently observed in practice. Few Jewish men arrange for a Torah scroll to be written, and virtually no nonscribe ever acquires the skills, and invests the 1,500 to 2,000 hours of labor required, for writing a scroll. Maimonides was the exception. He fulfilled the obligation to the letter and wrote a Torah scroll for himself which met all halakic specifications.[15]

In a letter to Pinḥas, the rabbinic judge of Alexandria, he rebukes Pinḥas for stating publicly that rabbinic law requires a male who has a seminal emission to bathe before either reciting his prayers, entering the synagogue, or studying the Torah. Someone of Pinḥas's standing should have instructed his flock that bathing after a seminal emission is not obligatory, although Jews in Muslim countries do have the custom to bathe in one of the three instances, namely, before reciting their daily prayers. After berating his Alexandrian colleague for failing to expound the legalities correctly, Maimonides assures Pinḥas that he was himself faithful to the custom of his fathers and was careful to bathe before praying after a seminal emission, unless illness prevented him from doing so.[16]

In his code of law, Maimonides sets down the talmudic regulations for the meal preceding the ninth day of the month of Ab, the fast day commemorating the destruction of the Holy Temple: The meal must be restricted to one cooked dish. He thereupon adds that the pious of earlier generations went beyond the fixed rules and would eat nothing but bread dipped in ashes as their meal before the fast, and scholars should follow the supererogatory practice. As for himself, he writes: "I never ate a cooked dish on the eve of the ninth of Ab, not even a dish of cooked lentils [the food of mourning par excellence], unless the eve of the ninth of Ab happened to occur on the Sabbath," when mourning rituals are not permitted.[17]

While there is no evidence that Maimonides lived the philosophic ideal, he plainly lived the rabbinic ideal to the fullest.

Did two incompatible personas then jostle in his breast, one a devotee of rabbinic law and the rabbinic ideal, and the other a devotee of philosophy? Or was he perhaps a full-fledged philosopher who lavished decades and boundless effort on his rabbinic writings, who observed the ritual regulations to the letter and beyond, merely in order to create a smokescreen for concealing his revolutionary philosophic ideology and a surreptitious vehicle for advancing it? Or was he, on the

[14]Maimonides, *Book of Commandments*, positive commandment #18, based on BT *Sanhedrin* 21b. (The list of commandments in *Halakot Gedolot* does not recognize such a commandment.) Rabbinic authorities speculate about whether the obligation is incumbent only on males or also on women.

[15]Maimonides, *Mishneh Torah*: *H. Sefer Torah* 8.4; 9.10; *Responsa*, pp. 261, 293.

[16]I. Shailat, *Letters and Essays of Moses Maimonides* (in Hebrew) (Jerusalem 1987–88) 437–38.

[17]*Mishneh Torah*: *H. Ta^{c}anit* 5.7, 9. The commentators give Maimonides' sources.

contrary, a halakist, whose philosophic interests remained firmly under the thumb of his dominant rabbinic persona? Readers in recent years have endorsed each of the three positions,[18] but none of the three reflects what Maimonides himself tells us. He avers in a dozen different ways that science and philosophy are not disciplines standing apart from the scriptural and rabbinic worldview and certainly not disciplines in conflict with it.

Prophets and philosophers alike, he states in his introduction to the Commentary on the Mishna, agreed that everything in the lower world inhabited by man exists for a single purpose, to bring forth men who excel in "knowledge and practice"; and by knowledge, he makes clear that he means philosophic knowledge.[19] In the *Mishneh Torah*, he reads the first two positive commandments of the Written Torah as the obligations to *know* that God exists and that He is one; those two propositions can be properly known solely through mastery of the demonstrations certifying their truth, and hence solely through the study of philosophy.[20] When expounding the scriptural commandment to study the Written and Oral Torahs, he makes the startling statement that the rabbinic subject known as *gemara* includes philosophy; the ancient rabbis themselves thus embraced philosophy as an integral part of their curriculum.[21] He was convinced that the biblical *account of creation* and its rabbinic elaboration are identical with the philosophic science of physics, that the biblical *account of the chariot* and its rabbinic elaboration are identical with the philosophic science of metaphysics, and that the rabbis ranked the study of metaphysics higher than immersing oneself in the dialectic argumentation of the Babylonian and Palestinian Talmuds.[22] He asserts that rabbinic aggada contains the metaphysical truths "that men of science have opined and on which the philosophers have spent ages."[23] Only someone who has perfected himself in science and philosophy can hope for the gift of prophecy.[24] The *world to come* of the rabbis is, in Maimonides' hands, the immortality of human intellectual thought of the supernal incorporeal realm; and the rabbis themselves realized that the subrational levels of the human soul have no part in that postmortal state.[25] The prophets and ancient rabbis looked forward to the days of the Messiah because it

[18]For example: W. Jawitz, *Toledot Yisrael* 12 (Tel Aviv 1935) 40–41 (the first position); A. Ginzberg, "*Shilṭon ha-Sekel*," in *Kol Kitebe Aḥad ha-ᶜAm* (Jerusalem 1956) 361a, 364b, 365b; English translation: "The Supremacy of Reason," in Achad Ha-am, *Ten Essays on Zionism and Judaism* (New York 173) 186–87, 201, 205 (the second position); B. Benedikt, *Asuppat Ma'amarim* (Jerusalem 1994) 190 (the third).

[19]Above, p. 163.

[20]Above, pp. 235–37.

[21]Above, p. 244.

[22]Above, p. 245.

[23]Above, p. 126.

[24]*Guide for the Perplexed* 2.38.

[25]Above, p. 242.

will be a period when human beings dedicate themselves to acquiring knowledge of their Creator to the extent that they are capable of doing so, as is written: 'For the earth shall be full of the knowledge of the Lord, as the waters cover the sea.' "[26]

In the vision that Maimonides unfolds, philosophy and the Written and Oral Torahs once formed a single, unified domain in which the study of metaphysics constituted talmudic study at its pinnacle. The unity had been rent during the millennium-long exile, and he was the instaurator who would reestablish it and thereby do justice not so much to philosophy as to the twin Torahs.

Maimonides the Man. The impression that one quickly forms of Maimonides is of an austere, self-confident elitist; an uncompromising rationalist; at the same time, a pious Jew who was meticulously observant of the niceties of scriptural and rabbinic law; and a driven writer who took as his sacred calling the education of his coreligionists and particularly the small number of like-minded, but inadequately trained souls capable of rising to his level. He had ascetic leanings and advises readers to allow themselves "physical pleasures only to the extent necessary for maintaining the body," to look upon the human sense of touch, which "bids [us] to pursue food and sex," as a shameful aspect of human nature, to regard the satisfying of one's physical needs as a distasteful and embarrassing chore comparable to carrying buckets of manure from one place to another.[27] He forbids the reading of books of history and poetry or of any other secular work that serves neither a scientific nor practical purpose; reading for recreation is a "mere waste of time."[28] He heaps opprobrium on persons who abuse God's gift of speech by employing it in obscene talk or song,[29] and in legal contexts, he records the talmudic prohibition against listening to music now that the Temple has been destroyed.[30]

Here and there, we are nonetheless afforded glimpses that soften and humanize the picture. Maimonides was so attached to his brother David that, he later wrote to an acquaintance, news of the brother's death left him bedridden for a year.[31] A snippet preserved in the correspondence between him and Joseph ben Judah reveals warm paternal feelings. He writes that apart from his intellectual pursuits, his only consolation was his son, Abraham, a winsome young man, "very modest, of high

[26]Above, p. 259.

[27]Maimonides, Commentary on the Mishna (=*Mishna ᶜim Perush R. Moshe ben Maimon*), Arabic original and Hebrew trans. J. Kafah (Jerusalem 1963–68), introduction 42; *Abot* 4:22; *Guide for the Perplexed* 2.36; 3.8; 49 (quoting Aristotle, *Nicomachean Ethics* 3.10).

[28]Commentary on the Mishna, *Sanhedrin* 10:1, p. 210.

[29]*Guide for the Perplexed* 3.8; Commentary on the Mishna, *Abot* 1.16; *Responsa* (n. 13 above) 224.

[30]*Mishneh Torah*: *H. Taᶜanit* 5.14, based on BT *Giṭṭin* 7a, and *Soṭa* 48a, and *Responsa* §224, without mention of the destruction of the Temple.

[31]Above, p. 72.

character, and possessed of a sharp mind. . . . May God give him a long life. . . . With God's help, he will surely acquire a name 'like that of the great ones [that are upon the earth.]' I pray to God that He should watch over him and bestow His goodness on him."[32]

In his code of law, Maimonides instructs rabbinic judges and communal leaders to behave toward their communities with "modesty and awe," and he himself made a point of addressing nonscholars with sympathy and courtesy.[33] Soon after arriving in Egypt he became the central figure in the collection of funds to redeem Jewish captives of war. In later life, he would return from the royal court each afternoon to find Jews and non-Jews of every class waiting in his courtyard with their medical problems and he would write prescriptions into the evening hours while overcome by fatigue.[34] In actual life, he plainly did not behave toward ordinary human beings as if they were animals of prey to be shunned or cattle to be exploited.[35]

In the same work in which he bans books of history and poetry, he concedes that listening to poetry and music and amusing oneself in other ways does, after all, have a legitimate role in human life: Persons suffering from debilitating melancholy and able to extract themselves from it through music and the like should do so—with the ultimate aim, of course, of returning to a healthy state in which they will mobilize all their powers toward the goal of "knowing as much of God as is possible."[36]

Then there is a letter in which someone reports back after having delivered a written message to a man of aristocratic status named "R. Moses," whose son was named "R. Abraham." The messenger informs the person who sent him that he had taken his own young son along on the errand. The two had been received in so warm and affable a fashion that "a book" would not suffice to give a full account of what occurred: Refreshments had been served, and R. Moses had himself eaten lemon cakes! R. Moses had then invited the visitor to sit down for a private conversation, while R. Abraham amused the boy. And as the two were leaving, R. Moses called the boy back to exchange a final pleasantry.[37] If the R. Moses in the report is indeed Maimonides, as the scholar who published the letter assumes, an appealing stroke would be added to our portrait of Maimonides. The names *Moses*

[32]Moses ben Maimon, *Epistulae*, ed. D. Baneth (Jerusalem 1946) 95–96, with an allusion to 1 Chronicles 17:8 (assuming that the attribution to Maimonides is genuine).

[33]Above, p. 486.

[34]Above, pp. 52, 69.

[35]See above, p. 541.

[36]*Shemona Peraqim* (=Commentary on the Mishna, introduction to *Abot*) chapter 5, p. 388. English translation: Moses Maimonides, *Eight Chapters*, ed. and trans. J. Gorfinkle (New York 1912). On music as a therapy for depression, see above, p. 466.

[37]P. Fenton, "A Meeting with Maimonides," *Bulletin of the School of Oriental and African Studies* 45 (1982) 1-4.

and *Abraham* were, however, common in the Middle Ages; the city, country, and century in which the delivery of the message took place are not identified; and since the title "R." is not necessarily equivalent to "Rabbi," the Moses in the story need not have been a scholar. We are unfortunately left only with the hope, not the certainty, that Moses Maimonides was being described.

In his rabbinic works, Maimonides endorses the Aristotelian definition according to which each ethical virtue is a characteristic in the soul lying midway between two extreme characteristics, the two extremes being defined as vices. A passage in the *Mishneh Torah* recognizes a pair of exceptions to the rule.

"There are," Maimonides writes, "psychological characteristics in which it is forbidden to follow the middle way and in which a person must instead go to the opposite extreme." One is pride. "The good way is not that someone should be merely modest, but that he be meek. . . . The Rabbis consequently enjoined [in the Mishna]: 'Be very, very lowly in spirit'; and they said: 'Everyone who is haughty denies the existence of God.'" When Maimonides expands on the instruction to be "very, very lowly in spirit" in his Commentary on the Mishna, he retells with approval the Arabic anecdote of the pious man who was traveling in the hold of a ship and on whom a wealthy fellow passenger urinated deliberately. The man called that day the happiest in his life because he was able to submit to the humiliation with equanimity.[38]

The other psychological characteristic in which it is forbidden to follow the middle way is anger. Anger, in Maimonides' words, is "an exceedingly bad quality, and a person should flee from it to the opposite extreme. He should train himself not to become angry even about things that justify becoming angry," and when someone in authority has to deter unacceptable conduct by demonstrating anger, he should merely feign the quality without allowing himself actually to be affected by it. "The ancient rabbis said: 'When someone gets angry, it is as if he worships a false deity.' They also said: 'When someone gets angry, if he is a wise man, his wisdom deserts him, and if he is a prophet, his prophecy deserts him.'"[39] We can hardly help asking how far Maimonides lived up to the standards that he prescribes.

Letters written in the early 1190s to Joseph ben Judah take up Joseph's complaint that he had been the subject of false tales spread by his enemies. Maimonides tries to persuade his former student to stop giving heed to

[38] Above, p. 94.

[39] *Mishneh Torah*: *H. De*ᶜ*ot* 2.3; there is an inconsistency between what Maimonides writes here and *H. De*ᶜ*ot* 1, where he includes pride and anger among the intermediate psychological characteristics which constitute virtue. The ethical stance he takes in his rabbinic works is, further, more moderate than his stance in the *Guide for the Perplexed*. On both points, see H. Davidson, "The Middle Way in Maimonides' Ethics," *Proceedings of the American Academy for Jewish Research* 54 (1987) 31–72.

"foolishness" and to concern himself solely with personal moral and intellectual development.

He contrasts himself with Joseph: Thanks to the passage of time and experience, and through study, he had become "very forgiving," whereas the younger man obviously had a way to go before attaining that level.[40] Maimonides further explains that the "anguish and anger" suffered by Joseph at the hands of the slanderers were ultimately due not to the slander itself but to his youth. And he thereupon makes a confession: "When I was your age and even older, I suffered still more intensely from the emotions that affect you now. I would employ my tongue and pen without restraint to take revenge against men of standing and knowledge who had the temerity to disagree with me. . . . You have undoubtedly heard what occurred between me and R. Judah ben Parḥon ha-Kohen, of blessed memory, on two questions regarding defects that render an animal ritually unfit for consumption, between me and the judge of Sijilmasa regarding [the validity of] a [certain] divorce document, between me and Abu Joseph ben Joseph, may he rest in peace, regarding [the legal status of] a woman who had been a captive [of the gentiles], and many other incidents of the same kind. I would please my friends and make my adversaries weep with my tongue and pen—wielding my tongue against those in the immediate vicinity and my pen against those who were at a distance."[41]

Maimonides does not say when he finally learned to control his temper. But we learn from another letter, this one to Pinḥas of Alexandria, that about ten years before offering the good advice to Joseph, and when already in his forties, he had not yet succeeded.

Pinḥas had written to him expressing fear that he was falling out of favor. Maimonides had failed to answer previous letters and had reportedly made uncomplimentary statements about Pinḥas. The latter, for his part, suspected that Maimonides had been swayed by reports of uncomplimentary remarks supposedly made by him about Maimonides. He pleads not to be forsaken.

Maimonides replies in a conciliatory tone, addressing his Alexandrian junior colleague as "his glory, honor, eminence, and holiness, our master, Rabbi Pinḥas—may God protect him—the great judge, the fortress, the tower, the outstanding scholar." He explains that he had failed to answer previous letters because of his illness and not because of anything he had heard. He assures Pinḥas that he never paid attention to rumors and was above reacting even when he knew for a fact that someone went as far as to curse him. And he promises that he would not forsake Pinḥas; for God "forbid that I should uproot what I have planted and tear down what I have built." Then he turns to an issue that I mentioned a few paragraphs earlier.

[40]Moses ben Maimon, *Epistulae* (n. 32 above) 49–50.

[41]Moses ben Maimon, *Epistulae* 49–50, 89–90.

Pinḥas had learned that one of his previous letters made Maimonides "very angry." Someone, it seems, had announced to the Alexandrian Jews in the name of Maimonides that Jewish law does not require a man who had a seminal emission to bathe before praying, entering the synagogue, or reading from the Torah. Pinḥas, in the previous letter, informed Maimonides that the entire populace of Alexandria, "from one end to the other, young and old" came to protest: "We cannot put up with what you rabbis tell us, with your permitting whatever you want and prohibiting whatever you want. We have an ancient tradition from our forefathers saying that a Jewish man who has a seminal emission must not pray until he washes in the bathhouse or in the sea. . . . If you now permit us to pray, enter the synagogue, and read the Torah without washing and purifying ourselves, . . . we'll go and tell the gentile authorities."

Maimonides responds that the report of his having become angry at the time was correct. The letter arrived when he was "sick, on the verge of death." He knew from a separate source that Pinḥas had blown things out of proportion, that the hubbub was raised by just a few ignoramuses and not by the entire Jewish population of Alexandria. Instead of telling the troublemakers that they were misinformed, that bathing after a seminal emission was only a custom observed by Jews in Muslim countries and not a religious obligation, and that the custom was limited to prayer and did not apply to the other activities, Pinḥas had concurred and egged them on. "How," Maimonides writes, "could I have failed to be angry?" Pinḥas's letter and behavior would have angered "even Hillel the elder," who was renowned for his even temper and imperturbability.[42] When in his forties, Maimonides could thus still admit to becoming "very angry."

He never confesses to the quality of pride. In the letter to Joseph in which he recalls the days when he wielded his tongue and pen out of anger, he stresses that he always tried to act with humility (*ᶜinwetanut*); and in the letter in which he speaks of his forgiving nature, he reminds Joseph that he behaved with "humility toward everyone" and placed himself on an equal level with "the smallest."[43]

A description of Maimonides by a Muslim scholar has been preserved, however, which is at odds with his depiction of himself. ᶜAbd al-Laṭīf al-Baghdādī visited Egypt a few years before 1193 and arranged to have Maimonides come to meet him; what he perceived was not humility but rather a "consummately erudite man, whose predominant quality was love of headship and of service to the important men of the world." ᶜAbd al-Laṭīf did not possess the sweetest of personalities and he does not hide his antipathy to Maimonides, which Maimonides may well have reciprocated on the occasion. What he says may, therefore, be taken with a grain of salt. But we have also seen Maimonides writing with satisfaction that he had "achieved great fame in medicine among the nobles, such as the chief *qāḍī*, the emirs, and the

[42]Shailat, *Letters and Essays of Moses Maimonides* (n. 16 above) 436–38.
[43]Moses ben Maimon, *Epistulae* 61, 89–90.

house of the [vizier] al-Fāḍil, as well as other prominent people of the land."[44] ᶜAbd al-Laṭīf's impression may therefore contain a grain or two of truth.

Be that as it may, humility is not the quality that stands out when Maimonides talks about his literary achievements.

He completed his Commentary on the Mishna at the age of thirty and he there directs us to read "over and over what I have written here [about the foundations of Jewish belief] and contemplate it well. If you let yourself suppose that you have gotten to the heart of it in one or ten readings, then, God knows, you have been led into an absurdity." "I did not write it haphazardly, but after . . . investigating correct and incorrect opinions, distilling out which of them should be believed, and seeking arguments and proofs relative to each point."[45] When his Commentary takes up the Order of the Mishna dealing with impurity law, Maimonides disparages what "great teachers" of the posttalmudic period had said as "long in words, light in usefulness." "If you go to heads of today's rabbinic academies . . . you will find, . . . as a consequence of our many sins," that they fail to understand even relatively clear and straightforward aspects of the subject. Of his own introduction to the Order of impurity law, he writes: Only someone who has "agonized days and sleepless nights" over the statements on the subject scattered through the rabbinic corpus and then opened Maimonides' introduction will appreciate "what has been accomplished here." To read his introduction "even a thousand times without memorizing it" will be "insufficient; it must be as fluent on your tongue as the Hear O Israel prayer." He would later apprise readers that his commentary on the Order of impurity law allows those desiring to understand "anything within the area of impurity and purity" to dispense with the study of any other book.[46]

In the course of his Commentary on the Mishna, Maimonides asks that careful attention be given to his explanation of a certain mishnaic passage, because the passage has "not been clarified, prior to me, by any of the *geonim* whose words I have seen."[47] Of another mishnaic passage, he writes that "most of the *geonim*" found it problematic, but "the [correct] explanation is as follows. . . ."[48] Of yet another passage: "Everyone about whom I have heard and whose words I have seen" failed to grasp the matter, "but God has enabled me to understand it."[49]

He was no less pleased with the "fourteen chapters containing important rules and numerous principles," which form the introduction to his *Book of Commandments.* Those rules "are like mountains upon which everything depends"; they are "important rules, . . . which a person must know, whereupon he will clearly see the error of everyone, from the author of *Halakot Gedolot* until today, who

[44]Above, p. 35.
[45]Above, p. 159.
[46]Above, p. 153.
[47]Commentary on the Mishna, *Yoma* 2:1.
[48]Commentary on the Mishna, *Baba Batra* 2:4.
[49]Commentary on the Mishna, *Negaᶜim* 1:4.

enumerated the commandments except for me."[50] He ventures that his *Mishneh Torah* has no equal "since the time of Judah the Prince and his holy collaborators," who compiled the Mishna corpus.[51] Its value will be recognized solely by "just men, men of religion and science," who have the ability to appreciate what was involved in fashioning a work of its magnitude.[52] "In the time to come, when jealousy and ambition disappear, all Israel will use only my composition, and every other will undoubtedly be abandoned except by persons looking for something with which to keep themselves occupied . . . even though they derive no benefit from it."[53] As for the *Guide for the Perplexed*, it is "a pearl that has no price."[54]

Maimonides took pride in another quality, which goes hand in hand with extreme equanimity and humility. He writes to Samuel ben Eli, the principal of the Baghdad rabbinic academy: "You must have imagined that I am like most men, who are disturbed when someone contradicts what they say," but "God, be He praised, has freed me from that. The Creator knows that should the least of my students, a colleague, or an adversary rebut me and the rebuttal be correct, it makes me happy; I am glad that he called my attention to something I overlooked. Even if I find that the person rebutting me is mistaken, I do not despise him, God forbid, or reproach him for daring to offer a rebuttal that is baseless."[55]

He expresses the sentiment in similar words to Joseph ben Judah[56] and in one of his letters to Joseph makes an additional point. Self-respect, he writes, prevented him from reacting to those in Baghdad, including Samuel ben Eli, who belittled the *Mishneh Torah* while refusing even to admit that they had looked at it: "Out of self-dignity and because of my character, I do not answer fools; [the rabbis have told us that] the Holy One undertakes to defend a scholar's honor."[57] About the same time, he received a letter from Joseph Ibn Jabir, an uneducated Iraqi Jew, who, he heard, had stepped forward to defend him and the *Mishneh Torah* against disparagers in Baghdad.[58] Maimonides answers in a friendly and courteous vein and in the course of his reply writes: "I forgive everyone who speaks . . . ill of me . . . through stupidity." He then makes a wry allusion to a rule in talmudic

[50] Above, p. 185.

[51] Above, p. 197.

[52] Maimonides, *Treatise on Resurrection*, Arabic text and Medieval Hebrew translation, ed. J. Finkel, *Proceedings of the American Academy for Jewish Research* 9 (1939) 4.

[53] Letter to Joseph ben Judah, in Moses ben Maimon, *Epistulae* 52.

[54] Letter to Joseph ben Judah, in *Epistulae* 16.

[55] Maimonides, *Responsa* (n. 13 above) §310, p. 572; 4.21.

[56] Letters to Joseph ben Judah, in *Responsa*, 3.144–45, and *Epistulae* 58.

[57] Letter to Joseph ben Judah, in *Epistulae* 56, quoting BT *Berakot* 19a.

[58] Ibn Jabir wrote to Maimonides that he was uneducated (*ᶜam ha-areṣ*) and unable to understand Hebrew; see Maimonides' letter to Joseph Ibn Jabir, in Shailat, *Letters and Essays of Moses Maimonides* (n. 16 above) 404, 408–9. Judah ben Judah expressed surprise that Maimonides had taken the trouble to write a letter to a person such as Ibn Jabir; see Maimonides, *Epistulae* 88, 90.

commercial law which probably was above the head of Ibn Jabir, the person to whom he was writing.

The talmudic rule states: When one party will suffer no monetary loss or inconvenience by making a concession that will benefit a second party, the first party is legally bound to make the concession; it was the inhabitants of biblical Sodom who refused to accommodate others where there was no cost to themselves.[59] Since the men who belittled Maimonides did so in order to inflate their standing in the eyes of their supporters, whereas they were sufficiently beneath Maimonides that nothing they said or did could possibly cause him harm—since the belittlers had something substantial to gain, and Maimonides had nothing to lose—talmudic law mandated that he let them bark to their hearts' content. Furthermore, Maimonides goes on, undoubtedly still smiling to himself, the unjustified attacks not only did him no harm; they actually benefited him. For to suffer injustice without responding redounds to a person's moral and religious credit. He therefore asks Ibn Jabir to avoid quarrels and refrain from intervening on his behalf.[60]

On one occasion, we can observe Maimonides living up to the standard that he set. After a circle of talmudists in southern France who were well disposed to him and to whom he was well disposed questioned him about a number of legal rulings in the *Mishneh Torah*, he thanks them for the care with which they had read the work. He acknowledges that they had uncovered an error, grants that their position on a second issue where they disagreed with him was possible, and encourages them to "examine and scrutinize" everything he wrote.[61]

He did not, however, always suffer criticism gladly. In an earlier chapter, we saw him branding critics of the *Mishneh Torah* as "evil, jealous" men, "unlettered ignoramus[es]," "deluded, confused tyro[s]," and "blockheaded, dull-witted pietist[s]"[62] We cannot be certain that Samuel ben Eli was one of the ignoramuses or dull-witted pietists whom he had in mind, but Samuel's criticisms were among those that rankled.

In an exchange of letters, also referred to in earlier chapters, Samuel challenged Maimonides on the question whether Jews are allowed to travel by riverboat on the Sabbath. A member of the Baghdadi community had solicited Maimonides' opinion on the question, and Maimonides had explained in an unusually lengthy responsum why river travel is permitted. The Baghdadi Jew was apparently a stalking horse, because Samuel quickly wrote to Maimonides informing him that he

[59]BT *Baba Batra* 12b, and parallels: *kofin ᶜal middat Sedom.*

[60]Letter to Joseph Ibn Jabir, in Shailat, *Letters and Essays of Moses Maimonides* 417–18. Regarding the moral and religious credit that results from suffering injustice without responding, see BT *Rosh ha-Shana*, 17a, parallels, and Maimonides, *Mishneh Torah*: *H. Deᶜot* 7.7–8 (where Maimonides ignores qualifications placed on the principle by BT *Yoma* 23a).

[61]See *Responsa* 3.56–57.

[62]Above, p. 209.

had been shown the responsum, as Maimonides undoubtedly realized he would be. Samuel opens with polite, complimentary language, expresses confidence that Maimonides would not be offended by having his errors corrected, and offers his critique. Maimonides replied in a surrejoinder that is again atypically long. This was the context in which he assured Samuel that unlike most men, he was not offended by criticism, no matter who the critic was.

Although Samuel was a personage of "high repute," whose degree of mastery of the Talmud was "well known," an "elder" and "man of stature," and consequently someone who should not commit elementary blunders, Maimonides would not blame him for his slip. The fault undoubtedly lay not in a lack of intelligence and understanding on Samuel's part but in too hurried and superficial a reading of Maimonides' words. Whereupon the tone shifts enough to confirm the suspicion that we are being treated to a good dose of sarcasm.

Samuel had, in his critique, quoted passages from the Babylonian and Palestinian Talmuds for support, and Maimonides chides his opponent for imagining that he would have been unfamiliar with the passages in question; Samuel should at most have alluded to them rather than quoting them in their entirety. Maimonides further chides Samuel for failing to examine what he wrote about the issue in the *Mishneh Torah*. He had, after all, been informed that the *Mishneh Torah* was available in Baghdad and indeed that most Baghdadi rabbinic courts were using it to decide legal and ritual questions[63]—although he had also heard that certain persons there belittled the code without bothering to read it. "If this *gaon*, may God grace him with long life," had taken the trouble to peruse what was said in the *Mishneh Torah*, he would have seen at once whether or not Maimonides was familiar with the pertinent talmudic sources.

Maimonides then goes to the core of the matter by exposing the error in Samuel's reasoning. Samuel had missed something that somebody who studies Talmud just one day a year (*bar be rab de-ḥad yoma*) would understand. Maimonides had not spelled out the nub of his argument in more detail in the original responsum—notwithstanding the responsum's length—because, "may the Creator be my witness, I never supposed that rabbinic scholars [*talmide ḥakamim*] would fail to grasp" the point and would need to have it hammered home. The implication is unmistakable: Samuel was not a genuine rabbinic scholar and, at least in the present instance, understood less than is understood by a person who studies the Talmud one day a year.

Samuel had indicated in his rejoinder that he had reservations about additional statements in Maimonides' "noble text" but had refrained from raising them. Maimonides now "requests, pleads, and urges" that the Baghdadi *gaon* withhold nothing out of pity for him. He entreats Samuel: Scrutinize every word in my

[63]Perhaps these were courts under the control of the exilarch, who was at loggerheads with Samuel.

original responsum, in my subsequent surrejoinder, and in anything else I wrote, "so that I shall benefit" from your critique. "For the Torah attains its object only through the raising of objections . . . and the meticulous examination of everyone's words, *on the condition that the objections have substance*." Maimonides plainly relished the prospect of uncovering further blunders that even a beginner in rabbinic studies would not have committed.[64]

In the previous chapter we saw that the two men clashed as well on the issue of the world to come. When Joseph ben Judah sent Maimonides a copy of Samuel's treatise on resurrection, which tacitly attacked Maimonides' position, Maimonides wrote back: "I am amazed at you, my son; how could you have sent it [that is, the treatise] to me? In order to let me see how little the man knows?" "God knows, I was genuinely amazed that he could speak such . . . ridiculous and disgraceful . . . nonsense." Samuel was a "poor soul" possessed of "little knowledge," who had achieved his status in Baghdad thanks to genealogy, the absence of persons of discrimination there, and a gift for feeding people a "noxious pottage."[65]

Instead of treating the baseless arguments of the poor soul with forbearance and ignoring his adversary out of a sense of self-dignity, Maimonides sat down and composed his own *Treatise on Resurrection*, a work in which he expresses himself even more bitterly and sarcastically than he did in the dispute about river travel. He takes Samuel to task for compiling rabbinic homiletic exegeses verbatim and without expounding their inner sense, although "*everyone* knows that men of science" do not proceed in that fashion. He laughs at Samuel for presenting homiletic materials in the way that "women recite to one another in a house of mourning." And he explains that his own *Treatise on Resurrection* addresses only the "masses," "women, and the ignorant," leaving it to Samuel, the target of the *Treatise*, to select the category in which he wished to classify himself.

Maimonides, in sum, characterizes himself as "very forgiving," while admitting that he had been irascible in his youth and that he could, even in his forties, become "very angry." He takes credit for placing himself on an equal level with "the smallest," whereas his writings show him to have been a supremely proud man. He assures us on several occasions that he was unaffected by criticism, yet he displays hypersensitivity to the criticisms of the head of the Baghdad academy, whom he dismissed as a purveyor of nonsense. Genius though he was, he was much "like most men" in his inability to view himself in a clear light.

There were other complexities in his character. While his *Guide for the Perplexed* preaches the solitary life more forcefully than his rabbinic works—in the *Guide*, he recommends separating oneself from society and avoiding contact with

[64]Maimonides, *Responsa* §§308–10; 3.171–77; 4.11–22.
[65]Above, p. 523.

other human beings as far as one possibly can[66]—he wrote the book around the time when he emerged from his study to spend long days in the company of nonintellectuals at the royal court and at home. He denigrates the "bestial" pleasures of food, drink, and sexual intercourse, and describes the sense of touch as something of which to be ashamed about the time that he accepted a commission to write a manual on enhancing sexual prowess.[67] He insisted that the date of the coming of the Messiah cannot be predicted and he warned against attempts to make the calculation. In the next breath, he discloses a closely held family secret regarding the date of the renewal of prophecy, which will herald the Messiah's coming; and the closely held secret turns out to be a variation of a midrashic comment recorded in the Palestinian Talmud for all to see.[68] He stressed the secret character of the biblical accounts of creation and the chariot; a few pages later he explicates the two scriptural accounts in easily decipherable language, and what he uncovers in the biblical texts turns out to be commonplaces of medieval Arabic Aristotelianism which he expounded elsewhere without hesitation. The nature of divine attributes, the essence of prophecy, and the operation of divine providence are listed by him among the "secrets of the Torah" which must not be divulged to the ordinary run of mankind.[69] He nonetheless discusses each of those subjects openly and in detail in his *Guide for the Perplexed.*

Perhaps the complex and contradictory nature of the man helps to explain how he was capable of viewing the rabbinic and philosophic ideologies, which would appear to be no more compatible than oil and water, as a homogeneous unity.

Concluding Note. Before taking leave of Maimonides we should be careful not to forget his accomplishments.

His first thirty years saw him departing Cordova, the city of his birth, undertaking a number of trips by sea, residing for a time in Fez, visiting Palestine, and settling in Egypt.[70] It is reasonable to suppose that his travels were in some way connected with the conquest of Andalusia by the fanatical Almohads, although neither he nor his father ever mentions having personally suffered harassment at Almohad hands. During these migratory years, he was able to master the vast body of rabbinic literature, attain expertise in medieval Arabic mathematics and astronomy, study medicine with experienced Arab physicians, acquire a basic knowledge of Arabic Aristotelian philosophy, serve as an apprentice under rabbinic judges in the lands of the West, and, above all, compose commentaries on two-thirds of the Babylonian Talmud and on the Mishna corpus.

[66] *Guide for the Perplexed* 3.51, p. 125a.

[67] Above, pp. 467–68.

[68] Above, p. 491.

[69] *Guide for the Perplexed* 1.35; above, pp. 373, 375.

[70] Above, pp. 14, 21, 28, 31.

Upon arriving in Fustat, he was recognized as the foremost rabbinic scholar in the country, quickly became president of the local Jewish law court, and was a prime mover in the promulgation of a number of far-reaching public edicts. After completing his Commentary on the Mishna, he produced, in a remarkably short time, what became the most influential work on the subject of the 613 commandments believed to have been given by God to Moses at Sinai. At the age of forty, he completed his monumental code of Jewish Law, one of the two most significant and influential works produced in the medieval Jewish world. Necessity impelled him into gainful employment, and his aptitudes demonstrated themselves in that area too; he developed a broad and highly successful medical practice, which extended to the royal court itself. All the while, he continued to serve as a rabbinic judge and to answer questions regarding rabbinic law. The demands on his time and further periods of illness did not prevent him from writing the *Guide for the Perplexed*, the most influential and widely read philosophic work of the Jewish Middle Ages, as well as a series of medical compositions, the last of which he was still working on when death overtook him.

Maimonides made fun of pretentious titles[71] and, we saw earlier, there is no evidence to sustain the conjecture that he ever held the grandiose official title of Head of the Egyptian Jews. He nevertheless was, in a true sense, head of the Jews not only in Egypt but throughout the medieval Jewish world.

[71] Above, pp. 59–60, 523, 525.

INDEX